115

W9-CFF-276

# BRITAIN AND THE HOLY LAND

MORDECHAI ELIAV

# BRITAIN AND THE HOLY LAND

## 1838–1914

*Selected Documents*
*from the British Consulate in Jerusalem*

YAD IZHAK BEN-ZVI PRESS
JERUSALEM

THE MAGNES PRESS
THE HEBREW UNIVERSITY, JERUSALEM

DS
125
.B75
1997

ISBN 965–217–139–5

Printed in Israel

# CONTENTS

# PREFACE

In 1939–1941, Albert M. Hyamson, historian and senior official of the Palestine Government, published an extensive, two-volume collection of documents entitled *The British Consulate in Jerusalem in Relation to the Jews in Palestine, 1838–1914*. This pioneering work, meticulously edited, pointed the way to the use of consular records as an important source for the history of Palestine and its Jewish populace.

Hyamson systematically went through the relevant files in the Public Record Office (PRO), particularly those in two classes: FO 78 and FO 195. The former includes primarily drafts of despatches sent to consulates throughout the world and the original despatches and correspondence forwarded by the consuls to the Foreign Office. FO 195 contains the correspondence between the British Embassy in Constantinople and the various consulates in the Ottoman Empire over which it had jurisdiction. Even Hyamson, however, was forced to admit that "documents which are known to have existed and whose contents should have proved of interest for the present purpose cannot be found." (Hyamson, *British Consulate*, Introduction, p. x).

It is now evident that the relevant documentation preserved in classes FO 78 and FO 195, despite its great quantity, is far from complete. Even without the missing documents, Hyamson's publication of 465 items, replete with many appendices, can only be considered a sampler of this important material.

What befell the archives of the British Consulate in Jerusalem? Unfortunately, on 30 October 1914, the day on which diplomatic relations were severed between Turkey and Great Britain, William Hough, the last British consul in Ottoman Jerusalem, set fire to an important part of these papers — especially those marked "Confidential" — upon instructions from his superiors. When his exit from the city was delayed, he burnt the rest of the classified material (see Hough, and Doc. 135 in this volume). What remained was transferred to the American consulate for safekeeping. When the United States joined the war against Turkey and Germany in April 1917, the British documents were moved once again, this time to the Spanish consulate, from where Hyamson retrieved them in the name of the newly-established Mandatory administration.

Even these remnants of the British consulate archives suffered loss during the several transfers, with only a very small part surviving, as Hyamson testifies: "These records were sparse and very few survived. But they included a few useful documents of which no copies are to be found in London."(Hyamson, ibid.) With the end of the British Mandate over Palestine, they were transferred to the Israel State Archives (ISA), but we do not know how many of them were lost or vanished under the difficult conditions during Israel's War of Independence. Indeed, scrutiny of the British consulate archives in the ISA has produced disappointing results when compared to the consular archives of Germany and Austria, from which I have previously edited and published selected documents (Eliav, *German Policy*; idem, *Austrian Protection*).

Obviously, then, the vast majority of the Jerusalem consulate papers have been lost over the years. The surviving documents in the ISA include lists and registers of British citizens and protégés dating from different periods; some correspondence with vice-consuls and consular agents in Palestine's port cities, also from various periods; remnants of the consulate's correspondence with the local Ottoman authorities; files dealing with the acquisition of land and other property by consul James Finn and his wife; drafts of despatches to the Foreign Office and the embassy in Constantinople (for 1911–1912 alone); and papers dealing with a few other matters. All of these are random files, without chronological continuity.

What is missing? Most of the correspondence with British citizens and protégés in Jerusalem; the majority of the consulate's correspondence with the Jewish communal leadership, other foreign consuls, the Turkish authorities and the English missionaries in the city; documents dealing with cases brought before the consular court and such which touch upon the personal status of individuals. It is only natural that correspondence with the Foreign Office and embassies, which has survived, is devoted in the main to political matters or to the consuls' reports on events in Palestine. It is documentation of a local nature, dealing with a wide spectrum of economic and social matters as well as having relevance to questions of a religious and legal nature, or describing the consulate's activities, which has unfortunately been lost. This is a serious loss in its own right and also in comparison with the archives of other foreign consulates in Jerusalem. As a result, anyone dealing with the documents of the British consulate must of necessity limit himself primarily to the political arena, though it is possible to widen the scope of the discussion from time to time thanks to other documents which have survived under some fortuitous circumstances. There is yet another difficulty. The latest files in FO 78 date from 1905, while FO 195 contains but a few which hold material from 1906 onwards. Documents originating in or relating to the Jerusalem consulate are scattered through the hundreds of files in classes FO 369 (Consular Correspondence from 1906) and FO 371 (General Political Correspondence from 1906). Unlike record groups dealing with earlier periods, these are arranged chronologically, rather than geographically, so that correspondence from all over the world is interfiled. Any attempt to locate in them documents relating to the Jerusalem consulate is a very difficult task. Moreover, the old card index for 1906–1914 in the PRO is not very helpful. This probably accounts in part for the fact that Hyamson published only 20 documents dating from February 1906 until the end of 1914, most of them from FO 371 and the rest from the remnants of the consular archives which were in his possession.

Thus, it is all the more regrettable that drafts of consulate correspondence to London and Constantinople in the material found today in the ISA have survived for but two years -1911 and 1912.

Another small group of documents, about 70 in number, is today in the Manuscripts and Archives Department of the Jewish National and University Library in Jerusalem. These may be items that were once in the consulate's archives, which at some time probably came into private hands and were then acquired by the JNUL. Most of them are originals and include various reports, lists of protégés from different years, and letters, some of which were published by Hyamson.

From a systematic rechecking of the relevant files in the PRO, I soon realized that they include several important and interesting documents which Hyamson omitted from his work. This is understandable when one recalls that Hyamson strictly limited his selection to items which related to the Jews of Palestine in general and to the British protégés in particular. Furthermore, he believed that in many cases an extract from the document, or a summary of its content, would suffice. All this notwithstanding, his selection is at times questionable, since important documents which fall within the limited scope of his volume are missing from it.

This state of affairs led to the conclusion that Hyamson's two volumes are insufficient to gain an accurate sense of the consulate's wide spectrum of activities. A broader selection is called for, one which would include documents that shed light on the general development of Palestine and its inhabitants, on relationships among the foreign powers in the Holy Land, on economic and commercial activity, and the marked development of Jerusalem in the nineteenth century — all as reported by the British Consul in Jerusalem. Only such a corpus can throw light upon the unique attraction exerted by the Holy Land and Jerusalem, and the development of foreign political and religious interests therein during the nineteenth century.

The documents published in the present volume testify to the multi-faceted subject matter included in the reports of the consuls, who followed events in Palestine and deemed it their duty to faithfully report to their superiors in detail on developments in various fields of activity. It should be noted, however, that we have also published documents dealing specifically with the Jewish community which for some reason were omitted from Hyamson's selection. These deal, inter alia, with important topics such as plans for Jewish settlement at El-Arish and in the Rafah area, the Anglo-Palestine Bank, Jewish colonies throughout the country, Arab-Jewish relations, and Arab opposition to Zionism.

In the course of preparing this corpus for publication, I systematically examined scores of files in record groups FO 78 and FO 195, and also sought out documents filed in record groups FO 369 and FO 371. The search for items related to Palestine in the latter two groups was often a long and tedious procedure which, however, produced positive results: 34 of the documents date from 1906–1914. I have also published in their entirety, or with but a few omissions, several documents from which Hyamson saw fit to select but a few passages, which I deem to be of great importance. Documents 6, 7, 9 and 11 have been published previously by Nathaniel Katzburg, "Some Early Despatches by the First British Vice-Consul in Jerusalem (1839–1841)," H.Z. Hirschberg (ed.)., *Vatiqin*, Ramat Gan 1975, pp. ix–xxix (Hebrew).

Most of the documents are kept in the various record groups of the PRO, while the minority are in the other repositories listed in the Bibliography appended to the volume. For the reader's convenience, I have added five appendices: lists of Turkish Governors of Jerusalem, Foreign Secretaries, Ambassadors at Constantinople, Consuls and Consuls-General at Beirut, and a table showing the number of British subjects and protégés in Palestine at different periods of time.

Every effort has been made to reproduce the document faithfully from the original. We have generally omitted some of the official titles with which the despatches open, and some of the the repetitive closing phrases. Very few omissions have been made in the text of the despatches, and these have been marked by three dots [...]. No changes have been made in spelling. The call number of each document has been recorded as it appears on the original. The detailed Bibliography is arranged according to the abbreviations used in the notes to the historical essay and the annotations appended to the documents.

Each document is preceded by a short introduction which provides the reader with background information and sets the despatch in its relevant historical setting. At times, the reader is referred to further letters and documents which are not included in the present volume. Annotations to the documents add relevant clarifications or biographical information. The historical essay and the introductions and annotations to the documents have been expertly translated by Mr. Edward Levin, to whom I am most grateful for his considerable efforts. Responsibility for the accuracy of quotations and information in the annotations, of course, rests with the author.

The 135 documents included in this volume contain much important information on Palesine and its inhabitants from the 1840s until the closure of the consulate after the outbreak of World War I. They form an important historical source which contributes to a better understanding of the political, economic and social processes of nineteenth-century Palestine. Above all, these documents testify to the beneficial contribution of the British consuls to events in Palestine by means of their influence, aid and guidance. They are also evidence of the great efforts expended by the consuls in representing the interests of a world power which evinced much interest in the Holy Land and persisted in its efforts to enhance its status and influence in Palestine.

*

An expression of gratitude is in order to the many persons involved in this volume, from its planning stage until publication. I should first like to thank my friend and colleague Prof. Yehoshua Ben-Arieh, presently Rector of the Hebrew University of Jerusalem and former Head of the Institute for Research of Eretz Israel at Yad Izhak Ben-Zvi, from whose advice, initiative and support I have benefited from the very outset of the project until its completion. My thanks, too, to Prof. Ephraim Stern, the incumbent Head of the Institute, who helped to bring this project to fruition during its final stages.

I owe a great debt of gratitude to Mr. Yohai Goell, director of the library of Yad Izhak Ben-Zvi and coordinator of its English publications, who carefully edited the manuscript, unstintingly sought to solve questions of content or of bibliographical notation, suggested emendations to the translation wherever necessary, and rendered me invaluable help throughout the entire process of editing and producing the volume. My thanks to the staff of the Yad Izhak Ben-Zvi Library for their support of my efforts to prepare the manuscript and their important bibliographical help.

I express my sincere gratitude to Mr. Jan Kevlin, Senior Copyright Office at Her Majesty's Stationery Office, who graciously granted permission to publish the documents which are in the possession of the Public Record Office, thus making them accessible to readers everywhere interested in the history of the Holy Land and its inhabitants.

Last, but definitely not least, my heartfelt thanks to Yad Izhak Ben-Zvi — first and foremost to Director Dr. Zvi Zameret and Deputy Director Mrs. Channah Biderman, who spared no efforts and undertook a considerable financial obligation to make this volume possible. Dr. Zameret and Mrs. Biderman, who have been involved in all stages of this project, encouraged me to continue in my work and devoted much effort to bring it to a successful conclusion.

Many thanks to the Magnes Press of the Hebrew University of Jerusalem, which has joined Yad Izhak Ben-Zvi as co-publisher, and to its director, Mr. Dan

Benovici. To Mr. Hananel Goldberg, who capably handled the technical aspects of seeing the volume through the press, my sincere thanks.

It would be impossible to name all of my friends and colleagues from whose advice and comments I have benefited during the various stages of work on the volume, and with whom I consulted to solve several problems of fact. To all of them I express my sincerest gratitude.

Jerusalem, 1996 *Mordechai Eliav*

# THE BRITISH CONSULATE IN JERUSALEM

## 1838–1914

# Introduction

Great Britain was the first foreign Power to establish a consulate in Jerusalem, soon to be followed by others. Within a decade, the Holy Land hosted six consulates: that of Britain opened in 1839, Prussia in 1842 (later becoming the German Consulate); France and Sardinia, both in 1843, the United States in 1844 (for a very short period; its activity was renewed only in 1856), and Austria in 1849. Russia was the only Great Power to limit itself for the present to a vice-consulate in Jaffa, establishing its Jerusalem consulate only in 1858.

The opening of six consulates within such a short period of time would prove to be of great significance. The exalted and special status enjoyed by the Consuls, the representatives of the Powers, who vigorously defended the rights of their subjects and protégés and zealously demanded the punishment of those who harmed their charges, forced the authorities to bear in mind the fundamental change in the status of foreign subjects and religious minorities. The terms of the Capitulations agreements enabled the Consuls to attain positions of great influence, compelling the Ottoman governors in Jerusalem to treat them with respect and take their wishes into account.[1] The status of foreign subjects, thus, underwent a fundamental transformation, and Jerusalem became the main arena for the activity of the Consuls, who looked to the interests and spiritedly developed the influence of their countries, and sought to increase their political and commercial vantage in the region.

The authority and status of the Consuls rested on the Capitulations, the agreements which, from the sixteenth century, the Turkish authorities had made with various foreign powers: first with France and various Italian cities, then in 1580 with Britain, and, in the course of time, with most of the Powers.[2] These treaties

---

1  In 1859, Henry Bulwer, the British Ambassador to Constantinople, wrote about the commanding status of the Consuls: "Many of the foreign Consuls, including our own, have been in the habit of assuming the function of government, of dictating to the pashas arbitrarily the line of conduct to be pursued in internal affairs ... [all of which] has gone towards annihilating the power of the provincial Governors" (FO 78/1637), cited by Maoz, p. 25. The German Consul Friedrich Rosen, who had grown up in Jerusalem, wrote regarding the second half of the nineteenth century: "... for after God the Consuls were the highest persons in Palestine, even the Pasha was not quite so revered by the inhabitants" (F. Rosen, *Oriental Memoirs*, London 1930, p. 9). M. Busch, who visited the city several times, described the Consuls as "partners in the rule" [*Mitregenten*] (Busch, p. 313).

2  For the Capitulations, see: A. Overbeck, *Die Kapitulationen des Osmanischen Reiches*, Breslau 1917; N. Sousa, *The Capitulary Regime of Turkey: Its History, Origin and Nature*, Baltimore 1933; J.C. Hurewitz, *The Middle East and North African World Politics: A Documentary Record*, New Haven 1975, vol. I: *European Expansion, 1534–1914*.

entitled them to open consulates throughout the Ottoman Empire which would enjoy extraterritorial status and granted their subjects and protégés freedom of movement, trade, and settlement, the right to freely practice their religion, and exemption from military service and from most of the financial liabilities and taxes imposed on Ottoman subjects. The residences of these protected subjects also acquired extraterritorial status, police and soldiers being forbidden to enter their homes without the approval of the Consul and even then only in the presence of his representative. The Consul was authorized to deal with all aspects of the personal status of his protégés: registration of births and deaths, issuance of marriage and divorce certificates, and execution of wills and bequests. He was further empowered to adjudicate all civil and criminal claims of those under his protection. Only the consular courts could judge foreign subjects. They had the power to impose punishments, including imprisonment and even deportation, and their judgments were unconditionally honored by the authorities. Foreign subjects were denied only the right to purchase lands and real estate, until the enactment of the Land Law of 1867/8, when the Powers accepted the Ottoman demand that in these matters their citizens and protégés would be subject to the Turkish courts.

Although the Capitulations were intended to put an end to the maltreatment and persecution of foreign subjects, each Consul could only provide effective protection and ensure the implementation of agreements within his specific area of jurisdiction. Foreign subjects who resided where no consulate had been established were defenseless, remaining at the mercy of the local authorities and population. For centuries, the Powers evinced no interest in the establishment of consulates in Palestine, thereby preventing foreign subjects resident there from exercising their rights. Various Consular Agents (usually local residents) were active during this period, mainly in the coastal cities. Their authority, however, was restricted mainly to commercial affairs, until the period of Egyptian rule in Palestine (1831–1840) prompted the Powers to consider the establishment of consulates. The British took the lead, opening their consulate before Egypt relinquished its control of Palestine, while the other Powers took similar decisions only after the restoration of Ottoman rule.

The Egyptian occupation was a watershed in the history of Palestine. The period of Egyptian rule was marked by the initiation of comprehensive reforms in a neglected and backward country, suddenly placing Palestine in the forefront of international diplomacy. The European Powers 'rediscovered' the religious, political, and strategic importance of the Holy Land. They would now strive to establish a solid basis which would enable them to increase their influence in the land, whose sanctity to the three monotheistic religions turned it into a sensitive and important region within the bounds of the Ottoman Empire. The penetration of the Powers into the Holy Land brought in its wake competition over the role of patron of Christian interests in Palestine and for influential status throughout the Empire. France was the traditional defender of Catholics, while Russia served as patron of the Greek Orthodox community. As the Consuls successively arrived in Jerusalem, they primarily regarded themselves as the representatives of Christian interests. They extended their protection to the Christian minorities and encouraged the establishment of religious, educational, and charitable institutions for the benefit of their coreligionists.

The Jews of Palestine, a sizable number of whom were foreign subjects, were also profoundly affected by the establishment of the consulates. They, too, were afforded protection by the prestigious and influential Consuls. These new conditions presented the Jewish community with the prospect of increasing its numbers and more firmly establishing its undertakings. The importance and significance of this turning point for the advancement of the *Yishuv* (the Jewish community) has been discussed in various studies.[3]

From its establishment, the British Consulate actively sought to extend its protection to the Jewish community. In the absence of a Protestant community in Palestine, the Consulate strove to create a firm basis for its activity by making the Jews the central object of their first endeavours. Thus, they freely granted protection to every petitioner, at least in the first decades of the Consulate's existence, fostering a mutual interest in closer ties. As time passed, the number of Jews benefiting from English protection increased, in turn enhancing British prestige within the Yishuv.

## Establishment of the British Consular Service

Following the signing in June 1580 of the Treaty of Commerce between the Ottoman Empire and England, which granted the latter special privileges under the Capitulations equivalent to those enjoyed by France,[4] the Levant Company

---

3  See, inter alia, Eliav, *German Policy*, Introduction; idem, *Yishuv*, pp. 49–56; idem, *Austrian Protection*, Introduction; Hyamson, *British Consulate*, Introduction; A. Schölch, "Europa und Palästina," H. Meijcher and A. Schölch (eds.), *Die Palästinafrage 1917–1948*, Paderborn 1981, pp. 11–46; Blumberg, *Zion*, pp. 91–136; Parfitt, pp. 127 ff.; Tennenbaum, Consul.

4  The treaty included twenty two articles, or 'capitulations', defining the liberties afforded to English subjects in the Ottoman Empire, based upon the terms of alliance with France (1535). The treaty was ratified in May 1583, and was renewed and expanded in 1603. The final treaty of Capitulations was signed in September 1675 and remained in force until the outbreak of World War I. Over the course of time, however, it was expanded by successive renewals and additions. See: J.C. Hurewitz, ibid., pp. 8–10, 34–41; Wood, chap. I; Marlowe, pp. 13–16.

was established in 1583 and granted a monopoly of all trade with the Ottoman Empire.[5] For almost 240 years, the Company appointed all the commercial and diplomatic representatives — Consuls and Consular Agents — in the area under Ottoman rule in the Levant, mainly in cities along the Mediterranean coast. These Consular Agents were usually local merchants, whose sole remuneration was in the fees they collected. From the very outset of the Company's activity, it appointed the first two Consuls, whose numbers increased as time passed. The latter were British subjects who albeit received a small salary, but whose livelihood depended mainly upon their business dealings.

In 1823 it was proposed that each Consul receive a fixed salary from the public purse. This led Foreign Secretary George Canning to abrogate the Levant Company's authority to maintain and supervise consulates. Under the Consular Act of 1825 the Company was obligated to transfer to the Foreign Office the appointment and maintenance of the Consuls, which led to the liquidation of the Company.[6] The Act also decreed that British Consuls would no longer engage, either directly or indirectly, in commercial activity, mainly to prevent conflict of interest; they would instead receive a salary from the Foreign Office.[7] An independent Consular Department was established in the Foreign Office, headed by John Bidwell as Superintendent of the Consular Service.[8] It soon became clear, however, that the prohibition of private commercial activity was unenforceable. The Consuls' salaries did not suffice for their needs, and the Consular Department took no action to ensure compliance with the interdiction. The main change, therefore, consisted of placing the Consuls under the supervision of the Foreign Office and turning them into civil servants. The Consular Department's entire staff consisted of four officials, and it was incapable of coping with the amount of work it was assigned. Clear criteria regarding the pay scale of the Consuls were not established, and despite being officially forbidden to engage in commercial activity, this provided the bulk of their income.

When Lord Palmerston was appointed Foreign Secretary in 1831, he initiated a sweeping reform of the Consular Service. He decided to decrease the number of Consuls, and to further cut their already low salaries. To offset these economy

---

5 The first Charter of the Levant Company had already been signed on 11 September 1581, but the Company started its activities only in 1583. For the history of the Levant Company, see: Wood.
6 Wood, p. 199.
7 Platt, *Finance*, p. 384; Bourne, pp. 448–450.
8 John Bidwell (1798–1853) was the first Senior Clerk of the Foreign Office until 1851, and served as Superintendent of the Consular Service until 1838. He was then succeeded by John Backhouse, the Permanent Under-Secretary of State, 1827–1842. (See Platt, *Cinderella Service*, p. 58, who describes Bidwell as "a capable man of wide experience.")

measures, the prohibition against private business activity was formally cancelled. These reforms patently impaired the efficiency of the Consular Service.[9] Moreover, Palmerston was also of the opinion that the post of Consul did not require any special training or experience, since the brief of the Consul was limited to representing the commercial interests of England. The denigrating attitude reflected in Palmerston's steps in 1831–32 would change within a few years, when the Foreign Secretary became convinced of the importance of the Consular Service, not only for business interests, but also for the enhancement of Britain's political stature throughout the world.

Palmerston expressed great displeasure at the signing of a mutual defense treaty between Russia and the Ottoman Empire at Unkiar-Skelessi in 1833. Apprehensive of Russian intentions, the British and the French lodged forceful protests against the strategic advantages the treaty afforded Russia. After several years of negotiations and 'explanations' by the Turks, an additional commercial pact between Britain and the Ottoman Empire was concluded on 16 August 1838 in Balta-Liman. This agreement in effect granted Britain primacy in the Ottoman Empire's foreign trade.[10] England's growing commercial interests, coupled with its anti-Russian policy and undeclared competition with France, motivated Palmerston to strengthen the consular service in the Levant and increase the number of consulates. The establishment of additional consulates was dictated primarily by England's commercial interests in the region. Salaries, however, remained low, and therefore limitations were not imposed on commercial activity by Consuls seeking to augment their income. After some time, however, the Foreign Office exhibited a greater degree of flexibility regarding salaries, even increasing them in several important diplomatic posts, but made the increase conditional upon a renewed prohibition of private commercial activity. In 1836, fourteen British Consuls served in the Ottoman Empire, their number rising to twenty five by 1842, including seven in Syria and Palestine.[11] The increase in the number of consulates and consular agencies reflected Palmerston's policy of developing commercial ties and increasing the English diplomatic presence as a means of enhancing British influence, the first step toward closer political cooperation with the Sublime Porte.

The Foreign Office maintained its tight-fisted policy with regard to consular salaries until the late 1850s, even though its senior officials were aware of the fact that a Consul could not live solely on his salary. Most Consuls were still 'amateur

9 Bourne, p. 449; Platt, *Finance*, p. 384. ("Denials of permisses to trade became rather the exception than the rule.")
10 Temperley, pp. 31–39; Webster, II, pp. 548–557; Platt, *Finance*, pp. 181 ff.; Horn-Elbaum, pp. 9–15.
11 Horn-Elbaum, p. 90.

diplomats', appointed on the basis of personal ties. No prior training or experience were required of British Consuls, unlike the case with the consular services of other Powers which demanded professional training and whose important consulates in the Ottoman Empire were staffed exclusively by experienced diplomats, very often fluent in the languages spoken in the region.[12]

Until the 1860s, transfers from one post to another were rare, generally coming at the initiative of the Consul himself or as a means to solve problems that had arisen in the Consul's current posting; accordingly, there were Consuls who served for many years at the same consulate.[13] This undoubtedly had its advantages, for the experience gained over the course of years enhanced the Consul's judgment and provided him with a deeper understanding of the problems facing the population which he served, even leading him to identify with the local populace. As the years passed, he also succeeded in developing good relations with the local Ottoman authorities. The reports of a veteran Consul were also considered more attentively in the Foreign Office, which placed greater value on his opinions and proposals.

Only in 1858 were Consuls forbidden to engage in commercial activity, accompanied by some improvement in their salaries. The advance, however, was slow and insufficient; the Consuls continued to complain about their livelihood, and even had difficulty in financing home visits while on leave.[14] Over the course of years various commissions were appointed to examine the Consular Service in the Levant, the most important of which being the 'Select Committee on Diplomatic and Consular Services' established in 1870 and headed by C.M. Kennedy of the Foreign Office. Assigned the task of examining the conduct and status of the Consuls, the Committee warned of the inappropriate quality of these diplomatic representatives, their meagre salaries, and the need for a general reform of the Service.

---

12  Tilley & Gasellee, pp. 232–235; Jack, p. 38. In the early 1850s, various salaries (per annum) were as follows: Beirut — £500; Jerusalem — £550; Damascus — £600; Smyrna — £750; Jaffa — £300; Dardanelles — £300 (Platt, *Cinderella Service*, p. 158).

13  Three Consuls each served 27 years in a single location: Eldridge (Beirut); Cumberbatch (Smyrna); and Moore (Jerusalem). Rogers served 24 years in Cairo, and Finn, 17 years in Jerusalem (see: Iseminger, pp. 302–305).

14  Consuls were entitled to only one month's leave at full pay per year. In 1870 N.T. Moore, the Consul in Jerusalem, complained that the Consul's salary was reduced by one half if he absented himself from his post on leave (i.e. for more than one month), and applied for modification of this rule. He added: "Under the present rule the possibility of such a visit becomes so restricted that few can avail themselves, except at very wide intervals, of this privilege" (cited by Iseminger, p. 304). Consul-General Eldridge in Beirut had not been back to England for ten years (ibid., p. 305). Cumberbatch wrote, after 27 years in service: "I have never absented myself from my post, as I could not sustain the loss" (ibid.).

A decision on reorganization, however, was not taken until 1877, when a separate Consular Service for the Levant was established, at which time new rules were laid down: only native-born Britons could be appointed after a competitive examination of the candidates, who also underwent suitable professional training and attained some proficiency in the relevant languages. The candidates who successfully passed this course were first assigned to junior posts at the various consulates, and only afterwards would be promoted to Vice-Consul or Consul. Salaries were gradually raised and the period of service in any one location was shortened, the Consuls being rotated from one posting to another, but the pace of their advancement remained slow.[15] The newly-professional Consular Service existed as a separate entity until World War I.

## Establishment of the Consulate in Jerusalem

One of the very first to suggest the establishment of a British Consulate in Jerusalem, if not the originator of the idea, was W.B. Lewis, a missionary who had spent some time in Palestine in 1823, when he witnessed the unsuccessful attempts by the first missionaries to establish a foothold in the city and undertake missionary activity among its Jewish residents. They encountered many difficulties in their endeavours, both from the Turkish authorities and from the indigenous Christian communities, who were clearly hostile to the Protestant missionaries. Lewis hoped that a British Consulate in the Holy City would provide protection for the mission, and might obtain for the missionaries the same rights enjoyed by the Catholic community.[16]

A few months later, the 'London Society for Promoting Christianity Amongst the Jews' sent a physician, Dr. George Dalton, to the Holy Land to open a missionary station in Jerusalem. The Society, founded in 1809 for the purpose, as its name implied, of gaining Jewish converts to Christianity, regarded the Holy Land as its prime target. Although it had begun its activity in London, in aptly-named 'Palestine Place', and during the course of the nineteenth century had developed an extensive missionary network throughout Europe, the Jewish *Yishuv* in Palestine remained the most important arena for its activity, to which end it spared no means or efforts.

The dispatch of Dalton constituted the Society's first attempt to establish a

---

15 N.T. Moore was promoted to Consul-General in Tripoli only after 27 years of service in Jerusalem.

16 *Jewish Expositor* (= *JE*) 1824, pp. 379–383; 1825, p. 100; 1826, p. 25; Gidney, *London Society*, pp. 118–119.

permanent station in Jerusalem. Dalton, however, first spent some time in the cities of Lebanon, coming to Jerusalem only on 26 December 1825. He soon fell ill and died there on the twenty-fifth of the following month. During his short stay in the country, he urged the Society to encourage the opening of a consulate in Jerusalem. He explained that though there was no economic justification for the establishment of a British diplomatic presence in the city, there were a considerable number of European subjects among the Jews, and travelers also were in need of protection; furthermore, a consulate would be able to advance the work of the mission and to assist it in overcoming the open hostility it encountered.[17]

His call for action went unheeded. Conditions were not yet ripe for the establishment of a consulate in Jerusalem, and no one gave the proposal serious consideration.

Beginning in 1831, however, conditions changed radically. The revolt of Muhammad Ali against the Turks resulted in his conquest of Palestine and the imposition of Egyptian rule for nine years. The reforms that Muhammad Ali instituted significantly changed the status of the Christian and Jewish minorities, freeing them from the maltreatment and humiliations they had suffered at the hands of the Ottoman authorities and the local population. The Egyptians sought to show the Christian Powers that they were considerably more tolerant than the Turks, and so, for the first time, Palestine was opened to Europeans. Thus the Powers were able to begin their activity in the Holy Land, and the way was paved for the establishment of diplomatic missions.

John William Perry Farren, the Consul-General in Damascus, was the first British diplomat to propose the appointment of a British representative in Jerusalem. Following a visit to Jerusalem to settle various disputes, he reached the conclusion that the city was in need of a Vice-Consul, and put forth the arguments in favour of such a proposal on 20 November 1834 in a despatch to the Foreign Secretary.[18] Farren even put forth his own candidate, who in practice he had already appointed — a local Armenian by the name of Merad. Farren's suggestion was received with reservations by the Foreign Office, especially since he himself was not a favourite of senior Foreign Office officials.[19] The Foreign Secretary

---

17  Tibawi, pp. 12–13; Gidney, *London Society*, pp. 119–121; *JE* 1826, p. 233.
18  FO 78/243. Farren pointed out that the number of British travellers in Palestine was constantly increasing, and that they had no one to whom they could turn in case of emergency. The interests of British residents and travellers, and those of British policy, made necessary the appointment of a Consular Agent in Jerusalem, "the chief and largest city in the extreme south of Syria." The details leading up to the establishment of the Consulate in Jerusalem have been thoroughly described by Vereté, pp. 316–345. For Farren's visit to Jerusalem, see: *JE* 1833, pp. 290–292.
19  For the negative attitude toward Farren, who was also suspected of taking bribes, see: Vereté, p. 321, and p. 325, n. 2.

decided to consult with Colonel Patrick Campbell, the Consul-General in Egypt, who had been appointed in 1833 as the senior British representative in all the countries conquered by the Egyptians. Farren, who was Campbell's subordinate, went over his superior's head, and did not even discuss with him the matter of Merad's appointment. In the meantime, Permanent Under-Secretary of State John Backhouse reprimanded Farren for appointing Merad without prior approval; in the same letter, he also cast doubt on the necessity of a Vice-Consul in Jerusalem.

In a quite tardy response to the Foreign Office, Campbell replied that such an appointment in Jerusalem would be superfluous, and Britain's needs could be met by the Vice-Consul in Jaffa, whom he had appointed two years earlier.[20] Palmerston had meanwhile returned to the post of Foreign Secretary; he did not regard the question of Jerusalem to be a matter of any urgency. In the spring of 1836 Campbell conducted a tour of Palestine and Syria in order to gain firsthand knowledge of their problems. Prior to his visit, he had circulated a questionnaire among the British representatives throughout Syria, in which he asked, inter alia, where it was desirable for additional Consular Agents to be appointed. Niven Moore, who had begun serving as Consul in Beirut the previous year, included Jerusalem in his reply.[21] He also put forth the name of a candidate for the post, the missionary John Nicolayson, who was resident in Jerusalem, and whom he thought would make an excellent British representative.[22] Campbell, however, immediately rejected this proposal: "The nomination of a Missionary to be Vice-Consul would, I think, be most objectionable in every point of view."[23]

Farren did not abandon this issue, despite the reprimand he received for his hasty appointment. In a letter of 18 September 1836 to Palmerston, he stressed the firmly entrenched position of Russia and France in the Holy Land as the respective defenders of the interests of the Greek Orthodox and Catholic communities. Farren added that he regretted that Merad's appointment had not been confirmed,

20  16 May 1835, FO 78I260.
21  FO 78/283. In reply to Question No. 33 ("Where you may deem it requisite that an Agent should be appointed with the reasons for such necessity?"), Moore wrote: "To Tyre, Sidon and Acre I would add Jerusalem as a place where a Consular Agent might advantageously be placed. The number of British Travellers visiting that city is considerable. Jerusalem is moreover a garrison of considerable importance and intelligence from there would frequently prove to be be useful and interesting."
22  "If Mr. Nicolayson would accept the appointment of Consular Agent, I know of no person better qualified for the office. He is a most respectable man, and to great intelligence adds the further qualification of a knowledge of the Arabic language" (ibid.). For Nicolayson, see below, Document No. 1, n. 3.
23  Campbell included the answers to the questionnaire in his despatch of 31 July 1836 to Palmerston (FO 78/283).

since the latter was the most qualified for the post, and that the establishment of a British representation in Jerusalem was most essential.[24]

Palmerston was now partial to the recommendation, which was supported by Moore, despite Campbell's rejection of it a year previously. On 6 November 1836 he instructed Backhouse, who also had opposed the proposal, to inform Campbell of the desirability of establishing a consulate in Jerusalem, and to seek a suitable candidate.[25] The latter undoubtedly was surprised by Palmerston's directive. Due to the difficulty he encountered in finding a suitable candidate, more than nine months were to pass before he replied to the Foreign Secretary; it was only by chance that an acceptable nominee was found, based on the recommendation of Consul Moore in Beirut.[26]

When Moore had come to Beirut, he was supposed to serve exclusively as Consul, with no involvement in private commercial ventures. After some time, however, he realized that he could improve his financial condition by entering into a business partnership in Beirut or in England. While examining potential under-takings, he met W.T. Young, who had been in the region since late 1835, visiting various sites in Syria and Palestine, apparently to explore commercial possibilities. During his travels he had met with Nicolayson in Jerusalem and with Campbell, who was in Syria at the time. Moore offered Young a partnership and commercial ties. He then conceived of proposing Young for the post of Vice-Consul at Jerusalem, probably believing that such an appointment was quite likely to advance their joint trade ventures. He therefore advised Young to offer his candidacy for the position if he were interested.

Young, who in the meantime had returned to London, gladly agreed to this proposal, and on 27 June 1837 wrote to Campbell offering his candidacy for the post. Campbell was only too happy to accept this offer, and so informed Young in a letter dated 5 August 1837. Young now applied directly to the Foreign Secretary. Campbell, at the same time, also addressed himself to Palmerston, formally proposing Young for the post in Jerusalem, apparently without knowledge of Young's direct communication with the Foreign Secretary.[27] Campbell's letter

---

24  "I very much regret that your Lordship did not confirm my appointment of Mr. Merad to Consular Agent at Jerusalem for I am convinced that ... [an Agency] would have a favourable tendency towards our influence and certainly no individual in the country could be better calculated to support those subjects than Mr. Merad" (FO 78/292).

25  "Request him to select a person; query what pay" (FO 78/295). Meanwhile Campbell had sent another despatch, opposing an appointment in Jerusalem (7 October 1836, FO 78/295), not knowing of Palmerston's decision to establish an Agency in the city. On 29 November 1836, Bidwell transmitted Palmerston's instructions to Campbell (FO 78/295).

26  For Niven Moore, see below, Document No. 1, n. 2.

27  See below, Document No. 1; Vereté, pp. 337–339. All the correspondence appears in FO 78/322.

also attests to a change of opinion by the Consul-General, who now distinctly supported the establishment of a consulate in Jerusalem.

The proposal was accepted by the Foreign Secretary, and the Ambassador in Constantinople was instructed to apply to the Sublime Porte for a firman authorizing the appointment of a British Vice-Consul in Jerusalem.[28] The approval of the the Turkish authorities proved to be difficult to obtain, however. The Sultan only confirmed the firman in June 1838, thus removing the last obstacle hindering the creation of the new post. On 19 September 1838 Palmerston officially informed Young of his appointment as Vice-Consul "in Palestine," and that he would be subordinate to Campbell. He would be paid a salary of £300 per annum, and would be permitted to engage in private commercial enterprises, as Young himself had requested in his first letter to the Foreign Secretary. That same day Young was sent instructions emphasizing the importance of commercial ties and his role in the fostering of amicable sentiments towards Great Britain.[29] These instructions were augmented by directives from Campbell in his letter of 21 November 1838 to Young, who was already in Egypt. After delineating Young's area of jurisdiction, from Jaffa to Sidon, with authority over all the Consular Agents in the ports along the coast, Campbell stressed that "many of the Consuls-General in Alexandria will request you to afford protection to the numerous subjects of their Country of the Hebrew persuasion resident there... and you are therefore authorized to afford such protection if demanded," in accordance with the Capitulations, as Young was at the present "the only European Consul in Jerusalem."[30]

This was the first time that the extension of protection to the Jews in Palestine was specified as one of the duties of the Vice-Consul at Jerusalem. This initiative was taken by Campbell, because the instructions of the Foreign Office made no mention of Jews. It may be assumed that Campbell's opinion on the matter directly influenced the well-known directive by J. Bidwell, in the name of the Foreign Secretary, to the effect "that it will be a part of your duty as British Vice-Consul at Jerusalem to afford Protection to the Jews generally."[31]

This summary description of the course of events would not be complete without an examination of what lay behind Palmerston's decision in late 1836 to establish a consulate in Jerusalem, a city not regarded as possessing any economic

---

28  Palmerston to Ponsonby, 11 November 1837, FO 78/300; Bidwell to Campbell, 18 November 1837, FO 78/322. See below, Document No. 1, n. 6.
29  Documents 2, 3.
30  Hyamson, *British Consulate*, Encl. to No. 3, Campbell to Palmerston, 10 December 1838, FO 78/344.
31  Ibid., No. 2, 31 January 1839.

importance, and at a time when Great Britain had as yet on the whole shown no specific interest in Palestine.

Vereté correctly concludes, on the basis of a thorough and precise study, that Palmerston was motivated primarily by political considerations.[32] Palmerston, who shaped Britain's foreign policy during the 1830s and served as Foreign Secretary throughout the entire period (except for four months in late 1834-early 1835), adopted a policy aimed, first and foremost, at preserving the integrity of the Ottoman Empire, England's traditional ally, and which was blatantly anti-Russian, regarding the empire of the Tsars as England's most dangerous rival.[33] Accordingly, he addressed the need to curb the growing influence of Russia, which had been growing stronger in the region, as the patron of the Greek Orthodox community, the largest of the Christian sects in Palestine in general, and in Jerusalem in particular. In their latest letters, Farren and Moore had also warned of increasing Russian penetration, but at the same time pointed to the military and strategic importance of Jerusalem, which necessitated a British presence in the city to observe and report on the course of events. Palmerston was displeased by, and even hostile to the conquests of Muhammad Ali and his attempts to deal a fatal blow to the Ottoman Empire. This, together with his fear of a Russian-Egyptian alliance, led to Palmerston's firm resolve to extend military aid to the weak Ottoman Empire and to put an end to the Egyptian conquest, when circumstances permitted.[34] To further these goals, he sought to strengthen the network of consulates throughout the Empire, and especially in Syria, of which Palestine formed the southern section. Palmerston accordingly felt that his policy would be served by the establishment of a consulate in Jerusalem. In addition to his concern over growing Russian influence in the region, Palmerston was also troubled by the increased activity of France as defender of the Catholics, and as the only Power that supported Muhammad Ali and provided the Egyptian ruler with valuable diplomatic assistance. This French policy was also damaging to the long-standing Anglo-French friendship, and aroused suspicions regarding France's intentions in the Middle East. The amicable relationship between the two European states was replaced by surreptitious competition for primacy in the East and for the ad-

---

32  Vereté, pp. 328–333.
33  J. Ponsonby, who in 1832 took up his post as the new Ambassador to Constantinople, regarded his main mission as the strengthening of the Ottoman Empire and curbing the inroads made by Russia, which he viewed as highly menacing. His influence was considerable. In 1839–41, however, he disagreed with Palmerston's policy and constantly opposed him, even undermining the latter's actions. He was replaced in 1842 by Sir Stratford Canning.
34  For Palmerston's policy during the Egyptian conquest, see: M.S. Anderson, *The Eastern Question*, New York 1966, chap. IV; Temperley, pp. 89 ff.; Webster, pp. 594 ff.

vancement of each country's economic interests. The cooling of relations between Britain and France caused Palmerston to restrain his anti-Russian policy, and paved the way for Anglo-Russian cooperation to put an end to the Egyptian occupation.

As noted above, the Jews do not figure in any of the correspondence preceding Palmerston's decision, nor do they play any role in the contacts concerning Young's appointment, including the instructions he received from the Foreign Office and from Campbell before assuming office. In much of the historiography and the scholarly literature, however, it is argued that the Jewish question was the central motive that led to the decision to establish the Consulate.[35]

The first document supporting this hypothesis is the diary entry for 29 September 1838 by Lord Ashley, later the Earl of Shaftesbury,[36] regarding his meeting with Young before the latter set out to assume his post.[37] This diary notation tends to indicate that Ashley played a significant role in the appointment of the Vice-Consul at Jerusalem. This entry, however, was made some two years after the decision to establish the Consulate, and approximately a year after Young's candidacy was raised. The relatively long period of time that elapsed between the events and the written account makes it difficult to accept the conclusion that Ashley was party to the decision, or that there was any connection to the Jewish issue.[38] Ashley's relationship with the London Society had already begun in 1835, and he may well

---

35  See, inter alia: N. Sokolow, *History of Zionism*, London 1919, vol. I, chap. 23; Hyamson, *British Projects*, 1917; idem, *British Projects*, 1918, pp. 138–143; idem, *Palestine*; idem, *British Consulate*, Introduction, p. xxxiii; Tuchman, chap. X. Additional books and articles are listed by Vereté, p. 318, n. 2. Vereté consistently rejects this interpretation. See also: Tennenbaum, Consulate, pp. 84–85; Friedman, Palmerston.

36  Anthony Ashley Cooper (1801–1885), from 1851 the seventh Earl of Shaftesbury, a prominent statesman and philanthropist, was a highly influential parliamentarian. He was very active in missionary work, serving for 37 years as president of the London Society (1848–1885). His contacts with the Society had antedated his presidency; in 1835 he became its vice-president. He was a fervent supporter of the Restoration of the Jews to Palestine and the revival of the Jewish People on its land. In June 1830 he married Emily Cowper; her mother was the intimate friend of Palmerston for thirty years and was to become his second wife in 1839 (Bourne, pp. 200–201). See the three-volume biography by Hodder.

37  "Took leave this morning of Young, who has just been appointed Her Majesty's Vice-Consul at *Jerusalem*! ... If this is duly considered, what a wonderful event is this! The ancient city of the people of God is about to resume a place among the nations, and England the first of Gentile Kingdoms that ceases 'to tread her down' ... I shall always, at any rate, remember that God put it into my heart to conceive the plan for his Honour, gave me influence to prevail with Palmerston, and provided a man for the situation" (Hodder, I, p. 233). Ashley began his diary in September 1838 "with extreme care" (ibid., p. 230).

38  Vereté, pp. 335–336, but see: Morgenstern, Perushim, p. 130, n. 97, who contests Vereté's views. See also: Friedman, Palmerston, pp. 23–24; idem, British Schemes, pp. 42–44; Lipman, *Americans*, p. 13.

have utilized his family ties with Palmerston to discuss at a very early stage with the Foreign Secretary the need to establish a consulate in Jerusalem. Ashley may have played some part in Palmerston's decision, but it cannot be determined whether he served as the missionary society's agent to further its request to found a church in Jerusalem and to establish a consulate there to aid the Society in its work. This hypothesis remains, therefore, unproven.[39] On the other hand, only in 1839 did Ashley begin to formulate his views on the Jewish question and the plans for their Return to Zion, and especially after the London conference in July 1840.[40] During this period he met frequently with Palmerston, to whom he revealed his views and plans regarding the Return to Zion and the restoration of the Jewish People to its ancestral homeland.[41] These conversations, which were preceded by Campbell's proposal, apparently convinced Palmerston that granting protection to the Jews in the Holy Land and the proposals for the Restoration of the Jews were likely to further British interests. To this were added the humanitarian considerations involved in the extension of aid to persecuted Jews.[42] This does not imply that Palmerston intended to make cynical use of the Jewish question for purely political ends, but rather that he truly sought to treat the Jews kindly and to aid them in returning to their land. The Jewish question, therefore, supplemented

39  Tibawi, pp. 33–34. This opinion is rejected by Vereté, p. 319.
40  In January 1839 Ashley published a review of Lindsay's *Letters from Egypt, Edom and the Holy Land*, London 1838. He noted in his diary: "At the time that I undertook the article, I knew nothing of the Jewish Question save and except the appointment of a Vice-Consul" (Hodder, I, p. 242; see also Tuchman, p. 123). After the London Conference, Ashley believed that the time was ripe for the fulfillment of the prophecies on the Return of the Jews to Palestine, and thought that it was now possible to establish an Anglican Bishopric in Jerusalem (Hodder, II, pp. 310, 364 ff.). On 1 August 1840, after dining with Palmerston, he wrote in his diary: "Palmerston has been chosen by God to be an instrument of good to this ancient people and to recognise their rights without believing [in] their destiny. And it seems he will yet do more. But though the motive be kind, it is not sound. I am forced to argue politically, financially, commercially; these considerations strike him home" (ibid., p. 310).
41  See the entries in Ashley's diary (Hodder, II, pp. 310–315). Ashley believed that if the five Powers would be "induced to guarantee the security of life and possessions to the Hebrew race, they would now flow back in rapidly augmenting numbers" (ibid., p. 310, 24 July 1840). See also: Document 5, n. 2. On 25 September 1840, Ashley sent Palmerston a 'Memorandum on the Return of the Jews to Palestine', "which may refresh his memory and exist as a record both of the suggestion and the character of it" (full text: ibid., pp. 313–315; Hyamson, *British Consulate*, II, pp. lxxi–lxxxiii). In 1854 Ashley returned to his project, asking the Foreign Secretary, Lord Clarendon, to use his influence, "that the Sultan should be moved to issue a firman granting to the Jewish people power to hold land ... [Palestine] is a country without a nation, and God now ... directs us to a nation without a country" (Hodder, II, p. 478).
42  Charles Webster, Palmerston's biographer, states: "Palmerston seems to have had a genuine desire to protect the Jews in Palestine for humanitarian reasons as well for the advantage which he thought might thus be obtained both for the Sultan and for Britain" (Webster, p. 761).

the political considerations which motivated the Foreign Secretary to establish a consulate in Jerusalem.[43] Palmerston adopted these proposals, and instructed the Ambassador in Constantinople, who was not an enthusiastic supporter of the project, to recommend them to the Sultan, stressing the benefit that was likely to accrue from them to the Ottoman Empire.[44] These overtures were not crowned with success and were soon abandoned by Palmerston, who nonetheless did not rescind his directives that the Vice-Consul extend his protection to the entire Jewish community. Palmerston was undoubtedly aware of the significant advantage to be gained by Great Britain from extending protection to all the Jews in the Holy Land, who would thus provide it with a firm basis, there being no Protestant community in Palestine.

Just as the Jewish factor was not influential when the decision was taken to establish a consulate in Jerusalem, it similarly cannot be assumed that the request of the mission was of significant consequence in Palmerston's decision. The London Society had no contact with the Foreign Secretary regarding the opening of a consulate, even though it looked to such a step to provide protection and aid to the mission. The files pertaining to this period contain only the London Society's request to establish a church in Jerusalem, which was granted by Palmerston (see below). Nor may it be assumed that Palmerston, the realist and rationalist, would have accepted the theological and eschatological arguments,[45] that the Return to Zion and the Redemption of Israel constituted a necessary precondition to the final phase in which they would accept the Christian faith in anticipation of the Second Advent of Christ and the Millennium. Nevertheless, the missionary society would later claim credit for the establishment of the Jerusalem Consulate.[46]

---

43  Even Ashley confesses in his diary: "The growing interest manifested for these regions and the confluence of British travellers and strangers from all parts of the world have recently induced the Secretary of State for Foreign Affairs to station there a representative of our Sovereign in the person of a Vice Consul" (Hodder, I, pp. 240–241).

44  On 24 August 1840 Ashley wrote in his diary: "Palmerston tells me that he has already written to Lord Ponsonby to direct him to open an intercourse with Reshid Pasha at Constantinople respecting protection and encouragement to the Jews" (Hodder, II, p. 311). Ponsonby was instructed to point out to the Ottoman potentate that the plan would be "highly advantageous to the Sultan," but the British diplomat gave this initiative little support, and the Sublime Porte did not respond (Webster, pp. 762–763). Temperley speaks of the "immovable obstinacy of the Porte" (p. 444). See also: Friedman, British Schemes, pp. 57–59.

45  "Palmerston was not a man to be moved by any mystical ideas about the future of Palestine" (Webster, p. 763).

46  "The missionaries were the main promoters of the project of the consulate" (Tibawi, p. 34; Blumberg, Zion, pp. 37–39). "Efforts by missionaries to get the appointment of an English Consul were crowned with success so as to ensure safety and freedom to the establishment of the Mission" (Gidney, Sites, p. 64).

In the final reckoning, neither the Jewish question nor the aspirations of the London Missionary Society played a definitive role in the decision to establish a consulate in Jerusalem; rather it was Palmerston's political and pragmatic considerations that decided the issue.[47]

## The Consulate over the Course of Time

During the seventy five years of its existence (April 1839–November 1914), the Consulate in Jerusalem was staffed by eight Consuls, one of whom served for twenty seven years, while the last held the post for only three months. Personal connections were instrumental in the appointment of the first two Consuls, who lacked prior diplomatic experience and served only in Jerusalem. All the others were professional diplomats, serving in a consular capacity in other postings both before and after their term in Jerusalem.[48]

The terms in office of the Consuls were as follows: W.T. Young — 1839–1845; J. Finn — 1846–1863; N.T. Moore — 1863–1890; J. Dickson — 1890–1906; E.C. Blech — 1906–1909; H.E. Satow — 1909–1912; P.J C. McGregor — 1912–1914; W. Hough — 1914. Dickson was the only one to die in office, and was buried in Jerusalem.

### Consular Jurisdiction

Changes occurred in the jurisdiction of the Consulate during the period of its activity. Young, who was initially appointed Vice-Consul before his promotion to Consul in 1841, was responsible for "Jerusalem and Palestine," with his jurisdiction extending to Sidon in Lebanon, and holding authority over the Consular Agents in the coastal cities.[49] As long as Syria and Palestine were under Egyptian rule, Young was subordinate to the Consul-General in Alexandria. Beginning in 1840, the Consul-General in Beirut became the senior British representative in the region, and for some years the Consul in Jerusalem was under his authority. As time passed, however, Jerusalem was granted the status of an independent 'political' consulate, authorised to maintain direct contact with the Ambassador at Constan-

---

47  For the establishment of the Consulate as a counterbalance to Russian and French expansionist tendencies in the region, see: Vereté, p. 334; Schölch, p. 50; Horn-Elbaum, pp. 298–302; Friedman, Palmerston, p. 28; Jack, p. 42; Barclay, p. 602.

48  See below for biographical details of the Consuls.

49  Campbell to Young, 21 November 1838, FO 78/368, copied in Hyamson, *British Consulate*, Encl. to No. 3; Campbell to Palmerston, 10 December 1838, FO 78/344.

tinople and with the Foreign Office in London, so its subordination to Beirut became a mere formality.

The area of its jurisdiction, however, did not change until the 1860s. Finn notes in his memoirs that his jurisdiction "embraced the whole of Palestine, from Egypt to the Lebanon," and in another version: "from the northern boundary of the Vice-Consulate of Saida, that is to say the river Damoor, to the Egyptian frontier on the South, and from the Mediterranean on the West to the river Jordan on the East."[50]

The extensive scope of the Consulate's jurisdiction aroused the displeasure of the Turks, who were highly suspicious of increasing Western presence in Palestine which, they feared, was possibly intent on turning the Holy Land into a Christian state. Accordingly, the Ottoman authorities demanded that the bounds of the Consulate's authority be changed to correspond with the administrative division of the region, i.e., the various Pashaliks. Northern Palestine, including the consular agencies in the coastal cities in the region, was consequently placed under the authority of the Consulate-General in Beirut, while the jurisdiction of the British Consulate in Jerusalem was restricted to the boundaries of the independent Sanjak of Jerusalem, like the other consulates.[51]

The frequent changes made by the Turkish authorities in the administrative status of the Jerusalem district also are indicative of their apprehensions.[52] All attempts by the representatives of the various Powers to expand the jurisdictions of their consulates at Jerusalem to include all of Palestine proved fruitless. The Ottoman Government clearly and consistently refused their request; from the 1880s onward, they also suspected that a Jewish national question was evolving and found it expedient to maintain the administrative division of the country, even though this greatly hindered the work of the consulates, mainly due to their detachment from northern Palestine. Consequently, no change took place in the jurisdiction of the British Consulate at Jerusalem until it was closed down in 1914.

---

50  Finn, J., *Stirring Times*, I, pp. 90, 267. The Consul's wife states: "His district included half of Lebanon, all Palestine as far south as the Egyptian boundary and as far eastwards as any English people chose to go" (Finn, E., *Reminiscences*, p. 61).

51  "The Consulate is now curtailed to the dimension of the Pasha's jurisdiction, as then were those of the other European countries" (Finn, J., *Stirring Times*, I, p. 268 n.). Upon Niven Moore's promotion to Consul-General at Beirut, Finn received a despatch from the Foreign Office stating: "I have to instruct you to obey any orders which you may receive from that office" (25 February 1854, FO 78/1024). The Agents at Soor [Tyre], Saida, Acre, and Haifa were concurrently subordinated to Beirut.

52  See Introduction to Document No. 62.

## Consular Status

The Consuls enjoyed superior status in Jerusalem. The first Consuls, especially Young, were received with some hostility by the Governor of Jerusalem, who often placed obstacles in their path. From the early 1850s, however, especially following the Crimean War, their standing improved, with a corresponding rise in their influence. They vigorously defended their protégés, and were on their guard to ensure the full observance of the Capitulations. Not only were the Consuls shown great respect; due to their all-powerful status, they were also the object of fear. Many of them tended to intervene in anything that occurred in the Holy Land, even playing an active role in certain events.[53] The Consuls began to make their presence felt in every issue, freely flew their national flags,[54] and stood on every point of protocol and every honour which was their due as representatives of the Great Powers. Over the course of time, they also established medical, educational, and charitable institutions, which further elevated their standing and increased their influence. Virtually no Governor of Jerusalem in the second half of the nineteenth century dared refuse the demands of a Consul, knowing full well that such a refusal would cost him dearly, if the Ambassador were to support a Consul's complaint to the Sublime Porte.

The combined action of the Consuls often saved the population during time of trouble and crisis: in the wake of plagues, wars or tribal revolts, and in times of economic crisis, when the spectre of famine raised its head. The Jewish community especially benefitted from such aid, and on many occasions found relief through consular intervention on its behalf.

Consular cooperation, however, was evident only during crises. In general, the Consuls were in covert or open competition for primacy and to enhance their own national interests, each Power creating for itself a basis within a segment of the local populace. France and Austria vied for the role of protector of Catholic

---

53 Noteworthy is the evaluation of an eyewitness who lived for many years in Jerusalem: "The Consuls at Jerusalem are not only much respected, but greatly feared, and indeed may be said to exercise an all-controlling influence, when they can be brought to co-operate, but they are often in a state of hostility to each other.... As far as his own subjects are concerned, a Consul is virtually 'King in Jeshurun', and plays the despot with perfect impunity" (Barclay, pp. 600–602); see also: Horn-Elbaum, p. 89; Warren, p. 82. See also n. 1, above. But cf. a negative opinion regarding the Consuls: "Britain had a Consul in Jerusalem for 3 years before any other nation except Prussia [this is incorrect — the Prussian Consulate was established only in 1842 — M. E.], but no sooner did she send a bishop, then France, Russia and Austria sent Consuls forthwith. Five Consuls of the Great European Powers sit, looking at one another; it is difficult to say why and wherefore." (Herschell, p. 188).

54 See below, Documents Nos. 13, 35 and 36.

interests, Russia served as patron of the Greek Orthodox, enhancing its presence in the Holy Land with a multiplicity of institutions and undertakings. The Germans, too, could look with pride upon their establishment of religious and educational institutions and their role in the economic development of the country, in addition to the German settlements, the only such Christian enterprise to successfully take root in Palestine. Consular activity also contributed to the overall economic progress of the country, especially after 1900, when representatives of the Powers vied with each other in attempting to secure the local market for their home country. All this diverse activity contributed greatly to increase the standing and influence of the Consuls.

In this respect, Great Britain found itself in a paradoxical situation. On the one hand, as the mightiest Power of the nineteenth century, with an empire extending over lands and seas, and the first to open a Consulate in Jerusalem, it was only natural that the British representative would enjoy an exalted status and a great deal of prestige. On the other hand, it did not have a basis of support within the population, nor did it initiate the establishment of many institutions or other undertakings. True, the London Society's mission could claim credit for many accomplishments, including the establishment of the first hospital in Jerusalem, and, as time passed, a network of educational institutions and workshops in Palestine. These projects were not, however, the fruit of any initiative undertaken by the Consulate or the British government. Conflicts of interest generated frequent confrontations between the Consulate and the mission, as we shall see below. Nor did the British government approve of the activities of the mission, which often led to unpleasant complications. From Palmerston's time onward, the British regarded the granting of protection to the Jewish *Yishuv* as the key which would provide them with a base in the form of loyal and grateful populace in the city. Thus, such protection became one of the primary functions of the Consulate. Throughout the entire period, however, there were incessant complaints regarding the unsatisfactory level of British initiatives, which harmed efforts to compete with the other Powers for influence in the Holy Land.

While Young had been compelled to carve out a position for himself in the face of Turkish hostility and the competition of the Russian Consul for the role of defender of the Jews, Finn's demeanour was completely different. Throughout his term in office, profoundly aware that he represented the most powerful of nations, he believed himself to be the equal of the Governor.[55] He strove to emphasize

---

55  Finn states in his memoirs: "The rank of the Consuls had been defined to be equal with that of the Turkish Governor and they are not in any case subordinate to the Pasha or under his jurisdiction" (Finn, J., *Stirring Times*, I, p. 92; see also: Blumberg, *View*, p. 81).

Britain's superiority in his contacts with the authorities and with his fellow Consuls. He was deeply offended whenever he felt that Britain's prestige had been compromised, or if his country were not treated with the honour it deserved. He was prepared to pursue his rivals to the bitter end, never forgiving them for any real or imagined slight. Finn acted high-handedly, and did not hesitate to interfere in anything that happened in Palestine — all in order to increase the prestige of Great Britain.[56] He consequently complained in his despataches to the Foreign Office that insufficient steps were being taken to strengthen Britain's status in the Holy Land.

The Consuls who succeeded him refrained from intervening in affairs in Palestine, unless those under British protection were involved. Nevertheless, they continued to dutifully report the increasing influence of any of the various Powers resulting from their establishment of institutions and other enterprises. The British, in contrast, could only point to progress in missionary activity, and to the establishment in 1883 of an English medical institution, the Opthalmic Hospital of the Order of St. John.[57] Several Consuls did, however, report a striking growth in the volume of British trade with Palestine in the late nineteenth and early twentieth centuries.[58] In all other areas, the British lagged far behind their European counterparts, despite the great esteem in which they were held by the local population. Complaints of a lack of British initiative did not cease even in the last years of the Consulate's existence.[59] It should be stressed, however, that this lack of British initiative did not impinge upon the lofty status of Her Majesty's representatives in Palestine, and the Ottoman authorities were attentive to the wishes and demands of the British diplomats.

Noteworthy among the efforts to enhance the Consulate's standing were the attempts to elevate it to the rank of a Consulate-General, which were not favourably received in London. In a letter to the Foreign Office dated 28 June 1903, Dickson noted that there were already five Consulates-General in Jerusalem. A

---

56 Reporting on his intervention in the disturbances caused by intertribal hostility, Finn concluded: "I am happy in having been able to do something for the preservation of the district from anarchy" (10 August 1853, FO 78/962). The Consul's wife later remarked, in 1854: "Mr. Finn had to go off again in December to quell some of the popular disturbances. He really was the Government at that time, for there was no one else to represent law and order" (Finn, E., *Reminiscences*, p. 102).

57 See below, Document No. 69 and n. 6 there.

58 See the Commercial Reports, Documents 82, 99, 116, 124 and 132.

59 See the severe critique by Goodrich-Freer, pp. 64 ff; E. Blyth, the daughter of Bishop Blyth, who lived for many years in Jerusalem, wrote in her memoirs: "It was often mortifying to us ... to note how far behind all the other Great Powers there was our own country" (Blyth, p. 145); "British work in Palestine, alone of all foreign work there, received no aid and very little backing from its own Government" (ibid., pp. 149–150).

few months later, when he proposed affording similar rank to the British representation in Jerusalem so as not to lag behind the others. Dickson received a negative response, since there were insufficient reasons for the proposed change.[60]

The matter was raised a second time by Consul Blech, who complained of the "inferiority of rank," and asked O'Conor, the Ambassador at Constantinople, to use his influence to elevate the Consulate to the level of a Consulate-General.[61] The Ambassador supported the request, and in his letter to the Foreign Secretary he stressed: "Jerusalem is now in my opinion of quite sufficient importance to justify its being ranked as a Consulate-General, and our interests make it desirable that our representative should have as high rank as his French, Russian and Italian colleagues and I would ask you to recommend this change to the Lord Commissioners of H. M.'s Treasury."[62]

Officials in the Foreign Office supported the Ambassador's recommendation, but the Chief Clerk disagreed and instructed that the Ambassador be informed that the matter would be discussed at a later date.[63] The proposal was repeatedly postponed, until on 20 December 1913 it was finally raised once again by the Ambassador, Sir L. Mallet, who recommended elevating the Jerusalem Consulate to the rank of Consulate-General. Once more, however, the change was rejected by the Foreign Secretary, who noted: "I fail to see the reasons for giving added importance to Jerusalem,"[64] thus putting an end to the subject. The British Consulate retained its inferior status, for in 1914 Germany had also raised the level of its Consulate. The issue of the Consulate's status further attests to the attitude of

60  28 June 1903; 4 November 1903 (FO 78/5285); Foreign Office to Dickson, 10 December 1903, ibid. The five Consulates-General in Jerusalem at the time were those of France (1892), Russia (1893), Greece (1902), Italy (1902) and Persia (1901) (FO 195/2127).

61  "I can assert that excluding political matters, in no one of them so many important cases occur as I have had occasion to handle since my arrival here.... Great Britain is the only great power which has contented itself throughout with an inferior rank for its consular representative" (16 November 1907, FO 195/2225).

62  O'Conor to E. Grey, 4 December 1907, FO 369/107. The Ambassador added: "The difference in expense ... will be nil and the eventual increase only £100 a year. Blech receives at present £800 a year, considerable [sic] less than the salary of his Russian and French colleagues." See below, n. 71.

63  The Foreign Office stated: "It would certainly assist the Consul in dealing with such cases if he was raised to the rank of Consul-General. The case is put forward by the Ambassador on his own initiative, an unusual proceeding, and that shows that Sir N. O'Conor had good reasons for the suggestion." The Chief Clerk, however, instructed his officials: "Postpone this question and tell Sir O'Conor that it will be considered with other cases when the time comes for preparation of the Estimates for 1909–1910" (2 January 1908–11 January 1908, FO 369/107; 9 January 1908, FO 195/2225).

64  FO 369/629.

the Foreign Office toward its representation in Jerusalem, which, was forced to make great efforts to maintain its status in relation to other foreign consulates.

## Remuneration of the Consul

The meagre salary of the Consuls, insufficient for their livelihood, was a painful issue. Although gradual raises were granted throughout the years, they never met the rising cost of living and the many expenses incurred by the Consuls, whose complaints did not cease until the Consulate was closed. Young was allotted an annual salary of £300 and was permited to engage in trade.[65] His successors did not enjoy similar privileges. Finn was initially allocated an annual salary of £550, a sum totally insufficient for his needs. He found himself in financial arrears, his condition becoming more severe after 1854, when the income tax was doubled. Finn also engaged in real estate ventures, which greatly increased his debts. He reiterated his request for a raise several times, stressing the higher wages received by the Anglican Bishop and the other Consuls in Jerusalem,[66] but only in 1860 was his salary increased to £600, and once again to £700 a year later. Similarly, the annual allocation for Consulate expenses, initially fixed at £120, was raised to £250 only in 1861. This sum was supposed to cover all expenses, including staff salaries. N.T. Moore was granted Finn's last salary — £700 and an additional £250 for expenses. He, too, protested the low salary and allocation for expenses, which was quite insufficient. He specifically complained that his salary did not enable him to visit England while on leave.[67] Despite his complaints, he did not receive a raise throughout his long term of service.

Dickson, appointed in 1890, also was awarded an annual salary of £700 and £250 for expenses. However, as long as as H. Amzalak served as Consular Agent at Jaffa without pay, Dickson received an additional allowance of £100 "for supervision of the Agency." When the Foreign Office decided in 1903 to raise the level of its representation in Jaffa to a Vice-Consulate, with the appointment of J. Falanga as Vice-Consul, the additional payment received by Dickson was cancelled. Embittered, he requested that this matter be reconsidered and that his salary not be reduced, noting "the difficult position in which I am placed by the reduction of my

---

65  See below, Document No. 2, n. 3.
66  Bishop Gobat's annual salary was £1450. In his letter of 8 July 1854, Finn complained that the Pasha received ten times more than he did, and all the Consuls were paid higher salaries and allowances. Consequently, "the Prussian, Austrian, French and Spanish Consuls are men of considerable standing in society and are entitled to keep up more of outward state than I am" (FO 78/1024).
67  See above, n. 14.

income by the amount in question".[68] His request was not fulfilled, and when he died in Jerusalem, his widow was left penniless.[69] Blech, who succeeded Dickson, assumed his post with a salary of £800 (of which £100 was "a personal allowance"). One year later, he complained that malaria was common in Jerusalem and that his family had been hard hit by the disease.[70] He requested that Jerusalem be added to the list of "unhealthy places," with the accompanying benefit of two months' paid vacation. Blech emphasized, however, that his request was raised mainly in the interests of his successors, "as my means would not permit of my availing myself of the two months' leave."[71]

The Consul's salary was not raised — Blech's successor, Satow, received the same remuneration. The next Consul, McGregor, did not even benefit from these conditions, being paid only the sum of £700, albeit with a raise of £100 in the allowance for expenses, to £350.[72] The last Consul, Hough, who served only a few months, did not have time to deal with the issue of his salary.

By way of conclusion it may be said that in contrast to their fellow Consuls, Great Britain's representatives received a meagre salary which did not enable them

---

68  10 October 1903, FO 115/2149. Dickson added in his letter to the Ambassador: "I would earnestly beg that Your Excellency will kindly see fit to support my application to the Marquess of Lansdowne, so that my standing as the Representative of H.M. in Jerusalem may be somewhat on the same footing as that of my Colleagues of France and Russia and the Anglican Bishop."

69  See the following characteristic example of the British policy of austerity: Acting Consul J.C. Freeman asked the Foreign Office to grant Dickson's widow a pension as she had been left without any means and with considerable debts (4 July 1906, FO 195/2225). On 7 August 1906, the widow wrote to Foreign Secretary Sir Edward Grey, applying for a pension, as she was without private means, and had a son in the army and three unmarried daughters. In a marginal note Grey wrote: "There is nothing to be done for Mrs. Dickson officially ... inability to obtain pension for her — E.G." When the widow received the negative reply on 3 September 1906, British residents in Jerusalem and Jaffa intervened on her behalf. The Foreign Office made a disappointing gesture: on 28 December 1906 Mrs. Dickson acknowledged the receipt of a sum "equal to three months salary [£175] to cover all claims" (FO 369/105). She remained for many years in Jerusalem.

70  See Document No. 107: "Since my arrival here in June not one week has passed without one or more of my family attacked by this insidious and debilitating malady."

71  Ibid. This request was granted. On 16 November 1907 Blech informed the Foreign Office of the salaries of the various Consuls at Jerusalem: Russian Consul-General — £1294; French Consul-General — £1094; Italian Consul-General — £748; German Consul — £741; Austrian Consul — £696 (FO 369/107). He also stated: "I can confidently assert that whereas in 1872 a Consul could have lived here in comfort for £300 a year, it would [now] cost him at least £750 to maintain the same standard. Almost every article has trebled or quadrupled in cost" (FO 195/2255). Blech was certainly mistaken about the cost of living in 1872.

72  ISA 123/1/11, Letter of Appointment, 26 January 1912, "to be H.M. Consul for Palestine, to reside at Jerusalem." Even in 1912 it had to be stated in the letter that the Consul "is restricted from engaging in commercial pursuits."

to maintain a proper standard of living similar to that enjoyed by the other European diplomats. Throughout the entire period, the British Consuls complained of financial difficulties and their unfavourable treatment in comparison with their colleagues. The Foreign Office remained unresponsive to their repeated requests for a raise in salary. Britain's parsimonious policy seriously hampered the Consuls' efforts to live in dignity and maintain their status as the representatives of a powerful empire.

## Consulate Facilities

Whereas the other Powers took pains to provide their recently-established consulates with proper physical facilities, including a spacious and representative office, in this matter, too, London exhibited frugalness. All the requests by its Consuls, who declared that the prestige of the British Empire required the purchase or construction of a suitable building, so as not to lag behind the other Powers, were rejected. This would remain official policy throughout the entire period under discussion.[73]

When Young arrived in Jerusalem, he was initially compelled to live in Nicolayson's home in the Armenian Quarter. After construction of Christ Church began, he moved to a small rented house nearby. Although this building did not meet the needs of the Consulate, Young remained there throughout his term of office.

Since there was no hotel in Jerusalem, Finn also lived at first in the Nicolayson home, before moving to the residence of Bishop Alexander, vacant in the interim between the Bishop's death and the arrival of Bishop Gobat. Acting on the advice of the Armenian Patriarch, Finn then moved to a rented house in the Armenian Quarter, all this before the end of his first year in Jerusalem. During this period, Finn had already recommended the establishment of a Consulate building to be financed by Her Majesty's Government. The Foreign Office was not receptive to such a proposal, instead instructing him to take up residence in the mission building adjoining the church under construction, because the building permit was officially conditional upon the establishment of a church to serve as the chapel for the Consul and his family.[74] Having no alternative, Finn moved into the cramped

---

73 See a description on the final years of the Consulate: "The Governments of other Countries either bought or built houses for their consulates; England alone left her representatives at the mercy of any landlord from whom they were able to hire a dwelling-place" (Blyth, p. 147).

74 For the permit to build the Church on condition that it would be regarded as a Consular Chapel, see: Newbolt to Aberdeen, 4 November 1845/3 January 1846, FO 78/626; Tibawi, p. 74; Finn, E., *Reminiscences*, p. 35. For the different houses, see: ibid., pp. 49, 56; Tibawi, p. 123.

building which was totally unsuitable for his family and offices.[75] Finn was afforded some relief when work was completed on the Church and adjoining buildings, as he then received a new apartment and offices.[76]

When relations between the church and the Consul worsened, and it was no longer necessary to maintain the pretense of the 'Consular Chapel', late in 1853 the mission demanded rent for the Consulate offices and the Consul's living quarters.[77] Relations further deteriorated, and when the heated quarrel between Finn and Gobat erupted in 1856 (see below), the Consul was ordered to evacuate the building, a demand with which Finn was forced to comply on 28 October 1857.[78] The Consul and his family wandered from one lodging to another for a period of several years. In 1860 he once again urged the Foreign Office to establish a Consulate building in Jerusalem. When this appeal met with no greater success than its predecessor, Finn was forced to avail himself of rented quarters.[79]

A substantive change occurred only when Moore assumed the role of Consul. In his first year in the city, he moved the Consulate and his residence to a spacious building, also rented, near the Austrian Consulate, in the vicinity of Damascus Gate.[80] In the 1880s Moore resolved to construct a building, in the area later to be

---

75 "The parsonage is ill adapted for the Consulate, — only 6 rooms (3 bedrooms); no accommodation for servants and officials" (Finn, J., *Stirring Times*, I, p. 99). Finn remarked that the other Consuls housed the servants in their houses, and complained that there is no waiting room for the numerous applicants. His wife also noted that they were asked to take possession of the house adjoining the church, which was designed to be a "consular chapel." The house was very small and not suitable, "but we had to comply" (Finn, E., *Reminiscences*, p. 71). According to Platt (*Cinderella Service*, p. 85), the family had only a single living room, while two rooms were occupied by the Consulate. Finn wrote in his diary: "During the first year we resided in three separate houses; now in a fourth" (8 April 1847).

76 "A new home near the Church" (Finn's diary, 21 July 1848); "Removed into the new Consulate house, besides the Church" (ibid., 1 February 1849).

77 20 December 1853, FO 78/963.

78 See Document No. 38.

79 Document No. 43. After the evacuation of the house in October 1857, Finn moved to one near Damascus Gate "at almost the lowest level of the City, in the Tyropean Valley." It was a large house, "but the situation was most unfavourable, not only on account of the lowness of the site, but because it was close to an open drain." But he had no choice, because there was "no other house to be found that would hold us" (Finn, E., *Reminiscences*, p. 171). In 1859 they moved to another house "at the extreme north-west corner, close to the city wall, well situated and the only we could get." It was small, but "more healthy" (ibid., p. 186). Finn wrote: "We have been 16 months in the very lowest house of Jerusalem and are now removed to the very highest house" (Finn's diary, 16 February 1859).

80 Finn, J., *Stirring Times*, II, p. 384 n. This house had already been offered to Finn, but he did not rent it: "A house was offered us above the Austrian Consulate. It is a palace compared to any house that we have yet inhabited in Jerusalem and within the compass of the Government's allowance for rent, but the air is not so good as where we are now and the distance considerable

known as 'Mahané Yehudah'. He built an impressive two-story structure, with six spacious rooms on each floor.[81] This building would serve Moore and all successive British Consuls. After the British conquest of Jerusalem in December 1917, it became a police station, a function it fulfills to the present day. This building, however, served only as the residence; the Consulate offices were located in a small structure on Ethiopia Street, totally unsuitable to represent Great Britain.[82] This state of affairs remained unchanged until the closure of the Consulate.

## Consular Pursuits

No occurrence in Palestine escaped the attention of the Consuls. The Consulate's activities may be divided into three main areas: (1) diplomatic; (2) consular/juridical; (3) commercial. Since Jerusalem was regarded as a 'political' Consulate, the first two realms overshadowed the third,[83] at least until the last decade of the nineteenth century, when the political importance of the Consulate waned, with a corresponding rise in commercial interests. Not only did the Consuls monitor the activities of the other Powers and provide detailed reports, the first two Consuls (especially Finn) actively intervened in various events, taking initiatives that often exceeded their authority. Moore and his successors refrained from such active involvement, restricting their activity primarily to reports.

The consular activity of the Consulate, firmly grounded in the Capitulations, entailed vigorous defense of the rights of British protégés and a continuous dialogue with the Turkish authorities.[84] The Consuls persistently demanded the safeguarding of rights and the correction of wrongs done to those under their protection, and did not rest until their claims had been met. The Jewish *Yishuv* also benefitted from this vigorous consular intervention, which positively influenced its security, status, and development. The judicial functions also included the operation of a Consular Court, which tried disputes between the British

from Church" (Finn's diary, 7 March 1861). It seems that the distance from the church did not bother Moore.

81 "On either side of the entrance stood pillars topped by two lions. Behind the house was a large garden and a stable for horses and donkeys" (Ben-Arieh, II, p. 146).

82 See Document No. 127: "The British Consulate ... situated in a back lane and in a poor looking place, surely it should present an appearance which can fairly be compared with the Consulates of other Countries."

83 "The press of political & judicial business tended to overshadow the commercial functions which are the essential work of Consuls generally" (Lipman, British Consulate, p. 13).

84 "Consular work had grown more and more into the settling of disputes, normal routine of protection of British subjects and interests, but had lost much of its political importance" (Hough, p. 11).

protégés, heard civil cases, and even tried those under British protection who faced criminal charges. Other spheres of consular activity included the granting or revocation of protection, in accordance with the directives of higher authorities; the issuance of passports and *laissez-passers*; the registration of changes in personal status, such as marriages, divorces, births, and deaths; and the execution of wills and estates. The Consul registered those under his protection and periodically updated these lists, usually once a year. All these endeavours entailed a great deal of paperwork, which took much of his time.

The surveys and reports of the Consuls dealt with the political, religious, economic, and social condition of various groups within Palestine, and especially that of their protégés. These reports provide a broad range of information regarding the country, its inhabitants, and various events that occurred from the establishment of the Consulate until its closure in 1914. Like consular activity, the Consuls' despatches generally fall into one of three categories: political, consular, or commercial, with the second category including the juridical activity of the Consulate.

The Consul faced a difficulty when he was required to make an urgent decision or to take a stand on a certain issue. At least three weeks would pass before his despatch reached London or two weeks before it arrived in Constantinople, with a corresponding delay before he received a reply, usually about a month to a month and a half after the despatch of his letter (about two weeks if the reply came from Beirut). In the interim, the Consul was on his own, and compelled to act as best he saw fit. It later transpired that in some cases his superiors did not confirm the steps he had taken. This state of affairs changed upon the inauguration of the Jerusalem-Constantinople telegraph line in 1865, which facilitated communications. Furthermore, Britain did not operate a regular steamship line or a postal service of its own,[85] thereby forcing the Consul to rely upon foreign services. The operation of the telegraph obviously detracted from the Consul's freedom of action, since he would now be subservient to precise instructions which arrived quickly, with a consequent decline in his political importance.

The Consulate employed an extremely limited staff, because, as noted above, the Consul's meagre allowance had to suffice for all his office expenses. This forced the Consul to personally undertake a great deal of work, unlike his fellow Consuls who had recourse to a larger number of employees. It should be borne in mind that all correspondence with the Foreign Office, the Embassy, the Consulate-General in Beirut, the Ottoman authorities, etc., was conducted in handwriting. This required the preparation of a draft, which would be kept in the Consulate's

85 See below, Documents Nos. 97 and 112.

archives and from which an original despatch or report would be copied and sent to its destination. The great deal of work this entailed can easily be conceived, especially since many of the communications were rather lengthy, comprising numerous pages. In the second half of the nineteenth and the early twentieth centuries, there was a gradual decrease in the quantity of correspondence, being limited to routine reports and urgent matters requiring action. Due to budgetary constraints, the Consuls also restricted their travel throughout Palestine to essential trips. Finn was exceptional in this respect as well. He made frequent journeys, paying no heed to the cost, which led to the accumulation of large debts for consular expenses.

Though Young, as the first British Consul, had to deal with many issues that suddenly cropped up, the number of letters and reports he wrote during his six years in office did not exceed one hundred. Finn, by contrast, was a copious and stubborn correspondent. An examination of the archives of the Foreign Office and of the Embassy in Constantinople reveals that hardly a single day passed in which he did not send a despatch to one of them, and at times even more than one; furthermore, he frequently provided the Embassy with copies of his missives to London. Not only was Finn a frequent correspondent, his letters often extend over many pages, in an outstanding display of loquacity and tenacity. If the reply was tardy or not to his liking, he tirelessly continued to engage in the same topic without respite. A great deal of patience was required by the recipients of his correspondence. Even at the height of his quarrels with the Bishop or the Prussian Consul (see below), he would immediately reply to communications he received; at times letters and replies would be sent twice in one day. Finn apparently devoted a considerable portion of the day, and even more of the night, to writing.[86]

. By his own testimony, in 1853–56 he wrote 761 despatches to London, Beirut, and Constantinople, in addition to weekly letters to all the Consular Agents in his area of jurisdiction, all the documents and correspondence relevant to cases brought before the Consular Court, letters relating to queries by tourists, and the routine correspondence pertaining to the granting of protection.[87] Finn also

---

86 "The British Consul alone of all Consuls in Jerusalem had to do the work of his office single-handed" (Finn, J., *Stirring Times*, I, p. 98). After Rogers left his post in Jerusalem in 1853, to assume the role of Vice-Consul at Haifa, "Finn had to do all Consular work with the help of his wife, single-handed" (Finn, E., *Reminiscences*, p. 115).

87 Finn, J., *Stirring Times*, I, p. 98. In 1861 the Foreign Office sent Finn 19 despatches and received 96 from him (Lipman, British Consulate, p. 6). In his report from 23 June 1856, Finn complained: "The English Consulate holds the meanest position of all in the aspect it presents to the public, though it was the earliest in this city and although the amount of the work exceeds that of all the rest put together" (FO 195/524).

implied that the burden of this correspondence and the effort involved were deleterious to his health.[88]

Highly sympathetic to the Jews and their predicament, Finn exerted great efforts to alleviate the suffering of the *Yishuv* by extending vigorous protection, creating employment, and bestowing aid upon the poor (see below). Much of his correspondence was devoted to the Jews, in whom he patently exhibited greater interest than his fellow Consuls, although this concern also led to unpleasant confrontations and blatant interference in the internal affairs of the Jewish community. Jewish affairs, however, did not constitute the decisive element in his correspondence; his keen interest in political developments and other events in Palestine is reflected in his despatches.

The Consuls who succeeded Finn engaged to a lesser degree in Jewish issues, unless they too were required to intervene or provide protection, which they did quite forcefully. It would be an exaggeration, however, to argue that the Jewish question played a central role in the activity of the Consulate, or that it accounted for most of its time and efforts.[89] Jewish matters certainly constituted a considerable, but not the major part of the Consulate's activity. In fact, they occupied the British Consulate to a lesser degree than its German and Austrian counterparts, who had a larger number of Jews under their protection.

Though Moore did not defend his protégés with the same fervour as his predecesor, he successfully removed many hindrances faced by Jewish travelers and immigrants. Beginning in the 1880s, the Consulate was also required to intervene in weighty political issues: restriction or even prohibition of Jewish immigration, and limitations on land acquisition by Jews. Moore adopted a policy of quiet diplomacy. The Turkish governors were sympathetic to his requests, and he also took joint action with his fellow Consuls against the restrictions on immigration and land purchases, although the British Consul had fewer Jewish protégés who suffered from the hostile Turkish policy. When the need arose, he protested every injustice, as did his successor, and whenever necessary, turned to his superiors to intervene for the redress of wrongs committed by the Ottoman authorities. Moore evaded any quarrel or dissension, and was highly respected in all circles. He wrote less than his predecessor, producing fewer despatches and reports than did Finn. He also kept his distance from the mission, whose activities

---

88  "The public office work by day, and all this mass of writing chiefly by night — what health or strength could endure the strain of all this labour, anxiety and responsibility during seventeen years of unbroken work in harness?" (Finn, J., *Stirring Times*, I, p. 99).
89  See, inter alia, Hyamson, *British Consulate*: "... almost monopolised the time and attention of the Consul and his staff" (Introduction, p. xxxiv); "Jews and their interests absorbed the greater part of the attentions of the Consuls" (ibid., p. liv).

are hardly mentioned in his reports. Moore similarly refrained from interfering in the affairs of the Jewish *Yishuv*, restricting the Consulate's interest to those Jews under his protection. Moore limited his activity to matters requiring his care or in which he was instructed to intervene, in addition to the filing of routine reports. His annual report was often virtually a copy of its predecessor, including population figures.[90] There is no basis, however, for the claim that Moore wrote only infrequently or that he took no interest in current events.[91] Foreign Office files contain many reports by Moore on the activity of the foreign Powers in Palestine, economic and commercial problems, visitors, and the development of Jerusalem. His communications foster the impression of peace and stability in the region. The Foreign Office's satisfaction with the manner in which he carried out his duties was attested by his extended term of office in Jerusalem and by the promotion he received upon the end of his service in the Consulate.

The growing importance of the commercial sphere toward the end of the nineteenth century was reflected in the work of the Consulate, which encouraged and fostered business ties. Moore and the Consuls who succeeded him sent detailed commercial reports, containing a multiplicity of specific information regarding imports and exports of various goods, maritime traffic at Jaffa port, the success of crops in Palestine, the financial state of the Jewish settlements, etc. These reports constitute primary sources for the economic history of Palestine and are extensively quoted in the documentary section of this volume.[92] Many of them have also been published in the *Diplomatic and Consular Reports* (*DCR*) series.

Dickson continued the policy adopted by his predecessor, intervening in every matter concerning his protégés and sparing no effort until these issues were successfully resolved. Dickson also wrote sparingly, possibly even to a greater degree than Moore,[93] which may have been a consequence of his poor health. He, too, enjoyed the respect of the entire local population.

---

90  His report on trade in Jerusalem during 1867 was unfortunately found to be "almost a copy of the preceding year." The Foreign Secretary, Lord Stanley, reprimanded him severely, mentioning the "meagerness of your reports" (17 April 1868, FO 78/2048). See also Tibawi, pp. 153, 193.

91  See the unjustified opinion of Carmel, Competition, p. 124; Tennenbaum, Consulate, pp. 92, 98; Tibawi, p. 154. Even the claim that "his despatches make very dull reading" (Hannam, Britons, p. 63) is unfounded. But we can agree with judgments such as: "Moore was certainly more reticent, answering questions briefly and reporting only on what could not be ignored" (Tibawi, p. 152); "He adopted a much lower profile. His despatches were less frequent, his interpretations less dramatic" (Lipman, *Americans*, p. 16).

92  See below, Documents Nos. 68, 71, 78, 82, 90, 99, 116, 124 and 132.

93  "Dickson's despatches are even more barren than those of Moore ... Dickson came with the rubber stamp and the printed form" (Tibawi, p. 213). This verdict, too, is overly harsh; see Dickson's various despatches in this volume and in Hyamson, *British Consulate*, II.

The succeeding Consuls served for relatively short periods of time and were not noted for much activity. Indeed, their intervention in local affairs progressively decreased. They sent fewer and fewer reports to London and Constantinople, a tendency which continued unabated until the closure of the Consulate.

By way of summation, one may say that the Consuls at Jerusalem were very attentive to events in Palestine and developments affecting the local population. No important occurrence in Palestine was absent from the reports of the Consulate, reflecting the point of view of the Consul, the representative of a great Power. These documents, accordingly, constitute a primary and important source for the history of Palestine in this period.

## The Mission, the Bishopric, and the Consulate

In the nineteenth century, missionary societies played an integral role in the process of European expansion in Asia and Africa. The diffusion of Christianity was carried out side by side with the imperialistic policy of the European countries, which sought to expand their spheres of influence and gain new protectorates and colonies. The mission frequently served as the vanguard, establishing its presence in a foreign country and laying the groundwork for a diplomatic foothold. The process of European penetration reflected both Great Power competition and the congruence of religious interests and political goals.

Every Power sought to increase its influence and presence by means of religious-cultural penetration and by extending its protection to existing minorities or those taking shape in the Levant. Accordingly, the European Powers considered aid and encouragement of the missionary and cultural endeavours of their subjects as a means to achieve this goal. To the status of France as the defender of Catholicism and of Russia as the protector of the Greek Orthodox community was now added that of Britain as the patron of the nascent Protestant community in the Holy Land and of the Jewish *Yishuv*. Missionary activity received a political seal of approval, to a degree unprecedented elsewhere, and interests of state became intertwined with religious, social, and cultural concerns.

The British mission, which would constitute a firm base for British presence in Palestine, sought to undertake extensive activity. It was ideologically motivated by the movement for the Restoration of the Jews, which had come into being in late eighteenth-century England, with the objective of encouraging the return of the Jewish People to its ancestral homeland, in the hope that the Jews would there accept Christianity, as a precondition to the Second Coming of Jesus.[94] The London Society therefore regarded the Jewish *Yishuv* as the prime object of its efforts, becoming in effect the sole mission to the Jews of Palestine until the end of the nineteenth century. It consistently supported sundry programs for the return of the Jews to the Holy Land and for the advancement of Jewish settlement in Palestine. The history of the London Society has already been discussed at length in the literature;[95] the following discussion shall be restricted to outlining its relationship with the Consulate.

After several unsuccessful attempts to establish a foothold in the land, John Nicolayson founded the London Society's permanent station in Jerusalem in 1833 and headed it until his death in 1856. Commencing his activity with much vigour, he soon encountered many obstacles, as well as increasing suspicion on the part of the Jewish community. He soon concluded that a Protestant church must be built in Jerusalem to serve the nascent community. It was not until 1838, however, that the London Society authorised him to purchase land for the church and the mission buildings.[96] He acquired a plot of land near the Citadel of David for the sum of £800. Construction began in February 1840, only to be halted a year later by the Turkish governor in the absence of a *firman*, a royal writ, from the Sublime Porte. Diplomatic efforts to obtain such permission were initiated, but the pro-tracted diplomatic pressure exerted in Constantinople was crowned with success only on 10 September 1845. The *firman* was granted on condition that the building would serve only as a chapel for the Consul and his entourage.[97] Construction was renewed, but the Ottoman Governor did not cease his obstruction, continually finding new excuses to stop it. Additional strenuous action had to be taken in Constantinople until the matter was finally resolved. The church was not conse-crated until 21 January 1849, in the presence of Consul Finn.[98] In reality, Christ Church was an imposing edifice intended to serve the entire community, especially the converts. Officially, however, the Governor regarded it solely as a chapel for the adjoining Consulate. In 1850 a *firman* was issued granting the Protestant congregation the status of an independent community.

94  See: M. Vereté, "The Idea of the Restoration of the Jews in English Protestant Thought," *Middle Eastern Studies* 8 (1972), pp. 1–50; Le Roi, *Christenheit*, I, pp. 75 ff.; F. Kobler, *The Vision Was Here*, London 1956.

95  See, inter alia: Gidney, *London Society*; ibid., *At Home*; ibid., *Sites*, II; Halsted; Hannam, *Jerusalem Bishopric*; Ginat; Tibawi; Richter; Schwake; Blumberg, *Zion*.

96  *JI* 1838, pp. 38, 53–54; 1839, p. 141; Le Roi, *Christenheit*, III, pp. 177–180. Consul-General Campbell supported Nicolayson's efforts to buy land and erect a church.

97  "A special Protestant place of worship within the British Consulate." Blumberg, *Zion*, pp. 40–41; Halstead, pp. 151–153; Finn, J., *Stirring Times*, I, p. 99; Gidney, London Society, pp. 180–181, 235–236; Horn-Elbaum, pp. 289–290; *JI* 1846, p. 26.

98  See below, Document No. 21.

As early as 1837 the London Society had sent several missionaries to Jerusalem to aid Nicolayson in his proselytizing work among the Jews. From the very first, and throughout the entire period, the London Society preferred to send converted Jews as missionaries, since they were familiar with Jewish sources and spoke Hebrew. Singularly qualified to engage in polemical debate with Jews, they attempted to utilise their rhetorical skills and tendentious interpretations of the Bible and the Talmud to persuade them to abandon their faith and find shelter in the bosom of the mission. Since the end justified all means, they frequently engaged in debate in Jewish homes and in synagogues. The missionaries were not deterred by the energetic opposition of the lay and rabbinical leadership of the *Yishuv*. They took advantage of the severe financial distress of the Jewish community, and provided sundry material support to draw Jews nearer to Christianity. They did not attempt to refute Jewish tradition and values; to the contrary, they sought to strengthen them and to emphasize that the Jews were the Chosen People, while tying these beliefs to the acceptance of Christianity and Jesus as the Messiah. In July 1838 Nicolayson also instituted daily prayer in Hebrew, using the rendition into this language of the Anglican liturgy that had been published in December 1836.[99] The daily Hebrew prayer occupied an increasingly central place in church services as the number of converts increased, except on Sundays, when prayers were conducted in English.

Throughout the years, the mission invested unflagging effort and tremendous resources to persuade the Jews in the Holy Land to convert. The results, however, were meagre and disappointing. The missionaries could not point to impressive results, despite their exploitation of the horrendous economic straits of the Jewish community. Nicolayson was unable to convert even a single Jew until 1839, when the first Jewish family was baptized. For many years, the average annual number of Jewish conversions did not exceed four or five, though it did increase as time passed. By the end of the nineteenth century a total of 450 Jews had converted, after sixty years of missionary labours.[100]

99 Strauss, p. 253; Bartlett, p. 28; Ewald, pp. 55, 219; Gidney, *London Society*, pp. 179–180; Gobat, p. 289; Halsted, p. 152; Warren, p. 105. See also Ashley's statement: "[The missionaries] have designed the establishment of a Church at Jerusalem, if possible on Mount Zion itself, where the order of our service and the prayers of our Liturgy shall daily be set before the faithful in the Hebrew language" (Hodder, I, p. 240). Some visitors were mistaken, stating that the Jewish prayer book was used in the Hebrew service (Frankl, p. 70; Busch, p. 300 n.).

100 The London Society spent £7000 annually in Palestine. Even if there were seven or eight converts each year, the mission expended approximately £900–1000 on each proselyte. See the negative opinions regarding the efficacy of the mission: Braun, pp. 219–225; Bremer, II, p. 102; Busch, p. 300; Goodrich-Freer, pp. 64–65, 373; Rhodes, pp. 460–462; Tristam, p. 170; Thomp-

The mission viewed the appointment of Young to the Consulate in Jerusalem as an act cf Divine Providence, hoping that the new Consul would aid and defend the missionaries in their efforts in the holy city.[101] Young's first steps were taken in complete harmony with the mission, and he strongly supported the plan to erect a church.

Shortly after Young's appointment, Lord Ashley conceived the idea of establishing a Protestant bishopric in Jerusalem,[102] but the time was not yet ripe for such a program. Conditions changed only after the Powers forced Muhammad Ali to withdraw from Syria and Palestine, and Ottoman rule was restored to these areas, mainly as a result of Britain's uncompromising stand. For the first time since the Crusades, European public attention was directed to the Holy Land during the negotiations between the Powers. It was their initial intent not to reinstate Ottoman rule in Palestine; they even proposed a plan, mainly at the initiative of the King of Prussia, for the internationalization of Jerusalem and the Christian holy sites. These plans were shelved due to the inability of the Powers to reach a consensus. Following protracted discussions regarding the future of the Holy Land, Palestine was returned to its former rulers, who explicitly guaranteed the rights of the non-Muslim minorities and promised to improve their status.

Prussia now proposed the establishment of an Anglo-Prussian Bishopric in Jerusalem whose jurisdiction would encompass the entire Near East. The Prussian monarch sent the diplomat C. von Bunsen, who initiated the plan, to London to further its realization. Von Bunsen's forceful efforts were well suited to the aspirations of Ashley and the London Society, in which the latter played a prominent role. All this naturally coincided with British aspirations to create a basis for British influence in Palestine as a counterweight to the danger of spreading

---

son, p. 189; Titmarsh, p. 119; Tobler, *Dritte Wanderung*, p. 295; idem, *Topographie*, pp. 386–390; Plitt, p. 82; Ginat, pp. 115–118; Scult, p. 3. For the first baptized family, see: Eliav, Shimon Rosenthal.

101 See above, n. 37 and below, Document 5, n. 2; Tibawi, pp. 33–34. Young was a devout Evangelist, and before his departure he visited A. McCaul, the head of the Mission to the Jews in London (see below, n. 107). In July 1838 Young was elected as a member of the General Committee of the London Society, but he never attended its meetings. McCaul's later statement that Young professed "great interest in the cause of Jewish conversion" is undoubtedly exaggerated (Vereté, pp. 336, 342–343. Gidney, *London Society*, does not even mention him.

102 "Could we not erect a Protestant Bishopric at Jerusalem and give him jurisdiction over all the Levant, Malta, and whatever chaplaincies there might be on the coast of Africa?" (Hodder, I, p. 235, entry for 8 October 1838). After the treaty of London was signed in July 1841, Ashley reaffirmed his belief that the Jews were to return to their "inheritance," and that the time was ripe for the fulfillment of the prophecies. Now it was possible to establish an Anglican Bishopric in Jerusalem (ibid., pp. 309–310).

Russian influence in the region. An agreement was quickly obtained, especially since Prussia agreed to give the Anglican church primacy within the Bishopric.

On 6 August 1841 it was agreed that the two countries would jointly finance the establishment of the Bishopric. It was also stipulated that the Bishops would be appointed alternately by the British and Prussian governments and would be subordinate to the Archbishop of Canterbury. The agreement assured the Anglican church predominance within the new Bishopric. It also received the blessings of the London Society, which anticipated the Bishopric's support for its activities.[103]

On 9 December 1841, in a "Statement of proceedings relating to the establishment of a Bishopric of the United Church of England and Ireland in Jerusalem,"[104] the Archbishop of Canterbury declared that the agreement constituted a step toward the unification of the Protestant churches, explicitly stressing the proselytising of the Jews as a primary goal ("chief missionary care will be directed to the conversion of the Jews, to their protection and to their useful employment"). The Archbishop, however, also stated that the other Christian communities would have to be convinced that there was no intention to interfere in their activity; rather the objective of the joint Bishopric was to provide a basis for Protestants who would settle in the Holy Land.[105]

Lord Ashley was the driving force throughout the negotiations until their successful conclusion, just as — so he claimed — he had succeeded in persuading Palmerston to lend his backing to the plan.[106] Indeed, the Foreign Secretary was quick to comprehend the advantage that could accrue to British political interests from the establishment of the Bishopric and the creation of an active British foothold in Palestine. Palmerston anticipated that the attainment of Protestant religious goals would serve his political objectives, just as he believed that the proposal to extend protection to the Jews in Palestine, in general, would further British interests.

The establishment of a joint Anglo-Prussian Bishopric reflected the aims of the two Protestant Powers to found a community of their own in the Holy Land, while

---

103  *JI* 1841, p. 383.
104  For the entire text see: Tibawi, pp. 82 ff.
105  For the history of the Bishopric, see: W. Hechler, *The Jerusalem Bishopric*, London 1883; R.W. Greaves, "The Jerusalem Bishopric 1841," *English Historical Review* 64 (1949), pp. 328–352; Horn-Elbaum, Part III; Tibawi, pp. 43 ff.; Hannam, Jerusalem Bishopric; Eliav, *German Policy*, Introduction; J.M. Hornus, "L'évêché anglo-prussien à Jérusalem (1841–1881)," *Proche Orient Chrétien* 13 (1963), pp. 130–149, 234–250; 14 (1964), pp. 184–201.
106  "Really it is wonderful to trace the finger of God ... Palmerston went forward with the zeal of an apostle (howbeit, I fear, he thinketh not so), did in three weeks what at another time, or so it seems, under any influence but mine, he would not have listened to in twelve months" (Hodder, I, pp. 375–376, entry for 28 September 1841).

lending support to the efforts of the missionaries. Such a community would enjoy their protection but would also give them a status similar to that of France and Russia, the traditional defenders of the large Christian communities, or at least curb the growing influence of those two European states.

The post of Bishop was first offered to Alexander McCaul, who had devoted his entire life to missionary work among the Jews.[107] McCaul rejected the offer, believing that this position should be filled by a person of Jewish origin, who would know how to approach the Jews of Jerusalem and draw them to Christianity.

Upon his recommendation, M.S. Alexander was selected and installed as Bishop on 7 November 1841.[108] By this time, however, there had been a change of government in England. Lord Aberdeen, the new Foreign Secretary, adopted a different Near Eastern strategy and sought to improve relations with France and Russia, instead of continuing the hostile policy of his predecessor. He did not favour the very idea of the new Bishopric, which was likely to arouse the ire of the two continental Powers. Since its establishment had already been ratified by Parliament, he therefore sought to restrict it to a religious basis, stripping it of any political significance. He did not prevent Alexander's departure for Jerusalem, despite his apprehensions as to possible complications with the Ottoman Governor and with Russia and France. Palmerston had made no attempt to obtain Turkish approval for the establishment of the Bishopric, nor did the mission in Jerusalem enjoy official recognition.[109]

Alexander arrived in Jerusalem on 21 January 1842 and immediately began missionary efforts among the Jews, according to plan. He served as Bishop for only three years until his sudden death while on a trip to Egypt. Despite his overly

107   Alexander McCaul (1749–1863) was devoted to the idea of the conversion of the Jews. He was well-versed in Hebrew and Rabbinical literature, and — together with M.S. Alexander — he translated the New Testament and the Anglican liturgy into Hebrew. After ten years of successful missionary work in Warsaw, he became the central personality in the London Mission at Palestine Place and headed the college for the training of missionary-converts, of whom there were a total of 255 in the nineteenth century. His daughter Elizabeth Ann married Consul Finn in January 1846.

108   Michael Salomon Alexander (1799–1845), born in Schönlanke (Posen), received a strict Jewish Orthodox upbringing. In 1820 he left for England to become a teacher, and later served as a rabbi in Norwich and in Plymouth. It was in Plymouth that he took an interest in Christianity and was dismissed from his position. He was baptised in 1825, ordained, and became actively involved in the activities of the London Society. In 1832 he was appointed Professor of Hebrew and Rabbinical Literature at King's College, London, filling this position until his nomination as Bishop in Jerusalem. His wife and six children accompanied him to Palestine.

109   Horn-Elbaum, pp. 246–253, 313–314. For Aberdeen's policy, see: Temperley, p. 444; Tuchman, p. 132; Tibawi, pp. 54–57. The Sublime Porte protested against the appointment of the Bishop, probably following Russian pressure. The appointment became a veritable nuisance to the British Foreign Secretary, who saw no political merit in it.

energetic efforts and uncompromising obstinacy, Alexander had little to show for his endeavours. If it could be said of Young's first three years in Jerusalem that they were marked by correct relations with the missionaries, this rapport was interrupted after Alexander's arrival in Jerusalem, and the relationship cooled to a considerable extent. The Foreign Secretary had specifically warned Young not to become involved in any way with Alexander's missionary activity.[110] The Bishop, who naturally also headed the mission, adopted methods too aggressive and too blunt to influence or convert Jews. His activity created a dilemma for the Consul. On the one hand, he was required to defend the Jews, who bitterly complained of the means employed by the mission and demanded Young's intervention. On the other hand, the Bishop and the missionaries were British subjects, who insisted upon consular protection for their activity, though they did not always accept his authority. The main point of contention revolved around the status of the converts and the candidates for conversion, foreign subjects whom the missionaries had assured of British protection and whose entry under the aegis of the mission was liable to create unpleasant diplomatic incidents.[111] These confrontations would eventually turn into open disputes, with the Consul often expressing his displeasure at the doings of the Bishop and the mission.[112] Young was supported in these clashes by the Foreign Secretary and the Consul-General in Beirut, although he was requested to tone down his statements and prevent a further deterioration of relations with the Bishop and the missionaries.[113]

Relations did not improve, however, and Alexander continued to regard Young as his main adversary, who only placed obstacles in his path. Faithful to the instruction he had received, Young refused to extend British protection to converts and even to missionaries who were not British subjects. Alexander could not boast of impressive achievements for his proselytising efforts, especially since he himself,

110  "You will carefully abstain from identifying yourself in any degree with his mission and from assisting to promote any scheme of interference with the Jewish Subjects of the Porte, in which Bishop Alexander may possibly engage. You will clearly understand that H.M.'s Government will not sanction ... any attempts, directly or indirectly, to interfere with the religious tenets of any class of the Sultan's subjects" (3 May 1842, FO 78/501 — Hyamson, *British Consulate*, No. 30).

111  Aberdeen explicitly instructed Young: "You will most carefully abstain from affording to persons who may associate themselves to Bishop Alexander's congregation any protection as British Dependents, to which, under other circumstances, they could not properly lay claim" (ibid.). See also Hyamson, *British Consulate*, Introduction, p. lvi.

112  For his conflicts with the Bishop, see: Hyamson, *British Consulate*, No. 31 and Enclosures, Nos. 32, 36, 38 and 41; *JI* 1843, pp. 60–61; Tibawi, pp. 61–64, 68. Alexander was even criticised in the House of Commons, where he was described as a failure (ibid., p. 70). See also: Horn-Elbaum, pp. 276–278.

113  Hyamson, *British Consulate*, Nos. 32–33.

as a converted Jew, aroused stiff opposition among the Jews.[114] The appointment of a convert as Bishop of Jerusalem had proven to be erroneous. Lacking governmental or consular support, he found it difficult to win over souls to Christianity. His standing had changed completely. The Bishop, unwelcome in Jerusalem, became a burden to the Foreign Office. Nicolayson, who was the de facto head of the mission, kept his counsel in all these disputes, and apparently did not approve of the Bishop's methods.

In the meantime, the mission continued to establish new undertakings for prospective converts. In 1842 it founded the 'House of Converts' to train future missionaries. In 1843 a 'School of Industry' was opened, in order to teach various crafts to the young, an institution that played an important role in directing Jews to productive trades. That very year was also marked by the inauguration of the 'Enquirers' Home' which provided candidates for conversion with free food and clothing, along with systematic religious instruction.

The mission's crowning achievement, however, was in the field of medical assistance. As early as December 1838 a free clinic had been opened by Dr. Gerstman, aided by the pharmacist Bergheim who dispensed medicine free of charge; both were themselves converts. The opening of a clinic at a time when there were many ill in Jerusalem, which had no hospital at all, enhanced the mission's standing, and Jews began to avail themselves of its services.[115] When ill health forced Gerstman to retire, he was replaced by Dr. E. Macgowan, who opened a hospital at the end of 1844 which by 1846 had expanded into an institution with twenty four beds. Despite the ban placed by Jerusalem's rabbis on the hospital (which was conducted in accordance with Jewish law, with *mezuzot* affixed to the the doorposts and providing kosher food and even small *talitot* — prayer shawls — for the patients), Jews continued to avail themselves of its services, in the absence of any other medical facility. The missionary hospital proved to be a great success,[116] and was openly supported by the Consul.

The harsh disputes between Consul Young and Bishop Alexander were eclipsed by the ferocity of the quarrels between their successors, Finn and Gobat.[117] It could have been anticipated that the new Consul's relationship with the missionaries and the Bishop would be correct, even friendly, for Finn had joined the London Society in his youth, had been elected to its Committee in July 1841, and had

---

114  Horn-Elbaum, pp. 263–267, 286–288; Hannam, Jerusalem Bishopric.
115  See: *Jerusalem Medical Mission*; Horn-Elbaum, pp. 280–283.
116  For the hospital, see: *Jerusalem Medical Mission*; Schwake, I, pp. 108 ff.; Gidney, *London Society*; Halsted, pp. 164 ff.; Tibawi, pp. 208–210.
117  "It is a curious fact that neither Consul could suffer his bishop for very long" (Tibawi, p. 134).

become close to Lord Ashley, who was a leading member of the Society. Finn expressed great interest in the Jews, published several books about them, engaged in missionary activity, and married Elisabeth Ann, the daughter of A. McCaul, on the eve of his departure for Jerusalem.[118] Before setting out to assume his new post, he severed his ties with the London Society, being cognizant of the conflict of interest between this activity and his duties as Consul, especially his instruction to protect the Jews in Palestine. It could have been assumed that Finn would not have engaged in any missionary activity in Palestine. Almost throughout his entire term in office, however, harsh charges, both justified and not, were raised about his missionary efforts, until it was claimed that these accusations played an important role in his dismissal.

He undoubtedly keenly desired the success of missionary endeavours,[119] as he had declared at the last meeting of the Committee of the London Society, which he attended before setting out for Jerusalem, that he was always ready to assist in the dissemination of Christianity among the Jews.[120] But Finn never applied direct pressure to convert, preferring instead to act indirectly and to gently persuade those under his protection. Throughout his term as Consul he invited converts to his home, attempted to care for their needs, was present at baptisms and confirmation ceremonies, and in great measure considered himself to be their leading patron.

The close relations between the converts and Finn highly displeased the missionaries, who regarded themselves as the natural mentors of the proselytes. This was one of the main causes of disagreement between the Consul and the representatives of the London Society, which developed into an open struggle for power and influence.

Even in the philanthropic enterprises founded by Finn and his wife, such as 'Kerem Abraham' in Jerusalem and at Artas, to the south of Bethlehem, Finn's original missionary intentions should not be overlooked, together with his sincere desire to train Jews for agricultural work and thereby provide them with a livelihood dependent upon their own labors.[121] Finn did not allow the London

---

118  For details of his biography and his relationship with the mission, see: Eliav, Finn.
119  "Both Finn and his iron-willed wife remained convinced that their life's work was the conversion of the Jews" (Blumberg, *Zion*, p. 63); "[They] felt a natural duty to promote Christianity to Jews" (Hannam, Britons, p. 60); "There may have been some hope of conversion at the back of their minds" (Lipman, *Americans*, p. 15).
120  This meeting took place on 13 January 1846 (Tibawi, p. 123).
121  Finn wrote in his diary: "My great object and desire being to see the land of Israel cultivated by Christian Israelites, preparatory to the time when the land will be restored to their nation" (entry for 18 December 1850). See also his memorandum to Foreign Secretary Clarendon, 15 September 1857 (Hyamson, *British Consulate*, No. 186).

Society a foothold in any of his projects, thereby arousing the wrath of its representatives. The missionaries regarded his activities to be overt competition, leading to a further deterioration in their relations.

In several episodes involving the struggle between the Jewish community and the missionaries over prospective converts, Finn did take a strong stand in favour of the missionaries and the proselytes, thereby exceeding his authority, which even led to a reprimand by the Foreign Office.[122] A few years later, however, the missionaries would claim that Finn sought to play a central, independent role in proselytising efforts and that he intended to infringe upon their sphere of action. Not surprisingly, almost all the missionaries, including the doctors at the hospital, sided with the Bishop in his fierce dispute with Finn (see below), in practice virtually isolating the diplomat and his wife.

Actually, as time passed, Finn abandoned his overt proselytising, possibly because he comprehended the essence of his role as Consul. He gradually refrained from any personal involvement in missionary activity, but the charges levelled against him did not abate. Even though he undertook many initiatives for the welfare of the Jewish community, the *Yishuv* continued to suspect him of having missionary intentions.

Most grave was his relationship with Bishop Gobat, who arrived in Jerusalem in December 1846, closely following Finn's assumption of his duties.[123] To Finn's aspirations to control the affairs of the mission, which was subordinate to the Bishop, was added a clearly nationalist motive. Gobat, who — in accordance with the agreement — had been appointed by the Prussian king, was a product of German culture. Finn obviously surmised that the Bishop did not have English interests at heart,[124] especially since Gobat found a common language with Prussian Consul Rosen, Finn's outstanding rival.[125] Over the years, Finn thought — at times justifiably and more often without any justification — that the two had plotted against him and against Great Britain, and that the Bishop was excessively inclined toward Prussia. Though Finn and the Bishop enjoyed correct relations at

---

122  See: Eliav, Finn, pp. 46 ff.; below, Document No. 22; Hyamson *British Consulate*, No. 76 and Enclosures, Nos. 81, 85–86 and 122.

123  See below, Document No. 30, n. 2. The volume of Gobat's life and works includes his biography and various letters and documents.

124  "Gobat's position among the English Christians was not easy; He was too English for Germans and too German for the Anglicans" (ibid., pp. 346–347); "The Bishop was a French-speaking Swiss with strong German propensity and connexions" (Tibawi, p. 133); "Bishop guards the interests of the German Church" (Warren, p. 83).

125  See below, Document 32, n. 7. For Finn's quarrels with him, see: FO 78/1217; Eliav, Shimon Rosenthal; Eliav, Finn, pp. 68–69; Blumberg, *View*, pp. 214–217, 240, 247; Files 491, 494 in the Israel State Archives, Record Group 67 (German Consular Archive).

the beginning of the Consul's term in office, they had deteriorated after only a few years, culminating in a severe crisis. Both men were forceful personalities, each regarding himself as the head of the Protestant community. Finn, furthermore, was a quarrelsome and contentious individual who bore grudges and was always ready to engage in an uncompromising struggle to maintain his standing.

Gobat looked with displeasure upon Finn's attempts to intervene in mission and church affairs. The proselytising policy he adopted from the very outset of his time in office, unlike that of his predecessor, constituted an additional cause of tension between the Bishop and the Consul. Gobat did not take great pains to persuade Jews to convert, nor did he believe in the sincerity of the converts' motives. He encouraged the activity of the Church Missionary Society (CMS), with which he had cooperated in his previous posts and which had recently become active in the Holy Land as well. The objective of the CMS was to convince the members of other Christian denominations, especially the Greek Orthodox, to become Protestants.[126] This policy was not acceptable to Finn, who had always endeavoured to bring the message of Christianity to the Jews, and especially since Gobat's policy led to a deterioration of relations with the other Christian communities, which complained of the unexpected competition, in contradiction to the assurances which had been given upon the establishment of the Bishopric. As time passed, Gobat's efforts gave rise to unpleasant quarrels into which the British Consulate was unwillingly drawn. Relations between the Consul and the Bishop worsened. Although the missionaries of the London Society did not advocate Gobat's policy, they unreservedly supported him throughout his protracted conflict with Finn. The Consul sent letters to London critical of Gobat and his activity. The tension between the two men was compounded by the rivalry between their strong-willed wives for senior status within the community. The two women were ambitious and domineering. They intervened in public matters, and were responsible in large measure for the deterioration of personal relations between their husbands and the creation of an irreconcilable crisis.[127]

---

126 The Church Missionary Society (CMS), founded in 1799, was first active in Africa and the East. It later established missions in Malta, Greece, Egypt, and Abyssinia. The mission in Malta included Gobat, who urged the CMS to found a Palestine mission after the Ottoman government in 1850 had legalised the conversion of Christian Ottoman subjects to Protestantism. Now, thanks to Gobat's initiative, a new field of activity was opened for the CMS.

127 An eyewitness wrote: "Both Mrs. Gobat and Mrs. Finn are highly gifted women, each in her own way ... they are now separated, do not see one another, do not speak to each other, because their husbands have become enemies" (Bremer, p. 104). Similar opinions: "Hauptursache-Ehrgeiz einer Frau ... wollte eine Rolle in der Gemeinde spielen, die Erste in derselben sein, in die Geschäfte des Bischofs hinein reden ... Gobat ging darauf nicht ein, und seine Gemahlin verhielt sich nicht immer ganz laut der Etiquette ... der Consul ... vom Willen seiner Missis abhängig"

Relations between Consul and Bishop worsened over the course of a decade until they were severed completely. All the efforts of various mediators, first and foremost the missionaries, to effect a reconciliation were fruitless. The confrontation reached its peak in November 1857, when Finn attempted to appoint his Dragoman and confidant, the infamous convert Shimon Rosenthal, as his temporary replacement. The two sides conducted a lengthy correspondence with the Foreign Office. At Finn's urging, Rosenthal finally filed a libel suit against the Bishop and his supporters. Finn wanted to judge the case, and summoned his opponents to appear before him. When they ignored his demand, he decreed on 2 March 1858 that they were not to leave Jerusalem for more than two hours.[128] A scandal ensued, and Finn received an explicit order from London to cancel all legal proceedings against the Bishop. This was a crushing blow to Finn's prestige, which caused severe damage to the Consul's standing.[129] The affair came to an end a year later, with a strongly-worded directive from Foreign Secretary Malmesbury to Finn, ordering the Consul to end his conflict with the Bishop. The Foreign Secretary threatened to depose Finn if he should disobey.[130]

The animosity between the two continued unabated until the end of Finn's term, totally undermining the Consul's relations with the church and the mission. When the Bishop and the missionaries learned that Finn was to be relieved of his post by the Foreign Office, due mainly to the tremendous debts which had driven the Consul into bankruptcy, they made no attempt to conceal their joy. Thus came to an end the tenure of Consul Finn, who had initially granted his full patronage to

(Busch, p. 307); "Finn unter überwiegender Einfluss seiner willensstarken Gattin; kein Herz für den Bischof" (Gobat, p. 404); Hornby, p. 131 and below, Document No. 53.

128 See the voluminous correspondence in FO 78/1295, 78/1384, and 78/1448; Eliav, Shimon Rosenthal; Gobat, pp. 405–406.

129 See the following entries in Finn's diary: "This was an unpalatable medicine to take" (13 April 1858); "I do not know if I ever in my life felt so much depressed" (14 April 1858); "I never could have imagined formerly that I should ever be in such a position as at present, with my people under me rebellious, as a hinderer of missionary operations and reviled by the religious people in the name of Protestant religion" (22 May 1858).

130 "It is the desire of H.M.'s Government that, if you cannot remain on good terms with the bishop, you should abstain from all communications with him.... I have to inform you that if I should hear any more complaints against you, with regard to this matter, it will become my duty to recommend to the Queen, that you should be removed from your post as H.M.'s Consul at Jerusalem" (28 April 1859, FO 78/1448). Upon receipt of this warning, Finn wrote in his diary: "When will there be an end to the distress which I and my family feel in attending services. Bishop suddenly staring at us ... I fear that exemption from distress is only to be attained when the threat of Lord Malmesbury's Despatch of yesterday is accomplished ... when I call to my mind all that I and mine have done for the Jewish Mission, for the services of Christ Church, Bishopric and for the individuals during the last 18 years" (Entry for 15 May 1859). It is difficult to understand Finn's reference to "18 years."

the activities of the mission, supporting it in various ways, and had at first acted quite civilly toward the new Bishop. Finn's difficult character and domineering manner led to the crisis in their relations. Finn fell into disfavour with the Foreign Office, while Gobat received its full support.

The approach adopted by Noel Moore was completely different from that of his predecessors. He had never been affiliated with any missionary society, nor was he a zealous fighter for British prestige. As a young diplomat, he sought to remain within the bounds of his function as Consul. During his lengthy term of service he did not intervene in the affairs of the Bishop and the mission, other than the granting of protection when necessary and responding to requests for assistance in certain instances. He thereby avoided any confrontation with the missionaries and the Bishop, with whom he maintained correct relations. Consequently, few of Moore's reports deal with the mission and its religious and educational activity.

During his years in Jerusalem, the London Society greatly expanded its medical and educational operations, both in Jerusalem as well as in Safed and Jaffa. The missionaries also established a network of educational institutions in various cities. The second missionary society, the CMS, successfully increased its activities among the Arab Christian population, but could not point to similar achievements among the Muslims, due mainly to the opposition of the local authorities. Moore barely mentions all this activity in his reports.[131] The joint Anglo-Prussian Bishopric was disbanded after the sudden death in 1882 of the third incumbent, Joseph Barclay. The Germans established an independent congregation, while the mandate of the new Bishop, Blyth, extended only to the Anglican community.[132]

One instance in which Moore intervened in the proselytising of the London Society is indicative of the Consul's careful attitude. In October 1876 E.B. Frankel, who was temporarily in charge of the mission, affixed placards to the walls of the mission building, in clear view of the public, containing a Christian interpretation of Biblical verses arguing that the Jews erred in their belief that the Messiah had not yet come. Infuriated by this provocative act, the *Hakham Bashi* (Chief Rabbi) and the leaders of the *Yishuv* first turned to the Governor of Jerusalem, demanding the removal of the placards which were an affront to the Jewish religion and were detrimental to public safety. They pointed to a precedent in 1871, when a spirited protest by the heads of the Jewish community compelled the missionaries to take down similarly offending placards and those responsible were punished. The

---

131 For the activities of the societies, see: Tibawi, pp. 151–170, 206–212.
132 See below, Document No. 103, n. 1; Blyth, introductory chapter. For the negotiations prior to his appointment, see: Tibawi, pp. 217–222. Instead of Bishop of Jerusalem, Blyth's title was now "Bishop in Jerusalem and the East."

Governor justified their complaint and demanded that Moore take forceful steps to remove the placards in order to prevent "quarrels between the two communities." Moore acceded to the Governor's demand and firmly "advised" the removal of the placards, which presumably offended the religious sensibilities of the Jews by "implying that a very large section of the population of the city, professing a religion recognised and protected by the State, misbelieve or misunderstood their own scriptures."

The mission was, of course, compelled to comply, and when Moore reported his action to his superiors, his behaviour was supported and confirmed by London and Constantinople.[133]

Moore's successor, Dickson, maintained this policy of noninterference. He acknowledged the Bishop as the head of the Protestant community, and had no interest to clash with the prelate. As evidence of the warm relationship the two enjoyed throughout Dickson's term, in 1904 a delegation of British subjects, both Christians and Jews, headed by Bishop Blyth presented the Consul with a gift as a token of their appreciation for his devoted service.[134]

Far-reaching changes had taken place during this period. Blyth, the first Anglican Bishop, led the community in a high-handed manner. He established his own missionary society, to the displeasure of the two existing missionary groups.[135] Unlike Gobat, Blyth operated in concert with the Greek Orthodox church and concentrated his proselytising efforts among the Arab population, focussing his efforts upon the strengthening of educational activity, and not upon conversions. Thus, he established a network of schools which were open to members of all faiths.[136] When, however, a girl's orphanage was inaugurated in 1888, Jewish girls were required to undergo baptism before their acceptance.

Dickson was involved in several confrontations with the London Society, when it was charged with unlawfully holding Jewish girls and even refused to return

133  See: Hyamson, *British Consulate*, Nos. 290–292.
134  FO 78/5352. The address was signed by 109 British subjects, and a silver service and two watch chains were presented to Dickson. See below, Document No. 103, n. 3. The letter by Bishop Blyth to the Foreign Secretary, Sir E. Grey, (Document No. 103) was written after Dickson's death and includes a warm appreciation of the late Consul.
135  Blyth, who opposed the independence of the LJS and the CMS, unsuccessfully attempted to assert his authority over them. After some time he founded the "Jerusalem and East Mission," concentrating his missionary work in this organisation (Tibawi, chap. 9; Crombie, pp. 124–128).
136  Blyth maintained that the missionary schools should be open to Jews, Christians, and Muslims together, and that they should not be used to detach children from their parents (Tibawi, pp. 259–261). At his initiative, an impressive new church, St. George's Cathedral, was erected in 1898, near Damascus Gate, to serve as the main church of the Anglican community. "The very location of St. George's is evident of trends ... to make approaches to the Arab population, at the cost of relations with the Jews" (Ben-Arieh, II, p. 327).

them to their parents. The Italian Consulate intervened in one case, which threatened to develop into a diplomatic incident. Dickson, who acted decisively but graciously in all these instances, succeeded in restoring the girls to the custody of their parents.[137]

Forceful action was required of the Consul in April 1897, when the London Society inaugurated its new hospital, in a magnificent building outside the walls of the Old City. This sparked vigorous protests by Jews against the mission and the hospital, accompanied by a rabbinical decree forbidding hospitalization in the new institution or supplying it with kosher meat. These protests were accompanied by acts of violence, and the Consul sought to defuse the charged atmosphere and defend the hospital.[138] Dickson even requested the Governor of Jerusalem's assistance in protecting the missionary institutions. Once more, Dickson acted in a quiet and gracious manner throughout the entire episode, without being overconspicuous. Acts of violence against the hospital ceased within a few months, although the rabbinical bans remained in effect. Dickson continued to foster amicable relations with the missionaries, and was even invited as a guest of honour to the dedication of their institutions and to their yearly celebrations.

The Consuls who succeeded him served in Palestine for short periods, and did not develop any relationship with the various missionary societies, nor did they intervene in the latter's activities.

## Consular Policy on the Granting of Protection

Granting British protection to Jews was undoubtedly one of the central issues that occupied the Consulate throughout its entire existence. It involved much work: examination of the requests and the eligibility of the petitioners, maintenance of records and the issuance of certificates, and — above all — defense of the protégés. These activities were the core of consular efforts, greatly occupying the Consul and his staff during long periods of time.

At first, protection was extended to Jews in general, without granting individuals the official status of protégé. This was Young's interpretation of the well-known directive of 31 January 1839, and he acted accordingly, providing succor and

---

137  For the various incidents, see: Hyamson, *British Consulate*, Nos. 350, 372, 384 and 385; Tibawi, p. 262.
138  See: Hyamson, *British Consulate*, Nos. 385, 386 and Enclosures, Nos. 387–390 and 393. When a Jewish woman died in the new hospital, she was refused burial in the Jewish cemetery. Dickson even asked for the removal of the Chief Rabbi (S.J. Eliachar), "who is said to be instigated by several European Jews of Socialist tendencies." See also Crombie, pp. 128–135.

defense to the entire Jewish *Yishuv* as well as to individuals who had fallen victim to persecution and attacks. Young forcefully devoted himself to this task, even at the cost of confrontations with his superiors.

This policy changed during the Finn's term in office. He initiated the granting of personal protection to Jews who were subjects of foreign Powers (primarily Russia) and had lost their citizenship. Following negotiation, it was decided to extend protection to Jews from Russia on condition that the Russian Consul would agree in writing to transfer them to British protection. Finn extended this arrangement beyond Jerusalem, seeking to increase the number of protégés as much as possible by placing Russian Jews in Hebron, Jaffa, Safed, and Tiberias under his protection, obviously with the consent of his superiors.[139] Over the course of time, Finn undoubtedly exceeded the instructions he had been given. On the one hand, he granted protection to former Russian Jews who had not received the written approval of the Russian Consul or who did not possess documents attesting to their former citizenship. On the other hand, he attempted to extend British protection to foreign subjects following their conversion to Christianity.[140] Though these efforts were the cause of many confrontations with Finn's superiors, they did not prevent a constant increase in the number of British protégés.

In 1859 even Finn realised that he had gone too far in extending protection to too many individuals of doubtful eligibility. Accordingly, he resolved to follow the directives which instructed him to cancel the protection that had been granted to all those not possessing a certificate of dismissal from the Russian Consul. In practice, the number of protégés did not significantly decrease. Finn was aware of the fact that many of the protégés of Russian origin had passed away and their certificates of protection had been transferred to individuals who were ineligible for British protection.[141] In the wake of this abuse, Finn proposed in 1862, shortly before his ouster, to limit the validity of the documents, but his recommendation was not accepted.

New regulations were instituted in 1864 upon the receipt of directives from London. An annual check and registration of certificates of protection was introduced applicable to British subjects and protégés alike, for which a certain sum would be collected from all except the indigent. Every head of household enjoying British protection was required to appear in person before the Consul or a duly

---

139 See the memorandum, "Protection of Jews in Syria and Palestine," Hyamson, *British Consulate*, No. 274; ibid., Introduction, pp. xxxviii–xlii.
140 See the Appendix for details on the number of protégés during the entire period.
141 See the complaint of the Jews in Safed and Tiberias regarding Finn's conduct: Hyamson, *British Consulate*, No. 234 and Enclosures.

authorised official. Despite these measures, the number of protégés did not decrease, because many individuals who were ineligible for protection obtained the certificate by improper means, chiefly by acquiring those of deceased protégés. It was similarly unclear whether protection was granted only for an individual's lifetime, or whether it also unlimitedly devolved upon his descendants.

The protection extended to the Jews of Safed and Tiberias proved to be extremely problematic. Unlike his predecessor, Moore did not trouble himself to visit northern Palestine, so the Jews resident in the region were required to present themselves at the Vice-Consulate in Haifa to renew their certificates. This entailed a long and arduous journey, a requirement which many of the protégés, especially the elderly and the chronically ill, were incapable of meeting. In an attempt to solve the problem, semi-consular agents who were authorised to renew the certificates were appointed from among the Jews of these cities. As a consequence, the registration of protégés was unreliable, reports of the number of individuals under British protection in Safed and Tiberias being based more on estimates than on accurate records. The Ottoman authorities also took advantage of this situation, refusing to recognize the validity of many certificates of protection, since they did not acknowledge the local agents who had not been formally appointed. The Turks maltreated Jews in Safed and Tiberias on the pretext that they were not in fact British protégés. The situation was aggravated during periods in which there was no consular representative in Haifa to provide protection to these Jews. When northern Palestine was placed under the aegis of the Consulate-General at Beirut, this office would periodically send a special representative to the region to examine and renew the certificates, but this was not done every year, thereby providing the local authorities with a pretext for further maltreatmeant of the Jews. In one instance, in 1871, the British Consul at Damascus, Richard Burton, personally renewed certificates in Safed and in Tiberias, although they were not under his authority, to the great displeasure of the Consul-General in Beirut. Burton also reported of the disorder he found there relating to the certificates of protection.[142]

The policy of granting long-term protection arose after a visit to northern Palestine in 1872 by Consul-General J. Eldridge to inspect the registration of protégés. Eldridge took the trouble to personally examine the certificates in Acre, Haifa, Tiberias, and Safed and drew up a new list of their holders, after these individuals presented themselves before him and signed the documents in his presence. In his report Eldridge raised fundamental questions: how long would protection be extended to Jews of Russian origin, and how long would their

---

142 Hyamson, *British Consulate*, No. 263 and Enclosure; see also below, the introduction to Document No. 68.

descendants be automatically entitled to such protection. Eldridge hinted at the need to conduct a complete revision of the matter, in order to limit the list of protégés, whose number had grown over the years despite the fact that protection had not been granted to new cases.[143] Eldridge noted that he had issued certificates to 188 persons, of whom only seventeen were "really British," three were of doubtful citizenship, and 168 were of Russian origin. The total number of protégés was 776, only 68 of whom were British subjects. Foreign Secretary Granville concurred with him, replying that

> "a term must be put to the protection of those Jews, because if continued indefinitely the result would be that a considerable and annually increasing number of persons who have been in Turkey and therefore properly owe allegiance to the Turkish Government would be withdrawn from their natural allegiance.... These protected Russians are already ten times more numerous than the bona fide British subjects."

The Foreign Secretary also stressed, however, that protection should be withdrawn only gradually, after suitably informing the interested parties, and after an interim period of several years in which they could prepare for the loss of protection.[144] This reply clearly reflected the strategy of a gradual limitation of protection which would eventually lead to the revocation of this status from the majority of former Russian Jews.

Upon receipt of this response, Eldridge drafted a detailed proposal according to which heads of households of Russian origin who were thirty five year of age or older on a specific date would enjoy lifetime protection, as would their widows, their sons until they reached the age of twenty, and their daughters until they wed. Protection would be withdrawn from those under the age of thirty five only five to seven years hence, in order to enable them to obtain the protection of another Power or to become Ottoman subjects. He felt that this proposal would lead to a considerable reduction in the number of protégés, "provided that all above 35 are alive at that time, which is hardly probable."[145]

The Foreign Office did not respond speedily to the proposal. Meanwhile, Eldridge fell ill, so that no progress was made on this issue. On 11 November 1873

---

143 Hyamson, *British Consulate*, No. 267. Eldridge stated in this document: "The question of the continuance of protection to future generations is one of considerable importance, and with a view to avoid future difficulties, should it be decided upon, I have enregistered the names and ages of all the members of the different families, the heads of which are recognized as under British Protection."
144 1 July 1872, Hyamson, *British Consulate*, No. 269.
145 13 August 1872, Hyamson, *British Consulate*, No. 270.

the Ambassador in Constantinople, Sir Henry Elliot, suggested certain changes in the proposal, mainly raising the age of eligibility for lifetime protection to fifty, while protection would be withdrawn from all those under this age after three years.[146] Interestingly enough, Moore did not express any opinion in the matter, notwithstanding the fact that this pertained to a considerable number of protégés within his jurisdiction, though he did almost totally refrain from granting protection to new individuals over the years. In the meantime, the problem of effectively providing protection to the Jews of Safed and Tiberias had intensified. The protégés in these cities were distant from the consular representation in Haifa and consequently suffered at the hands of the local authorities.

Once again, a few years passed without a decision. In the early 1880s, as immigration from Eastern Europe increased, the number of those seeking British protection increased. Even though the directives relating to the granting of protection had not been changed, and such requests were generally refused, the number of protégés rose considerably, after certificates of protection had been obtained in various manners. The issue now became more pressing. Following Eldridge's suggestion, at the end of 1884 Foreign Secretary Granville approved the amended proposal put forward in 1873. All those of Russian origin above the age of fifty who had received approval for protection in 1849 and had continued to be British protégés after this date would enjoy lifetime protection, as would their widows and their children to the age of twenty. Those who were not of Russian extraction, held certificates of protection, and were over fifty years of age, would enjoy the same rights. All others would lose their protected status after five years, i.e., on 1 January 1890. Any future request for protection would be forwarded to the Ambassador for his decision.[147] This arrangement met with the approval of the Ottoman government, which demanded once again that Britain revoke its protection from foreign Jews and from ineligible native born Jews, claiming that there was no longer any reason for such protection.

Publication of the new regulations set off a tempestuous response within the Jewish *Yishuv*, but all requests to postpone their implementation were rejected, although in isolated cases the Consulate at Jerusalem did not rigorously enforce them.

Accordingly, 1890 was a watershed. On 1 March of that year Moore reported that close to 400 souls had ceased to enjoy British protection, 91 of whom were heads of household, while only 35 elderly individuals, 50 years of age and older, would continue to enjoy protection for their entire lives, along with the members

---

146 Hyamson, *British Consulate*, No. 277.
147 Hyamson, *British Consulate*, Nos. 308, 309, 311–314, 321, and 335; Introduction, pp. xliv–xlvii.

of their families. The Consul appended a complete list of those of Russian origin whose protection had been rescinded.[148] Within a short period of time, protection had been revoked from 1,456 Jewish protégés, including those in northern Palestine.[149] The lists of protégés in Jerusalem, as well as in northern Palestine, were drastically reduced, and the Consuls who served from 1890 onwards did not accept new Jewish protégés of Russian origin.[150] The lists continued to decrease, until in 1911 Consul Satow reported a total number of 394 adult British and naturalized subjects and protégés, including 21 who had been granted protection for life.[151] It may be assumed that, including children, the total number in 1911 did not exceed 1,200, similar to that in 1849. The goal had accordingly been attained: the granting of protection to those of Russian origin had gradually been revoked, until only a few such protégés remained.

## The Consuls and their Activities

### The First Consul

**William Tanner Young**, the son of a Highbury underwriter, came to this post by chance (see above). When he set out on a business trip to Syria and Palestine, nothing was further from his thoughts than a diplomatic career. When offered the position, however, he willingly agreed and took steps to attain it. He was honest, well-educated, courteous, and a devout Protestant, but his lack of diplomatic experience proved to be a major drawback.[152] On 19 September 1838 he was appointed Vice-Consul, receiving instructions which were insufficient to prepare him properly for his duties,[153] the most important of which was gaining support and sympathy for England.

---

148  FO 195/1690.
149  On 4 July 1890, the Embassy reported to the Foreign Office that 1456 persons had lost their protection, according to reports from the Consulates at Beirut, Damascus, and Jerusalem. It is difficult to determine how many of them had been under the protection of the Consulate at Jerusalem, but certainly more than one third of that number (FO 83/1723; Hyamson, *British Consulate*, No. 341).
150  In 1890 the Russians reversed their policy, claiming the right to protect their Jewish subjects in Palestine.
151  Satow to Lowther, 4 April 1911, ISA 123/1/27.
152  There are no biographical data about him. For his evangelical devotion, see above, n. 101. For his appointment, see below, Document No. 1.
153  See below, Documents Nos. 2 and 3. He was instructed: "It will be your duty to avail yourself of every favourable opportunity for collecting and transmitting to me any useful or interesting information relating to Commerce, Navigation, Agriculture and any other branch of Statistics."

He set out for his posting on 3 October 1838, arriving in Alexandria on the ninth of the following month. On 21 November 1838 Consul-General Campbell gave him the firman confirming his appointment as Vice-Consul for "Jerusalem and Palestine," together with a letter of authorisation from the Sublime Porte to the Governor of Jerusalem.[154] This was the first time that Campbell had expanded the duties of the Consulate to include the granting of protection to Jews at large, as he would reiterate a month later in his letter to the Foreign Secretary, noting: "I should suppose that one great and perhaps the chief object of his duties will be the protection of the Jewish Nation in general."[155] Palmerston approved of the suggestion, as is attested by his sweeping directive of 31 January 1839 "to afford protection to the Jews generally."[156]

On 4 February 1839 Young informed the Foreign Office of his arrival at Jaffa, which was under quarantine due to an epidemic currently raging in the country. The quarantine was lifted on 24 February, but Young was careful to remain in the port, since the gates of Jerusalem were still closed because of an epidemic rampant in its environs. He visited Jerusalem for the first time only on 10 March 1839, despite the quarantine. He was met by Nicolayson, who accompanied him on his first visit to the Egyptian Governor. His reception by the latter was intentionally humiliating, and only after the new Vice-Consul raised his voice and demanded an explanation did the attitude towards the British representative change. He was given an apology for the insults he had suffered. This incident made Young aware of the difficulties he could expect in his contacts with the authorities.[157]

The quarantine of Jerusalem was lifted two days later, and Young returned to Jaffa. During his short stay in Jerusalem he despatched his first letter to Palmerston, apparently under Nicolayson's influence, in which he stressed the need for a Protestant cemetery.[158] He returned to Jerusalem on 16 April 1839 and opened the Consulate. He was received joyfully by the Jewish community and its leaders, who

---

154 Ashley wrote in his diary: "This gentleman set sail for Alexandria at the end of last September. His residence will be fixed at Jerusalem, but his jurisdiction will extend to the whole country within the limits of the Holy Land. He is thus accredited as it were to the former kingdom of David and the Twelve Tribes" (Hodder, I, p. 241).
155 Below, Document No. 5, dated 10 December 1838.
156 Hyamson, *British Consulate*, No. 2.
157 Below, Document No. 6. Young added that he had been informed that his appointment "is by no means liked by the Authorities there and that I must be prepared for every opposition and many difficulties." Nicolayson's report mentioned only that Young "was duly acknowledged and received as the British Vice-Consul in this city" (*JI* 1839, p. 174). See also: Horn-Elbaum, p. 100.
158 Hyamson, *British Consulate*, No. 4. Young added an interesting note: "There are two parties here, who will doubtless have some voice in the future disposition of affairs. — The one is the Jew, — unto whom God originally gave this land for a possession and the other the Protestant Christian, his legitimate offspring." See also: Tibawi, pp. 36–37.

now looked to his protection against the oppression they suffered at the hands of the local population.[159]

Young's first steps are indicative of his empathy for the severe distress of the Jews. He sent a detailed report on their condition which painted a chilling picture of their profound poverty and humiliation, emphasising: "What the Jew has to endure, at all hands, is not to be told."[160] He praised the gratitude of the Jews, and stated his conviction that they were deserving of protection. The Vice-Consul adopted an aggressive stance towards the Governor, refusing to receive him in his office after that official had ordered that an innocent Jew be tortured to death.[161] A month later, he had already dealt with the cases of Jews who, as foreign subjects, demanded exemption from the poll tax. His spirited defense of the Jews and actions on their behalf were not favourably received by Campbell, who reprimanded the Vice-Consul for exceeding his authority. The disagreements between the two reached such a degree that on 13 August 1839 Young complained to Palmerston of the lack of support by his superior,[162] especially since as sole Consul in the city he was in need of support and encouragement to be able to carry out his duties with the required decisiveness.[163] The clashes continued, however, until — to Young's relief — Campbell retired and was replaced by Col. Hodges. Young was informed that Palmerston had instructed Hodges "to give you all proper support in your official character of British Vice-Consul at Jerusalem."[164]

As if Young's isolation as the only Consul at Jerusalem, his confrontations with his superior, and the hostility of the Governor were not enough, he also had to contend with a blunt attempt by the Russian Consul at Beirut, K. Basily, whose brief also included Palestine, to undermine Young's status as defender of all foreign Jews. Arriving in Jerusalem in September 1839, Basily took several forceful steps and appointed a distinguished Jew as his *Vakeel*, a sort of consular agent bearing responsibility for all Russian Jewish subjects (who constituted the decisive majority of the Ashkenazic Jewish community), and in practice assuming the role of patron to all European Jews in the city. When Basily informed the

159 "When the Jews have heard that an English Consul was going to be stationed here, they were full of joy; a great many say, now we shall have more liberty and will be able to work for our own bread and no more depend on others" (*JI* 1839, p. 180).

160 Hyamson, *British Consulate*, No. 6 (25 May 1839). See also his remarks on the difficult conditions in the country: below, Document No. 7.

161 Hyamson, *British Consulate*, Enclosure 2 to No. 6 (25 May 1839); Bonar & McCheyne, p. 132.

162 Hyamson, *British Consulate*, No. 7; Enclosures 1–4 to No. 7; Enclosure 1 to No. 9; No. 10.

163 "Standing alone as I do here, without any European Colleague and my appointment not very favourably looked upon ... I have in a peculiar manner needed the support and encouragement of my superior officer, that I might act with the firmness and decision which my position has required" (ibid., No. 10).

164 Backhouse to Young, 23 November 1839, FO 78/368 (Hyamson, *British Consulate*, No. 16).

Governor of Jerusalem of the appointment, he emphasised that only his *Vakeel* was authorised to act on behalf of the European Jews.[165] Young reported that this surprising appointment placed him in an embarrassing situation and did not enable him to properly fulfill his role as defender of all Jews.[166] In response, the Foreign Office instructed him to appoint as a counterweight a *Vakeel* for the "British Jews," ignoring the fact that such a group was virtually nonexistent. Young nevertheless searched for a suitable candidate. When none could be found, he stated that he would reconsider the matter, for "should the British Jews become more numerous, the appointment of a Vakeel will be very desirable."[167] The consequences were quite harsh. British prestige had suffered a severe blow, and Young's activity on behalf of all the Jews was limited, although he continued to deal with the problems of foreign Jews, if they requested his assistance, while persistently warning of Russia's growing influence, which was intended to frustrate Palmerston's policy.[168]

In the fall of 1840, following British intervention on behalf of Turkey, the Egyptian Governor of Jerusalem ordered Young to leave the city. He travelled to Jaffa, continuing from there to Acre aboard a warship. He returned to Jerusalem only at the beginning of 1841, after the Egyptian army had withdrawn from Palestine and Ottoman rule had been restored.[169] It is noteworthy that even during this difficult time Palmerston did not abandon his support for the Restoration of the Jews, to great degree under the influence of Ashley, and had the Ambassador at Constantinople exert pressure on the Sublime Porte, but to no avail. His renewed proposal to extend British protection to the Jews generally, reiterating the benefits that would obtain to the Ottoman Empire, met with a categorical refusal.[170] Palmerston was finally forced to shelve his plans regarding the Jews.

---

165 Below, Document No. 8 and Hyamson, *British Consulate*, Nos. 13 and 14. Basily's letter of appointment mentions only the Russian Jews, but Young in his report speaks about all the European Jews, who should look "to the Russian Consul as their protector." This appointment "leads them to dispute the right of the Russian Consul to take cognisance of others, than his own subjects."

166 The instructions of Bidwell and Campbell "have been comparatively nullified" and the new situation is "injurious to British influence among the Jews" (below, Document No. 8).

167 Hyamson, *British Consulate*, Nos. 17 and 18 (21 December 1839, 31 January 1840, FO 78/360).

168 Ibid., Nos. 19 and 20 (27 February 1840, 28 April 1840, FO 78/413). The FO files 78/390, 78/413, 78/444 and 78/501 contain many warnings by Young about the growing influence of Russia.

169 FO 78/444; Tibawi, pp. 37–41; Hajjar, p. 190; JI 1840, p. 360. The Scottish missionaries noted in their report: "When it was lately reported, that he was to be removed on account of the war that threatened, many Jews came to him with tears running down their cheeks, entreating him to remain" (Bonar & McCheyne, p. 149).

170 Hyamson, *British Consulate*, Nos. 22a, 23a–b, 24–26. See also: Friedman, British Schemes,

On 1 June 1841 Young requested home leave, due to his flagging health, but was granted six months' leave only in September. Meanwhile, in July, he was compelled to report that he had been publicly insulted and that the Governor had not punished the offenders, just as he ignored various requests by the British representative.[171] He left for England, after being promoted to Consul, on 2 September 1841, returning to Palestine early in 1842. In his absence, Bishop Alexander had arrived in Jerusalem to assume his post.

A new situation had developed. Young and Alexander soon became open rivals, as described above in the chapter on the mission. Young's reservations regarding the Bishop's exploits were reinforced by the explicit instructions he received from the new Foreign Secretary, Lord Aberdeen.[172] The Foreign Secretary forbade him to intervene in the affairs of anyone who was not under British protection, and the Consul was clearly not authorised to extend protection to converts who were foreign nationals. Young also believed in limiting missionary activity, which was liable to lead to confrontations with the representatives of the other Powers and with the Turkish authorities.[173] Alexander complained about Young, seeking to circumvent the Consul by appealing directly to the Consul-General at Beirut and the Ambassador at Constantinople, but Young had the full backing of his superiors. The tension and rivalry between the two degenerated into palpable hostility, with Alexander regarding Young as the main obstacle to the fulfillment of his goals and even as a personal foe.

In addition to reports of increasing Russian influence, Young also described events in Palestine: the rebellion in Hebron, the tribal warfare that seriously undermined public security, the serious incident sparked by the raising of the national flag by the first French Consul in the city and the inability of the

pp. 42–57; Hodder, I, pp. 310–315 ("Palmerston has already been chosen by God to be an instrument of good to this ancient people and to recognise their rights with believing in their destiny"); Temperley, pp. 443–444. See also below, Document No. 10 for his intervention in the Damascus Affair.

171 Below, Document No. 11 (27 July 1841, FO 78/444). Young complained that he had gotten no satisfaction from the Governor, and "I have not been at all satisfied with his method of treating my applications." It seems that the Ottoman Governor was no better than his Egyptian predecessor. Young stated in his request for leave: "I am very far from being strong and equal to the energy which my position here requires" (FO 195/170).

172 See above, nn. 110–112. Tennenbaum erroneously claims that Young retired in October 1842 with Newbolt then being appointed as acting Consul (Tennenbaum, Consulate, p. 88). Young left his position only in 1845.

173 In November 1843 Aberdeen once again instructed Young to limit consular protection (15 November 1843, FO 78/540); see also: Tibawi, pp. 62–68; Hajjar, p. 439; Horn-Elbaum, pp. 271–275. Also see Hyamson, British Consulate, No. 45 for the last conflict between Young and the mission in 1845.

authorities to control the ensuing disturbances even at the beginning of 1845, a state of affairs which Young described as total chaos.[174]

Just as Young had not seen eye to eye with Campbell at the beginning of his term, so, apparently, he was no more successful in developing good relations with his superior, Colonel Rose, the Consul-General at Beirut. The situation so deteriorated that in June 1844 Foreign Secretary Aberdeen found it necessary to reprimand Young for his outspoken style and baseless recriminations.[175] Relations apparently did not improve, and on 4 January 1845 Young tendered his resignation to the Foreign Secretary. His disagreements with Rose undoubtedly contributed to the decision to relinquish his post, just as he must have tired of the incessant clashes with the Bishop and the mission, and of the complaints lodged by the leaders of the Jewish community.[176] Only on 7 August 1845 was Young informed that his resignation had been accepted. Rose was directed to select a temporary Consul, so that Young could leave without further delay. The Consul-General appointed Henry Newbolt as Acting Consul until the arrival of the replacement. Newbolt did not come to Jerusalem before 16 October of that year. Young presented him to the Governor and then left Palestine.[177] He resigned from the Foreign Service and was not heard of again.[178]

## The Exceptional Consul: James Finn

Although his seventeen-year term in office was not the lengthiest of the British Consuls, **James Finn** became the most prominent and famous of all the Consuls sent by the Powers to serve in Jerusalem. This was due to his prodigious activity, which enabled him to surpass all the diplomats serving in the city with or after him.[179] He was no career diplomat, Jerusalem being the sole post he filled during

174  See below, Documents 9, 11, 13–15. In the last Despatch, Young stated: "In the absence of all power in the Local Government to redress grievances, it is in vain to apply to the Authorities for redress." See also reports in FO 78/581.
174  "I regret to have now occasion again to disapprove of your conduct and I trust that this admonition will be a sufficient warning to you and will induce you to be more guarded for the future" (6 June 1844, FO 78/581). Col. Hugh Henry Rose (1801–1885) was Consul-General at Beirut in 1841–1851.
176  FO 195/210; FO 78/625.
177  FO 78/626. Newbolt served in Jerusalem for only about six months, but nevertheless had also to intervene in missionary affairs. Hyamson, *British Consulate*, Nos. 48–50 and Enclosure.
178  According to Hannam, Young took a position with the Tithe Redemption Society (Hannam, *Britons*, p. 59). Finn met Young only after his own retirement. He noted in his diary that Young visited him for the first, and probably last, time: "I was very much pleased. I have often wished to see him. I liked him better than I expected to do" (entry of 5 February 1866).
179  For details of his biography and activities, see: Eliav, Finn.

his lifetime. Furthermore, he was a contentious and quarrelsome individual, arrogant and pretentious, and as Consul he waged harsh battles with all and sundry. His relations with the Turkish Governors, several of his fellow Consuls, and the Bishop and heads of the mission were marked by tension and dispute. Of the many Consuls to serve in Jerusalem in the last decades of Ottoman rule, he was the only one to be deposed.

James Finn was born in London in 1806 to a poor family. Fortunately for the lad, he came to the attention of Lord George Clarendon, a future Foreign Secretary, who assumed the financial burden of Finn's education. In 1832 he obtained the position of private tutor in the home of Lord George Aberdeen, who also would serve as a future Foreign Secretary. His lengthy employment in the Aberdeen household had important consequences for his future. During this period he had already begun to take an interest in the religion and practices of the Jews, and even the study of Hebrew. He would later publish two books on Jewish topics.[180] He meshed his fervent Protestant faith with concern for the Jews by joining the London Society for Promoting Christianity amongst the Jews and participating in its activities.[181]

When Lord Ashley learned in 1845 of Young's intention to resign, he considered Finn a suitable candidate to replace him, despite his total lack of experience in the Foreign Service. Bunsen, the Prussian Special Ambassador and architect of the joint Anglo-Prussian Bishopric, counseled Finn to submit his candidacy. Finn took his advice, at the same time cancelling his membership in the London Society. Since the Foreign Office had difficulty in finding a suitable candidate, it accepted Finn's application, publishing his appointment on 26 November 1845. The Foreign Secretary asked that he set out with all expediency and specified the financial terms accompanying his appointment.[182]

On 18 April 1846 Finn and his young wife arrived in Jerusalem. Newbolt transferred the consular functions to Finn, thus beginning the latter's term in office in Palestine.

Any description of Finn's career should be preceded by brief mention of his character and personality, which in great measure account for his actions as Consul at Jerusalem. The sudden transition from a simple private tutor to an all-powerful Consul representing the mighty British Empire, greatly affected his

---

180  *The Sephardim: History of the Jews in Spain and Portugal*, London 1841; *The Jews in China*, London 1843.
181  See above, in the chapter on the mission.
182  10 December 1845, FO 78/626. The salary was fixed at £550 per annum, with the proviso: "You will consider yourself as restricted from engaging in Mercantile pursuits." Finn received £175 for "outfit."

conduct. During his entire term in office he was unable to escape his sense of inferiority to educated people or members of the upper classes whom he encountered among his fellow diplomats. He consequently tended to be overly self-confident and to scrupulously defend his honour and standing through haughty and unyielding behaviour that stood on every formality.

He was guided, on the one hand, by a profound sense of religious and moral purpose, expressed in his intense interest in the Jews and his incessant efforts on their behalf. But he also sought, on the other hand, to emphasise his country's superiority in his contacts with the authorities and his fellow Consuls, being deeply affronted by any seeming attack on Britain's standing, or if England were not afforded the proper honour. He never forgave any real or imagined slight. Convinced of the correctness of his conduct and deeds, he was prepared to do battle for that which was just, or which he believed to be just. Compulsion to dominate his supporters and aides was one of his traits; he was unable to accept contradictory or opposing views. Some scholars argue that the source of his stubborn and uncompromising behaviour can be traced to his ambitious and assertive wife, the daughter of the missionary McCaul, who wielded much influence over her husband.

Finn also zealously guarded the full judicial authority over his protégés which he deemed to be his right. He was not willing to yield in this matter, even if his uncompromising stand led to disputes over his authority. In the end, he was severely reprimanded and unwillingly forced to back down.

James Finn possessed an extraordinary degree of personal courage. He aspired to become involved in all that took place in Palestine and thereby flaunt his status as the representative of Great Britain. This led him to set out, unhesitatingly, for dangerous places, being deterred neither by tribal disputes or uprisings against the Turkish authorities. He jeopardised his personal safety to mediate between the opposing parties, to restore the peace, and to ensure the punishment of rebels and brigands. No other Consul exhibited such a degree of involvement in current events or took such an active part in the efforts to restore public order and security, even when this greatly exceeded his authority. His excessive action generated a plethora of reports on tribal warfare and his attempts to intervene, peppered with complaints against the indifferent and impotent government.[183] The Crimean War

---

183  See above, n. 56 and below, Documents 19, 32–33 and 36; Hyamson, *British Consulate*, Nos. 134–136; Blumberg, *Zion*, pp. 71–72; Finn J., *Stirring Times*, I, pp. 248 ff., 305 ff.; numerous reports in files FO 195/292, FO 78/803, and FO 78/962. On 10 August 1853 Finn remarked in his report: "I am happy in having been able to do something for the preservation of the district from anarchy" (FO 78/962). An eyewitness described Finn as the "uncrowned monarch of Southern Palestine," as the "very embodiment of the British Lion — courageous, persevering and alert to maintain his country's dignity" (Lambert, *Time Is at Hand*, p. 43).

led to a marked increase in his intervention and influence. Each of his reports mentioned the impotence of the authorities which, he argued, compelled him to take action. He sometimes acted impulsively, but even when cognisant of having overstepped his authority he was not prepared to admit his error, lest this undermine his dignity.

Finn travelled extensively throughout Palestine, both to demonstrate his presence and to gain first-hand knowledge of the land and its inhabitants, and even published a book on his travels.[184]

He did not allow himself to leave the country even once during his entire seventeen-year tour of duty in Palestine, in contrast to his colleagues, who would absent themselves from their posts for many weeks. Undoubtedly, his severe financial straits also prevented him from spending a leave of absence in England.[185] He neglected his health in his zealous attention to his work and his many travels. It is hardly surprising that he developed a heart condition, in light of his strenuous activity and the endless number of disputes in which he was embroiled. His health steadily deteriorating, Finn returned to England mortally ill.

Finn's entire term in office was marked by his efforts to increase the number of Jews under British protection and to aid them, although his activities raised suspicions of concealed missionary intent. As early as March 1847 he inquired whether he could extend protection to Austrian and Russian Jews whose passports had expired and who had no intention of returning to their homelands, being in fact stateless persons and without protection. The Consul-General in Beirut was cool to the proposal regarding Austrian nationals, but did report hints dropped by the Russian Consul in Beirut, Basily, that his government presumably would not object to the granting of British protection to former Russian subjects. Palmerston, unwilling to turn this into an issue involving the European governments, instructed that protection be extended only in cases in which the foreign subjects were not protected by their own Consul, or, alternatively, that the relevant Consul had no objection to the granting of protection by his British counterpart.[186] This marked the beginning of one of the major elements of the British Consulate's activity, which would foment unrest until the end of the nineteenth century: the granting of protection to Jews who were former Russian subjects. Finn was the first to

---

184  Finn J., *Byways*. See also the descriptions in Finn J., *Stirring Times*.
185  In 1860 he requested a special allowance in order to go on leave, but he received "a very discouraging answer from London." The Foreign Office told him that there is "no probability of the rule being relaxed in my favour, with regard to expenses paid or half-salary" (Finn, Diary, entry for 3 February 1860). See also above, n. 14.
186  See below, Document No. 16; Hyamson, *British Consulate*, Nos. 52, 54, 56 and 58; ibid., Introduction, pp. xxxix ff.

instigate the transfer of these Jews to British protection, and this group later constituted a significant portion of the Consulate's protégés.

Suspicious of Finn's missionary ardour, Jews from Russia would soon ask Basily to abrogate this comprehensive arrangement. They preferred, inter alia, Austrian protection, which was not suspect of missionary designs. Niven Moore, the new British Consul-General at Beirut, stressed in a private letter to Finn that he was to refrain from interfering in religious matters.[187] Finn hotly denied these accusations, but declared in his reply: "although were I not a Consul, it would be impossible for a Christian Gentleman residing here to be silent as I have been on so important a subject and yet I know of no reason why I should not ... express my preference of the religion that I profess."[188]

The extension of protection to former Russian subjects was accompanied by crises from time to time, due to Finn's suspected missionary intentions, despite the Consul's vigorous denials. Such apprehensions accompanied Finn's entire tenure, even though he did not openly try to persuade Jews to abandon their faith. At any rate, in the first years of his consular service, Finn supported proselytising activities, befriended converts, and aided the mission, even when difficulties arose with other Consuls and Finn's intervention was liable to impair relations with the representatives of the Powers.[189] Even in later years Finn took steps — at times extraordinary — to extend British protection to as many Russian Jews as possible. He was reprimanded by the Foreign Office for his over-zealousness in this matter.[190]

Scholarly opinion is divided regarding Finn's involvement in missionary activity. Some argue that he undoubtedly engaged in such undertakings, but this definitive claim is questionable. Certainly, he was pleased by every instance of conversion, which corresponded to his view that the Jews should be attracted to the truth of Christianity. As noted above, however, his efforts to draw the proselytes to him and to attend to their needs undermined his relations with the missionaries; these differences of opinion would exacerbate into a fierce conflict.

---

187 Below, Document No. 22. See also: Moore to Finn, 18 June 1849, FO 78/2068 (Hyamson, *British Consulate*, Enclosure 4 to No. 76); Moore to Palmerston, 2 July 1849, FO 78/2068 (ibid., No. 76); Moore even mentioned suspicions raised by the Austrian Vice-Consul Pizzamano regarding Finn's zeal for the conversion of Jews; Finn to Moore, 27 July 1849, FO 78/2068 (ibid., Encl. 2 to No. 76), denying all accusations and concluding: "I have never used Consular influence as a means of proselytizing or have any intention to do."
188 27 June 1849, FO 78/2068 (Hyamson, *British Consulate*, Enclosure 2 to No. 76).
189 See Hyamson, *British Consulate*, Nos. 72 ff.; Eliav, Finn, pp. 46–48; Neumann, p. 232; Frankl, II, p. 67; Hannam, Britons, p. 60.
190 Hyamson, *British Consulate*, Nos. 92, 105, 116–117, 125, 133, 147, 209–210 and many more. Finn was reprimanded by Foreign Secretary Malmesbury on this matter (ibid., No. 145, 8 November 1852).

Finn continued to take an interest in the Jewish people and its religion, dutifully studied Hebrew, struggled to read chapters of the Bible in the original, and succeeded in gaining a certain degree of expertise in Jewish culture and in the literary sources of Judaism. Blessed with an outstanding linguistic ability, he taught himself several languages; in this he greatly surpassed the other British Consuls.[191]

As time passed, his desire to convert the Jews lessened, although his opinion regarding the need to reveal to them the "light of Christianity" remained unchanged.

James Finn and his wife Elizabeth established important projects to aid the Jews. These were an open manifestation of his aspiration to train the Jews to till the land and provide them with a livelihood from the labour of their own hands, but also expressed hidden missionary designs.[192] In 1850 he purchased a plot of land in Talbieh, outside the walls of Jerusalem, for the construction of a summer residence.[193] Finn was the first European to dare live with his family at some distance from the city walls, spending the summer months and more in this new location. Faithful to his desire to have Jews engage in productive labour, he employed many of them in the construction, expansion, and maintenance of his estate.

Two years after the purchase of Talbieh, a considerable area to the north of the city known as Kerem el-Halil (Kerem Avraham) was acquired, mainly at Mrs. Finn's behest. A 'colony' was established on this land, where many Jews would be employed in construction and agriculture without having to leave their homes. This was an outstanding philanthropic enterprise, which alleviated to a considerable degree the distress of hundreds of families, while also making a major contribution to education for productiveness.

A severe crisis faced the *Yishuv* with the outbreak of the Crimean War, as Jews were cut off from their European sources of financial support. Many families were on the brink of starvation. Finn and his wife began to distribute bread and coal, while a women's association founded by Mrs. Finn, the Sarah Society, dispensed clothing and extended aid to the sick and to new mothers. The major form of

---

191 In his report to the Foreign Office (20 November 1851, FO 78/874) Finn stated that he reads, writes, and speaks English, French, Italian, Spanish, "and a little German," vernacular Arabic, and "Hebrew more than Arabic." He omitted Greek and Latin, in which he was also fluent, as is reflected in his diary.

192 "My great object and desire being to see the land of Israel cultivated by Christian Israelites, preparatory to the time when the land will be restored to their nation" (Finn, Diary, entry for 18 December 1850).

193 Documents 24–26; Tibawi, pp. 123–124.

assistance, however, consisted of providing employment at Kerem Avraham, which even supplied 'public relief works' in order to increase the number employed for a daily wage. This undertaking made a major contribution during the crisis, and even afterwards. The farm at Kerem Avraham continued to function for many years, even after Finn had left Palestine and after his death. His widow ensured monetary support and the ongoing employment of Jews. Kerem Avraham continued to function until the beginning of the twentieth century, this time with the full support of the missionaries.[194]

The Finns' third undertaking, at Artas, to the south of Bethlehem, would have far-reaching consequences.[195] Their first two ventures had already laden them with a heavy debt burden, now further compounded by the considerable losses they incurred due to the Artas project, which also entangled them in a severe diplomatic incident with the United States, from which they extricated themselves only with great difficulty. Finn set two goals for himself at Artas: to prove that with European initiative and guidance, agriculture could prove successful in Palestine, simultaneously transforming wasteland into a fertile and prosperous farmstead; and to create a farm where Jews, primarily actual or prospective converts to Christianity, would be able to engage in productive work and refute the claim that they avoided physical labour.

John Meshullam, a convert and a British subject,[196] was the central figure in the settlement at Artas. In 1850 he and his family moved to the site and began to develop the farmstead with the encouragement of the Finns. Artas soon prospered and could point to considerable success in its fields and plantations. In time, however, Artas was plagued by many troubles: incessant attacks by a Bedouin tribe that plundered and destroyed the settlement's crops, causing damage to the farm and the plantations; a serious dispute with a group of American Adventists who attempted to settle there, which brought in its wake the first demand for Finn's ouster, since he revealed partiality in the cases which came before him for trial. Following the desertion of the place by the Americans, Mrs. Finn gained control of their property and became Meshullam's partner.[197] Her relations with

---

194  Eliav, Finn, pp. 56–60; Ilan; Finn E., *Reminiscences*, pp. 117 ff.; Shepherd, p. 129; Finn J., *Stirring Times*, chaps. 20, 28; Yellin, p. 13. There is no mention at all of this project in the Consular correspondence.

195  For Artas see: Rubin; Eliav, Finn, pp. 60–62; Hanauer, pp. 124–133; Finn E., *Reminiscences*, pp. 165 ff.; Blumberg, *View* (index); Finn J., *Stirring Times*, chaps. 11, 19, 27.

196  For Meshullam see below, Document No. 26, n. 4.

197  See below, Document No. 52; Hyamson, *British Consulate*, Nos. 187 and Enclosures, 188 and 189; Lipman, *Americans*, pp. 119–126; ibid., America-Holy Land, pp. 29–32; Blumberg, *View*, pp. 146–147, 207–210; Schur, Finn, pp. 86–87.

Meshullam deteriorated after the Finns purchased adjoining lands, increasing their debts once again.

Meshullam was well aware of the intent to dispossess him. His partnership with Mrs. Finn was dissolved, accompanied by charges and countercharges regarding debts and fraudulent accounts. These accusations came before the Consul in his judiciary capacity; Finn did not bother to disqualify himself, and decided in favour of his wife. Meshullam was forced to leave Artas in 1862, losing all his property and the fruits of his labour. He settled in Jerusalem, loudly denouncing the injustice he had suffered and the Finns' scheme to dispossess him. This affair, which was brought to the attention of the Prince of Wales (the future Edward VII) during his tour of Palestine, also hastened the end of Finn's tenure as Consul.

Finn's Artas project, his efforts to grant protection to former Russian Jews, and his other undertakings on behalf of the Jewish community in distress all indicate that he considered the extension of aid to Jews to be the central goal of his activities. His efforts to serve as benefactor to the Jewish community exceeded those of any other Consul in the nineteenth century. Though among the other Consuls there were some who tended to philosemitism and engaged in activities on behalf of the *Yishuv*, none exceeded his authority or went into debt in order to help the Jews.

Nonetheless, the suspicion in which he was held by the leaders of the *Yishuv* did not abate, and prohibitions forbidding Jews to take advantage of his aid were published even in times of distress. These decrees were not efficacious, nor did they reduce the number of Jews who sought the Consul's assistance. Despite the aid he extended, relations with the leaders of the Jewish community deteriorated. Finn sought to place the *Yishuv* under his authority; he intervened in its internal affairs, which lay completely beyond his authority, and thought that his forceful protection obligated the Jews to fully obey his directives. Accordingly, he was not deterred from challenging the heads of the *Yishuv*, especially its rabbinical leadership, which he termed "zealous" and "tyrannical." In this arena he was handed a sounding defeat. He was compelled to nullify incarcerations which he was not duly sanctioned to implement and to cancel directives detrimental to the *Yishuv* leadership. When complaints against Finn increased and he ignored warnings and reprimands, his days as Consul at Jerusalem were numbered.[198] It was characteris-

---

198   For Finn's disputes with the rabbinical authorities, see: Hyamson, *British Consulate*, Nos. 179, 208–214, 219–224; below, Document No. 51. On 12 December 1861 Lord Russell reprimanded him: "You have nothing to do with their religious tenets, or with the internal regulations of their community ... you are not entitled to extend your protection or jurisdiction over Jews who are not British Subjects or to interfere directly or indirectly in their concerns" (FO 78/2068 [Hyamson, *British Consulate*, No. 213]).

tic of Finn that it was precisely his relationship with the Jewish leadership, on which he prided himself throughout his tenure, that would finally become an important factor in his downfall.

Finn's vigorous efforts on behalf of the Jewish *Yishuv* cannot, however, be discounted. In March 1847, soon after his arrival in Jerusalem, he was the only Consul to forcefully intervene in a blood libel, successfully causing the false accusation to be retracted.[199] He rose to the defense of Jews who suffered from acts of violence, and demanded punishment of the guilty parties. He intervened on behalf of Jews in Tiberias, Safed, and Hebron, mediated disputes concerning inheritances and burial, succeeded in preventing the Pasha's obstruction of Jewish ritual slaughter, and closely followed the actions of Sir Moses Montefiore during his visits to the Holy Land. Finn supported the request of the Ashkenazic Jews to build a central synagogue, and similarly intervened on behalf of Maghreb Jews when they sought to erect a synagogue of their own. He also attempted to extend his protection to Jews from Algeria, and exhibited great interest in the Samaritans.[200] In all these he frequently, and consciously, exceeded his authority, since he sought, as the representative of mighty Great Britain, to aid Jews under any circumstances, irregardless of the limitations of his position.

Finn closely followed the activities in Palestine of the Great Powers, both the Catholic nations as well as Russia and Prussia, at times cautioning his superiors that others were enhancing their power and influence while England lagged behind.[201] The British Consul's persistent goal was to attain primacy in Jerusalem, exhibiting extreme sensitivity to any possible affront to the prestige or interests of his country.

Protection for Jews of Russian origin, as already noted, was the source of much discord between Finn and the representatives of Russia during the British Consul's first years in Jerusalem. Conflicts with the American Consuls began in 1855, springing from the disagreement over the American property in Artas and the complaints lodged against Finn in this respect. The British Consul's relationship with the first Austrian Consul, Pizzamano, was significantly influenced by Finn's sense of inferiority vis-à-vis the educated nobleman. Finn had no qualms about charging the Austrian Consul, behind his back, of secretly conspiring with his Prussian colleague to support the rebels in Hebron against the Sultan, and this in

199  Hyamson, *British Consulate*, Nos. 53 and 59; Finn's diary, entry for 11 March 1847.
200  Hyamson, *British Consulate*, Nos. 129, 156, 157, 169 and 170; below, Document No. 45.
201  Below, Documents Nos. 27, 34, 35–37 and 39. In his report dated 11 March 1847 he remarked ironically: "Of England and her political position it is somewhat difficult to give a description, except by comprising the topics of my despatches into an Essay" (Document No. 37).

the midst of the Crimean War.[202] The charge would prove to be baseless. This tense relationship further deteriorated in 1857 when Pizzamano was promoted to the rank of Consul-General and granted the title of Count. Finn, doyen of the diplomatic corps and sensitive to matters of protocol, could not reconcile himself to the advancement of the Austrian Consul, which in effect negated Finn's senior status.

By far the most severely strained relationship, and a source of protracted hostility, was that between Finn and the Prussian Consul, Dr. Georg Rosen. Good relations and cooperation could have been expected between the representatives of England and Prussia, partners in the joint Bishopric and in the leadership of the Protestant community. Finn, however, could not see eye to eye with Rosen, the educated scholar and experienced Orientalist, and his jealousy got the better of him. In 1855 Finn, without foundation, charged Rosen with supporting the rebels in Hebron, and some time later accused him of adopting a pro-Russian stance in the Crimean War. The Foreign Office forwarded these allegations to Berlin, leading to a lengthy correspondence culminating in Rosen's innocence being clearly manifested. Finn was ordered to come to terms with his rival after the unprecedented attacks he had made against his fellow diplomat. Finn's defeat only deepened the enmity between them, the strain in their relationship reaching critical proportions when Finn learned of Rosen's support of Bishop Gobat. Finn's position became untenable when the Foreign Office also expressed its support for the Bishop. Rosen's victory was complete in April 1862, when the Prince of Wales visited Palestine. Rosen, an archaeologist and Orientalist, was clearly preferred to the British Consul by the royal visitor. He accompanied the Prince on his travels and completely overshadowed the deeply affronted Finn. The Prince of Wales was presented with petitions demanding Finn's removal, possibly at Rosen's instigation, thereby causing the Prince to gain a negative opinion of Finn.[203]

Nevertheless, it was Finn's serious monetary entanglements that were the main cause of his dismissal. He was incapable of managing his financial affairs. Throughout his tenure he complained of his meagre salary, insufficient for his needs.[204] He took no heed of the limits of the budget at his disposal when

---

202  Blumberg, *View*, pp. 214–216; Eliav, *Austrian Protection*, pp. 25–91.
203  For the various disputes and confrontations between the two Consuls, see: Blumberg, *View*, pp. 214–217, 240, 307; idem, "The British and Prussian Consuls of Jerusalem and the Strange Will of Rabbi Hershell," *Zionism* 1 (1980), pp. 1–8; Eliav, Shimon Rosenthal; Hyamson, *British Consulate*, No. 180; FO 78/1217. Relations with the first Prussian Consul, Dr. Gustav Schultz, and Acting Consul T. Weber, were, however, very cordial. Both asked Young and Finn to attend to the affairs of the Consulate in their absence (9 July 1844, FO 78/581; 29 January 1849, FO 78/803).
204  On 8 July 1854, Finn asked for a raise in his salary, stating: "The foreign Consulates in Jerusalem

expending funds for the Consulate, and the deficit increased from year to year. The loans he took at high interest to finance the expenses of the Consulate, his travels throughout Palestine, and the purchase of lands caused his debts to grow unchecked. He continued taking loans to cover his expenses, and found himself in an inextricable financial crisis.

Following the visit by the Prince of Wales, Jerusalem was rife with rumours of Finn's impending dismissal. No one would loan him more money, and his creditors demanded the immediate repayment of his debts, which totalled thousands of pounds sterling. Finn was reduced to penury, unable even to purchase firewood for heating in the winter, or even the most basic foodstuffs. He was virtually bankrupt, and the entire city knew of his desperate situation. The Foreign Office, which had already decided to remove Finn from his post, despatched Judge Sir Edmond Hornby to Jerusalem, to prevent the British Consul from being officially declared bankrupt. Hornby succeeded in considerably lowering the rate of interest charged on the loans, thereby reducing Finn's debts by half to approximately £2350, and compelled the Consul's creditors to accept a repayment schedule extending over a period of years. All the Finns' landed assets were mortgaged, and Finn was required to pay off his debts at the rate of £200 per year, out of his salary.[205] The agreement was drawn up and signed by Hornby on 26 June 1863, after having received the consent of the creditors and Finn, and deposited in the archives of the British Consulate.

Hornby's report treated Finn in a forgiving and understanding manner, casting the blame for the Consul's troubles upon his inflexible character, which gained him enemies instead of friends. Regarding the dispute with the mission, here too the judge vindicated Finn, although noting that he had erred in his behaviour towards the Bishop and the mission. Hornby also emphasized that Mrs. Finn contributed considerably to these developments by expending vast sums in order to improve the condition of the Jews, impoverishing her husband in the process.[206]

---

have been increased in number and raised in estimation since 1845. The Prussian, Austrian, French & Spanish Consuls are men of considerable standing in Society, and are enabled to keep up more of an outward state than I am" (FO 78/1024). On 30 March 1857 he complained of the "inadequacy of income" and stated: "Every year augments my difficulties.... What to do I do not know unless I retire during the working period of my life upon the pension to which I am entitled, to reside at the cheap port of Caiffa and support my children by the labour of my hands" (Document No. 38). In a long letter dated 30 August 1859 Finn described his financial situation and his heavy debts (FO 78/1448). See also: Finn J., *Stirring Times*, p. 98; Shepherd, pp. 129–130.

205   See below, Document No. 53; Eliav, Finn, pp. 70–74. See also op. cit., p. 77, a facsimile of the last page of the agreement.

206   In his autobiography, written many years later, Hornby specifically accused Mrs. Finn, "a lady

In addition, Finn undoubtedly exhibited lack of judgement and intervened in affairs which exceeded his brief as Consul.

Not only was Finn reprimanded and harshly warned by four Foreign Secretaries, he was also the only Consul whose actions led to the despatch of investigators to Jerusalem on three occasions to conduct an inquiry into his doings and to draw conclusions. The first, Francis Napier (the future Lord Napier of Ettrick), was instructed in March 1855 to examine the charges raised against Finn by the government of the United States concerning the Artas affair. Although Napier was sympathetic to the Consul, he noted that the accusations against him were not unfounded, and that his nature and conduct were in bad taste. Colonel A. Frazer, sent in July 1862 to investigate the charges raised in petitions submitted to the Prince of Wales in Jerusalem, issued a scathing report which led the Foreign Office to decide, once and for all, to remove Finn from his post.[207] Finn was informed of the recommendation to appoint him as Consul to the Dardanelles, with an annual salary of £600. Though he argued that this was a decrease in both rank and salary, the official announcement of his new posting and of the appointment of Noel Moore to replace him as Consul at Jerusalem was issued on 29 December 1862.

Finn had no choice but to accept his deposition; moreover, he was compelled to inform the Foreign Office that he would have to forego the leave in England which he had been granted, being unable to afford it. Moore arrived in Jerusalem on 3 March 1863, and assumed his post a week later. Finn ceased to be the Consul at Jerusalem, but did not make haste to leave the city, because he had not yet come to an arrangement with his creditors, who harrassed him greatly. Only after Hornby's arrival in June 1863 and his success in reaching an agreement with the creditors was Finn ready to leave Jerusalem. In the meantime, it was proposed that he should exchange positions with the appointed Consul to Erzerum, who preferred the post in the Dardanelles. Finn resolved to accept the alternative proposal, which would not entail a reduction in salary since the Consulate in Erzerum was regarded as a political Consulate, with a salary matching that of the Consul in Jerusalem: £700.

Due to the poor state of his health, Finn decided to first take leave in England.

---

of very considerable energy and ability and of a masterful temper, in the exercise of which she managed to involve her husband in serious pecuniary difficulties" (Hornby, pp. 131–132).

207 But already on 13 June 1862, James Murray, Assistant to the Under-Secretary of State and the official in charge of the consular service, stated in a memorandum: "Every Secretary of State has felt that Finn ought to be removed and I have been derived to try and effect an exchange so as to let him down easy, but I have never been able to persuade anyone whose place was at all equivalent to Jerusalem to go there.... If the Dardanelles becomes vacant, Finn might be sent there and Noel Moore to Jerusalem" (FO 78/4782).

On 17 July 1863 the Finn family set sail for Great Britain. He returned to his homeland mortally ill, broken in body and in spirit. The Foreign Office decided to forego his services. Finn's state of health further deteriorated. He passed away on 29 August 1872 a lonely man, impoverished and depressed.

Various factors influenced the decision to remove Finn from his post in Jerusalem and to dismiss him from the Foreign Service. In his years of isolation in London he continued to long for the Holy Land and held fond memories of Jerusalem, firm in his conviction that he had suffered an injustice.[208]

## The Professional Consuls

In contrast to the first two Consuls in Jerusalem, all those who succeeded them were career diplomats. **Noel Temple Moore** (1833–1903), son of the Consul-General at Beirut, Niven Moore,[209] had served in the Beirut Consulate from 1851 to 1862, and had accompanied the Prince of Wales on his tour of Palestine in April 1862.[197] Quite likely, he caught the attention of the Prince, who may have recommended him as the future Consul. At any rate, his candidacy was already proposed in June of that year, [210] and he was officially appointed Consul at Jerusalem on 29 December 1862. Moore would fill this post for the next twenty-seven years — a longer term in office than any other Consul. Nevertheless, he was less well-known, both because he was overshadowed by the dominant character of his predecessor, and because he scrupulously observed the limitations of his post. He did not exceed the framework of his brief, nor was it of his nature to take the initiative in various matters. He may also have been influenced by the troubles of his predecessor, and therefore carried out his duties with extreme care, avoided becoming involved in any imbroglio, and refrained from unnecessary intervention in the affairs of the Jews, although he was quick to extend aid and protection to them when necessary.

Moore arrived in Jerusalem on 3 March 1863. Finn presented him to the Pasha, and after receiving possession of the archives of the Consulate, he assumed the post of Consul on the 10th of the month.[211] Like his predecessors, Moore was a superb linguist, fluent in English, French, Italian, Arabic, Turkish, and Persian.[212] He was also an Orientalist of note.

His assumption of duties, however, was not without difficulties. Finn, who was

---

208   For his last years, see: Eliav, Finn, pp. 79–81.
209   See below, Document No. 1, n. 2.
210   See above, n. 194.
211   FO 195/761; FO 78/1692.
212   FO 78/1449.

still conducting negotiations with his creditors, was in no hurry to leave. His very presence in Jerusalem proved burdensome to Moore, for Finn, as was his wont, continued to intervene in affairs, writing Moore almost daily, because he could not reconcile himself to the fact that after so many years he was no longer Consul. On 2 April 1863 Moore wrote quite frankly to the Foreign Office that he had indeed been cautioned not to assume his post until Finn had arranged his affairs and left the city, lest complications ensue. Indeed, there were many difficulties, and he requested that someone be appointed to examine the allegations and financial claims that had been raised.[213] This request led to the dispatch of Consular Judge Hornby, as described above. In the meantime, there was growing tension between Moore and Finn, who was critical of the new Consul. As a general rule, Moore preferred not to respond, merely ignoring Finn's criticism. This tense situation prevailed until Finn left Jerusalem for good.

In his first years in office, Moore dealt with the issue of granting protection to Jews of Russian extraction, after they once again applied for British protection. The Foreign Office replied favourably to this appeal, but only on condition that the Russian Consul would agree in writing to such an arrangement.[214] Moore, quite sympathetic towards the Jewish community, provided aid to the victims of the plague in 1865.[215] He also took forceful action in the dispute between the Ashkenazic and Sephardic communities in 1867 over ritual slaughtering of meat, and was praised for his intervention.[216]

Moore, who had been instructed not to intervene in religious matters, did not show much interest in mission affairs; in fact he treated them with some reservation.[217] He was a man of restraint and lacking in inspiration. Consequently, his reports are matter of fact and concise, certainly inferior to those of Finn, who was capable of filling tens of pages with a single report. Moore was not an outstanding correspondent, limiting his reports primarily to the most important and essential

---

213  FO 78/1775. Moore mentions "pecuniary claims of Foreign & British subjects; complaints of illegal acts in his judicial capacity and of local land speculations." He did not want to complain, but Finn's behaviour is problematic, and he does not know when he will depart.

214  Hyamson, *British Consulate*, Nos. 241–251. The main petitioner, Hirsch Berliner, stated in his letter to the Foreign Secretary that the applicants who could produce the formal letter of dismissal "were kindly received under British Protection by H.M.'s Consul, Noel Temple Moore, who dealt very kindly with us, giving gratis the paper of Protection to those who had not the means to pay; indeed he is always prepared energetically to protect us and even personally to interfere with the Pasha" (No. 246).

215  Below, Documents 55–56; Eliav, *Austrian Protection*, Nos. 135–142.

216  Hyamson, *British Consulate*, No. 252.

217  It is very characteristic that the missionary effort to settle Jewish immigrants in Artouf in 1883 is not mentioned in Moore's dispatches.

matters, and even these did not merit lengthy treatment. He did, however, exhibit great concern for British travellers and pilgrims and sought to ensure their safety.

In January 1866 the Consul-General at Beirut, George Jackson Eldridge, was instructed to evaluate the quality of Moore's work. After visiting Jerusalem, Eldridge wrote a very favourable report, which undoubtedly raised Moore's standing in the Foreign Office.[218]

When Assad J. Khayat, the British Consul at Jaffa, died on 19 November 1866, Moore took advantage of the opportunity to request that the Consul at Jaffa be placed under his authority.[219] This request was approved, and upon Moore's recommendation, Khayat's son was appointed to succeed his late father.[220] When the Governor, Izzet Pasha, concluded his term in office, Moore saw fit to emphasise in his reports the good relations he had enjoyed with the Governor, in a document markedly different from the complaints by Finn against the various Governors.[221]

Foreign Office satisfaction with Moore was reflected in an announcement by the Foreign Secretary in 1882 of the intention to appoint the Consul Companion of the Order of St. Michael and St. George after nineteen years of service in Jerusalem, the only Consul in Jerusalem to receive such recognition.[222] Moore had successfully avoided confrontation, forged amicable relations with everyone with whom he had come in contact in his role as Consul, and in general was held in high esteem by all circles in the city.

Noteworthy is Moore's attempt to intervene in a controversy within the Jewish community that erupted in 1879. It followed in the wake of a contribution by Moses Montefiore and British Jewry to finance the study of Arabic in Ashkenazic educational institutions, especially in the Etz Hayyim religious school. The dona-

---

218 "Moore is a most efficient public servant and is animated with great zeal for the public service, while at the same time he performs the duties of his delicate position as H.M.'s Consul at Jerusalem with much tact and prudence, taking great care to avoid mixing himself in party quarrels that are so frequent at Jerusalem" (Eldridge to Clarendon, 29 January 1866, FO 78/1952).

219 29 November 1866, FO 78/1875. For Assad Khayat, see below, Document No. 21, n. 1; Tibawi, pp. 142–145.

220 12 May 1866, FO 78/1929. See also below, for the Consulate at Jaffa.

221 "I feel it is my duty to record my own high sense of the conduct of Izzet Pasha towards H.M.'s Consulate. During the whole course of his administration extending 4 years, nothing occurred to interrupt the best understanding between us, whilst immediate attention to my representations and requests and prompt settlement of all claims have characterised my official relations with His Excellency" (11 April 1867, FO 78/1979).

222 "The Queen upon my recommendation has been graciously pleased to approve of your being appointed a companion of the most distinguished Order of St. Michael & St. George as a mark of approbation of your services as H.M.'s Consul at Jerusalem" (17 February 1882, FO 78/3421).

tion had been made with the approval of Rabbi Samuel Salant, the rabbi of the Ashkenazic community, and of other rabbis in the community. Once teaching of Arabic began, however, a vehement controversy erupted, resulting in violent opposition among the religious extremists, who demanded that the lessons cease immediately. They regarded them as damaging to their protracted struggle against the modernisation of education in Jerusalem, and especially against the incorporation of secular studies. When their demands were not met, they forcibly broke into the school, causing much damage and demanding that the money be returned to the donors. The Consul unsuccessfullly attempted to intervene.[223] Most of the religious zealots enjoyed the protection of the Austrian Consulate with which Moore sought to avoid a confrontation. The British Consul also sought to influence the *Hakham Bashi*, Rabbi Abraham Ashkenazi, to intervene in the affair, but the latter limited his response to expressing his sorrow, noting that "The British Consul was also grieved to see men rejecting their welfare with their own hands"; he termed Moore "a friend of Israel and desires our welfare." The heads of Etz Hayyim capitulated to the terror and were forced to return the money to the contributors.[224]

During the struggle against the anti-immigration decrees in 1887–1890, Moore participated in the coordinated activity of the European Consuls to bring about their cancellation, as they believed them to be contrary to the rights granted by the Capitulations and detrimental to the interests of their protégés. The diplomatic campaign, the brunt of which was borne by the Ambassadors in Constantinople, bore fruit, and the Sublime Porte was forced to back down, step by step. As the struggle progressed, Moore periodically reported of the maltreatment of Jews under British protection who sought to enter Palestine. He forcefully intervened on their behalf, and totally rejected the demands of the Governor of Jerusalem to help in locating and deporting the illegal immigrants.[225]

Moore did not ignore the growing influence and presence of the various Powers. In a despatch in 1879 he listed the achievements of the Russians, the Germans, and the French in the establishment of buildings and institutions, as well as in other spheres. One of his letters written in 1880 was devoted to a description of growing

223  Hyamson, *British Consulate*, Nos. 295, 296 and 298.
224  Ibid., Enclosure 2 to No. 298.
225  M. Eliav, "Diplomatic Intervention Concerning Restrictions on Jewish Immigration and Purchase of Land at the End of the 19th Century," *Cathedra*, no. 26 (December 1982), pp. 117–132 (Heb.); idem, Yishuv, pp. 262–264; Hyamson, *British Consulate*, Nos. 322–326, 328–331. The Ambassador's clear instruction to Moore was: "The right of British subjects to go and come within the Ottoman dominions is secured by the Capitulations.... British subjects enjoy alike the same rights and privileges and no creed or other distinction can be admitted as regards British subjects or protégés whatever religion they profess" (ibid., No. 324).

French influence, and in 1890, in a report on Jerusalem, he wrote of the increased numbers of foreign institutions and the open rivalry accompanying their establishment, stressing the progress made by the Germans in the economic sphere and in settlement, in addition to the gains achieved by the Russians and the French. In this letter Moore also mentioned the British institutions: the various missions and their operations, as well as the Ophthalmic Hospital that had been established in Jerusalem in 1883 ("an excellent institution"), which faithfully served the public at large and served in a way as a British national institution.[226] His emphasis on the hospital's importance was in characteristic contrast to his tendency to ignore mission institutions, which he apparently did not hold in high regard. In August 1890 N.T. Moore was transferred to Tripoli, with the rank of Consul-General.

The fourth Consul was **John Dickson** (1846–1906), who was appointed to the post on 10 September 1890,[227] with an annual salary of £700 and an additional £250 for the expenses of the Consulate, the same salary received by Moore and which had not changed over the course of twenty-seven years. Dickson was a veteran member of the Consular Service, having served in the 1870s as Vice-Consul in Mosul, Damascus, and Beirut. In the early 1880s he replaced the Consul-General in Beirut when Eldridge suffered from a protracted illness, filling this post for eighteen months. When Eldridge returned to his post he warmly praised Dickson, who had discharged his duties "in an admirable manner," and described his understudy's character in favourable terms.[228] Between 1882 and 1890 Dickson served in Beirut, for the first two years as Vice-Consul before being elevated to the rank of Consul.

Dickson arrived in Jerusalem on 16 March 1891 to assume his duties as Consul, after William Henry Khayat had served as Acting Consul in the interim. Shortly afterwards, tragedy befell him: his eldest son died of diphtheria. The main problem, however, was that Dickson himself was sickly, and was frequently compelled to take sick leave when his health failed him.[229] He nevertheless made every effort to

226  See below, Documents 65, 66 and 69. Upon the opening of the Ophthalmic Hospital, Moore remarked in his report to the Ambassador: "it approaches more closely to a British national institution than any other at present existing at Jerusalem" (3 July 1883, FO 78/3532). Tibawi's claim that Moore ignored the vigorous French and Russian activity in Jerusalem (p. 211) is unfounded.

227  10 September 1890, FO 78/4294.

228  Dickson "displayed great discretion and tact as well as firmness, in dealing with the various matters which came before him and he gained the good will and esteem of all" (FO 195/1369).

229  On 4 November 1892, Dickson asked for leave for "medical reasons" (FO 78/4432). In 1894 he complained of malaria and other diseases (4 May 1894, FO/78/4558). In 1895 and 1896 he received three months sick leave (FO 78/4742), and the same in 1900, because of malaria fever, from which he apparently was a constant sufferer. In 1894, 1895, 1896, and again in 1900 an Acting Consul was appointed in Dickson's absence. It seems that since 1900 he was affected by

fulfill his duties in the best possible manner, until poor health got the best of him.

Unlike Moore, who acted with restraint, limiting his activity to the formal duties his position imposed upon him, Dickson was obviously emotionally involved in all that he did during the sixteen years he served in Jerusalem. He attempted to foster friendly relations with all circles in the city, both Christians and Jews, and was held in great esteem.[230]

During Dickson's term of office, Jerusalem underwent considerable modernisation, a fact which was also reflected in the reports of the Consul.[231] He generally despatched short reports, concentrating on the essence of matters, but despite his many absences from his post he wrote a great deal concerning events in the region.[232] He also submitted annual commercial reports, based mainly on information from Jaffa. From 1900 onwards, following instructions received from the Foreign Office, he wrote quite routine quarterly trade reports, accompanied by several general observations. It is noteworthy that, in contrast with the practice of his predecessors, Dickson corresponded mainly with the Ambassador in Constantinople, and refrained from directly addressing the Foreign Office.

The main issue that occupied Dickson throughout his term as Consul was the ongoing confrontation with the Ottoman authorities regarding the restriction of Jewish immigration and land purchases by Jews. From his reports it is evident that he vigorously opposed the prohibitions, which were contrary to the Capitulations, and forcefully protested the denial of entry to Palestine to British subjects and the attempts to expel them. They also reveal his empathy, on humanitarian grounds, with the plight of the unfortunate and defenseless Jews who had been left at the mercy of the Turkish police and authorities.[233] In all these efforts Dickson acted in coordination with the representatives of the other Powers, who also opposed the new regulations and forcefully rejected the authorities' harassment of the Jews.

heart disease, which increased in severity from year to year until he died in 1906 from heart failure. See also below, the introductions to Documents No. 76 and No. 103.

230 See below, Document No. 103, especially the introduction and n. 3.

231 See, e.g., below, Document No. 74, for the Jaffa-Jerusalem railway; Document No. 76 for city's the water supply; Document No. 100 for street lighting; and Document No. 84 for the general development of the city.

232 On 3 August 1893 Dickson reported that a total number of 958 despatches had been received and sent out during the last year (FO 78/4498). Some harsh verdicts regarding Dickson's correspondence would seem to be unjustified. See above n. 93 and inter alia: Dickson who, "to judge from the scope and infrequency of his reports, showed even less interest in what was happening around him" (Carmel, Great Powers, p. 59); "equally unremarkable" (Hannam, Britons, p. 63).

233 See below, Documents 75, 79, 86, 87 and 98; Hyamson, *British Consulate*, Index to Documents, part II. On 14 February 1892 Dickson described the ill fate of Persian Jews, who were to be expelled (ibid., No. 360).

Dickson was in constant conflict with the Governor of Jerusalem, informing him from time to time that he could not accept the various restrictions imposed by the Governor. This happened whenever he was required to cooperate in deporting illegal immigrants, whenever the requirements for entry to Palestine were made more stringent; or whenever the Turks maliciously attempted to deny entry to Jews who were British subjects, whom the local authorities were not authorised to detain.[234]

He took especially vigorous action against any attempt to prevent land acquisition by Jews. If Dickson's demands were not accepted by the Governor, he would immediately turn to the Ambassador, who would intercede with the Sublime Porte or even request the intervention of the Foreign Office. Dickson received the full cooperation of the Ambassador, N. O'Conor, who supported the various steps taken by the Consul and acted forcefully to have the unjust decrees abrogated. In many instances, the central Turkish government claimed that actions had been taken without its knowledge, and even ordered the Governor of Jerusalem to revoke his decree. Encouraged by the positive attitude of the Ambassador, Dickson continued in 1898–1904 to successfully act against the aggravation of the regulations concerning the Jewish *Yishuv*, a true benefactor of the community.

Dickson's amicable attitude was also exhibited in his strong defense of the A.P.C. (Anglo Palestine Company) Bank which had been established in Jaffa in 1903. When the Turks sought to obstruct the bank in its early stages, the Consul came to its aid, since it had been properly registered as a British institution.[235] He took similar steps on behalf of the Evelina de Rothschild school, which also enjoyed his protection as a British institution. His comprehensive reports on the Jewish National Fund, too, were written in a sympathetic spirit, though without adopting a political attitude.[236]

Dickson's entire term in office was marked by financial difficulties, since his meagre salary did not enable him to properly maintain his family, which included four children, especially in view of the continually rising cost of living in the developing city, while his wages remained constant throughout all these years. Dickson refrained from openly asking for an increase, but his various requests to

---

234  Even Miss A. Landau, who arrived in 1899 to take up her appointment as Headmistress of the Evelina de Rothschild School, was prevented at Jaffa from proceeding to Jerusalem. Only after firm intervention in Constantinople, the Governor of Jerusalem was instructed "to leave her unmolested" (ibid., Nos. 423, 427–430). See also below, Document No. 125.
235  See below, Documents 94–96; see also Document No. 106.
236  See below, Document No. 101. Dickson remarked that "if a company is formed under English protection for the acquisition of territory in Palestine and the eventual creation of a Jewish state, important political questions must arise between the British and Turkish Governments."

have the Consulate elevated to the rank of Consulate-General, similar to the representations of the other Powers, were undoubtedly also motivated by the hope that their acceptance would entail a considerable improvement in his salary. These petitions, however, were rejected.[237]

Dickson's strenuous activity aggravated his physical condition. On 4 July 1906 the Consul died of heart failure and was buried in Jerusalem, mourned by all sectors of the city's populace.[238]

A few weeks later, when news of Dickson's death became known, **Edward Charles Blech** (1861–1919), a Dragoman in the Embassy in Constantinople, tendered his candidacy for the now-vacant position of Consul, accompanied by the warm recommendation of the Ambassador.[239] After his appointment was confirmed on 15 November 1906, and his salary increased to £800 per annum, (of which £100 was for "personal allowance"), Blech already assumed the post two days later. Only a year would pass, however, before he would complain about Jerusalem's difficult climate, and especially of the malaria to which Europeans fell prey. The Consul successfully requested that Jerusalem be "added to the list of unhealthy places," since this would entitle those serving in the city to lengthier leaves of absence than the customary two months.[240]

Blech tried once again to have the Consulate become a Consulate-General, in light of its markedly inferior status in comparison with the six Consulates-General in Jerusalem. In the same letter he complained that his remuneration was insufficient to meet the high cost of living in Jerusalem, again comparing his income to the higher salaries enjoyed by his colleagues.[241] Ambassador O'Conor supported his Consul's request,[242] but the head of the Eastern Department noted in the

---

237   See above, n. 60. On 4 November 1903 he asked to be promoted to the rank of Consul-General, but received a negative answer: "there are no sufficient reasons" (FO 78/5285). On 8 October 1904 he tried again (FO 195/2175).

238   See above, n. 69 for the financial arrangement with his widow. See below, Document 103, and the appreciation of the Palestine Exploration Fund: "He always took a keen interest in the work of the Fund, and was ever ready with sound advice and help in his official capacity.... His loss will be deeply felt by all British residents in Jerusalem" (*PEFQ* 38 [October 1906], p. 268). Upon the announcement of Dickson's death, Sir Eric Barrington, the Assistant Under-Secretary, remarked: "I have known his work for many years. He was an excellent Consul" (FO 369/44).

239   27 July 1906, FO 369/45. O'Conor emphasized his "exceptional ability, remarkable powers of memory, proficiency in foreign and oriental languages."

240   Below, Document No. 107.

241   "Great Britain is the only power, which has contented itself throughout with an inferior rank for its consular representative.... I can assert that excluding political matters, in no one of them [British Consulates in Turkey] so many important cases occur as I have had occasion to handle since my arrival here" (16 November 1907, FO 195/2255).

242   See above, n. 61.

margin of O'Conor's letter: "I do not think that there are any political reasons for raising the status of the Consulate."

Senior officials in the Foreign Office, however, supported the request.[243] This time as well, the answer was evasive. The Chief Clerk instructed that the matter be deferred to "next year." In effect, the question was permanently shelved.[244] It is highly likely that this evasiveness may have influenced Blech's decision to conclude his term of service in Jerusalem after three years.

Very few despatches remain from this short period. Most interesting is a detailed letter regarding the development of the Jewish *Yishuv* in which the Consul attempts to provide quantitative estimates and which also surveys the transition of the Jewish colonies from the custodianship of Baron Rothschild to the administration of the Jewish Colonisation Association. The Consul was also cognisant of the attempt by Baron Hirsch to settle Jews in Argentina, of the Zionist movement's plan for Jewish colonisation at El-Arish, and he even mentions the 'Uganda scheme', a British proposal for Zionist colonisation in East Africa. In his opinion, however, the economic absorptive capacity of Palestine was no more than twice the number of its present inhabitants.[245] In other letters Blech discusses the Arab issue and also reports of the clashes in Jaffa between Jews and Arabs in March 1908.[246] Blech had reservations about granting British protection to Jewish companies, since this would only add to the workload of the Consulate, with the exception of industrial corporations, which were likely to increase British prestige and be of economic benefit to Palestine.[247] The Foreign Office, however, did not agree with him, and established unequivocally that every company registered in England was entitled to the protection of the Consulate.

On 2 December 1909 Blech was appointed Consul-General at Port Said and was succeeded in Jerusalem by the sixth Consul, **Harold Eustace Satow** (1876–1969), who arrived at the beginning of 1910, only to go on leave a few months later. In his absence James Morgan served as Acting Consul until Satow's return on 19 December 1910.[248]

An interesting letter from 1910 over Morgan's signature describes how men

---

243  2 January 1908, FO 369/107: "The case is put forward by the Ambassador on his own initiative, an unusual proceeding, and that shows that Sir N. O'Conor had good reasons for the suggestion."

244  See above, n. 63.

245  11 November 1907, Hyamson, *British Consulate*, No. 450. For the El-Arish project, see below, Documents Nos. 92 and 93.

246  Below, Documents Nos. 105, 109–111. See also his despatches on the boycott of Austria, below, Documents Nos. 114 and 115.

247  Below, Document No. 113.

248  Blech served as Consul-General in Port Said and afterwards in Genoa. Satow (later Sir Harold) was Vice-Consul at Uskub before his appointment to Jerusalem.

were inducted into the Turkish army. One hundred and ten new recruits, 34 of whom were non-Muslims (i.e., Christians), set out for Adana. Of the 69 Christians who had been called up, 20 had ransomed themselves, and 15 had fled. Thirty-six Jews had been drafted; 10 paid the ransom while an additional 10 ran away. The Acting Consul added: "No enthusiasm was manifested by the Non-Moslems. The Jews, however, are far from happy and totally opposed to serving as soldiers."[249]

Another important letter written by Morgan deals with various plans for the development of Jerusalem. It is informative about new programs for water supply, about negotiations concerning investments for the installation of an electrical system and even for electric tram cars.[250] The central issue during Satow's term in office was the attempt to purchase lands for Jewish settlement in the Rafah region, in which the British Consular Agent at Gaza, Knesevich, played a central role. The Consulate had reservations about the venture and was not pleased with the initiatives taken by the Consular Agent, although it provided detailed reports of the various developments in the matter.[251]

Only two years passed before Satow left Jerusalem.[252] His successor, **P.J.C. McGregor** (1865–1936), was appointed on 26 January 1912. His letters reflect a reserved, even hostile, attitude towards the Jews. He was especially ill at ease regarding Jews from Russia who had immigrated to England to be naturalised there, in order to immigrate to Palestine with a British passport. The Consul demanded that their British citizenship be revoked, but the Foreign Office rejected his claims.[253]

The proposal to elevate the Consulate at Jerusalem to the rank of Consulate-General was raised again during McGregor's term in office, this time on the initiative of the Ambassador at Constantinople, Sir L. Mallet, and was once more rejected by the Foreign Office.[254] McGregor wrote very few letters, making almost no mention of the important events preceding World War I, except for the

249  23 September 1910, FO 195/2351.
250  Below, Document No. 118.
251  Below, Documents Nos. 122–123, 126 and 127. See also Eliav, Rafah.
252  After Jerusalem, Satow served as Consul in Trebizond and Salonica, as Consul-General in Tripoli, and was afterwards employed in the Foreign Office. After World War I he served as Consul-General in Beirut and Tunis, before retiring in 1937. Peter James Colquhoun McGregor entered the Levant Consular Service in 1885, was Vice-Consul in various countries, and served as Acting Consul at Jerusalem in 1894 and in 1895. During World War I he was employed in the Foreign Office.
253  Below, Document No. 126. Naturalised Jews who immigrated to Palestine and enjoyed British protection were already mentioned in Dickson's despatches, but in a neutral manner. See also Hyamson, *British Consulate*, Nos. 459 and 462.
254  FO 369/629.

cancellation of the 'red paper' and increasing Arab opposition to Zionism.[255]

The state of the Consul's health deteriorated until he suffered a breakdown and was no longer capable of fulfilling his duties. The Vice-Consul at Jaffa, **William Hough**, was called to Jerusalem, first as Acting Consul and then, in the final months, as the last British Consul.[256] After Turkey declared war, he burned an important portion of the Consulate archives. On 16 November 1914 he left the city. His arrival in Cairo on 19 November 1914 marked the end of seventy five years of British Consulate activites in Jerusalem.

## Consular Officials

### Jaffa

The British consular representation at Jaffa was the first to be established in Palestine. As a commercial Vice-Consulate, it was subordinate to the Consulate-General in Beirut, until, at the request of the Consulate, it was transferred to the authority of the Jerusalem Consulate in 1866. Beginning in the 1870s, the number of regular commercial reports sent from Jaffa to Jerusalem increased, and would later constitute a significant portion of the Consulate's reports.

The following is a listing of the representatives, most of whom bore the rank of Vice-Consul.

**Guiseppe (Yussuf) Matback** was the first Vice-Consul, apparently appointed by Campbell on 16 July 1834 and holding this post until 1847.[257] He is mentioned in several books by travellers which describe the extensive and effective assistance he extended to them upon their arrival in Palestine. In several instances his name is given as "Madbuck." It may be assumed that he did not receive a salary as Vice-Consul, but engaged in commerce. It cannot be determined whether or not he resigned of his own will.

---

255 Below, Documents Nos. 130–131 and 133.

256 William Hough joined the Consular Service in 1904, and was appointed Vice-Consul at Jaffa in 1912. He was the first and only career officer to ever hold that post, his appointment reflecting Jaffa's increasing commercial importance. McGregor was still the titular Consul at Jerusalem at the outbreak of hostilities. He fell ill in the summer of 1914, and Hough, on leave in England, was rushed out to relieve him. On 6 September 1914 Hough took charge of the Consulate in Jerusalem, where he remained until 16 November. After World War I, Hough returned to Mandatory Palestine to serve as Deputy Controller of Light Industries until the end of the British Mandate.

257 In the list of Vice-Consuls in the District of Beirut dated 1 January 1838, he is mentioned as "Madbuck," Vice-Consul since 30 August 1836 (FO 78/340). But in the list of 1 January 1847, his appointment is dated from 16 July 1834 (FO 617/2).

**Assad Jacob Khayat** (1811–65) was a native of Beirut who completed his medical studies in London, where he received British citizenship. He was an educated person, well-acquainted with Palestine and its population. He was appointed Consul on 18 June 1847, and held this post — as the only representative in Jaffa to bear this title — until his death on 19 November 1865. He was allocated an annual salary of £300, was subordinate to Beirut and despatched his reports to the Consulate-General there; many of his reports were also received by the Consul in Jerusalem.[258]

When Khayat passed away, Moore requested the Foreign Office to place Jaffa under his authority, arguing: "Jaffa being the port of Jerusalem and the Turkish Authorities there are subordinate to the Governor of Jerusalem."[259] The Consul-General in Beirut did not express any opposition. The Foreign Office approved Moore's proposal and asked him to recommend a suitable candidate for the post of Vice-Consul, with an annual salary of £100 and permission to engage in commercial activity, thus indicating that after Assad's death the Foreign Office decided to lower the level of British representation in Jaffa to that of Vice-Consul, with a corresponding decrease in salary. Moore proposed the son of the deceased Consul, who was a naturalized British subject,[260] and his recommendation was accepted.

**Habib A. Khayat** was designated for the post in 1866, but the Ottoman authorities refused to confirm the appointment, since they did not recognise his British citizenship. Negotiations continued for some three years, but the Turkish authorities maintained their refusal. On 18 September 1869 he resigned his post, after being highly commended for the manner in which he carried out his duties. Moore implored him to withdraw his resignation. Habib made one further effort by travelling to London to obtain British citizenship. His quest proved unsuccessful, and at the end of March 1870 he tendered his final resignation, all attempts to persuade him to continue in his post proving fruitless.[261]

In 1869, after Khayat's first resignation, Moore had suggested replacing him with H. Amzalak, "a Jewish merchant of Gibraltar origin, who has some knowledge of Italian, but none of English," but who was "the only eligible British Subject residing at that port."[262] The Foreign Office, however, delayed its response,

---

258  See below, Document No. 21, n. 1 and Document No. 41; in FO 78/705, the announcement of his appointment also mentioned that his father and uncle had previously been Consular Agents.

259  See above, n. 206.

260  12 May 1866, FO 78/1929; below, the introduction to Document No. 63.

261  FO 78/2697.

262  "This appointment is liable at any time to revision if hereafter a properly qualified person for the appointment should be found" (see below, Document No. 63); FO 195/994; FO 78/2514.

apparently because it was reluctant to appoint a representative who was not proficient in English. It seems that no more qualified candidate could be found, and on 26 October 1871, for lack of a better alternative, Moore raised his proposal once again. Only one year later did the Foreign Office agree to the appointment, but merely as an unpaid Consular Agent, this after some two years in which there had been no British representative at Jaffa. The Foreign Office apparently believed that this would be no more than a temporary appointment, and could not imagine that Amzalak would fill this post for about three decades.

**Haim Amzalak** (1828–1916). His letter of appointment dated 14 November 1872 was conditional, emphasising the temporary nature of the appointment. Despite these limitations, Amzalak served longer than any other consular official at Jaffa. His reports attest to his vigilance in protecting British interests and his devoted activity to counter attempts by the local authorities to obstruct the Jewish immigrants of the First Aliyah (the first wave of Zionist immigration, 1882–1903). Amzalak did all that was in his power to prevent the arrest or deportation of Jews and called upon the Consul to help in any instance of a clash with the authorities. He was mainly concerned with land and property, and was indeed successful in his economic endeavours. His relations with Moore were correct, the Consul apparently resigning himself to the fact that no better representative could be found in Jaffa.

Consul Dickson, however, at first deemed Amzalak unsuitable for the post of Vice-Consul, believing that the latter's lack of fluency in English would burden him with additional work.[263] Dickson would later change his mind. In 1899 he reported that Amzalak had already served for seventeen years as an unsalaried Consular Agent and had been highly commended. Nevertheless, Dickson concluded, a more suitable representative was needed at Jaffa.[264] The Foreign Office, however, did not respond, so Amzalak retained the position despite his limitations, with which the Consul was forced to acquiesce. In 1902 Amzalak tendered his resignation, after thirty years of service, on account of his age, finally retiring on 17

---

263 "It was necessary to either correct or rewrite Amzalak's letters and to handle personally all British business in Jaffa" (27 August 1891, FO 78/4367).

264 FO 78/4218. In his report to O'Conor on trade at Jaffa in the same year, Dickson remarked that "it is very essential that Great Britain should be represented at that port by a person whose education and attainments would be more suitable to the present requirements." Amzalak was now seventy years old, "entirely ignorant of the English and French languages, but speaks Judeo-Spanish, Italian, Arabic and Hebrew, although he can only read and write the two last. He is at the mercy of his employé, who writes his letters in English." All this notwithstanding, "I would state that as far as his integrity and zeal in wishing to discharge his duties are concerned, I have found him blameless" (below, Document No. 78).

October 1902, when he turned seventy-five.[265] Amzalak requested suitable compensation after having served for such a long period of time without salary. Following Dickson's lengthy negotiations with the Foreign Office, Amzalak was awarded a severance grant of £250 and reimbursement for expenses.[266] After his resignation, the Foreign Office announced that, in view of the growing importance of Jaffa, a salaried Vice-Consul would be appointed.[267]

**John Falanga**, who served from May 1903 as acting Vice-Consul, was appointed Vice-Consul in December 1903 with an annual salary of £300. In July 1911 he asked to be relieved of his duties due to his advanced age and ill health, retiring one month later.[268]

**Nasri Fiani** served as a Dragoman to the great satisfaction of his superiors. He was appointed Vice-Consul on 13 November 1911, but with an annual salary of only £200. He served in this position for less than a year.

**William Hough** was an Englishman, the only professional diplomat to serve in Jaffa. He was appointed Vice-Consul on 18 April 1912, and on 6 September 1914 was summoned to assume the duties of Consul at Jerusalem . Fiani was called upon once again to administer the Vice-Consulate at Jaffa for the remaining two months before its closure.[269]

## Haifa / Acre

Whereas the Vice-Consulate in Jaffa operated continuously throughout the entire period, with the exception of two years, that at Haifa was closed down several times, not being regarded as essential as its counterpart at Jaffa. Only in the second half of the nineteenth century did the importance of Haifa increase, when the office in Acre was abolished and the Vice-Consul at Haifa assumed responsibility for the entire north of Palestine. Before this, however, arguments in support of diplomatic representation at Haifa were met with a considerable amount of derision, and

265  FO 195/2127; FO 369/105.
266  FO 195/2149. On 31 December 1906, however, Amzalak applied to the Foreign Secretary Sir E. Grey and asked again for a pension or gratuition. The grant of £250 was made, in his opinion in settlement of expenses, but he received no gratuition or allowance for the period until the new Vice-Consul arrived. He therefore claimed an annual pension of £66 (FO 369/105). But Sir E. Barrington's reply on behalf of the Foreign Office was negative. The office "is unable to consider a gratuition beyond the sum of £250 already been issued" (18 January 1907, FO 369/105). Amzalak stated in his application that since his appointment in 1872 he had received a salary of £100, but in all the despatches he is mentioned as an unpaid agent.
267  "The unpaid post at Jaffa will be abolished and a salaried Vice-Consul will be appointed" (5 August 1903, FO 78/5285).
268  FO 78/5285; FO 195/2377; FO 369/416.
269  FO 195/2377; FO 369/775.

serious efforts had to be undertaken to persuade the Foreign Office to reestablish it, after the post had remained vacant from 1865 to 1879. In November 1863 all of northern Palestine came under the authority of the Consulate-General in Beirut, which for years had tried to convince the Foreign Office of the need to appoint a representative in Haifa. A listing of Haifa's British officials follows.

**Paolo Malagamba**, apparently of Italian extraction, was appointed on 18 May 1837 as an unpaid Consular Agent. He was dismissed on 10 February 1848 by Finn, who came to the conclusion that Malagamba was unsuited for the post.[270]

**Moise Abraham Finzi** (born 1803) was a Jew and a subject of Tuscany. He served as a Consular Agent at Acre from 18 May 1837, after having held a similar position in Safed. In 1849 Finn increased his jurisdiction to include Haifa as well, until the appointment of a Vice-Consul there in 1853, following which Finzi resumed his position as Consular Agent at Acre. He remained in this post until 1879, when he was forced to retire due to advanced age.[271] During this long period of service, Finzi expended much effort, with great dedication, on behalf of the Jews of Galilee.

Finn regarded the extension of Finzi's authority to Haifa to be but a temporary measure and resolved to take steps to establish a Vice-Consulate there which would be subordinate to himself. In his letters, the Consul emphasised the increasing importance of Haifa, which necessitated British representation of more substance. The candidate for such a position, however, must be an Englishman, rather than a member of the Jewish faith, thus ruling out Finzi. To avoid offending the latter, he would continue to serve as Consular Agent at Acre.[272] The best candidate, Finn informed the Foreign Office, was E.T. Rogers, who was definitely capable of filling the post in Haifa. Though Finn's proposal was rejected, he raised the issue once more by informing the Foreign Secretary that he had appointed Rogers, and recommended that he be given the rank of Vice-Consul.[273] Although Finn had acted on his own accord, his recommendation was accepted.

**Edward Thomas Rogers** (1830–1884) had served from 1848 as Cancelliere in the Jerusalem Consulate. Finn's proposal to appoint his as a salaried Vice-Consul in Haifa was rejected by the Foreign Office. Rogers agreed to accept the appointment without pay, engaging in commerce for his livelihood. Two years later he requested

270 FO 78/340; FO 78/755.
271 FO 78/340; FO 78/803. In a letter of 20 November 1851 Finn wrote that Finzi reads and writes only Italian, speaks Arabic, Turkish, and Yiddish, "but only a little French and even less English" (FO 78/874). For his resignation, see: 12 April 1879, FO 78/2375A; see also below, Document No. 28, introduction and n. 3.
272 Below, 29 November 1851, Document No. 28.
273 Below, Document No. 31. The appointment was confirmed in May 1853 (FO 78/963).

the Foreign Office to pay him a salary, and he was apparently allocated an annual wage of £200. Rogers filled this post for eight years (1853–1861), until he was transferred to Damascus.[274] When he left Haifa, the Foreign Office replaced him with a professional Vice-Consul.

**Thomas B. Sandwith** (1831–1900) was officially appointed on 23 July 1861, serving at Haifa for only four years. The amount of his salary was not recorded, but in May 1863 he requested Moore, who was still responsible for Haifa, to ask London for a "special allowance" to cover his office and travel expenses, since his jurisdiction covered all Galilee (excluding the Acre region), and his duties included periodic visits to British protégés in Nazareth, Safed, and Tiberias.[275]

When Sandwith left his post, no Vice-Consul was appointed to succeed him. In 1867 Sir Moses Montefiore appealed to Permanent Under-Secretary Hammond, stressing that the abolishment of the British representation in Haifa had left the Jews of Safed and Tiberias without protection, and that the reopening of the Vice-Consulate was a matter of urgency. The Foreign Office rejected Montefiore's request,[276] stating that the presence of the Consular Agent at Acre, Finzi, was sufficient.[277] In 1872 Eldridge once more raised this matter, advising the Foreign Secretary to appoint a Vice-Consul who would be stationed at Acre: "Finzi is too old and should be retired," wrote Eldridge, but he knew of no one in the region who was suitable for the post. He nevertheless counselled reestablishing the Vice-Consulate at Haifa, which had been abolished in 1865. "This would give efficient protection, of which they [i.e., the Jews] are now almost deprived. One might be found who with the right to trade would undertake the duties with an allowance of £50–100 p.a." Granville totally rejected the proposal. He opposed the

274  FO 78/963; Hyamson, *British Consulate*, No. 172; below, Document No. 28, n. 4. He later served as Consul in Damascus (1861–1868) and in Cairo (1869–1875). After this, he was Director of the Ministry of Public Instruction in Cairo.

275  20 May 1863, Hyamson, *British Consulate*, No. 227. Sandwith reports that there are 600 Jews in Safed and Tiberias who enjoy British protection, and that there are "numerous questions." In 1865 he was transferred to Cyprus, afterwards serving at Damascus, Beirut, and Odessa.

276  Montefiore to Hammond, 18 December 1867 (Hyamson, *British Consulate*, No. 253): "no one on the spot to appeal for aid in case of necessity." Hammond to Montefiore, 3 January 1868 (Hyamson, *British Consulate*, No. 254): There is a British Consular Agent at Acre (Finn). With the transfer of Sandwith to Cyprus, "the post was abolished as a paid appointment." Before this letter, Murray stated in a memorandum of 31 December 1867 that there is no sufficient reason for a Vice-Consulate; there are no British interests; and "the main if not the only thing which the Vice-Consul had to do was to assist Foreign Jews" (FO 78/2375A).

277  Eldridge already stated in his despatch to Foreign Secretary Granville on 14 June 1871: "Since the abolition of the Vice-Consulate at Caiffa, the protection is more nominal than effective. Finzi is now very aged and does not possess the weight with the local authorities necessary to protect the large number who may be considered as within his district, while Beyrout is too far distant" (Hyamson, *British Consulate*, No. 263).

employment of a salaried official, since there were no British interests in Haifa.[278]
A solution to the problem was found only in 1879, when an unsalaried candidate
was proposed and Eldridge forced Finzi to retire.

**Dr. Johannes Schmidt** (1850–1910) was a physician and a Russian subject of
German origin. He was appointed Vice-Consul responsible for all of northern
Palestine by Consul-General Eldridge in March 1879, with the approval of the
Foreign Office.[279] The Russian Consul-General at Beirut initially raised difficulties
for the new appointee, but withdrew his objections after negotiations, and Schmidt
was granted British protection. He faithfully executed his duties, without pay,
while continuing to practice medicine for his livelihood. When in 1888 he requested
a modest salary, his petition was rejected by the Foreign Office.[280] Schmidt
resigned in 1892, but continued to reside in Haifa.

The post remained vacant during the next six years, with no British representative either in Haifa or in Acre. The British protégés became the responsibility of the
Consulate-General in Beirut, which limited itself to despatching a representative to
the region once a year, primarily to examine eligibility for certificates of protection
and their renewal.

**James Henry Monahan**, appointed in 1898, served as Vice-Consul at Haifa for
seven years, until 1905.[281] A member of the professional staff of the Levant
Consular Service since 1888, before coming to Haifa he had filled junior positions
at several posts. Upon his transfer from Haifa, Monahan was not replaced by a
professional diplomat.

**Pietro Abella**, a local resident, also apparently of Italian extraction, was appointed in 1905 as unpaid Acting Vice-Consul and promoted to Vice-Consul in
1909. He filled this post until the closure of the Vice-Consulate in November 1914.


*Safed*

In consequence of the large number of Jews in this city enjoying British protection,
the idea of appointing a British Consular Agent had already been considered in
1872, following the visit by Eldridge to Safed. He intended to appoint **Joseph
Miklasiewicz**, a Polish Christian resident of Safed who had served from 1858 as the
Austrian Consular Agent, to represent British interests as well. When Eldridge

278  10 May 1872, Hyamson, *British Consulate*, No. 267; Granville's reply of 1 July 1872 (Hyamson,
      *British Consulate*, No. 269).
279  Eldridge to Granville, 12 April 1879, FO 78/2375A. See Schmidt's report to the Foreign Office
      of 19 June 1883, below, Document No. 67.
280  4 January 1888, FO 78/4122.
281  See his despatches: below, Documents Nos. 81 and 88.

learned, however, that Miklasiewicz was at odds with the Jewish community and that various charges had been raised against him, he withdrew his proposal.[282] Only later in 1890 was he appointed as unsalaried British Consular Agent, probably because no other candidate could be found. The need to care for the British protégés was pressing, due to their tenuous links with the Vice-Consul in Haifa; moreover, the latter had resigned in 1892, and the post remained vacant.

Miklasiewicz served as British Consular Agent from 1890 to 1894, and once again from 1897 until his death in January 1907. On 1 July 1907 his son **Carl Ladislaus** was appointed in his stead, filling this post until the end of 1914.[283]

*Gaza*

In 1899 Consul Dickson proposed the establishment of a Vice-Consulate at Gaza, in light of the increasing economic importance of this port city. The suggestion was rejected by the Foreign Office, which was willing only to appoint an unpaid Consular Agent. It was not until February 1902 that Dickson could report to the Foreign Office that he had found a suitable candidate who was willing to serve as Consular Agent without remuneration.

**Alexander Anton Knesevich**, a Polish Christian and Austrian subject, was not appointed until January 1905. He dealt with the protection of the Jews in Gaza, also playing a key role in land transactions in the Rafah area.[284] He moved to Alexandria during World War I.

Throughout this entire period the Foreign Office clearly tended to scrimp as much as possible on the expense of maintaining representations in various cities. It preferred to appoint local residents who consented to fill the positions without pay, until the despatch of a career diplomat from outside the region, who had to be paid a salary. This policy undoubtedly seriously undermined the efficiency of these representations, even leading to temporary closures, as in Haifa. Other Powers, such as Germany, Austria, and France, adopted an opposite policy. From the

---

282  "I thought at first it would be advisable to name him as British Agent, but when I found that the Community complained very much of his proceedings, I renounced that idea. Many grounds of complaint against him were brought to my attention, but I believe the great objection against him is that he acts in some way as a sort of agent to the mission establishment at Jerusalem for the conversion of the Jews" (Hyamson, *British Consulate*, No. 267). Miklasiewicz served as the Austrian Consular Agent for 48 years (1858–1906), and there were indeed many complaints about his behaviour, but he was not active on behalf of the missionaries. See: Eliav, *Austrian Protection*, pp. 33, 111–112, 234–235.

283  FO 78/5205; FO 369/105.

284  See below, Document No. 83, introduction and n. 1; Documents Nos. 108, 122–123, 126–127.

1880s onwards they appointed professional, salaried representatives, both in Jaffa and in Haifa, thus overshadowing Great Britain, which continued to practice a policy of parsimony and economy. It should be noted, however, that in many instances the 'volunteers', who were even compelled to struggle for reimbursment of their expenses, faithfully and honourably represented British interests.

## The Jerusalem Consulate Staff

A complete listing of all the Consulate employees would exceed the scope of this work, especially since there was a frequent turnover. Accordingly, only the most important employees will be mentioned.

**Raphael Abraham Bekhor Miuchas** was the son of Joseph Yom Tov Miuchas, one of the leading Sephardic rabbis of Jerusalem. He was appointed by Finn on 11 May 1846 as Dragoman for Hebrew, serving in that capacity until the end of Finn's term in 1863. He formed a close relationship with the Finn family, which visited his home on holidays and learned from him about Jewish practices. As the subordinate of Finn, who was suspected of missionary intentions, Miuchas suffered from poor relations with the Sephardic community, which on several occasions demanded that he resign, and even published broadsheets attacking him. Miuchas paid no attention to these calls and continued to serve Finn loyally. When the leaders of the community imposed a ban on Miuchas in 1858, Finn compelled the rabbis, led by the Rishon le-Zion (the Sephardic Chief Rabbi), to come to his house and publicly proclaim the lifting of the ban. In 1862 Miuchas headed a group that sought to purchase lands in order to engage in agricultural labour. After a broadsheet on this matter had been published, however, the community leadership warned the public to beware of Miuchas, since they believed that the initiative was connected to Finn's plans. After his retirement, he was one of the first Jews to settle in 'Mishkenot Sha'ananim', the first neighbourhood outside the walls of the Old City of Jerusalem, which had been established by Montefiore. He apparently died late in 1873.[285]

**Moussa Tannous,** a Christian Arab of Egyptian origin, was appointed by Finn

---

285  For Miuchas, see: Finn's diary, entry for 11 May 1846; Blumberg, *View*, p. 57; Finn E., *Reminiscences*, pp. 51, 195–199; Yellin, p. 37; M.D. Gaon, *Oriental Jews in Eretz-Israel*, Jerusalem 1938, vol. 2, p. 403 (Heb.); A. Ben Yaacob, *Jerusalem within Its Walls : The History of the Meyuhas Family*, Jerusalem 1976, pp. 25–28, 190 (Heb.). A report in the Hebrew newspaper *Hamaggid*, 6, No. 18 (1862), on the efforts to purchase land for agricultural work contained the warning: "The writer is subservient to Consul Finn ... and this Miuhas has become as an axe in the hands of the Consul, whether consciously or unwittingly." For the lifting of the ban, see Finn's dairy, entry for 3 March 1858.

on 1 March 1848 as senior Dragoman in the Consulate. He, too, became very close to the Consul. He engaged in the sale of lands and was also a moneylender. In time, he grew wealthy, owning many plots of land immediately outside the city walls. He acquired those of Talbieh and Kerem Avraham on behalf of Finn.[286] In 1853 he became embroiled in a land sale involving the American missionary Dr. James T. Barclay, who accused Tannous of fraud and deceitful acts after having lost his money. His claim against Tannous was adjudicated by Finn who was partial to Tannous and ruled in his favour, thus arousing the ire of the Americans.[287] Charges of corruption were raised against Tannous in later years as well.

He apparently resigned in 1880, but continued to represent Mrs. Finn's interests, for a fee, in her suit to restore the property that had been mortgaged for the repayment of the Consul's debts. This litigation continued for about thirty years, without result; Tannous apparently stood to gain by the protracted proceedings. Only after his death in 1907 were all the financial affairs suddenly resolved to the satisfaction of Mrs. Finn.[288]

**Constantin N. Tadrous**, a Greek Christian, was appointed by Moore as senior Dragoman in 1880. Proficient in many languages, he served until January 1910. He gained the confidence of the Consuls, but his integrity also left something to be desired. Tadrous played an important role in the lawsuit of Mrs. Finn.[289]

**Edward Thomas Rogers** was appointed Cancelliere (bureau chief) in 1848, holding this position until 1853, when he was appointed Vice-Consul at Haifa (see above). He served as Finn's right-hand man: the Consul trusted him unquestioningly and even sent him on many tours throughout the land on his behalf, including to northern Palestine to examine certificates of protection and report on

286  Finn's diary entries for 1 March 1848; 17 June 1850 ("Tannous purchased Talbijeh after months of negotiations. Yet it remains in his name"); 26 August 1850 ("Tannous bought the land estate called Kerem el Khalil"); Tibawi, p. 139; Yellin, p. 13; Finn E., *Reminiscences*, p. 51. On 10 March 1897, Tannous compiled a detailed memorandum on the history of the Talbieh estate, which was sent by Dickson to the Foreign Office (FO 78/4972).
287  For the Barclay-Tannous affair, see: Lipman, America-Holy Land, pp. 28 ff.; ibid., *Americans*, pp. 109 ff.; Blumberg, *Zion*, pp. 99–100; ibid., *View*, pp. 99–100, 146–148, 279.
288  "Tannous has lived upon it for 30 years.... Tannous died last month and the case was settled in a fortnight ... greatly to Mrs. Finn's advantage" (Blech to O'Conor, 24 November 1907, FO 195/2255). On 24 October 1907 Mrs. Finn thanked the Foreign Office for the return of the estate of Talbieh. She mentioned that she had paid off her husband's debts, and concluded: "I have been consoled in these long sad years by repeated testimonies from strangers to myself ... that his memory is still cherished and revered all over the country as that of a just, upright officer and never failing succourer of the oppressed and defender of British interests" (FO 195/2349).
289  In 1893 Dickson wrote that Tadrous knows Turkish, Arabic, English, French, and Greek, and that his services are "indispensable" (3 August 1893, FO 78/4498). He ceased to be a Dragoman on 12 January 1910 (FO 195/2351).

events in different places. Even after his transfer to Haifa, he continued to carry out various assignments at Finn's request.[290]

**Peter Meshullam** was the eldest son of John Meshullam, owner of the farmstead at Artas (see above). In November 1860 Peter was appointed by Finn as Cancelliere, a post he held for only two years. He obtained this position after having cultivated a close relationship with the Finns, who trusted him completely and treated him as a member of the family. But Peter was arrogant and haughty, and in the course of executing his duties at the Consulate tyrannised the peasants and persecuted them, thus making many enemies among the rural population. Finn and his wife ignored the harsh accusations raised against Meshullam; the Consul even proposed his candidacy for the post of Vice-Consul at Haifa after Rogers had been transferred to Damascus — a suggestion which was totally rejected by the Foreign Office.

Faced by the serious charges and evidence against Meshullam, Finn fired his Cancelliere on 19 August 1862. On 6 March 1863, a few days before Moore assumed his duties as Consul, Peter Meshullam was murdered, and the effort to find the assailants and bring them to justice occupied Moore for many years.[291]

**William Henry Khayat** (1850–1907), second son of A.J. Khayat, the Consul at Jaffa, became a naturalized American citizen. He was appointed as Cancelliere by Moore in 1881, and in 1885 was granted the title of Pro-Consul. He served as acting Consul in Moore's absence on several occasions. Dickson wrote a very favourable evaluation of him in 1893. On 1 October 1906 he resigned from his position at the Consulate, apparently due to poor health, passing away on 29 June 1907.[292]

Within seventy five years, through the establishment and activities of the Jerusalem Consulate and its dependent Consular Agencies, the foundation of the Anglican

---

290  Rogers began to function as a Cancelliere on 29 March 1848; see Finn's diary for that date. A bachelor, he brought his sister with him. She later published an interesting book about her experiences (Rogers). See also: Blumberg, *View*, pp. 57, 128, 151; Finn E., *Reminiscences*, pp. 52, 115; Finn J., *Stirring Times*, I, pp. 352, 477.

291  For the proposal to appoint him to Haifa, see: 1 March 1861, FO 78/1605. On 16 June 1862 Lord Russell instructed A.J. Frazer "to proceed to Jerusalem and to make enquiries of serious imputations against the conduct of Peter Meshullam." Frazer's report confirmed all the accusations (FO 78/4782), and Finn dismissed Meshullam. See also: below, Document No. 52; Eliav, Finn, pp. 62–63, 75; Schur, Finn, pp. 80–85. Files FO 78/1676 and FO 78/1952 contain a vast amount of despatches and correspondence on the murder and the efforts to bring the perpetrators to trial. The affair ended with an acquittal of the suspects by the Supreme Court in Constantinople on 25 February 1869 (FO 195/761).

292  See: Tibawi, p. 146; FO 78/3781; FO 369/45; FO 195/2349. On 3 September 1893 Dickson described him as "very competent and with a considerable experience" (FO 78/4498).

Bishopric and the missions, and the achievements of various medical and educational institutions, Great Britain established a firm political presence in the Holy Land, a presence that grew steadily in importance throughout the entire period and contributed significantly to the welfare and progress of Palestine and its inhabitants.

# SELECTED DOCUMENTS
from
## THE BRITISH CONSULATE IN JERUSALEM

# LIST OF DOCUMENTS

| 17 | J. Finn<br>to Viscount Palmerston | Arrival of the Latin<br>Patriarch | 29 January 1848 |
|----|-----------------------------------|----------------------------------|-----------------|
| 18 | Proclamation of the Turkish Government Precautions against Pestilence | | August 1848 |
| 19 | J. Finn<br>to Viscount Palmerston | Arrest of Sheikh of Abu<br>Ghosh | 13 September 1848 |
| 20 | J. Finn to Sir S. Canning | Jewish Converts to Islam | 15 January 1849 |
| 21 | J. Finn<br>to Viscount Palmerston | Consecration of Christ<br>Church in Jerusalem | 22 January 1849 |
| 22 | Niven Moore to J. Finn | Finn's Zeal for Conversion of<br>Jews | 18 June 1849 |
| 23 | J. Finn to Sir S. Canning | Attack on a Russian Jew | 25 June 1849 |
| 24 | J. Finn<br>to Viscount Palmerston | Purchase of Lands | 10 July 1850 |
| 25 | J. Finn to Adhem Pasha | Lease of Land at Talbieh | 5 August 1850 |
| 26 | J. Finn to Sir S. Canning | Purchase of Lands | 14 August 1850 |
| 27 | J. Finn<br>to Viscount Palmerston | Catholic Interests in<br>Palestine | 25 September 1850 |
| 28 | J. Finn<br>to Viscount Palmerston | Appointment of a Vice-<br>Consul at Haifa | 29 November 1851 |
| 29 | J. Finn<br>to Malmesbury | Austrian Lloyds Company | 9 October 1852 |
| 30 | S. Gobat to J. Finn | Complaints on Mail Service | 28 December 1852 |
| 31 | J. Finn<br>to Lord Malmesbury | Importance of Vice-Consulate<br>in Haifa | 1 January 1853 |
| 32 | Declaration of Consuls | Deteriorating Situation in<br>Palestine | 19 May 1855 |
| 33 | J. Finn<br>to Earl of Clarendon | Hostilities in Hebron | 25 June 1855 |
| 34 | J. Finn<br>to Earl of Clarendon | The Growing Influence of<br>Austria | 3 August 1855 |
| 35 | J. Finn<br>to Earl of Clarendon | Hoisting Flags of<br>Consulates | 20 August 1855 |
| 36 | J. Finn<br>to Earl of Clarendon | Political Situation during<br>the Year 1855 | 7 January 1856 |

| | | |
|---|---|---|
| 74 J. Dickson<br>to Earl of Rosebery | Inauguration and Importance<br>of the Jaffa-Jerusalem Railway | 4 November 1892 |
| 75 Foreign Office<br>to Sir F. Clare-Ford | Prohibition of Land Purchase | 14 June 1893 |
| 76 J. McGregor<br>to Foreign Office | Water-Supply for Jerusalem | 29 January 1895 |
| 77 J. Dickson<br>to Sir Ph. Currie | Fanatical Attitudes in Jaffa | 16 September 1895 |
| 78 J. Dickson<br>to Sir N. O'Conor | Report on Trade at Jaffa | 31 January 1899 |
| 79 N. O'Conor<br>to Marquess of Salisbury | Prohibition of Jewish<br>Immigration | 18 July 1899 |
| 80 J. Dickson<br>to N. O'Conor | Establishment of Caza<br>Beer-Sheba | 20 November 1899 |
| 81 J.H. Monahan<br>to Drummond Hay | Report on Jewish<br>Colonization and J.C.A. | 5 February 1900 |
| 82 J. Dicksonto N. O'Conor | Quarterly Report | 11 May 1900 |
| 83 M. Berouti<br>to J. Dickson | Establishment of a Vice-<br>Consulate at Gaza | 25 September 1900 |
| 84 J. Dickson<br>to M. de Bunsen | Report on Jerusalem<br>(Extract) | 13 November 1900 |
| 85 P. Wheeler / W.<br>Masterman to J. Dickson | Sanitary Conditions in<br>Jerusalem | 13 November 1900 |
| 86 Wainer Bros.<br>to J. Dickson | Complaint on Confiscation of<br>Passports | 26 February 1901 |
| 87 J. Dickson to N. O'Conor | Demand for Expulsion of Jews | 17 April 1901 |
| 88 J.H. Monohan<br>to Drummond Hay | Purchase of Atlith | 25 October 1901 |
| 89 Lord Cromer to<br>Marquess of Lansdowne | Plan for a Jewish Settlement at<br>El-Arish | 29 November 1902 |
| 90 J. Dickson<br>to N. O'Conor | Report on the German<br>Colonies | 8 December 1902 |
| 91 J. Dickson<br>to N. O'Conor | Quarterly Report; Effects of<br>Cholera | 27 January 1903 |

| | | | |
|---|---|---|---|
| 112 | E.C. Blech to G.H. Barclay | Proposal for Establishment of a British Post Office at Jerusalem | 20 May 1908 |
| 113 | E.C. Blech to G.H. Barclay | British Protection for Jewish Companies | 29 June 1908 |
| 114 | J. Falanga to E.C. Blech | Hostilities against Austria | 13 October 1908 |
| 115 | E.C. Blech to Sir G. Lowther | Boycott of Austria | 15 October 1908 |
| 116 | J. Falanga to H.E. Satow | Commercial Report on Jaffa for 1909 | 9 March 1910 |
| 117 | H.E. Satow to G. Lowther | Purchase of Property by Jews | 21 May 1910 |
| 118 | J. Morgan to Foreign Secretary | Water-Supply for Jerusalem and other Schemes | 11 August 1910 |
| 119 | J. Morgan to Foreign Secretary | Distribution of Charity from South Africa | 14 December 1910 |
| 120 | H.E. Satow to G. Lowther | Difficulties of the Anglo-Palestine Company | 28 February 1911 |
| 121 | G. Lowther to Sir E. Grey | Anti-Zionist Resentments in Turkey | 7 March 1911 |
| 122 | H.E. Satow to G. Lowther | Purchases of Land at Rafah | 27 April 1911 |
| 123 | H.E. Satow to G. Lowther | Purchases of Land at Rafah | 23 August 1911 |
| 124 | H.E. Satow to Sir E. Grey | Annual Report on Trade for the Year 1911 (Extracts) | 12 March 1912 |
| 125 | H.E. Satow to Sir E. Grey | New Building for E. de Rothschild School | 19 March 1912 |
| 126 | J. McGregor to Ch. Marling | Purchases of Land at Rafah | August 1, 1912 |
| 127 | G. Lowther to Sir E. Grey | Purchases of Land at Rafah | 20 November 1912 |
| 128 | G. Lowther to Sir E. Grey | Ottoman Opposition to Zionism | 17 March 1913 |
| 129 | Sir J. Gray Hill to Foreign Office | Suggestions for Enhancing British Influence at Jerusalem | 21 July 1913 |

# 1 Colonel Campbell to Viscount Palmerston
## Appointment of a Consular Agent at Jerusalem

On 3 November 1836, Foreign Secretary Palmerston decided to appoint a Consular Agent in Jerusalem, despite the unfavourable memorandum sent on 2 November 1836 by John Backhouse, Permanent Under-Secretary in the Foreign Office, and of the long-standing opposition of Colonel Patrick Campbell, Consul-General in Egypt (1833–1841). In response to Backhouse's memorandum, Palmerston wrote: "I think it would be expedient to have an English Consular Agent at Jerusalem. State this to Col. Campbell and request him to select a person" (FO 78/295).

On behalf of the Foreign Secretary, John Bidwell, the Inspector of the Consular Service, wrote in a similar vein to Campbell on 29 November 1836, as is mentioned in his letter, below. Campbell's response, however, was delayed for nine months, apparently because no suitable candidate could be found for a long period of time.

On 27 June 1837 William Tanner Young tendered his candidacy for the post to Campbell, apparently upon the initiative of Niven Moore, the consul in Beirut and his business associate (see below). He asked Campbell to recommend him for the position. The latter responded favourably, expressing his pleasure at the request in a letter to Young dated 5 August 1837. Young now directly addressed the Foreign Secretary, attaching a copy of Campbell's recommendation to his letter to Palmerston of 21 September 1837 (FO 78/322). He pointed out that he had spent about a year in Palestine, thereby becoming acquainted with conditions in that country and with its inhabitants. At the same time, Palmerston received the following letter, which dealt with the same matter. Campbell apparently was unaware of Young's direct communication with the Foreign Secretary. For the further development of this matter, see: Vereté, pp. 319–339, and also the introductory essay to this volume.

FO 78/322 (Cons. No. 28)                    Alexandria, the 19th September 1838

My Lord,

In obedience to Your Lordship's Despatch N° 18, of 29th November 1836, relative to the appointment of a British Consular Agent at Jerusalem, I have the honour to report to Your Lordship that I had, after much enquiry, been able to select a gentleman, who appeared to me to be in every way fit for that situation.—

This gentleman is a Mr. William Young, now in England, who had been some time in Syria, where I made his acquaintaince[1] — and he has since been strongly recommended to me both by Mr. Consul Moore[2] and by the Revd. Mr. Nicolayson.[3] —

On mentioning to the Pacha of Egypt the desire of the British Government to have a Consular Agent at Jerusalem, he told me that, Jerusalem being one of the Holy Cities, he could not take upon himself to sanction such an appointment there, unless he (the Pacha) should have a Firman to that effect from the Sultan, who, he said, he did not think from motives of Religion, would grant it — and that, at any rate, he himself had it not in his power to sanction it without such Firman.[4] —

It is true that there is not a Consular Agent of any other Power in Jerusalem — but there are Catholic and Greek Convents, protected by France and Russia, to which travellers of those different Persuasions resort, and which, in some measure, serve to travellers for the purposes of Consulates, as they have Dragomans and Janissaries attached to them.—

English travellers generally go to the Catholic Convent, and have the

1    Young visited Syria and Palestine in 1836, apparently to investigate commercial possibilities. During his travels he met Campbell, who was in Syria at the time.

2    Niven Moore (1795–1889), a veteran member of the Levant consular service, served as Consul at Beirut from 1835 to 1853, when he was promoted to Consul-General. He retired in 1862. Moore maintained commercial ties with Young, and believed that the appointment of the latter as Consular Agent in Jerusalem was likely to advance their joint business ventures. Accordingly, he advised him to apply for the post, should he be so inclined.

3    John Nicolayson (1803–1856), a native of Schleswig and a Danish citizen, first arrived in Jerusalem in January 1826 as a missionary, in order to assist Dr. George Edward Dalton, the first physician in the city, acting on behalf of the Protestant mission. After Dalton's untimely death, Nicolayson left Jerusalem and engaged in missionary activity in Lebanon, Syria, and Egypt. He married Dalton's widow. In 1833 he returned to Jerusalem, where he founded a permanent station of the 'London Society for Promoting Christianity amongst the Jews'. He was quite active in founding the Protestant 'Christ Church' in the city and in establishing the Protestant community in Jerusalem. He headed missionary activities among the Jews until his death. Nicolayson was accepted by all the religious and ethnic groups in the city.
     When the proposal to appoint a Consular Agent in Jerusalem was raised in 1836, Moore first suggested Nicolayson, but Campbell rejected his candidacy, arguing that the appointment of a missionary was not desirable (see Vereté, p. 320)

4    Campbell's formal recommendation of Young was deferred for the time being, since the Consul-General first wished to obtain the consent of Muhammad Ali, the ruler of Egypt, who controlled Syria and Palestine at the time. Muhammad Ali evaded giving a clear answer; to avoid damaging his relations with England, he referred Campbell to the Sultan, without whose consent, so he claimed, the request could not be granted.

same Protection — and particularly during the period when I was there, when the Bishop of Jerusalem was a Maltese and therefore a British Subject.[5] — But if a British Protestant Chapel be established at Jerusalem, it appears to me the appointment of a British Consular agent there will be a matter of necessity to insure a proper respect and support to the Clergyman and other desservants of that Chapel, as from what I know of the Spirit of Religious disputes in Jerusalem, the Protestant Establishment, which I trust to see formed there, will meet with every possible opposition, not on the part of the Turks, but on that of the Catholic, Greek and Armenian Convents and their Inmates.—

This is the principal reason which leads me to believe that the Establishment of a British Consular Agent in Jerusalem will be highly desirable.—

Campbell[6]


# 2    Viscount Palmerston to W.T. Young
Appointment as Vice-Consul in Palestine

The negotiations with the Sublime Porte regarding the establishment of a consulate in Jerusalem continued for approximately ten months, after which more than a year elapsed before the British Ambassador in Constantinople, Lord Ponsonby, informed Foreign Secretary Palmerston that the Sultan had indeed given his confirmation of the Firman (FO 78/331, 30 June 1838). Now that the main obstacle had been removed, Young was officially informed of his appointment as Vice-Consul.

It might be concluded from the corrected date at the beginning of the letter that it had already been prepared in August, but was sent only in September. It was preceded by the letter of Young to Palmerston of 16 August 1838 (Hyamson, No. 1), in which he requested permission to visit the northern part of the country from time to time, "to obtain information as to the state of the

5    We do not know to whom he is referring. There is no information concerning a Catholic bishop in Jerusalem during this period. This may possibly refer to the head of the Franciscan Order and the monasteries, who was appointed every three years by Rome as head of the Latin church, bearing the title, 'Custos of the Holy Land' or 'Guardian of the Hill of Zion and Keeper of the Holy Land', (see Ewald, p. 50). Acccording to Rhodes, p. 67, the Custos was appointed for a six-year term, and was required to be an Italian. See also: Salzbacher II, p. 93.
6    On 18 November 1837, Bidwell informed Campbell: "I am directed by Viscount Palmerston to acquaint you that his Lordship has communicated to H. M.'s Ambassador at Constantinople the substance of your Despatch (Cons. No. 28) and has instructed His Excellency to apply to the Porte for permission for a British Consul to reside at Jerusalem" (FO 78/322).

people and to cultivate a friendly feeling towards the English." He made explicit mention of his ties with Jews in Safed and in Tiberias, whose acquaintance he apparently had made during his previous stay in Palestine.


FO 78/340 — No. 1                                    F.O. Sept. (August) 19th 1838
Draft

Mr. Wm. J. Young
Jerusalem[1]

Sir,
       HMGov. having had under their consideration the expediency of stationing a Consular Agent in Palestine, have come to the determination of appointing a British Vice Consul to reside in that Country; and I have the satisfaction to acquaint you that you have been selected for that situation.
       You will accordingly make immediate preparations for your departure, and you will proceed to your Post by way of Alexandria, where you will receive from Colonel Campbell the proper Document constituting you British Vice Consul, together with the Firman of the Porte, which is in his Possession.[2]
       You will lose no time in making yourself conversant with the details of the Consular Service, and with the nature & extent of your Duties. The General Instructions to the Consuls, of which a Copy is herewith inclosed, contain full directions for the guidance of your official conduct on all ordinary occasions, and special Instructions on particular Points will be given to you from time to time, as occasion may require.
       I also inclose to you Copies of Circular Despatches dated 30. Sept. 1833 & 1. of Oct. 1836; & I have to call your particular attention to the directions contained in those Despatches, enjoining the careful preservation of the Archives of the Consulate.
       You will be punctual in forwarding to this Dept. at the regular periods, the Returns required by the General Instructions; & it will be your Duty to avail yourself of every favourable opportunity for collecting & transmitting to me any useful or interesting information relating to Commerce, Navigation, Agriculture, & any other branch of Statistics.
       The Volume hereunto annexed, & mentioned in a Circular dated the 12. of Aug. 1833, will make you acquainted with the nature of the statistical

1    This is a strange error, because Young clearly was in London at the time.
2    The Firman was sent by the Ambassador in Constantinople to Campbell in Alexandria, the intended superior of the new Vice-Consul.

information which HMGt. is desirous of obtaining, & to the acquirement of which they attach considerable importance.

Permission is given to you to engage in Commercial Pursuits; and a Salary at the rate of £300 a year has been assigned to you during the period of your employment as Vice Consul;[3] but you are distinctly to understand that this Appt., which is only held during pleasure, will give you no further claim upon HMGt., & that you will not be entitled to any Pension or Allowance upon the termination of your Services under this Dept.

Your Salary will commence ten days previously to your embarkation from England, & will be paid to you in the usual way by the Lord in Council of HMTreasury.

Palmerston

## 3    Viscount Palmerston to W.T. Young
Instructions for the Vice-Consul

The following instructions were sent together with the preceding letter. Thus, here too the date is corrected and it was erroneously addressed to Jerusalem. The instructions emphasise the role of the Vice-Consul in the collection of information and in the fostering of possible commercial ties. They also expressly state that he shall be subordinate to the Consul-General in Alexandria. Regarding the sphere of responsibility of the Vice-Consul, on 10 December 1838 Campbell informed the Foreign Secretary that Young would be responsible for the entire country: "As Mr. Young is appointed Vice-Consul for all Palestine, I have directed him to take under his charge and jurisdiction the several parts in Palestine where there are British Consular Agents, and I

3    An internal Memorandum of the Foreign Office dated 22 August 1838 (FO 78/340) attests: "Colonel Campbell stated in a letter to Mr. Young, that he does not believe, that the salary will exceed £100–150 per annum with the liberty to trade." The Memorandum further states that the Vice-Consuls in Alexandria and in Tarsus receive £200 per annum, and the Vice-Consul in Beirut, £300; all three were permitted to engage in trade. The author of the Memorandum continues: "It is presumed that the Vice-Consul of Jerusalem will be of superior importance to Alexandria and Tarsus, but inferior to Beirout, where there is a great deal of responsible Consular-Work to be performed." The Foreign Secretary, however, did not agree with the author of the Memorandum, and ruled in a marginal note from 23 August: "Allow £300 & Liberty to Trade," thus equating the salary of the Vice-Consul in Jerusalem to that of his colleague in Beirut. As is stated here, however, the term of service in Jerusalem did not impart any rights at the conclusion of the Vice-Consul's service.

have made a communication to that effect to Consuls at Damascus and Beyrout" (FO 78/344, Cons. No. 33).
Campbell was referring to five sea ports: 1. Jaffa (Consular Agent Yusuf H. Madbuk); 2. Caiffa (CA Paolo Malagamba); 3. Acre (CA Moise Abraham Finzi); 4. Sidon (CA Joseph Abella); 5. Tyre (CA Georgio Abella). This indicates that his jurisdiction, as defined by Campbell, extended to Tyre and Sidon.

FO 78/340 — No. 2                                             F.O. Sept. (August) 19 1838
Draft

Mr. William Young
Jerusalem

Sir,
    You will fix your principal residence in Palestine at Jerusalem, which will be the seat of your Consulate, from whence you will report to me upon the state of affairs within your District. In order however to enable you to obtain accurate information respecting the whole extent of the Country which is placed under your Jurisdiction, it may be desirable that you should occasionally visit the several Districts round about Jerusalem;[1] & you will accordingly consider yourself authorized to take journies [!] for that purpose from time to time; & to reimburse yourself for the expences of such Expeditions by inserting the amount as Items of Charge in your accounts current with the Lords Commissioners of HM's Treasury. You will not fail however to keep your expences upon those occasions within the lowest possible limits.
    You will make it your business to cultivate a friendly feeling towards Great Britain amongst the Inhabitants of the Country, & you will use your best endeavours to introduce a desire for British Commodities; & to extend the Commercial Relations between the two Countries: you will always bear in mind that there has been considerable difficulty in procuring you your permission to act as British Vice Consul; you will therefore take care to conduct yourself upon all occasions, & in every description of Persons, whether Natives or Foreigners, with mildness & moderation.[2]
    You will address yourself direct to me, but you will transmit your Despatches under flying seal to Col. Campbell; whose Instructions you will at

1    This constitutes a response to Young's letter of 16 August 1838 (Hyamson, No. 1); despite its stating "round about Jerusalem," the intent is to all of Palestine.
2    This paragraph is copied verbatim from the above-mentioned letter by Young.

all times obey; & you will maintain an unreserved Correspondence with HMConsuls at Damascus & Aleppo,[3] whenever there may be occasion so to do.

Palmerston

## 4  W.T. Young to Colonel Campbell
## Request for Appointment of a Dragoman

On 21 November 1838 the Consul-General presented Young with the Firman confirming his appointment as Vice-Consul, noting that the Consular Agents, who previously had been under the authority of Beirut, would now be subordinate to Young. He was to vigilantly defend British interests and take the necessary steps whenever his intervention would be demanded. Furthermore, he was to extend his protection to Jews holding foreign citizenship if requested to do so by the Consuls-General in Alexandria, as the sole European representative in Jerusalem, all in accordance with the Capitulations agreement.

Young responded to this letter by seeking, in the following missive, the support of the Consul-General for his request for the allocation of a Dragoman and Janissaries for the Consulate in Jerusalem, in consideration of the many tasks it was required to perform.

FO 78/344                                      Alexandria 24th November 1838
Copy

Sir

As there is no allusion made by Viscount Palmerston in my instructions, respecting an allowance for a Dragoman and Janissaries; I am desirous of seeking your advice before I venture to take upon myself, the responsibility of engaging such assistance.

From your thorough knowledge of the position I shall stand in, in my new appointment, I feel it is quite unnecessary for me to trouble you with any detailed instances, of the necessity of such appendages to the Vice Consulate at Jerusalem and Palestine.

---

3    For some reason Beirut is omitted here, although there undoubtedly were closer ties with it than with Aleppo.

I would merely take the liberty of calling your attention to the great and increasing influx of Travellers in Palestine. — The fact that I shall be the only European recognised Authority there, will throw upon me a very considerable responsibility, and much more extended intercourse with Foreigners, than perhaps most other Consulates in the Levant; and besides, my occasional absence in visiting the various districts comprised within the limits of my jurisdiction; I would humbly suggest as forming considerable claims, on which I may found a hope that, you can recommend Viscount Palmerston to take into His Lordship's consideration the expediency of making me some allowance to provide myself with a Dragoman and two Janissaries, for the more efficient performance of the Public Service, in the Consulate to which His Lordship has done me the honour to appoint me.[1]

W.T. Young

## 5   Colonel Campbell to Viscount Palmerston
## Protection of Jews in Palestine

In this despatch, Campbell reported of his instructions to Young. Including Young's letter (No. 4, above), he recommended approval of an annual budget of £120 for the employment of a Dragoman and two Janissaries. This allocation was approved on 31 January 1839.

Campbell repeatedly stressed his directive to Young to fulfill the requests of the Consuls-General in Alexandria, to place the Jewish subjects in Jerusalem and Palestine under his aegis, with the consequential well-known instruction of J. Bidwell on behalf of the Foreign Secretary that the responsibilities of the British Vice-Consul included affordance of protection to Jews in general. This was accompanied by a request to report on the present condition of the Jewish population in Palestine (31 January 1839; Hyamson, No. 2).

FO 78/344 (Consular ° 33)                                    Cairo 10th December 1838

My Lord

Mr Vice Consul Young has informed me that he has had the honour to communicate to Your Lordship the details connected with his arrival here, as

1    Campbell also sent Young a copy of the Capitulations, as well as confirmation that he was granted an allowance of £100 for "Outfit." (FO78/368, 26 November 1838).

120

also the instructions which I have given to him, and which I hope may meet Your Lordships approbation.

As Mr Young is appointed Vice Consul for all Palestine, I have directed him to take under his charge and Jurisdiction the Several Parts in Palestine where there are British Consular Agents, and I have made a communication to that effect to Her Majesty's Consuls at Damascus and Beyrout.

I have now the honour to inclose to Your Lordship the copy of a letter addressed to me by Mr Young on the subject of an allowance being made to him for a Dragoman and two Janissaries —

Mr Young's duties in Palestine will not be merely commercial, but I should suppose that one great and perhaps the chief object of his duties, will be the protection of the Jewish Nation in general.

A great number of Jews, not only British; but also Austrian, Dutch, Prussian, Russian and Tuscan resort to Palestine to pass the latter part of their lives in the land of their Forefathers, and generally reside in Jerusalem, Nazareth,[1] Tiberias or Saffet.

Many of those Jews are wealthy and respectable, and as they have not a Consular Agent of their own nation in Palestine, they will naturally place themselves under the protection of Mr Young, and which in conformity to established usage in the Levant, he is bound to accord to them, and indeed some of the Consuls General in Alexandria have already asked Mr Young to protect their Jewish subjects.[2]

It is therefore indispensable for the discharge of Mr Young's duties that he should employ a Dragoman and two Janissaries, and under that view, I take the liberty to recommend to Your Lordship the request of Mr Young.

As the Consular fees in Jerusalem will be a mere trifle, I should think that the sum of 120 Sterling per annum would be required to defray the expence of salary for a Dragoman and two Janissaries in Palestine. —

Campbell

---

1    This is a surprising mistake, because Campbell could have known that there were no Jews in Nazareth. Hebron, by contrast, is not mentioned in the letter.

2    Noteworthy is the response to Young's appointment by the representatives of the London Missionary Society: "The presence of a British officer and the increased security of property which his presence will confer, may invite them from these islands to the cultivation of Palestine, and the Jews, who will betake themselves to agriculture in no other land, having found in the English Consul a mediator between their people and the Pasha, will probably return in yet greater numbers and become once more the husbandmen of Judah and Galilee. This appointment has been conceived and executed in the spirit of true wisdom" (*Jewish Intelligence*, 5 [1839], p. 37). This passage is almost identical to the entry in Lord Shaftesbury's diary for 29 September 1838 (Hodder, p. 240), and it may assumed that Shaftesbury was also the author of the article in *Jewish Intelligence*.

# 6 W.T. Young to Viscount Palmerston
## First Visit to Jerusalem

Although Young was now provided with all the necessary documents, he still remained in Alexandria, due to the cholera epidemic then raging in Palestine. The epidemic broke out at the end of 1838 ("Plague just beginning" — 20 October 1838, *Jewish Intelligence* 5 [1839], p. 7), and reerupted with even greater force in mid-January 1839 (Spyridon, pp. 129-130). The gates of Jerusalem were locked, and each person arriving in Jaffa was required to remain in quarantine for twenty-one days. Only after a stay of two months in Egypt did Young finally set out — even though he knew that the plague had broken out again — arriving in Jaffa on 4 February 1839 (Hyamson, No. 3), where he remained in quarantine until the twenty-fourth of the month. Entry to Jerusalem was still forbidden, however, and Young decided to exhibit extra caution and delay his coming to the Holy City (FO 78/368, 4 March 1839). It was only at the end of March that he dared set out for Jerusalem and, as he relates in the following letter, met with the Governor and his entourage close to the entrance to the city. He was received with hostility, but Young's forceful reaction caused his hosts to apologize.

FO 78/368 — No. 10                                   Convent of Santa Croce near
                                               Jerusalem[1] 26th March 1839

    I have the honor to report to Your Lordship that I have visited Jerusalem.

    In consequence of the repeated complaints I continued to receive of the maladministration of the Quarantine — I concluded to come up that I might ascertain from personal observation the state of the City — and also for the purpose of presenting myself to the authorities at the Gate, with my credentials as Her Majesty's servant.

    Accordingly I procured myself a health guardian that I might accomplish my purpose without subjecting myself to quarantine.

    I found the position of the City most distressing; there has however been no new case of Plague for 15 days, but the sufferings of the people from the long confinement within Gates have been very severe. But I am happy to be

---

1    The monastery in the Valley of the Cross, west of the city. See below, No. 40, n. 1.

able to state to Your Lordship, that the day after my arrival, the Governor in Council resolved in consequence of the distressed state of the city, to open the Gates the following day. It was accordingly proclaimed, but, that the City was still to be considered in Quarantine, and that soldiers would be stationed at some distance on the several roads to prevent any one from passing without a tescare.[2]

I think it my duty to inform Your Lordship, that my reception at Jerusalem was, in the first instance, far from satisfactory, but the consequences I trust will prove advantageous to British influence.

Although Mr. Nicolayson[3] — a British subject who was in quarantine, waited on the Governor to intimate that in consequence of the unhappy state of the city I was unable to wait upon him as I would wish, I therefore begged the Governor would do me the honor to appoint a place where I could present myself as Her Majesty['s] Vice Consul.

When I entered the Gate, where the Governor had appointed, and was sitting in Council, no one took the slightest notice of me, nor was there even a chair provided for me, nor one handed to me, when I came forward with my Firmans in my hand, though every one was seated. In finding myself in this position, My Lord, I considered it my duty to assume an air of some importance. I therefore requested to know the meaning of such a reception, at the same time refusing the chair when at length it was offered to me for I could look at it in no other light than a direct insult offered to Great Britain, and I further explained to the Governor that if Her Majesty's servant who was the bearer of a Firman from both Constantinople and Egypt, was not considered worthy of the commonest civility in Jerusalem, he must withdraw himself. This said in rather an exalted voice and determined manner, had, I have the honor to inform Your Lordship, the happiest effect. The Council rose simultaneously and the Commandant leaped off his Divan, and himself brought me a chair, nor would any one be seated before I had sat down. A thousand apologies were offered, when I assured the Governor how much I regretted what had occurred for my Country's sake, nevertheless I was willing to believe that the mistake arose out of the unhappy position in which quarantine had placed every thing.

The usual compliments of Pipes, Coffee etc. were then offered and I am happy to be able to assure Your Lordship, that it is the opinion of all the British subjects present, that this trifling circumstance will be the means of

---

2    Travel permit.
3    See above, No. 1, n. 3. Nicolayson, who had been the first candidate for Vice-Consul, was among those recommending Young.

placing the British Consulate in the City of Jerusalem on the most advantageous feeling.[4]

[Young]

[p.s.] With Your Lordship's permission I will take the liberty of adding in postscript what I have since been informed privately, that the appointment of a Vice Consul in Jerusalem, is by no means liked by the Authorities there, and that I must be prepared for every opposition and many difficulties, as I shall be looked upon quite as an intruder.

# 7   W.T. Young to Viscount Palmerston
## Remarks on the State of the Country

On 25 May 1839 Young sent the Foreign Secretary a detailed report on the condition of the Jews in Palestine (Hyamson, No. 6), in which he emotionally described their distress. His following despatches also attest to an increasing interest in the status of the Jews and his efforts on their behalf (see, e.g., Hyamson, No. 6, Enclosure 1; No. 7 and Enclosures; No. 9). Palmerston also allocated Young a budget for the employment of a Dragoman who knew Hebrew to strengthen his ties with the Jewish community, despite Campbell's opposition to such action (see: Hyamson, p. 15 — FO 78/368, FO Minute; Hyamson, No. 12 — FO 78/368, 20 September 1839).

In the following despatch, Young relates for the first time to the general state of the country. He reports on the continuing epidemic and on other events in Jerusalem and in Hebron.

FO 78/368 — No.                                      22 Jerusalem, 24th July 1839

      I beg permission to make a few general remarks on the state of this part of the country.

4    Young's visit and meeting with the Governor were also described in a letter by Nicolayson from 1 April 1839 to the journal of the missionary society. According to Nicolayson, the quarantine was lifted two days after the meeting with the Governor, and Young returned to Jaffa, "fully determined to return the week after, to take up his residence here" (*Jewish Intelligence, ibid.*, p. 174).
Young returned to Jerusalem with his family in the second week of April, and on 14 April 1839 was present at the baptism of the Rosenthal family, the first Jewish family to convert to Christianity in Jerusalem under the auspices of the British mission (see: Eliav, Shimon Rosenthal, pp. 113–132).

124

The plague still continues with us — contrary to the experience of all previous years. This however, I am happy to say, is not so fatal in its attacks as it was two months back. Notwithstanding all the precautions of the Latin Convent — yesterday one of the monks was declared to have it — it has in consequence thrown them into considerable consternation lest others may be seized. This disease has been peculiarly fatal to young people from 30 years of age and under and also to infants. The quarantine regulations, I am happy to say, have been removed from this neighbourhood — for such as they were, better calculated to extend than diminish the evil — and were admirably adapted to vex and annoy the people as they are every where, to the suppression of industry and commerce, but they may be often made to serve a Political purpose.[1]

We have still a Quarantine of seven days at Mount Carmel in passing by land northward — and in passing by sea, from Jaffa to Beirout, seventeen days are required.

This week certain coins passing for 21 piasters, 9½ piasters, and 4½ piasters, have been cried down to 20, 9, and 4 piasters each,[2] and after thirty one days, they are no longer to be current, but will be received at the Treasury at the intrinsic value of the metal; and further, the proclamation states, that gold and silver are not to be transported either by land or water from one part to another, under pain of confiscation, and again a coin named "Altli" of Constantinople — which has been for some years passing for 6 piasters, is now to pass for 4, and after 31 days, to pass no longer in the Bazaars at any rate.

The city is perfectly tranquil. I am informed however that in the neighbouring mountains this is not the case but considerable disaffection is evinced. Ten days back the Governor was called to Hebron where a Mountaineer Sheik had alarmed the neighbourhood by his movements — and according to a report I received, this individual did not hesitate to declare that the Mountains generally were enemies to the present government — and of the truth of this, My Lord, I believe there can be little doubt.[3]

---

1    According to another source, 2,000 died in the renewed outbreak of the plague (Spyridon, pp. 130–132). For the sufferings of the Jews, see the above-mentioned report by Young dated 25 May 1839.
2    Devaluation was not uncommon under Egyptian rule. An American traveler in those years mentions that an "edict proclaimed ... changing the value of the current coin, reducing the tallahree or dollar from 21 to 20 piasters, commanding all the subjects of Mohammed Ali to take it at that value" (J.L. Stephens, *Incidents of Travel in Egypt, Arabia, Petrae and the Holy Land by an American*, II, New York 1837, p. 147).
3    The reference is to Abd-el-Rahman, who had a long-standing dispute with the Governor of Jerusalem over some matter. See below, No. 9.

On the Governor's return from Hebron he assured me that everything had been satisfactorily settled, and that it had only been some difference between the above mentioned Sheik and the Governor of Hebron.

On the 30th of last month the Guns of the Castle were fired to announce, as was officially given out, a victory of Ibrahim Pacha over the Sultan's troops[4] — but by the people this was not by any means generally believed — but rather, the Guns were only for the ears of the disaffected in the mountains.

On the 21st the Castle Guns were again fired — which lasted till yesterday, the Governor giving out, that a decisive victory had been gained over the Turkish troops — and that the Sultan[5] had died at Constantinople — and his son had offered Mehemet Ali Egypt and Syria, and that any hostilities were to cease. As this intelligence is not confirmed by any private communication, no one is disposed to believe it, and moreover, they are unwilling to believe intelligence so contrary to their own wishes.[6]

A steam boat under Austrian colors has commenced running between Smyrna and Alexandria calling at Jaffa twice in each month.[7] This, My Lord, may prove a great convenience in many respects; at present however the Quarantines offer a serious obstacle, and must always absorb half the benefit which would arise from this improved method of communication.

[Young]

# 8  W.T. Young to Viscount Palmerston
# Activities of the Russian Consul

During his first year as Vice-Consul, Young endeavoured to comply with his instructions to provide aid and extend protection to all European Jews, regardless of nationality (see, e.g., Hyamson, Enclosures to No. 7; Nos.

---

4   The battle of Nezib, on 24 June 1839, endangered the Ottoman Empire and expedited the intervention of the European Powers.
5   Mahmud II (1808–1839). His son Abdul Mejid (1839–1861) was a sixteen-year-old boy when he became Sultan.
6   Muhammad Ali was offered the continuity of his hereditary pashalik of Egypt, while Palestine and Syria were to be governed by his stepson Ibrahim Pasha during his father's lifetime. The Egyptian ruler rejected this proposal, and the Egyptians were driven out of Palestine. Ottoman rule was restored throughout Syria and Palestine.
7   The "Austrian Lloyd" was established in August 1836, and began to call regularly at Mediterranean ports, becoming a central factor in shipping and passenger service (see below, No. 29).

9–10), but such activity was not to the liking of Russia, whose citizens constituted the majority of the European Jews in Palestine. The Russian government accordingly resolved to hamper the activities of the British Vice-Consul, and to appoint a Wakiel (local consular representative) who would be authorized to deal with all the affairs of Jews who were European subjects and to represent them vis-à-vis the authorities. This official also would be granted judicial powers. Rabbi Israel Bardaki, the leader of the Perushim community and an Austrian subject, was appointed to fill the position. Bardaki evidently did not restrict his activity to Russian subjects, but also dealt with Austrians (until the establishment of the Austrian consulate in 1849). These activities dealt a severe blow to the prestige of the British consulate in the eyes of the European Jews. Few of them, except for British protégés, continued to seek Young's assistance. The appointment of the Wakiel for Russian Jews consequently undermined the standing of the Vice-Consul as the protector of all the Jews.

The following letter is published in its entirety, although Hyamson has already published an abstract (Hyamson, No. 13).


FO 78/367 — No. 31                                      Jerusalem 10th October 1839

My Lord,

From the political state of this Country, I feel it is important to acquaint Your Lordship of what otherwise it might be unnecessary to report viz.: The result of the Russian Consul's visit to Jerusalem, who purposes to reside half the year at Beirout, and the other half in this City or at Jaffa as his duties may require.[1] His proceedings were marked by a great confidence in the extent of his powers. He banished for life one of the principle Priests of the Greek Church to a Convent in the Desert. He made repeated visits to the Synagogues of the European Jews,[2] and there he addressed them upon the Authority he had, to depose their present Wakiel, whom he put in prison, and appointed

---

1    Constantin Basily was born in Constantinople. After his father had been executed for supporting the Greek uprising, he and his family found refuge in Russia. He joined the diplomatic service in 1833, being appointed Consul at Jaffa in 1838. The following year, however, the Consulate was transferred to Beirut, and its jurisdiction included Syria, Lebanon, and Palestine. In 1843 Basily was promoted to the rank of Consul-General, and ended his career upon the outbreak of the Crimean War in 1853. His book, *Memoirs from Lebanon, 1839–1847*, was published in Russian (Odessa 1862), and in Hebrew translation (Jerusalem: Yad Izhak Ben-Zvi, 1984). Despite what is stated in this letter, Basily spent most of his time in Beirut.

2    The reference apparently is to the 'Menahem Zion' synagogue, which was founded after the 1837 earthquake in Safed, within the bounds of the Hurva synagogue in the Old City of Jerusalem.

another in his place,[3] and he informed them, that all who did not submit would be sent out of the Country.

This arbitrary manner of proceeding with the Jews, has caused great confusion, and widened the breach which already existed among them. With regard to any political motive for this interference, I will only observe to Your Lordship, that the effect had been to lead the European Jews in a body under the new Wakiel, to look to the Russian Consul as their protector, had not their divisions led them to dispute the right of the Russian Consul to take cognisance of others, than his own subjects. The local Authorities were advised of this change, and were ordered to recognise no interference in behalf of the European Jews but through the New Wakiel.[4]

Some other difficulties arose out of this business between the son of the French Consular Agent at Jaffa, who happened to be present in Jerusalem, and during an interview, the Russian Consul took away the sword of the son of the French Consular Agent, and ordered his attendants to put him out of his presence. I was applied to by the latter, but I declined all interference whatever. Some French travellers of distinction who were in Jerusalem, I believe, have taken the matter up, and have represented the case to their Consul General in Egypt.

On the arrival of the Russian Consul in Jerusalem, I took occasion to make him a visit, and I had the pleasure to offer him such hospitality as I was enabled to do. In conversation I learned that for the Priest whom he had banished, he had received an intimation from the Metropolitan at St. Petersburgh that the said Priest was a dangerous and troublesome person, and that his influence on the Pilgrims did not give satisfaction.

He prepared me for what he knew would come to my knowledge, of his movements among the Jews, by stating, that he had full instructions from the

---

3    The identity of the Wakiel who was deposed and arrested is unknown. According to Basily's letter of appointment (Hyamson, Enclosure 7 to No. 14), the previous Wakiel was the leader of the Perushim community, Rabbi Israel [Ashkenazi] of Shklov, Bardaki's father-in-law, who had died in an epidemic in Tiberias in the summer of 1839.
     Rabbi Isaiah Bardaki (1790–1863) emigrated to the Holy Land in 1810, leading the Perushim community and the entire Jewish *Yishuv* (community) for more than twenty years. Bardaki fulfilled his consular duties in a high-handed manner, as if he were an actual Consul. Already in 1849 Consul James Finn had written about him: "Rabbi Yeshaiah has his official Dragoman and official Kawass and makes visits of ceremony like a Consul. He is a learned Talmudist, and is commonly reported to have combined his political influence with his influence as a Rabbi" (Hyamson, No. 71). Bardaki did not refrain from clashing with Young regarding candidates for baptism, as if he were a full-fledged Consul (see Hyamson, Nos. 31–36).

4    It would seem, therefore, that according to the directives from Egypt to the Governor in Jerusalem, the Wakiel's duties referred to all European Jews, and not merely to Russian subjects.

Consul General at Alexandria and he expressed his astonishment that I had not likewise received the same instructions.

I immediately desired the English Jews not to pay the slightest attention whatever to any of the injunctions or instructions of the Russian Consul. In respect to other European Jews, it had been too plain to them My Lord, that I have not had the support of my Superior in Egypt. Hence, my General instructions authorising me to afford protection to Strangers, Mr Bidwell's despatch N° 2, desiring me "to consider it part of my duty to afford protection to the Jews generally"[5] and the Instructions of Her Majesty's Agent and Consul General himself, to afford protection to European Jews, have been comparatively nullified, and I cannot but feel My Lord, that this has proved injurious to British Influence among the Jews.[6]

W.T. Young

# 9 W.T. Young to Viscount Palmerston
# Rebellion in Hebron

Sheikh Abd-el-Rahman from the village of Durra, the head of the Aamar clan, took control of the entire Hebron region, ruling the area for more than twenty years in a forceful and cruel manner. He rebelled against the central government, and was the cause of much suffering to the population, especially to the Jews. The Governor in Jerusalem occasionally attempted to depose him by the use of military force, but even if he succeeded in this goal for a time, Abd-el-Rahman would once again impose his rule on the area and declare its independence (for Abd-el-Rahman, see: Zvi Ilan, "The Exploits of Abd-el-Rahman ben Aamar of Durrah in the Hebron Hill-Country," *Nofim* 11–12 [1979], pp. 58–71 [Hebrew]; Eliav, *Austrian Protection*, Nos. 5a, 6–8, 23).

In 1834 the members of the Aamar clan led the revolt against the Egyptian army. Even after the Egyptian conquest of Hebron, Abd-el-Rahman did not lay down his arms, openly challenging the occupying forces (see also below, No. 33).

5  Hyamson, No. 2; see also Enclosure to No. 3.
6  Young was ordered to appoint a Wakiel for the Jews under British protection, as a counterbalance to Bardaki, but was unsuccessful in finding a suitable candidate (Hyamson, Nos. 17–18).

My Lord,

I have the honor to report to Your Lordship, that this district continues in a very unsettled and disturbed state. In Hebron, and in the neighbouring mountains, there have been during the past week some open demonstrations of rebellion, in which two lives have been taken by the insurgents.

In consequence of this, the Governor of Jerusalem has gone out with four hundred of the irregular Cavalry, and I am informed by the Commandant of the city — who is at present laid up with the fever — that he only awaits his convalescence to join the Governor, who has taken up a position in the Hebron road by the Pools of Solomon, when active steps will be taken to put down the insurgents.

The town of Hebron is quite deserted by all except the aged and the Jews; the latter, many of them being Europeans, have applied to me for protection.[1] They are in a state of great alarm, and have already been pillaged.

I have addressed an official letter to the Commandant on the subject and I have his assurance, that the most speedy relief shall be afforded to them, and that in case there should be fighting, he will give to his soldiers the necessary instructions to protect their property.

Should the Government party not prove sufficiently strong, I fear that there will scarcely be security in Jerusalem, unless there be additional aid sent from Headquarters.

W.T. Young

## 10   Viscount Palmerston to W.T. Young
## Deputation to Investigate the Damascus Affair

The blood libels and savage persecutions of the Jews that occurred in February-March 1840 in Damascus and in April 1840 in Rhodes aroused Jews everywhere. Even before English Jewry took action on behalf of their suffering brethren, Palmerston, true to his liberal-humanistic views, had expressed his horror at the libels. He was not inclined to accept the opinion of

---

1   The Jews of Hebron apparently preferred to turn in their distress to the British Vice-Consul, and not to the Wakiel appointed by the Russians. Young, of course, immediately undertook vigorous measures.

the British Consul in Damascus, who upheld his French colleague's open support of the accusations and the severely repressive measures taken against the Jews. Already on 30 April 1840, Palmerston had promised Moses Montefiore, the President of the Board of Deputies of British Jews, that he would use his influence with Muhammad Ali, the Egyptian ruler, and with the Sultan in Constantinople, to put an end to the cruel treatment of the Jews and to conduct a thorough investigation to reveal the truth. When British Jewry decided to send a high-level delegation to investigate the causes of the persecutions in Damascus and Rhodes and to extend assistance to their suffering coreligionists, Palmerston quickly complied with their request for aid, ordering all British diplomatic representatives to assist the delegation. Palmerston's stance in this affair clearly attests to his positive attitude towards Jews and his sympathy for the victims of the libel, which he did not believe for a single minute, and of his intention to present himself as a defender of the Jews wherever they may be. It is highly probable that political considerations influenced his position, for energetic action against the libels and on behalf of their victims was likely to undermine the status of the French and their protégé, Muhammad Ali.

For this affair, see: A.M. Hyamson, "The Damascus Affair — 1840," *Transactions of the Jewish Historical Society of England*, 16 (1945–1951), pp. 47–71; Friedman, Palmerston, pp. 27–28; Montefiore, pp. 208 ff.

FO 78/413
Draft

27th June 1840

I have to acquaint you that it has been represented to me that it was determined at a meeting held by several congregations of the Jews in London at their great Synagogue on the 23rd June,[1] that a Deputation should proceed to the East for the purpose of obtaining a full and fair investigation of the unhappy circumstances which have led to the recent persecutions of the Jews at Damascus and at Rhodes, in the confident expectation that the result of this enquiry will prove to the world the injustice of the accusations which have been brought against that people, and which have been followed up by most barbarous outrages committed upon them with the sanctions of the local Authorities of those places.

I have now to inform you that Sir Moses Montefiore accompanied by the Gentlemen named in the margin (Mr. David Williams Wire, and perhaps Dr. Madden)[2] proceeds to the East on behalf of the Jews of this country for

1    Montefiore, pp. 214–215.
2    Mr. D.W. Wire was Montefiore's former Under-Sheriff and afterwards Lord Mayor of London; Dr. Madden was a well-known author and traveler in the East (*ibid.*, p. 216).

the purposes stated in the beginning of this Despatch, and I have to instruct you to afford to these Gentlemen all the countenance and protection which your official character will enable you to give them, and to use your utmost influence with the authorities in your District to obtain for these Gentlemen who are British subjects every facility for the prosecution of their enquiries, and to secure them from all injury or molestation during their residence in the East.[3]

In conclusion I have to acquaint you that Her Majesty's Government feel the deepest interest in the welfare of the Jewish Community in the East, and are anxiously desirous that the result of the mission of the Gentlemen mentioned in this Despatch may be satisfactory to themselves, and may tend to secure for their brethren in religion who inhabit the Turkish Empire, the peaceable enjoyment of their property, and freedom from all personal injury or molestation from the local Authorities.

Palmerston

P.S. July 2nd. Sir Moses Montefiore will be accompanied by two other Gentlemen, Mr. Adolphe Crémieux and Mr. Louis Loewe,[4] who are not British subjects, and therefore are not entitled as a matter of right to the protection of H.M.'s servants in the East. But I wish that you should extend to those Gentlemen such protection as you may be able properly to afford to them, as persons who although not British subjects are engaged in an undertaking in which the British Government feel an interest.


## 11   W.T. Young to Viscount Ponsonby Deteriorating State of Country

The end of Egyptian occupation and the return of Ottoman rule was accompanied by a serious deterioration of security in Palestine. Once again, the weakness of the Turkish government was revealed, as was its inability to enforce order and impose its will on local sheikhs and notables. Internal security was undermined, and tourists and travelers faced increased dangers.

3   Similar instructions were sent simultaneously to the Consuls in Alexandria, Damascus, Beirut, Aleppo, Rhodes, Smyrna, and Constantinople.
4   Adolphe Crémieux (1796–1880) was the Vice-President of the Central Consistory of French Jews. Louis Loewe (1809–1888), Montefiore's secretary and the editor of his *Diaries*, was a Prussian subject.

As is indicated by the following letter to the British Ambassador in Constantinople, even the status of the British representative was not inviolate, nor was the Governor himself capable of dealing with Young's complaints and extending the necessary assistance.

FO 78/444 — No. 17

Jerusalem 24th July 1841

Before this part of the Country becomes in a still more disorganised state, I consider it my duty to call your Excellency's attention to the apparent inability of the Local Authorities to control the Sheiks of the surrounding Country.

The laboring peasantry are now in danger of being much more oppressed by the Sheiks than they were even by the Egyptian Government, and the general security to the traveller which there was at one time on the most secluded roads, now no longer exists on those most frequented. The system of travelling in Caravans is again restorted to.

Scarcely a week passes [?] we have intelligence of some fighting between the neighbouring sheiks, whose aim seems to be to aggrandize themselves by making the neighbouring villages tributary to them.

At this moment the village of Abu Goush is engaged in open war with Beni Zait — many lives have been lost, but the Authorities take no notice of these things, and it is a matter of general remark, that the Country is in a state of complete insubordination.

Your Excellency is aware that the peasants are all armed, and they do not fear even to menace even [sic] the tranquility of the City. The whole aspect of the Country is changed. The wholesome fear of the Galleys, and of other punishments held over them by the Egyptian Authorities is at an end.

I should be sorry, My Lord, to reflect unnecessarily, on any public functionary, but I feel I should not be doing my duty were I not to state to Your Excellency, that I believe our present Governor, Osman Agar, to be totally unqualified for the duties of his office, which from the attitude of the Sheiks, and their partisans in the City, as well as in the surrounding Country, are daily becoming more responsible.[1]

To-day for the first time since my residence in Jerusalem, I have been personally insulted in the streets. My Janissary, who was walking before me,

---

1   In a later despatch, Young penned an even harsher condemnation of the Governors: "They are perfectly incapable of governing the country ... they appear afraid to act with firmness on the most trivial occasions ... they neither speak the language of the people, nor are they alive to their charlatanisms" (Young to Palmerston, 16 September 1841, FO 78/444, No. 28).

enquired of the fellah, who commenced abusing me without the slightest provocation, the reason for his attack upon me, he was answered by having a loaded carbine presented at him — which caused some confusion, but terminated by my Janissary's succeeding with the aid of the bystanders in securing the person, whom he took to the Seraglio, where he found Abu Gosh, his Sheik, who in the hearing of the Governor, and in the presence of a large number of people commenced an attack of abuse on me (whom he had never seen) and my Government. This, My Lord, is the family who gave up my Janissary to the Egyptian Authorities during the late war, when he was the bearer of the Sultan's proclamation, and I would respectfully submit that so long as this family is permitted to proceed in the lawless way they are doing, there can be no tranquility for this part of the Country. They are desperate characters and there seems to be but one opinion among all classes here concerning them. Their village has for many years been known by the name of the "Robbers Village" — as their chief means of subsistence is by plunder and exactions on Pilgrims.[2]

In Ibrahim Pasha's time the elder of the family was never allowed to quit Jerusalem, other two were kept as hostages attached to the army.

I regret to say, My Lord, the Governor gave me no satisfaction, but without hearing the case released the fellah, and thus, My Lord, encouragement is given to future, and maybe serious outrages. For I would submit to Your Excellency, that if I am unable to obtain respect to myself personally and to my official representations when made to the chief local authority — I fear British subjects can expect but little assistance at my hands in the case of them requiring it.

I do not trouble Your Excellency with a report of every trifling application to the Governor which I have to make, but I may here take occasion to observe to Your Lordship that on two or three occasions I have not been at all satisfied with his method of treating my applications. Nevertheless, from the embarrassed state of the local administration, I have refrained from urging to the utmost my requests; but I would humbly entreat Your Excellency to take my representations into your Excellency's consideration — with permission to add, that the greatest vigilance and the most active measures are continually requisite on the part of the Governor here, to keep this district in tolerable tranquility. The difficulties are not only in dealing with the Sheiks and Fellahs, but with the effendis of the City, who are all more or less connected with the various sheiks in the neighbourhood.

[Young]

2    Complaints about the conduct of the inhabitants of Abu-Ghosh were also raised in the following years, during Consul James Finn's term of office.

134

134

# 12 Sir Stratford Canning to Lord Aberdeen
## Protection of Dutch Subjects

In the absence of a Dutch Consul in Jerusalem, the first immigrants from Holland sought Prussian protection, since they were affiliated with the Dutch-German Kollel (community), which had been founded in 1837 and included immigrants from both Germany and Holland. The decisive majority of Dutch immigrants in the following years enjoyed Prussian (and later German) protection, until ca. 1880. See the file of the German Consulate: ISA 67/115: "Verordnungen betreffend dem Schutz der Holländer."
Already in 1842, however, the Dutch Ambassador in Constantinople had requested the British Ambassador to extend his protection to Dutch subjects in Palestine. This request, the subject of the following letter, received a favourable response. Consequently, some Dutch subjects were under Prussian protection, while others were under the aegis of Great Britain. Furthermore, the lists of protégés of the British consulate for the years 1854 and 1856 include Dutch subjects who also appear in the list of those receiving the protection of the Prussian consulate; they were apparently protégés of both powers (see the lists of subjects under the protection of the British consulate, ISA 123/1/6–8).
Consul Finn would later became embroiled with two of his protégés, and this situation would be among the factors leading to his dismissal (Hyamson, Nos. 211–214). In 1861 a Dutch Consul-General was appointed at Beirut, with a jurisdiction that included Palestine. In July 1862 the Dutch Foreign Office directed that all its Jewish subjects in Palestine be placed under the protection of the Prussian Consulate, thus putting an end to British involvement with their protection (see the above-mentioned file of the German Consulate, the letter of A. Lehren from 11 November 1862 to the Prussian Foreign Ministry, and the letter of 24 December 1862 from the Prussian Embassy in Constantinople to Consul Rosen in Jerusalem).

FO 78/2068 — No. 250

Buyukdere, December 10, 1842

My Lord,
I think it proper to inform your Lordship that in consequence of an official application from the Dutch Charge d'Affaires, I have authorized Her Majesty's Consul General in Syria, to extend the British Protection to ten individuals of the Jewish persuasion, subjects of the King of Holland, who are residing, partly in Jerusalem, and partly in other cities of Syria, where His Majesty has no Consul or Consular Agent. This circumstance and the protec-

tion afforded to British subjects in this Country on the departure of the Ambassadors in the year 1827, by Mr. le Baron de Zuyler, at that time Ambassador from the Netherlands, are the grounds stated by Signor Testa[1] for his application to me, and I hope that your Lordship will approve the assent which I have given to it, subject to the confirmation of Her Majesty's Government.[2]

Stratford Canning

## 13   W.T. Young to Colonel Rose
Hoisting the French Flag

The British Consulate in Jerusalem was joined in 1842 by the Prussian Consulate, and in 1843 by that of Sardinia (Italy). These Consulates refrained from flying their national flags in public in order to avoid arousing the anger of the xenophobic Muslim population, just as churches were forbidden to ring their bells. Therefore Young and his two colleagues were shocked when the first French Consul ignored their practice and boldly displayed his country's flag, without asking permission of the authorities. This act aroused great turmoil, as described in the following report, and the French Consul was forced to forego the flying of the flag to prevent a serious incident. It is possible that the French Consul was aware of the ban, but sought to emphasize his country's preferred status as opposed to that of the other powers. At any rate, this was the first time that the flag of a European power was flown in Jerusalem (see also: Finn J., *Stirring Times*, I, p. 76).

FO 78/540 — No. 28                                         Jerusalem 24th July 1843

Copy

Sir,
        I have the honor to report to You by special Messenger that M. le Comte de Lantivy arrived in this City on the 20th Instant to take up his residence as French Consul.[1]

1   The Dutch Ambassador in Constantinople at the time.
2   Permission was granted; see: FO 78/2068, 20 January 1843, Lord Aberdeen to Sir Canning.

1   Gabriel Marie Jean de Lantivy (1792–1866) was appointed to his first diplomatic post here, and served in Jerusalem for approximately a year and a half, until December 1844.

Mr Lantivy's arrival at Jaffa and the probable hour of his arrival in Jerusalem was officially notified to my Colleagues and to myself by the Native French Agent. We each sent our Interpreters and Janissaries to wait Mr Lantivy's arrival at the City Gate — and they accompanied him to the Latin Convent, where he alighted to attend a Religious Service — . The Pacha sent an Officer and party some distance to meet him and to conduct him into the City —

The following day we paid our new Colleague a Congratulating visit in due form, and afterwards he made his introductory visit to the Pacha, which the Pacha returned on the 22nd when to the surprise of every one the French Flag was hoisted, on the French Agent's house where Mr. Lantivy is residing—

As soon as I discovered this I immediately saw my Colleagues Mr Lenchautin and Dr Schultz[2] on the subject, whom I found, like myself without the slightest notification from Mr Lantivy of his instruction to hoist his national Flag. — There had been a faint rumour of such an intention, and some preparations had been made at the "Casa Nuova" but which the Superior of the Convent I believe had not approved of, lest they should be compromised.

The fact of the French Flag having been hoisted very soon spread through the City, and caused the greatest excitement amongst the Musulmans. — The Effendies assembled at the Mekhamé, and after deliberating with the Kadi, — it was notified to the Pacha that the Flag must be immediately lowered and not rehoisted. The Pacha sent to the French Consul to request that the Flag might be taken down however the Flag was kept flying from 2 Poles until Lunch, during which time the excitement continued, and during the Evening until a late hour an intercourse was kept up between the French Consulate and the Mekhamé, which resulted in the matter being referred to Beyrout[3] and the French Consul consenting not to rehoist the Flag the following day, which was Sunday.

Thus the French Flag has been hoisted in Jerusalem, without being saluted, and lowered by direction of the local Authorities[4] —

2   The Consuls of Sardinia and of Prussia. The Consul of Sardinia, appointed in 1843, was Lenchentin. In 1846 he was succeeded by Castellinari, but the Consulate was closed down in 1849. The Prussian Consul was Ernst Gustav Schultz (1811–1851), who was appointed in April 1842 and arrived in Jerusalem shortly thereafter. He served until 1851, when he fell ill, passed away in Jerusalem and was buried on Mount Zion. He was the first consul to die and be buried in the city.

3   Since the matter was referred to Beirut for decision, Young addressed his report to the British Consul-General in that city.

4   If the flag had been raised with the permission of the authorities, it would have been accompanied by a twenty-one-gun salute. The flag was lowered by order of the authorities, not torn down by an enraged mob, as stated in one study (Schölch, p. 249). This incident is also mentioned by: Tibawi, p. 72; Parfitt, p. 217.

Owing to the Sardinian and Prussian Consuls having only vizirial Letters,[5] they were unable to do more than to report the fact to their respective Superiors. — Being thus left to act alone, my first impulse on seeing the French Flag hoisted, was to send to His Excellency Rachid Pacha to know, if the British Colors would be saluted, should I hoist them, — but on mature consideration I thought that my Instructions would not jusfify me in such a procedure, especially if any commotion should be the result. — I therefore resolved on taking the same course as my Colleagues, the Sardinian and Prussian Consuls. —

During the following day, we heard that serious excitement had been manifested among the Musulman population — The Pacha had been summoned to the Mekhamé, and notified, that if the French Flag was rehoisted, the Musulman population would rise and destroy his own, as well as the French Consul's houses — and threats were held out against all Europeans, but especially against the Consuls. Many proceeded to the Mosque, and there swore on the Koran that they would die for their faith, which they considered to have been attacked. —

This sudden demonstration on the part of the Musulmans I presume must have caused the French Consul to pause before he proceeded further to exasperate the largest and most influential portion of the population.

Sunday was spent by the French Agents in visiting the Effendies, and in endeavouring to convince them of the superior claims of France to peculiar privileges, but as far as I am enabled to learn, but little impression was made on them —

The Pacha has however declared that in consequence of the Superior force of the French Consul's Credentials from Constantinople, he is ready — if the French Consul insists on it — to uphold the French Flag at the point of the sword, but he recommended him to give way for the present, as otherwise bloodshed must be the Consequence —

The Sardinian Consul has it from the Pacha, that Mr Lantivy's Barat states, that he is to be treated with more consideration than the other Consuls residing in Jerusalem, in short that he is to be regarded as being charged by his Government with a special mission, and it states also that he will be accompanied by several subordinate Officers, and that he has permission, and is to have every facility afforded him to build to any extent to which he may require accommodation.

---

5   The standing of the Consulates was initially determined by the nature of their credentials. It seems that the credentials issued by the authorities in Constantinople to the Consuls of Sardinia and Prussia were inferior to the Firman of the Sultan held by Young and to the documents in the possession of the French Consul.

I have to day visited one of the most influential of the Effendies here, with a view to ascertain the state of their feelings. — It is always difficult to know how far it is prudent to rely on the assurances [!] of any here, who take a leading part in the affairs of this place, — owing to the jealousy which prevails. — But I am assured by this person that the Pacha has not the power to uphold the French Flag if the Effendies are opposed to its being hoisted[6] — And I believe this to be correct.

They all refer to the fact of my having been here for some Years, and the hoisting of the British Colors has not been made a question, and they state that at all counts the English have a prior and stronger claim, where any favor is to be shown, to any other nation, when they consider how often the English Government has aided the Sultan in his difficulties —

Thus the matter at present remains.

In conclusion, I would respectfully call Your attention to the fact, that neither myself nor my Colleagues received any communication from the French Consul as to his intention on this important matter — He has acted independently of us, and has overlooked that Courtesy, which in a matter of common interest, we considered was due to us as his Colleagues —

The consequence of his proceedings might have been serious — if persisted in, even fatally so, to others, as well as to himself and those connected with him, for there is no saying when a fanatical mob once beginning, would end their work of destruction, in Jerusalem. Of course the Fellahs of the surrounding Country would take part against the Christians, and would be only too glad of such an opportunity. —

There is no precedent for hoising a Flag in Jerusalem, and there appears to be no local advantage to be gained — under present circumstances — in urging the point, but rather the contrary. Slow as the movement may be — yet there is an inclination towards improvement, which I would submit, it would be unwise to check by needlessly rousing the prejudice of the Musulman population.

W.T. Young

6    The power of the effendis apparently was greater than that of the Pasha, who feared to oppose them. Nevertheless, when the incident became known in Constantinople, the Governor of Jerusalem was deposed (see below, No. 14). For this incident, also see: R. Neuville, "Heurs et malheurs des consuls de France à Jérusalem," *Journal of the Middle East Society* 2-3 (1948), pp. 34–36; *Jewish Intelligence* 9 (1843), pp. 351–352; Tibawi, p. 72.

# 14  W.T. Young to Lord Aberdeen
## Suspension of the Pasha of Jerusalem

The incident surrounding the raising of the French flag had far-reaching consequences. The French Consul, who had been affronted by the stance of the Governor and the threat of the Muslim effendis, complained to the French Embassy in Constantinople, which registered a stiff protest with the Sublime Porte about the humiliation inflicted upon the Consul and the French flag. France's strong standing in Constantinople apparently compelled the Ottoman government to take forceful measures — the Pasha was deposed and five effendis were exiled — to mollify the French (see also: Finn J., *Stirring Times*, p. 31). Despite these steps, however, the French Consul refrained from further attempts to fly his country's flag; only after the victory at Sebastopol in the Crimean War would the national flags of the various Consulates, not only that of France, be raised. After this, the flag would routinely be flown at any official event observed by each Consulate (see below, No. 35).

FO 78/540 — No. 41                                    Jerusalem 2nd October 1843

My Lord
    I have the honor to report to Your Lordship that I received a Visit from Mr de Lantivy[1] on the 29th Ultimo to announce to me that His Excellency Rachid Pacha had been superseded in the Government of Jerusalem, and that five of the Effendies are to be banished in consequence of his representations to the French Ambassador at Constantinople on the subject of the French Flag. —
    Yesterday on paying a friendly visit to the Sardinian Consul in company with Dr. Schultz,[2] I met there Mr de Lantivy —
    Dr Schultz informs me that after I had left, the French Consul read to them a Despatch which he had just received from the French Ambassador at Constantinople, informing him of the measures which had been taken at the Porte respecting the French Flag Affair, and approving of his conduct in the strongest possible terms. —
    I am entirely ignorant of the motive of the French Consul, in allowing

1   See above, No. 13, n. 1.
2   See above, No. 13, n. 2.

me to quit the Sardinian Consul's house before he would read this Despatch to his Colleagues.[3]

I have shown every disposition to state my opinion to Count de Lantivy frankly and openly on all matters which I have considered to be of a general and mutual interest, but I have not remarked a similar disposition on his side towards me, but rather the reverse.

W.T. Young

## 15   W.T. Young to Colonel Rose
## Unsafe Conditions in the District

The following despatch, one of the last sent by Young as Consul in Jerusalem, indicates that the serious lack of security described above (No. 11) had not improved during the past four years, but rather had worsened. The authorities were powerless to impose order or provide security in the country.

FO 78/626 — No. 32                                      Jerusalem, 7th May 1845

Sir,

I have the honour to inform You that the affairs of this District continue to be in the most disturbed and unsatisfactory state.

The intercourse with Nablouse is entirely interrupted, and the efforts of the Pacha[1] to accommodate matters with the Sheiks there have hitherto proved abortive — They have declared their intention not to receive the Turkish officer who has been recently appointed their Governor; he remains for the present in Jerusalem.

It is most difficult to obtain correct information, as to what measures the Authorities are actually taking, and what is really going on around us. But it is evident that the Neighbouring Sheiks are under no sort of control.

---

3   The behaviour of the French Consul indicates covert competition with the British representative for premier standing.

---

1   Ali Pasha succeeded Reshid Pasha, who had been deposed in the aftermath of the French flag incident (above, No. 14). Throughout the entire period, this district (Nablus) was noted for its rebelliousness and agitation against the Turkish authorities.

The roads are everywhere insecure, and rumours are continually being brought to the City, of some fresh outrage being committed on passengers by the Fellahs whose insolence and temerity know no bounds. —

In the absence of all power in the Local Government to redress grievances, it is in vain to apply to the Authorities for redress.

I beg therefore to report to You that in the present state of the affairs of the Province I cannot answer for what may happen to any of her Majesty's Subjects. — I can only caution them to endeavour to avoid falling into difficulties as I cannot be responsible for the issue.

W.T. Young

## 16 Colonel Rose to James Finn
## British Protection for Jewish Subjects
## of Foreign Powers

In April 1846 James Finn arrived in Jerusalem to serve as the second British Consul in Palestine. By March 1847 Finn had already written a letter to Palmerston in which he raised the question, whether he was permitted to afford protection to Jews, Austrian and Russian subjects, whose passports had expired and did not intend to return to their homelands (Hyamson, No. 52). Consul-General Rose had reservations regarding the very proposal, especially as it pertained to Austrian subjects who were under the protection of the Austrian Consul-General in Beirut, but he reported the hints dropped by the Russian Consul, Basily, to the effect that his government would not oppose the British government's granting of protection to former Russian subjects (Hyamson, No. 54). Palmerston, however, was not inclined to make the issue a subject of negotiation between the governments, so as not to arouse suspicion. He informed Rose to advise Finn that in any instance in which any foreign subject was in distress but was not protected by his own Consulate, the British Consul could extend such protection, provided that the relevant Consulate consented (Hyamson, No. 56). The following is the text of the directive Rose was requested to send to Finn.

In the end, Finn's initiative led to an official provision for the granting of British protection to Jewish subjects from Russia, who had in practice lost their citizenship.

FO 78/963                                                                Beyrout June 30. 1847

Copy — Circular

Sir,

        Her Majesty's Consul at Jerusalem submitted a question to Her Majesty's Principal Secretary of State for Foreign Affairs, as to the propriety of his affording British Protection to the Jewish Subjects of Foreign Powers who might have forfeited their claim to be protected by the Consular Agents of their own country.

        I have received Instructions from Viscount Palmerston on this subject, and in obedience to them I have the honor to instruct you that whenever an Austrian, Russian, French or other Jew shall be suffering under persecution or injustice and shall be repudiated and refused protection by his own Consul, you upon ascertaining the fact may ask the repudiating Consul, whether he has any objection to you as British Consul interposing your good offices in behalf of such Jew, in compliance with the general Instructions under which you are authorized to interfere in favor of Jews generally, and unless the repudiating Consul should assign some strong and sufficient reason for objecting to your doing so, you will take steps in accordance with those Instructions.[1]

                                                                        Hugh Rose


# 17  J. Finn to Viscount Palmerston
## Arrival of the Latin Patriarch


In 1841 Britain and Prussia agreed to the establishment of a joint Protestant diocese in Jerusalem. This was followed in January 1842 by the arrival in Jerusalem of an apostate Jew, Michael Alexander, who had been appointed as the first Protestant Bishop. In 1845 the Greek Orthodox Patriarchate was transferred from Constantinople to Jerusalem. Patriarch Cyril II (1845–1872), took vigorous steps to enhance the activity of this community, and in 1847 he even established a central Greek Orthodox church. Although the Greek Orthodox Patriarch cooperated with the Russians, this did not satisfy them. Shortly after his appointment, an Archimandrite of the Russian Orthodox church was dispatched to Jerusalem.
After the appointment of the Protestant Bishop, the Catholics exerted pres-

1    Rose copied Palmerston's orders verbatim (Hyamson, No. 56).

sure for the appointment of a Catholic Patriarch. This was opposed by the Franciscans, who until then had controlled the affairs of the Catholic community in Palestine and whose head, the Custos of the Holy Land, to all intents and purposes had the status of a bishop (see above, No. 1). The Franciscans feared the loss of their hegemony and the imposition of limitations upon their activities, but were unsuccessful in preventing the appointment for any length of time. When it was learned that both a Greek Orthodox Patriarch and a senior Russian ecclesiastic had come to Jerusalem, France pressured the Pope to reestablish the Latin Patriarchate, already existent in the city, as a center for well-defined Catholic activity and as a counterweight to the intensive activity of the Protestants and the Greek Orthodox. France viewed with displeasure the enhanced status of its rivals England and Russia by means of the churches, and sought to reassert its premier status as the defender of Catholic interests in general and of the Latin Patriarchate in particular.

Joseph Valerga (b. 1814) filled this post until 1872, and was quite actively involved in establishing churches, monasteries, and educational institutions for the local population. This energetic churchman was noted for his initiative and courage (see also: Finn J., *Stirring Times*, chap. II; Colbi, pp. 94–96; Rhodes, pp. 68)

FO 78/755 — No. 4                                      Jerusalem 29 Jan 1848

My Lord

I have the honor to report the arrival of a Latin Patriarch in Jerusalem, on Monday the 17th Instant, with great demonstrations of honor —

The French and Sardinian Consuls rode out in full uniform to meet him:[1] and in the train were the French and Sardinian Vice Consuls from Jaffa — The Pasha sent as a Deputation, his Dragoman, the Revenue Collector, and the Chief of the Police.

When within the city, His Clergy and the monks met the Patriarch in vestments and with lighted tapers, opposite the door of the Latin Hospice, where he also assumed robes and mitre, and proceeded under a canopy to the Convent Church chanting the Te Deum.

In the afternoon I paid a visit of congratulations, and His Seigneury has since returned the Compliment.

There can be no doubt that Roman Catholic Interests in this country have suffered hitherto from having remained stationary under the rule of

1    The two Catholic Consuls then serving in Jerusalem. The Austrian Consulate was opened only in 1849.

ignorant monks, while the Greeks and Protestants have had their affairs administered by high ecclesiastical dignitaries.[2]

The monks from having so long had exclusive rule over the natives of their Communion, are much annoyed at this change in affairs, but the people have easily learned to transfer their allegiance to the Patriarch and his officers: which they do with enthusiasm.

The Patriarch enjoys a reputation for considerable knowledge in Oriental languages, having spent much of his previous life in Persia and Turkey. His age is said to be 34, and He wears a long beard, — a circumstance supposed to be of some consequence in these countries, though I believe not really so, for a European in these days.

J. Finn

## 18  Proclamation of the Turkish Government Precautions against Pestilence

The following document is included, even though it did not originate with the Jerusalem Consulate, because it sheds light on the treatment, and presumed medical care, of cholera victims in this period, and the means for preventing the spread of the disease. The Consul reported of the epidemic on 28 August 1848: "50 persons were attacked with cholera, of whom eleven died. No other cases had occurred up to the date of the 25th" (FO 195/292, No. 22).

FO 78/755              Translation of a Proclamation published in Jerusalem, August 1848

It appears that this year is a year of pestilence which has existed in some countries, and even in Damascus [namely] the Cholera — and the most necessary thing is confidence in God the supreme, and to take care against this pestilence.

1st — It is necessary for every man to be always clean about his clothes and body, and [to keep] his house from dirt and filthings.

---

2    The Consul also was aware of the fact that the appointment of the Latin Patriarch came in the wake of the establishment of the Protestant diocese and the transfer of the Greek Orthodox Patriarchate to Jerusalem.

2nd — It is necessary to abstain from heavy food such as yellow melons, apples, plums, quinces, the two sorts of cucumbers, pears, bad meat, salads, food cooked with oil, doughy pastry etc. — to abstain from indigestible food, and from drinks that bring on blood, as spirits, wines etc. and to forbear from women.

But what are praiseful for human health are good meat, rice, pumpkin, koosa, bamy and green beans —, [and] of the fruit sort, apples and quinces cooked with sugar alone, and even that very moderately.

3rd — If God permits one to fall into such a complaint, at its commencement he will surely feel either cramp or diarrhea, but at that moment without hesitation and without the least delay he must drink a drop of camphor, or half a finjan (small cup) of peppermint, or from 5 to 8 drops of the spirit of peppermint with water. But if the diarrhea is very strong, then to take 60 drops of Laudanum with hot water and to clyster with it the patient. — And if vomiting follows and is very strong, and cannot be stopped, take 6 or 8 drops of the spirit of camphor in a finjan of water, or half a finjan of peppermint or balm.

During this complaint the patient is not to eat any thing.

So after all these remedies, if he is no better before the cold enters his sides, it is necessary to take blood about 200 drachms and upwards until the blood changes, — and also by the side of the patient ought to be men to rub his body with course woolen stuff with very great force.

After that if the complaint is not stopped, to place upon the stomach leeches, according to the state of the patient; and if the complaint is not cured by that remedy, then to place upon his feet and sides mustard with flour.

And the supreme God is the healer, who works as he will.

## 19   J. Finn to Viscount Palmerston
## Arrest of Sheikh of Abu Ghosh

In the incessant warfare between the two main camps in the Arab population, the Kais and the Yaman, the allegiance of families and tribes was determined, in most instances, by tradition and by political interest. This violence undermined security in Palestine, leading to acts of robbery and destruction. The Kais faction was led by the Samhan family, and the Yaman camp by the Abu Ghosh clan. The latter was presumably entrusted with the safeguarding of travellers along the main road to Jerusalem, which also entailed the collection of a toll. Wayfarers were terrified by the members of the Abu Ghosh clan, who even instigated the peasants to rebel against the authorities (also see above, No. 11).

Tribal feuds and the lack of security on the roads continued throughout the following years The various Consulates, led by the British, sought to make peace between the rival camps, but without success (see also: Eliav, *Austrian Protection*, No. 24; Finn J., *Stirring Times*, chap. IX). File FO 195/292 contains much correspondence dealing with the tribal warfare in the years 1847–1850.

FO 78/755 — No. 29                                        Jerusalem 13 September 1848

My Lord,

I have the honor to report that on Wednesday last the 6th Instant, Yusuf the responsible Sheikh of Abu Gosh, was arrested in Jerusalem, and conveyed by night to Jaffa.

The cause of this arrest was the disturbance in which the country has lately been kept by that restless clan. The Pasha had not forgiven his recent defiance of the Turkish soldiery by summoning the peasantry by letters to defend themselves — by throwing his people of Kariet el Aneb[1] into Lifta[2] — by having the roads patroled [!] at night with armed peasants — and by challenging the Pasha to come out of Jerusalem and fight, offering that if His Excellency were not well supplied with ammunition he would lend him some.

But the Pasha kept silence and the affair seemed blown over so that Yusuf had several times since entered Jerusalem.

The manner of the seizure was this. — Abu Gosh had gone to dine with the Colonel of the Garrison. While washing hands, previous to eating, his arms were tied by eight soldiers — and he was driven to the Seraglio.[3] Upon the way he shouted aloud the Moslem Confession of Faith, whereupon one of the soldiers struck him on the back of the neck and said — "What then! you have now learned that there is a God" —

His celebrated rival, Ibn Simkhan being in the city, the Pasha ordered him to convey Abu Gosh through his territory, avoiding the Abu Gosh territory, with an escort of twenty or thirty men. This was done in the night.

So deliberately had the scheme been planned that the gates of the city

1   The present-day Jewish settlement of Kiryat Anavim. See also the description in: Schulz, p. 89.
2   An Arab village at the entrance to Jerusalem.
3   The residence of the Governor.

were shut earlier than usual, that is at Sunset, the universal hour of dining —
to the temporary inconvenience of some Europeans outside the gates,
depending upon the usual time.

In the same night seventeen men called by the title of Sheikh were seized
in Bethlehem during their sleep, and sent away in company with Yusuf Abu
Gosh.

The first effect upon the country was that of stupor — except in those
villages such as Bethlehem and Ain Karim where the population are usually
divided in nearly equal numbers between the two factions. In these villages the
half favoring Abu Gosh either escaped to the hills with their families, or fled
for a kind of refuge to Kariet el Aneb.

These are now returned fully armed — and in all such villages as well as
Batteer, and Beit Safafah, are fighting once more.

Bahri Pasha[4] has sent out Bash-Bezuk[5] and Infantry into the villages
and is now seizing Camels for the transport of provisions for the troops.

J. Finn

# 20  J. Finn to Sir S. Canning
## Jewish Converts to Islam

The Ottoman government forbade all missionary activity among its Muslim
subjects ("Rayahs"), and a Muslim who converted to Christianity or to
Judaism was liable to be punished by death. Finn had already dealt with cases
of Jewish Ottoman subjects who had converted to Christianity, without the
Sublime Porte expressing opposition (see Hyamson, Nos. 51 and 58). This,
however, was an instance of a Jew who had converted to Islam and later
returned to Judaism; if his Muslim past were to come to light, his life would
be in danger. In this case as well, Finn exceeded his authority, for this
involved a Rayah who was not entitled to the protection of the Consul. The
following letter was abstracted by Hyamson (No. 69), but is cited here in full,
due to its cardinal importance.

4    The Governor of Jerusalem, 1848–1849.
5    Irregular local cavalry, recruited by the Pasha.

Sir

I have the honor to apprise Your Excellency that a case has been mentioned to me of a Jew in Jerusalem who under constraint of circumstances some years ago embraced the Moslem religion at Aleppo.

He has now lived some time in Jerusalem practising the Jewish religion but having been recognized recently by a Moslem from Aleppo has concealed himself ever since, within a house in a state of utmost terror. Though a Rayah subject of the Sultan, he has appealed to me for protection.

Knowing what efforts Your Excellency has already made in resisting Mohammedan fanaticism, I venture to bring his case before Your Excellency's notice, and to request directions on the subject.

Aware of the measures taken in 1844 concerning the Armenians executed in Constantinople and Brussa for Apostasy from Islamism, and understanding that the Sultan's declaration to Your Excellency that — "The Sublime Porte engages to take effectual measures to prevent henceforward the execution and putting to death of the Christian who is an Apostate" — has been since interpreted to refer only to cases of persons not born of Moslem parents, but who having embraced Islamism from another religion had reverted to their first religion — I beg to remind Your Excellency that this is such a case, only substituting the word Jew for Christian.[1]

I beg also for copies or Translations of such public declarations as His Majesty may have made during his reign, in favour of religious toleration, as I often wish to have such documents to refer to.

J.F.

## 21.  J. Finn to Viscount Palmerston
## Consecration of Christ Church in Jerusalem

Already in 1838, Nicolayson had purchased the plots facing the entrance to David's Citadel on behalf of the London Society (see: *Jewish Intelligence* 4 [1838], pp. 52–53). They were intended for the construction of a church and

---

[1]  In a later letter (5 February 1849), Finn informed the Ambassador that the Turk left Jerusalem. The danger had passed, and the Jew came out of his hiding place, free to engage in his own affairs.

mission headquarters. In 1839 the foundations were laid for the church building and its cornerstone set in place in 1840, but construction could not continue apace due to the machinations of the Governor and the negative policy of the Sublime Porte, which forbade the establishment of new churches. Over the course of time, the representatives of Britain and Prussia strove to pressure the central government in Constantinople to change its stance, and in September 1845 the Firman for the building of the church was confirmed. The Governor of Jerusalem and the leaders of the local Muslim population sought, however, to prevent any further construction work; moreover, the Firman restricted the construction of a church to within the bounds of the Consulate. The mission members understood that space for the Consulate would have to be allocated within the church precinct, so that the church under construction could be linked with the Consulate. Construction work was renewed in 1846, after a considerable sum had been donated for the building project, and was completed at the end of 1848. The new church and the surrounding precinct would serve from then on as the center for British activity, both of the Consulate and of the mission.

FO 78/803 — No. 2                                    Jerusalem 22 January 1849

My Lord
    I have the honor to report that yesterday the new English Church in this City was consecrated by the name of Christ Church.
    Acting as Registrar for the day I read the Petition for Consecration.
    Dr Kayat, Her Majesty's Consul for Jaffa,[1] and Mr Weber the Acting Consul for Prussia in Jerusalem,[2] were present. The Syrian Bishop of Jerusalem, Some Clergy of the Greeks and Greek Catholics, Some Laity of the Latins and numerous Armenian Pilgrims were also in the Church.
    On this occasion were read for the first time, the Prayers for the King of

---

1    Assad Jacob Khayat (1811–1865), a native of Beirut, served as a Dragoman from 1830. In 1839 he began his medical studies in London, but did not complete them. After engaging in missionary activity on behalf of the Christ Missionary Society (CMS), he returned to London and resumed his studies until he received his medical degree in 1846, obtaining British citizenship upon the completion of his studies. In July 1847 he was appointed Consul in Jaffa, serving in this capacity until his death on 19 November 1865. The Consulate in Jaffa was subordinate to the Consulate-General in Beirut (see: FO 78/705, Palmerston to Finn, 18 June 1847). For Khayat see: Tibawi, pp. 142–145; Salibi, pp. 135–158; see also a description from 1841: Egerton, pp. 3, 133.
2    In the absence of Consul Schultz from Palestine from 1848 to the summer of 1850 (see above, No. 13, n. 2), the position was filled by Theodor Weber, who was the Secretary in the Prussian Consulate in Beirut (1848–1855). In 1855 he was promoted to the rank of Consul in Beirut, serving afterwards as Consul-General (1866–1875).

Prussia, and the Sultan, of which the enclosed are Copies,[3] and which will be continued in use.

Ministers of the Evangelical Church of Prussia are permitted to hold Divine Service in the Church upon certain conditions: but there are no such Ministers here at present.

The Consulate house erected by the London Society beside the Church, is not yet completed: but I have kept my Office in one of its rooms for some months past.[4]

J. Finn

## 22   Niven Moore to J. Finn
## Finn's Zeal for Conversion of Jews

In May 1849 the Russian Consul-General in Beirut formally informed Niven Moore, the British Acting Consul-General in that city, that the Russian government had agreed to place under British protection Jews whose Russian citizenship had been revoked (see above, No. 16). Not a month passed, however, before serious accusations were raised in Jerusalem regarding Finn's missionary intentions. The Jews, former Russian subjects, were not pleased with the prospect of coming under the protection of Finn, who, as rumour had it, sought to encourage them to convert to Christianity. Basily was asked to cancel the overall arrangement transferring them to British protection. After he spoke with Moore, the latter emphasized to Finn that he was not to interfere in the religious affairs of those under his protection (see: Hyamson, Nos. 74, 76; Eliav, Finn, pp. 46–48). Finn, for his part, totally denied all the allegations raised against him (see: Hyamson, Enclosure 2 to No. 76, 27 June 1849).

FO 78/2068                                                      Beyrout 18th June 1849

Copy — Confidential

My dear Sir,
    With reference to my official letter of this date,[1] I beg to say that I have

3   Not enclosed here.
4   Finn was compelled to maintain his office there, in only a single room, because the Firman for the church building required that the church adjoin the seat of the Consulate.

_____

1   See: Hyamson, Enclosure 1 to No. 76. Moore wanted to stress the severity of the matter by sending him a personal letter the same day.

had a long private conversation with Mr. Basily on the subject.

He spoke with great frankness. He said he could not do otherwise than address the Instruction to Mr. Marabutti,[2] which at my request he deferred sending till I hear from you.

Mr. Basily gave it as his opinion that if you give the Jews clearly to understand that you had instructions not to interfere with their religion, in your official character, no reluctance would exist on their part to apply for British protection.

I must in candor tell you that Mr. Basily spoke of your great zeal in the conversion of the Jews, and that this was the cause of the difficulty they made in applying to you.

Sir Moses Montefiore is now here and will shortly visit Jerusalem. He was delighted to learn from me of the transfer of the Russian Jews to our protection. But should his suspicion once be roused that there is an intention of making the arrangement subservient to conversion, I am persuaded that he would be the first to encourage the Jews not to accept it.[3]

Mr. Basily did not overlook this circumstance, he said, he was sure that Sir Moses would on his arrival at Jerusalem be beset with complaints of the Jews that such was the intention.

I thought it friendly to give you in the present private and confidential form the substance of Mr. Basily's conversation.

N. Moore[4]

## 23 J. Finn to Sir S. Canning
## Attack on a Russian Jew

Not long after the extension of protection to Jews who were former Russian subjects, the Consul was required to come to the aid of one of them who had been attacked in the street. When Finn sent his Dragoman to the Pasha, the latter initially refused to deal with the complaint, claiming that in accordance with Islamic law he could not accept the testimony of a Jew regarding the incident. When, however, Finn demanded this in writing, the Pasha retreated from his initial position, and ordered the imprisonment of the assailant.

2   The Russian Vice-Consul at Jaffa.
3   For the response of Montefiore, see Moore's despatch to Palmerston of 2 July 1849 (Hyamson, No. 76).
4   See above, No. 1, n. 2.

This episode reflects Finn's forceful defense before the Pasha of those under his protection.

A summary of the report was published by Hyamson (No. 75). It is reproduced here in full, as sent to the Ambassador in Constantinople with a copy to the Foreign Secretary.

FO 195/292 — No. 22                                    Jerusalem, 25th June 1849

Sir,

I have the honor to report to Your Excellency that a Russian Jew named Simon Tob Mordochai Oglio, whose term of Russian passport was expired, having applied to me last week for redress against a Turk who had beaten him in the street and torn his clothes, I sent the case to the Pasha.

My Dragoman having understood His Excellency to say that he could not receive Jewish evidence, I wrote to enquire if this were true. Upon which the Pasha confined the offender in prison, and sent his Secretary to request me to withdraw my letter.

I pressed however the necessity of an answer; when His Excellency replied that he had not said that he would not receive Jewish evidence.

The offender having been then two days in prison, I consented to his release.

J. Finn

# 24  J. Finn to Viscount Palmerston
## Purchase of Lands

Serious problems of security forced the inhabitants of Jerusalem to dwell solely within the walls of the Old City. It was only in the 1840s, after the Egyptian occupation had ended, that the first daring attempts were made to purchase land outside the walls, and even to take up residence there. Initially, lands were acquired for agricultural ends, mainly for vegetable gardens and plantations. The first to venture out were members of the Greek Orthodox church, headed by the Archimandrite Nikophoras, who also served as Secretary to the Orthodox Patriarch. Nikophoras was quite active, systematically purchasing many tracts to the southwest of the walls, where thousands of trees were planted upon his initiative. The intent was to give the Greek Orthodox church a monopoly on land acquisition in this area. The

153

Greeks' anger knew no bounds, therefore, when they learned that the British Consul had purchased land in the Talbieh area, in order to build a summer residence for himself and his family so that they might escape the oppressive heat and deadly climate within the walls (see: Ben-Arieh, p. 59; Tobler, *Topographie*, II, pp. 42–43). Since the Greek Orthodox were Ottoman subjects, they were permitted to purchase land, unlike the Europeans to whom this was forbidden. Their resentment of Finn's initiative developed into open hostility.

FO 78/839 — No. 13 Jerusalem 10 July 1850

My Lord

I think it my duty to make a report to Your Lordship about certain purchases of land recently made about the city of Jerusalem.

For nearly four years past, finding the health of my family seriously affected by the miasma[1] of the city during a great part of the year, I have wished to procure a simple residence for them outside the city, but at an easy distance. I applied to natives offering them to rent such a house if they would build it,[2] but in every case their demands were too high for me to entertain them. — I therefore set myself to purchase a small piece of land through my Dragoman, in order to build for myself, as several Consuls and other Europeans have done in these countries.[3]

On commencing such a negociation lately, I have been surprised to find to what an extent the Greek Convent (a term used familiarly to denote the property and affairs of the Orthodox Greek Church under its ecclesiastical rulers) has bought up land around Jerusalem.

I began with a spot of very rocky ground on an eminence South-West of the city, which I preferred on account of its extensive prospect and convenient distance. There I failed, and in every direction that we proceeded, it was discovered that the Greek Archimandrite Nikephori had been before us.

At length we obtained a piece near the first piece enquired for, and just behind his plantation, to be mentioned presently.[4] The rage of the Archiman-

1 Miasma — infectious germs floating in the air, causing infections and fever.
2 Until the promulgation of the Lands Law of 1867/8, foreign subjects were forbidden to purchase real estate (immobilia).
3 Finn was the first European who sought to build a home for himself outside the walls. Due, however, to the restrictions of the law, he was forced to employ his Dragoman as a straw man, who presumably owned the property. The reference to other Consuls does not relate to Jerusalem, rather to other locations within the Ottoman Empire.
4 The land in Talbieh had apparently already been purchased in 1849. On 14 August 1850, Finn wrote to Canning, the Ambassador in Constantinople: "The plot is already cleared of stones and surrounded by a wall" (FO 78/839).

154

drite was in consequence shewn by his causing to be displaced from his office, the Sheikh of Malhhah[5] who had assisted in our purchase, and by his invectives against all the peasantry concerned in it, for allowing a Nattûr to be placed among his property.

A Nattûr in the Arabic language signifies a watchman placed in a rude turret among vineyards during the time of ripening of grapes, whose business it is to spy around him continually for detection of thieves.

An immediate rise took place in the prices of land, so that now by a wonderful idea propagated, that Franks[6] are competing for purchase of land, it can scarcely be obtained for six times the value which it bore two months ago. But certain Effendis of the city have threatened the peasants with severe penalties, such as imprisonment, the public works of Acre, or being sent for soldiers, if they dare to sell land to the Dragoman of the English Consulate.

Yet this does not arise from zeal for the laws or established customs of the country, — on the contrary they have allowed and still allow the Archimandrite to purchase land, though a Christian and a European, in such remarkable situations as ought to excite alarm in men of real patriotism. Nearly the whole city is now environed by pieces of land purchased by him, ostensibly for cultivation, but forming a perfect circle, — not of the best soil for agriculture, sometimes far otherwise, but just such as serve to fill up that ring; which by a remarkable coincidence forms nearly the identical line where the famous circumvallation of Titus[7] must have been — Some of these fields have been bought within the last fortnight. — and for others to complete the circle he is now in treaty with the peasantry —

In every instance his grounds command a clear view of the city at about three musket shots distance.

But the most remarkable work is what has been done at the small Convent of St George directly opposite the Castle — Three years ago this was a ruin which the Greeks attempted to rebuild, but Mehemed Pasha[8] (now Ambassador in London) would not suffer it — assigning military reasons for his refusal — the ground about it was rocky in the extreme, and strewed with ashes, and other rubbish.

Soon after the departure of Mehemed Pasha, we learned that the Greeks

5    Malhah — the only Arab village between the walls of the Old City and Ein Karem. The villagers of Malhah were hired by the Greek Orthodox monks to work the plantations and vineyards. Even though they were in the employ of the Greek Orthodox church, their sheikh agreed to aid Finn in the purchase of lands.
6    Europeans.
7    The encompassing of the city with a dike by Titus before the conquest of the city and the destruction of the Second Temple.
8    Mehemed Pasha was Governor of Jerusalem, 1845–1847.

had bought that ground, and we saw rocks blasted, walls built, terraces and straight walls constructed, and during the last winter many thousands of mulberry trees were also planted within the enclosure and potatoes grown. Those who have walked within the Walls assure me that immense chambers are sunk into the rock, said to be intended for cisterns and granaries. The little Convent has been covered in — and many people have been delighted to witness the improvement that can be effected in so unpromising a spot by Christian industry. — This site is upon an eminence across the valley of Hinnom, directly commanding the Castle and the principal gate of the city. [...]

Meanwhile I believe that the Pasha has no idea of being surrounded by a Russian line of property, — though no one doubts that the Town Council of Effendis is largely and frequently remunerated from the Greek Convent.

I ought to mention that it is commonly calculated, the Greeks possess one third of the city itself, — and wherever their houses are not immediately contiguous to each other, they are connected by arches thrown across the streets, or when it is considered necessary, by raising the houses a story higher, and then throwing an arch over the intervening house which is not yet bought.

It is frequently said in Jerusalem that the whole army in Russia are obliged to appropriate one day's pay in the year for support of the Convents etc. in Jerusalem. It is certain that the riches of the Greek Convent here, are prodigious.

I have to report also that not only have the Greek pilgrims been unusually numerous this year, but that several Russian ships of war have landed bodies of men wearing a white uniform, with foraging caps, and polished black belts, — whether these are soldiers, sailors, or marines I know not, or even men serving in each capacity alternately, — but they always keep together in a corps, and march in step. They come ostensibly on pilgrimage, and go to the Jordan etc. like other pilgrims; but their military appearance attracts some attention.

There is a body of 40 in the town at present, who arrived yesterday.

What has created at least equal surprise, is the arrival here of Russians of high rank; — within the first four months of this year, we had —

1. Prince A. de Lieven. 2. Count P. de Boutouslin. 3. A. de Mouravief. 4. Prince Wiasemsky.

The two latter are Chamberlains of the Emperor's Court. — There was also an Admiral of the Fleet, whose name I have not remembered.

These matters I have thought proper to report to Your Lordship.

J. Finn.

156

## 25 J. Finn to Adhem Pasha
## Lease of Land at Talbieh

Adhem Pasha (July 1849–October 1851) supported the Greek Orthodox, and at their bequest attempted to cancel the British Consulate's purchase of land by intimidating the seller. It was clear to all, including the Governor, that although the Dragoman appeared as the buyer the Consul stood behind the transaction and provided the funds. Finn saw fit to send the Pasha a strongly-worded letter indicating that should the Governor continue in his attempts to frustrate the transaction, he would turn to the Sublime Porte.

FO 195/292                                                      5 August 1850
Copy

His Excellency Adhem Pasha of Jerusalem
    I wish to inform Your Excellency that I have lately leased a piece of land called the Talibiyeh near Jerusalem for the term of four years from a Rayah of His Imperial Highness the Sultan — and his name is Moossa Tannoos.[1] He is at present employed as my first Arabic Dragoman which however does not prevent him from being a Turkish Subject.
    But the Seller has come to the said Moossa and informed him that the sale is invalid, because Your Excellency has sent for him and threatened him greatly that he should return the price to the buyer.
    I have the honor to inform Your Excellency that he is not desirous to restore the land which he has lawfully bought, but is ready to answer before You by my Order, as to whether or not he has transgressed the laws of His Imperial Majesty the Sultan.
    And with respect to the Fellahheen who sold the land, I have a right [to demand] that Your Excellency will cease from persecuting or threatening them on that account.
    It cannot be said that I have no right to interfere in a matter which concerns only Rayahs of the Sublime Porte — for this matter does concern me

---

1    Moussa Tannous served for decades as First Dragoman in the British Consulate and was Finn's confidant. Tannous also was a property owner in his own right, engaged in commerce with the peasants, and was involved in many real estate transactions (see: Tibawi, p. 139; Yellin, p. 13). Finn officially appeared as the lessee of the land from Tannous. It is only at the end of his letter that he mentions his intention to build a house for his family on the plot (also see: Eliav, Finn, p. 55).

in part — because I have hired the land as above said. And if it did not, I am sure that the Supreme Government would listen to my statement of the injustice which has been done in this matter by Your Excellency, and by others in your presence.

It is not entirely a new thing to improve waste places near Jerusalem or near Jaffa, or near Beyrout — And now I hope to have a residence for the health of my family at a short distance outside the city.

J. Finn, Consul


## 26   J. Finn to Sir S. Canning
## Purchase of Lands

Finn did not limit his initiatives to the acquisition of land in Talbieh. He also aided in the purchase of lands in Artas (Urtas) near Solomon's Pools, where a model farmstead was to be established, in which Finn also invested sizable sums of money and much energy (see: Eliav, Finn, pp. 60–64; Rubin, pp. 325–331; Hanauer, pp. 127 ff.). Tobler also describes the project in Artas in most favorable terms, referring to it as "Paradise" (Tobler, *Dritte Wanderung*, pp. 86–87).

As in Talbieh, the Greek Orthodox clergy also interfered with the purchase of lands in Artas, trying in every way possible to obstruct the British initiative there. Finn acted in an extremely forceful manner, opposing the efforts of the Greeks until he succeeded in putting a stop to them. On 29 April 1851 Finn reported once again of the purchase of lands by the Greek Orthodox for astronomical sums, including rocky, long-abandoned tracts which they turned into olive and berry orchards (FO 78/874).


FO 78/839 — No. 11                                    Jerusalem 14 August 1850

Copy

Sir,

I have the honor to report to Your Excellency that the threats mentioned in my Despatch N° 13 to Viscount Palmerston,[1] as used by Effendis of the City Council towards the peasantry on account of the piece of land bought by my

---

1    See above, No. 24.

Dragoman and leased from him to me, were followed by further proceedings—

On the 2nd Instant, the Pasha sent for those who had been concerned in that transaction: and having in presence of the Council threatened them for selling land to the English — they denied the charge — and he remanded them till the next day.

On their reappearance the whole Corps of Effendis present, at one moment shouted at the poor men in order to terrify them — The Pasha commanded them to restore the money to the Dragoman, under the menace of being chopped in pieces.

His Excellency then informed the Council that the English were going to build Castles all over the country — and described how they had taken India; first there came a street-sweeper earning a few paras; he inhabited an old sepulchre, then built a dome over it, then added a chamber, then wrote home to his Government, who sent others, and so at last the English conquered India.

One of the Council enquired what the peasants were to do, if the Dragoman should demand several thousand piastres' compensation for the works he had commenced, of clearing stones and building a wall around the place? — The Pasha sentenced that they were to pay that too, as a punishment for their offence —

The men asked what they were to do if the Dragoman should refuse to take back the money? — and His Excellency replied by peremptorily ordering them out of his presence.

Finding the people much alarmed at such proceedings, which had commenced in private threats, and advanced through Greek ecclesiastical denunciations, and menaces of Effendis in the streets, to the climax above described I wrote to His Excellency the letter of which Copy is here enclosed,[2] — to which he sent an oral reply, that there was one word in it which displeased him. — I therefore wrote again, requesting that his Secretary and my Dragoman might confer in my presence as to the Arabic words employed. — but I heard no more of the matter.

I have another case of a kindred nature to report to Your Excellency.

About two hours' distance from Jerusalem, near Solomon's pools, there is a small valley with a fine Spring of water, and a village utterly ruined named Urtas. — A population is nominally attached to it, but the people sleep in a ruined Khan near the Pools, and work by day at some small patches of ground in the valley.[3]

---

2    See above, No. 25.
3    The inhabitants of the village had abandoned it because of problems of security and taxes, and lived in the nearby fortress of Solomon's Pools.

An English Subject named Meshullam[4] conceived the project a few months ago, of putting more of this valley into cultivation: by entering into partnership with the Sheikh of the place, on the terms of himself to enjoy three fourths of the produce, and the Sheikh the remainder, — besides a yearly rent to be paid.

They petitioned the Pasha for leave in this affair, — when His Excellency countersigned the paper, and sent it to the Makhkameh. — There a lease was made out in full legal formality for a term of five years.

Upon this Mr Meshullam set to work with his family, hired peasants at good wages, cleared portions of ground, sowed kitchen vegetables and grain, bought cattle and built two chambers separate from each other, against the face of the rock.

All went on prosperously, — a wild waste becoming a beautiful farm and garden in a very short time, until the Greeks and Effendis commenced their interference with my hired ground near the city. Then Greeks came into the valley, and purchased those pieces of land on which the peasants had ignorantly toiled before. Thus dissensions began, and I have myself heard the peasants use the party designations of Abu Kalusch (monks' caps) and Abu Bornetah (Frank hats). Taamri Arabs came with guns into the place and disturbed Meshullam's labours; diverting the water course in favor of the new comers, though contrary to the terms of his lease.

One of Meshullam's labourers was thrown arbitrarily into prison in Jerusalem in this manner. The Pasha summoned him to the city, together with another, and asked why they had allowed the English to cultivate that valley? — "By Your Excellency's own permission" — they replied — and without another word they were carried off to the dungeon — but released after some days on my remonstrance.

A very respectable Sheikh of the Great Mosque, who was lately with me at Urtas, overheard peasants there saying that they had received gold gazis

4    John Meshullam (1799–1878) was born in London to a respected Jewish family. In his youth, the family moved to Salonika, while he was sent to study in London. In the British capital he began to take an interest in Christianity. In his twenties he spent three years in Jerusalem, before traveling through many countries, where he acquired the knowledge of more than ten languages. He was baptised in 1840 in Malta by Samuel Gobat, later to become the Anglican Bishop in Jerusalem. He and his family immigrated in 1841 to Jerusalem, where he opened the city's first European hotel. In 1845 he came for the first time to Artas and was greatly impressed by its fertility and abundant water. He began to rent lands from the village's inhabitants and on 12 June 1850 resolved to move with his family to the village. Over the course of many years Meshullam and Finn and his wife enjoyed amicable relations which took a turn for the worse at the beginning of the 1860s, leading to Meshullam's dispossession from his holdings in Artas (see the detailed discussion in Eliav, Finn).

from the Archimandrite Nikephori, with directions to be civil to Meshullam "until the time" —

Meanwhile we hear constantly of this Archimandrite having bought fresh pieces of land, — and it is supposed that the Greeks now possess an uninterrupted line between Jerusalem and Bethlehem. The Pasha who never leaves the city knows nothing but what the Greek-paid Effendis tell him.

A few days ago, the Archimandrite was negociating for a piece of land that is indisputably *Wak'f*:[5] Thereupon one of the Council went to remonstrate with the Pasha, against allowing *the English* to get it. So His Excellency indignantly forbade the sale of it to the English.

The day before yesterday, some Germans were endeavouring to take on lease a small piece of ground on a wild stoney hill near Beit Jala. The Greek convent interfered, and they were baffled.

Such were the attempts made by the Effendis and Pasha, no doubt at the instigation of the Greeks, to prevent any effort for improvement being made in the country, except by the latter, — but as usual in such proceedings they have had no practical result. We now hear no more about them. —

I am told, however, that the peasantry in this neighbourhood have offered much more land to European cultivators in expectation of regular employment under improved systems of agriculture —

It is still deplorable to see the millions of acres of fine land lying waste throughout Palestine, from which the Turkish Government derives no revenue whatever — and in travelling over which, among deserted villages, the wish rises perpetually in the mind — "O that the Sultan would allow me to turn some wilderness into a fruitful field and make numerous people happy, even though double Miri were paid for the opportunity of doing so" — but then it must be somewhat distant from the conceptions and intrigues of Jerusalem.

J.F.

## 27  J. Finn to Viscount Palmerston
## Catholic Interests in Palestine

France's traditional role as defender of Catholic interests was not universally accepted (see above, No. 17). The Franciscans, in particular, complained about the haughty attitude of the French, on the one hand, and their inactivity,

5  Land owned by a religious trust which could not be sold.

161

on the other. The Sardinian Consul also objected to the actions of France and its representatives. With the establishment of the Austrian Consulate in Jerusalem in 1849, a representative of another Catholic great power appeared on the scene, claiming the right to protect Catholic interests. This led to rivalary, both hidden and open, between the representatives of the two Catholic powers for premier standing. The traditional British reservations against the French also found expression in Finn's support for the Austrian Consul, who was quite well accepted by his colleagues (see: Eliav, *Austrian Protection*, p. 22, n. 78).

FO 78/839 — No. 19                                      Jerusalem 25 Sept. 1850

My Lord

I have the honor to give Your Lordship the substance of one recent conversation in particular with the Austrian Vice Consul, Mr Pizzamano,[1] combined with the result of general observation for some time past, on Roman Catholic interests in Palestine.

The Latin communities are dissatisfied with the inefficiency of French Protection for a long time past, but especially within the last few years. — They complain that the French have suffered the Greek ecclesiastics to usurp by gradual encroachments, most of the sacred localities in Jerusalem and Bethlehem. They shew by documents and old maps that a century ago the Greeks had scarcely any property in the Sanctuaries about the Holy Sepulchre — whereas now they possess the largest proportion — and that the same is the case in Bethlehem, although at the period above-mentioned, they had not even a chapel for worship there.

The great cupola over the Church of the Holy Sepulchre remains in a state of shameful dilapidation on account of dispute as to who shall repair it, — because the fact of reparation would according to usage of the country, confer the right of property. The Latins even accuse the Greeks of occasionally stripping lead from the dome, in order to bring it the sooner into a state of absolute wreck.

Complaints of French inefficient protection are not novel — The late

---

1    Josef von Pizzamano (1809–1860), a native of Venice, was appointed Vice-Consul at Jerusalem in September 1847. Various occurrences, however, prevented him from arriving before 1 March 1849, when the Consulate began to function. In February 1852 he was appointed Consul, and in November 1857 he was granted the personal rank of Consul-General, to the displeasure of Finn, who was a more senior diplomat in Jerusalem and the doyen of the diplomatic corps in the city. Pizzamano eventually fell ill, dying in Jerusalem on 22 July 1860. He was buried on Mount Zion.

162

Sardinian Consul[2] was always in an attitude of hostility to the French Consulate on behalf of the Convents.

Now, however, the Austrians are about to assume the lead with vigour; they ridicule the pretensions of Sardinia, a petty power without even a single Treaty with the Ottoman Porte, and scoff at the title of "Protector of Christianity" held by the French, who contribute nothing to the Jerusalem Treasury and have not one monk in any of the Palestine Convents, while Austria has several monks, and has rendered this year no less a sum than 35.000 crowns to the Terra Santa Treasury.[3]

The title of "Protector of Christianity in the East" has been so far resisted by other Roman Catholic Powers that it now confers no precedence on French Consuls in the religious processions etc.

Austria is therefore about to take up the Conventual and Sanctuary interests here with real influence — not as the French, who commenced and failed twice within the present century — I think the dates are 1812 and 1829.

Mr. Pizzamano is a military man of resolute character. Mr. Botta, the Consul of France, is an amiable and retiring scholar in delicate health.[4]

I have observed that within the last year, the Latin monks of Jerusalem are mostly new arrival, and of a class of men superior to those who resided here on my first coming into the country. — Sisters of Charity are multiplied — and the schools of the Latin Community are better conducted than formerly.[5]

J. Finn

2   The Sardinian Consulate was opened at the beginning of 1843, but was closed down in August 1849. Finn's report states: "Sardinian Consulate suspended ... Management of business entrusted to the French Consulate" (FO 78/803, 3 September 1849; see also above, No. 13, n. 2).

3   For the raising of funds in Austria on behalf of the Holy Land, see: "300 Jahre General-Kommissariat des Heiligen Landes in Wien," Oesterreichische Pilgerbriefe, April–Juni 1933; Eliav, Austrian Protection, pp. 4–6.

4   Paul Emile Botta (1802–1870) was the third French Consul in Jerusalem, serving between 1848 and 1855. He was a renowned scientist, linguist, and archaeologist, and published many studies (see also: Finn J., Stirring Times, I, p. 77).

5   Three years later, Finn would write in this respect: "Count Pizzamano has taken frequent occasions of representing to me the hollowship of French pretension to the Protectorate of Christianity in the east, while France supplies neither monks, nor priests nor money to Palestine. Finally the French Consulate is industriously circulating the belief that the French Empire is stable and mighty, while England is on the very brink of a fearful socialist revolution and bankruptcy." (FO 78/962, 3 December 1853).

## 28   J. Finn to Viscount Palmerston
## Appointment of a Vice-Consul at Haifa

For many years British Consular Agents were employed in Haifa and in Acre. The Consular Agent in Haifa, Paolo Malagamba, a local Christian of Italian descent, was appointed on 18 May 1837. This post was a "hereditary" one, and he had been preceded in it by his father and by his uncle (FO 78/340, 1 January 1838, List of Vice-Consuls, District Beyrout). Finn considered Malagamba unfit for the position, dismissed him on 10 December 1848 (FO 78/755) and placed the representation in Haifa under the jurisdiction of the Consular Agent in Acre, Moses Abraham Finzi, a Jew of Italian origin. Finzi had initially served as Consular Agent in Safed (1831–1837) from where he was transferred to Acre on 18 May 1837. He was quite active on behalf of the Jewish community in Galilee, and tried to be of assistance in time of trouble. Now Finn reached the conclusion that the time had come to once again appoint a consular representative in Haifa. This time, however, he was not content with a Consular Agent, but rather intended to appoint a Vice-Consul in the growing city. Finzi remained the consular representative in Acre.

FO 78/874 (Consular No. 19)                                      29 November 1851

[...] I take this opportunity of reminding Your Lordship that in February 1849 (N° 8) I recommended the port of Caiffa to particular attention. — Since that time I have pressed it upon the notice of Colonel Rose,[1] in consequence of the increased grain export from Europe.

But I have now to add that within the last twelve months that little town is greatly enlarged, and some of the most expensive dwelling houses in all Palestine have been erected there by native merchants, besides whole streets rebuilt by the Latin Convent of Carmel, which has purchased much of the land around and a part of the town. I have not been furnished with details but am informed that the Russian and Austrian Agents there (the former an Ionian subject) are carrying on trade upon a large scale for this country.

It therefore seems to me desirable that a native Englishman should be placed with a small Salary, and leave to trade (at least at the beginning) who might be able, not only to superintend Trade, but to give prompt aid to the

1   Colonel Hugh Henry Rose (1801–1885) served as Consul-General in Beirut in 1841–1851. The reference here is merely to cooperation, for during the period of Finn's service, Galilee was included in his jurisdiction, as it had been during the tenure of his predecessor, Young.

numerous Jews under British protection in Safed and Tiberias, reporting however to the Consulate in Jerusalem.[2] I am sure that such a person would be fully occupied.

I am not more disposed than before to recommend Mr. Finzi for the post,[3] — the person should be an Englishman and not of the Jewish religion. Mr. Finzi might however be left still in Acre, to avoid the appearance of dismissal or disgrace after long service but in truth, the British interests in these days require to be represented by a superior class of persons to that which might be sufficient in former times.

Your Lordship was pleased on December 22. 1848, to instruct me, that "if in my opinion a fresh appointment should be made at that post, I should recommend another person for that place" —

In compliance with that direction I now beg to recommend my Cancelliere, Mr. Edward Thomas Rogers for Vice Consul of Caiffa, as a person peculiarly well fitted to fulfil the duties I have described above.[4]

He has been nearly four years in my service, accustomed to its routine, inured to the climate — fluent in vernacular Arabic, besides French and Italian, — and has in the course of deputed service from me, made himself greatly esteemed by the Jews in Safed and Tiberias, with whose peculiar dialect he is already somewhat conversant. He is also acquainted with the principal personages in Caiffa and Acre

I know of no other Englishman in the country that could accept the office, and I confidently recommend him for that post.[5]

J. Finn

2   Finn sought to ensure that even with the appointment of a Vice-Consul in Haifa, Galilee would remain under his authority.
3   According to Finn, Finzi was unsuitable for such an important post. On 14 May 1860 Finn wrote to the Foreign Office (apparently at Finzi's request), noting that Finzi had already served for 24 years without salary, that he was 57 years old and had a large family. In consideration of his dedicated labours during the Crimean war, Finn proposed offering him the modest salary of £80 per annum, as a token of gratitude for his long service.
4   Edward Thomas Rogers (1830–1884) was Finn's chief assistant in the Jerusalem Consulate from 1848 onward. On 26 February 1852 he was appointed Vice-Consul at Haifa and held this post from 1853 to 1861.
5   See his appointment as Vice-Consul on 26 February 1852 with a salary of £200 per annum (FO 78/914); but see below, No. 31.

## 29   J. Finn to Lord Malmesbury
## Austrian Lloyds Company

In 1833 several Austrian insurance companies in Trieste united and began to dispatch steamships to the Levant. After the trial sailings proved successful, the Austrian Lloyd Company was founded on 2 August 1836, with a capital of 2,500,000 francs and began to operate regular shipping lines in the Mediterranean. The ships also dropped anchor in Haifa, initially only once per month, and not until the 1850s did they begin to stop at Jaffa as well. The Austrian Lloyd ships accounted for a significant proportion of the regular passenger and cargo transportation in the Mediterranean. In the second half of the century Austrian Lloyd became the largest commercial line in the region. In addition to the Austrians, the French and the Russians also maintained regular shipping lines in this period.

FO 78/913 — No. 10                                           Jerusalem, 9 October 1852
Political

My Lord,
    I have the honor to report to Your Lordship that I have been recently informed by Count Pizzamano, Austrian Consul in Jerusalem and Palestine, that a line of Austrian Steamers will shortly commence plying between Tarsous and Alexandria touching at all the principal ports on the coast, and making one voyage, each way, every fortnight.
    Count Pizzamano also informed me that he has made application to Austrian Lloyds Company and to a banking House in Vienna to beg them to set about to repair the road between Jaffa and Jerusalem,[1] as they have done in other parts of the Levant where an important inland town was ill connected with the coast at which their steamers touched, such as across the isthmus of Corinth.

J. Finn

---

1   The construction of the road from Jaffa to Jerusalem would begin only fifteen years later. When the Sultan learned that the Austrian Emperor Franz Josef was to visit the Holy Land on his way to the gala opening of the Suez Canal (1869), he ordered (in 1867) that the road between the two cities be paved, so that it could accommodate carriages. Work progressed slowly, although it was carried out with forced labour. The road which resulted was far from serving as a real highway, causing much difficulty and inconvenience to those who travelled it. Only in 1888 was the fundamental renovation of the road completed.

# 30 S. Gobat to J. Finn
## Complaints on Mail Service

The following letter, signed by the Anglican Bishop and twenty-eight local British protégés, describes the long and complicated route taken by mail sent from England to individuals in Jerusalem. It was sent aboard French ships and, due to the unbelievable inefficiency of the French, much time elapsed before the letters and other items reached their destination, thus causing much suffering and inconvenience to the residents of Jerusalem. The appeals to the English authorities apparently were to no avail; they did not even receive a reply. Accordingly the Consul had been requested to try have mail sent on Austrian Lloyd ships, even though it would be preferable "to the honour of the British nation" to employ a British steamship for this purpose. The Austrian mail service, the first in Palestine, was established at the end of 1853, and although several other European Powers followed the lead of the Austrians in the ensuing years and opened their own postal offices, the Austrian mail service was renowned for its quality and reliability.

FO 78/914
Copy

Jerusalem 28 December 1852.

Sir

We have the honor to bring before your notice the serious inconveniences which we have experienced more or less for the last eighteen months from the extreme irregularity in the transmission of our letters between Europe and this country. Our letters arrive in Jerusalem at such *various intervals of time*, and by such various means, that we can never feel perfectly assured that they all even eventually come to hand.

Under the present circumstances, when our letters and newspapers are carried by the French steamers, those for Jerusalem via Marseilles are sent on to Beyrout although the steamer touches at Jaffa, which is within ten hours of this City — At Beyrout the letters lie until a convenient opportunity occur for their being sent back to Jaffa, and it has more than once happened that the first ensuing opportunity has been the same French steamer on her return after ten days from Smyrna, by which they were then again carried to Alexandria before being delivered in Jaffa.

We do not know where the original cause of irregularity may lie, but we believe that there exists a careless and culpable negligence on the part of those

Officers who have charge of the English mails on board of the French Steamers.

In January last we had the honor of addressing a petition to Col. Maberly which you were kind enough to forward for us to him in hopes that he would remedy the then existing evil. But as we have received no answer, nor has any intimation been given that the petition was even received by him, and the irregularity having considerably increased, we take the present opportunity of begging you, Sir, to use your influence in the right quarter that the losses of time and money which have been recently experienced here may be prevented for the future, either by a Contract being entered into with (as a suggestion) the Company of the Austrian Lloyds'[1] or what would be *far* more *to the honor of the British nation*, by placing a British Steamer on the coast for the *certain* conveyance of the British mail between the various ports in the Levant.

(Signed by the Anglican Bishop[2] and twenty-eight other Protestant residents in Jerusalem, chiefly British Subjects)

# 31   J. Finn to Lord Malmesbury
## Importance of Vice-Consulate in Haifa

Although Finn had already requested in November 1851 the appointment of a Vice-Consul at Haifa (above, No. 28), and the Foreign Office had given its consent on 26 February 1852 to the appointment of Rogers to this post (see *ibid.*), official confirmation of the appointment was not forthcoming, and Rogers remained for the while in his post at the Jerusalem Consulate. Finn consequently once again urged the Foreign Secretary to confirm Rogers' appointment, based upon the urgency of the matter, due to Haifa's increasing importance. The appointment was finally confirmed in May 1853 (FO 78/963).

1   See above, in the introduction to No. 29. This letter was written before the establishment of the Austrian postal service in Palestine.

2   Samuel Gobat (1799–1879) was the second Protestant Bishop in Jerusalem, arriving in December 1846. Over the course of time he was involved in serious altercations and disputes with Finn, whom he charged with pro-German proclivities (see Eliav, Finn, pp. 64 ff.; Eliav, Shimon Rosenthal, pp. 113-132). See also the testimony of a German clergyman, from 1851: "Der Bischof Gobat ist übrigens sammt seinem ganzen Hause, obwohl in allen Sprachen sehr bewandert, nach Charakter und Sprache, durch und durch deutsch und in seiner Familie ist die deutsche Sprache die herrschende." (Schulz, p. 120).

FO 78/963                                    Jerusalem 1 January 1853
Separate

My Lord,

I have the honor to enclose Returns of trade in the principal Ports within the district of this Consulate N° 1 — of the British trade at the Ports of Caiffa and Acre — and N° 2 — of the British and Foreign trade in Gross, at those two ports —

And I have the honor to state that I have felt regret that so much British trade should be carried on in Caiffa without the presence there of a British Officer of any description whatever.

The Station has been unoccupied since November, 1848.[1]

Under these considerations, I have appointed[2] Mr Edward Thomas Rogers, a British subject who has been in the service of this Consulate as Cancelliere for nearly five years and is well acquainted with the language and customs of the country, to the port of Caiffa and would venture to urge Your Lordship to take into consideration the importance of a British born person there from the following circumstances. But I have to recommend that whereas the place was formerly held by a Consular Agent (a foreigner) the rank of the Office be now that of a Vice Consulate.

1st The great increase of British trade there —

2nd The rising importance of the port as a place of Commerce in general, it being in such immediate communication with the most fertile district of Palestine viz. Galilee, and the famous wheat district of the Hauran.

3rd Other European Powers have already appointed their own subjects natives of Europe, as Vice Consuls there.[3]

4th The fact that the Austrian Steamer has for a second time been obliged to leave the mail for Jerusalem at Caiffa not being able to get into the port of Jaffa; the former being universally acknowledged as the better and safer harbour.

5th So many residents in Safed and Tiberias (each within a day's journey of Caiffa) have lately obtained British Protection, who with the Station of the Church Missionary Society now at Nazareth will need occasional visits for information and protection, which could easily be afforded by a British Vice Consul in Caiffa.

1  Finzi's appointment to the Consular Agency in Haifa (see above, No. 28) was also only temporary, a state of affairs which Finn did not regard as desirable.
2  A boastful exaggeration, since Finn proposed — but it was the Foreign Office that appointed.
3  Here, too, Finn exaggerated: most of the Powers had only Consular Agents in Haifa, and only later did some of them become Vice-Consuls.

6th The welfare of British interests would be much promoted by having a respectable representative in communication with the Pasha of Acre; Caiffa being within so short a distance of Acre, that a degree of influence might be established and kept up by a British Vice Consul there.

J. Finn

# 32   Declaration of Consuls
# Deteriorating Situation in Palestine

The various Governors of Jerusalem were unsuccessful in enforcing law and order in the region. Incessant tribal warfare undermined the state of security, despite the efforts to subdue the clans. Several of the Consuls, especially the British and the French, unsuccessfully endeavoured to make peace between the rivals (see above, No. 19). The outbreak of the Crimean War led Turkey to withdraw almost all of its troops from Palestine. The tribes took advantage of this development to rebel, completely undermining security in the country. In 1855 the armed skirmishes in Palestine intensified, leading to chaos in the land. Many villages were destroyed, their inhabitants killed, and the cultivated areas turned into wasteland. Highway robbers controlled the roads, with none to stop them (see Finn's description: Finn J., *Stirring Times*, chap. XXIV). Abd-el Rahman el Amer, the sheikh of the village of Durra, who for years had held the populace in his dread, rose up in open revolt and terrorized Hebron, which was under his control (see below, No. 33). Nablus also served as a focal point of constant rebellion and unrest. Kiamil Pasha, the new Governor, was compelled to ask the consuls to support his plea for immediate aid from the Sultan. At his request, the consuls sent a joint declaration to their ambassadors in Constantinople, asking for their vigorous intervention to have the Sublime Porte despatch troops to the area to quell the riots. Finn took upon himself to mediate between the warring tribes and attempt to bring about a peace. Despite his endangering himself in these efforts, while exhibiting exemplary courage, his actions did not have positive results.

FO 78/1120                                                      Jerusalem, 19 Mai 1855

A l'invitation de S. Ex. Kiamil Pasha Gouverneur de Jerusalem,[1] les

1   Kiamil Pasha (1832–1915) arrived in Jerusalem on 15 February 1855 and ended his term of service in March 1857, but later served twice more as Governor. He was also thrice the

Consuls résidant en cette ville se sont réunis auprès de lui pour lui prêter leur concours dans les circonstances difficiles ou se trouve aujourd'hui la Palestine.

Les rivalités personnelles entre divers chefs et les inimitiés de tribu à tribu qui depuis un certain nombre d'années entretiennent le pays dans un état de guerre civile permanente n'ont fait que l'étendre et s'envenimer dans l'administration des prédecesseurs de Kiamil Pasha, par suite de certains abus et faute d'une repression, — impartiale et energique. Les efforts de Kiamil Pasha depuis plus de 3 mois dans le but de pacifier la contrée par les voies de douceur et de persuasion n'ont eu pour résultat que d'obtenir quelques trèves à chaque instant violées. De plus il est evident pour qui connait l'état des choses et l'esprit des populations de la Palestine que ce système dès aujourd'hui impossible à pratiquer est de plus dangereux, en ce qu'il donne aux gens du pays la conviction de l'impuissance où se trouve le gouvernement de faire respecter les ordres — De nouvelles concessions pour concilier les parties ne réussiraient pas à empêcher une explosion génèrale, et achèveraient de détruire la force morale de l'autorité. Le Canton de Nablous s'est levé en armes pour repousser un Caimacam[2] nommé et envoyé par la Sublime Porte; celui d'Hebron est en pleine révolte[3] et l'un des chefs ose même faire des sommations au gouverneur en lui indiquant un délai de cinq jours pour le satisfaire sous menace de tout ravager; les Bedouins de la rive orientale du Jourdain sont tout prêts à envahir le pays des que les chefs des differents partis les appelleront. — Enfin, plusieurs villages ont déjà été détruits dans ces dernieres années, des arbres nombreux ont été coupés, des moissons ravagées, et les revenus du tresor en ont éprouvé une perte considerable.

Il a fallu à Ibrahim Pasha une armée nombreuse pour dompter les populations turbulantes de la Palestine et les maintenir en tranquilité. — Aujourd'hui le Gouverneur de Jerusalem n'a dans les mains aucune force matérielle pour faire respecter l'autorité de la Sublime Porte, puisque toute la garnison de la province se compose d'un bataillon incomplet dont il ne peut pas disposer, et d'environ 600 irréguliers qui n'imposent aucun respect aux

Governor of Beirut and served four terms of office as Grand Vizier (i.e., Prime Minister). He achieved a reputation as a superb administrator and as one of the outstanding politicians in the government. He possessed liberal views, was educated, and had pro-British sympathies. Finn, however, who at first had showered praises on him, soon found himself in conflict with Kiamil. Finn accused him of favouring the French, and expressed his satisfaction when Kiamil was removed from his post in 1857 (see Eliav, Finn). Kiamil's openness toward Europeans was unprecedented. During his term in office, the Consulates were allowed to fly their national flags and non-Muslims were permitted entry to the Temple Mount (see also: Blumberg, *Zion*, pp. 73–74).

2    Regional governor.
3    See below, No. 33.

paysans. De plus les règlements du Tanzimat paralysent toute action energique, et encouragent les rebelles dans leur audace.[4]

Les Consuls réunis sont unanimés à reconnaître qu'il est impossible et dangereux d'essayer plus longtemps le système de conciliation et les voies de douceur; que les moyens de répression dont dispose le Gouverneur sont évidemment insuffisants, ce qui augmente l'audace des insoumis qu'il ne peut y avoir de sécurité si la province n'est pas pour quelque temps mise en état de siège avec suspension des règlements du Tanzimat; si le Gouverneur ne peut prendre rapidement les mesures qu'il juge convenables sans en référer à ses supérieurs éloignés, si l'on ne met pas à sa disposition une force militaire d'au moins d'un régiment.

Ils rendent justice aux bonnes intentions de S. Ex. Kiamil Pasha et aux efforts qu'il a tentés, mais comme ils en reconnaissent l'inutilité ils l'engagent à demander à ses supérieurs d'autres instructions et l'appui d'une force matérielle, offrant de faire appuyer sa demande par leur Ambassadeurs respectifs à Constantinople, puis que l'état actuel du pays menace la sécurité de tous.

P.E. Botta[5] / Pizzamano[6] / G. Rosen[7] / de A. Garcia[8]/[9]

4   The reforms instituted by the Ottoman government in 1839, due mainly to pressure by the Powers, apparently were considered too liberal by the Consuls, who believed that the changes encouraged the rebels. In the course of time, the reforms had little permanent effect.

5   See above, No. 27, n. 4.

6   See above, No. 27, n. 1.

7   Dr. Georg Rosen (1820–1891), a noted Orientalist and archaeologist, was the Prussian Consul in Jerusalem during 1852–1867. A fierce rivalry clouded his relations with Finn (see Eliav, Shimon Rosenthal; Eliav, *Yishuv*; Eliav, Finn, pp. 68–69).

8   Pio de Andres Garcia was the first Spanish Consul in Jerusalem. The Consulate was opened in March 1854 (see FO 195/445, 18 April 1854).

9   Finn reported about the meeting of Consuls to the Foreign Office on 28 May 1855, noting that it was held in his absence from the city, and therefore he was not a signatory to the protocol. He wrote, "My First Dragoman was invited in my place but did not consider himself empowered to sign so important a document." Finn had his reservations concerning the content of the declaration, possibly because he was angry at their not waiting for him. He emphasized: "It is true that the present condition of Palestine is such as to prevent its commerce, its agriculture and general civilization from advancing with the progress which the Great Powers of Europe have a right to expect, but I am far from participating in the fears entertained by the signers of the document" (FO 78/ 1120).

# 33 J. Finn to Earl of Clarendon
## Hostilities in Hebron

On 6 June 1855, Finn reported about Abd-el-Rahman's takeover, once again, of Hebron. This was the last attempt at open rebellion by the sheikh, who had troubled the Ottoman authorities for years (see above, Nos. 7, 9, 32). It was only after the events described below that the Governor of Jerusalem succeeded during the course of the year (in contrast to the harsh verdict Finn had pronounced on him) to subdue the rebels and restore the rule of law. Abd-el-Rahman himself, however, succeeded in escaping and continued to engage in rebellious acts against the government until he was finally taken capture in 1863 and exiled to the island of Rhodes (see Finn J., *Stirring Times*, II, chap. XXVII; for the events in Hebron, see also: Eliav, *Austrian Protection*, pp. 91–96 and notes; Blumberg, *Zion*, pp. 79–89).

FO 78/1120 — No. 16                                      Jerusalem June 25, 1855
Political

My Lord
    I have the honor to report that this country still remains in a very disturbed state.
    The hostilities of Hebron are suddenly stopped, all parties remaining under arms, and watching each other.
    On the 12th Inst. Abderrahman demanded and took a toll of five dollars from three travellers coming from the desert — they were Americans, but represented to him — by their Dragoman as English. This is the first time that he has ventured to take so decided a step against the English name, — they were afterwards during the day, twice stopped by peasants of his faction, and threatened with total plunder.
    On the same day H. E. Kiamil Pasha invited the Consuls to a meeting at the Seraglio[1] — He produced a Mazbata[2] just then signed by the regular

1    It was stated in the Consulate diary that the purpose of the meeting of the Consuls with the Pasha on 12 June 1855 was "to deliberate on the expediency of declaring war against Abderrahman, the Infantry and Artillery headed by the Pasha to proceed to Hebron" (Blumberg, *View*, p. 195). See also: Finn J., *Stirring Times*, II, pp. 286–289. It should be noted that these events took place during the Crimean War, and consequently the Pasha wanted the approval of the representatives of the Powers.
2    The Consulate diary (*ibid.*) states: "The Civic Council having already recommended this measure." *Mazbata* = official report, protocol.

City-Council unanimously requesting him to resort to military measures for suppression of the rebellion, and to carry into execution the orders of the Sublime Porte still extant and valid for apprehension of Abderrahman alive or dead.

His Excellency requested the expression of our opinions on this matter, and the Consuls (speaking according to Seniority) pronounced unanimously in favor of military force.

I have the honor to enclose Copy of the document drawn up and signed on the occasion.[3]

This Minute or Protocol has been (as the Pasha informs me) forwarded by him to his official superiors: but we know of no answer received as yet.

On the 17th the Pasha sent Hadj Mustafa and Besheer Abu Gosh[4] to parley with the rebel — proposing the meeting to take place among the tents of the Taamri Arabs on the wild hills.[5] He refused to come, and they repaired to him at the village of Halkhul:[6] the very place where he had two days before torn up a Buyuruldi[7] of the Pasha ordering that ten of the regular infantry should be stationed in the Jewish Quarter of Hebron.

I have the honor to enclose Copy of a letter addressed by me to His Excellency on the subject.

On the 15th I had addressed to His Excellency a letter on the subject of powder and lead being sold in considerable quantities in Bethlehem, — this being on the verge of a desert country on one side, and of the hill-paths to Hebron on another. Especially that two men whose names I gave, of the faction of Abdurahhman had made these purchases, as well as of arms of all kinds during three days and boasted: "now we shall see what will become of the English travelling along the road"[8] —

3    Not enclosed with the original document.
4    The reference is to the leader of the Abu-Ghosh tribe and to his uncle Besheer (see Finn J., *Stirring Times*, II, pp. 206 ff., 218). This mission aroused Finn's wonder and even ire, because the Pasha had not mentioned this plan for reconciliation with the rebels at the meeting of the Consuls. Finn immediately sent a written protest to the Pasha. Kiamil Pasha later explained to Finn that the intent was to apprehend the sheikh: "The treacherous design, so characteristically Turkish, was, of course, one in which the Consuls never could have participated" (Finn, *ibid.*, p. 290).
5    The Ta'amri tribe dwelled to the east of the Bethlehem-Hebron road, near Artas, and over the course of time caused much trouble for the farm that had been established there, which was very dear to Finn and his wife.
6    It is highly likely that Abd-el-Rahman was suspicious of the purpose of the meeting, and therefore preferred to meet in Halkhul, which was close to Hebron, where he felt more secure.
7    Decree.
8    The reference is to all the visitors in Artas — the Consul, his family, and other British subjects.

174

I have the honor to reiterate my opinion of Kiamil Pasha — that he is a man without decision of character — without energy — and whose chief virtue consists in exceeding politeness of manners.

He is not accused of receiving bribes openly, but few people doubt that he takes money from native parties indirectly, through the hands of even Europeans in the form of rewards for services rendered.

James Finn

## 34   J. Finn to Earl of Clarendon
## The Growing Influence of Austria

In his incessant efforts to strengthen Britain's preeminence, Finn initially regarded France as the primary rival for consular hegemony in Jerusalem. But the increasing influence of Austria since the establishment of its Consulate in 1849 was an additional thorn in the British diplomat's side. With a hint of jealousy, Finn saw fit to report of the enhanced status and deeds of the Austrian Consulate, which added greatly to its prestige. Although Finn maintained friendly relations with the Austrian Consul in the first years, being assured of his position as the doyen of the diplomatic corps, relations took a turn for the worse when Finn charged the Austrian Consul — and his Prussian colleague — with supporting the rebel Abd-el-Rahman (see Eliav, *Austrian Protection*, p. 25; Blumberg, *View*, pp. 214–216). Although Finn quickly withdrew this accusation, relations between the two Consuls cooled and Finn became increasingly critical of the activities of the Austrians.

FO 78/1120 — No. 22                                   Jerusalem August 3, 1855
Political

My Lord.

I have the honor to report the increasing feeling here that Austria is a Power to be guarded against in Palestine.

Travellers arriving from Europe have frequently spoken to me of the high tone which Austrian Agents and Officers are assuming throughout the Levant, — and the events which occur in Jerusalem are sufficient to warrant my bringing them before Your Lordship's notice.

The visits of two Royal Princes to Jerusalem within a few months have served to enhance the influence of the Austrian Consulate which is at the same time Belgian. — His Royal Highness the Duke of Brabant has married an Austrian Princess[1] — and His Imperial Highness the Archduke Maximilian has promised to return hither shortly[2] — The latter is noted for a fervid devotional turn of mind, and his naval occupation cannot fail to impart vigor and decision to acts resulting from his habitual feeling.

I am informed by a person who was present at a quiet conversation between them in Jerusalem that His Imperial Highness referring to the present war,[3] assured the Consul Count Pizzamano[4] that it would not last long, for his brother (the Emperor) would soon arrange it all.

The Pasha was honored by a strictly private interview with His Imperial Highness for half an hour.

I have already reported to Your Lordship the incident respecting the flag over the Convent at Mount Carmel[5] — and the dispute between the Spanish and French Consulates here on the subject of the official jurisdiction over persons who are inmates of the several Latin Convents: in which the Austrian Consul took a strong though indirect part. I have also reported the offence taken by Count Pizzamano at the administration of the Holy Sacrament on Maundy Thursday, by the precedence awarded to the French Consul in presence of the Archduke.

For a few months past the Patriarch[6] and the Austrian Consul have been on such unamiable terms toward each other, that upon an occasion of

---

1    Duke Leopold of Brabant, the Belgian Crown Prince (later Leopold II, 1835–1909), and his wife Maria Henrietta, the daughter of Archduke Josef of Austria, visited Palestine 30 March–9 April 1855. The Austrian Consul hosted the royal couple, due both to the origins of the Duke's wife and to the fact that the Austrian Consulate represented Belgian interests (Finn J., *Stirring Times*, II, pp. 220–257). The couple were the first Europeans granted permission to visit the mosques on the Temple Mount, by a special Firman issued by the Sultan (but see below, No. 65, n. 2). The consular corps, headed by Finn, took advantage of this opportunity to visit the Temple Mount for the first time.

2    Archduke Ferdinand Maximilian (1832–1867), the brother of Franz Josef, the Crown Prince at the time, was the Commander of the Austrian army. In 1864 he was chosen to be Emperor of Mexico, but suffered a bitter fate: after a general insurrection against him, he was executed in June 1867. He visited Palestine from 30 June to 5 July 1855 (Finn J., *Stirring Times*, II, pp. 258–261).

3    The Crimean War (1853–1856). England and France, joined later by Austria, came to the aid of Turkey, which had been attacked by Russia. The decisive allied victory was at Sebastopol on 9 September 1855.

4    See above, No. 27, n. 1.

5    The Duke refused to enter the Carmelite monastery, because it flew a French flag, demanding that it be replaced by the Austrian standard during his visit. This led to great embarrassment: the monks refused to lower the French flag, and the Duke did not enter the monastery. For a description of the incident, see: Finn, *ibid.*, pp. 259–260; FO 78/1120, letter to Foreign Office, 4 July 1855.

6    Joseph Valerga. See above, introduction to No. 17.

the latter making a call and sending-up his card, His Grace sent word that he was very busy; and then wrote a note expressing his desire that at all his visits Count Pizzamano would limit his conversation to official matters.[7] [...] Large funds are placed at his disposal by the Imperial Government, as he himself told me not many days since, to the amount of a million and a quarter of florins (about £150,000) for the erection of an Hospital, a Hospice for pilgrims, and a Consulate house — all three on one site within the city. For this purpose he has already completed the purchase of a piece of ground near his present house. He has complained to me that the four rooms which form his official Cancellaria (and which very nearly equal the whole of my Consulate house together) are quite inadequate for the purpose.

About four years ago the Austrian Consul informed me that he had received a sufficient sum of money from Vienna to erect a Palace in Jerusalem for the Archbishop of that Capital, but I have heard no more of it since.

I ought not to omit that the Archduke Maximilian has promised Count Pizzamano to have his rank raised to that of Consul General.[8]

The Austrian Lloyds' Company[9] are very successful competitors against the French in the Levant Seas, and Count Pizzamano expresses himself so surely, that that energetic association is about to repair the wretched road between Jerusalem and Jaffa, that Sir M. Montefiore though desirous to do it himself for the general good, leaves it for them to accomplish.[10]

Count Pizzamano never hesitates to speak disparagingly of French promises, French exaggeration, and the inefficiency of French negociations in the matter of the Holy places, — and boasts that his Empire advances more securely, by deeds not by words.

Such is my representation of the phasis which Austrian affairs now present in this country.

J.F.

7    The dispute erupted due to Pizzamano's efforts for the establishment of a hospice for Austrian pilgrims. At first the Consul sought to found an Austrian hospital. Despite Valerga's objections, a plot was purchased in 1855 and its preparation begun. When, however, the Patriarch continued to oppose the project, the Austrians decided to content themselves with a hospice (see Eliav, *Austrian Protection*, p. 27). The hospice still serves this function today.
8    The awarding of the personal rank of Consul-General to Pizzamano on 7 November 1857 put Finn in an embarrassing position, for the Austrian Consul now bore the highest diplomatic rank in Jerusalem.
9    See above, No. 29.
10   For Pizzamano's activity in this regard, see: Eliav, *ibid.*, p. 25 and notes; Hyamson, No. 184.

## 35  J. Finn to Earl of Clarendon
## Hoisting Flags of Consulates

The Consulates refrained from raising their national flags, in the absence of governmental permission to do so. The official reason for the ban was the reaction of the Muslim population, which was likely to cause disturbances. The first French Consul had already experienced this in 1843 (see above, No. 13), when he managed to fly the flag for one single day. As a result, the Pasha had been deposed for supporting the act of the Consul (see above, No. 14). This state of affairs angered the Consuls who waited an opportunity to hoist their flags, and even to maintain the practice of a twenty-one-gun salute by Ottoman troops on festive occasions. They were not successful, however, until the Austrian Consul violated custom and raised the flag over his residence in Bethlehem on the Emperor's birthday (18 August 1855). He thus set a precedent, but the Consuls nevertheless did not dare to hoist the flag in Jerusalem until reports of the victory at Sebastopol (9 September 1855) reached the city. The Austrian and British Consulates unfurled their flags, with the other Consulates following their lead. The two Consuls were absent from the city on this day, and it is difficult to determine who was the first to raise his flag; at any rate, the French flag was hoisted only afterwards (see: Finn E. *Reminiscences*, pp. 142–143; Blumberg, *View*, p. 203). From then on, the flying of the national flag on official occasions became standard practice, and neither the authorities nor the Muslim population posed further objections.

FO 78/1120 — No. 24                                           Jerusalem August 20, 1855
Political

My Lord,

    I have the honor to report that since my Despatch Political N° 10 of May 26th,[1] the French and Austrian Imperial Fete days have occurred, the former on the 15th Instant, and the latter yesterday — on each of these occasions the Castle guns fired a salute of twenty one. —

---

1    In this letter, Finn writes: "I requested by official letter a Salute of the Castle guns might be fired for celebration of Her Majesty's birthday. Accordingly Salute of guns was fired and the Castle flag kept flying all day. The Moslems are angry of this innovation — its having occurred during the month of Ramadan" (FO 78/1120).
    A year earlier, Finn had already thought of flying the flag, and thus he writes in his diary: "The Pasha sent a warning not to raise the flag at Talbiyeh house without a license from Constantinople. I replied that I shall certainly put up the British flag over the Consulate house" (Diary, 22 September 1854).

The Austrian Consul having taken a Country house in Bethlehem for the summer, raised his flag there yesterday.[2] This step in advance is one which Count Pizzamano has long resolved to accomplish either in or out of town. At one time he proposed to all the Jerusalem Consuls that they should appeal to their respective Embassies, by some one and the same post, for permission to raise flags. —

Being an inland town, it has not been usual hitherto to have Consular flags at Jerusalem although the native Agents in Ramlah near three hours inland have them, — and we are informed that it is usual to have them at the Consulates in Aleppo. The Austrians have now raised a flag in Bethlehem, a town second only in importance to Jerusalem as a religious centre, and as much inland as this. —

It is on this ground of the importance of the holy city that all Consuls here seem anxious to have their flags, this being not a mere place of passage, but the terminus of a pilgrimage for persons of all nations and religions. And if such be considered as a sufficient reason for effecting a change, I can represent that the English Consulate has more reason than any other to require it. We have this year had travellers from Canada, West Indies, Australia and China. — Indian officers came frequently, and even Moslem gentlemen from Delhi and Agra, all attracted to Jerusalem as the focus or object of their long pilgrimage, and we have a kind of Convent for Indian Moslem pilgrims, of course British subjects, an ancient establishment in the city.

And the circumstance of Royal and Imperial princes coming on pilgrimate to the holy city, might seem also to point out Jerusalem as a proper station for national flags.

I might remind Your Lordship that if it be judged expedient to allow flags in Jerusalem, although with other nations it would be a novelty, it would not be so for us. When Sir Sidney Smith marched into the Jaffa gate of Jerusalem with drums and pipes, the British flag was borne before him, and he hoisted it over the Latin Convent.[3]

---

2     The reference is to the hoisting of the flag on the birthday of the Austrian Emperor. A week later, Finn visited Pizzamano in Bethlehem, and in his honour the Austrian and Belgian flags were run up. In his report of the visit, Finn mentions that he obviously would have to return the honour and raise the British flag when Pizzamano would visit him. He adds: "I am told that the hoisting of the Austrian flag in Bethlehem created great sensation ... The population were in raptures of joy, which they exhibited by firing of guns, singing, dancing" (FO 78/1120, 28 August 1855; see also Finn's diary, 21 August 1855).

3     Sir William Sidney Smith commanded the British fleet that in May 1799 forced Napoleon to lift the siege of Acre. After Napoleon's withdrawal from Palestine, the British army entered Jerusalem.

I have myself seen the lower half of the flag-staff remaining pointed out to me with exultation by the monks. — And the same was done in Bethlehem.[4]

James Finn.


## 36   J. Finn to Earl of Clarendon
## Political Situation during the Year 1855

At the beginning of 1856, Finn saw fit to evaluate the changes that had taken place in Jerusalem in terms of European influence. In his opinion, the city was infused by a liberal spirit and prejudices were waning. As a prime example of this he cited the permission granted Christians and Jews to visit the mosques on the Temple Mount, as well as the new practice of the raising of national flags. In contrast with his optimistic views regarding the implications of European influence, he does not heap praise on his fellow Consuls. A few lines from the following report were published by Hyamson (No. 178), but due to its importance, it is reproduced here almost in its entirety, except for a few passages which are not relevant.

FO 78/1217 — No. 1                                        Jerusalem, January 7, 1856

Political

My Lord,

So many new occurrences have taken place in this country during the past year that I take the liberty to place a digested Summary of them on record in a new-year Despatch.

1. I have first to remark on the tranquility and diminuation of fanaticism in this country. At the commencement of the war,[1] the natives, inexperienced in European influence, were apprehensive of an outbreak of Moslem fury. They

---

4   For the raising of the flag when news of the victory at Sebastopol arrived on 27 September 1855, see: Finn, ibid., pp. 362–364; Blumberg, *View*, p. 203; Finn E., *Reminiscences*, pp. 142–143; Eliav, *Austrian Protection*, p. 27. In a later letter, Finn stressed that the British Consulate was the first to hoist its flag, followed by all the other Consulates, except for the Prussian Consulate (FO 78/1121, 27 October 1855).

---

1   The Crimean War.

feared for their property and for their lives. [...] To my surprise when in Acre, I found the military governor using the word *Giaour* for *Christian*.[2] To this I instantly put a stop, although my own Consular Agent and that of the U.S., expressed their opinion aloud that there was no great harm in the expression.

—

I gave the offender a long lecture on the subject, and had a proclamation made over the town as well as in the barracks to forbid the use of the word.[3] [...]

2. Old prejudices are abating and liberality of sentiment greatly increased in Jerusalem also, which has been ever since I know of, in advance of other places with respect to toleration of non-Muslim religions, inasmuch as the Moslems live by the trade created by pilgrimage and letting of houses to Europeans.

The Jews also greatly exceed the Moslems in number.

But the opening of the Sanctuary of the Great Mosque to Christians by Firmans in open daylight has been the great event of Jerusalem this year. Four times has this occurred, namely by the coming of H.R.H. the Duke of Brabant, that of His Imperial Highness the Archduke Maximilian, that of Sir Moses Montefiore, and that of the Sardinian Duke of Vallombrosa.[4] It was reported lately that the Pasha had offered the Jews permission to pray for rain in the Temple enclosure, which they declined on religious grounds, but requested leave to pray at the Tomb of David.[5] This rumour did not however turn out to be well-founded; but such an idea could not have obtained currency a few years ago.

Twelve years ago the green paint was scraped off the door of the Anglican Bishop during the night, because of the sacredness of the colour. Now, not only have the English and other ladies worn green veils for some years past, but I have lately remarked a young Jew upon Sabbaths, enjoying himself at the principal gate of the city in a complete dress of the most peculiarly Moslem shade of green.

3. The Europeans effect upon Jerusalem as a centre during the past year, has been very great, produced by the visits of the Royal and Imperial Princes, with expectations of others to come and by the hoisting of national flags over the consulates, together with the new practice of the Sentinels presenting arms to Consuls on their going in and out of the city. The two decorations of the Pasha

---

2   See also Blumberg, *View*, p. 162.
3   A description of his visit to Lebanon is omitted here.
4   See above, No. 34, and also: Finn J., *Stirring Times*, II, pp. 421–423.
5   This "report" also appears in the entry for 17 December 1855 in Finn's diary, in the very same wording.

received from Austria and Belgium have also served to mark a new epoch in Jerusalem.[6]

4. The politics of the respective consulates towards each other are deserving of attention.

I am perhaps incapable of perceiving correctly the feeling of others towards H.M.'s Consulate, but the Austrian and Prussian have sufficient grounds of jealousy for watching each other, and for separately making remarks on each other to me.[7]

We all regret that in the Consulate of France we have lost the gentleman and scholar M. Botta, whatever may have been his merits as a consul.[8] The French and English support each other on important questions, but nothing more than a political friendship can be expected when the immoralities of persons employed by the French Consulate are published as much scandalous in printed documents from the Court of Rome. [...] From all the above observations Your Lordship will perceive that the importance of Jerusalem is considerably enhanced since the commencement of the war.

In conclusion I should observe that with all his faults, Kiamil Pasha is as tolerant and conceding to Europeans as can be fairly expected.[9] For our Protestant community it was a notable event that the Pasha attended our English Church service yesterday.[10] — A few years ago it would have seemed incredible to have the bell ringing, the British colours flying, and a Pasha going to church, all upon the few yards of ground which form the Mission premises.

In a doctrinal point of view it was looked upon as a remarkable coincidence for Epiphany day that in a church with the Commandments and

---

6  See Finn, *idem*, p. 386: "The long-expected Grand Cordon of the Order of Francis Joseph, destined for the Pasha, arrived at last (October 28). It furnished the wished-for opportunity for inaugurating the Austrian flag over the Consulate.... In another month the Grand Cross of Leopold of Belgium came to the Pasha... Mr. Pizzamano was a Commander of this Order and was acting Belgian Consul." The event is also described in Finn's diary (28 October 1855). On the occasion of the presentation of the decoration, the city was illuminated and all the Consuls appeared in their formal attire, except for Finn, who would not wear a uniform on a Sunday.

7  This refers mainly to the Austrian Consul, who would from time to time discuss with Finn their Prussian and French colleagues. Finn's relations with the Prussian Consul, however, were strained, due to serious disagreements between them (see also FO 78/1120, 1217).

8  See above, No. 27, n. 4.

9  This is a surprising evaluation, since he always complained about Kiamil Pasha's pro-French stance (see above, No. 32, n. 1). Also, in his memoirs he expressed a balanced opinion (Finn, *ibid.*, pp. 453–456), but see his scathing criticism of the Pasha's weakness in the following document (No. 37).

10  See: Finn, *ibid.*, pp. 406–407; Finn E., *Reminiscences*, pp. 150–151.

Creed inscribed in Hebrew[11] there should be a Turkish Pasha standing at the *Te Deum* with our Prayerbook in Turkish in his hand, at Jerusalem.

James Finn

## 37 J. Finn to Earl of Clarendon Remarks on Political Conditions during the Year 1856

As in his previous annual report (above, No. 36), Finn also surveyed political conditions and the status of the Powers in Jerusalem during the course of 1856. This time he severely criticized the governmental chaos in Palestine — a veritable state of anarchy, while the Pasha was powerless to impose law and order (see also: Finn J., *Stirring Times*, chap. XXX). His survey of the activity of the Consulates reflects some jealousy of various institutions that had been established by the representatives of the European Powers in Palestine and which contributed to their enhanced influence, while Britain could not point to many achievements. Indications of his anti-German bias also appear in the following report.

A few passages from this lengthy report were cited by Hyamson (No. 183), but the omitted sections deserve to be published in their entirety, especially those dealing with the activity of the Consulates; only a small section of the previously-published passages appears here.

FO 78/1294 — No. 1                                               Jerusalem, 1st January, 1857
Political

My Lord,

I have the honour to present to Your Lordship the following remarks on the political condition of this country during the Year 1856. [...]

The Turkish Government does nothing but collect taxes for itself in as loose a manner as formerly; — it returns no protection, and allows of no improvement.

11  In 1851 plaques were installed in the Anglican church on which the Ten Commandments, the Apostle's Creed, and the Lord's Prayer were inscribed *in Hebrew*, for most of the worshippers were apostate Jews. The Hebrew plaques are in the church to the present day.

Within the city the Pasha's rule is a shadow. The butchers refuse when they please to slaughter cattle for food, — the corn dealers raise their commodity to any price they please, and the kitchen vegetables are kept out of the market by the Effendis in order to enhance the value of the land, on which they grow. The prices especially of corn, fuel, and vegetables have been during the last three years raised by a system of monopoly which is most injurious to the city. The wealthy Moslems residing in Jerusalem prevent peasantry from bringing in their stores on their own account. They buy from them outside the walls, and permit no peasant to sell excepting through their Agents. By this means though the crops are good, the prices in Jerusalem are exorbitant, and there appears to be no remedy. The Pasha is powerless, and the municipal Council with their relatives, are themselves the culprits. There are no foreign merchants here of wealth sufficient to offer a check to these proceedings. [...]

The main protection in this country is found in wearing European costume — and if to this one can add a knowledge and manners, so as to avoid ever having recourse for aid to Turkish authority, the security is complete.

I should add that I believe there are few countries in the world where in spite of appearances to the contrary, there is so much of practical religious toleration as in Palestine.

The entrance to the Haram, commonly called the Mosque of Omar, is now principally a matter of paying a pound for each person on the application of a Consul, — and of the many parties, whom I have escorted thither during the last five years, the most remarkable have been the Jewish company with Sir Moses Montefiore, and a party of Russians last week, the first of that nation so privileged.[1] [...]

I now beg to draw Your Lordship's attention to the politics of European nationalities resident in Jerusalem.

The Austrian Consulate is busily engaged with its erection of the Hospice and getting on in general matters as well as can be easily done till that work is finished.[2] Count Pizzamano tells me that he considers he has sufficient reason to expect a Turkish decoration in return for the Pasha's two decorations, — one Austrian, the other Belgian,[3] — besides valuable presents of firearms through his hands. But he added to me lately, it is one object to get on with the

---

1 See above, Nos. 34 and 36. Montefiore's visit to the Temple Mount, which aroused a tempestuous reaction within the Jewish community, was omitted from his diaries. A ban was proclaimed against him in Jerusalem, but when he expressed his remorse, the Jewish circles merely censured him, and removed the ban. Finn reported of the visits of foreigners on the Temple Mount for a fee in his letter dated 8 May 1857 (FO 78/1294).

2 See above, No. 34, n. 7. The work continued for a few years, the Hospice being dedicated only in 1863.

3 See above, No. 36.

hospice, the Pasha might, if he were ill-disposed, check on operations, or cause us needless expenses. We shall therefore not press him about the insults at Gaza or anything of the sort, till that work is done, — meanwhile our flag is flying close to the Hharam, and we have put one at Ramlah, all quietly. [...] The line of Austrian steamers also in the coast and the parade of purchasing Cavalry Horses, maintain an Austrian reputation among the nations,[4] while we Europeans are informed of a great project for an Austrian submarine telegraph throughout the Levant.

The Austrian influence is of course considerable among the labouring population of Jerusalem and Bethlehem, from the number of men kept in unemployment, — the purchase of large rocks for quarrying, the cutting of stones of greater size than for any period since that of the Romans, and the conveyance of these on carts to the city. It is but lately that the first ruts of wheels were seen about Jerusalem since unknown centuries.

Russia is only represented in Jerusalem by an annual visit of the Vice-Consul from Jaffa.[5] This blank is somewhat surprising, seeing that at such period of the Year as this, the Russian pilgrims are numerous. — This lasts four of five months in the year. — They have also no church, so that a Russian gentleman now here, named Olsoufieff complains to me of the ignorant people being obliged to attend services in the Greek language. The convent rulers of the Greek Orthodox Church in this country dread the approach of a regular Russian establishment as there can be no doubt that such an organization would interfere with their old irregular practices of life, as well as with their financial concerns.

The United States are unrepresented, except by an Armenian, who knows no language but Armenian, Turkish and a little Arabic. He is Deputy for his brother, the Vice-Consul at Jaffa.[6]

German interests divide themselves into two recognized forms. All Germans who are Roman Catholics naturally apply to the Austrian Consulate, while German Protestants even when subjects of Roman Catholic states, attach themselves to the Prussian.

Prussia is in Jerusalem inclined to adopt a high tone. It has a population of steady mechanics, not all Prussians, but under that protection, — just as the

---

4    Surprisingly, Finn makes no mention here of the establishment of the Austrian postal service, which was undoubtedly the most important Austrian achievement.

5    The Russian Consulate was opened only in 1858. The first Consul, Dorgobuzhinov (Dorgobouginev), served only two years. Blumberg erroneously wrote that the first Consul was Kozhevnikov (Blumberg, *Zion*, p. 103); actually, he succeeded Dorgobuzhinov.

6    Jacob Serafin (Serapion) Murad. For the conflicts between him and Finn, see: Blumberg, *View*, Index. Murad also served for many years as the Prussian Consular Agent in Jaffa. He died on 31 December 1858 in Jerusalem.

Consul himself is a Hannoverian and the Pastor a Dane.[7] It has its regular religious congregation with an Hospice for Travellers, and also an Institution of Deaconesses comprising an Hospital and a girls' school[8] — The Prussian Consul is purchasing houses in various parts of the city; it has already secured a good number, said to be bought from the King's privy-purse.

Out of Jerusalem the influence of the Prussian Consulate would be scarcely felt, were it not for the fact that the Agents of the Church Missionary Society under the direction of the Anglican Bishop,[9] are Protestant Germans, and such is the case in Jerusalem itself as well as in Jaffa, Caiffa, Nablus and Nazareth. The Agents and the interests of an English mission are thus brought under the control of the Prussian Consulate. [...]

France has increased her influence in Jerusalem by the recent acquisitions, first for the Armenian Catholics and secondly of the Church of St. Anne.[10] A new order of French religious ladies of rank, termed "Dames de Sion", has been established here in the course of the past year. Their object is to give education of high order to females of all religions. The other Consulates of course bear especially ill will against that of France for its having monopolized all the power of Turkish administration here and having used the Pasha like a puppet.

It has been a troublesome task and often painful to keep up the public alliance with such Agents of France as these, but I laboured to do so and have heard it remarked by strangers, that they have seldom seen so much amity existing between French and English Consulates as in Jerusalem.

7   Rosen (above, No. 32, n. 7) was a subject of Hanover, which was annexed to Prussia only in 1866. Friedrich Peter Valentiner, born in Schleswig-Holstein, was a Danish subject who arrived in Jerusalem in January 1852. He was the first clergyman of the German community, and also the first to deliver sermons in German.

8   The Hospice was established in 1851. The Kaiserwerther Diakonissen order began its activity in Jerusalem in 1851, founding a hospital and a school for Arab girls. These two institutions later moved to new buildings outside the Old City walls: the first, the Augusta Victoria Hospital, in 1894 (currently the site of the Ziv Hospital), and the second, the Talitha Kumi school, moved to the New City in 1868/9 (this building is no longer standing).

9   After Gobat (see above, No. 30) came to Jerusalem, the Church Missionary Society (CMS), on whose behalf Gobat had worked in other countries before his appointment as Bishop in Jerusalem, began its activity in Palestine. In contrast to the London Society for Promoting Christianity amongst the Jews, the CMS restricted its activities to the Arab population. It initially functioned among Christians belonging to other communities, seeking to convert them to Protestantism, later widening its activities to include Muslims. Here as well Finn accused Gobat and his society of pro-German tendencies, which added to the status of the Prussian Consulate. For the activity of the CMS, see: Sapir, chap. 2.

10  The Armenian Catholic Church was established in Jerusalem in 1855. The Church of St. Anne, near Lions' Gate, was built over the ruins of an ancient church. In October 1856 the site was given to the French, who erected there an imposing Catholic church.

Of England and her political position it is somewhat difficult to give a description, except by comprising the topics of my Despatches into an Essay.

In spite of the delay of justice in Nablus[11] and consequent infavourable impression on some minds, I believe that in general influence over the country, the name and character of England are respected and looked up to, as ever. Yet, the position taken up by the other Consuls in Jerusalem, makes it impossible for the British Consulate to be at present regarded as holding that rank in external appearance to which it is entitled in the East and has formerly been accustomed to hold.

Meanwhile I endeavour to proceed upon a straight forward life of duty, believing to be the surest road to eventual goodness and greatness for my country.

James Finn

## 38  J. Finn to Earl of Clarendon
## Financial Difficulties of the Consul and
## the Consulate

When Finn set out for Jerusalem, he was allocated a yearly salary of £550 and £150 for the expenses of the Consulate. He soon realized that his salary was insufficient, and that Consulate expenses had in practice been fixed at only £120 per annum. Finn was incapable of supporting his family and maintaining the Consulate on these sums, all the more so since income tax and other sums were deducted from his salary. A deficit was created, which increased from year to year. Finn was compelled to take loans at exorbitant interest rates to cover the Consulate's and his personal expenses, especially after he had invested much money in the purchase of a plot in Talbieh and the construction of his summer home there, in the establishment of the Kerem Abraham farmstead, and in the purchase of lands in Artas (see Eliav, Finn, pp. 58–62). His financial distress increased in the course of time while all his pleas for an increase in salary and expenses went unheeded. In his desperation, he declared in the following letter that he would be forced to leave his post and earn his livelihood by his own hands.

11   For these events in Nablus, that began after the installation of the bell by Bishop Gobat and the flying of the flag over the school he founded in the city, and in the wake of a serious incident in which a Muslim was killed by a missionary, see: Finn J., *Stirring Times*, II, chap. XXXIII.

An additional problem was posed by the Consulate building. His office and residence were located in the courtyard of Christ Church, in the precinct owned by the London Society for Promoting Christianity amongst the Jews. As a consequence of his quarrels with the missionary society, already in 1853 the latter demanded rent for the Consulate offices (FO 78/963, 20 December 1853). When the severe dispute with Bishop Gobat and the members of the missionary society broke out in 1856 (see Eliav, *ibid.*, pp. 64ff.; Eliav, Shimon Rosenthal), the missionaries demanded that Finn vacate the Consulate offices and his residence, while the Foreign Office refused to allocate funds for the purchase of a building for the Consulate, as was the practice for most of the other Consulates.


FO 78/1295 (Consular No. 13)                                    Jerusalem, 30th March 1857

My Lord,

[...] I have already on several occasions been compelled to address your Lordship on the inadequacy of my income for provision of almost the necessaries of life, not reckoning the sums which I am necessitated to supply out of my salary for carrying on an official establishment upon a lower scale than that of any other Consul in Jerusalem.

The British Consulate is the earliest one established in Jerusalem, and I am the Senior Consul as I have long been. Other Consulates having special objects of aim, have gone before us in expense for convenience, hospitality, or display. — Besides these some of the English in Jerusalem are far before me in these matters,[1] and to me it seems that Her Majesty's Consulate appears to undue disadvantage by the side of the Episcopate, — and I beg to represent further, as I have formerly alluded to the circumstance, the disadvantage at which I stand in comparison with Jaffa and Caiffa.

The territory of my jurisdiction in Her Majesty's service, extends from Egypt to within sight of Bayrout,[2] comprising races and classes of people of great diversity, and political interests demanding talents and learning to cope with them, not to mention peculiar temper in dealing with our own people in Jerusalem, and travellers of rank complaining of want of hospitality.

But every year augments my difficulties, — my family is increasing, prices are higher, and what to do I do not know unless I retire during the

---

1    An allusion by Finn to the fact that Gobat received a yearly salary of £1450, more than twice the sum paid to Finn.
2    The Consular Agents in Tyre, Sidon, and Acre were still subordinate to Finn, as was the Vice-Consul in Haifa.


188

working period of my life, upon the pension to which I am entitled, to reside at the cheap port of Caiffa and support my children by the labour of my hands.

My enclosure N° 1 will partly shew the difficulty of obtaining a house in Jerusalem,[3] but the difficulty will appear yet more distinct from the fact that the late Consul General for Spain, resided most of his sojourn here, being unmarried, in a hotel, such a one as Jerusalem could furnish and had his flag flying over it.[4] The present Consul General is residing in the Hospice (Casa nuova) of the Terra Santa Convent until a house which he has leased at a high rent for five years can be put into repair for him.

On the other hand I should mention that the Prussian Consulate with its Hospice and Pastors house are bought property, and occupy, besides the irregularities of form, a clear straight line of 250 feet.[5]

The large influx of pilgrims this year has affected the rents of houses to so extraordinary a degree that besides filling their convents nearly 30 in number, and numerous dwelling houses in the city, they have been known to engage a small house recently at 7000 Piastres for a period of 30 days at the utmost. The Armenians besides erecting wooden sheds with tiled roofs over the spacious courts and gardens of their Convent have taken a small house of two rooms for 35 days at £2 a day.

These unusual proceedings will of course only last during the Pilgrim season, but they cannot fail to leave a permanent effect afterwards. — If such prices are to be obtained during the season, it will be worth while for the owner to retain them empty during the rest of the year, unless they can procure such rents for longer periods as will counterbalance the profits to be had from keeping them in abeyance, — or at least they will demand from settled residents here, rents higherto unprecedented.

With respect to the house at present occupied by me, I gather from the contents of Despatch Consular 9 of August last, that the London Society had applied in due formality for it — And alltho' I could not consider that Despatch as an authoritative notice to quit, I am desirous to meet their wishes at as early a period as possible.[6] But what to do in the matter I am entirely at a loss to divine.

---

3    The enclosure is not attached. Finn mentions the high prices of buildings and the many expenses entailed in the renovation of a house and adapting it to serve as an office and residence.

4    The first Consul was Andres Garcia (see above, No. 32, n. 8). He was succeeded by Don Miguel de Tenorio, who arrived in Jerusalem on 7 March 1857.

5    The Prussian Consul dwelled in Aqabat et-Takiye, a lane leading off Khan-ez-Zait, with the Prussian Hospice on the other side. The buildings were joined by the roof extending over Khan-ez-Zait.

6    Finn left the mission building on 28 October 1857 (FO 78/1295).

I cannot take Her Majesty's Office, with its archives, I cannot betake myself and family of four children[7] into tents among ruined houses. — Were I to engage the very best conditioned house that I have yet seen for a residence, it would require enlargement (for there is none large enough) and repairs, and cleansing, that would occupy the space of several months.[8]

James Finn.

## 39   J. Finn to Earl of Clarendon
## Remarks on Political Conditions during the Year 1857

In his report for 1857, Finn wrote at length of the activities of the Powers during the year. With a trace of jealousy, he reviewed their achievements (see above, introduction to No. 37), emphasizing the contrast with the inferior standing of England, which could not pride itself on similar accomplishments. The sections dealing with Jews and with Muslims were cited by Hyamson (No. 190); the following passages discuss the activities of the Powers.

FO 78/1383 — No. 1                                          Jerusalem, January 1, 1858
Political

My Lord,
        I have the honor to give the following summary of political affairs in Jerusalem for the year 1857. [...]

7    His children at that time were Alexander (b. 5 November 1847), Constance Mary (b. 12 October 1851), Arthur Henry (b. 11 November 1854), and Emily Louisa (b. 7 February 1857). Emily Louisa died after twenty-two months (12 December 1858). The first infant, born in 1847, died a few days later in Haifa and was buried there. Alexander later joined the diplomatic service. He died in 1919, while holding the post of Consul-General in Chile. Arthur became a minister, serving, *inter alia*, in India and in Burma; he died in 1921. Constance was blessed by longevity; in 1929 she published her mother's memoirs.
8    His request to purchase a house was rejected. After additional appeals, the Foreign Office answered him on 30 August 1860: "I am directed by Lord Russell to state to you that after consideration of your suggestions, H.M.'s Government are not prepared to bear the expense of purchasing land and building a Consular Residence at Jerusalem" (FO 78/1537). The British Consulate was forced to make do with rented buildings, moving from one location to another during its existence. The only immediate consequence of this letter was the approval of the Foreign Office on 11 May 1857 for a one-time sum of £.100 "for office-expenses."

I may now proceed to make some observations upon the several Consulates of Jerusalem.

*Russian*: It is remarkable that with the increase of Russian subjects not only the Pilgrims but occasional crews of ships of war, and resident ecclesiastics (I ought not to omit the recent influx of Russian Jews) besides the property of a Convent and the purchase by permission of land, for a hospital and a hospice outside the Walls, that we have as yet no Russian Consul in Jerusalem,[1] it is difficult to suppose that this deficiency can much longer exist.

*Prussian*: The Prussian Consulate is the Protectress of an increasing number of well-conducted industrious mechanics and shopkeepers — of a lodging-house and of the excellent Deaconesses' Institution, which is both school and hospital,[2] besides having its joint protection of the Episcopate.

But it is to be observed that among the objects of Prussian protection but few are Prussians, — the persons are Protestants of any German country, who naturally look up to Prussia as their defender and helper. [...]

*Austrian*: The elevation of the Austrian Consulate into a Consulate General[3] has imparted a tone of something like victory to the language and conduct of the persons composing that establishment. This is a natural reaction after the recent elation of the French party, who had not only given out in conversation, but had published in a French Gazette of Constant the probability that the prolonged absence of the Austrian Consul was owing to a reprehension on the part of his Government for faults of official conduct.[4]

It is clear that Austria is resolved to assure and maintain a high position in this country, as I have on several occasions had the honour to report,[5] neither should this be a matter of surprise, when we consider the geographical contiguity of Austria and Turkey and the religious interests which attach Austria to Jerusalem.

---

1   The reference is to the purchase of lands for the complex later known as the 'Russian Compound'. A portion of this area had been given as a present by the Sultan to Tsar Alexander II after the signing of the Treaty of Paris in 1856. For the Russian Consulate which was opened in 1858, see above, No. 37, n. 5. In the course of time, Russia became the European Power which owned the greatest quantity of land in Palestine (see also Tristram, pp. 167–168; FO 78/2191, Moore to Foreign Office, 18 December 1871).

2   See above, No. 37, n. 8.

3   On 23 December 1857 Finn reported, with displeasure, of Pizzamano's promotion to the rank of Consul-General (FO 78/1294, No. 1).

4   Finn wrote in his diary: "Rumours were circulated that he was dismissed for inefficiency" (Diary, 5 June 1857). In actual fact, Pizzamano was absent from the country for an extended period because of ill health.

5   On 23 December 1857 Finn wrote to the Foreign Office: "On the whole, the Austrian Government is the one which spends most money and comes most prominent before the public, of all others represented here" (FO 78/1295, No. 41).

I have on several occasions reported the avowed determination of the Austrian Consul to lower the tone of French assumptions as: "Protectors of Christianity in the East". A ludicrous illustration of this conflict for Patronage took place in June last, when the Austrians suddenly set up a bronze statue of the Empress Helena on the site of the Invention of the Cross. The French Consul repaired in anger to remonstrate at the Austrian Consulate and exclaimed: "Why you even ventured to do it without first informing me of the intention!"

With respect to the principles and proceedings in Jerusalem, I beg to call Your attention to the consideration, that every nation having interests concerned here, has during the past year steadily made advance in concentrating influence upon Jerusalem.

[...] Austria has its Hospice progressing; the large sums spent upon which give considerable influence throughout the city. - It has established a Consulate-General and besides the Lloyds' Agency has set up an Imperial Post Office in immediate connection with the Government.

*French*: The French cause in Jerusalem has sustained real loss in the removal of Kiamil Pasha.[6] — The persons of the French Consulate are charged with advantage to the interests of morality and of honest public principle; but the present Pasha[7] entertains a disposition hostile to everything French, though I believe this is no guarantee against his acting on any occasion under the influence of fear, should France be able to bring motives of that nature to bear upon him.

It is distressing to see influence thrown away from us into the hands of Roman Catholic countries, because those alone are coming forward to bestow that education which the people are determined to have at any cost. [...]

Prussia may boast of her landed acquisitions and the increasing stability of her institutions.

The United States of America have now raised the banner for the first

---

6    When Kiamil Pasha was deposed, Finn noted that this was greeted with satisfaction, because he had been "a weak Governor," indifferent to the public, and was totally under French influence: "His whole career here has been simply that of blind obedience to the dictation of the French Consulate." Finn claimed that he had not received the cooperation or help of the Governor when these were requested (FO 78/1294, No. 7, 14 March 1857). See above, No. 32, n.1.

7    Sureya Pasha first arrived at Jerusalem on 2 May 1857 and served as Governor until 2 April 1863. If Finn had raised any complaints against the preceding Governor, his successor was motivated by open anti-Western hostility, and he quickly became the Consul's enemy (see also: Eliav, Finn).

time in Jerusalem, having this year sent a Consul to reside here.[8]

Russia has made important landed acquisitions for public purposes and revived a Clerical Mission to be increased shortly by a Bishop[9] and a large train of ecclesiastics already arrived in Beyroot, besides pursuing without intermission her ancient policy. All these are making progress, leaving the only exception of that nation, England, which first began the movement and whose principles if made known and acted upon, would be the most beneficial to the Ottoman Government and the general population of the East.

English inferiority is shared likewise by H.M's Consulate as compared with those of other nations, but it has the single advantage of having a larger number of subjects, and consequently a larger amount of business to be transacted, business involving the most mighty interests.

J. Finn

# 40   J. Finn to Lord Russell
# Roads and Buildings Outside the City Walls

Road construction projects, as well as the accelerated pace of building in the Russian Compound — the first European construction outside the walls of the Old City — greatly impressed the Consul, who was a keen observer of developments in Jerusaelm. All this transpired before the building boom that resulted from the enactment of the Lands Law in 1867/8, which permitted foreigners to purchase lands and construct buildings on them, thus constituting the beginning of the development of the New City outside the walls. Hyamson published only a few lines of the following document (No. 200).

8   John Warren Gorham, the first American Consul in Jerusalem, came to the city in March 1857, serving in this post until 1860. Even before this, however, in 1844, an eccentric individual, Warder Cresson, had been confirmed by the Senate as Consul in Jerusalem. This, however, had been without the knowledge of the diplomataic representative in Constantinople and without the approval of the Sublime Porte. Cresson's appointment was cancelled after one month (due to "insufficient business in Jerusalem"), but the would-be Consul remained in Palestine and converted to Judaism in 1848. (See: Ruth Kark and J. Glass, "United States Consuls in Jerusalem," *Cathedra*, no. 70 (January 1994), pp. 170–173 [Hebrew]).
9   Cyril Naumov (1823–1866) was appointed Russian Orthodox Bishop in Jerusalem and set out for his bishopric at the head of a Russian delegation, with the aim of enhancing Russian presence in the Holy Land. He arrived in Jerusalem at the beginning of 1858 (Derek Hopwood, *The Russian Presence in Syria and Palestine*, Oxford 1969, Index; see also: Finn E., *Reminiscences*, p. 177).

FO 78/1448; FO 195/604                                   Jerusalem November 17 1859
Consular No. 44

My Lord

On my arrival in Jerusalem, I could not but be surprized at the greatly increased stir prevailing in the suburbs of the city, arising from the employment of hundreds of men in blasting rocks, erecting walls and levelling for the wide road which is to be made from the city to the Convent of the Cross distant about two miles.[1]

The Pasha was riding out to inspect the erection of one of the numerous little towers which are intended for stations of Bashi Bozuk[2] on the high roads. His Excellency[3] observed to me on the spot that I must now confess at least, the Turkish Empire has some vitality in it —

I could not but thank him for the improvement made in the road from Jaffa; — which I have since learned he had effected at his own expense, but in haste, on learning the probability of the Sultan's visit, in August last.[4]

I see that the Russians have already done much in enclosing their recent possessions with strong walls[5] — Their property outside the walls is mostly concentrated about the North West corner. Rumors are afloat of their intention to erect four Hospices instead of one, besides their other establishments.

The Greek Convent property along the way to Bethlehem[6] is being rapidly enclosed for mulberry plantations, — but the charitable works of Sir Moses Montefiore are still prohibited by authority.

James Finn

---

1    This indicates that Mamila Road and its continuation, Gaza Street, constituted one of the main transportation arteries outside the walls. The Monastery of the Cross was an ancient structure, which apparently had been first built as a Greek Orthodox monastery during the period of Byzantine rule in Palestine. From 1855 the Holy Cross seminary for Greek monks was active in the monastery building.

2    See above, No. 19, n. 5.

3    Sureya Pasha (see above, No. 39, n. 7).

4    This was an unfounded rumor; in fact, the road was paved only in 1867–9, in anticipation of the visit to Jerusalem of Austrian Emperor Franz Josef on his way to the dedication of the Suez Canal. Sureya built a a series of small towers (forts) along the way, including a few Bashi-Bazuks, in order to protect the travellers from bandits. For the Austrian proposal to Montefiore to join the project of paving the Jaffa-Jerusalem road, see: Hyamson, No. 202; below, No. 59.

5    See above, No. 39, n. 1. In a letter dated 4 January 1860, Finn explained why the Russians required many hostels for their pilgrims: "The French and Austrians do all they can to get up large caravans of Pilgrims to the Holy Sepulchre, but the Russians far surpass them and bring so many of their people into the country as Christian Pilgrims at cheap rates in the Steamers, that they are only allowed to remain for three weeks at Jerusalem, thus making room for others" (FO 78/1521).

6    The Greek Orthodox monastery Mar Elias, at the exit from Jerusalem on the way to Bethlehem.

# 41 A.J. Khayat to Lord Russell
## Situation of the Peasants

The Consul in Jaffa, who had served in this post for eighteen years, also was accustomed to write directly to the Foreign Office, in addition to the reports he sent to Beirut and Jerusalem. In the following letter he criticizes the attitude of the Ottoman government towards the peasants. A copy of this letter was sent to Finn, who expressed his displeasure at the direct correspondence between the Consul in Jaffa and the Foreign Office. For the Consul, see above, No. 21, n. 1.


FO 78/1537                                             Jaffa January 17th 1860
Separate

My Lord,
    I have the honor to inform your Lordship that the great fear of the people of this country which was caused by the want of the early rain is now subsided, for within the last and the present week it has rained enough, and the country-people have began ploughing and sowing, but I am sorry to remark that in several districts, the peasants are short of the usual quantities of Corn for seed, on account of high prices and they have applied to the Authorities for assistance from the Government stores, but without success; this is much to be regretted, for the Government in one way and another takes from growers nearly one third of their produce, by taxes; and common sense would suggest that a Government the more it helps its subjects, the more benefit it receives, but the Turkish Authorities seem to prefer selling their stores in cash than lending or helping their agriculturists. Consequently farmers and peasants must be left to borrow money at 20 or 30 per cent interest for a short time to buy seeds.[1]

                                                          Assad Kayat


---

1    Khayat also initiated attempts to plant cotton in order to alleviate the condition of the farmers in the vicinity of Jaffa. He imported the seeds and encouraged the peasants to sow them. He reported four years later to Foreign Secretary Lord Russell of the successful results (FO 78/1834, 15 March 1864).

## 42  A.J. Khayat to Lord Russell
## Changes of Currency Rates

Toward the end of Ottoman rule in Palestine, the coins of the major Powers were legal currency, enjoying greater circulation than the Turkish denominations. Foreign merchants and subjects, in particular, used the carried on transactions in European coins. Exchange rates were generally determined by money changers and market demand, rather than by the government, and therefore were very fluid. There also were significant differences in the rates of exchange in effect in Jaffa, the chief commercial city, where rates were higher, and those in Jerusalem, which in those days was not a major commercial center. On occasion, however, the government attempted to intervene in the monetary realm; the following attests to an official devaluation of the foreign currencies in the amount of approximately twenty percent. This caused loss only to the foreign merchants, as is reflected in the following letter.

For the problematics of exchange rates toward the end of the Ottoman Empire, see: Shimon Rubinstein, *The Coins, Measures, and Weights in Use in Eretz Israel at the End of the Ottoman Period*, Jerusalem 1988 (mimeo; Hebrew). The information provided by the sources regarding rates of exchange in the course of the nineteenth century indicates a great deal of fluctuation in the rates.

FO 78/1537 — No. 8                                          Jaffa 8 May 1860
Draft

My Lord,
    I have the honor to inform your Lordship, that last week the Governor of this place issued a Proclamation, based upon orders from the Sublime Porte, lowering the rates of the currency of coins, as follows — £stg from 130 Piastres to 110.[1] French 20 Franc pieces from 102 to 87 Piastres,[2] Turkish

---

1    In the midnineteenth century, the rate of exchange of the £ sterling ranged between 120 and 140 piastres. After this devaluation, the value of the pound rose once again, and in 1882 its rate had returned to 133 piastres (A.M. Luncz [ed.]. *Jerusalem*, I, Vienna 1882, German section, p. 9).
2    The common French gold coin was called the Napoleon d'Or, and was worth 20 francs. In 1882 its rate was 106 piastres in Jerusalem and 120 piastres in Jaffa.

Liras from 117 to 100 Piastres,[3] Spanish Dollars from 28 to 23 Piastres, and so on all the coins.

This policy has been received most unfavourably by all classes, for it is injuring commerce and trade as well as those who have fixed salaries.

It is working against commerce and shipping in the following ways.

For example — An English Merchant, used to buy before the Proclamation, say 8 kilos of wheat for 320 Piastres, paying his sovereign[4] or £stg at 130 Piastres, whereas now he pays the same price, giving his £s. at 110 Piastres, in other words, he now gets the same quantity of produce, and must pay about 20% more money — i.e. he must pay 24£ now for what he had given 20£ formerly; and it works also against the Merchant in his expenses; for British and Foreign Commerce here is chiefly in the export trade, such as in Corn, Oil, Wool, seeds etc etc, so the Merchant now in paying porters, lightermen, Camel-drivers, taxes etc. (as he pays them in piastres), his Pound or Shilling goes for less value, for instance 2 weeks ago he paid duty, say 400 Piastres on a Ton of Olive Oil, and paid his £stg at 130 Piastres, and now he pays the same duty, and only pays his £s at 110 Piastres. Again a merchant paid his porters 2 weeks ago 100 Piastres for carrying 100 bales of good from his warehouse to the shipping wharf which 100 Piastres were equivalent to 15s.. 4d, but now he must pay for the same work, 100 Piastres, which are equivalent to 18s.. 2.

It is especially working very hard against those who have fixed salaries. It destroys indirectly nearly one fourth of their income, i.e. they pay now for their living and expenses the same prices, and in many instances higher, while their money or coins are ordered to be received at 20% under their value, so now we can only obtain with our English pound 20% less quantities of food etc.

Assad Kayat

---

3    The rate of the Turkish pound (the gold coin) was set in 1843 at 100 piastres, but as time passed its value dropped to 110–120 piastres. An attempt was made here to once again determine its value at 100 piastres, but this rate did not remain in effect for long. According to Luncz (above, n.1), the value of the Turkish lira was 121 piastres.
4    One £ sterling contained 20 shillings, but the sovereign (guinea) comprised 21 shillings.

## 43  J. Finn to Lord Russell
## Building for the Consulate

This and similar letters followed No. 38 (30 March 1857), after the Foreign Office failed to respond to Finn's entreaties to sanction the construction of a British Consulate building in Jerusalem. This had become necessary due to his forced vacation of his chambers and residence in the Christ Church compound at the demand of the missionary society, as a result of the antagonism that reigned between them. Although three years had passed since then, the problem was still unresolved and Finn and his family were forced to endure temporary housing solutions, which did not add to the standing of the British Consulate. This letter was preceded by a detailed despatch from 30 August 1859, in which he described to the Foreign Office his serious financial situation and pressing debts (FO 78/1384).

FO 195/604 (Consular No. 13)                                    Jerusalem May 9 1860
Copy

My Lord
    I had the honor in the year 1857 to receive notification that only under very rare and exceptional circumstances could the Government build a Consulate House.
    Since that time Her Majesty's Government has made me an annual allowance of One Hundred Pounds for house rent, but under the peculiar circumstances of Jerusalem, I venture again to represent the necessity for a National Consulate House.
    The lease of the house I now occupy[1] will expire in February next and I have reason to expect that then the rent will be largely augmented, on account of the desirable situation of the house, although it is very small.
    The great increase of Political consideration attached to this city and especially the amount of Russian purchases,[2] has altered the value of all house

1    After leaving the quarters of the mission in October 1857, he could not find suitable housing. He recorded in his diary on 16 February 1859: "We have been 16 months in the very lowest house of Jerusalem, and are now removed to the very highest house." He took up residence in the new house in February 1859, and since contracts for apartments and houses were generally for a period of one year, he feared that in February 1861 the rental would rise considerably (see the description of the house: Finn E., *Reminiscences*, p. 186).

2    See above, the description in No. 39. A few months later (12 November 1860), Finn noted in his diary: "I walked to inspect the progress of the Russian buildings, and am surprised at the advance that has been made."

or land property to such a surprizing degree that within one year past, almost every rent is doubled, and I know one instance in which it has been nearly quadrupled.

I beg leave to suggest that it will be more advantageous as well as economical for Her Majesty's Government to have a house of its own, as other and less important nations already have, such as Prussia and Spain. The Russians are building a new house for their Consulate adjoining the Church of the Holy Sepulchre; and the French Consul is recommending to His Government the purchase (for the same purpose) of an ancient house formerly the palace of King Baldwin, adjoining the Church of the Holy Sepulchre, at the opposite end from the Russians; this is well situated also for general business.

I would submit to Your Lordship as a rough estimate, the purchase of the ground which has been offered me, between the new Russian buildings and the City walls[3] for One Thousand Five Hundred Pounds and for a plain substantial house Three Thousand five Hundred more. Total, Five Thousand.[4]

I am obliged by this Post to draw upon the Treasury for Seventy Five Pounds, on account of House rent advanced by me a year and a half ago, and which I can no longer obtain on interest as hitherto.

The Pasha has put all money affairs of Jerusalem into confusion by depreciating the currency suddenly, from twelve to fifteen per cent,[5] and money is at present not to be had.

James Finn

# 44   J. Finn to Sir H.L. Bulwer
## Complaint on the Conduct of the Pasha

The inimical relations between Finn and Sureya Pasha deteriorated further (see above, No. 39, n. 7). The hostility of the Governor bothered the Consul and led to much friction between them. Finn sent frequent letters of complaint about the Pasha to the Foreign Office and to the Embassy in Constantinople, hoping that they would support him in his quarrels with the Governor, and

---

3   The site Finn earmarked for the Consulate building was at the western end of the large "Parade Square" separating the Russian Compound from the small buildings adjoining the Old City wall. The Turkish Post Office would later be built on this site.

4   The negative reply of 30 August 1860 was already cited above (No. 38, n. 8).

5   Simultaneously with the devaluation implemented in Jaffa (above, No. 42), a similar devaluation was carried out in Jerusalem.

perhaps even take steps to have him removed. In the following letter, Finn protests the Pasha's arbitrariness, as in other letters from this period (see, e.g., Hyamson, Nos. 194–204).


FO 78/1537 — No. 14                                    Jerusalem May 10 1860

Sir

I have the honor to represent to Your Excellency another of the violent proceedings of H.E. Sureya Pasha at variance with the equitable laws of H.I.M. the Sultan, and the propriety of conduct which so high a functionary ought to maintain.

The complainant (as it seems there is no reason to doubt) is of Russian origin, but unprovided with the document of dismissal from Russian Consulates to entitle him to be received under English protection.

He was formerly protected for a time by the Prussian Consulate, but on that ceasing the Pasha regards him as a Rayah, i.e. without European exemption from his tyranny.

Mr Hilpern is a Convert to Christianity from Judaism, and a member of the English Church here.[1] Some years ago he was directed by Dr Mendelsohn not to wear a Tarboosh on account of his liability to severe headache, and I have seen a recent certificate of the present surgeon of the English Hospital in Jerusalem pronouncing it improper for him to wear a Tarboosh.

---

1    Finn saw fit to intervene especially on behalf of Hilperin not only because he was an apostate, but also because he was one of the moneylenders who had aided him in his financial distress, in return for exorbitant interest. Hilperin would be one of Finn's main creditors two years later, when his debts reached new heights. Thomas Murad (Mordecai Joshua) Hilperin was born in 1823 in Bialystok, Poland, immigrated with his family to Jerusalem at the age of thirteen, and was baptized by the Anglican mission. According to P. Grajewski, he had a store for gold jewellery and precious stones in the main street of the market, and wielded great influence among the apostate community. Grajewski writes that his wife, who converted together with him, prided herself on actually remaining Jewish: "She was happy to always light the Sabbath candles in their proper time, and she maintained a kosher kitchen, which was difficult to believe." On 28 February 1862 the Foreign Office asked Finn for a clarification of how Hilperin merited British protection. Finn replied that for years Hilperin had been an Austrian protégé, but when he was no longer afforded this status he had requested British protection from Finn. Since this was a "case of persecution," as this document presents the matter, "I felt myself bound to afford him British protection" (see Hyamson, Nos. 215–216). According to a letter by Acting Consul McGregor dated 22 July 1895 (FO 195/1848), Finn had granted Hilperin British protection in 1862 ("for reasons unexplained"). McGregor continued: "On 18.6.1889 he was dismissed by Consul Moore, but [Moore] did not inform the Turkish Authorities. Hilperin died on 8.9.1889. He had nine children, all converts. Two of his daughters were married to British subjects."

Your Excellency will doubtless remember the conduct of Sureya Pasha as reported by me on the 22nd March in endeavouring to drive my Dragoman to wear a Tarboosh on the ground of his being a Rayah, and the insulting expression used towards the European hat.[2]

There is a good deal of excitement in Jerusalem on the subject, as numerous Armenians, and other Rayahs from Constantinople and the Turkish islands, are in the habit of wearing hats.

It seems difficult to imagine that we are living in the times of Turkish reforms — once allow this proceeding of the Pasha and it is but an easy step to the middle age barbarity of stigmatizing sects of religion by different colored head dresses.

It would also be observed that H.E. imprisoned the complainant from mere personal arbitrariness without accusation or examination for a crime — and that too in a dungeon of the most horrible description.

J. Finn

# 45    J. Finn to Lord Russell
## Samaritans at Nablus

The small sect of Samaritans in Nablus was under the protection of Finn, who took an interest in the group's history and practices (see: Finn J., *Stirring Times*, chap. XXVI). On 29 December 1851 he had already addressed the Foreign Office regarding the Samaritans (Hyamson, No. 129), and when he learned in 1852 that for years they had been unable to conduct the rite of the Paschal sacrifice on Mount Gerizim due to the enmity of the Muslims, he interceded on their behalf. Thanks to the intervention of the British Ambassador in Constantinople, they were once again able to perform this ceremony ("to celebrate the sacrifice of the Passover"; see: Finn E., *Reminiscences*, pp. 101, 109). From then on Finn regarded the members of the sect as being under his protection. In 1855 he succeeded, by means of the Embassy, in obtaining for them a royal edict recognizing them as a separate sect with religious autonomy, and at a later stage they were granted the same status as Christians regarding the payment of taxes (see: Blumberg, *View*, pp. 186, 192, 231). Finn

---

2    He refers to the letter of complaint of 22 March 1860 (FO 195/604), most of which was published by Hyamson (No. 204). This passage, however, which relates to the wearing of the tarbush by the Dragoman Raphael Meyuhas, was omitted by Hyamson. See also: Finn E., *Reminiscences*, pp. 215–216.

was present at the offering of the Paschal lamb in 1852 (*ibid.*, p. 127), visited the Samaritans on various occasions, and dealt with their requests. In a letter dated 22 November 1854 to the Foreign Secretary, he declared, "I have never failed to render good offices to the Samaritan Sect" (see: Finn J., *Stirring Times*, p. 370; Hyamson, Nos. 170, 173). In later years, the British Consulate also dealt with the affairs of the Samaritans (see, e.g.: Hyamson, Nos. 258, 294, 310).

FO 78/1521 — No. 31                                          Jerusalem August 14 1860
Political

My Lord
    I have the honor to represent to Your Lordship that I have this day forwarded to Mr Consul General Moore of Bayroot[1] a Petition from the Samaritans at Nablus describing a case of unfair trial and the employment of actual torture by the Kaimakam upon two of their community in default of witnesses in a cause instituted against them. I have already during two weeks employed my efforts in their behalf, but in vain, but as during these times of confusion and business in Syria, it is possible that the subject may be somewhat overlooked, I take the liberty of mentioning it to Your Lordship.
    In 1854 Lord Palmerston[2] recommended the Samaritan sect to such good offices as we can properly employ for Ottoman subjects, and in consequence Lord Stratford de Redcliffe[3] procured a strong Vizirial order in their behalf addressed to the Musheer of Bayroot.
    The Russian Bishop and his learned friends here are taking a deep interest in the ancient Scriptures and histories of the Samaritans, into which profound researches are being made — and the Bishop is this day appealing to his Consul General in Bayroot on their behalf. His Lordship tells me that he intends to take up this case in earnest and from what I can see and hear I am persuaded that the Russians are likely to work much more effectually for their benefit than English authorities feel justified in doing.
    Hitherto they have looked up to us as their natural protectors and in gratitude for the books which I have obtained from them for the British Museum, I have been always desirous to do them good, but this subject is one of those in which English influence in this country is falling to the rear, in

1    See above, No. 1, n. 2.
2    This mistake is surprising, for in 1854 Lord Clarendon was the Foreign Secretary.
3    Sir Stratford Canning, who had served as Ambassador at Constantinople a number of times, was awarded the title of Viscount Stratford de Redcliffe in 1852 (for an evaluation of him, see: Finn E., *Reminiscences*, p. 185). At the time of the writing of this letter, the Ambassador was Sir Henry Lytton Bulwer.

consequence of our keeping honestly to our old point without advancing in proportion to the march of others.

I have the honor to enclose a translation of a petition from the Samaritans in their own language to the Russian Professor here,[4] requesting the Bishop to procure from 'the king of the nations in Constantinople' a document in their favour, and to allow one of their number to be placed in the Town Mejlis. They also complain that they are commanded to perform their divine service in a low voice, so as not to be over-heard by others.

This small sect of people now numbers about thirty families only but are exposed to peculiar vexations, as not belonging to either of the large and usually understood bodies, the Christians or Jews, and any friendly offices which can be employed in their behalf will be very gratefully appreciated.

James Finn

# 46  J. Finn to J. Lewis Farley
# Establishment of a Bank in Jerusalem

When Finn learned of the establishment of the Bank of Turkey in Constantinople, with a British subject serving as Accountant General, he asked the latter to open a branch of the bank in Jerusalem. In his letter, Finn emphasized the importance of his proposal in terms of influence on the money market and financial conditions in Jerusalem. He also provided important details concerning the harmful practice of extending loans at exorbitant interest rates, in the absence of any financial institution in the city capable of providing credit at reasonable terms. An abstract of this letter was published by Hyamson (No. 207), but it deserves to be printed in full.

FO 78/1605                                          Jerusalem January 13. 1861
Copy

Sir,

It is with much pleasure, that I learn from you the establishment of the Bank of Turkey in Constantinople and most anxiously wish to see a branch of the same in Jerusalem.

Jerusalem is not an imperium of commercial trade, but it is a place into which money is continually being poured from without.

4    Not enclosed with the letter.

The great religious Establishments as Convents, Patriarchates, Episcopates, not to mention the seven Consulates[1] — all have money dealings, and would be benefitted by a Banking Institution with a good capital and character.

At the Russian buildings now in progress, and which will continue four years more, they were lately paying for mere cutting of stone, £500 weekly. — Those works began with a capital in hand of above a million Sterling.

The Greek Convents also are spending considerable sums in agricultural works about us: —

But almost all the money affairs here are in the hands of some petty firms of Jews, who transact their business at enormous interest.

The only person with pretension to be any thing like a European banker is Mr Bergheim, who acts as Correspondent for the Ottoman and some London Banks.[2]

At the present time all Jewish and Christian owners of money are keeping it carefully concealed, from an unfounded apprehension of insecurity in the country.

The recent failures of harvest in the country for two years have brought on great distress,[3] so that numerous very respectable families are reduced to sell property of all kinds at quarter of its value, and money when obtained on loan often costs at the usurious rates of 50 to 60 per cent per annum. — 24 per cent per annum is considered very moderate.

Your Bank here would prove a great blessing to such families, and under its operation I should expect to see credit generally revived; trade enlarged even in lines not yet tried; coins of foreign currency (as they mostly are) less fluctuating in value,[4] and more uniform between one town and another in Palestine — with less possibility of Pashas playing tricks with the currency.

Any Bank that would lend money at moderate rates on security of jewellery or lands, might have a large business here.

James Finn

1     The Consulates of England, Prussia, France, Austria, Spain, the United States, and Russia.
2     Melville Peter Bergheim (1813–1890), a native of the Poznan district, converted to Christianity in London, and in 1838 was sent to Jerusalem by the London Society as assistant pharmacist to the Society's physician. In 1852 he left his position and opened a private bank in Jerusalem which would later wield great influence in the city. When Finn's financial situation deteriorated, he was compelled to make use of Bergheim's services; with Finn's help, the banker also became one of the trustees of the diplomat's properties, which were given over as sureties for the payment of Finn's large debts (for Bergheim, see: Eliav, Shimon Rosenthal; Eliav, Finn).
3     See below, Nos. 47–48.
4     See above, introduction to No. 42.

# 47 J. Finn to Lord Dufferin
# Economic Crisis in Palestine

The following letter describes the economic distress of the population, especially the rural elements, of Palestine, resulting from two years of drought which led to crop failures and the impoverishment of the peasants. The urban population suffered less, but it also experienced want and distress; many individuals were forced to sell their possessions, one after the other, in order to obtain food.

FO 195/675 — No. 7                                            Jerusalem January 23. 1861

My Lord[1]

I have the honor to report that the failure of two harvests is telling fearfully upon the peasantry of this country, especially in that district which is always much depended on for supplies of grain, the plain extending from Jaffa to Gaza and inland to Hebron.

In one part of that district I have heard of sixteen continuous villages being abandoned by the inhabitants who have retired either to Egypt or to the district of Nablus.

In our own neighbourhood also, especially Southward of Jerusalem the peasantry have had to make extraordinary sacrifices to obtain a small amount of seed-corn for the present season.

In Bethlehem I hear that there are four hundred souls dependant upon charity for subsistence — and our streets are crowded with mendicant fellakheen in the most abject rags.

---

1    Lord Frederick Temple Dufferin (1826–1902) joined the Foreign Office in 1855 as the British representative to a joint commission of the Powers. In 1860 he was appointed to investigate the Lebanese-Syrian massacres of Christians initiated by the Druze and Muslims. Lord Dufferin stayed in Beirut until May 1861, when an agreement between the Powers was achieved and the French force withdrew from Lebanon.
It is surprising that Finn sent the following report to the special emissary of the Foreign Office, and not to the Ambassador in Constantinople or to the Consul-General in Beirut. Lord Dufferin served as Ambassador in Constantinople, 1881-1884. Lady Dufferin's visit to Jerusalem in 1860 led to friendly relations with the Finn family, which would have important implications later, when her husband would come to Finn's aid in his time of trouble. Regarding this friendship, Finn noted in his diary on 8 December 1860: "The friendship struck up among us all is almost romantic, and I think it will prove as really beneficial to us."

In the city itself however the price of bread is not extravagantly high owing to supplies of flour brought from Odessa.

The standard of the staff of life being thus disturbed, every thing else has fallen in value, as riding horses, farm-cattle, clothes, jewellery. —

And capitalists have now the opportunity of buying up all kinds of property cheap. — I know of families whose means of livelihood have been injured from other causes, now reduced to real distress by the lowness of price offered for articles which they are obliged to dispose of. Capitalists here, still keep their money very close, having not yet recovered from the panic produced by the calamities in the North during the Summer.[2]

And the usual trade of Jerusalem is this year greatly diminished, indeed the pilgrim trade scarcely exists, on account of the failure in pilgrims arriving: who are generally by this time of the year, several thousands in number and they remain till Easter.

I have the honor to enclose Copy of a letter which I lately addressed to Mr Farley, replying to his Enquiry as to the prospect of establishing here a branch of the Bank of Turkey.[3] Still we remain in perfect security which is a great blessing.

J. Finn

## 48   J. Finn to Lord Russell
## Hunger and Starvation in Palestine

Following his earlier report to the special emissary, Lord Dufferin (above, No. 47), Finn also reported to the Foreign Secretary of the terrible conditions in Palestine which had taken a turn for the worse over the past few years, especially for the rural population. After two years of crop failures and the death of much livestock, the desperate, starving peasants could not provide for their families. The shocking description provided by the Consul accurately reflected conditions in Palestine in 1861.

2   The reference is to the massacre of Christians during the summer of 1860 in Lebanon and in Syria and to the panic-stricken atmosphere in Jerusalem. See also: Finn E., *Reminiscences*, pp. 218–223.
3   See above, No. 46.

FO 78/1608 (Consular No. 15)     Jerusalem March 1, 1861

My Lord

I have the honor to report that distress and hunger are on the increase among the rural population of Palestine, even after the cessation of the inclement wintry weather.

Such wretched objects as now meet our view in the streets and on the roads, have perhaps never been seen before[1] — They are generally peasants from the South whose harvests have failed for the last two years. — They wear a few squalid rags, and beg from door to door, some sleeping at night in the caves at Acceldama.

People who have themselves been bountiful dispensers of Arab hospitality away from town and high roads, are craving morsels of bread among us, and devouring the refuse of the vegetable market, such as orange-peelings, and the outer leaves of cauliflowers, raw.

I have been assured by persons who have had opportunities of judging, that there is no such distress known in Bayroot, as what we witness among such persons as the above in Jerusalem and Bethlehem — in the latter town I have heard of some deaths from starvation.

I believe that the Latin Convents have been very liberal in doling out food to the hungry.

The town's people are not so badly off, except that there is a good deal of poverty in the Jewish Quarter.

There has been an enormous loss of cattle of every kind, particularly of camels and sheep among the peasantry. Only in the villages around Hebron I have been told of two thirds having perished, partly from cold during the deep snow, but more from want of fodder, which their owners were unable to supply at such a time. — The estimate of loss for the South of Palestine amounts to two hundred thousand head, in fifteen days.[2]

A tale which I long refused to believe, seems to be really true, that of a

1    In an additional despatch to the Foreign Office, written after travelling along the road from Jerusalem to Jaffa, Finn wrote: "I was struck with the deplorable and famished looking of the peasantry all along the road. [...] They are living on bitter and unwholesome roots dug out from the ground" (FO 195/675). Finn further relates in this despatch that he had unsuccessfully intervened with the Pasha in order to lessen the tax burden; the Pasha did not extend any substantial aid to the unfortunate. The moneylenders took advantage of the situation, lending money at the rate of ten percent monthly interest, or even more. Many among the rural population emigrated to Egypt, and in recent months 26,000 left via Gaza alone.

2    Finn wrote in his diary on 16 February 1861: "We hear frightful accounts of distress among the peasantry this winter, and enormous losses of camels, cows, sheep & goats from the severity of the weather."

peasant from the South, coming to the village of Bait Jala near us, and placing his three infant children in a cavern to perish, blocking up the entrance with stones, and leaving them there. They were however discovered by means of their cries, and he was found on the road. — He said that he had done it on account of starvation.

I do not hear of any measures being taken by the Government to alleviate this calamitous state of things.

Difficulties must continue to increase till the next harvest, but how are the people to subsist during the two months' interval?

Money is so scarce that it is only to be borrowed with great difficulty in Jerusalem, at an interest of from 80 to 90 per cent, per annum.[3]

James Finn

# 49   A.J. Khayat to Lord Russell
# Construction of a Railway

Montefiore was involved in a project to lay a railway line between Jaffa and Jerusalem. He met with Lord Palmerston on this matter in April 1856 to request his support. Palmerston regarded the proposal favourably, and even initiated the first contacts with the Turkish government (see: Montefiore, 2, pp. 58–63; FO 78/1221, 14 April 1856, A. Khayat to Clarendon). During his visit to Palestine in 1857, Montefiore presented his plan to Finn, but when the Austrian Consul Pizzamano learned of the proposal he expressed his reservations regarding the laying of a railroad line, suggesting instead the paving of a road for carriages ("a good carriage road") (see: Hyamson, No. 184; Eliav, *Austrian Protection*, p. 25). The Governor apparently did not look with favour upon the construction of a road by European partners (see Finn's report to the Foreign Office dated 3 January 1860, FO 78/1521). Montefiore retreated somewhat from his project, nor was he successful in finding partners to finance it. An additional attempt was made in 1862 — without Montefiore's participation, although his name appeared in the prospectus of the plan. Chief among the initiators were General Francis Chesney and Sir John McNeil (see: Kurt Grünwald, "Origins of the Jaffa-Jerusalem Railway," *Chapters in the History of the Jewish Community in Jerusalem*, II, Jerusalem 1976, pp. 255–260 [Hebrew]). The entrepreneurs met with Montefiore on 18 June 1862, but once again the needed funds could not be raised and the proposal was shelved. This time, too, the Consul in Jaffa saw fit to report directly to the Foreign Secretary (see above, No. 21, n. 1).

3   For the interest rates, see above, No. 46.

FO 78/1692

Separate

Jaffa August 25th 1862

My Lord,

I have the honor to report that the news which has just reached this,[1] that the Firman has been lately obtained by an English Company for constructing a Railway between Jaffa and Jerusalem has excited general interest among the Natives and Foreigners of all classes in these parts; and I have often been asked by Chiefs of districts and others when it will commence.

The inhabitants of this place seem also delighted at the report that it is the intention of the Company to construct a sheltered harbour or breakwater in connection with the Railroad;[2] if so, it will be the only harbour on the Coast of Syria, and consequently will greatly increase the commerce and prosperity of this place.

The native Christians as well as the Mahomedans and Jews look upon such undertaking as directed from Heaven inasmuch that it will facilitate the Pilgrimage to the Holy City Jerusalem, and beleive [sic!] that God will bless this movement and the Railway will be made.

But the Moslems seem to look upon it in another view and favor, they think this Railway somehow or other will undo the project of the present work of the Suez Canal,[3] and I find the Moslems of this part of the country in Palestine are adverse to that undertaking.

I am sure that nothing can do more good to this Country in developing its resources, and promoting its civilization and prosperity than a Railroad and a harbour, and as far as I know of the interior (almost every part of it), after the road is completed to Jerusalem, there will be no great natural difficulties to extend it through Nablouse, Nazareth and so on to Damascus and thence to Homs, Hama and Aleppo, and so joining the south extremities of this part of the Ottoman Empire in a direct line with the Capital, and taking the commerce of the Interior to and fro.

Assad Kayat

---

1    The word "Consulate" is apparently missing here.
2    The scheme also called for the establishment of a deep-water harbour in Jaffa (at this time, there was no suitable port along the coast of Palestine and Lebanon). Two years later, the Vice-Consul reported of "three improvements: 1) a second gate was opened in the city wall; 2) a landing place and a lighthouse were constructed at the port; 3) Jaffa was connected with Europe by a telegraph" (FO 78/1834, 15 March 1864).
3    According to Grünwald (*idem*, p. 260), Chesney was the first to envision the possibility of digging the Suez Canal.

## 50   Lord Russell to J. Finn
## Dismissal of Peter Meshullam and the Duties
## of the Consul

Peter Meshullam, the firstborn son of John Meshullam (see above, No. 26, n. 4) greatly impressed Finn and his wife with his capabilities, charming manners and way with words. He succeeded in winning their hearts and became the Consul's confidant. In 1860 Finn sent him on an official mission to Galilee and Lebanon. When, however, he reported to the Foreign Office of this commission and its results, he was severely censured for exceeding his authority and jurisdiction, while in the process wasting the Consulate's money on a superfluous task. Despite this reprimand, Finn appointed him as Cancilliere in the Consulate, to the displeasure of the Dragomans (see Finn's diary entries for 2 November and 5 November 1860). When Rogers, the Vice-Consul in Haifa, was appointed Consul at Damascus (see above, No. 28, n. 4), Finn proposed his protégé Peter for the post that had been vacated (FO 78/1605, 1 March 1861). This suggestion was rejected, and the Foreign Office appointed another Vice-Consul for Haifa. The exceptional fondness of the Finns for Peter Meshullam led them to overlook his shortcomings. He was arrogant and overbearing, domineering, and irrepressible, and he acted cruelly to the peasants, whom he dispossessed of their property. He caused grave damage to the Consulate's relations with the rural population. Finn did not pay heed to the various complaints lodged against Peter, always finding his protégé to be innocent. Peter's relations with his parents also deteriorated into a serious dispute and they accused him of helping Mrs. Finn in her policy of evicting the peasants (see below, No. 52). Many complaints against Peter's conduct were lodged with the Prince of Wales during his visit to Palestine in April 1862. When Colonel Frazer arrived in Jerusalem to examine the charges against Finn and Peter Meshullam, Frazer demanded that Meshullam be relieved of all his duties in the Consulate. In response, Finn fired Meshullam on 19 August 1862, although he continued to claim that the charges were baseless. Frazer, surprised by Finn's compliance, reported to the Foreign Secretary that he believed there was ground for the claims against Meshullam (FO 78/4782, 10 September 1862). For a detailed discussion, see Eliav, Finn; see also: Platt, *Cinderella Service*, pp. 161 ff.

FO 78/4782                                          Foreign Office, October 23, 1862

Sir,

I have received and considered your volumnious despatches from the

27th August to the 25th September, in defence of Mr. Meshullam, your late Cancellier, [...]

I am at loss, indeed, to understand that it should not have occurred to yourself that Mr Meshullam's official position and intimacy with your family might be turned to account by a person so mixed up with local questions, or at all events might cause those with whom he might have dealings to connect Her Majesty's Consuls with his proceedings. I need not, however, pursue these considerations further. It is sufficient for me to confirm your dismissal of Mr Meshullam from employment in your Consulate; and in order to prevent any further misapprehension in regard to his connection with this Consulate, it is my direction that if Mr Meshullam is a native of Syria, he should no longer be considered as under British protection.[1]

I cannot, however, refrain, after having perused your despatches, from remarking that you appear to be under some misapprehension as to the precise nature of your duties as Her Majesty's Consul at Jerusalem. Those duties are limited to the protection of British interests, and it is no part of your duty to interfere in local disputes, or to meddle in the petty intrigues and misunderstandings among the inhabitants of the country in which you reside. But it is very clear, from your own statements, that you have allowed yourself to be involved in local squabbles[2] to such an extent that, I am constrained to say, that however innocent your intentions have been, it is desirable, on account of the public service, that on the earliest opportunity you should be removed to some other post.[3]

Russell

1    On 19 August 1862, the day of his dismissal, Peter Meshullam wrote Lord Russell that he is an Englishman by birth, as his father was born in London (Peter himself was born in Malta) (FO 78/4782). In another letter he denied all the charges and claimed that he was the victim of an injustice.
2    This alludes, *inter alia*, to his imbroglio with the leaders of the Jewish community, especially the rabbinic courts, in the wake of the Joseph Shalom episode and the imprisonment of two Jews, Dutch subjects, whom he was forced to free in the end (see Hyamson, Nos. 209–214; Eliav, Finn).
3    Already on 28 April 1859, following the severe censure by Foreign Secretary Lord Malmesbury in connection with his dispute with Gobat, Finn was told: "I have to inform you that if I should hear any more complaints against you with regard to that matter, it will become my duty to recommend to the Queen that you should be removed from your Post as H.M.'s Consul at Jerusalem" (FO 78/1448). On 31 December 1862, Finn was appointed Consul at the Dardanelles (FO 78/1678), but he never assumed the position.

# 51   J. Finn to Lord Russell
## Denial of Accusations

In response to the harsh letter from the Foreign Minister, in which he was also informed of his imminent dismissal (see above, No. 50), Finn attempted to refute all the charges raised against him. He denied his involvement in quarrels with the various Consuls and other religious denominations, attempting to limit his disagreements to his rival, the Prussian Consul Rosen (see the detailed discussions: Eliav, Shimon Rosenthal; Eliav, Finn) and to a few Jews. Finn concealed the fact that he had become involved in a serious disagreement regarding the religious leadership of the *Yishuv*, and even had attempted to incite various individuals against it. He did not know that these matters had already led Montefiore to turn to the Foreign Office, an initiative which led to the decision to depose the Consul (see Hyamson, No. 219 and footnotes; *ibid.*, Nos. 220–222). Unaware that his fate had already been sealed, Finn continued to try and revoke the sentence that had been passed. If, however, his transferral was irrevocable (he did not conceive that his actual dismissal was intended), then this had to be done in a proper manner, and he should be given his choice of the vacant posts. The reply of the Foreign Secretary, dated 20 November 1862, however, was unequivocal; it had been recommended that he be transferred to the Dardanelles (FO 78/1692).

FO 78/4782 (Cons. 51)                                                                Nov. 14, 1862
Copy

My Lord,
    In the Despatch N° 12 of 23rd Ultimo, lately received, Your Lordship gives me a notification that because I have allowed myself to be involved in local squabbles to a great extent, it is desirable on account of the public service, that on the earliest opportunity I should be removed to some other post — and this, after having perused my Despatches.
    I have the honour to assure Your Lordship that I am involved in no local squabbles whatever.
    With Greek and Latin, Armenian & Syrian Patriarchs & Communities I have not one subject of difference — Neither with the French, the Austrian, the Russian, the Spanish, the American and Greek Consulates — nor with any British residents — nor with the great body of Jews.[1] — I intend to send Your

---

1    What is written here is far from the truth. Finn himself had reported to the Foreign Office of "the tyrannical interference of the rabbinical Courts" and of his quarrel with them

Lordship translation of a Hebrew Address numerously & respectably signed which I have lately received.[2]

Unfortunately my recent Despatches have been voluminous from the necessity of refuting exaggerated versions of matters which must shrink into nothing if placed impartially against the weight of my real position here — and of the respect shown me by all but the Prussian Consul and two or three persons under his influence.

A great noise was made on purpose to involve me in small matters, yet I did nothing but simply rely for support & assistance on Your Lordship.

Having supposed however Mr Peter Meshullam to be possessed of inherent rights as an Englishman I have always felt bound to entertain his claims for redress of grievances equally with those of any other Englishman. — The cases mentioned in those Despatches are those of various robberies of Mr P. Meshullam's property committed before his becoming Cancellier. [...] Also the lawsuit of Joseph Shalom and Rabbi Kimchi which will form the subject of a separate Despatch[3] —

Each of these cases was pressed upon me, as I had supposed, by the direct interests of born British Subjects — but the appointment of a legal Vice Consul for Palestine would of course relieve me at once from the necessity of hearing & entertaining such cases.

My removal from this Consulate under present circumstances, with the stigma of having encouraged an Englishman in my service to plunder peasantry, to abuse women, & intimidate witnesses, is not I trust Your Lordship's intention — But Dr Rosen[4] and still more Colonel Fraser[5] have made this

(Hyamson, No. 209, and Enclosures). Finn sent harsh letters to the rabbis and heads of the community, who imposed a ban on those making use of consular jurisdiction; he even delivered an ultimatum calling for the cancellation of the threat of the ban (see also the continuation in Hyamson, No. 210, and his censure by the Foreign Secretary, *ibid.*, No. 213). In their distress, the rabbis even turned to the mission for aid against Finn (Finn's diary, entry for 19 June 1861).

2   The declarations in favour of Finn's remaining in his post were translated and sent to the Foreign Office on 13 December 1862 (see Hyamson, No. 225 and Enclosures).
3   See the letter by Lord Russell, 24 November 1862 (Hyamson, No. 224).
4   See above, No. 32, n. 7.
5   Colonel A.J. Frazer, Commissioner for Syria. On 16 June 1862 he was asked by Lord Russell "to proceed to Jerusalem and make inquiries of serious imputations against the conduct of Peter Meshullam" (FO 78/4782). He also was requested to examine the conduct of the Consul himself. Frazer arrived in Jerusalem on 23 July 1862, and secretly began his investigations. On 28 July 1862 Finn was surprised to hear from him about the purpose of his mission and of the petitions submitted to the Prince of Wales during the latter's visit to Jerusalem (see below, No. 52). For the testimonies against Meshullam and the Consul, see Finn's entries in his diary for 28 July 1862, 7 August 1862, and 9 August 1862. Finn himself was summoned to a meticulous interrogation on 11 August 1862 (also see above, the

view of the case so public that no attempt of mine here can do away with that stigma, if I am now sent away after 17 years of honourable estimation.[6]

For myself I prefer Jerusalem to any other post — not only as being Jerusalem, but as being a Political and rising Consulate, held high in English and foreign consideration — And I have devoted years of labour to acquiring the difficult languages daily needed here.

Nevertheless if it should be decided by Your Lordship after reconsideration, that it is indispensable for the good of Her Majesty's Service that I be appointed to another post, then that my removal be effected in such a manner, as to do away with the idea of disapprobation, giving me a choice among vacant Consular posts, so that I may leave Jerusalem without sacrifices of self-respect, and of the honourable standing which has been my only recompense after so many years of laborious service and severe privations.

J.F.

# 52 John Meshullam to N.T. Moore
## Expropriation of Meshullam's Property in Urtas

The end of 1862 was marked not only by Finn's dismissal from his post of Consul, but also by John Meshullam's (see above, No. 26, n. 4) loss of his property in Artas. After having purchased a portion of the lands of Artas in 1856, over the course of time Elizabeth Finn, with the discreet help of her husband, gained control of various plots in the vicinity of the village. In March 1861 the couple acquired the lands of Fa'our, a village southwest of Artas, and began to restore it with the aid of Peter Meshullam. The relations between the Finns and Peter's father, John Meshullam, reached a crisis, with Mrs. Finn and John trading accusations of financial debts and fraudulent accounting. When the charges were brought before the Consul for judicial decision, he did not disqualify himself from sitting in judgment and rendering a decision in favour of his wife. In the auction of the properties of Artas, Mrs. Finn bought the entire farmstead with all its contents and lands, this at a time

introduction to No. 50). Frazer's severe report sealed Finn's fate, and the Foreign Office resolved to depose him. Even before this, however, rumours of Finn's impending dismissal had swept through Jerusalem.

6   On 29 October 1862 Finn recorded in his diary: "The 'Levant Herald' recently arrived announces my going to the Dardanelles and Mr. Noel Moore, the Vice-Consul in Beyrout, going to Jerusalem in my place." On 7 November 1862 Finn wrote: "It is wonderful, how the city is full of expectation on the subject, waiting from post to post, and in money affairs this affects us very seriously, but not less in official dealings with the local government."

when the Finns experienced severe financial distress, being forced to pawn jewellery to support themselves. Meshullam was compelled to leave Artas, being reduced to penury as his life's work collapsed (for a detailed discussion, see: Eliav, Finn).

The following letter was found among the remains of the consular archives preserved in the Israel State Archive and which apparently never reached the Foreign Office. It was already written to the new Consul, Noel Temple Moore, who was officially appointed in December 1862 and arrived in Jerusalem at the beginning of March 1863. It contains Meshullam's version of the affair and is patently one-sided, but nevertheless casts grave doubts upon the conduct of the Finns. At the time the letter was written, the Finns were still living in Jerusalem, leaving the city only on 22 May 1863. Obviously, they knew nothing of the content of the letter. It may be assumed that it was formulated by another person, since Meshullam himself was incapable of writing such a missive.

ISA 123/1/27                                            Jerusalem, March 26th 1863
Draft

Sir,

You may probably have heard of my agricultural undertaking in the valley of Urtas near Bethlehem, where as the first European Colonist in Palestine, I have resided with my family for the last fifteen years.[1] [...] In 1856 Mrs. Finn, the Consul's Lady, proposed to enter into partnership with me in certain waste lands situated in the eastern portion of the valley. By means of my influence with the native proprietors the land was obtained and an agreement entered into between myself and Mrs. Finn regarding its cultivation.[2]

Meanwhile my deceased son Peter[3] began to behave rudely and lawlessly

---

1   In actual fact, he and his family settled there only on 12 June 1850. Henry Baldensperger, wishing to engage in agriculture, had settled there before him, in October 1847. With the good offices of Bishop Gobat, he entered into a partnership with Meshullam but left Artas in 1851. See: Baldensperger, Introduction and pp. 113–114.

2   Here Meshullam ignores the settlement of a group of Americans in Artas in the early 1850s, which ended in an intense quarrel that almost caused a diplomatic incident. It was after this that Mrs. Finn purchased a portion of the village's lands (see Eliav, Finn, pp. 61–62).

3   Peter Meshullam, who was hated by the Bedouin tribesmen and the peasants because of his crooked deeds, was murdered on 5 March 1863, in the very same period in which Finn transferred the Consulate to Moore. The new Consul was charged with the investigation of the murder, but since Finn was still in Jerusalem, he intervened quite a lot, causing much discomfort for Moore. The correspondence regarding the murder and Finn's dismissal were submitted to Parliament, upon its request, in 1880. All this appears in FO 78/4782, entitled: "Case of Consul & Mrs. Finn — Correspondence respecting the Murder of Mr.

towards my Arab neighbours which threatened to bring upon me their resentment, destroy all feelings of friendship which had existed between me and them, endanger his own life and imperil my residence amongst them. — I made repeated representations of the danger to the Consul, but found that instead of aiding me to reclaim my son within the province of reason, the Consul made him his Chancellor and took him under his especial protection, which encouraged him in his lawless and disorderly career[4] and subsequently entered into partnership with him, in certain lands of which the inhabitants of a village about an hour distance from Urtas had been most unjustly deprived of by the Consul and my son.[5]

A scene of conflict and disturbance ensued, my complaints to the Consul remained unanswered; the natives persecuted by my son crowded my residence, some presenting a threatening attitude, others demanding justice and bitterly complaining of the various losses and damages entailed upon them and of the indifference of the local Government towards them.

It was under these circumstances that I ventured to present a petition to General Bruce during the sojourn of H.R.H. in this country.[6] Colonel Frazer was subsequently here in order to investigate my case, but I have had no intimation as to the result of that investigation.[7] [...] Previous to the events

Peter Meshullam and the Removal of Mr. Finn from the Consulate of Jerusalem," Presented to the House of Commons by Command of Her Majesty (Turkey No. 8, 1880).

4   On 21 October 1861 Finn wrote in his diary: "His Mother and Father are outraged, screaming against the Consul for not restraining Peter, but allowing him to resort to sanguinary measures, and so entailing murder upon himself. Thus the Consul is guilty of the blood of my son."

5   The reference is to the purchase of the land of the village of Taghoor [Fa'our]. The contracts were signed on 4 December 1860, with Peter as an active partner, afterwards acting as an agent of the Finns and dealing in this capacity with the restoration of the village, the building of houses, and the cultivation of the fields. When Finn's dismissal became known, Bedouin attacked the village and destroyed it (diary entry for 28 November 1862; see also Eliav, *ibid.*, p. 62).

6   The Prince of Wales, later to become Edward VII (1841-1910), visited Jerusalem in April 1862. During his visit, he was presented with petitions against Finn and his arbitrary behaviour, and against Peter Meshullam for his cruel actions. The appeals led to the investigation by Col. Frazer (see above, No. 51, n. 5).
    General Bruce was the official escort of the young Prince of Wales. Noel T. Moore, later to succeed Finn, served as the Prince's translator and escort. His tour with the Prince may possibly have influenced his appointment. The Prince of Wales was the first European in modern times who entered the mosque in the Cave of Machpelah in Hebron, openly and without disguise.

7   In the summary of his report to the Foreign Secretary, Frazer wrote: "I came to the conclusion that the charges contained in the Petitions presented to the Prince of Wales were in general well founded; that Mr. P. Meshullam had been able to carry out a system of oppression and spoliation towards the unfortunate peasantry through the power he derived from his position in the British Consulate on the one hand, and from a servile

described above, the Eastern Valley, by mutual consent of both parties was divided between me and Mrs. Finn, and a document was drawn up and signed by the latter, that she had no further claims upon me. This document, although the Consul has tried to deprive me of it, under various pretences, is still in my possession. Certain accounts however remained pending between me and Mrs. Finn, the balance of which although clearly in my favour, I was condemned by a most unfair process to pay to this lady the sum of Pia. 32,208 — about £260. The Consul knew that I did not possess this amount in cash, his demand was however imperious. England too far off, the spirit of revenge stirred against me, was too powerful to be encountered by feeble means, my property would be sequestered, sold and my family reduced to the most abject poverty.

In this defenceless condition I found no other alternative but to pay the amount. I proposed therefore to pay it by annual installments with legal percentage and ample security, but this offer was refused. I then asked for my deeds of the land, deposited in the British Consulate, in order to raise the money upon security of those deeds, but they were denied to me. I endeavoured by various legal means to borrow the whole amount on interest, but found that Mr.& Mrs. Finn have caused a prohibition to be issued against any one who might feel disposed to lend me money upon security of my lands. Seeing she had succeeded in closing my way, Mrs. Finn now drew bills upon me. In order to meet these bills, I went to a Banker in Jerusalem (Mr. Bergheim)[8] and proposed to him the sale of a plot or two of land. He accepted the proposal of one plot only for £100. I immediately wrote to Mrs. Finn, requesting her to accept either the transfer of the money or the land, promising to pay the remaining amount at the end of one year with interest and security. But this proposal was also refused; the bills drawn upon me were protested, neither bearing my signature nor acceptance and the whole of my property, worth of £2000 subsequently sequestered by the Consul. [...]

Mr. Finn then sold to Mrs. Finn my property for the paltry sum of Pia. 45,000 (about £400),[9] the cost alone of my house, not to speak of my gardens, the most valuable land under cultivation, which brought me an annual income of from £150 to £200. My Winter crops in finest cultivation, worth about £100, were also sequestered together with my stores of provisions, of all I was not allowed to remove a single straw. — My cows, donkeys, mules, house

deference to that position, displayed by the local Governor" (FO 78/4782, 10 September 1862).

8   See above, No. 46, n. 2.

9   On 9 December 1862 Finn wrote in his diary: "Consular order for sale of Meshullam's property." The following day, a "Public Note" appeared, and on 15 December 1862, Elizabeth Finn purchased all the properties "at public auction" for the sum of 45,000 piastres, a ridiculously low amount. Afterwards, all the contents were sold.

furniture, mill, kitchen and garden utensils, worth about £300, were all taken in order to defray about £33 of Consular fees! The announcement of the sale of my household furniture etc. was effected by means of a public crier, sent through the streets of Bethlehem to declare, that this had happened to me by order of the English Government, adding mockery and recrimination to the announcement.

I was now brought to extremes, my mind no longer able to bear such sudden and unexpected reverses partially effected one abberation succeeded another, until I was taken into the Latin Hospital in Jerusalem almost bereft of reason, my family meanwhile were dispersed in various quarters, while my son Peter was placed to constitute the Consul's guardian over the property of which I had been so unjustly deprived.[10]

The whole population of Jerusalem, of all denominations are panic stricken at the unparalleled persecutions, I have and am still enduring but what could Mr. Finn do more!! He has ruined me and my family and brought me on the borders of insanity and being an unlettered man myself, he has taken all possible advantage of the distracted state of my mind, in order to force me to acts of insubordination and to make use of expressions by which he might entangle and condemn me.

Such is but a brief and imperfect sketch of my history. — I have written both to Col. Frazer and Lord John Russell an account of these facts as they happened upon the period of the sequestration of my property,[11] but I have had no answer.

Now it is nearly four months that I and my family are left to the mercy of a kind friend, who continues to supply us with board and lodging. But it being impossible to continue longer in this state, I therefore most earnestly recommend my case to your humane consideration. I ask that Justice should be done to me, in conformity to the laws of my country, and I recommend myself to the kind acceptance of this my humble appeal.

And looking forward for a favourable reply,[12]

I am, Sir, etc.

[John Meshullam]

10    On 24 December 1862 Finn recorded in his diary: "Peter would be left [at Artas] as Agent for rectifying of documents [...] if old Meshullam should return, then merely as our guest, out of respect to him as an old man."

11    Letter to Lord Russell blaming the Finns for his ruin (ISA 123/1/27, 27 November 1862).

12    Even before arriving in Jerusalem, Moore was ordered by the Foreign Ministry "to investigate Meshullam's claims" (ISA 123/1/27, Murray to Moore, 22 January 1863). In the wake of the official investigation of the Finns' actions and his debts (below, No. 53), the purchase of Artas by Mrs. Finn was set aside, and the property reverted to its owners. Meshullam returned to his holdings and began to restore his property; he apparently lived here until shortly before his death in 1878.

# 53   E. Hornby to Lord Russell
## Report on Investigation of Finn's Affairs (Extracts)

On 31 December 1862 Finn was officially appointed Consul to the Dardanelles, but he was in no hurry to leave Jerusalem, even though his creditors
began to harass him and demand the repayment of his debts. This situation
was highly embarrassing for Moore. The new Consul asked the Foreign
Office to send a person of authority to examine Finn's debts and thus prevent
his predecessor from being publicly declared bankrupt.
Sir Edmond Hornby (1825–1896), who in 1856 had been appointed Chief
Judge in the Supreme Consular Court in Constantinople, was sent to Jerusalem to examine the situation and to engage in negotiations with the creditors.
Arriving in Jaffa on 1 June 1863, he ordered Finn, who was about to leave for
the Dardanelles, to return with him to Jerusalem to facilitate the investigation.
Finn quite willingly agreed and accordingly postponed his departure from
Palestine. Hornby successfully reached an arrangement with the creditors
which included a drastic reduction in the sum of Finn's debts and a payment
schedule (see Eliav, Finn). The detailed, 36-page report, extensive sections
of which appear below, indicates that the judge related favourably to the
Finns, even finding some points of merit in connection with their behaviour
and actions, while displaying contempt for the creditors. The arrangement
included the sale by auction of all of Finn's possessions, with his properties in
Talbieh and in Artas being mortgaged for the payment of the debts. Finn left
Palestine impoverished, after having been compelled to sign the agreement.

FO 78/1951 — No. 60

Supreme Consular Court
Constantinople 23th July 1863

My Lord
    I have now the honour to report to Your Lordship the result of my
inquiry into Mr Consul Finn's affairs.
    On my arrival in Palestine, and indeed previously, I heard a great deal
against Mr Finn, and I fully expected that my task would not only be an
extremely troublesome and painful one, but that the result of it would prove
most unfavorable to Mr Finn.
    A little investigation on the spot however, satisfied me, that a very great
portion of the scandal that had reached me, was unfounded, and that most of
it, could be distinctly traced to a feeling of opposition that had its root in
differences of a personal and I might almost say, religious character, which

had first shown itself, many years ago, and which had continued ever since.[1]

I do not acquit Mr Finn of being free from blame. I think, a more conciliatory manner, — greater judgment in the exercise of his authority, and in the general performance of his duties, and a more lenient mode of viewing the faults, weaknesses, and conduct of others, should have enabled him to make friends instead of enemies, while it would undoubtedly have made his Consular position more respected.

As far as I could learn it would appear that on the establishment of the Jewish Mission in this City, a Dr Macgowan who was the Medical man attached to it, assumed its direction. This Gentleman died some time ago.[2] He appears to have possessed very considerable energy of character, but at the same time to have been one of those men who are extremely useful so long as they are allowed to govern everybody, and no one ventures to question their authority, or to express an opinion different to one which they may have formed. His object was evidently to make the Jewish Mission an all powerful body in Jerusalem and an engine of quasi Political as well as Religious Authority. To accomplish this he was willing to avail himself of Consular assistance and to respect it so long as the Consul did, and said what he, Dr Macgowan, desired. The Mission was wealthy, and most of the English residents were more or less allied to it or dependant on it. The Shop-keepers, were most of them, converted Jews — of English or of Anglo-German Nationality, and so long as they were content to be dependant on the Mission, so long the Mission was willing to assist and support them.

The Society, however, had no ideas of opposition. Its orders were to be obeyed — its advice followed, and any one venturing to dispute the one, or to decline following the other, was forthwith to be ejected from Jerusalem.

Having converted men to Evangelical Protestantism, the least that was expected of the Proselytes, was a surrender of all right of self-assertion.

In the course of time however, and as some of these Proselytes became thriving Traders, a feeling on independence began to manifest itself — and from the Society, persons who felt themselves aggrieved or annoyed, naturally appealed to the Consul. The Consul was at least bound to listen to their complaints, and if possible to see justice done them, and the justice which the

---

1    Hornby alludes here to the incessant quarrels with the Bishop and the missionaries.
2    Dr. Edward Macgowan had been sent to Jerusalem in 1842 by the mission, and in 1844 he opened the missionary hospital in the city. Very successful in the provision of medical assistance and in firmly establishing the hospital, he was favourably accepted by all the communities in Jerusalem. He supported Gobat in his severe dispute with the Consul. Hornby's evaluation of the role played by Macgowan in the dispute is exaggerated and based on hearsay, for Macgowan was no longer alive at the time of his investigation. He had died in 1860 in Jerusalem and was buried there.

Civil Officer felt inclined to make out, was not always of the character that suited the Religious Society. Hence the first breach.[3]

Men of Dr Macgowan's stamp cannot understand how other men can venture to differ from them, and he accordingly construed the natural protection given by the Magistrate as a direct intentional offence to himself, and the Society which he represented. Hence all those who felt inclined to be independant or to respect the Consular Office, were treated as enemies, and placed beyond the pale of the Society —its influence, protection or countenance.

Unfortunately the Bishop was not an Englishman,[4] or he might have exercised a useful influence in preventing this schism among the British Community. Many of the Proselytes were Germans under British Protection. The Bishop, in every way, an excellent man, but unaccustomed to business, soon fell under the influence of Dr Macgowan's energetic chracter, and naturally enough consulted the Prussian Consul, a man of considerable talents and excessively ambitious of power and authority.[5] Dr Rosen saw the influence which the Mission would give him, and therefore allied himself closely to the Bishop and to Dr Macgowan. Even then an open conflict might have been avoided, had Mr Finn possessed more tact and less touchiness, but altho' far weaker in mind and character, he had quite as great a love of power as Dr Macgowan, and the price of the Consul's protection partook a good deal of the character of that exacted by the Mission. Hence arose two parties. In the struggle that ensued, — the Mission would undoubtedly have soon gained the upper-hand, but fortunately or unfortunately, the Consul's wife was more than a match for Dr Macgowan, the Prussian Consul and the Bishop. She was not only a highly educated woman, but possessed naturally great talents especially for acquiring languages and marvellous courage and strength of character. Extra-ordinary weapons soon became necessary, and were freely used on both sides.

Finding the field of conversion already occupied, Mrs Finn determined not to try to convert Jews, but to raise their social condition and influence as Jews. The Mission made proselytes; Mrs Finn endeavoured to convert lazy Mendicants living on the charity of Europe into laborious work-people. Hence another fertile cause of opposition.[6]

---

3    Here, as well, Hornby defended Finn, who took steps to draw the apostates closer to him, to the displeasure of the mission.

4    Hornby accepted Finn's claim that the Bishop had acted in concert with the Prussian Consul, had defended German interests, and did not properly represent the Anglican church.

5    See above, No. 32, n. 7.

6    In his previous letter Hornby had written: "Both he and Mrs. Finn have been extremely sanguine, as to the success of their plans for raising the social condition of the Jews and like

In means however, the Mission was rich, while Mrs Finn had only to trust to chance subscriptions and her own energy — where she spent hundreds, the Mission spent thousands, and the result was, that her husband's means were soon exhausted, and the Jews repaid the philanthropy manifested for their race by the wife of the British Consul by purchasing her husband's bills at a discount of 50 and 60 percent [...]

It is undeniably true that his late Cancellier,[7] in some respects a remarkable man, was the immediate cause of much of the local irritation against Mr. Finn. The Consul could see no faults in him. [...] I can easily conceive that to a man of Mr. Finn's nervous temperament and to Mrs. Finn's masculine energy of mind he was eminently attractive and useful.

That he abused his position is certain; he did great mischief, — the greater portion of what he did was unknown to Mr. Finn [...] The notice taken of the Petitions presented to His Royal Highness the Prince of Wales when at Jerusalem, and the consequent mission of Colonel Frazer[8] were also instrumental in bringing about a crisis in Mr. Finn's affairs. Immediately on Colonel Frazer's arrival, a general idea prevailed that Mr. Finn would inevitably be dismissed. From that moment Mr. Finn's supplies of money stopped.

There has been nothing fraudulent or criminally improper in Mr. Finn's conduct, although there has been undoubtedly much to blame and regret. I determined to endeavour to put his pecuniary affairs into something like order and after reducing the exorbitant demands for interest, I have induced the majority in value of the Creditors to consent to an arrangement which when carried out, will, I hope, relieve Mr. Finn from his difficulties.[9] [...]

I have seen numbers of Jews, Arabs and Christians. Most of the persons with whom I was in communication, only spoke of Mr Finn's embarrassments and of his conduct by report, — of their own knowledge few, if indeed any of them, knew anything. Reports had been circulated from mouth to mouth, losing nothing in their transmission, and a very little investigation and examination convinced me, that it would be most dangerous to attach any credence to them. In no single case was any charge of misconduct, oppression, corrup-

---

most people who indulge in such transcendental schemes of philosophy, they have been grossly taken in, and in several instances those who have benefited most by their assistance, have been the most violent in their reproaches and abuse. — Mr. Finn is a strange contradiction of no great mental power, — he is extremely obstinate and one-sided in his views, particularly of men" (FO 78/1952, 12 June 1863). He characterized Finn as one who did not understand people, put his trust in the wrong persons, and distanced himself from those who warned him, ignoring their cautions.

7    Peter Meshullam (see above, No. 52).
8    See above, No. 51, n. 5.
9    For details, see: Eliav, Finn.

tion or injustice made by any person,[10] although many told me of what they had heard from others, and when I called upon those from whom the information has been received, they referred me to other persons, and then again to others, and so on ad-infinitum, but in no one instance, although I waited patiently and gave every proper encouragement, did any sufferer present himself.

I failed therefore to discover that Mr Finn in the sense of direct official misconduct, has been to blame. Undoubtedly in some instances he has shown a want of judgment and decision, and he has meddled with matters with which in his position of British Consul, he had no business to meddle; but as his motives have never been otherwise than fair and right, and as I do not find, that in endeavouring to realize any object, that he has had in view, he has acted unjustly or corruptly, I have not thought it necessary to do more than point out to him the errors he has committed.

In the Law suit in which Mrs Finn acting as the Agent of the Jewish industrial association was engaged with Mr Meschullam the sub-Agent, — and which was heard and decided by Mr Finn in his capacity of Consul.[11] The fact of his wife being one of the litigants was a misfortune, and it placed him in a false position, because the mass of the Community here insisted that he was acting as Judge in his own cause. They refused to recognise the character in which Mr Finn stood towards the Defendant, altho' all the chief differences between them were purposely submitted to four indifferent Arbitrators. Mr Finn in his character of Consul giving only an executory effect to the award given in his wife's favour.

It is true that even in so acting — he exceeded his powers, and I have had to review his decisions, and to set aside his Orders, but I do not think, that the mistakes he committed were intentional or intended to favour his wife, nor do I think that had any other person than his wife been the party benefited, any one would have thought of suggesting any impropriety of intention or conduct.

In concluding this Report, I would call Your Lordship's attention to the peculiar character of the resident English and English protected Community, and to the difficulties which will, I fear, always exist in its relations with the Consular Officer. It consists almost entirely of people, who whatever may be their business or trade, reside here from peculiar religious convictions. In other places, social and business ties are the principal bonds which connect Society together. Here it is simply a matter of Religion.

10  A strange statement, for there were many complaints about Finn and his arbitrary behaviour. Finn wrote in his diary on 12 June 1863: "Hornby told us, he has written to Earl Russell, that he has found nothing dishonourable respecting me in his investigations."
11  See above, No. 52. Here Hornby admits that Finn acted improperly.

There is one class who think that the great end and aim of life ought to be to convert Jews to Christianity so that on the second coming of the Messiah, he may find the good work accomplished and reward those through whose instrumentality it has been brought about. Another party think that Jews ought to remain Jews, but that they ought to be morally and intellectually raised for the future that is in store for them. To agree with one party is to give mortal offence to the other. To be indifferent to either is to give offence to both. In all times toleration in such matters has been rare. In Jerusalem it would seem to be impossible. Which ever side a Consul espouses he is certain to be overhelmed [sic!] with abuse by the other — every action will be misrepresented, and no little ingenuity will be exerted to find some flaw in him or in some member of his family, and if he steer an even course, I greatly fear he will be a general object of dislike and suspicion to all. Of all Communities those which are the growth of Religious opinions, are it would appear, the most difficult to manage. [...]

I have endeavoured, so far as I could, to point out the folly of this course of thought and action to everybody with whom I have been brought in contact. For the moment all promises well. The removal of Mr Finn is looked upon as a concession to justice and the Mission, and it is impossible to convince anybody to the contrary. The Community are therefore graciously inclined to friendliness and good humour. If anybody can maintain and keep alive this good feeling, it will be Mr Moore and his wife — and the Incumbent Mr Barclay[12] will, I feel certain, assist him.

The Bishop is well-disposed, and I hope Mrs Gobat is also now that Mrs Finn is leaving,[13] and the other members of the Mission cannot fail to be conciliated by the frankness and amiability of both the Consul and his wife; but at all times the position of Consul here will be one of difficulty, requiring unbounded good nature and good temper with no little firmness and discretion, — all which qualities Mr Moore appears fortunately to possess.[14]

Edmund Hornby, Judge

12  Dr. Joseph Barclay was the head of the mission in Jerusalem in 1861–1870. After Gobat's death, Barclay was appointed the third Protestant Bishop of Jerusalem, but died shortly afterwards, in October 1881.
13  Hornby alludes to conflicts between the two women, who were responsible for fanning the flames of the quarrel (see Eliav, *ibid.*).
14  In his memoirs, which he wrote many years later, Hornby had harsh things to say about Mrs. Finn: "[...] a lady of very considerable energy and very masterful temper, in the exercise of which she managed to involve her husband in serious pecuniary difficulties [...] [She had] strong financial instincts and was not overscrupulous in using them. [...] [Finn] was ordered to remain in Jerusalem until my arrival. This did not at all suit Mrs. Finn, and she hurried him and herself down to Jaffa, hoping to leave before I got there. [...] She had

## 54 N.T. Moore to Sir H. Bulwer
## License for Printing Press and Newspaper for J. Brill

Jehiel Brill (1836–1886), one of the pioneers of the Hebrew press, together with his friends Michal Cohen and Joel Moses Salomon, published the first Hebrew newspaper in Palestine, *Ha-Levanon*. His two colleagues returned in the autumn of 1861 after training in the printing profession in Königsberg, bringing with them a lithograph machine, and opened a print shop. They brought in Brill, who already had some experience in journalistic writing, to become the actual editor. The first issue appeared on 19 February 1863. Lacking a license, the publishers apparently bribed the local officials. The following letter indicates that Brill was forced to suspend publication, and he asked the British Consul to intercede for him through the offices of the British Ambassador (see: Sh. Halevy, "First Steps of the Hebrew Press in Palestine," *Chapters in the History of the Jewish Community in Jerusalem*, II, Jerusalem 1976 pp. 239–254 [Hebrew]).

FO 295/761 — N° 27                                      Jerusalem. November 24. 1863
(Not sent Home)

Sir,
       I have the honor to enclose to Your Excellency a Copy of a letter addressed to me by Mr Jechiel Juda Lip-Bril,[1] a British subject, native of

borrowed from every Jew in the town and entered into engagements to pay [which were] impossible of performance. [...] Mrs. Finn never forgave me, and for years after she was abusing me as if I had robbed and ruined her" (Hornby, pp. 131–135).
Hornby also introduces an antisemitic overtone when referring to the Jews of Jerusalem, especially regarding the creditors.
A later book by an expert on the British foreign service stated: "Hornby investigated and suspended the Consul at Jerusalem, whose wife amongst other things, was conducting an ingenious land fraud, selling plots in the Holy Land to credulous Anglican clergymen" (Platt, *Cinderella Service*, p. 155). The author erred by attributing Finn's suspension to Hornby; he also incorrectly wrote that Finn was transferred to Trabizond (*ibid.*, p. 161).

---

1    Jehiel Brill (the son of Judah Leib) appears here as a native of India. S.J. Finn, who knew him well, also states this (*Knesset Yisrael* 1886, p. 520; see also: *Jewish Encyclopedia* 3:385). In most of the literature, however, the Ukrainian city of Tulchin appears as his birthplace. According to this letter, he clearly was a British subject, apparently due to his

India, applying for a Licence from the Porte for opening a Printing Press and publishing a Hebrew Newspaper, called "Halbanon", at Jerusalem. I have also transmitted a copy of Mr Bril's application to the Pasha of Jerusalem, requesting him to take the necessary steps to procure the Licence, which His Excellency has promised to do.

Mr Brill having opened a Printing Press and published his Newspaper without a Licence, in consequence of alleged ignorance of the Regulations on this subject, he has been under the necessity of suspending the publication of his Journal;[2] an early receipt of the Licence would therefore save him much loss and inconvenience.[3]

Noel Temple Moore

# 55 N.T. Moore to Foreign Office
## Outbreak of Cholera

Difficult sanitary conditions in Palestine, severely overcrowded housing, great poverty, the poor diet and lack of water sources led to a high incidence of sickness and mortality. From time to time epidemics would sweep the land and claim many victims. The most severe was the cholera epidemic that hit Palestine in the summer and fall of 1865. The epidemic originated in Mecca, where 12,000 Muslim pilgrims died. From there it spread to Egypt, Lebanon, and Syria, and also to Palestine. Hardest hit were the large cities, but hardly any village or settlement was left untouched. Refugees from Jaffa brought the

birth in India. It is also possible, however, that he became an Indian subject on one of his journeys. In 1855 he immigrated to Palestine and, together with his father-in-law Jacob Sapir, served as the scribe of the Kollel of the Perushim. *Ha-Levanon* also was intended to serve as the journal of the Perushim community. Brill published *Ha-Levanon* in Paris from 1865 to 1870. After the Franco-Prussian War he moved to Mainz, where he published the newspaper as the Hebrew supplement of the Orthodox *Israelit*. In 1884 he settled in London, and in 1886 resumed publication of the newspaper, for a short time, until his death.

2    Apparently due to a denunciation to the Ottoman officials, as a consequence of the stiff competition with the newspaper *Havazzelet*, which was established a few months after *Ha-Levanon* began to appear.

3    This appeal bore no fruit. Brill also sent his letter directly to the Grand Vizier in December 1863, after the last issue (No. 12) appeared on the 19th of that month. Two months passed without a response, and Brill set out for Constantinople to attempt and attain his request. He remained there for four months, until he received a final, negative reply. He then moved to Paris, where he resumed publication of *Ha-Levanon* exactly one year after the last issue in Jerusalem.

plague to Jerusalem, despite the quarantine. On 28 July 1865 the epidemic erupted in Jerusalem, continuing for a month. All municipal services collapsed, and whoever could do so fled the city. The epidemic erupted once again in September, even more virulently, continuing until December of that year. It was estimated that more than 800 people died in Jerusalem, including several hundred Jews (see: Eliav, *Austrian Protection*, Nos. 135–142, and sources listed there).

FO 195/808 — N° 4
Copy

Jerusalem October 20th 1865

My Lord,

Adverting to my dispatch N° 3 of the 23rd of August last, I regret to have to report that Cholera has within the last fortnight broken out at Jerusalem and the neighboring villages — happily as yet on a limited scale. It is not possible to obtain accurate returns of the number of cases daily. The reports I receive are very contradictory. Comparing one with the other, the number of attacks ending fatally may be, on an average, between five and eight a day.[1] The greatest number of cases are occurring amongst the poorer classes of Mehometans — next come the Jews. The troops have also suffered.

It is not surprising that the malady should have broken out. The present is the most unhealthy season of the year for Jerusalem — add to which a fierce sorocco wind has been blowing for the last twelve days, causing intense heat.[2] The sickness usual at this season has turned into the Epidemie so generally prevalent this summer.

It is confidently hoped that a change of weather, which, in the ordinary course, cannot now be long delayed will rid us entirely of this scourge, which under the circumstances is most likely.

Noel Temple Moore

P.S.

October 23rd — The deaths have risen to about forty five a day since the 21st.[3]

1    According to a letter by the Austrian Consul (Eliav, *Austrian Protection*, No. 136), ten to fourteen people died every day.
2    The Austrian Consul also wrote about the east wind, "that it raises the temperature to the highest levels" (*ibid.*). He also noted that he was the only Consul who remained in the Old City, while his colleagues and many wealthy residents had gone to the villages or slept in tents outside the city walls, from where they tried to extend aid to the stricken.
3    According to a report by the Austrian Consul, "Deaths increased with the appearance of the cholera, and the disease only worsened" (*ibid.*, No. 137). He noted that there were 43 fatalities on the 22nd of October, 75 on the 23rd, and more than 60 lost their lives on the 24th.

The population is quitting the City; about one half have left, principally for the Coast. —

## 56  N.T. Moore to Lord Russell
## Outbreak of Cholera

During November 1865, there was a decline in the number of those who died due to the epidemic, probably because a sizable portion of the population had fled. The Pasha, accompanied by most of the senior officials, went to Jaffa. In the absence of any governmental action to aid the stricken or to stop the epidemic, the European consuls initiated the establishment of an Aid Committee, which organized medical assistance and the free distribution of basic supplies. These activities were financed by contributions from the Consulates, and by charitable organizations in Europe. This was the main source of relief for the suffering population, in contrast with the helplessness exhibited by the Ottoman authorities, who did nothing to alleviate the distress of the city's inhabitants. For the epidemic, see also the reports in: Carmel, *Palästina-Chronik*, I, pp. 86–88.

FO 195/808 — N° 7                                   Jerusalem November 13th 1965
Copy

My Lord
    The mortality from Cholera here since my last report, rose to seventy per day,[1] on a population thinned by the flight of probably the third of the inhabitants, which would leave about twelve thousand people in the City. This happily proved to be the culminating point, after which the epidemie commenced gradually to decrease, — with, however, occasionally — renewed virulence. Yesterday six cases occurred, that I have heard of.
    Soon after the first serious outbreak of the Malady, my foreign Colleagues and myself constituted ourselves into a Relief Committee,[2] which, at

1    According to the report of the Austrian Consul, the highest number of deaths occurred on 24 October, gradually decreasing afterwards, and by the end of the month, it had gone down to 30 per day (Eliav, *Austrian Protection*, No. 139). According to the despatch reproduced below, the decline in the number of deaths continued, decreasing significantly.
2    The Aid Committee was headed by the Prussian Consul, Dr. Georg Rosen, the senior of the consuls, who did everything in his power to augment the assistance rendered to the populace.

our invitation, the Pasha joined,[3] and we have been dispensing such relief, principally in the form of wholesome foods (rice and meat) to the poor of every creed and sect, as the funds which had reached us respectively from benevolent Associations and persons in Europe, enabled us to afford. Twelve hundred portions of meat and rice were daily distributed, under the supervision of the Committee, for twelve consecutive days, when the sum devoted to this purpose was exhausted. The same sanitary measures suggested by ourselves and the Medical Gentlemen, were adopted, and from yesterday fires will be lighted in the different parts of the City for a number of days, to purify the Atmosphere.

Only three Europeans have been attacked by the Cholera, two of whom died; but several Mehometans of the highest class have been carried off by the epidemie, amongst others the Mufti and three members of his family, and the President of the Criminal Tribunal.

It is calculated that about six hundred persons have fallen victims to the scourge in Jerusalem.[4]

Although it is hoped that the Malady will now soon disappear, the continued draught, no rain having as yet fallen, beyond one or two light showers, is an unfavourable circumstance.

Noel Temple Moore


# 57   N.T. Moore to Foreign Office
# Plague of Locusts

In the summer of 1865, when the cholera epidemic broke out, Palestine also suffered from a severe locust infestation. In addition to the extreme drought in Palestine, the population also suffered from the swarms of locusts that had begun to appear in late April. Fields and orchards in various regions suffered grievous damage from the pests, which devoured all in their path. This natural disaster brought famine in its wake, and many people died of starvation in the streets of Jerusalem. In an unusual recurrence of infestation year after year, the plague of locusts that struck the land in the summer of 1866 was even more severe than its predecessor. The peasant economy collapsed;

3   Izzet Pasha arrived in Jerusalem at the beginning of 1864 and served in this post until February 1867.
4   But see the introduction to No. 55, above.

they could not meet their tax payments, were even incapable of purchasing seed to renew their crops and, as a consequence, also suffered hunger. There were serious shortages in Jerusalem, with many having nothing to eat (see: Eliav, *Austrian Protection*, No. 135; Carmel, *Palästina-Chronik*, I, pp. 83–84, 91, 96). According to the Consul, this infestation of locusts exceeded in severity any other such plague in the past.

FO 78/1929 170558
Consular N° 14
Copy sent to Embassy

Jerusalem, June 11th 1866

My Lord,
I much regret to have to report, for Your Lordship's information, the destruction by Locusts of all the Crops, trees and plants of every description in this district, with the exception of the grain Crops, which happily had, for the most part, been gathered in, or are too far advanced in maturity to be devoured by these Insects. Of the Olive Crop, which, with the grain, is our staple product, not a vestige remains; and it is feared that the Trees themselves will be injured for some time to come, — for the Locusts, after baring them of every leaf, commenced strapping the bark off the younger branches. Nor is this all, for the probability is that these swarms, having laid their eggs in the country, will reappear next year in increased numbers.

Within living memory, no such visitation of Locusts as the present has been known in the country. On looking abroad, the scene that presents itself is sad in the extreme, — the fields bare, the trees leafless and stark as in mid-winter. Accounts received from other parts of the country state that the scourge is there as well.[1]

Should the apprehensions above referred to be realised, great distress will, I fear, prevail.

I purpose urging the Pasha to remit the tithes and land tax from the present year.

Occasional measures were taken to destroy the Locusts by the Authorities and the people but they were inadequate; and although more energetic

1    See the description of the locusts in Jaffa and its environs on 24 August 1865. It was then that tens of thousands of eggs were laid, from which the locusts hatched, to consume all the crops in the fields at the beginning of the summer of 1866. According to the writer, the locusts also invaded homes, and it was impossible to dispel them. As a "cure", the authorities ordered that every person would have to hand in five ounces of the pests, dead or alive, every day, under pain of fine (Carmel, *Palästina-Chronik*, I, pp. 84–85). Cf. a similar "treatment" for the locust infestation of 1915 (Eliav, *Austrian Protection*, p. 425); in this case, however, the requirement was to collect ten kilograms of locusts in five days.

means will probably be adopted, after this severe lesson, to destroy the eggs against next year, yet such are the countless myriads of these animals that one cannot be sanguine of success.

Noel Temple Moore

## 58   H.A. Khayat to N.T. Moore
## Establishment of an American Colony

Habib Assad Khayat was appointed Acting Vice-Consul in 1866 upon the death of his father (see above, No. 21, n. 1), but since this was not confirmed by the Ottoman authorities he was forced to resign in 1869.

The attempt to found a modern American colony on the outskirts of Jaffa was taken upon the initiative of George James Adams (1813–1880), who upon his arrival in Jaffa symbolically changed his first and middle names to Washington Joshua. Adams, who for several years had been a Mormon and had also been influenced by Millenarists, claimed in 1859 that God had called upon him to work for the revival of the Holy Land in anticipation of the imminent Second Coming of Christ and the return of the Jews to the land of their forefathers. In 1861, on the east coast of the United States, he founded the 'Church of the Messiah', through which he intended to realize his beliefs and plans. In 1862 he began to publish a periodical, *The Sword of Truth and the Harbinger of Peace*, as an informational organ, in which he also published many articles about events in Palestine. In 1865, accompanied by a friend, he set out for a tour of the Holy Land, arriving in the middle of the cholera epidemic. After visiting Jerusalem and other places, he decided that the Jaffa area was more suitable for the establishment of the colony. Before leaving Palestine, he asked Hermann Loewenthal, a German Jewish convert to Christianity, banker and businessman, to purchase lands for his society, the 'Palestine Emigration Association'. Upon his return to the United States, the American government requested of the Sublime Porte a Firman to enable the acquisition of land for settlement purposes, but the request was turned down. The negative reply was received after the colonists' ship had already sailed, and upon disembarking in Jaffa they were stunned to hear that the settlement had not been approved.

Adams, who referred to himself as the President of the 'Church of the Messiah', was a forceful and domineering person, who did not tolerate opposition or criticism, imposed his will on his followers and demanded total obedience. At the same time, however, he was a confirmed alcoholic, and the amounts of liquor he consumed dulled his senses and fueled his aggressive

231

behaviour. For the American colony in Jaffa, see: S. Eidelberg, "The Adams Colony in Jaffa 1866–1868," *Midstream* 3 (Summer 1957), pp. 52–61; P. Amman, "Prophet in Zion: The Saga of George Adams," *The New England Quarterly* 7 (1964), pp. 477–500; R.H. Holmes, *The Forerunners*, Independence MO 1981; R. Kark, *Jaffa — A City in Evolution*, Jerusalem 1990, pp. 84–88; Lipman, *America-Holy Land*, pp. 32–33; Lipman *Americans*, pp. 140 ff.; Carmel, *Palästina-Chronik*, I, pp. 87, 96–98.

FO 78/1929                                                       Jaffa 26 September 1866
Copy

Sir
I have the honor to report to you the arrival here on the 22nd Inst of an American Clipper the "Nelly Chapin" of 600 Tons, W Wass, Master, direct from Jonesport (near Boston) in 41 days.[1]
This Vessel brought 156 American Emigrants.[2] They belong to different states but the majority come from the state of Maine. They come to settle near Jaffa, with the object of cultivating the soil; the most of them are Farmers, Carpenters, Blacksmiths and Tradesmen, and they bring with them their implements, and wooden Houses all ready made, and easily put up.[3] They landed on Monday last the 24 September on the beach on the North side of the Town, where they have pitched tents temporarily until the whole of the Cargo is discharged from the Ship. They purpose in a few days to remove to a plot of land outside the Town which was purchased for them some months ago from Mr Loewenthal the United States Vice Consul here.[4] They intend to erect their houses on the ground and to cultivate the adjoining land which belongs to them and thus to maintain themselves.
The Colony is headed by the Revd Adams who is obeyed by all the

1    For a description of the ship, see: Holmes, *ibid.*, p. 135, and of the journey: *ibid.*, pp. 161–180. The captain of the vessel was Warren Wass.
2    According to Holmes, *ibid.*, p. 165, there were 167 passengers and crew on board. See also the passenger list, including 155 names, to which Adam's wife and daughter must be added (*ibid.*, p. 181).
3    After the passengers sold all their belongings, Adams had in his possession the sum of $43,000. Beside what is mentioned here, they also brought with them beasts of burden, tools, seeds, and furniture — all with the intention of founding a modern agricultural colony, from which nothing would be lacking.
4    Loewenthal, who had recently been appointed American Vice-Consul, was aware that the settlement had no license, and that the purchase of land would not be approved either. He tried his hand as well, hoping that in the end the Firman would be granted. He resigned his position in 1867, when the complete failure of the settlement attempt became clear.

Bretheren, as they call themselves Bretheren of the Church of the Messiah.

The ostensible and declared object of their leaving their Country (where they sold all they possessed) is out of a strong and earnest desire to live and die in the Holy Land, as they beleive [sic!] that ere long, great changes will take place i.e. as I hear from them, the gathering together of the Jews from all parts to this country and the advent of Christ.

They say that they do not come as Missionaries, but only to cultivate the land, to set a good example in Agriculture and trades, and to earn their livelihood, to live peaceably, and to submit to all the local Regulations and taxations.

They beleive [sic!] that some of them are part of the tribe of Ephraim,[5] and their chief the Revd Mr Adams is of Jewish descent,[6] he is a very energetic and enthusiastic man, and is respected and obeyed by all the bretheren.

The Local Authorities made no difficulties on their landing, the Mudir has been very civil to them, and has sent several Zabliehs[7] to guard their Tents. The Inhabitants seem pleased at their coming, and anticipate an opening and increase of trade in these parts.

It will be my duty to keep you informed of the further movements of the Colony.

H.A. Kayat

# 59  N.T. Moore to Embassy, Constantinople
## Construction of a Jaffa–Jerusalem Road

There were no paved roads in Palestine. In 1857, when Montefiore raised his proposal to lay a railroad line between Jaffa and Jerusalem, Austrian Consul Pizzamano made a counterproposal to pave a road between the two cities, which would constitute the main highway of the country, as a joint effort with European initiative (see above, No. 40, n. 4; Eliav, *Austrian Protection*, p. 25). Attempts were made to carry out the road project, and security along the route improved, but actual construction was never undertaken. Nevertheless, a large church bell was successfully brought from Jaffa to Jerusalem in 1864: the bell was put in a cylinder, which was rolled all the way by 150 Russian pilgrims.

---

5    For this belief, see: Holmes, *ibid.*, pp. 138–139, according to which some of the descendants of the tribe of Ephraim were dispersed among the peoples of the world.
6    This "report" is baseless, and is not mentioned in reliable sources.
7    Gendarmes.

Nazif Pasha, who became Governor in April 1867, resolved to pave the road without the aid of engineering experts, using conscript labour from Jerusalem, Jaffa, and the villages along the route. It was possible to be exempted from this forced labour upon payment of a "redemption" fee. The Jews of Jerusalem sought to free themselves from the construction work. In order to pay the "redemption", the Hakham Bashi, the chief rabbi, imposed a special tax on the purchase of kosher meat, as an addition to the *gabella* (the regular meat tax paid to the community). The Ashkenazim (Jews of European origin) rebelled against this decree because, as foreign subjects, they were exempt from the levy in any event. This opposition led to a dispute regarding the ritual slaughtering of meat, with the Ashkenazim demanding the right to conduct their own ritual slaughtering (see Hyamson, II, No. 252; Eliav, *German Policy*, Nos. 11–14; Eliav, *Yishuv*, pp. 158–159; Eliav, *Austrian Protection*, Nos. 49–50).

The road was completed within two years, but only a year later it was already pitted and barely passable for carriages, necessitating repairs. The roadway sank and the repairs were of little avail. Only in 1878 did regular public transportation begin along the Jaffa-Jerusalem road, though repairs were not completed until the end of 1888 (see: S. Avitzur, *One Hundred Years of the Jaffa-Jerusalem Road*, Tel Aviv, 1970 [Hebrew]).

FO 195/808 — N° 20                                   Jerusalem November 28th 1867
Copy sent Home (FO 78/1991)

Sir,

I have the satisfaction to report that at length a carriageable Road is being constructed between Jaffa and Jerusalem by the local Administration, on the system of "prestation", by which every male inhabitant of the two towns and of the intervening and neighbouring villages, between the ages of 15 and 60, is called upon to contribute five days gratuitous labour or thirty Piastres in lieu thereof.

Considering that little more than two months has elapsed since the works were commenced I found, on my recent return to Jerusalem, that very considerable progress had been made thanks to the impulse given to the works by Nazif Pasha,[1] who personally superintends and directs them with an amount of zeal and self-sacrifice worthy of high commendation, spending as His Excellency does the greater part of his time on the Road directing and encouraging the workmen.

1    Nazif Pasha served as Governor of Jerusalem from April 1867 to September 1869. The paving of the road apparently was his personal ambition, in anticipation of the expected visit of the Austrian Emperor, Franz Josef.

An expression of satisfaction on your part to the Pasha would I venture to think be very gratifying and encouraging to His Excellency, who has received expressions of commendation from the different foreign Embassies through their respective Consuls here.

It may be hoped that by next spring the road will be completed. It will then be open, I understand, to any company or private individual to establish a service of diligences, but under what conditions is not yet known.

N.T. Moore

# 60 Ch. Warren to N.T. Moore
## Excavations on the Temple Mount

The Palestine Exploration Fund (PEF) was established in London in June 1865 (see: V.D. Lipman, "The Origins of the Palestine Exploration Fund," *PEFQ* 1988, pp. 45–54). Over the years the emissaries of the Fund, all leading archaeologists, conducted many excavations which changed in great measure the knowledge of the Holy Land's past. The activities of the PEF also significantly strengthened Britain's political influence. The first expedition, headed by Charles Wilson, engaged in the mapping of Lebanon and Palestine. The second expedition, in 1867, was led by Lieutenant Charles Warren (1840–1928) of the Royal Engineers. Its main objective was the study of the Temple Mount and Jerusalem. Warren arrived in Jerusalem on 15 February 1867, bearing a letter from the Grand Vizier empowering him to conduct excavations everywhere, with the exception of the Temple Mount area and sites holy to Christians and Muslims. This limitation was used by the Governor to place obstacles in Warren's way. Consequently, Warren was not capable of fulfilling his original program, despite the long period of time he waited. He accordingly concentrated on excavations and research around the Temple Mount, in the study of the structures and the city walls. He published a summation of his activities and discoveries in his: *Underground Jerusalem*, London 1876. Warren's achievements laid the foundation for the archaeological and historical research of ancient Jerusalem. See also: Tibawi, chap. 8; Palestine Exploration Fund, *Our Work in Palestine*, London 1873.

JNUL 4°1513/66                                              Jerusalem 12th May 1868
Confidential

Sir,

With reference to the attitude assumed by the Local Government of

Jerusalem with regard to the excavations of the Palestine Exploration Fund[1] — I have the honor to make the following remarks which I request you will have the goodness to forward to the British Ambassador to the Porte together with your own view of the subject which I understand to be in coincidence with mine.

It appears from the Correspondence in the Consular Office that in the Vizierial letter authorising the agent of the P.E. Fund to make excavations in and about Jerusalem, an exception was made to the Haram Area under the misapprehension that it was inaccessible to Franks in general and that H.R.H. the Prince of Wales alone had entered there;[2] the fact being that Christians of all denominations are allowed to examine and walk about it.[3]

After fifteen months experience in Jerusalem, I find that there are no real obstacles to our digging openly in the Haram Area provided the Pacha is inclined to help us.

I have sounded the principal Effendis and local Officials and find that there is nothing at present to prevent our working in the Haram Area except the fanaticism of Nazif Pacha the Governor of Jerusalem.[4]

1    Warren describes Nazif Pasha as "an honest and weak man [who] became the willing tool of his advisors" (Warren, p. 9). According to the archaeologist, the members of the Governor's entourage tried to extort money from him for permission to conduct his excavations. Warren was forced to pay large sums of money, yet he was allowed to excavate around the Temple Mount only after exhausting negotiations which continued for two years. At first they attempted to stop his excavations on various pretexts (see the letter from the Pasha to Consul Moore, 22 February 1868, *ibid.*, pp. 387–390). After writing the letter published below, Warren decided to go to England and involve the Foreign Office, but no progress was attained in this manner as well (*ibid.*, pp. 392–395). Upon his return to Jerusalem, Warren attempted to come to some arrangement with Nazif that would allow the work to continue, even in a limited format, but neither Constantinople, and certainly not Jerusalem, were prepared to grant approval for Warren's program.

2    The first non-Muslim apparently was the American physician and missionary James Turner Barclay, who in 1854 had been summoned by the royal architect to advise him on repairs to the structures on the Temple Mount (see: Barclay, pp. 477, 483–383; Lipman, *Americans*, p. 100). Barclay took advantage of this opportunity to conduct a thorough survey of the Temple Mount, publishing his findings in his book (*ibid.*, pp. 485 ff.). Afterwards, Kiamil Pasha permitted the Duke of Brabant and the Duchess to visit the Temple Mount at the beginning of April 1855, also allowing entry to the Mount to the Austrian heir presumptive Maximilian (see above, No. 34, n. 2). The tour of the Prince of Wales was conducted in 1862 (see above, No. 52, n. 6); in the interim, other individuals, including Montefiore, were also granted permission to visit the Temple Mount. Warren utilized the erroneous claim that the Prince of Wales had been the first Christian to visit the Temple Mount "alone" to indicate that precedents had already been set, and that in practice the Mount was open to visitors and tourists.

3    It already was the practice to allow any Christian to visit the site, upon payment of a certain sum.

4    As a pious Muslim, Nazif Pasha sought to reinstate the prohibition against visits to the Temple Mount by non-Muslims, just as he tried to delay Warren's excavations.

One Effendi who has behaved most liberally and in whose grounds I am working tells me "I am getting into difficulties, the Pacha tells me that if I do not stop your work, he will made difficulties for me next time I go to the Serai." —

All the Effendis of any note have given me to understand that they have no objection to our working in the Haram Area. I have asked them to put it in writing, they say they cannot as the Pacha would get their names and crush them one by one.

The whole difficulty comes from this Pacha nominated by the Porte and it appears that if pressure were put upon him he must yield; even if the strongest Vizierial letter were sent out here, he, if he does not get private instructions from his Government to assist, can call up each Effendi separately and terrify him into making statements which would obstruct the work.

Nazif Pacha is acknowledged by his own creed to be a fanatic and it is quite hopeless and too expensive for Europeans to try and bring him round to look with indifference on our digging in the Haram Area so long as his own Government does not attempt to cause him to alter his views.[5]

Charles Warren[6]
Lieut. Royal Engineers

# 61   N.T. Moore to Foreign Secretary
Failure of the American Colony

The American colony, initially founded in September 1866 (see above, No. 58), was doomed to total failure. The first settlers were forced to contend with many difficulties. They suffered from a climate to which they were not accustomed and from agricultural problems unknown to them. They were soon in the throes of disappointment and despair, blaming Adams and his

5    The negotiations continued for about a year. This file contains additional letters from Warren to the Consul from 1869, in which the archaeologist complains of the Governor's interference with the excavations. In practice, Warren never received permission to excavate on the Temple Mount and was forced to content himself with excavations in its vicinity. He faced not only with the opposition of the Governor but also the hostile attitude of the Muslim populace, which was enraged by excavations of holy sites. Despite all the obstacles and delays, Warren nevertheless can claim impressive achievements.

6    Warren conducted the first methodical archaeological survey of Jerusalem. In addition to *Underground Jerusalem*, he co-authored *Recovery of Jerusalem*, London 1871, with C.R. Conder, and together they conducted the monumental Survey of Western Palestine, later published in several volumes.

domineering wife for their failures. Adams' alcoholism grew more severe, he borrowed sums of money he was incapable of repaying, and his despotic behaviour led to fierce quarrels with his fellow colonists. In the meantime, the United States government also had begun to investigate the entire venture. The magnitude of the failure became clear from the reports it received, especially since a Firman permitting settlement had not been obtained. As conditions deteriorated, fueled by the disappointing crop, some of the settlers slowly began to leave the site. Many of the children died. By the spring of 1868 only the Adams family and twenty three additional people, half of them children, remained. At the beginning of July the Adams family also left, on the pretext of going abroad to raise funds to rehabilitate the colony, as this letter also reports. Twenty-two souls remained. The German Colony was founded on the ruins of the Adams venture (see the sources cited above, in No. 58).

FO 78/2048                                           Jerusalem, July 2nd 1868

My Lord,
    I have the honour to state that Mr. Adams, the organizer and president of the late American colony at Jaffa has left that place in order, as he has announced, to proceed to England with the object of inducing by means of public meetings and lectures, English people to come out to Jaffa to revive the Colony.
    I deem it my duty to report Mr. Adams' intentions to your Lordship. Mr. Adams has not proved himself by his management of the Jaffa colony a fit person to carry out a scheme of this nature; nor is public report or the opinion of his own Consular Authorities favourable to him in other respects.[1] It would be deplorable were he to succeed, by misrepresentations, in bringing out a number of our countrymen to encounter troubles, loss and disappointment, to which be added the loss of health in a climate very trying, during the intense heat of summer, to natives of a cold northern country.
    The failure of the American settlement at Jaffa, indeed, is but a repetition of the fate of previous similar experiments made under better auspices. In present circumstances, both as regards the country itself and the still unsettled question of land tenure by foreign subjects in Turkey — a question naturally of primary importance to the settlers — there seems little hope of success attending these enterprizes.

                                                        Noel Temple Moore

1    Adams continued with his family to Philadelphia, where he had spent his youth. He
     attempted to restore the Church of the Messiah, and abstained from drinking alcohol. He
     died there on 11 May 1880.

## 62 N.T. Moore to Sir H. Elliot
## Palestine as a Separate Eyalet

Palestine had been divided into seven Sanjaks since the restoration of Ottoman rule in 1841. The largest Sanjak was that of Jerusalem. Its eastern border was the Jordan River, its northern boundary extended to the northern extremity of the Sharon Plain, near Caesarea, and in the south it included the former Gaza district, the Negev, and the Sinai Peninsula up to the border delineated in 1841. The Consuls, the representatives of the Great Powers in Jerusalem, were not pleased with this administrative division of the country. It posed difficulties for consular efforts throughout the whole of Palestine, since some of the northern Sanjaks were subordinate to the Vali of Beirut and others to the Vali of Damascus. In 1854 the Jerusalem Sanjak was officially declared an independent province, directly subordinate to Constantinople, but its administrative autonomy was cancelled shortly thereafter. Now, in 1872, the provinces were redefined. The Sanjaks of Acre (including all of northern Palestine) and of Belka (comprising Nablus, Samaria, and Transjordan) were added to that of Jerusalem. According to this redivision, the Sanjak of Jerusalem was to be an independent province (Eyalet of Palestine) headed by a Vali. The Consuls were quite satisfied with this administrative change, which was likely to make their work significantly easier. However, after a short time the Sublime Porte in Constantinople reversed its decision and once again separated the Sanjaks of Acre and Belka from the Jerusalem district, which, however, retained its autonomy and from 1874 on was directly answerable to Constantinople (see Schölch, pp. 21–22).

FO 195/994 — N° 6; FO 78/22427                                   Jerusalem, July 27th 1872
Copy sent Home

Sir
     Your Excellency is doubtless cognisant of the recent erection of Palestine into a separate Eyalet by the addition of the Liwas of the Balka and Acre to that of Jerusalem, and the appointment of Surreya Pasha to be its Vali.[1]
     That functionary arrived a fortnight ago, and had hardly assumed the Government when he was apprised by a telegram from the Porte that the

---

1    Sureya Pasha, who had already served as Governor of the Jerusalem district in 1857–1865 (see above, No. 39, n. 7), was Vali in Aleppo during that year, and he now agreed to serve as Governor of the new province. After the Jerusalem province returned to its former dimensions, Sureya refused to continue as Governor of Jerusalem, leaving his post two months later.

annexed Liwas had been again severed from Jerusalem in consequence of some new scheme for the Government of Syria.[2]

The first mentioned decision of the Porte has long been looked forward to as a most desirable improvement in the administration of Palestine — a view I fully share.[3] The Balka, at least, which includes the district east of the Jordan, naturally appertains to the Government of Jerusalem from its immediate contiguity thereto, the constant close commercial and general intercourse between the two districts, and the community of their interests. Their separate administration is therefore fraught with serious public inconveniences. So much is this felt, that on the receipt of the above-mentioned intelligence, my German, Russian, Austrian, and Italian[4] Colleagues (the French Consul is absent) at once communicated by telegraph with their respective Embassies with a view to endeavour to maintain the decision of the Porte constituting the Eyalet of Palestine, — a step in which I was asked to join, but content myself with offering these observations to Your Excellency.[5] Many British travellers and explorers visit the country east of the Jordan, starting from, and generally returning to, Jerusalem; in case of any difficulty, I have to address myself to the Vali at Damascus.[6] A case in point, amongst others, as to the inconvenience of the present system, is furnished by the detention of the Revd Dr Tristram and his party, in February last, at Kerak,[7] which is so near to Jerusalem as to

2    The two districts were included in the province of Beirut; afterwards they were made subordinate to the Vali of Damascus, while in 1888 they were once again transferred to the Vali of Beirut, upon the reestablishment of the province of Lebanon.

3    The Consuls not only regarded this as alleviating their activity, they also claimed that it was the desire of the population and that the new administrative framework would advance the development of Palestine. The Sublime Porte, however, acted on different considerations. There apparently arose opposition to the concentration of all Christian and Jewish holy sites in a single district, thus furthering the activity of the European Powers, and possibly also creating a Jewish national problem. It may be assumed that administrative division was intended to enable the Ottoman authorities to increase their control and also to prevent the unification of the districts into a single national unit.

4    The Italian Consulate was established in 1872, with Rege de Donato serving as the first Consul. In the words of the British Consul, "France has persistently opposed the establishment of an Italian Consulate ... [but] the heads of the Latin religious establishments, who are all Italians, have been strongly urging. There can be little doubt that [the establishment of the Consulate] will have the effect of weakening to a certain extent the paramount influence of France in respect of that Protectorate" (FO 78/2242, 15 March 1872; FO 195/994).

5    Even regarding such an important issue, Moore preferred to be cautious, and not to act without the advance approval of the Ambassador.

6    The district of Belka-Nablous, which included Transjordan, was subordinate to the Vali of Damascus.

7    See: H. B. Tristram, *The Land of Moab*, New York 1873, pp. 99 ff.). Henry Baker Tristram (1822–1906), clergyman, archaeologist, and naturalist, devoted his researches to Palestine. He visited the country several times. His *magnum opus* is *The Land of Israel: a Journal of Travels with Reference to Its Physical History*, London 1865 and many later editions.

240

be visible from it,[8] and yet the Governor has no jurisdiction there, and the affair has to be treated with the Vali at Damascus; five months have elapsed since the occurrence but I have not yet been able to obtain from Soubhi Pasha restitution of the money extorted from the travellers or punishment of the guilty parties.

Personally, Surreya Pasha has the advantage of long previous experience of the country, having already been Governor of Jerusalem for several years, and his re-appointment has been received with general satisfaction. I understand that it is his intention to resign the post if its reduction is maintained.

Noel Temple Moore

## 63   N.T. Moore to H. Amzalak
## Appointment as Consular Agent at Jaffa

Upon the death of Assad J. Khayat on 19 November 1865 (see above, No. 21, n. 1), Moore recommended that his son Habib Assad Khayat be appointed to succeed him (see above, introduction to No. 58). Consul Moore took advantage of this opportunity to demand that the diplomatic representation in Jaffa be made subordinate to that of the Consulate in Jerusalem, arguing that "Jaffa being the port of Jerusalem, and the Turkish Authorities there are subordinate to the Governor of Jerusalem" (FO 78/1875, Moore to Clarendon, 28 November 1865). Moore's suggestion was approved on 12 May 1866, and Habib Assad Khayat was appointed Vice-Consul. He was given a yearly salary of £100 and permission to engage in commerce, and made subordinate to the Consulate in Jerusalem (FO 78/1929). The Consulate regarded Habib as "a naturalized British subject," but the Turkish authorities refused to recognize him in any official capacity, claiming that technically he was an Ottoman subject. As a result, Habib resigned in August 1869. Moore then decided to recommend the appointment of the Jewish merchant Haim Amzalak ("the only eligible British subject residing at that port [...] He has some knowledge of Italian, but none of English" — FO 78/2697, 18 September 1869) as a Consular Agent serving without salary. Moore also tried to persuade Habib to withdraw his resignation; since, however, the Sublime Porte refused to confirm his appointment, Moore dropped the matter and,

8   Kerak, the ancient Qir-Moav, the largest city in south Jordan, 282 km. distant from Jerusalem. It is difficult to accept the Consul's claim that the town could be seen from Jerusalem.

on 26 October 1871, once more raised his proposal regarding Amzalak. It was approved on 4 September 1872 (FO 78/2514), followed by the issuance of these credentials.

ISA 123/1/14                                            Jerusalem, November 14th, 1872

Mr Haim Amzalak, Jaffa[1]

In virtue of the Authorisation which I have received from Her Majesty's Secretary of State for Foreign Affairs I hereby appoint and constitute you to be British Consular Agent at the Porte of Jaffa, acting under my immediate directions.

The Imperial Berat recognising you in that capacity having been presented to the Governor of Jerusalem, I transmit to you herewith a letter from His Excellency to the Kaimakam of Jaffa, giving him the necessary instructions in that regard.

As you are unacquainted with the English language,[2] you will understand that this appointment is liable at any time to revision, if hereafter a properly qualified person for the appointment should be found, and that it gives you no claim on Her Majesty's Government when your services cease.[3]

You will keep some person in your office during the travelling season, who is conversant with English [...]

Not doubting the zeal and assiduity which you will display in the discharge of your duties,

                                                            Noel Temple Moore

1    Haim Amzalak (1828–1916), born into a wealthy family, settled in Jaffa at the end of the 1850s and engaged in international trade, banking, and real estate. In 1871 he was appointed Portuguese Vice-Consul. He agreed to Moore's proposal, and represented British interests with honour for a long period of time, dealing also with Jewish immigration and commercial activity. In 1889 he was presented with a medal as a mark of satisfaction with his service. He remained in his post until May 1903, when he reached the age of 75 (see: Glass & Kark, pp. 114 ff.; see also below, No. 78).

2    This was Amzalak's main drawback. In 1891 Dickson requested a special allowance for himself, "because it was necessary to either correct or rewrite Mr. Amzalak's letters," and the Consul was obliged to personally handle part of the British business at Jaffa. Dickson referred to Amzalak as "Acting Vice-Consul," even though he was only a Consular Agent.

3    On 14 November 1872 Moore informed the Foreign Office of Amzalak's appointment as Consular Agent (FO 78/2697).

# 64 N.T. Moore to S. Locock
## Murder of a Jew and the Trial

Hyamson devotes only two lines to the trial of Simeon Sakolin, a Russian
Jew under British protection (Hyamson, No. 279). Since, however, the trial,
the verdict, and its repercussions shed light upon Ottoman judicial practice,
the following despatch deserves to be published in its entirety. The Consul
relates the entire episode to the Ambassador in Constantinople, requesting
that he take action in order to ensure the proper pension for the widow and
four orphans who were left penniless upon the death of the head of the family.

FO 195/1047 — N° 2                                Jerusalem February 4th 1874
Copy to be sent Home

Sir,

I have the honour to inform you that in the month of July last, a Jew
under British protection, of the name of Simeon Sakolin, was shot by a
Turkish Zaptie and died on the following day. Sakolin had been a Russian
Jew who had passed under British protection under the arrangement of 1848.

The deceased was a milkman by trade; on the morning of the day on
which he met his fate, at about 1 o'clock A.M., he was going from his house,
situated outside the City, to a neighbouring village to get a supply of milk. On
passing by the guardhouse, close to one of the City Gates, he was fired at by
the Zaptie on duty there, Ibrahim El-Birawi, with the fatal effect already
mentioned. It was established in evidence that he carried a lantern.[1]

I attended the trial; the culpability of El-Birawi was established on his
own previous confession at the preliminary inquiry immediately after the
event, and by the evidence, and he was sentenced by the Turkish Tribunal to
fifteen years penal servitude in the bagnio, conformably to Art. 174 of the
Criminal Code. At the trial he denied his own confession, evidently having
been taught to do so.

The reason assigned by El-Birawi for the deed was that he challenged
Sakolin three times but received no answer, that he then fired upon him,
taking him to be a robber or a hyena, and because he had understood that if no
answer was returned to a challenge thrice repeated it was the duty of a sentinel

---

1    The authorities required every person walking about at night to carry a lantern.

to fire. There was no previous acquaintance between the men, so there could have been no malice prepense.

The case was next removed to the Mehkeme for judgment according to the Sheriat, with a view to obtain the compensation of the Diyyé, or blood money, for the heirs. The Cadi decided that the case was not proved against El-Birawi according to the requirements of that law, without, however, stating the grounds for this decision. Thus we have the anomaly of two verdicts in the same case contradicting on another.

The Cadi left Jerusalem, his term of office having expired, immediately after issuing his Ilam. The new Cadi, who arrived a month after the trial, and of course had taken no part in it, has thought fit to append to the sentence an opinion that the punishment inflicted is excessive, and suggesting two years' imprisonment in accordance with Art. 182 of the Criminal Code. But not only is this article not applicable to the circumstances of the case, but the Cadi has conveniently ignored the clause in that article providing for the rights of the heirs under the Sheriat law. With the Ilam of his predecessor, however, he declines to interfere.

The Sentence and all other documents have been submitted to the Porte, as required by regulation.

Even should the Ilam of the late Cadi be valid, the case is one in which, under the circumstances, the Porte might think fit to grant a compassionate allowance to the unfortunate widow and four young children of Sakolin, who are left destitute by his death.

Noel Temple Moore

# 65  N.T. Moore to A.H. Layard
# Deplorable Situation of Palestine

The severe economic crisis that hit Palestine in the wake of the Turkish-Russian war of 1876–78 left its mark in all areas, not passing over the Jewish community which is mentioned only incidentally in the following report. Only a few lines were published by Hyamson (No. 297); however, due to the importance of the matter, the main passages from the Consul's survey of the situation are cited here.

Sir,

I have the honour to report to Your Excellency that at no former period of my sixteen years' residence in Palestine has the condition of the country been so deplorable as at present.

Various causes contribute to this depression. The drain of nearly all the able-bodied men for the late war, scanty harvests, insufficient rain, high prices, and the ruinous loss inflicted on hundreds by the stoppage of the payment of the interest on Turkish Government securities, have produced their natural consequences, in wide-spread destitution and industrial and commercial stagnation. Wheat and grain are at double their normal prices; this year's crops are again meagre; of the 12,000 conscripts and Redif who were sent to the seat of war from this Liwa, probably not more than a quarter have returned. Thus the prospect of better times coming in the natural course of things is unpromising in the extreme.

Instead of combatting these evils by remedial measures, the conduct of those in authority greatly aggravates them. The corruption and endless abuses in every branch of Turkish administration are too well known to Your Excellency to need any description from me. These are as rife as ever. The greatest sufferers thereby are incontestably the Mussulman rural population, the bone and sinew of the country, and whose numbers, as compared with that of the non-Mussulman inhabitants, is as four to one. Whilst every other community can, and does, in case of need, appeal to the protection and sympathy of powerful advocates, the Mussulman has no one to look to.

The actual Governor, Raouf Pasha,[1] is a well-intentioned and, as all believe, an honest man, but he is deficient in energy and initiative; but even were this otherwise, the task of reforming abuses which are traditional and systematic in the various departments of the administration is more than any one man can accomplish, unless under a thorough change of conditions. To give one or two instances of passive maladministration and improvidence; the one carriageable road in the whole Liwa, — that between Jaffa and Jerusalem, constructed some years ago by Nazif Pasha, — has been allowed to fall into such disrepair that it is now dangerous to travel on it in the strongest-made

---

1    Mehmed Raouf Pasha served as Governor of Jerusalem from June 1877 to April 1889, the longest term held by any Governor of the district. He was a nationalist Turk, who strictly enforced the decrees regarding Jewish immigration and the restrictions on land purchases by Jews, and adopted a hostile attitude towards the *Yishuv*. In 1889 he was appointed Vali in Beirut. The Consul's negative opinion of the Pasha is surprising, because the latter was known to be a talented administrator.

cart,[2] and yet the income of the road from the toll levied on all animals going over it, as well as wheeled conveyances, is between £600 and £700 a year. — The country having been denuded of trees which are cut down and sold for fire-wood, the peasants next took to digging up the roots which now constitute the common fuel of every house and establishment in the town, and this has been going on for years unchecked by the authorities. It is believed that this deforestation, which is further helped by the flocks and herds which roam over every hill and valley and crop up every green shoot that shows itself above the ground, reacts upon the climate and contributes to the short rainfalls now become so frequent, with all their attendant evils.

In strong contrast with this inertia of the rulers of the country is the activity displayed by foreigners. I have already reported on the Russian establishment which dot the neighbourhood of Jerusalem and elsewhere in Palestine.[3] The several German settlements are prospering;[4] whilst the influx continues of foreign Jews, mostly Polish and German, who, availing themselves of the right now professed by foreigners of holding real estate in Turkey, are buying land and building houses in all directions. At this moment the French are particularly active; four imposing new Latin edifices are rising simultaneously, three at Jerusalem and one at Jaffa, for educational and charitable purposes, namely (1) an orphanage and school capable of accommodating 200 boys, building with money collected in France and other Roman Catholic Countries; (2) a boarding school of the French fraternity of Frères de la Doctrine Chrétienne; (3) a Hospital building by a French philanthropist; and (4) a vast Hospital at Jaffa, also by a French body.[5]

It is not known whether the scheme of reform for Syria, which it is understood Midhat Pasha[6] has prepared and submitted to the Porte, includes

2    See above, No. 59.
3    In a report from 18 December 1871, Moore notes that the Russians were purchasing properties on a large scale and establishing many institutions. Their acqustions included land in Hebron, Beit Jala, on the Mount of Olives, and in Ein Karem. They also founded hostels for pilgrims in Jaffa, Haifa, Nazareth, and Ramla.
4    The Templars, a pietistic sect from Württemberg in southern Germany, set as their goal the "ingathering of the People of God" in the Holy Land. With this in mind, they began to settle in Palestine in 1868. Their first colonies, in Haifa and Jaffa, were founded in 1869, the colony of Sarona in 1879, and that in Jerusalem in 1873. The German colonists were pioneers in the introduction of modern agricultural techniques to Palestine.
5    For the French institutions in Jerusalem, see: Ben-Arieh, II, pp. 139–140, 285–290. The orphanage was founded in 1874 by Alphonse Ratisbonne. The hospital is the St. Louis Hospital. The cornerstone for the new building outside the walls was laid in May 1879. The hospital in Jaffa was founded in 1876 and conducted by the St. Joseph Sisters.
6    Midhat Pasha (1822–1884), an important statesman, was appointed Grand Vizier in 1876 by the new Sultan, Abdul Hamid II, who promised important reforms for the empire. After a short time, however, he was dismissed, and even exiled. In 1878 he was appointed Governor of Syria and once again proposed reforms in the provinces, but was again

the Liwa of Jerusalem, which is politically and administratively independent of Damascus.

N.T. Moore

## 66  N.T. Moore to Earl Granville
## Increase of French Influence

In the second half of the nineteenth century, the quiet competition between France and England in the region intensified, mainly in Syria and in Palestine. The British Consuls apprehensively observed French attempts at economic penetration and new initiatives, while it was difficult to point to similar British activity. The following document reflects the concern of the Consul at Jerusalem in the light of increased French activity and influence, in addition to the matters mentioned above (No. 65).

FO 78/3131 — N° 5                                              Jerusalem May 19th 1880
Political — Confidential

My Lord,
    I have the honour to report that for the last year or so there have been rumours of projected French enterprises in Palestine on an extensive scale. Various movements and proceedings from time to time seemed to lend colour to reports which have now assumed a tangible shape. The local Administrative Council has recently reported favourable to the Central Government on a French scheme for the navigation of the Dead Sea by means of steam vessels for the transport of the produce of the regions lying to eastward of it, to this side by direct transit from shore to shore, instead of the present circuitous and expensive carriage round it by beasts of burden.[1]

deposed after only twenty months in office. In May 1879 he was arrested, tried, and banished. He died in exile (see also below, No. 66).

1    The French had already exhibited interest in the Dead Sea during the journey in 1850/1 of the French officer de Saulcy, who published the results of his research in *Voyage au tour de la Mer Morte*, Paris 1858. In 1864 a special expedition, including a geologist, an architect, and a naval officer, set out for the Dead Sea region. This expedition conducted a comprehensive study of the area, which it later published in four volumes. The following

The rumours above alluded to include in these projects the construction of a harbour at Jaffa and a Railway to Jerusalem[2] and other parts of the country, and the conception now reported would seem to be a link, as it were, in the chain, for it cannot be supposed that the passage of the Dead Sea represents the whole or final extent of the enterprise into which most probably enters the exploitation of the minerals — bitumen, sulphur, petroleum etc. — to be found on the shores of the Dead Sea.

Yesterday Captain de Sorcy, Military Attaché to the French Embassy at Constantinople, left Jerusalem after a visit of about ten days, to resume his tour in Syria; he travels in his uniform and is transported from place to place on the sea-board in a man-of-war. His visit is generally believed to be in the nature of a mission to Syria; that the projects above referred to engaged his attention during his stay here is highly probable. He obtained from Midhat Pasha a promise of an early expedition of troops to be stationed at Kerak, a considerable town on the east of the Dead Sea, now in a condition of lawlessness and therefore a menace to the success of the Scheme in question.[3]

Raouf Pasha the Governor of Jerusalem is known for his French proclivities.[4]

M. de Sorcy is very unfavourably impressed by Midhat Pasha, whom he accuses of plotting to secure for himself eventual supreme and independent domination in Syria.[5]

I am informed that a short while ago a remarkable article appeared in the Globe Newspaper, of Paris, advocating, from a political point of view, the founding by France of such enterprises and interests in Palestine in view of increased British influence in these parts arising from the preponderating interest of England in the Suez Canal, and the acquisition of Cyprus.[6] In

planned navigation on the Dead Sea apparently never came to fruition, and it was not until the 1890s that the Turks instituted a sort of ferry in the Sea; this attempt, however, was short-lived.

2   The plan to build a harbour in Jaffa was presented only in 1882 by an Austrian engineer, who had previously built the harbour in Trieste; the project in Jaffa, however, was never implemented. In the early 1870s a French engineer was granted a Firman for the laying of a railroad line from Jaffa to Jerusalem, but the line was not built, and the Firman was revoked eighteen months later. The French did not despair and continued to survey the route of the planned railroad. Only in 1888 did Joseph Navon, a Jerusalem Jew, receive the concession for the railroad. Due, however, to a lack of funds, he was forced to sell the concession to a French corporation (see below, No. 69). The Turks undoubtedly preferred the Jewish entrepreneur from Jerusalem to the representatives of foreign Powers, of whom they were apprehensive.

3   See above, No. 62, n. 8.

4   See above, No. 65, n. 1.

5   See above, No. 65, n. 6.

6   Cyprus was bought by Britain in 1878, after the conclusion of the Russo-Turkish War and the Congress of Berlin.

former despatches I have drawn attention to the recent marked extension of French establishments and institutions and influence here, and the high ground taken by French agents in their dealing with the local authorities.

Noel Temple Moore

# 67 J. Schmidt to Earl Granville
# Report on Haifa

The Vice-Consul at Haifa, Dr. J. Schmidt, took advantage of his visit to London to report to the Foreign Secretary on the problems of his post. Not only did Schmidt serve without salary, he did not even receive an allotment to cover his expenses, which included postage, travel, and rent. He describes some of the extensive activity in Haifa of the representatives of the other Powers, especially of France, who had at their disposal Dragomans and Kavasses, while he had to make do with only a single Dragoman, who also did not receive any salary — for a jurisdiction that covered all of northern Palestine. His description is formulated as a memorandum, which does not even bear Schmidt's signature; it may be assumed that an official in the Foreign Office drafted it at Schmidt's request, because the Vice-Consul was not fluent in English.

FO 78/3536                                    London, June 19th 1883

Memorandum to the Right Honourable Earl Granville K.G.
Secretary of State for Foreign Affairs etc. etc. etc.
presented by Dr Schmidt, British Vice-Consul at Caiffa.[1]

Caiffa, on the Syrian Coast between Beyrout and Jaffa, is a seaport

---

[1] Vice-Consul Rogers served in Haifa until 1861 (see above, No. 28, n. 4), when he was succeeded by Thomas Backhouse Sandwith (1831–1900), who filled this post for four years, from July 1861 to 1865. A new Vice-Consul was not appointed to fill the position, and for fourteen years Finzi (see above, introduction to No. 28) was also responsible for Haifa. Not until 1879, upon Finzi's resignation, did the Consul-General in Beirut, Eldridge, renew the post of Vice-Consul in Haifa, appointing Dr. Johannes Schmidt (1850–1910), a physician of German extraction born in the Caucasus, bearing a Russian passport, as Vice-Consul for Haifa and all northern Palestine (FO 78/2357a, Eldridge to Salisbury, 12 April 1879). According to Eldridge, the Russian Consul-General at first raised difficulties because of the fact that Schmidt was a Russian subject, but he later dropped his opposition. Schmidt became a British protégé and was appointed Vice-Consul, serving without pay.

town with six thousand inhabitants and from its situation and other advantages is rapidly increasing in population and commerce. Its harbour is the best upon the Coast of Syria and is so well protected by its surrounding hills as natural Breakwaters that it is constantly resorted to in stormy weather as a Harbour of Refuge. British Men of War come in, whilst the Mercantile vessels of such lines as Papayanni's, Moss', Bell's Mail steamers and others call here to load cargoes of Grain, Cereals and other articles of exportation. The Austrian Lloyd steamers also call regularly in passing from Alexandria to Beyrout. — The commercial and industrial prospects of Caiffa and the neighbouring country are increasing every year, there is a thriving German Colony of 72 families numbering about 350 souls — which has been remarkably successful in bringing its land into cultivation, possessing also both steam-and wind mills and a soap manufactory.[2] They have also effected a great improvement in the District by the making of Roads, especially in the construction of a good highway for carts and other vehicles to Nazareth,[3] by which not only that ancient town has now been brought into communication with the Seaboard but also the important district round Galilee, Tiberias and Safed, where we have at the present time more than one thousand souls British subjects and protéges entitled to British protection, and it would be a great advantage to these people if our Agents at Tiberias and Safed would be officially recognised by the local authorities as the Agents of some other European Powers are, and if possible they should also have one dragoman and one cavass; at Nazareth where there are large English Schools and Missionary Establishments we have *no* local British Representative as the French Convents possess. —

Dr Schmidt, who has the honour to present this memorandum to Lord Granville, has been eight years resident at Caiffa, the last four years as British Vice-Consul, — and being now in England for a short time he ventures to ask His Lordship's kind attention to the facts thus brought to His notice, — and especially would Dr Schmidt ask for Lord Granville's kind consideration of the position the British Vice Consulate occupies at Caiffa. The increasing commerce and mercantile importance of that Port requires continual and often arduous attention on the part of the Consul, his advice, assistance or intervention being frequently requested, and it is highly important in these Eastern Countries that the position and prestige of a Consul be adequately maintained.

2   The German Colony in Haifa was established in 1869 and developed at a rapid pace. It exerted great influence upon the development of the city as a whole, thanks to the Germans' superb technical knowledge and economic initiative. Their soap factory was equipped with modern machinery, and in fact was the first industrial enterprise in Haifa. It produced high quality soap, some of which was exported to Germany and the United States.

All the other European Vice Consuls at Caiffa — the French, German, Austrian, Prussian, Greek, Belgian and Spanish as well as the American and Persian — have dragomans and cavasses attached to their respective Consulates either two or three dragomans and two or three cavasses both for Caiffa and Akka, — whilst the British Consulate is only allowed one! for Caiffa and none for Akka — the residence of the Mutessarif and of the Courts of Appeal for the whole Sandjak of Akka. The difference is especially marked in the case of the French Vice Consul who has not only three Dragomans and three cavasses since many years but is also allowed ten thousand francs pro annum, — whilst the British Vice Consul receives no salary whatever! All our dragomans and cavasses are *unpaid* and selected of the better and quieter class of the population so that an augmentation of our Consular staff would cause to H.M. Government neither expenses nor much trouble and such an increase is accorded by the treaty with the Sublime Porte. Having continually a large correspondence in Arabic with the five local authorities of Caiffa, Akka, Nazareth, Tiberias and Safed, being compelled to see personally some of these authorities and to send often a Dragoman with our British claimants to the Courts of Justice — especially if there is any case of appeal to Akka: it is quite impossible to fullfill all the Consular duties with only one dragoman who — being unpaid — is often abroad occupied by his own business. All the other Vice Consuls that live at Caiffa have a dragoman and a cavass at Akka so that the Sublime Porte could not reasonably refuse the appointment of a Dragoman at a place which is not the Consul's residence. —

Dr Schmidt would also respectfully and earnestly draw Your Lordship's kind attention to the fact that he not only receives no allowance whatever — even for necessary expenses — but hitherto he has been obliged to find at his own cost such requisites as flags, and also to pay out of his own pocket the charges for postage and telegrams transmitted on the business of the Consulate.[4]

Her Majesty's Government would do a great act of humanity if they would continue to accord their precious protection to the poor Russian Jews as during the last 30 years, without this powerful British protection this poor people would be nearly lost considering the great abuses etc etc of the local Turkish authorities.[5] —

3    In 1873 the Germans, pioneers in public transportation in Palestine, laid the road from Haifa to Nazareth at their own expense, and introduced the use of wagons for passengers and freight. They also maintained regular transportation to Acre and to Tiberias.
4    In response to this memorandum, which is limited to the question of expenses, he was informed of the decision to provide him with a flag and to authorize the Consulate General in Beirut to reimburse him for expenses (FO 78/3536, 30 June 1883). Nothing was mentioned about staff.
5    The reference is to the hundreds of Russian Jewish immigrants who had arrived at the

It may perhaps be allowed to observe, that Dr Schmidt never issued any new Certificate of Registration to persons not entitled to British protection — as well proved by the Archives of the Consulate. —

Dr Schmidt trusts that Lord Granville will be willing to consider kindly the points thus brought to His Lordship's notice, and that He will give such instructions on the matters referred to as will secure what is requisite to maintain the position of the Vice Consulate at Caiffa;[6] he was encouraged by Lord Edmund Fritz Maurice, H.M. Under-Secreaty of State for Foreign Affairs and by Mr Heel of the Consular Department to expose the before mentioned questions to Your Lordship. —

# 68   Ch. Eyres to J. Eldridge
## Report on a Visit to Northern Palestine

In 1885 new regulations were issued governing eligibility for British protection by former Russian Jews, with the object of significantly limiting their numbers (see Hyamson, Nos. 311–314). One requirement was that each protected individual report once per year to the nearest British Consulate to renew his status. On 8 January 1885 Consul-General Eldridge, the author of the new regulations, proposed that his official representative tour northern Palestine, especially Tiberias and Safed, to issue renewed documents of protection, because the majority of the many Jews living in these cities under British protection were infirm and impoverished, and they could not be required to make the exhausting journey to Haifa for this purpose (Hyamson, No. 314). This trip either was not undertaken, or did not produce results. The local Turkish governors took advantage of the situation and refused to recognize British protection for these Jews, demanding that they produce valid, authorized documents. The protests of the Consul-General and of the Ambassador in Constantinople were to no avail; the Sublime Porte supported the position of its local officials.

Not before March 1888 would Eyres go to the north to renew the documents

outset of the wave of immigration known as 'the First Aliya' in 1882–83 and had settled in Haifa and northern Palestine.

6   On 4 January 1888 Schmidt requested that he be paid a salary, since his duties as Vice-Consul had greatly expanded and took much of his time. He emphasized that all the other Vice-Consuls received a salary. The Foreign Office refused his request (FO 78/4122, 30 November 1888). Schmidt resigned in 1892, and once again Haifa was left without a British Vice-Consul.

of protection. Sir Henry Charles Eyres (b. 1856) was Vice-Consul in Beirut, 1885–1890. During 1890–1896 he served as Consul in Damascus, and in 1896–1914 as Consul-General in Constantinople.

FO 195/1613                                                          Beirut 12 April. 1888
Copy

Sir,

I have the honour to report that in accordance with your instructions I left Beirut on the 14th Ultimo for the purpose of visiting the district of Acre in order to register British Subjects and Russian Jews under British Protection residing in that district. I followed the usual route along the the coast to Caiffa returning by Nazareth Tiberias Safed Nabatieh and Sidon, the whole journey occupying 16 days.

I issued in all 183 certificates of which 44 were given gratis, more persons than usual being unable to pay the fee on account of the increasing poverty of the Jewish population of those places and also owing to the fact that the feast of the passover was just about to be celebrated.

It is hardly necessary to make a full report of my proceedings, as it would simply be a repetition of the reports of previous years, no change having taken place in the situation.

The only point which I should especially wish to bring to your notice, is that the local Authorities of Tiberias and Safed still have instructions to refuse to recognise holders of British Certificates as British Subjects,[1] and consequently the Russian Jews under British Protection and British Indian Subjects were loud in their complaints on the point affirming, what is indeed the truth, that it was absolutely useless for them to go on with the farce of renewing their Certificates year by year when the only result accruing from it is that they are maltreated by the Local Authorities on account of their claims to foreign protection. It was impossible for me to urge the Caimmakams of Tiberias and Safed to act contrary to their instructions but they both denied the ill treatment and promised justice to all such as claimed British Protection. At Tiberias I do not think that they have much to complain of as far as the Caimmakam is concerned as he is an honest and well meaning man, but his subordinates are mostly very fanatical Moslems, more especially the Census Official (Tahriri

---

1    The Ottoman authorities and the British representatives disagreed regarding the validity of British certificates of protection (see Hyamson, Nos. 318, 319, 321). The Embassy in Constantinople zealously defended the right of Russian Jews in Tiberias and Safed to British protection, but the local officials apparently held the upper hand.

mufuss memouri) whose business it is to grant tezkeres to travellers etc. The latter positively refuses to obey any orders from the Caimmakam on the question of foreign subjects as he says he has his own orders. This he stated in the presence of the Caimmakam.

At Safed the Caimmakam is a Governor of ordinary type and I do not place much trust in his promises.

I trust that you, Sir, will once again press on Her Majesty's ambassador the desirability of obtaining from the Sublime Porte a settlement of this question as it is clearly impossible to arrange the matter sur place.[2] [...]

Ch. Eyres

## 69 N.T. Moore to Sir W. White
## Report on the Situation in Jerusalem

Consul Moore was not in the practice of writing comprehensive accounts, generally preferring to send short, laconic reports. From this aspect, the following report is of great interest. It mainly surveys the intensive activity of the European Powers in Jerusalem, especially the pronounced competition between Russia and France. The general progress of the city and its environs also can be ascertained from the report, which praises the German contribution to its economic advancement.

Hyamson published only a few lines of the report (No. 336), which is cited here in full.

FO 195/1690 — No. 3                    Jerusalem, February 15th, 1890
(Sent in Duplicate)

Sir,

At the Commencement of a new year, I venture to think that an apercu of the general situation at Jerusalem at the present time may be of interest to Her Majesty's Government.

2    The Ambassador wrote in a letter to the Foreign Secretary on 30 November 1890, after the death of Eldridge, that the Caimakam of Tiberias continued to ignore the validity of British certificates of protection. He further stated that it had to be made clear to the Sublime Porte that regulations had been issued limiting British protection to former Russian Jews as of 1 January 1890, and that explicit instructions should be sent to local authorities to recognise British protection of those deemed worthy of this (Hyamson, No. 335).

For the last quarter of a century the condition of this City has been one of progress and improvement; for the first half of that period the progress was slow; it has proceeded much more rapidly during the latter half. Amongst the indications of this may be enumerated the very considerable increase of the population from 20,000 to 40,000, of whom more than half are Jews;[1] the springing-up of a large suburb of well built and handsome houses to the west of the City,[2] the rise in the price of land for building purposes in the vicinity of the City from 600 to 800 per cent; the making of a good carriage road to Jaffa, the port of Jerusalem, and to Bethlehem, Hebron, Jericho and Nablous; superior Hotel accommodation; good European shops etc. Most of these improvements followed the construction of the carriageable road to Jaffa.[3] As I reported at the time, the Porte has granted a concession to a Jewish active merchant of Jerusalem to construct a Railway between this City and Jaffa, and it is said the work is shortly to be commenced.[4]

From the utilitarian point of view, it cannot be doubted that the Railway, if constructed, will stimulate the material progress of the country.

The most striking feature of modern Jerusalem is the number and handsome appearance of the ever-increasing foreign establishments and institutions — religious, charitable and education, in and around the City. The Latins and the Russians continue to vie with each other in the number and grandeur of their establishments and it would not be easy to say which of the two had the most possessions.

Considering the disinclination manifested within recent years by the

---

1   This evaluation is plausible, although it may be assumed that the number of Jews already approached 25,000.
2   It is difficult to determine just what the Consul intended, but it is likely that he referred to the new Jewish quarters extending westward along Jaffa Road.
3   See above, No. 59.
4   Joseph Navon (1858–1934), a businessman and banker, dealt in real estate and the construction of neighborhoods outside the walls of the Old City, including Mahaneh Yehudah (literally, the "Camp of Judah", named after his brother). By 1885 he had already drawn up a scheme to lay a railroad line from Jaffa to Jerusalem, and he went to Turkey to further the project. On 28 October 1888 he obtained a concession for the railroad for 71 years, in return for the sum of 5000 Turkish pounds. He was not successful, however, in raising the funds needed to construct the line and in the end was compelled to sell the concession to a French corporation, the 'Societé Ottomane des Chemins', for the sum of 1,000,000 francs (£40,000). The construction of the railroad began in August 1889, the first tracks were laid in April 1890, and the initial 46 km. of tracks were completed by the end of that year, at great expense.
    Navon also tried to initiate the building of a deep-water port in Jaffa and electric trams in Jerusalem. In appreciation of his services on behalf of French interests, he was awarded the highest decorations and granted the title of Bey. For the railroad, see above, No. 66, n. 2 and below, No. 74. For Navon, see: Glass, pp. 87–110. Haim Amzalak (see above, No. 63) was Navon's uncle.

Turkish Government to sanction the foundations of such establishments by foreign subjects in Palestine — a disinclination for which, from the Turkish point of view, there is something to be said —, it seems curious that the Russians and French should be able to obtain permission to build edifice after edifice in rapid succession; but such is the fact. It is obvious that as these establishments increase, so do the interests and claims of the possessors in the Holy Land — a circumstance that may, at a given moment, have an important bearing on the relations of the two countries. [...] The German element has become so considerable, that it must in future be reckoned with. Although the German establishments are fewer than those of either the Latins or Russians, they have three prosperous Colonies at Jerusalem and Jaffa,[5] numbering about 1100 souls, owning the land and houses they occupy. Nearly all the foreign shopkeepers, bakers, tailors etc, both here and at Jaffa, are German. The German papers lately published an Imperial Edict formally organizing and liberally endowing the German Church at Jerusalem, of which a superior Ecclesiastic is to be appointed head.

With regard to ourselves there are some additions to note in British institutions during the period above mentioned. The Agents and institutions of the London Jews Society and of the Church Missionary Society continue to represent English Church Work in Palestine. In the year 1883 was established here the Ophthalmic Hospital of the British Branch of the Order of St John,[6] an excellent institution and an immense boon to the inhabitants of all creeds and races; while a number of ladies have come out to engage in various benevolent and educational work.

Turkish administration has generally improved under the wholesome laws, regulations and restraints enacted by the central Government; it is, however, still characterised by the vices of venality and religious bias, but foreign subjects at any rate, are generally protected from the effects of these vices by the safeguards provided by existing treaty arrangements.

N.T. Moore

5    The German colonies in Jaffa, in Jerusalem and Sarona (see above, No. 65, n. 4).
6    See the letter from Moore to the Foreign Secretary dated 3 July 1883, in which he reports that in the course of half a year 2,000 people had been treated in the hospital, and more than a thousand had been cured (FO 78/3532). The opening of a hospital "for the treatment of diseases of the eye" was timely, considering the widespread occurrence of eye diseases at the time. The hospital was open to all, irrespective of religion or sex, and patients streamed to it from throughout Palestine. The British Consul headed the Board of Directors. For this hospital, see: R. Izhaki, "The Opthalmic Hospital of the Order of St. John," *Cathedra*, no. 67 (March 1993), pp. 114–135 (Hebrew).

# 70  W.A. Khayat to Sir W. White
## Theft of the Siloam Inscription

The manmade tunnel from the spring of Gichon to the pool of Siloam, 530m. long, had been hewn out of the rock upon the order of King Hezekiah, and was already known from archaeological excavations of the nineteenth century. In 1880, however, archaeologist and researcher Conrad Schick discovered the 'Siloam Inscription', six lines in Palaeo-Hebrew, one of the most important finds in Biblical archaeology. (See his first report of the discovery: *ZDPV* 1880, p. 54; *PEFQ* 1880, p. 238). Prof. A.H. Sayce succeeded in partially deciphering the inscription, which had been placed to mark the meeting of the two teams of quarriers who had dug the tunnel from both ends (see his article: *PEFQ* 1881, pp. 141–154). Sayce's work initiated the research of the inscription. But in October 1890, the inscription had been cut out of its place and carried away. It was broken in two pieces in removal and the fragments were sold to a Greek in Jerusalem (*PEFQ* 1891, p. 2). On 1 November 1890 the Executive Committee of the PEF expressed "greatest regret and indignation on the clandestine removal and partial destruction of the Siloam Inscription" and demanded from the authorities "to recover the inscription and deposit it safely at the Museum in Constantinople" (FO 195/1727).

FO 195/1727 — N° 3                                      Jerusalem, February 18th, 1891
Sent in Duplicate

Sir,

I have the honour to inform Your Excellency that the Executive Committee of the Palestine Exploration Fund sent Mr Consul Dickson at Damascus,[1] a copy of a Resolution passed unanimously at a meeting held in London on the 18th of November last, of which I beg leave to enclose a copy.

Mr. Consul Dickson forwarded the copy to me with instructions to take any action I thought proper in the matter. At his suggestion I showed a translation of the letter to the Governor of Jerusalem,[2] who informed me that

---

[1]  N.T. Moore was appointed Consul-General at Tripoli on 10 September 1890. He was succeeded in Jerusalem by John Dickson, who had served until then as Consul at Damascus. For various reasons, however, Dickson remained in Damascus, arriving in Jerusalem only on 15 March 1891. Nevertheless, the Committee of the PEF sent its letter to Dickson in Damascus, because he was already formally serving as Consul at Jerusalem.

[2]  Ibrahim Hakki Pasha (1863–1918) was the Governor of the Jerusalem district from

he had also received telegraphic instructions from Constantinople to take such steps as would lead to the immediate recovery of the Siloam Inscription. A few suspected persons were imprisoned, but no positive information could be obtained.

Although not considering myself called upon to interfere in such matters, yet I exerted every effort in my power and by making private enquiries I happily discovered that the Revd J. Hanauer, and Dr Percy D'Erf Wheeler,[3] of the London Jews' Society here, had accidentally seen the missing Inscription at the house of a Greek, (Turkish subject) named George Patrides, by whom they were invited to see a Moabite stone, but this gentleman being absent, his wife by inadvertence showed them the Siloam one. On learning this I at once interviewed these gentlemen, but they refused to divulge the name without first seeing the Greek and advising him to give up the stone which he refused to do. On being informed of this I persuaded those gentlemen to give me his name. I then had a private interview with the Governor and informed him of my success in finding out the name of the perpetrator of this outrage, at which His Excellency was very pleased. By the Governor's orders, Mr Patrides was called upon to hand over the Inscription to the Local Authorities, and he did so stating that he had bought it for 35 Napoleons[4] from a Fellah whose name he could not remember.

I beg further to state, that Mr. Hanauer and myself have identified the stone to be the one which was stolen.

No steps have yet been taken to punish the offenders.

I regret to have to inform Your Excellency that the Inscription has been broken through its removal.

The Pasha is, I believe, awaiting instructions from the Sublime Porte as to its disposal.[5]

November 1890 to November 1897. After the revolution of the 'Young Turks', he served as the Minister of Education and the Interior, and Grand Vizier in 1910–1911.

3    James Edward Hanauer, the son of the Jewish convert C.W. Hanauer, who was baptised in 1844, began his missionary activities in Jaffa. In the 1870s he was transferred to the missionary station in Jerusalem, and in the years 1893–1903 he was again active in Jaffa. He later returned to Jerusalem, and after several years went as a missionary to Damascus. His important book, *Walks about Jerusalem*, was published by the London Jews' Society in 1910, and a second revised edition appeared in 1926, during the author's lifetime.
Dr. Percy D'Erf Wheeler was Director of the Missionary Hospital from 1886 until 1914. During his administration the main building of the hospital was erected outside the walls and consecrated in 1897. Dr. Wheeler left Jerusalem at the beginning of World War I, but returned in 1919 and resumed his activity as Director of the hospital.

4    700 francs = 35 Napoleons.

5    The Inscription was indeed transferred to the Museum in Constantinople, where it remains to the present (see also *PEFQ* 1891, p. 88).

I have the satisfaction to report to your Excellency that through my endeavours the stone has been as quickly restored to the proper Authorities.

W.H. Kayat[6]


# 71   H. Trotter to E. Fane
## Report on Haifa and Jewish Colonisation

The following report, located among the files of the Consulate in Beirut, was written by H.Trotter, Consul-General in Beirut in the years 1890–1894. It was sent to Sir Edmund Douglas Fane, who served as Secretary of the Embassy in Constantinople from 1886 to 1893. The passages in the report not referring to Palestine have been omitted; according to the author, however, the entire region is called "Syria", and the name "Palestine" is not mentioned even once.
The report notes the significant differences in the development of Haifa and of Acre. The second part of the document provides details about the Jewish colonies at the time, which Trotter had not personally visited, his information having come from the Vice-Consul at Haifa. The information, therefore, is secondhand, and accordingly is neither complete nor always accurate.


FO 78/4347 — N° 45                                     Beirut. — August 10.91.
Copy

Sir,
       With reference to my despatch N° 29. of May 28th last I have the honor to submit a short report on my recent visit to some of the Syrian Ports within my Consular Jurisdiction.
       As the object of my journey was principally to obtain a personal knowledge of the said Ports and to make myself personally acquainted with the Local Authorities and as far as possible with the chief inhabitants, — I do

6    William Henry Khayat, the second son of Assad J. Khayat (see above, No. 21, n. 1), was an American subject. He was appointed by Consul Moore as the Cancellier of the Consulate in Jerusalem, and in 1885 he was awarded the title Pro-Consul. Since Dickson had not yet arrived in Jerusalem, Khayat served as Acting Consul. In 1902 he retired from the diplomatic service.

not purpose writing lengthy descriptive accounts of what I saw but shall confine myself to notices of certain special subjects which I consider to be worthy of attention.

The ports visited by me were Haifa, St. Jean d'Acre, Tyre (Sur), Saida (Sidon), Tripoli, and Lattakia the whole of which are under the *direct* Superintendence of this Consulate General. — Circumstances did not permit me to extend my tour to Jaffa (Jerusalem Consulate) on the South or to Alexandretta and Mersina (Aleppo Consulate) on the North, which however I shall hope to visit on a future occasion.

*Haifa*. — We arrived at Haifa in Her Majesty's Ship Melita on the 13th of May. The Kamaikam, Ahmed Shukri Effendi, sent Officials on board to welcome us and was afterwards civil to us on shore.

The most striking object at Haifa is the German Colony which lies to the South of the town, stretching along the plain between the base of Carmel and the sea.[1] The township, which consists of about 60 houses and 400 inhabitants, is regularly laid out in two rows, parallel streets — each house having its garden and outbuildings, and in traversing it one might imagine oneself to be in the heart of Germany. German signboards, waggons, drivers, costumes, everything thoroughly national. To the South of the township is a large fertile plain about two miles in length and one in width every part of which is well cultivated and the whole presenting a most flourishing appearance highly creditable to the hard working colony which is composed entirely of the sect of the Temple, emigrants from Wurtemberg. There are three other similar colonies in Palestine, viz: at Jaffa, Sarona and Jerusalem (Refaim)[2] numbering in all about 200 souls. —

Although the Haifa colony has been established in Syria more than twenty years they keep entirely to themselves — and do not mix or intermarry with their Syrian neighbours. The fact that a German man-of-war (the "Loreley" from Constantinople) was at Haifa, during our visit, with the object of registering the adults of the colony for military service — and that German Sailors were parading the streets — almost completed the illusion that one was in a small flourishing German Seaport.

*St. Jean d'Acre*. — From Haifa we went across the bay to St. Jean d'Acre (Akka) where we landed and exchanged visits with the Governor Sadik Pasha, a brother of the Grand Vizir. — His Excellency kindly sent an officer to accompany us around the extensive but ancient fortifications which, although I believe Akka is considered a first class fortress, is practically in the

1    See above, No. 67, n. 2.
2    See above, No. 65, n. 4.

260

state it was left in after the bombardment by the British Fleet in 1840 — many traces of which are still visible. — Old smooth bore guns still lie dismounted on the massive ramparts, and the only modern guns it possesses are eight, — 9 centimetres — Breach Loading, Krupp Guns quite recently received from Constantinople — Its present garrison consists of about 300 Artillery men.

As the fiction of its being a strong fortress is still kept up, no one is allowed to build outside the ramparts and the place looks melancholy and deserted offering a strong contrast to the flourishing, prosperous and rapidly increasing town of Haifa on the opposite side of the Bay.

At both places great interest was naturally taken in the projected line of Railway to Damascus — the concession for which was recently given to Mr. Pilling, an Englishman.[3]

The projected line is from St. Jean d'Acre to Damascus (about 120 miles) with a branch from Mejdel to Haifa (10 miles) and other branch lines aggregating 90 miles in length to connect Banias (on the main line) with the Hauran and with Hasbeya.

Mr. Pilling was daily expected at Haifa while I was there but has never turned up and it would seem that the project has encountered unexpected difficulties and it appears doubtful whether it will even be carried out. —

Meanwhile French Capitalists have obtained a concession for a steam tramway from Beirut to Damascus — and engineers are daily expected from France to survey for the line. As the promoters of this railway have also the Beirut harbour works, and the existing Damascus and Beirut road in their hands, it is likely that this project will be energetically carried out and that in some four years time both harbour works and railway will be completed — in which case the Damascus traffic will probably be entirely lost to the Akka-Damascus line. —

From Haifa I made an inland excursion to Nazareth and Mount Tabor and thence across to Dalia the residence of the late Mr. Oliphant on Mount Carmel[4] and then back to Haifa. Much of our road lay across the plain to be

---

3   The British corporation headed by J.R. Pilling received the concession for the Haifa-Damascus railroad in 1890, but it was not until 1892 that the cornerstone laying ceremony was held in Haifa. The French made efforts to undermine the British venture, for they operated a carriage line from Beirut to Damascus and feared the competition. In 1891 the French obtained the concession to construct the railroad between these two cities, successfully completing it by 1895, while the British initiative encountered difficulties and came to nothing in the end, after only 8 km. of track had been laid. Only in 1903, after the Turkish government purchased the concession of the British corporation, did construction begin of the Haifa-Derah line of the Hedjaz railroad It was completed in October 1905, and from May 1906 this train ran through the Jezreel Valley and Zemah to Damascus. The description of the line in the report does not match the actual route of the railroad.

4   Laurence Oliphant (1829–1888) was a diplomat, mystic, and author. He was known in his

traversed by the proposed Haifa-Damascus railway — a large and fertile but very unhealthy plain — as is evidenced by the fact that there are hardly any towns or villages in the plain itself which is cultivated by the inhabitants of villages lying in the adjacent hills, — lately however there has been an enormous rise in the value of land in this plain — as well as in many other parts of Syria — mainly owing to land having been bought up by wealthy Jewish capitalists for purposes connected with Jewish immigration [...] I have already noted the great increase in the value of land in some parts of Syria principally due to the establishment of Jewish Colonies actual and prospective. —

Vice Consul Schmidt[5] at Caiffa has given me a good deal of information on the subject of these agricultural Colonies, which appears to be of special interest in view of the present exodus from Russia —

The principal Colonies are seven in number: —

1st — *Pesah-Tikweh* near Jaffa, commenced in 1879, is composed of 90 families (450 souls) 1600 hectares (N.B. one Hectare equals about 2½ acres) of land, of which 50 are under vine cultivation; these lands belong to the colonists who are very poor but receive occasional assistance from Baron E. de Rothschild of Paris.

2nd — *Rosh Pina* near Safed started in 1880,[6] 22 families (100 souls) 800 hectares of land under vines and orchards in equal parts.

3rd — *Yessod Amaila*[7] — started in 1882 on Lake Meron, 12 families, 600 hectares of land belonging to the colonists.

4th — *Zichrva Jacob*[8] near Cesarieh founded in 1882 — 100 houses, — 1500 hectares of which 300 planted with vines.

5th — *Richon el Zion* — 40 families — 1300 hectares, of which 250 are planted with vines.

6th — *Ecron* — near Jaffa — founded 1884 — 20 families — 600 hectares of very rich soil are plantged with fruit trees.

sympathy for the 'Hibbat Zion' (Lovers of Zion) movement, after having begun in 1878 to take an interest in the Jewish question and the Land of Israel. In 1879 he visited Palestine. He conducted research while in the country and published a book containing a program for Jewish settlement (*Land of Gilead*, Edinburgh and London, 1880). He aided Jewish immigrants in Palestine, and in 1882 he and his wife settled in Haifa and in the nearby Druze village of Daliyat el-Karmel.

5    See above, No. 67, nn. 1, 6.

6    Rosh Pinnah had its beginnings in the lands of the Arab village Ja'uni as the colony of Gei Oni. The lands of the abandoned first colony were purchased by the new settlers in July 1882, who established the colony of Rosh Pinnah. In 1900 its population numbered 500 souls.

7    Founded in 1883, Yessod ha-Ma'alah by 1900 had a population of about 230 inhabitants.

8    Zichron Jacob (Samarin). By 1900 its population numbered about 1500 souls.

7th — *Michemor*[9] — near Jacob's Bridge (Jordan) an independent colony started in 1890 — 20 families, 300 hectares, of which half are under vines. —

In Nos 2, 4, 5, and 6 the lands belong to Baron E. de Rothschild who spends large sums of money on them in providing workmen, plantations, stores, synagogues, medical dispensaries, schools, etc. etc.

As far as I can learn these Jews do not make good agricultural colonists and were it not for outside support would not prosper. They seem to prefer employing native labour to working themselves but as I have not yet had an opportunity of judging for myself it is perhaps unfair to trust too much to the statements of others. [...]

Lieutenant-Colonel Henry Trotter

# 72  J. Dickson to Dr W. Bailey
## Nablus Becomes Independent of Jerusalem

The following letter reflects the lack of logic in the administrative division of the country. The Nablus (Shechem) district, which was close to Jerusalem, was not included in the jurisdiction of the Consul in Jerusalem, but rather was subordinate to the Vali in Beirut. Consequently, the Consul was not empowered to intervene regarding events that occurred in Nablus, and was forced to refer the interested parties to the Consul-General in Beirut (also see above, the introduction to No. 62).

ISA 123/1/21
Copy

Jerusalem, August 19, 1891

Dear Mr. Bailey[1]

I beg to acknowledge the receipt of your telegram of the 17th instant informing me that the Government Zaptiehs had closed your dispensary, and

---

9    Mishmar ha-Yarden was established in 1891, and by 1900 its inhabitants numbered more than 100.

---

1    I was unable to find any information about him. He was a missionary and physician who also extended medical assistance.

also of your letter of the same date, giving me full particulars of the occurred.

I regret much that the Government of Nablous being independent of that of Palestine, I am unable to do anything with the Pasha here in the matter, but I at once telegraphed to Colonel Trotter, H.M. Consul General at Beyrouth[2] and requested him to represent the case to the Vali under whose authority the Governor of Nablous is placed. I telegraphed to you yesterday morning stating what I had done. I am also glad to see from your letter that you have sent a Copy of it to Colonel Trotter, as I am sure he will do all he can to obtain redress for you. Hoping soon to hear that the matter has been settled to your satisfaction.

J. Dickson

# 73   J. Dickson to Marquess of Salisbury
## Boundaries of Palestine

The following despatch delineates the boundaries of the province of Palestine, i.e., the extended Jerusalem district. After the short-lived attempt to turn the Jerusalem district into a large, independent province (see above, No. 62), the Acre and Nablus districts — in effect, the northern and central sections of the country — were first annexed to the province of Beirut, later transferred to the region of Syria, and when the province of Lebanon (i.e., the Beirut region) was reestablished in 1888, these districts were transferred to it once again, while the Jerusalem district ("Palestine") remained independent, directly subordinate to the Sublime Porte in Constantinople.

FO 78/4432
Commercial

July 19, 1892

My Lord,
    Mr. Pilling[1] appears to be entirely mistaken regarding the divisions of Syria and Palestine, as marked out by the Ottoman Government for administrative purposes. The stretch of country lying to the East of the Mediterranean

2    See above, the introduction to No. 71.

1    For Mr. Pilling, the railroad concessionaire, see above, No. 71, n. 3.

and generally known as Syria and Palestine, comprises the Provinces of Aleppo, Beyrouth, Damascus and Palestine.[2]

Until quite recently the Vilayets of Beyrout and Damascus were one province styled Syria, but in consequence of the growing importance of Beyrout, the district surrounding the latter place, including Acre and Haifa, was raised into a separate province. The Vilayet of Damascus, however, is still designated in Turkish official documents as the Province of Syria. The "Mutasereflick", a minor province, of Palestine, is bounded in the North by a line which runs from the river Awja (a little to the north of Jaffa) past the village of Sinjel (between Jerusalem and Nablus) and down to the fords of the Jordan, near Jericho, and is separated from Eastern Syria by the river Jordan and the Dead Sea.[3]

In my commission I am appointed Her Majesty's Consul for Palestine to reside at Jerusalem, as stated in the F.O. list. I am accredited by the Porte to the Governor of the Province of Palestine. My Consular District is, therefore, confined to the latter Province, Haifa and Acre are included in the District of the Consulate General of Beyrout.[4]

Mr. Pilling, however, seems to be under the impression that Palestine, as it at present exists, is the same as the Palestine of the twelve tribes of Israel, and it is surprising that, having obtained a concession from the Ottoman Government for such an important matter as a Railway from Acre to Damascus, should not have taken steps to ascertain what are the divisions of the country for administrative purposes.

John Dickson

## 74   J. Dickson to Earl of Rosebery
## Inauguration and Importance of the
## Jaffa-Jerusalem Railway

The Jaffa-Jerusalem railroad was inaugurated on 26 September 1892. The Consul's report on the inauguration stated that "the Opening of this line of

2   "Palestine" here refers only to the Sanjak of Jerusalem.
3   According to this division, Transjordan was within the area of Syria, and was subordinate to the Vali of Damascus. The northern boundary of the district passed along the Yarkon River and the Arab village Sinjil, located in the Samaria hill-country, on the border between the districts of Nablus (Shechem) and Jerusalem.
4   It is strange that the Consul finds it necessary to "explain" to the Foreign Secretary what is the jurisdiction of the Consulate.

railway caused the greatest sensation and the wildest excitement among the inhabitants of Jerusalem, and will probably be the beginning of a new epoch in the history of this City." (30 September 1892, FO 195/1765). The event turned into a festive occasion of great political and economic importance, since the travel time between the two cities had decreased from the 13–14 hours by carriage to slightly more than 3½ hours by train. This line went into operation three years before the more advanced railroad operating between Beirut and Damascus (see above, No. 71, n. 4). Rail transportation in Palestine was also the subject of stubborn competition between France and England. The Turks, who were suspicious of the efforts of the Powers, adopted various delaying tactics for years, and accordingly preferred to grant the concession to a Jewish Ottoman subject, Joseph Navon (see above, No. 69, n. 4). The British cast doubt upon the economic potential of the line, and whether it would indeed serve their interests. Thus Sir Arthur Slade, who was an admiral in the Ottoman fleet, argued that the railroad would indeed bring about an increase in the number of pilgrims, but they would not necessarily be Protestants(!): "The pilgrims would chiefly belong, as now, to the Roman Catholic Church and to the Eastern Churches, with a sprinkling of Hebrews. Protestants would be too few to influence opinion on the matter" (Paul Cotherell, *The Railways of Palestine and Israel*, Abingdon 1984, p. 2). Consequently, the French would eventually obtain the concession, buying it from Joseph Navon (see above, No. 69, n. 4).

A short section of the following report appears in Hyamson (No. 301).


FO 78/4432 — No. 17                                   Jerusalem November 4, 1892
Commercial — Copy


My Lord,

On the 26th of September last I had the honour to telegraph to Your Lordship reporting the inauguration of the Jaffa-Jerusalem Railway, and I beg to submit to Your Lordship a few remarks on the construction of the line and to enclose plans.[1]

---

1   The maps were not enclosed. Immediately following the inauguration of the line, Dickson wrote to the Foreign Secretary: "The opening of this line of railway caused the greatest sensation and the wildest excitement among the inhabitants of Jerusalem, and will probably be the beginning of a new epoch in the history of this City. As a commercial enterprise, it is difficult to predict at the present moment whether it will be a success or not. — On the other hand as regards the thousands of pilgrims and travelers who annually come to this city, either from a spirit of devotion or feeling of curiosity, the change will be momentous and the numbers of visitors will probably be greater now than it has been before [...] We cannot but consider the opening of the railway to Jerusalem as an event in the world's history" (FO 195/1765, 30 September 1892).

A few years back a native gentleman in Egypt, named Lutfy Bey, conceived the project of making a railway between Egypt and Palestine,[2] and the idea was taken up by a Jew in this city, Mr Navon, who placed himself in communication with Lutfy Bey on the subject. It was intended that the latter should obtain a concession for a line to El-Arish, on the Egyptian frontier, and that Mr Navon should undertake the construction of the remaining part to Jaffa and Jerusalem. This project, however, fell through, and Mr Navon then proceeded to make arrangements for procuring a concession from the Turkish Government for a line from Jaffa to Jerusalem, with a possible extension to Damascus and Aleppo. Negotiations were accordingly entered into with the Subline Porte, and in 1888 the concession, for a period of seventy-one years, was obtained, which Mr Navon offered to sell to various firms in London and Paris. It was, however, ultimately purchased for 1,000,000 francs by a Company in Paris under the name of "Société du Chemin de Fer Ottomane de Jaffa à Jérusalem et Prolongement", or shortly "Société Otto-mane Anonyme", the Director of which is a certain M. Collas, who is also President of the "Compagnie des Phares" (Lighthouse Company) in the Ottoman Dominions. In 1889 the Company entered into a contract with an Engineering Firm "La Société des Travaux Publics [!] et Constructions", for the construction of the works, which, according to the convention signed by the Porte, were to be completed in two and a half years from their com-mencement, and the first turf was cut at Jaffa on the 31st of March 1890. The terms of the contract were the payment of 10,000,000 francs (£400,000) to the "Société des Travaux", partly guaranteed by debenture bonds and shares,[3] and the right of the latter to work the line, after completion, for a period of five years for a stipulated sum to be paid annually to the Company. The works were proceeded with vigorously, and although many doubts were entertained as to whether the line would be finished in the time agreed upon, on account of the obstacles to be encountered in the mountains, yet they were completed on the 16th of September last, when the inauguration of the line took place, with considerable ceremony.

The line, which is a single one,[4] starts from the northern suburbs of the town of Jaffa, close to the sea shore, winds gradually round to the east and

2    Loutfi Bey was in fact the first to make an effort to be granted a railway concession, and afterwards Navon reached an agreement with him regarding the planned lines. See also: Glass, p. 102.

3    A considerable portion of the sum was raised by French Catholic religious institutions that were partners in the corporation.

4    For reasons of economy, the French chose a narrow-gauge line (only 1 m. wide), the narrowest gauge in the world. Similarly, they selected a route covering 87 km., while the straight-line distance between the two cities was only 60 km., and the carriage road was 65 km. long.

south past Ramleh and among the sandhills, until it reaches the torrent called Wady Surar, when it turns again to the east and follows the latter stream up the mountain gorge of that name, as far as the plain of Rephaim, situated to the south of Jerusalem. It then traverses the latter and terminates to the south west of Jerusalem, about half a mile from the Jaffa gate. There are five stations along the line, not including the two termini, namely, Lydda, Ramleh, Sejed,[5] Deir-Aban[6] and Bittir,[7] and their respective distances from Jaffa are as follows: — 19, 22, 39, 50 and 75 Kilometres, the entire length of the line from Jaffa to Jerusalem being 87 Kilometres or about 54½ miles. The different stations are well built, and are provided with all the material necessary for such places, such as telegraph apparatus, tanks for water etc. There is a double line of rails at each station. In reality there are only three important Stations in the line, namely, Lydda, Ramleh and Bittir, the two former being large villages, containing six or seven thousand inhabitants each, and the latter being the most prosperous mountain village on the line in the vicinity of Jerusalem, and well supplied with water. At Sejed a Station was built, as His Majesty the Sultan has a "Chiftlick", or farm close at hand, and another was placed at Deir-Aban for the convenience of the Latin convent situated in the hills a little to the South. Artuf, the Jewish Agricultural Colony, under English management, is also close to the latter Station.[8]

The line is of 1.04 metres gauge, and in some places is well built, though in others it has hardly had time to settle and is not sufficiently firm. There are 176 bridges in all, seven of which are of cast iron, the rest being of stone. [...] The villages situated in or near the route traversed by the railway are as follows: —

5   This station was closed down in 1915.
6   This is the present-day Beit Shemesh stop. The village of Deir-Aban was destroyed in October 1948 in the Israel War of Independence, after having served as a base for Arab bands.
7   The village and the station still stand today.
8   In 1883 the British mission, on the initiative of the missionary Friedländer, established an agricultural colony in Artuf, to settle Russian Jewish immigrants, with the goal of converting them to Christianity. The mission cared for this farm for many years, but these efforts were eventually unsuccessful, and in 1896 the plot was purchased by Jews, who established the settlement of Har-Tuv, which existed until the disturbances of 1929, when it was destroyed by the inhabitants of Deir-Aban (see Eliav, *Austrian Protection*, pp. 202–203); M.H. Kunstel and J. Albright, *Their Promised Land*, New York, 1990, ch. IV.

|  | Population |
|---|---|
| Yazur | 960 |
| Beit Dejan | 1044 |
| Safurieh | 940 |
| Lydda | 6540 |
| Ramleh | 5172 |
| Naaneh | 738 |
| Sidoun | 94 |
| Khulda | 60 |
| Artuf | 106 |
| Deir-el-Hawa | 154 |
| Deir-el-Sheikh | 134 |
| Er-Ras | 280 |
| El-Kabu | 88 |
| Bittir | 450 |
| Welejeh | 732 |
| Malhah | 626 |
| Sharafat | 84 |
| Beit Safafa | 384 |

At present there are only two daily trains for passengers, running one each way, and the times of arrival and departure are as follows:[9] —

|  | Arrival | Departure |
|---|---|---|
| Jaffa | — | 2.20 p.m. |
| Lydda | 2.56 | 2.58 p.m. |
| Ramleh | 3.5 | 3.7 p.m. |
| Sejed | 3.39 | 3.47 p.m. |
| Deir Aban | 4.7 | 4.9 p.m. |
| Bittir | 5.24 | 5.26 p.m. |
| Jerusalem | 5.55 | — |
| Jerusalem | — | 7.15 a.m. |
| Bittir | 7.44 | 7.46 a.m. |
| Deir Aban | 9.1 | 9.3 a.m. |
| Sejed | 9.23 | 9.31 a.m. |
| Ramleh | 10.3 | 10.5 a.m. |
| Lydda | 10.12 | 10.14 a.m. |
| Jaffa | 10.50 | |

9   Travel time on this line, even today, is almost three hours. For many years, however, the trip took longer than the official time. The tourist M. Thomas related that in 1895 the journey from Jaffa to Jerusalem took six hours (Thomas, p. 70).

The price of tickets is 1st Class 15 francs, 2nd Class 5 francs, for the whole distance, and 1st Class Return tickets 20 francs. Two goods trains also run one each way starting at night from Jerusalem and Jaffa respectively.

There will, however, never be any very considerable development in trade and consequent increase in the traffic of the railway, as long as Jaffa remains an open roadstead, and I would venture here to offer a few remarks on the construction of a harbour at that place.

As far back as 1862 Mr Zimpel, a German by birth, but a naturalized American, and an engineer by profession, drew plans for building a breakwater at Jaffa, and for constructing a railway from that port to Jerusalem.[10] The railway, as will be seen from the accompanying plan made by him, was to follow almost the identical route of the one just completed, and, indeed, the engineers, in making the present line, had carefully studied the plans drawn by Mr Zimpel. The line of railway projected by Mr Zimpel was to be continued from Jerusalem to Jericho, up the valley of the Jordan, and on to Damascus, but he foresaw that the traffic with the interior would never become very extensive unless a proper harbour could be built at Jaffa, where vessels could load and unload with safety, in all weathers. [...] The actual expenses, however, of working the line probably amount to much less than the estimated sum, particularly as the Company who constructed the line are obliged to maintain it in perfect working order until the 1st of April 1893, and consequently the "Compagnie & Exploitation" have a fair chance of reaping a profit as traffic increases.

The Company are now engaged, I understand, in trying to obtain further concessions for extending the line. They have already the power, it seems, to make branch lines from Ramleh or Jaffa to Nablous and to Gaza via Ascalon, but their intention is, it is stated, to prolong the line to El-Arish, and then possible to form a junction with the Egyptian railways.[11] Other projects for extending the line are also being discussed, but the most important of these is a Scheme for constructing a line from El-Arish to Akaba, and I am informed, on reliable authority, that negotiations are now actually in progress at the Palace at Constantinople for the purpose of obtaining a special concession for this line. If this is true a rival line to that from Alexandria to Suez

---

10 Carl Friedrich Zimpel visited Palestine in 1852 and published a small book: *Die Israeliten in Jerusalem* (*Eine Denkschrift*), Stuttgart 1852. He proposed a program for the productivization of the Jewish *Yishuv* in Jerusalem, which was later discussed in the Jewish press (Eliav, *Love of Zion and Men of Hod*, Tel Aviv 1970, pp. 176–177 [Hebrew]). In 1864 he presented a plan for construction of a Jaffa-Jerusalem railroad line and of a quay on the shore of Jaffa, even entering into negotiations with the Turkish government (see: Carmel, *Palästina-Chronik*, I, pp. 79, 83, 93).

11 These programs were implemented by the British only after World War I.

270

would appear to be in contemplation, and consequently a second route to India, running along the East side of the Suez Canal, and in the possession of a Power other than that at present occupying Egypt seems to be the object in view.

John Dickson

## 75 Foreign Office to Sir F. Clare-Ford Prohibition of Land Purchase

The anti-Jewish policy of the Ottoman government became more severe in the early 1890s. In June 1891 the prohibition against the immigration of Russian Jews was renewed and strictly enforced. On 21 November 1892 all Jews, including Ottoman subjects, were forbidden to purchase land or even to transfer land from one Jew to another. This led to a severe economic crisis, and all real estate transactions suffered a crushing blow. The various Consulates came to the aid of the Jews, some of whom had already made down payments. Local diplomatic representatives registered strong protests, demanding that the decrees be revoked, and requested the intervention of their Ambassadors in Constantinople (see: Eliav, *German Policy*, pp. 148–153; Eliav, *Austrian Protection*, pp. 102–103, 105–107). As a result of diplomatic pressure, the Sublime Porte backed down, and on 3 April 1893 announced that the purpose of the decree was to prevent the permanent settlement of Jews in Palestine, i.e., an explicitly political consideration. At the same time, however, foreign Jews would be permitted to purchase urban lands under certain conditions (see: Eliav, *Yishuv*, p. 264).
The British Consul also received complaints from the Jews under his protection and he, too, requested the intervention of the Ambassador (Hyamson, Nos. 362, 365). The Ambassador passed the complaints on to the Foreign Office and in response he received explicit instructions for vigorous intervention. The following is a draft of the official letter.

FO 78/4476 — No. 146                                    F.O. 14 June 1893
Draft

Sir,

  Y. Excl's Despatch No 199 of the 17th ult. enclosed copies of petitions addressed to the Consul at Jerusalem by certain British subjects of the Jewish faith, in which they complain of the regulations prolectating (?) Jews from buying & selling real Estate in Palestine, and appeal to HM.G. to protect their interests.[1]

The issue by the Porte of these regulations, if directed against Jews, on account of their religion is inconsistent with the spontaneous declaration in favor of the maintenance of the principle of religious equality made by the Porte on various occasions, especially by the Turkish P.P. at the Berlin Congress as embodied in Art 62 of the Treaty of Berlin. That Article states that in no part of the Ottoman Empire shall difference of religion be alleged against any person as a ground of exclusion or incapacity, as regards the discharge of civil and political rights, admissions to the public employments & the exercise of the various professions & industries.

If on the other hand, the Porte intends to prohibit foreigners from holding land in Turkey, the Turkish law of June 18 1867 which has been accepted by all the Great Powers, becomes a dead letter. By that law foreigners without any distinction as to their religion have been admitted on the same footing as Ottoman subjects or without other conditions, to the enjoyment of the right of holding urban and rural real property throughout the whole extent of the Empire with the exception of the Hedjas: on the faith of it British subjects of the Jewish persuasion as well as others have acquired real property in Palestine of which these regulations must tend to depose them. I am unwilling to believe that it is the deliberate intention of the Turkish Gov. to place foreign Jewish interests within the Empire upon a less favourable footing than Mahmetans and Christians, and I have accordingly to request Y.E. to take a favourable opportunity of representing to the Porte the hardship and injustice of a measure which is contrary to Treaty as well as to Turkish Law and of urging the importance of its early withdrawal.[2]

[unsigned]

1   See the enclosure to Dickson's letter (Hyamson, No. 366).
2   Although the Sublime Porte promised to right the wrong, the hostile Governor did not agree to ease the prohibition and continued to impede land acquisition by Jews. Since it was almost impossible to buy land during the 1890s, the building boom in Jerusalem and settlement activity came to a halt.

Jerusalem's water supply had always been extremely problematic. For the most part, the city's inhabitants were forced to rely upon cisterns and open reservoirs, insufficient for the needs of the rapidly growing population. In drought years the Arabs would transport water into the city on their backs, in leather bags, and sell it to the inhabitants at exorbitant prices, which many of the poor residents of the city could not afford. Later on, an aqueduct was built from the springs of Arroub (between the present-day Etzion Bloc and Hebron) and from Solomon's Pools, south of Bethlehem. The pipes had to be repaired from time to time, however, and the water supply was not reliable. After the railway line was laid and the railroad began operation, various programs were proposed for modernization and the improvement of the infrastructure of Jerusalem. Within this context, different plans for improving the municipal water supply also were discussed.

James Dickson, who served as Consul in Jerusalem beginning in 1891 (see above, No. 70, n. 1), was a sickly person. From time to time he would request sick leave, complaining of malaria and other ailments. Peter James McGregor, Vice-Consul in Beirut 1894–1896, would be sent on occasion to Jerusalem to serve as Acting Consul in Dickson's absence. He served in this capacity in Jerusalem during the first three months of 1895, and again in July-September 1895.

FO 78/4644B                                    Jerusalem, January 29, 1895
"Special"

My Lord,

I have the honour to report to Your Lordship that the Administrative Council of Jerusalem has recently had under consideration a scheme brought forward by a French Syndicate for supplying this City with water, and I understand that, as a favourable report on the subject has been sent to Constantinople, the promoters are confident of shortly obtaining a concession enabling them to take the work in hand.

The water supply of Jerusalem is for the present exclusively derived from cisterns, but, leaving out of account the disadvantages inherent to such a system, it has for some years been felt that the great increase in the population of this City imperatively called for some better means of ensuring a regular and abundant supply of pure water of which there is no want in the immediate neighbourhood of Jerusalem. The principal springs are at Arroub about 2½ hours ride from the City, and, considering the privations which must be imposed upon a large section of the population during the late summer and early autumn months when water is sold at as much as three piastres the "Kyrbe" (a goat's skin), and the public health suffers severely in consequence, it cannot be doubted that any scheme for obviating these crying evils would, if carried out with sufficient guarantees, be at once a profitable investment for the capitalist and a boon for the inhabitants of Jerusalem.

I believe that the first proposal to construct water-works was made by Lady Burdett-Coutts, who, however, failed to come to terms with the Municipal Authorities regarding the management of the proposed works and the terms for the repayment of the sums which her Ladyship was ready to advance.[1]

The same difficulties attended the realization of the scheme proposed in 1890 by the late Sir Edmund Lechmere in the name of a British Syndicate, the Municipality expressing its readiness to undertake the work with the capital to be advanced by Sir Edmund and his friends, but not seeing its way either to guarantee the repayment of the sums advanced or to allow the Syndicate to take the work with its own hands.

Sir Edmund Lechmere's proposal has been the subject of occasional correspondence and representations to the Sublime Porte ever since 1890, but owing to the Syndicate's persistence in its attitude towards the proposals of the Municipality, the matter seems to have reached a deadlock.[2]

Monsieur Thévenin, the promoter of the latest scheme, was the contractor for the Harbour works at Beyrout, and I learn that he is largely supported in this undertaking by influential capitalists in that town. He is now, I am told, in Constantinople endeavouring to prepare the way for the granting of a concession and it is generally believed here that he will be successful.

I have the honour herewith to enclose a Memorandum containing the principal features of the scheme proposed by Monsieur Thevenin.

James McGregor

1  In 1864, Lady Burdett-Couts, a British philanthropist, contributed £500 towards a survey of Jerusalem in an effort to improve the city's water system. This contribution made possible the mission of C.W. Wilson, who completed the survey in May 1865. In 1870 she intended to make another donation for the improvement of the water supply, but the authorities were opposed (see: C. Warren & C.W. Wilson, *Recovery of Jerusalem*, London 1871, pp. 236–237). M. Thomas, who visited Jerusalem in 1895, stated that the Turks turned down the offer, because the Lady refused to give them *baksheesh* (Thomas, p. 237). According to other sources, she offered a loan of £25,000. It seems that the version presented in this despatch is the correct one. See also: Henry Lumley, *Betrachtungen und Briefe zur Förderung des Baues einer Wasserleitung für Jerusalem*, Leipzig 1873.

2  According to one reliable source, G. Franghia, Engineer for Public Works, was engaged in 1894–1889 in the preparation of a program for a British syndicate, but the plan was not put into effect due to lack of funds (see below, No. 116).

274

*Memorandum*

1° Les sources devant servir à l'alimentation sont ARROUB, BOURRADI, MOUGARA³ et celles que le concessionnaire pourra découvrir.

2° La conduite maîtresse d'un développement de 22 Kilomètres a peu près sera libre en un tunnel sur environ 5 Kilomètres et forcée sur tout le reste de son parcours.

3° Le concessionnaire aura le droit de vendre l'eau à un prix variable à sa volonté mais qui ne dépassera pas 0 fcs. 50 centimes le mètre cube.

4° Le concessionnaire devra livrer gratuitement à la ville un volume de 25 mètres cubes d'eau par jour et il laissera un bassin alimenté par un robinet qui débitera 10 mètres cubes d'eau par 24 heures pour servir à l'alimentation publique.

5° Si le volume d'eau que l'on peut amener à Jérusalem sera supérieur à 4,000 mètres cubes, cette eau supplémentaire serait destinée jusqu'à concurrence de 25% à l'arrosages des rues.

6° Le concessionnaire paiera à la Municipalité la somme de 20,000 francs dépenses qu'elle a faites pour les études.

7° Le délai de la concession est de 75 ans.

8° Le concessionnaire est autorisé de former une Société qui prendra le titre de "Compagnie Anonyme Ottomane des Eaux de Jérusalem".

# 77 J. Dickson to Sir Ph. Currie
# Fanatical Attitudes in Jaffa

Arab nationalist efforts in the early 1890s against Jewish immigration and the purchase of lands for Jewish settlement, which had led to the imposition of more severe government restrictions on Jewish immigration and settlement, resulted in a rise in tension between Jews and Arabs in Jaffa. The ill feelings were the cause of several incidents. The increasing fanaticism of the Muslims began to express itself also in acts of violence, directed not only against Jews. The Consular Agent Amzalak informed the Consul of these acts, and the latter sent a comprehensive report to the Embassy in Constantinople. A few lines of this report, published below in full, were printed by Hyamson (No. 378).

3   Bourradi and Moughara are springs in Wadi el-Biar, near Solomon's Pools, which supplied Jerusalem with water for hundreds of years. This program too was not implemented.

Sir,

With reference to the concluding part of my Despatch No. 42 of the 3rd instant, in which I reported on the fanatical state of feeling existing among the lower classes of Mussulmans of Jaffa,[1] I have the honour to transmit herewith a Copy of a Despatch dated the 10th instant, which I have received from the Consular Agent Amzalak, stating that a Jew was murdered in the Jewish Colony of Mulabas near Jaffa,[2] by some Mussulmans connected with the tithe farming, the crime having apparently been committed without any provcation on the part of the victim.

I have further the honour to enclose herewith a list furnished to me by Mr. Amzalak in a Despatch No. 56, dated the 27th ultimo, showing the number of crimes and offences as well as breaches of the public peace, committed by the Mussulmans of Jaffa, and by Government Officials, during the last twelve or eighteen months.[3] The threatening attitude of the Mussulmans mentioned by Mr. Amzalak as having manifested itself on the 26th ultimo, confirms the reports which reached me from other sources respecting their recent excited state, but happily, so far, the general tranquility has not been disturbed, His Excellency the Mutessarif of Jerusalem being most anxious to prevent any disorder. The administration of justice, however, at Jaffa, is merely nominal; the police force most inefficient, there being only a few Zaptiehs and mounted gendarmes to maintain order, and the number of troops at the disposal of the Authorities (about 40 men with a Major and Lieutenant Colonel), being inadequate to quell a disturbance should such take place.

Considering that Jaffa is a town with from 25,000 to 30,000 inhabitants,[4] that it is the terminus of the railway to Jerusalem, and is increasing in prosperity on account of the brisk trade in oranges, which is yearly carried on

1    Dickson wrote in his letter of 3 September 1895: "I regret to report to Y.E., that I am informed from various sources, that a very bad feeling exists at present among lower classes of the Mohammedan population at Jaffa towards Europeans and Christians" (FO 195/1848).
2    The reference apparently is to Samuel Jacob Rosenzweig, who was shot to death in Petah Tikvah.
3    See the abbreviated list: Hyamson, No. 378.
4    According to Luncz, in 1895 Jaffa had a population numbering only 17,713, of whom about 3,000 were Jews, 11,630 Muslims, and the rest Christians (*Luah Eretz Yisrael* 1896, p. 28 [Hebrew]).

with England and other countries, it is necessary that some improvement should be introduced by the Authorities in the Government of the place.[5]

John Dickson

## 78 J. Dickson to Sir N. O'Conor
## Report on Trade at Jaffa

For years, the Consuls hardly reported about commercial activity, especially regarding imports and exports through the port of Jaffa. However, commerce through that port increased at the end of the nineteenth century. Several regular shipping lines docked there: those of France, Austria, Russia, Egypt, and the British "Anglo-Asian Steamship Company". Maritime transportation contributed to the increase in commercial activity, as well as serving the passenger trade. Besides the regular shipping lines, other ships struck anchor at Jaffa from time to time, including those flying the Turkish, Greek, and British flags. Trade increased from year to year and produced fine results. A comparison of the numerical data in the report with the charts provided by Avitzur (*Jaffa Harbor*, Tel Aviv 1972 [Hebrew]) indicates that the figures are accurate.

From 1886 on, the annual reports were published by the Foreign Office in the *Diplomatic and Consular Reports* series (DCR).

FO 195/2062                                     Jerusalem, January 31, 1899
"Confidential"

Sir,

I have had the honour to receive Your Excellency's Despatch of the 19th ultimo, with reference to the importance of Jaffa as a Commercial centre, and requesting me to furnish Your Excellency with a brief report of the trade of the Port, its progress, and a statement of any reasons that may seem to me to promise a further development in the near future of its imports and exports.

Your Excellency also desires to know whether, in my opinion, the present British Consular Agent satisfactorily fulfils the requirements of his post.

---

5    On 26 September 1895 Dickson confirmed that he had received the reply of the Ambassador, that steps would be taken and that the Pasha would be instructed to ensure tranquillity in the city.

I was hoping, before sending in the report in question, to have been able to procure statistics of the imports and exports for the past year, but, as yet, the British Consular Agent at Jaffa has not furnished these returns. No information can be obtained from the Custom House regarding the quantity and value of goods imported and exported. The British Consular Agent is, therefore, obliged to ascertain from the different steamship Agencies and Merchants, the number of packages of goods and merchandize brought into or sent out of the country in the course of the year, and the procuring of this information necessarily takes up a certain amount of time.

I have accordingly furnished Returns of the imports and exports at Jaffa, as well as Returns of Shipping, for the year 1897 and for the seven previous years; also for the years 1885, 1875, and 1862.[1] A comparison can be made between the Returns of these years and some idea may be formed as to the progress of the trade of Jaffa during the last 35 years.

From the annexed tables it will be seen that the amount of the imports has during the last eight years somewhat increased, but that the exports show an inclination to diminution; and it may be said that during the eight years referred to the trade of Jaffa has been fluctuating. Comparing, however, the Returns for the eight years ending 1897 with the Returns for 1885, 1875 and 1862 a marked increase in both the exports and imports is observable. The same may be said as regards the number of vessels that entered and cleared at the port of Jaffa, but the amount of tonnage shows during the last 35 years a steady increase, the total tonnage of all arrivals and departures in 1862 being 145,768 tons; in 1875, 334,851 tons; in 1885, 710,170 tons; in 1890, 908,515 tons; and in 1897, 1,029,004 tons. The total number of vessels that entered and cleared during the years above mentioned were respectively, 635, 485, 1938, 1434[2] and 1376, but it should be remembered that many of these were sailing ships of small tonnage which were afterwards replaced by steam vessels of considerable size.

As regards British trade it will be observed from the annexed Returns that it has declined of late years,[3] — due in a great measure to the active competition of other nations, the demand for cheap goods, the small profits realized, and the nature of the credit to be given. On the other hand British

1    The Enclosure is not published here (see the data in Avitzur).
2    The correct figure is 1,534. In 1898 a total of 1,485 ships entered the harbor of Jaffa.
3    Not mentioned in the Enclosure. The extent of British trade in Jaffa port, according to Avitzur (in £), is as follows:

|         | 1885   | 1892   | 1893   | 1895   | 1896   | 1897   | 1898   |
|---------|--------|--------|--------|--------|--------|--------|--------|
| Imports | 52,375 | 50,150 | 52,600 | 29,117 | 27,900 | 32,400 | 30,850 |
| Exports | 23,799 | 71,610 | 69,968 | 40,600 | 55,800 | 59,500 | 61,800 |

Shipping shows a very marked and steady increase, during the eight years ended 1897, as well as during the whole of the 35 years previous to 1897.[4] [...]

With reference to the question as to whether the present British Consular Agent fulfils the requirements of his post I would respectfully remark that Mr Amzalak was appointed on the recommendation of my predecessor, Mr Moore, in 1872, as being, at the time, the most suitable person available for the post.[5] He is a native of Gibraltar and a British Subject, and was engaged in commerce at Jaffa; and is now 70 years of age. He, however, is entirely ignorant of the English and French languages, but speaks Judeo-Spanish, Italian, Arabic and Hebrew, although he can only read and write the two last. He is, therefore, obliged, in order to carry on his official correspondence which is sometimes in English and at other times in French — the English being very deficient — to employ a Clerk, and as he is unable to revise what is written he is at the mercy of this employe as regards the mode of expression. It will thus be seen that his education, — although he is not naturally wanting in intelligence, — leaves much to be desired. At the date of his appointment in 1872, when there were only a few Jews under British protection at Jaffa, and not many British vessels called at that port, he filled the post of Consular Agent fairly well, but times have altered since then and Jaffa has become a very different place. It will be seen from the annexed Returns[6] that the Consular Fees collected at Jaffa have doubled during recent years, and that whereas in 1875 there were only 2, and in 1885 6 English born residents in the place, in 1897 they numbered 16. The number of English tourists who passed through Jaffa in 1890 (no record was kept before that date) was 802, and in 1897 there were 1305. Since 1872, the year of Mr Amzalak's appointment, the "Church Missionary Society" and the "London Jews' Society" have both opened Mission stations at Jaffa and in the neighbourhood, and in 1885 a handsome English hospital supported by private contributions was established in Jaffa.[7]

It will thus be perceived that Jaffa has made considerable progress during the last 35 years, especially so since the opening of the Jaffa–Jerusalem railway in 1892, and that under these circumstances it is very essential that Great Britain should be represented at that port by a person whose education and attainments would be more suitable to the present requirements of the post than those of the actual Consular Agent, and who would also have the

4    In 1886, 28 British steamships entered Jaffa; the numbers for 1891, 1893, 1894 and 1898, were 51, 69, 88 and 87 ships respectively.
5    See above, the introduction to No. 63.
6    Not attached to the report.
7    The Medical Mission Hospital apparently was founded in 1883. In its first year of operation, it treated more than 12,000 patients. For details, see: Bell, pp. 56–57.

same standing as the representatives of France, Germany, and Russia, who are all paid Officers of the Crown.

In considering this matter, however, it must be borne in mind that an English Company is now actively pushing forward the railway between Caiffa and Damascus,[8] and should a branch be made connecting this railway with the present line from Jaffa to Jerusalem, not a little of the traffic will be diverted from Jaffa to Caiffa, the latter post affording better anchorage in bad weather, and it may be doubtful whether the present Commercial progress of Jaffa will be maintained.

I have the honour to add that in making the above remarks respecting Mr Consular Agent Amzalak, I would state that, as far as his integrity, and zeal in wishing to discharge his duties, are concerned, I have found him blameless, and that he bears a very good name at Lloyds' whose Agent in Jaffa he has been for many years past.

John Dickson

## 79    N. O'Conor to Marquess of Salisbury Prohibition of Jewish Immigration

Ottoman policy regarding Jewish immigration to Palestine became stricter in mid-1898, and from then on individuals, not only groups, were detained at the port of Jaffa and prevented from disembarking. Since there were British subjects among them, protests were constantly lodged with the Sublime Porte (see Hyamson, Nos. 392, 397, 400, 404–406, 410). As time passed, however, the British position eroded to some degree. Her Majesty's Government was willing to accept the Turkish claim that the prohibition stemmed from considerations of "public health," as a precautionary hygienic measure, and that they had no objections to visits of thirty days, upon the posting of a security bond of 50 Turkish pounds, to be returned to the tourist when he left Palestine at the end of the month (Hyamson, Nos. 420, 422–426). It also became clear, however, that Russian Jews residing in Jerusalem sought to become naturalized British subjects, hoping thereby to obtain British protection against possible deportation from the country. The Ambassador in Constantinople expressed his displeasure with such actions, and even instructed Consul Dickson to cancel the registration of these people (*ibid.*, No. 418). Accordingly, the Ambassador also adopted a negative stance in the following matter.

8    See above, No. 71.

My Lord,

Before approaching the Sublime Porte on the subject of the action of the Turkish Consulate-General in London in refusing to affix a visa to the passport of Mr S. Brown to enable him to proceed to Palestine and reside there, as shown in the correspondence enclosed in Your Lordship's despatch no. 153 of the 1st instant,[1] I venture to revert to the point raised in my despatch to Your Lordship no. 650 of December 13 last,[2] as to whether it is fitting that British protection should be extended in Palestine to Russian Jews who have obtained British naturalisation with the object of evading the regulation excluding Russian Jews from the country.

I am still of opinion that it is not desirable to exercise pressure upon the Ottoman Authorities in favour of Russian Jews, naturalized in England, a category which appears to include Mr S. Brown.[3] If we do so in one case, numbers of Russian, Polish, and Roumanian Jews are likely to seek naturalisation in England solely for the purpose of subsequently establishing themselves in Palestine. That many such persons have already adopted this course is shown by Mr Dickson's despatch no. 67 of November 21,[4] enclosed in my despatch to Your Lordship already referred to. It appears to me that Her Majesty's Government have no interest in promoting the establishment of a Russian Jewish Colony in the Holy Land, and, unless otherwise instructed by Your Lordship, I am disposed to confine our representations to cases of interference with the treaty rights of bonafide British subjects only.[5]

As stated in my above-mentioned despatch, I understand that the claim of Russian Jews naturalized in England to enjoy British protection in Germany with a view to settling in portions of the German Empire where Jews are not permitted to reside was negatived by the Law Officers of the Crown, and that instructions were sent to Berlin accordingly.

N.R. O'Conor

---

1     Not copied. It was stated in a previous letter, dated 2 June 1899, that Saul Brown resides in England for thirty years (in Sheffield). He was over seventy years old and desired to immigrate to Palestine. In 1898 he was granted a visa by the Turkish Consul in London, but he did not go to Palestine, due to illness, and now, his request to renew his visa had been rejected (FO 83/1723).

2     Hyamson, No. 409.

3     The Ambassador ignored the fact that Brown had already been living in England for thirty years.

4     Hyamson, No. 408.

5     Brown's request to intervene with the Turkish government was refused.

# 80   J. Dickson to N. O'Conor
## Establishment of Caza Beer-Sheba

The Negev, including Beer-Sheba, was only formally under Ottoman rule; in practice, the Bedouin inhabitants of the region did as they pleased. Not until 1890 did the Turks in fact assert their authority over the Beer-Sheba district, when they sent a military contingent to take control of the area and keep the Bedouin in check. In 1894 the Turks established a small garrison force in the fortress of el-Jahir, to prevent warfare between the Bedouin tribes. After a few years, the Ottoman authorities saw fit to separate the area from the Gaza Caza and to establish an administrative unit that would ensure better control over the Negev.
The remarks of the Consul concerning the Turkish-Egyptian border are most interesting.

FO 195/2062 — No. 43                                      Jerusalem, November 20, 1899

Sir,

I have the honour to inform Your Excellency that, on the recommendation of the Mutessarif of this Sandjak,[1] an Imperial Trade was recently issued by the Sultan authorizing the erection of the district of Beer-Sheba into a Caza, to be governed by a Caimakam whose residence will be fixed at Beer-Sheba.[2]

Beer-Sheba is situated on the Wady Seba, a stream which, under the name of Wady Ghazzeh, empties itself into the Sea, a little to the South of Gaza. Its modern name is Bir-es-Seba, and it lies to the South East of Gaza at a distance of 26 or 27 miles but consists at present of merely a "Khan" or Caravanserai. It has, however, been considered that the position is favourable for the encouragement of trade with the Bedouin Arabs, who at certain times of the year assemble in large numbers in the locality to pasture and water their flocks. The surrounding country is under cultivation, crops of wheat and barley being raised by the Arabs, and there is an abundant supply of water which is drawn from seven wells, three of which are large and never dry.[3] The

---

1   The initiative came from the Governor of the Jerusalem district, Tewfik Pasha (November 1897–May 1901).
2   The first Caimakam was Ismail Kemal Bek. He came to Beer-Sheba accompanied by a company of police and gendarmes who were responsible for maintaining public order.
3   This alludes to the tradition that the name "Beer-Sheba" means seven (Hebrew: *sheva*) wells (sing., *be'er*). Archaeologists claim that the name derives from a well that was close to the Canaanite city of Sheba. According to the Bible, the source of the name is in the oath (*shvu'ah*) taken by Abraham and Abimelech (Gen. 21:31; but see also Gen. 26:33).

Arab tribes who mostly frequent the place are the Tayaha, the Tarabeen, the Azazmeh, the Jarrar and the Hanajreh. The climate is said to be very healthy.

As the creation of a new sub-province, under the administration of a Turkish Governor, near the confines of Egypt, may not be without interest, I would beg to submit a few remarks on the subject, but more especially in reference to the boundaries of Egyptian territory. The limits of this Mutessariflik southwards and to the South West, in the direction of Egypt, seem to be very vaguely defined, and the Turkish Officials, connected with the administration of this Province, have no precise ideas on the subject. El-Arish for instance is often spoken of, by the people of this country, as belonging to Turkey, and I have a map in my possession, published by the Turkish Authorities at Damascus, on which the town of El-Arish is marked as within the boundaries of this Mutessariflik.

According to the Firman addressed by the Sultan of Turkey to Mehemet Ali, Pasha of Egypt, on June 1, 1841, the Viceroy was granted the Government of Egypt "within its ancient boundaries (to quote the words of the Firman) such as they are to be found in the map which is sent unto thee by my Grand Vizier now in Office with a seal affixed to it." No such map, which no doubt since 1841 has been somewhat modified, seems to be known to any of the Turkish Officials of this Mutessariflik, and their ideas as to where the limits of Turkish territory end and Egyptian territory begins are, as I have already stated, extremely undefined. As far as I am able to ascertain from ordinary maps in my possession, the Egyptian boundary would seem to start from a place on the coast of the Mediterranean called Tell Refa, about 24 miles to the North of the town of El-Arish, curve slightly inwards, and proceed in a south-westerly direction to the 33° of East longitude, leaving a strip of country along the Mediterranean, together with El-Arish, as Egyptian territory. From the 33° East longitude the boundary line then appears to return eastwards as far as Jebel Magra, and then to bend almost direct Southwards to Akaba.

I am informed by the Mutessarif of Jerusalem that the details regarding the expenses of administration, the appointment of officials, the boundaries etc., of the new Caza of Beer Sheba, are now being settled by the Ministry of the Interior at Constantinople; and as the formation of a sub-Province within this Consular District, so far South in the direction of Egypt, renders it necessary that I should have somewhat more accurate knowledge as to the limits of Turkish territory towards the South and South-West of Palestine, I would beg that I may be furnished with some map giving the precise boundaries between Turkey and Egypt, for the use of this Consulate.

John Dickson

# 81 J.H. Monahan to Drummond Hay
# Report on Jewish Colonization and J.C.A.

Jewish settlement activity, which began in 1882, quickly reached a crisis. Only with the generous help of Baron Edmond de Rothschild were the settlements able to establish themselves and develop. As time passed, the Baron took settlement after settlement under his patronage. He invested great sums of money in their maintenance and development, and his officials took care of their every want. Despite these vast amounts of money, however, the colonies did not attain a firm economic basis under the direction of the Baron's officials. After having lost tens of millions of francs, on 1 January 1900 he transferred all his property in Palestine, which included about fifteen settlements and land encompassing tens of thousands of dunams, to the Jewish Colonization Association (JCA), adding an additional 15,000,000 francs to firmly establish the colonies. The JCA assumed the administration of the settlements with the goal of improving their economic state, and succeeded in this to a significant extent, while drastically changing the method of financial support and economic activity.

James Henry Monahan, a professional member of the Levant Consular Service since 1888, served as Vice-Consul in Haifa from 1898 to 1905. This report was sent to his superior, Drummond Hay, Consul-General in Beirut. On 13 February 1900 Hay passed on the report to the Ambassador, Sir Nicholas O'Conor.

FO 195/2075 — No. 8                                    Haifa, February 5, 1900

FO 78/5479

Sir,

I have the honour to report that much interest is excited here by pending changes in the administration of Jewish Colonies in Palestine, and by the proposed formation of new ones in this Vice-Consular district.

With the exception of one small, unprosperous, and unhealthy Colony of Russian Jews, called Khidera,[1] on the boundary of the Jaffa caza, the only Jewish Colony now established in this district is the important one in the caza of Haifa, namely, Samarin or Zichron-Jacob, including its three small dependencies.[2] It has hitherto been supported by Baron Edmond de Rothschild and

---

1    Haderah was founded in 1891. It suffered for years from malaria, which claimed many victims and halted the development of the settlement.

2    Zikhron Ya'akov was founded in 1882, and Baron de Rothschild purchased a large tract of

administered by his French nominees. Its lands are about 4,000 acres (15,000 dunums) mostly vineyards, and its population about 2,000 souls.

Samarin is now being transferred to a Society with an English title "The Jewish Colonization Association" (commonly known here as J.C.A.).[3]

Sajara, in Tiberias caza, between Hattin and Mount Tabor, consisting of a village about 4,000 acres of arable land, was sold four years ago by an Ottoman subject named Mudawar, to M. Simon Jourdain, a representative of Baron E. de Rothschild.[4] M. Jourdain has lately sold or transferred it to a representative of the same J.C.A. Three other villages near Sajara, having in all about 4,000 acres, are being sold to the same Society by Messrs. Sursok, of Beirout, though the official sale is not yet complete.[5] Two houses have been built on the Sajara lands, but no Jews appear yet to have settled either on these lands or on those of the three other villages. By Ottoman Law no foreign Jew is allowed to buy land in Palestine, but this difficulty is probably being surmounted in the usual manner. Such, in brief, are the changes and acquisitions in this Vice-Consular district.

I understand that the Jewish Colonies in Jaffa and elsewhere in Palestine are also being transferred to the J.C.A.

So far as I can learn this Society is now in one sense only nominally English. The Central Administration is in Paris, the Director-General being a M. Levin (? Levi), who is also at the head of the Alliance Israelite.[6]

I understand, however, though my information is not clear on the point, that the Society is legally a British one. A reason given for the transfer is that British Company Law is more favourable than French Law. Another reason given is the Anti-Semitism in France. I am informed that Baron de Rothschild has in fact never had recourse to the French Government for support or protection.

---

   land next to it. In 1889 Bat-Shlomo was founded, followed by Shfeia in 1891, in which an agricultural school was established; in 1893 a glass bottle factory, which would prove to be a failure, was founded in Tantura.

3    The Jewish Colonization Association was established in September 1891 by Baron Maurice de Hirsch and devoted its main efforts to the Jewish colonization effort in Argentina, which was inspired and maintained by Baron Hirsch. Only following the death of Baron Hirsch in 1897 did the JCA resolve to also support Jewish colonization in Palestine. Toward the beginning of the twentieth century it agreed to take over all the colonies which had been supported until then by Baron de Rothschild.

4    A farmstead was established on the lands of Sedjera in 1899 and the permanent settlement was founded there in 1901.

5    Kfar Tabor, Yavne'el, and Beit Gan were established on these lands in 1901–1902.

6    Narcisse Leven (1833–1915), a native of Germany, was among the founders of the Alliance Israélite Universelle, serving for many years as its Vice-President. In 1896 he was also appointed President of the JCA.

A commission sent by the J.C.A., to arrange the transfer, is expected here.

It is said that the Baron wishes that the Colonies should not depend on his individual life. I gather that he also probably wishes to get rid of the great sole responsibility for them, though under the new arrangement he takes a part in their management and guarantees the J.C.A. against pecuniary loss. His expenditure on Samarin must have been enormous. He has given it complete modern wine machinery and great cellars, in which I learn there are now as many as 18,000 barrels of wine. The French vines were destroyed by phylloxera, and have had to be gradually replaced at his expense by American ones. The white wine of Samarin is of very good quality, but the wine trade has hitherto not been a success. The Colony is supplied with good water, brought up a hill by steam power, another gift of the Baron. To his generosity are also due, mainly, if not entirely, the following advantages. There are some kilometres of excellent roads in different directions, and the hedges, wire fencing, and rows of trees have a most European appearance. There is the local salaried Administration, including a Director, secretary, accountant, engineer, wine expert, and doctor, with their houses and offices on an expensive scale. There are a good small hospital, a pleasant public garden, and a large store in which much business is done with natives and with colonists. The Baron, besides, gives a subvention of, I am informed, 12 fr. per month to every colonist until a living can be got from the land, the colonists being afterwards supposed to repay the Baron on easy terms and finally take possession of the land.

It is expected that this system of subventions will be largely modified by the J.C.A. and that the new Administration will be more economical.

The Samarin Jews seem to be mostly from Gallicia and Poland.[7] They are supposed and said to work habitually in the vineyeards, but personal observation inclines me to think that very little manual work on the land is done by any of them. The native fallaheen are employed for the purpose.

Foreign Jews are not supposed to be allowed to settle in this country, but Jewish settlers from Europe often arrive in Haifa where there seem to be exceptional facilities for their admission by pecuniary arrangement with the local officials.[8]

J.H. Monahan

7    Most of the settlers in Zikhron Ya'akov came from Roumania.
8    On 13 March 1900 the Ambassador sent this report to the Foreign Secretary, adding his regrets that the JCA "should have acquired the status of a British Company [...] It will, I fear, in the event of differences between the Association in its corporate capacity and the Ottoman Government, be incumbent on the Embassy to protect its interests, although as appears from Mr. Monahan's Report, its management and capital are French and the persons for whose benefit it exists seems to be mostly Polish Jews" (FO 78/5479).

# 82 J. Dickson to N. O'Conor
# Quarterly Report

For years the Consulate had been required to submit only an annual report on events in Palestine, mainly of economic activity, but from the beginning of the twentieth century the Embassy in Constantinople began to demand quarterly reports as well. In general, these were routine, and do not provide much fresh information. The following report, however, the first of the quarterly presentations, is of importance because of the great amount of detail it provides regarding the administrative bureaucracy of the Sanjak of Jerusalem, and for its data on the maritime traffic at Jaffa.

FO 195/2084 — No. 15                                        Jerusalem, May 11, 1900

Sir,

In reply to Your Excellency's Despatch of the 29th of January last, asking for a concise report, at the beginning of each quarter, on the administrative and economic state of this Mutessarifat, I have the honour to furnish the following observations: —

The Mutessarifat or Sandjak of Jerusalem is bounded on the north by a line which may be said to run from the Coast of the Mediterranean, near the mouth of the river Auja, eastward through the village of Sinjil, to the bridge over the river Jordan near Jericho; on the south by a line drawn from the Mediterranean midway between Gaza and El-Arish to the town of Akaba; on the east by the the river Jordan, the Dead Sea, and the valley running south from the latter to Akaba; and on the west by the Mediterranean.[1] It may be said to correspond very nearly with the ancient Roman Province of Judaea, as distinguished from Samaria and Galilee; but the boundaries are not clearly defined, and are traced in accordance with the bordering villages and lands belonging to them which come under the administration of the Mutessarifat.

The population of this Mutessarifat numbers about 300,000, and is made up of different sects as follows: — Mohamedans 195,000; Jews 70,000; and Christians 35,000.

The Mutessarifat is divided into three Caimakamliks or Cazas, namely: those of Jaffa, Gaza, and Hebron;[2] and into two Mudiries, Bethlehem and

1   The description of the borders corresponds to the details in No 73, above.
2   It is strange that no mention is made of the establishment of the Caza of Beer-Sheba, of which the Consul had already reported a half year previously (see above, No. 80).

Ramleh, the former being in the district of Jerusalem and the latter within that of Jaffa.

The capital of the Mutessarifat is Jerusalem containing about 65,000 inhabitants,[3] and is connected with the seaport of Jaffa by a railway, which was constructed in 1892. The distance between the two places, by rail, is 54 miles, but in consequence of the numerous abrupt curves on the line, which make a high rate of speed somewhat risky, the journey is performed in 3½ hours.[4] Jerusalem is also the Seat of Government.

The Governor of the Mutessarifat is Mohamed Tevfik Bey,[5] a young man of integrity and intelligence, and animated with a desire to ameliorate as much as possible the condition of the province under his rule, but his efforts in this direction are much hampered by his inability to obtain the necessary facilities from the central government. He holds the rank of Mutessarif, but has practically the powers of a Vali conferred upon him, for he is directly responsible to the Porte, and is not dependent on either the Valis of Damascus or Beyrout. The other officers of Government are the Cadi, who presides over the Court of First Instance, as well as over the Court of "Sheri", the Mufti, the Muhasebji (treasurer), the Chief of the "Vacoufs", the Mudir El Tahrirat (Chief Secretary), the Mamur El-Nufus (head of the Census Department), the Mamur El-Imlak (Director of the "Verghi" Department), Mamur El-Tabo (Chief of the land Registry Department), Mamur El-Tasakir (Head of the Passport Department), Amin Sanduk (Government Cashier) and Reis El-Baladie (Head of the Municipality). There is also a Military Commandant Rifaat Pasha, and a Chief of the Police Serwet Bey.

The Mutessarif is assisted in the Government of his district by the Administrative Council (Medjlis Idaret) which is composed of 12 Members, six Mussulman and six non-Mussulman. Of the Mussulman Members four are permanent, namely: the Cadi, the Mufti, the Mudir el Tahrirat and the Muhassebji; the other two are elected every two years. The non-Mussulman Members consist of four permanent ones, the spiritual representatives of their respective communities, namely: a Latin, a Greek Orthodox, an Armenian and a Jew, and two liable to election, namely, a Latin and a Greek Member. The Mutessarif is President of the Administrative Council. He is assisted by a Secretary and Interpreter, who is also a Medium of communication with the Consular Corps.

The Tribunals consist of the Court of First Instance, and the Court of

3   The figure is exaggerated. The population in Jerusalem in 1900 did not exceed 55–60,000, of which about 35,000 were Jews.
4   See above, No. 74. The travel time stated here is the official time; according, however, to memoirs and travellers' accounts, the journey usually took much longer, up to 5–6 hours.
5   See above, No. 80, n. 1.

"Sheri" or Ecclesiastical Court, which are presided over by the Cadi, who is appointed by the Sheik-ul-Islam. The Court of First Instance is divided into two sections, the Civil and Criminal, the former being composed of a Mussulman and Christian Member and four other Members (two Mussulman, a Christian and a Jew) who attend when Commercial cases are heard. [...]

The amount of the remittances to Constantinople was about the same as that in the previous year, namely: a little over £T. 43,000.

The total value of the exports from the port of Jaffa for the three months ended March 31, was £84,880 and of the imports £52,690.

The number of vessels which called at that port during the three months referred to was as follows: — British, 68 steam vessels, of a total tonnage of 62,777 tons; French, 16 of a total tonnage of 26,136 tons; Austrian 27, tonnage 37,261; Russian 23, tonnage 32,008; German 5, tonnage 8,763; Italian 3, tonnage 2,505; and Ottoman 3 steam vessels of an aggregate tonnage of 3,147 tons and 2 sailing vessels, total tonnage 77 tons.[6]

In my next Quarterly Report I shall have the honour to submit to Your Excellency further details respecting the administration of this Province and on its economic condition.

John Dickson

# 83  M. Berouti to J. Dickson
## Establishment of a Vice-Consulate at Gaza

As early as 7 February 1899, Dickson had pointed to the necessity of appointing a Consular Agent at Gaza, considering its growing economic importance: "Gaza is looked upon as the principal outlet in Palestine for the exportation of cereals, the grain being taken down to the sea-shore compiled up in heaps during the season for making shipments and the Turkish Authorities having established a Custom-House at the place of landing and embarkation. Gaza has of late years begun to assume more importance as one of the towns of Palestine, both commercially and as an English Missionary station. Very large amounts of barley are now annually shipped to England by British firms, who sometimes send out agents on the spot to look after the business

6   See above, No. 78, for the maritime traffic at Jaffa until 1897. The Consul reported in a letter from 11 May 1900 of a new shipping line: "Deutsche Levante Linie (Hamburg), which runs monthly a line of steamers on the Coast of Palestine and Syria" (FO 195/2084). Also in the yearly report for 1899, British ships head the list, at 180; the French are in second place, with 65, the Austrians next, with 60, and the Russians after them, with 44. Britain had a 14.6% share of the entire import-export trade ("Trade of Palestine for the Year 1899," *Diplomatic and Consular Reports*, No. 2405).

[...] Under these circumstances it may soon become necessary to appoint at Gaza a Consular Agent to look after British Interests" (FO 78/5008).
Michel Berouti had already been employed for several years as a British shipping agent at Jaffa; his duties included dealing with ships in Gaza. Accordingly, he indicated to the Consul the urgency of the matter.

FO 195/2084                                                    Jaffa, Sept. 25, 1900
Copy — Confidential

Sir,
    I have the honour to submit to you the following: —
Being the Agent of the 'Prince Line' of steamers for Jaffa & Gaza, I think it my duty to inform you that, as several of our steamers go to Gaza for the purpose of loading grain, barley etc., from that port, & have often to come back to Jaffa to go through certain formalities in presenting papers to be signed by the British Consular Agent in this place, I find it very inconvenient and very costly that this method should continue much longer, & I therefore venture to solicit that a British Vice Consulate may be established at Gaza for the convenience of our steamers & the interest of British trade in general. Several other British steamers call also at Gaza, & we often have difficulties with the Government which we are obliged to suffer for want of a Consul there. The trade between Gaza & the United Kingdom is very important, the export being of about £120,000 per year. The British flag shall have a better future, & a British Consulate should be established there before the other Powers who have almost no trade with that port.[1]

M. Berouti

1    It is clear that the Foreign Office rejected the proposal to establish a Vice-Consulate in Gaza, while agreeing to appoint a Consular Agent, if a suitable local candidate would be found who, like Amzalak in Jaffa, would agree to fill the post without pay. Dickson searched for such an aspirant for a long time, after having rejected Amzalak's suggestion to appoint his son Joseph to the position. Only on 16 February 1902 was he able to inform the Foreign Office that after a great deal of searching he had been able to find an acceptable local person. He proposed "Alexander Anton Knesevich, an Austrian subject [a Christian of Polish origin], who would be willing to accept the appointment. He was 22 years employed by the Missionaries as Dispenser in their Hospital, but is now engaged in business on his account. He is also Lloyd's agent in Gaza and a fit person for this post" (FO 195/2175, No. 73).
Once again, much time passed. On 16 January 1905 the Foreign Office finally announced that it agreed to Dickson's proposal and Knesevich was appointed Consular Agent at Gaza, without salary (FO 195/2199). Knesevich also dealt with the affairs of the Jews in Gaza, and took an active part in the purchase of land in Rafah (see below, Nos. 122–123, 126–127).

## 84  J. Dickson to M. de Bunsen
Report on Jerusalem (Extract)

The following is a section of the quarterly report pertaining to the third quarter of 1900, dealing with the administration of the city of Jerusalem, its officials and their salaries, and transportation problems in the city. As is his practice, the Consul provides full details of the administrative aspects and concludes with several data regarding trade via Jaffa port.
The Jerusalem municipality was apparently first established in 1867 as one of the first municipalities in the Ottoman Empire, but it started to function fully only in 1877, upon the promulgation of the Municipalities Law.
Sir Maurice de Bunsen served as the First Secretary of the Embassy in Constantinople, and at times as Chargé d'Affaires, from 1897 to 1902.

FO 195/2084 — No. 61

Jerusalem, November 13, 1900

Sir

[...] The rapid growth of Jerusalem during recent years has increased the labours of the Municipality and given more importance to its members as a body. The Municipal Council is composed of a President, Said Effendi,[1] who is assisted by a Chief Clerk and a Cashier, and, at present, five members (the nominal number being ten) — three Moslems, a Christian and a Jew.[2] The President receives a salary of P. 1200 per month; the Chief Clerk P. 600, and the Cashier P. 400; but the members are unpaid. There are besides, three under Clerks, each receiving a Salary of P. 300 per month; a Chief Inspector with a Salary of P. 600; two Inspectors with a Salary of P. 250 each; an Architect paid P. 600 and a Doctor P. 900. The revenues and expenses amount annually to between £T. 6000 and £T. 7000, the latter consisting mainly of expenses in paving and repairing the streets and water courses, macadamizing the carriage roads, funeral expenses of pauper Moslems, Salaries etc., a large margin being left for 'extraordinary' expenses, such as those incurred during the visit of the German Emperor in 1898, when the outlay was very considerable. Since then the Municipality has been in debt £T. 2000, which it has not yet

---

1    Said Effendi el Haldi was appointed to his position in 1902.
2    In 1898 Joshua Yellin was elected as a city councillor. In fact, another Jew — Rahamim Mizrahi — had also been elected, but the Governor refused to confirm the election of two Jews, appointing an Armenian in Mizrahi's stead.

been able to pay off. The ware [!] and tear of the carriage roads in consequence of the growing population and increase in traffic necessitates a proportionate consumption of water for the repair and watering of the roads and streets, and the want of a sufficient number of cisterms to furnish the required supply has driven the Municipal Council to great straits. The result has been that during the past summer the roads have been in a wretched condition, the dust excessive, and the accumulation of rubbish and dirt so great that in September last there was a severe outbreak of small pox which has decimated the lower classes of the inhabitants, and has recently broken out among the troops stationed in Jerusalem numbering about 500 men.

In my previous report I referred to the Collection of the tithes the exact amount of which had not yet been known. They amounted for the Turkish financial year 1316 to £T. 47,693, for the whole of this Sandjak, being less than the Government estimate, and a decrease of about £T. 2000 on the previous year.

The value of the imports through the port of Jaffa for the quarter ended the 30th September amounted to £142,210 or an increase of about £66,185 compared with the previous quarter. The exports for the same period reached £53,590, showing also an increase of £8,905.[3]

John Dickson

# 85  P. Wheeler / W.Masterman to J. Dickson
## Sanitary Conditions in Jerusalem

The following severe description of the catastrophic sanitary conditions in Jerusalem, and especially within the Old City, was written on the same day as the Consul's report regarding the administration of the city (above, No. 84). Two British physicians in Jerusalem felt the need to inform the Consul of the serious condition and to warn him of the danger of epidemics. The graphic description paints a quite chilling picture of poor sanitation in Jerusalem on the threshold of the twentieth century.

3     See the data for the first quarter of 1900, No. 82, above.

FO 195/2084
Copy

Dear Sir,

We the undersigned British Medical men practising in the city of Jerusalem, feel it our duty to call your attention, as H.M. representative, to the deplorable sanitary condition existing here. The present state of affairs is a standing danger to British residents and visitors but with the plague so near at hand to leave things as they are is to invite a disaster.

Jerusalem is extraordinarly well furnished with private Hospitals supported by various foreign Societies & there are many medical men of all nations, but such are the conflicting interests of the various nationalities & religions represented here & especially such is the entire indifference of the Ottoman Government, that nothing so far is being done or can by private individuals be done, to improve a condition of things which, considering the prominence of this city in the eyes of the World, is a disgrace to civilization.

As regards those things patent to all — the *streets* are kept in a state of constant filth,[1] with perhaps the exception of one or two of the carriage roads: piles of vegetable & animal substances in a rotting condition, are allowed to accumulate in every corner & are left there for days & often even months. In the Jewish quarter especially, being the largest & poorest of all, the state of things is deplorable. When, as is their custom on Fridays the Jews clean out their houses the house refuse is poured freely into the roads & we can testify that often it is left there uncleaned for many days. On the Jewish Sabbath (Saturday) the accumulated dirt in the streets is most objectionable.

Secondarily in all but the main streets & especially under archways (where foul air can specially accumulate) it is the custom for the people to answer the calls of nature whenever convenient to themselves. Several streets, frequently used by British visitors & travellers, and one in particular passing between British property on both sides of the road, are rendered almost impassable by the effluvia of the excreta against the walls & along the sides. No attempt appears to be made either to stop the nuisance or to clean away the filth, indeed in one of the worse places soldiers of the Government are among the chief offenders. Public urinals are practically unknown.

Coming to such large questions as *drainage & water supply* it is impossible to fully represent the state of affairs &, as things are, hopeless to expect much improvement. The drainage is utterly filthy, the stone lined channels are constantly getting blocked & overflowing & the distribution of the sewage in the valley leading to Siloam (Silwan) is one which no civilized municipal

---

1    See the report of the Consul above, No. 84.

Authorities would tolerate. The house drains are practically all untrapped and are constantly getting blocked.

The *water supply* by cisterns under the houses is most unsatisfactory especially as regards quantity. Among the poor during a great part of the summer water of, often, most questionable quality, has to be purchased in skins. As this city is steadily growing in population the water supply is becoming a question of increasing urgency. It seems to us that there can be no satisfactory solution short of restoring, as could be easily done, the supply of water which in olden times entered the city as a regular running stream from the springs at 'Solomon Pools' and 'Arub".[2] These supplies brought to the city in iron pipes, carefully guarded & looked after, would do much to make the city more healthy. It appears to us that the only possible way of getting this undertaking taken in hand would be by a joint representation to the Ottoman Government from the various Embassies or if necessary by the grant of a 'Firman' to a European Waterworks Company.

The above mentioned nuisances lay the inhabitants & visitors of this city open to constant attacks of Malaria, Dysentery, Diarrhoea & Enteric Fever, but they also directly & indirectly open the road for *Epidemics* of a serious nature. A large part of the city is now just in the condition which would give a most ready lodgement to the Plague or Cholera. The close crowding of the inhabitants, their general poverty & the condition of their constitutions undermined by poor living, the breathing of sewer gases, the drinking of foul water & the constantly recurring attacks of Malaria, Dysentery & Diarrhoea present a combination most favourable for such a visitation.

Such an epidemic being more than probable we ask what provision is there to meet it? We are now in the throes of an epidemic of Small-pox more severe than has been known here for many years.[3] Whole streets have been visited, house by house & a considerable proportion of the inhabitants have perished from malignant & confluent attacks. Our hands, as private medical men, are powerless to strike at the root, or roots, of the evil, & the municipal Authorities appear to us to have made no attempt whatever to cope with it. The two urgent necessities, the isolation of the sick & of infected households & the vaccination of the healthy has never been attempted. As regards the first there is not a single hospital bed in Jerusalem open to the poor for any infectious disease. The houses of the poor are invariably one room. The smallpox case lies in one corner while the children of the house, usually unvaccinated, the other relations & usually too the children & adults of other households freely pass in & out. We can testify from experience that there is,

2   See above, No. 76.
3   This epidemic is also mentioned in the Consul's report above, No. 84.

almost invariably, no attempt to keep visitors from other houses from the 'houses' of smallpox cases nor to prevent convalescent but still infectious cases wandering into other houses or promenading the streets.

Percy d'Erf Wheeler, M.D., Medical Superintendant
English Mission Hospital
Ernest W. Gurney Masterman, Dept. Public Health[4]


## 86    Wainer Bros. to J. Dickson
## Complaint on Confiscation of Passports

In the last decade of the nineteenth century, the Ottoman authorities more strictly enforced the prohibition against Jewish immigration and limited the duration of their stay to thirty days, demanding a deposit of 50 Turkish pounds to ensure that they would indeed leave the country at the end of this period (see above, No. 79). The Jews generally found ways to circumvent these decrees. In November 1900 the authorities changed the regulations. Henceforward, those entering the country were required to deposit their passports, receiving in return a temporary permit ('red paper') for three months. At the end of this period, they were required to leave Palestine, when their passports would be returned to them. Anyone found in the country after the end of the three-month period would be expelled.

The Consuls of most of the Powers expressed strong opposition to the total ban on residence in Palestine, claiming that this prohibition ran contrary to the Capitulations. The matter was discussed at length by the Consul and the Ambassador, who also opposed these restrictions (see Hyamson, Nos. 440–459).

It is possible that the writers of the following letter were unaware of the ban on immigration and that they were supposed to leave the country after three months. In any event, they had no intention of doing so, and therefore requested the assistance of the Consul.

---

4    For Dr. Percy d'Erf Wheeler, see above, No. 70, n. 3.
Dr. Gurney Masterman arrived in Jerusalem on 15 December 1892 and joined the medical staff in the Mission Hospital. He left the country after some years, returning in October 1899 as 'Assistant Medical Missionary'. He was also in charge of the Department of Public Health. Before the outbreak of World War I, he became the Director of the hospital. Masterman stayed in Jerusalem for many years after the war. His wife was the grand-daughter of Bishop Gobat.

FO 195/2106
Copy

Jaffa, February 26, 1901

Dear Sir,
   You will be aware about me Aaron Wainer and my brother Solomon, of Leeds, England, have established some time ago a business at Jaffa, Palestine, of English Machinery and ironmongery. Our family at Jaffa have managed the business until now, but it is on the increase, and we have had to come ourselves to Jaffa; we landed on the 24th of December 1900, but on the port, Jaffa, they have taken our passports and not returned to us yet. Now we hear that the Government of Turkey have given notice that we shall have to leave the country after the expiration of three months from our arrival. You may imagine, dear Consul, the loss we shall have when it comes to it, so we considered the best to let you know in time, so you may be able to get permission for us to stay here for regular, and to give us our passes back; hoping you will attend with success and awaiting your kind answer we remain etc.[1]

Wainer Bros.<br>British Subjects

## 87   J. Dickson to N. O'Conor
## Demand for Expulsion of Jews

After Britain totally refused to acknowledge the new Ottoman regulations for the deposit of passports and the receipt of a temporary permit for three months (see above, No. 86), Dickson strongly defended the right of the Wainer brothers to remain in Palestine, and even to settle there. Negotiations were conducted between the Consular Agent at Jaffa, Haim Amzalak, and the local Governor, who demanded that the two brothers leave the country. Dickson categorically refused this ultimatum and reported about it to the Ambassador, though he noted that this case, too, referred to a "new" British subject.

1   It transpired that the Consul did intervene on their behalf, and the matter was also the subject of discussion afterwards (see below, No. 87).

296

FO 195/2106 — No. 20                                   Jerusalem, April 17, 1901

Sir,

    I have the honour to acknowledge, with sincere thanks, the receipt of Mr Barclay's[1] Despatch of the 16th ultimo, enclosing, for my information, the draft of a Despatch which Your Excellency had addressed to the Foreign Office, on the subject of Jewish immigration into Palestine, and approving of the course I had proposed to pursue in the event of the Local Authorities seeking to expel the British Jews Messrs Aaron and Solomon Wainer.

    I have now the honour to transmit to Your Excellency herewith a Copy of a Despatch which I have received from Mr Consular Agent Amzalak[2] reporting that the Caimakam of Jaffa had asked the expulsion of the two Jews above referred to, in conformity with the recent regulations issued by the Porte respecting the admission of Jews into Palestine.

    I have instructed Mr Consular Agent Amzalak to inform the Caimakam that as the regulations in question have not yet been accepted by His Majesty's Government, he must decline to put them into force; and should any attempt be made by the Local Authorities to compel Messrs Wainer Bros. to leave the country I shall report the matter to Your Excellency by telegram.

    I beg to add that on enquiring carefully into the Nationality of Messrs Wainer Bros. I have ascertained that they are natives of Russia and were naturalized in England in 1894, which is another example of Jewish emigrants from Russia availing themselves of British naturalization with the object of eventually settling in Palestine under British protection.[3]

    The enclosure in Mr Barclay's Despatch above mentioned is herewith returned.

John Dickson

# 88   J.H. Monohan to Drummond Hay
## Purchase of Atlith

The Vice-Consul in Haifa reported to his superior, the Consul-General in Beirut, regarding the purchase of the lands of Atlith for Jewish settlement. A copy of the letter was sent from Beirut to the Ambassador in Constantinople.

1   Sir George Barclay, Attaché in Constantinople (1898–1902); Chargé d'Affaires in Constantinople (1906–1908).
2   Not attached here. The letter from 16 April 1901 is located in the same file.
3   The file contains no more information regarding the fate of the brothers.

This land, purchased by Baron de Rothschild's officials in the early 1890s, was initially cultivated by Arab sharecroppers, the inhabitants of the nearby villages of Atlith and present-day Ein Hod. In 1899 the tract, together with all lands possessed by Baron de Rothschild, was transferred to the JCA. When a dispute broke out with the Arab sharecroppers, there was some apprehension that the lands would be declared a *Mahlul* area, i.e., untilled land, and the rights of the owners would be revoked. About ten farmers from the colony of Zikhron Ya'akov and its offshoots moved in 1901 onto these lands and began to work them. In order to make things easier for them, for appearances' sake the land was leased to a German farmer from Haifa, and the ten Jewish settlers presumably tilled the lands for him. Two huts were erected, a well was dug, and the entire plot was sown with grain. Permanent settlement began only in 1903–1904.

FO 78/5479 — No. 50                                    Haifa, October 25, 1901
Copy

Sir,

I have the honour to report as follows in addition to the passage respecting Jewish colonies in my last Quarterly Report.

Fifteen years ago the wife of Rashid Pasha, Vali of Syria, bought the village of Athlit (the wellknown 'Castellum Peregrinorum'),[1] between Haifa and the great Jewish colony Zamarin, from the villagers for £T 15,000. Nine years ago the agent of Baron de Rothschild bought the village from her for £T 12,000.(?)[2] The Jewish colony, or the Baron, went on taking the customary share of revenues due to the owner, that is 1/5 of the produce, until the year before last when the villagers refused to continue payment alleging that the sale was irregular as the Vali's wife had carried out the transfer without their consent. However, the title deeds appearing to be in order, the villagers lost their case before the tribunal of Haifa, large sums as is said being paid by the Jews to the Cadi and members of the Tribunal, and a month or two ago they withdrew the appeal they had lodged at Acre. Accordingly the Jewish Colony has now secure possession of the village and its lands extending to 10,000 dunums, about 3,000 acres. Last year, before the judgment in Haifa has been

---

1    'Castrum Peregrinorum' (The Pilgrims' Fortress) — the magnificent Crusader fortress which was established in 1218 and destroyed by the Mameluke conquerors in 1291. During the Crusader period, Atlith was an important harbour. Precise archaeological excavations were conducted there during the British Mandate period. For a detailed description of the fortress, whose ruins are still visible today, see: C.N. Johns, *Guide to 'Atlit — The Crusader Town and Surroundings*, Jerusalem 1947.

2    It cannot be determined who added the question mark. The surprise is at the price, which was lower than the original purchase price.

given, the Jews put in a German subject as tenant, evidently in order to have foreign protection. The Ottoman military authorities still resist their claim to the ruined fortress and to the houses and some lands of the village, but there is no military port at Athlit and the case of the military authorities seems weak. No Jews have yet settled in Athlit.[3] The registrar of title-deeds at Haifa says that the judgment can not be extended until the sanction of the Vali has been obtained, but as the Jews are the actual holders of the title-deeds it would seem that this objection is not legal and that this important acquisition has now, according to Law, been definitely secured to the Jewish Colonization Association.

The French Consul here has lately asked me about the status of the Jewish Colonization Association.[4] The Jewish colonists have applied to him for Consular assistance which he has declined to give as he believes that the association is an English Company registered in London. I could only tell him that I knew nothing officially of the matter and that no application for assistance had ever been made to me.

J.H. Monohan[5]

## 89  Lord Cromer to Marquess of Lansdowne
## Plan for a Jewish Settlement at El-Arish

The plan for Jewish settlement at El-Arish was first proposed in a memorandum dated 12 November 1902 by Theodor Herzl (1860–1904), the leader of the Zionist movement, to the British Foreign Secretary (FO 78/5479). This missive was preceded by a conversation between Herzl and Colonial Secretary Joseph Chamberlain, who directed him to the Foreign Secretary, Lord Lansdowne. The latter requested that Herzl submit a written proposal. This was the first instance of direct negotiations conducted by the Zionist Organization with a Great Power. Herzl stated in this memorandum, *inter alia*: "Our proposal is to establish in the Sinai Peninsula a Colony or Settlement of Jews [...] In the South East of the Mediterranean a Country at present worthless and almost uninhabited, could be made by the influence of England, a place of refuge, a home for oppressed Jews, if England will favour the establishment of a Jewish Colony such as I have referred to."

3    The Vice-Consul also apparently regarded the Jewish "sharecroppers" as working for the German farmer.
4    See above, No. 81, n. 3.
5    See above, in the introduction to No. 81.

The negotiations over settlement in El-Arish have been described at length in various sources, including Herzl's own diaries and his biographies, as well as the extensive essay: Bein, pp. 179–220. Bein published much of the documentation, in English and in Hebrew translation, which was in the Central Zionist Archives at the time he wrote his essay. Below are several important letters not published by Bein (see also Eliav, Rafah). Quite surprisingly, Hyamson makes no mention of the El-Arish proposal.

The Foreign Secretary explicitly told Herzl that in considering the matter, he would rely especially on the opinion of Lord Cromer, the British representative in Egypt at the time. The following is Cromer's reply to Herzl's memorandum, in which he expresses his skepticism and reservations regarding the plan. The response was sent to the Foreign Secretary; its contents were transmitted to Herzl on 18 December 1902 in a letter from the Foreign Office (see Bein, p. 187).

FO 78/5479 — No. 164                                    Cairo, 29th. November 1902

Confidential

My Lord,

I have the honour to reply to Your Lordship's despatch No. 225 of the 21st. Instant.[1]

I should, in the first instance, remark that I find it somewhat difficult to believe that the Zionist movement will really find much favour in the eyes of the Sultan. It is certainly a fact that Mr. Friedmann's venture, to which allusion is briefly made in Dr. Herzl's letter, caused considerable anxiety at Constantinople.[2] I do not, however, propose to discuss this branch of the question any further. I turn to that portion of the subject with which I am more immediately concerned, namely, the proposal to establish a Jewish Colony in the Sinai Peninsula.

I see no political objection to the establishment of such a Colony, provided that due attention is paid to certain conditions which I will now explain.

In the first place, Your Lordship is aware that the Turkish and Egyptian

1   In a letter from 21 November 1902 accompanying the memorandum, the Foreign Secretary wrote: "I transmit a copy of the letter from Dr Herzl relative to his scheme for the establishment of a settlement of Jews in the Sinai Peninsula." Lord Cromer was asked to give his opinion, and also "to send out a Commissioner to examine the country and report upon its capacities" (FO 78/5479).

2   The reference is to the adventurous plan of Paul Friedmann, a convert to Christianity, who in 1891 sought to establish a Jewish State in 'Midjan', also referring to the Sinai Peninsula, which ended in total failure (see also: J.M. Landau, "Documents on the Attempted Jewish Settlement in Midjan (1890–1892)," *Shivat Zion* 1 [1950], pp. 169–178 [Hebrew]).

300

Governments are not agreed as to the frontier between El-Arish and the head of the Gulf of Akaba.[3] On this subject, I beg to refer to my despatch No. 41 of March 18th. 1902. It may be a long time before this dispute is settled. I think, therefore, that, both in the interests of the Jews themselves, and in order to avoid the possibility of trouble with the Turkish authorities, it would be desirable that the Colony, if it is founded at all, should be located wholly to the West, not only of the line claimed by the Egyptian, but also of that claimed by the Ottoman Government. It may be predicted with tolerable certainty that the colonists will fare better at the hands of the Egyptian, than at those of the Turkish authorities.

In the second place, I would strongly advise that, before going any further, those responsible for the movement should send, not a large Commission, but two or three qualified people to the spot, who would be able to report on the situation and form some opinion as to whether the project is, or is not, at all likely to succeed. I have never visited the Sinai Peninsula, but certainly all the accounts I have ever heard of the country from others preclude the possibility of entertaining any very sanguine expectations of success. Possibly I may take too pessimist a view of the case. I am, however, confident that much further investigation is required before any definite action can prudently be taken. I conceive that Dr. Herzl would not like to be associated with a project which is likely to end in failure, neither is it at all desirable that His Majesty's Government should give any encouragement unless a reasonable prospect of success can be entertained.

I think that a Commission of three persons would amply suffice. It might consist (1) of some one connected with the Zionist movement, who would be able to judge of the requirements of the colonists; (2) of an expert in agricultural matters, notably irrigation. I am inclined to think that this expert had better be some one who, although not unsympathetic to the Zionist movement, should not be connected with it. In fact, he had better not be a Jew at all. I would suggest that the third member of the Commission should be some one with a thorough knowledge of the language and of the locality. By far the best man would be Mr. Jennings-Bramly, now in the service of the Soudan Government.[4] He speaks Arabic perfectly. He has surveyed most of

---

3    In 1892 an attempt was made to delineate the border between Egypt and the Hedjaz province, since precise boundaries had not been drawn since 1841. When Lord Cromer intervened in the dispute, the Turkish government was compelled to agree that the entire Sinai Peninsula would be administratively annexed to Egypt, albeit while remaining under Ottoman sovereignty. No exact boundary was then delineated between Ottoman Palestine and Sinai, it being finally determined only after the dispute of 1906 (see below, No. 102).

4    W.E. Jennings-Bramley (1871-1960) was then a senior official in the Sudan government. Although Cromer proposed that he become a member of the Commission, he did not

the Sinai Peninsula, and he has a greater aptitude for dealing with Bedouins, and a more intimate acquaintance with their habits and customs than any European I know.

In the third place, I have to offer some observations on the nature of the conditions which the Egyptian Government would wish to impose before granting any concession. It would as yet be premature to discuss the matter in detail. Exemption from Taxation on any land brought under cultivation might probably be granted for a term of years. On the other hand, it will be necessary to organise some special force both to maintain order amongst the colonists themselves, and to protect them from the Bedouins, whose lawless habits are well known. The Egyptian Government would probably require that the leaders of the Zionist movement should, from the first, guarantee the payment of an annual sum sufficient to cover the cost of this force, as also the cost of any administrative and judicial establishment which it might be found necessary to create.

Lastly, I come to what is perhaps, in the present stage of the proceedings, the most important of all considerations.

I observe that, in his letter of November 12th., Dr. Herzl says that the 'greatness and future promise' of the proposed settlement 'lie in the guaranteeing of colonial rights'. I do not know what is implied by these words, or what would be the nature of the rights claimed by Dr. Herzl on behalf of the colonists. It is most necessary that there should be a very explicit understanding on this subject. I would suggest that, before going any further, Dr. Herzl should be asked to explain more fully his views and proposals on this important point. Even, however, before he does so, I can explain broadly the attitude which would be assumed by the various authorities here on this branch of the subject.

It is essential that the colonists should be wholly subject to Egyptian law, and that no rights should be accorded to them beyond those enjoyed by all other inhabitants of the country who are Ottoman subjects. I foresee that this condition may lead to difficulties of a nature calculated to threaten the further development of the project. The colonists will all be foreigners. Probably most of them will be of Russian, Austrian, or Roumanian nationality. Unless some special arrangement were made, they would be subject to the regime of the Capitulations. In civil affairs, they would be able to appeal to the Mixed Courts. As regards criminal affairs, they would only be amenable to the jurisdiction of their respective Consuls. I need not enter into the general

participate. In 1905 he was appointed Chief Inspector of Sinai, and in 1906 he took a decisive part in the determination of the boundaries. He would later become an authority on the Bedouin of Sinai.

question of the privileges enjoyed by Europeans in Egypt, as in other parts of the Ottoman Dominions. It is a subject on which much may be said on both sides. I am very far from advocating the abolition of those privileges. On the other hand, it cannot be doubted that they are frequently abused, and that the work of reform during the the last twenty years in Egypt, has been in some degree hampered and retarded by their existence. Whatever arguments may be advanced against the possession of these rights and privileges by Europeans resident in Egypt in the midst of the rest of the population, these would be greatly enhanced were similar rights and privileges extended to all the members of a heterogeneous and cosmopolitan body, living by itself in a somewhat remote part of the country.

The Egyptian Government would, very naturally, in my opinion, demur to the creation of a Colony of this nature, which would almost certainly cause much future trouble. And I venture to think that, unless this point can be satisfactorily settled. the project is not one which should receive any encouragement from His Majesty's Government.

The only solution possible is that the colonists should renounce their foreign nationalities and become Ottoman subjects. Unless they are to be wholly governed by Egyptian law, I do not think that the project should be entertained. I need hardly add that, in making this renunciation, they run no risk of being exposed to arbitrary or unjust action. They may feel assured that, at all events so long as the British occupation of Egypt lasts, they will receive at the hands of the Egyptian authorities treatment quite as just and impartial as any which would be extended to them by their Consular representatives etc.

I am not, however, sure that a simple renunciation of national rights on the part of the colonists would meet all the requirements of the case. I am not sufficiently acquainted with the laws of Russia, Austria etc. to say whether a renunciation of nationality can legally be made by the inhabitants of those countries. If there is any doubt on this point, then, besides the renunciation of the colonists themselves, their Governments should be made parties to the agreement, and distinctly signify their own renunciation of any right or claim to exercise jurisdiction over the colonists, or in any way to afford protection to them.

I beg to draw Your Lordship's special attention to this point. It is one of much importance.

Cromer[5]

---

5    Lord Evelyn Baring Cromer (1841–1917) was the British Chief Representative in Egypt during the years 1883–1907 and the actual ruler of that country. He played a decisive role in the failure of the El-Arish project. Herzl wrote in his diary after his first meeting with him: "Lord Cromer is the most unpleasant Englishman I have met till now."

## 90　J. Dickson to N. O'Conor
## Report on the German Colonies

The pretext for the submission of a report on the German colonies was a baseless report of a presumed concession granted to the Germans for a railroad and seaport in Palestine. The Consul found it necessary to write a detailed survey of the colonies, together with a description of the economic importance of German settlement in Palestine (see also above, No. 65. For a general description of the subject, see: Alex Carmel, *Die Siedlungen der württembergischen Templer in Palästina 1868–1918*, Stuttgart 1973).

FO 195/2127 — No. 79                                    Jerusalem, December 8, 1902

Sir,

Having observed in the 'Times Weekly Edition' of September 5th last, that it was reported that the German Ambassador at Constantinople had obtained a Concession from the Ottoman Government for a railway and a seaport in Palestine, I took the opportunity, during a visit which I paid to Jaffa in October last, of collecting some information from German residents and others in that place on the subject.

From all accounts the paragraph in the edition of the 'Times' above referred to was not confirmed, but it is possible that the securing of a concession such as that alluded to has been in contemplation.

There are four important German colonies at the present moment in existence in Palestine, a detailed description of which would necessitate a digression from the main object of this report. I shall accordingly allude to them briefly.

The largest and most flourishing is the Colony at Haifa, numbering some 500 souls,[1] which was founded by a certain Dr Hoffman,[2] who emigrated to Palestine about 40 years ago at the head of a sect consisting principally of

---

1　See above, No. 67, n. 2.
2　Christoph Hoffmann (1815–1885) belonged to the Templars, a sect founded by his father in 1819 in Korntal, near Stuttgart. He fashioned its character as an independent church and developed the ideology of the sect. After his first trip to Palestine in 1858, he headed the movement for settlement in the Holy Land. The first group set out, under his leadership, in March 1868. At first involved in the establishment of the colony in Haifa, he shortly later moved to Jaffa. In 1878 he transferred the sect's center to Jerusalem and was its undisputed leader until his death.

Wurtembergers, and in response to religious conviction which determined him and his followers to settle in the Holy Land.

The second is the German Colony of Jaffa, founded by a Mr Hardegg,[3] a companion of Dr Hoffman, and consists of about 230 individuals, most of them engaged in trade.

The third is an agricultural Colony at a place called Sarona situated somewhat over a mile to the north of Jaffa, and numbers 360 souls. With the exception of a few of its members who are engaged in the manufacture of wine, these Colonists are agriculturists, and since the creation of the Colony have wrought great changes and improvements in the surrounding country.

The fourth is the German Colony near Jerusalem, containing some 300 individuals, also followers of Dr Hoffman above mentioned. They are mainly occupied in earning a living as small traders and shopkeepers in Jerusalem.

A fifth Colony, however, is now being founded in the district of Jaffa, and has received the encouragement and support of the German Emperor, the King of Wurtemberg, and members of the German aristocracy. I am informed that the Emperor has contributed 10,000 marks towards its establishment, out of his private purse, the whole cost of founding the Colony being estimated at from £8000 to £10,000.

The situation of the new Colony is in the plain of Jaffa about 9 miles to the east of that town, and comprises lands purchased from the villages of Yahudiyeh, El-Tireh, and Rantieh.[4] 5500 'donnums' (a donnum — 224 acre) were bought from the inhabitants of the first of these villages; 1684 'donnums' from those of the second village; and 1700 from those of Rantieh in all 8884 'donnums' or 1995 Acres.

In order to avoid paying high prices, competition, and attracting public attention, the Germans purchased the above mentioned lands quietly through two influential natives of Jaffa, who acquired the property in their own names and afterwards transferred it to a Commission of Germans, whose president is

3     Georg David Hardegg (1812–1879) participated in the German revolutionary activity of the early 1830s; he was arrested and spent six years in prison. After his release, he joined the Templars and took part in bolstering the ideology of the sect, as Hoffmann's right hand man. A man of action, he played a major role in the materialization of the program for settlement in the Holy Land. He settled in Haifa, where, together with Hoffmann, he founded the first German colony. (Dickson erred on this point, because Hardegg remained in Haifa, while Hoffmann went to Jaffa.) After a disagreement with Hoffmann, Hardegg and his followers left the sect in 1874 and he limited his activity to Haifa.

4     The reference is to Wilhelma. The land was purchased in July 1902, and settlement there began the same year. The colony flourished, with impressive economic achievements, until it was conquered in November 1917 by the British, who deported all its inhabitants to Egypt.

a certain Christoph Hoffman.[5] The average price paid was about S 16/- per 'donnum'.

Several of the German Colonists from Jaffa, Sarona, Jerusalem and Haifa have invested capital and become landowners in the new Colony, besides other Germans who are expected to come from Germany and elsewhere. Already three families have arrived, two being German families settled in Russia, and the third a family direct from Germany. Others are expected to arrive soon; but the work of constructing farm houses or cottages, clearing the ground, etc. has begun, and ere long a new Colony equal in size, if not larger than the German Colonies already established, will come into existence. The Turkish Officials, I understand, hearing of the projected Colony endeavored to raise obstacles both in the way of the purchase of the land and its transfer to the Germans, which necessitated an appeal to the German Embassy at Constantinople, and orders, I am informed, were in consequence sent by the Porte to the Authorities in Palestine to offer the necessary facilities for the formation of the settlement.

The existing German Colonies at Haifa and in the Province of Jerusalem have, it cannot be denied, been of considerable benefit to the Country, by improving the state of agriculture, spreading civilized ideas among the natives, and promoting trade and commerce; and the creation of a new Colony of intelligent and industrious Germans will still further increase the prosperity of Palestine. Under these circumstances it is not unlikely that the German Government should desire to encourage German enterprise, by obtaining a concession for a railway and securing a suitable port on the coast as its terminus.

In my Despatch No. 46 of September 16, 1898, I had the honour to report that a rumour was current at the time with reference to the cession to the Germans of the ancient town of Caesarea on the sea coast for the purpose of founding a new Colony there. As, however, no port exists at Caesarea, it would be practically useless as the terminus of a railway, and the only place, where there is a good harbour, and which otherwise would be available, — in the event of the German Government seriously contemplating the acquisition of a seaport on the coast of Palestine, — is Haifa.

I beg to enclose herewith a map showing the position of the new Colony.[6]

John Dickson

5     Christoph Hoffmann Jr. (1847–1911) headed the Templar community from 1890 until his death. He was quite active in strengthening the sect and its colonies.
6     Not found in the file.

## 91 J. Dickson to N. O'Conor
## Quarterly Report; Effects of Cholera

Like the cholera epidemic that had plagued Palestine in the fall of 1865 (see above, Nos. 55–56), there was another outbreak of the disease at the end of 1902, which quickly spread from the south to the north of the country. It claimed many victims and paralyzed all economic activity; even maritime traffic was severely effected. The disease spread from Egypt, via El-Arish, due to the negligence of the border officials who did not properly inspect people and animals at the border crossing. The city of Gaza suffered greatly, and hundreds of its inhabitants died. From there the plague spread to Jaffa, Lydda, and Ramleh, even reaching the north where Tiberias was hardest hit. The aggressive measures immediately adopted by the authorities in Jerusalem were this time successful in preventing the spread of the epidemic to the capital, and Jerusalem was spared the horrors of the disease.

In the following report the Consul describes the spread of the epidemic and its decisive influence on economic life.

FO 195/2149 — No. 5                                    Jerusalem, January 27, 1903

Sir,

With reference to the administrative and economic condition of the Province during the quarter ended the 31st ultimo, I have the honour to report to Your Excellency that there has been an almost complete paralysis in all branches of trade, consequent upon the unexpected outbreak of Cholera in the month of October last, and that nearly all the Departments of the administration were, from the same cause thrown into a more or less state of confusion. The figures quoted below respecting the amount of shipping and the value of the imports & exports at the port of Jaffa will show the effect of the epidemic on trade and commerce generally.

The plague of Cholera, which had been for some months in existence in Egypt, gradually made its way across the border through the Egyptian Province of El-Arish, and suddenly showed itself into this Mutessarifat in the town of Gaza[1] and neighbouring villages. Cordons were established and

1    According to an article in the Templar newspaper *Die Warte des Tempels* of 27 February 1902, between 150 and 180 people died each day in Gaza (Carmel, *Palästina-Chronik*, II, pp. 253–257). Even if these figures are exaggerated, there was a very high number of casualties, as is also mentioned below. Since many people fled the city because of the epidemic, they oftentimes carried it to other locations.

communication prevented with other districts, but shortly afterwards the epidemic appeared in Lydda and Jaffa, having followed the usual trade routes of the country, but, as the result of strict sanitary measures, and the complete cessation of the running of trains and carriages to and from Jaffa, Jerusalem itself was spared a visitation.[2] Nevertheless the epidemic continued to rage until the end of December, when it passed on northwards into the provinces of Beyrout and Syria. The total number of victims of the disease according to official Return and information derived from private sources, was as follows. Official Return: Jaffa — 263 deaths; Gaza — 749; other places — 403, total 1415. According to private information: Jaffa — 273 deaths; Gaza — 2374, other towns and villages — 753 (approximately); Total — 3400 deaths during October, November and December.[3]

The total number of vessels that entered and cleared at Jaffa during the quarter ended Dec. 31st was 72 of an aggregate tonnage of 68,172 tons. During the corresponding three months of 1901, there were 188 vessels of 145,625 tons that entered and cleared at the same port, showing a falling off in the last quarter of 1902, of 116 vessels and 77,453 tons. Of these 72 vessels, 46 were steam of a total tonnage of 67,146 tons compared with 103 vessels and 143,140 tons during the corresponding quarter of 1901. [...][4]

The total value of the imports, through the port of Jaffa, during the quarter ended December 31st was £54,450 against £147,980 during the corresponding three months of 1901, showing a falling off of £93,530 or nearly two thirds of what they were in 1901. The exports also show a considerable diminution compared with the corresponding period of 1901. [...]

As regards the general state of the administration, I have the honour to report, that almost the entire attention of the Authorities was devoted to enforcing preventive measures against the spread of Cholera, whilst the ordinary routine duties in the different Government departments were little

2   The Muslim schools and the missionary educational institutions were closed for a few months. In addition to the measures adopted by the authorities, the Consuls and the Jews also took sanitary precautions. See the description of the preventative measures: Goodrich-Freer, pp. 53–54; Y. Shirion, *Memoirs*, Jerusalem 1943, pp. 173–175 (Hebrew); Luncz, *Luah Eretz-Yisrael* 9 (1903), pp. 185–186 (Hebrew).

3   There is a striking difference between the official figures and 'private' sources; it may be assumed that the truth lies somewhere in between.

4   In his lecture on commerce in Palestine in 1902 (published by Luncz, *op. cit.*, pp. 168–179), Consul Dickson stated that the epidemic was the main factor in the slowdown of business and maritime traffic. In 1902, 251 fewer ships dropped anchor in Jaffa than throughout 1901 and the value of the cargoes decreased by £20,760. Of the 330 ships that entered the harbour of Jaffa in 1902, 101 were British, 62 French, and 44 Russian. The export of barley to the beer industry in England from Gaza, which had been hard hit by the epidemic, dropped from 21,000 tons to only 2,940 tons. (See also: *Diplomatic and Consular Reports*, No. 2962, "Trade of Palestine for the Year 1902.")

thought of, and that in consequence of several of the outlying district having been cut off from the capital of the Mutessarifat by cordons, there was an increase of insecurity and lawlessness throughout the country. I would more particularly mention Hebron, which on account of the outbreak of Cholera in the place, was for a time completely isolated. I have been informed that in that town, where the inhabitants are noted for their fanaticism and turbulence, robberies and burglaries were of continual occurrence.

John Dickson

## 92 Foreign Office, Egypt to L. Greenberg
## Plan for a Jewish Settlement at El-Arish

The commission charged with examining the possibilities of Jewish settlement in Sinai toured the area in February–March 1903. Travelling about 1,000 km., it reached desolate locations previously unvisited by Europeans. Considering the matter as urgent, Herzl sent L. Greenberg to Cairo, "in order to confer on my behalf with the authorities as to the charter to be obtained from the Egyptian Government" (Herzl to Lansdowne, 22 January 1903; quoted in Bein, p. 212).
The Egyptian government, on its part, did not wait for the report of the commission of enquiry. In the following letter, it rejected the request for a charter, because this would contradict the terms of the Turkish Firman which determined the constitutional status of the Egyptian government. If, however, a Company would be established in accordance with Egyptian law, the government would be prepared to provide it with lands in the Sinai Peninsula. The settlers would be answerable to Egyptian law; preferably, they would become Ottoman subjects. It was explicitly stated that the Capitulations would not apply to them. Regarding the appointment of officials and judges, the needs of the settlers would be taken into account, "to the extent that this was possible." In effect, the Egyptian response expressed a negative reply to most of the requests of the Zionists.

FO 78/5479 — No. 181
Copie

Caire, le [22] Fevrier 1903

Monsieur,[1]
    Le Gouvernement de Son Altesse a pris connaissance de vos propositions

[1]   Leopold Greenberg (1861–1931), a journalist by profession, was one of the leading

tendant à obtenir pour une 'Jewish National Settlement Company' une charte en vue de l'établissement d'une Colonie Juive dans la Péninsule du Sinaï.

D'après les Firmans Impériaux, le Khédivat ne peut, sous aucun prétexte ou motif, abandonner en tout ou partie, aucun des droits inhérents au Pouvoir Souverain.

En conséquence, toute idée de concession d'une Charte doit être formellement écartée.

Mais si une Compagnie de Colonisation venait a se constituer, d'après les lois Egyptiennes, je suis autorisé à vous déclarer que le Gouvernement serait disposé a lui concéder dans la Péninsule du Sinaï des terrains dont la superficie ne pourra etre déterminée qu'après le retour de la Commission qui a été envoyée sur les lieux.

Les conditions de cette concession seraient fixées ultérieurement par le Conseil des Ministres; mais je tiens à vous informer d'ores et déjà, que le Gouvernement subordonne son consentement a l'acceptation expresse des clauses ci-après qui en constituent la condition essentielle:

1° Les colons amenés par la Compagnie doivent être sujets locaux. Tout colon qui ne serait pas sujet ottoman devra déclarer expressément par écrit accepter la compétence exclusive des Autorités indigènes tant administratives que judiciaires. Cette déclaration sera en outre accompagnée d'un certificat des Autorités de son pays d'origine attestant qu'il lui est loisible d'acquérir la nationalité ottomane, et qu'en tout cas, elles ne le réclameront jamais comme sujet ou protégé.

2° Les terrains concédés ainsi que les colons seront soumis en tout et pour tout aux lois et règlements qui régissent le territoire ainsi qu'aux Autorités indigènes, exception faite, bien entendu, pour les questions de statut personnel dont la connaissance appartiendra aux autorités religieuses dont relèvent les colons, dans les mêmes conditions que pour les autres Communautés non-musulmanes établies en Egypte.

Ces Autorités religieuses devront au préalable être reconnues par le Gouvernement.

3° Le Gouvernement, dans le choix et la désignation des juges, fonctionnaires et employés, s'inspirera (et tiendra compte) autant que possible, des besoins et des intérêts des colons.

4° Dès que les conditions de développement de la colonisation le per-

---

Zionists in England and a foremost advocate of political Zionism. He was Herzl's confidant, and was also very close to his successor, David Wolffsohn. He conducted the negotiations with the British government concerning the El-Arish and Uganda plans. He was a member of the Zionist Executive, 1905–1907; from 1907 he served as Editor of the *Jewish Chronicle*.

mettront, le Gouvernement se montrera disposé à prendre en considération toute demande d'établissement de municipalité sans que toutefois il puisse être porté atteinte aux principes ci-dessus.

[unsigned]

## 93 Lord Cromer to Marquess of Lansdowne
Plan for a Jewish Settlement at El-Arish

The report submitted by the commission of enquiry on 26 March 1903 (the complete report is in file FO 78/5479) stated unequivocally: "The result of the Commission's researches has been, that in their opinion, under existing conditions, the country is quite unsuitable for settlers from European Countries." Supplying water to an uninhabited desert territory posed the major problem. This would be difficult, because "the furnishing of which [water] would involve great capital expenditure." Cromer and the Egyptian government seized upon this determination. Relying upon their water expert, Sir William Garstin, they totally rejected the proposal. It transpired, however, that the decisive factor was political: total opposition to Jewish settlement in the Sinai Peninsula. The British Foreign Office thereby exhibited its total acceptance of the wholly negative position of Lord Cromer.

On 2 May 1903 the Foreign Office sent a secret cable to Cromer (in the same FO file) in which the Foreign Secretary noted about Herzl, in reference to the report: "He admits that it is in many ways discouraging but evidently desires that the project should be persevered with. He asks me to enlist your support." The following letter, not published by Bein, is in response to this telegram.

FO 78/5479 — No. 61

Cairo, 14th. May 1903

My Lord,

With reference to previous correspondence on the subject of founding a Jewish Colony in the Sinai Peninsula, I have the honour to forward (1) a report by Sir William Garstin,[1] and (2) a letter addressed by the Minister for

---

[1]   W. Garstin was Under-Secretary for Public Works in the Egyptian government and an expert on irrigation. His memorandum is in the same FO file.

311

Foreign Affairs to Colonel Goldsmid, who, on Dr. Herzl's departure from Egypt, remained behind as his representative.[2]

I think that Your Lordship is already in possession of the report made by the Commission which recently visited the Sinai Peninsula. It is, therefore, unnecessary for me to send a copy.[3]

Briefly, the matter stands thus.

The main requirement for bringing any of this desert land under cultivation is, of course, water. On enquiry, it appeared that two plans were worthy of consideration.

The first, which is by far the most important of the two, consists in bringing the Pelusiac plain, an area of about 60,000 acres, situated immediately to the East of the Suez Canal, under cultivation. The water would have to be supplied from the Nile. Syphons would have to be constructed under the Suez Canal.

When this subject was first mooted, Sir William Garstin was absent from Egypt. The various parties concerned were informed that the Egyptian Government must reserve its opinion on the technical aspects of the case until his return. I need hardly remind Your Lordship that Sir William Garstin can speak with unrivalled authority on all matters connected with Nile irrigation. His report, as Your Lordship will observe, is conclusive against the adoption of the project.

I may add that, even if this were not the case, the scheme could not be carried out without the consent of the Suez Canal Company, and it is more than doubtful if that consent could be obtained. Unless the works were carried out at a cost which would be almost prohibitive, the execution of the plan would entail the temporary closure of the Canal. This would appear to be quite out of the question.

Under the second of the two alternatives, it would not be necessary to rely on the Nile for water. No attempt would be made to irrigate the Pelusiac plain. The land lying along the sea-coast so far East as El-Arish would, under this scheme, be brought under cultivation by storing the rain-water, which descends from the northern slopes of the Sinai hills.

---

2     Albert Edward Goldsmid (1846–1904), a Colonel in the British army and a founder of the Hovevei Zion movement in England, was a member of the commission of enquiry on El-Arish. The letter of Egyptian Foreign Secretary Boutros Ghali was sent on 11 May 1903, and was published by Bein (pp. 216–217). It ends with an absolutely negative response: "J'ai donc le regret de vous informer que, pour toutes ces raisons, le Gouvernement de son Altesse ne peut donner une réponse favorable à votre proposition, qui doit être considéré comme définitivement décartée."

3     Herzl personally delivered the first copy of the report to the Foreign Secretary, as Lansdowne noted in the above-mentioned cable of 1 May 1903.

Your Lordship will observe that the Egyptian Government is not prepared to entertain this proposal, as they do not consider that it contains any probable elements of success.

I may remark that, from the commencement of these negotiations, I have, in the face of a good deal of opposition, used every endeavour to obtain a fair hearing for Dr. Herzl and those acting with him. I am, however, now decidedly of opinion that the matter should be dropped. I am convinced that nothing can be done in the direction of carrying out Dr. Herzl's wishes without the exercise, on the part of His Majesty's Government, of a far stronger pressure than the circumstances of the case would in any degree justify. I wish to explain that the Egyptian opposition is in no way due to anti-Jewish prejudice. It is based on two grounds. In the first place, none of the authorities here, whether British or native, believe in the possibility of success. They are unwilling to be associated with failure. They consider that not only would they be incurring some responsibility if they encouraged Dr. Herzl and his friends to spend more money, but that they might possibly lay the foundations of claims against the Egyptian Government when, as would almost certainly be the case, it was ascertained that the money had been expended uselessly. They think, therefore, that it is not only the wisest, but also the most considerate plan to abstain from holding out to Dr. Herzl hopes which cannot be realised, and to state definitely that the negotiation is at an end.

In the second place, the Egyptian Ministers have pointed out to me, with very great truth, that the machine of government in this country is already one of the most complicated in the world. To those who are intimately acquainted with its details, it is, indeed, astonishing that any good results can accrue from a system so replete with anomalies and imperfections. It is difficult to foretell what would be the precise results, if Dr. Herzl's plan were carried into execution. It can, however, scarcely be doubted that, whatever might be the conditions of settlement, if a large cosmopolitan society were allowed to settle in the Sinai Peninsula, for objects which are avowedly political and which are, to say the least, difficult to reconcile with the interests of the Sultan, who is Suzerain of Egypt, the existing complications might not improbably be materially increased.[4]

In conversation with Colonel Goldsmid, I have strongly urged him to allow the negotiation to drop altogether, and I venture to express a hope that

---

4    Cromer alludes here to the political considerations.

similar language should be used to Dr. Herzl should he, as is not improbable, apply to Your Lordship.[5]

Cromer

## 94　D. Levontin to J. Dickson
### Difficulties of the A.P.C. at Jaffa

As head of the World Zionist Organization, Herzl sought to establish a bank, the Jewish Colonial Trust, which would serve as a central instrument of the Zionist movement. In 1899 the JCT was incorporated as a company in London. Subscription for shares began after a minimal basic capital was ensured, which by the end of 1902 had reached the sum of only £226,000. The Anglo-Palestine Company (APC), registered as a company in London on 27 February 1902, was established as a commercial branch of the JCT. Levontin, who had already joined the JCT in 1901, was appointed Director of the first branch of the APC in Jaffa. Officially opened on 21 July 1903, it would eventually become the main branch of the bank throughout all of Palestine. Not many weeks passed, however, before the bank was confronted by difficulties, especially those created by the Governor of Jaffa.

Zalman David Levontin (1856–1940) immigrated to Palestine from Russia in 1882, and was among the founders of the colony of Rishon le-Zion in that year. A year later, he returned to Russia, where he entered the banking profession. In 1901–1903 he directed the JCT in London, and from then until 1924 he headed the APC in Palestine, thus playing a central role in the economic development of the country.

FO 195/2149　　　　　　　　　　　　　　　　　　　Jaffa, August 20, 1903
Copy

Sir,

I beg to acknowledge the receipt, with respectful thanks, of your favour of the 14th instant.

---

5　On 19 June 1903, the Foreign Office informed Herzl of the final negative response of the Egyptian government and Lord Cromer (Bein, pp. 218–219), which in effect is a summary of this letter. In an additional letter to Herzl dated 17 July 1903, the Foreign Office repeats the reasons which led to rejection of the program, concluding: "In these circumstances Lord Lansdowne regrets that he is unable to recommend that any further pressure should be exercised with a view of inducing the Egyptian Government to alter their decision in the matter" (*ibid.*, p. 219), thus putting an end to the affair.

I much regret my being obliged to trouble you again with the affairs of our Company. I beg to submit to you the following Statement: —

The Caimakam of Jaffa gathered today all the 'Moukhtars' of this town and in the presence of several officials and of a large crowd of other people, he declared that our Company has no permission to work here, and therefore every man that will do business with us will be punished by the local Authorities.

Further I beg to state that I was able to obtain a Copy of the warning issued by the Caimakam to the said Moukhtars as follows its translation: —

'As there was opened here an Anglo-Palestine Bank and the said Bank is not provided with a licence, therefore we notify you to give information that no man shall have to do with it; and he who will have anything to do with it we will fine him.'

I here beg to inform you of the following facts: —

I. Before I left London for coming and starting business here, I made enquiries at the Chambers of Commerce about the position of British Firms in Foreign Countries, and have been told that no special permission is required to a British Company for opening business in Turkey.

II. One of our Directors has received a letter from one of the Directors of the Deutsche Bank in Berlin, Mr Koch, dated May 22, 1902, in which he writes as follows: —

'"The Deutsche Palaestina Bank" has no concession and such is not necessary; it is only registered at the German Consulate in Jerusalem as a German Company Ld, and consequently enjoys all rights given to any German.'[1]

III. When I had the honour to be introduced by You Sir to the Governor General of Jerusalem,[2] H. Ex. has not asked me for any permission whatever, but even said that he is very pleased to give us work in Palestine, and promised us his assistance & even kindly gave us a letter to the Camaikam of Jaffa to whom I was introduced by Mr Consr Agent Amzalak.[3] In his presence the

---

1  The Deutsche Palästina Bank was founded in 1897 as a foreign bank in Palestine; as time passed, it became the most important financial institution in the country until the British conquest. The bank's premier standing was enhanced during World War I (see Eliav, *Austrian Protection*, p. 215). It operated without a special license, since it was properly registered with the German Consulate in Jerusalem, enjoying the protection of the Consulate and all the rights to which it was entitled under the Capitulations. Levontin expected a similar status for the APC, as a British company under the protection of the British Consulate.

2  The Governor of Jerusalem at the time was Osman Kiazim Bey (February 1902–Summer 1904).

3  See above, the introduction to No. 63.

Caimakam promised me all his assistance; he even proposed to build an Office for us here.

Under these circumstances I hired an Office for two years, and furnished it with all the necessary articles, have sent out our Circulars over the whole world, entered into large commercial transactions, and invested a large amount of money in Bills and other business in this Country.

Consequently not only the stopping of our business will cause a great loss of Capital, but even the aforesaid warning by the Caimakam to the Public, through the 'Moukhtars', will cause us great prejudice.

In conclusion I beg to state, that I have submitted to yourself what occurred and I feel sure you will kindly take the necessary steps for maintaining our position.

Should you find it necessary to apply to H.M's Ambassador at Constantinople so to kindly obtain for our Company the permission if necessary, you will always find me ready to comply to your instructions.

This forenoon I called at the Jaffa Consular Office and have acquainted Mr Agent Amzalak of what happened and he advised me to submit to yourself the whole matter.[4]

The Anglo-Palestine Co Ld<br>
D. Levontin<br>
Director

## 95   J. Dickson to N. O'Conor
## Intervention in Favour of the
## Anglo-Palestine Company

Dickson sent a copy of Levontin's letter (see above, No. 94) to the Embassy in Constantinople and requested its intervention, reporting of the hostile attitude of the local officials to the APC. It soon became obvious that the APC was a thorn in the side of the Turkish authorities, since it was a financial instrument of the Zionist Organization; the question was, to what extent was the British Consulate prepared to come to its defense as a British company.

For the early years of the APC, see: N. Gross et al., *A Banker for the Nation in Its Renewal*, Ramat Gan 1977, chap. 3 (Hebrew).

---

4   The Caimakam was not satisfied with the prohibition; he stationed policemen outside the office of the APC to deter people from entering the bank.

FO 195/2149 — No. 46
Confidential

Jerusalem, September 1, 1903

Sir,

I have the honour to inform Your Excellency that at the beginning of last July, Mr David Levontin arrived at Jaffa, as representative of the 'Anglo-Palestine Company Limited', with the object of engaging in business in that place. The 'Anglo-Palestine Company' was incorporated on the 27th of February 1902, and registered in London as a trading and banking company whose operations are to be mainly carried on in Syria and Palestine. Mr Levontin was appointed Director in Palestine, with a head office at Jaffa, as will be seen from the enclosed Circular,[1] and immediately after his arrival he came up to Jerusalem and I introduced him to the Mutessarif, who gave him a letter of recommendation to the Caimakam at Jaffa. Some days later Mr Levontin forwarded to me a letter from Sir Eric Barrington of which I have the honour to transmit herewith a Copy.[2]

Subsequently, however, I received complaints from both Mr Levontin and Mr Consular Agent Amzalak, as will appear from the enclosed copies of correspondence,[3] as marked in the margin, to the effect that the Caimakam of Jaffa was placing serious hindrances in the way of the legitimate carrying on of the business of the 'Anglo-Palestine Company', and accordingly on the 21st ultimo, I instructed Mr Amzalak to make representations to the Caimakam respecting Mr Levontin's complaint, and to request him to furnish him with a reply in writing stating the grounds on which he ventured to interfere with the business of an English trading Company. His answer was that he had been ordered to do so by the Mutessarif.

I therefore interviewed His Excellency Kiazim Bey[4] on the subject and also addressed to him a letter asking him to state his reasons for giving the orders above referred to, but His Excellency's reply both verbal and in writing (copy and translation of his letter are herewith enclosed) has been that he cannot allow the 'Anglo-Palestine Company' to carry on its business at Jaffa,

---

1    Not enclosed.
2    Not enclosed. Sir Eric Barrington was an Assistant Under-Secretary in the Foreign Office. The letter recommends that the Consul use his judgment in the assistance to be rendered to Mr. Levontin. This was more of a demurrer than a recommendation. Dickson, however, felt that it was his obligation to protect a British company, since this was a major part of his duties as Consul, as well as being essential to the maintenance of British prestige.
3    They are not enclosed, except for the letter by Levontin of 20 August 1903 (see above, No. 94). Levontin wrote another letter on this matter to Dickson on 27 August of that year (in the above-mentioned FO file).
4    See above, No. 94, n. 2.

unless the Company is licensed by the Porte, or presents a letter of introduction to His Excellency from the Ministry for Foreign Affairs.

I am aware that there is an Ottoman law dated 22 Rabi-ul-Awal 1305 / 25 Teshrin Sani 1303 (Novr 25 / Dec. 7 1887) prohibiting foreign Joint Stock Companies from establishing Agencies in Turkey without previously obtaining the permission of the Sublime Porte, but I understand that this law was not accepted by His Majesty's Embassy or the Representatives of other foreign Powers.

I have, however, reason to believe that, in consequence of the Company having, in their Circular above mentioned, stated that their Bankers are 'The Jewish Colonial Trust (Juedische Colonial Bank) Lted', London, and of its also being known that Mr Greenberg,[5] who is connected with the 'Zionist' movement, is the London Director of the 'Anglo-Palestine Company', the suspicions of the Turkish Authorities have been aroused that the establishing of a branch of the Company in Palestine has something to do with the movement in question; and these suspicions have no doubt been further excited in the minds of the Authorities by rival bankers and traders already doing business at Jaffa. Indeed I am informed, privately, that the Mutessarif reported his ideas about the matter to Constantinople, and is now acting under instructions received from the Sublime Porte.

In submitting, therefore, Mr Levontin's complaint to Your Excellency for such representations as Your Excellency may consider right to make to the Porte on the subject, I have ventured to report the above circumstances to Your Excellency.

John Dickson

## 96   D. Levontin to J. Dickson
## Thanks for Assistance

The British Ambassador decided to intervene on behalf of the APC, and his actions bore fruit. Harassment of the bank's customers in Jaffa ceased and Levontin was able to develop the company's activities. It soon became clear that the question of APC's legal status would surface from time to time. In November 1903 the Embassy received a Note Verbale from the Ottoman government declaring that the activity of the APC would no longer be obstructed, but this on the explicit condition that the company engage solely

5    See above, No. 92, n. 1.

in commercial transactions and not in banking. In response, the Embassy protested this limitation, which discriminated against a British company in favour of the banks of Germany and France that operated in Palestine. This protest went unanswered, however, and thus the Turks left open the possibility of hindering the bank's activity from time to time.

FO 195/2149                                                    Jaffa, December 28, 1903
Copy

Dear Sir,

We beg to acknowledge receipt of your favour of 26th instant, and hasten to express you our most hearty thanks for the assistance you have given us. We take the liberty of assuring you, most honored Sir, that we fully appreciate the generous support lent us by His Britannic Majesty's representatives in our collision with the local Authorities[1] and shall consider it as our duty to employ all means in our possession for the propagation of English importations in this country, as well as towards the development of commerce in general & English commerce especially.

The Anglo-Palestine Company Ltd
D. Levontin

## 97   J. Dickson to Marquess of Lansdowne
## Proposed Establishment of a British Post Office

The serious deficiencies of the unreliable Ottoman mail led the Powers, one after the other, to establish their own postal services, as part of their policy to create institutions and services for the inhabitants of Palestine and thereby enhance their political standing and economic influence. The first was Austria, which had already established a postal agency in 1852 in Jaffa, transporting the mail aboard the Lloyd's line steamships (see above, No. 29), and, in 1859, a post office in Jerusalem. A few months after the opening of the Austrian

---

1   On the same day, 28 December 1903, Dickson confirmed in his letter to Ambassador N. O'Conor that he had indeed received a "Note Verbale from the Porte in reply to Your Excellency's representations on the subject of the interference of the Local Authorities with the APC in Jaffa and to state that the Company would be permitted to conduct its affairs without hindrance" (in the above-mentioned FO file).

postal agency in Jaffa, France also appointed a postal agent in the city. As time passed, and especially in the early 1900s, other Powers, including Germany, Russia, and Italy, decided to open postal offices (for details, see below). The Austrian service, however, remained the best and most reliable mail system, used by very many residents. Throughout the nineteenth century, the proposal to establish a British mail service was not seriously considered, and only on 12 January 1904 was there a "Petition to Members of Parliament asking for Establishment of a British Post Office in this City" (Jerusalem). The petition was signed by Bishop Blyth, "Members of the Clergy," and other individuals. The immediate reason that lay behind the request was the claim of Miss Charlotte Hussey, who was at odds with the Consul and sought to undermine his standing, that her mail, which she received via the Austrian mail service, had been opened (see also below, No. 103).

Dickson wasted no time. On 22 January 1904 he wrote to the Foreign Office: "I could not but approve of the Proposal. Moreover, Austria, Germany, France & Russia having established post offices at Jerusalem and Jaffa, England could claim the benefit of the most favoured nation clause of Treaties." The question remained, however, whether this could be commercially justified, primarily in terms of expenses, especially since such a service would entail the operation of mail carriages between Jaffa and Jerusalem, due to "The conveyance of foreign mail by train being prohibited by the Turkish Authorities" (FO 78/5470).

The following letter is the second on this matter.

FO 78/5470 — No. 6                                        Jerusalem, February 14, 190·
Commercial

My Lord,

With reference to my Despatch (No. 6 Cons.) of the 22nd ultimo respecting the proposed establishment of a British Post Office in this city and at Jaffa,[1] I have the honour to enclose herewith to Your Lordship a statement of the expenditure incurred by the Austrian, German, French and Russian Governments in maintaining their Post-Offices in Jerusalem and Jaffa together with an estimate of the probable revenue which may be derived by H.M.' Government in the event of its opening a British Post-Office in the two places mentioned.[2]

1   See the introduction to this letter.
2   The "Statement of yearly expenses for maintaining Post Offices" includes the following details: Austrian P.O.in Jerusalem — £1072; in Jaffa — £346, totalling £1418. The German Post Offices in Jerusalem and Jaffa — £1178, sharing mail coaches with the French P.O. The French P.O. — £778, and Russia even less. Dickson estimated the cost of the British postal office as similar to those of the Austrians.

320

It will be perceived from the statement above referred to, that the total expenses of the Austrian Post-Office amount to over £1400 annually, and I understand, that its income is also considerably over that sum. The outlay therefore, for establishing and maintaining a British Post-Office in Jerusalem with a Branch Office at the Seaport of Jaffa, could not be much less than that occurred by the Austrian Government, if proper competition is to be kept up with the Foreign Post Offices.[3]

On the other hand I have endeavoured, as far as possible, to form a correct estimate of the probable revenue of a British Post-Office, and this would come to somewhat over £900 per annum. This figure, however, is based mainly on the sale of stamps, but some further income may be derived from transactions in Postal and Money orders.

I would beg to add that the establishment of Foreign Post-Offices in Jerusalem, an inland city, which does not seem to be entirely sanctioned by Treaty, arose in consequence of the German Government in 1900, followed by the Governments of France and Russia, claiming under the most favoured nations 'Treaty clauses', the same privilege which had been accorded to Austria many years ago, when the latter Power opened a Post-Office in Jerusalem for the benefit of Catholic pilgrims visiting the Holy Land. The Austrian, German & French Post-Office Authorities have not only now their different Offices in Jerusalem and Jaffa, but have recently put up Post Boxes in the main streets and thoroughfares of both towns, thus practically transferring the Postal Service of Jerusalem and Jaffa to Foreign nations and depriving the Ottoman Government of a source of revenue which she legitimately claims as her own.[4]

John Dickson

---

3    The German Post Office in Jerusalem was opened on 23 March 1900, the French office on 3 September 1900, the Russian on 10 September 1901, and the Italian on 1 June 1908.
4    On 27 February 1904 the General Post Office expressed its reservations about the opening of a post office in Jerusalem, and on 14 November 1904 the GPO informed Dickson: "there is no present intention of taking any action in this matter" (the above FO file), thus putting an end to the proposal to open a British postal service in Jerusalem (but see below, No. 112).

# 98  J. Dickson to N. O'Conor
## Acquisition of Land by Jews

The severe prohibitions against land purchases by Jews instituted in 1892 were only slightly alleviated as time passed. It became clear that mainly political considerations lay behind the restrictions: to prevent Jewish settlement and the establishment of agricultural colonies in Palestine. The only concession made by the Turks was that the prohibition did not apply to Jews who were Ottoman subjects, nor to immigrants who did not belong to the category of immigrants "en masse" (i.e., those from Eastern Europe). These Jews, however, were permitted only to purchase urban tracts, provided they would bring a Consulate certificate stating that they were not among the "type of immigrants whose entry was forbidden," that they had already been living in Palestine for at least thirteen years, and they committed themselves not to house immigrants on their property, nor to settle them on their premises. As regards rural lands, the purchasers were required to undertake an obligation not to establish Jewish colonies upon them.

This British Consul had do deal with this prohibition because Jews who had become naturalized British subjects had immigrated to Palestine and now sought to purchase land.

FO 369/247 — No. 64　　　　　　　　　　　　　　　Jerusalem, October 12, 1904
Copy

Sir

I have the honour to enclose to Your Excellency herewith copies of correspondence, as marked in the margin, which has passed between His Excellency the Mutessarif of Jerusalem[1] and myself respecting the acquisition of land by British Jews coming to Palestine.

The Mutessarif asks, with the object, I presume, of distinguishing between those Jews who are residents and those who are immigrants, how long the applicant for the purchase of real estate has been in the country.

I have replied to His Excellency, as to the definition of immigrant Jews, in the sense of the communications from the Sublime Porte to His Majesty's Embassy, copies of which were enclosed in Sir W. White's Despatch of October 6, 1688, and Sir Arthur Nicolson's Despatch of July 23, 1893 respectively.[2] It would be decidedly inconvenient, and the information may not

---

1　Ahmed Reshid Bey was Governor of Jerusalem from August 1904 to the end of 1906.
2　See: Hyamson, Nos. 331, 368.

always be correct, to acquaint the Mutessarif with the exact date of the arrival of British subjects of the Jewish faith in Palestine.

On the other hand it cannot be denied that foreign Jews naturalized in England and the Colonies come to Palestine with the express purpose of purchasing land and settling down for the rest of their lives. As regards those who are naturalized in the Colonies, as, in accordance with the instructions contained in Your Excellency's despatch of January 4, 1899, they are not registered in this Consulate, applications for the purchase of real estate by them are not transmitted to the Local Authorities through this Consulate. Foreign Jews, however, naturalized in the United Kingdom are registered in this Consular Office, and though when applying for naturalization they sign a declaration, in conformity with the Naturalization Act 1870, that their intention is to continue to reside in the United Kingdom, they almost immediately afterwards come to this country with the object of settling here. It is questionable whether this class of Jews ought not to be looked upon as immigrants.[3]

I have the honour to add that British born Subjects of the Jewish faith rarely, if ever, settle permanently in Palestine but come out either as visitors or to engage in trade.

J. Dickson

## 99   J. Dickson to Walter Townley
## Quarterly Report (Extracts)

Dickson's quarterly reports were usually routine and did not cover new ground. The following report is of interest for its description of the lack of security in Jerusalem: the absence of an effective police force was sorely felt, and there was no one capable of enforcing law and order in the city.
The report was sent to the Chargé d'Affaires in the Embassy at Constantinople.

FO 195/2199 — No. 6                                          Jerusalem, February 11, 1905

Sir,

In continuation of my Quarterly reports on the economic and administrative condition of this Province, I have the honour to state that, during the

3   Cf. No. 86, above.

three months ended the 31st of December last, the trade of this Consular district may be said to have been fairly flourishing. The total value of the exports and imports together showed, it is true, a diminution of about 13 per cent, when compared with the value of the exports and imports in the similar period of 1903, but there was a considerable increase as against those in the immediately preceding Quarter. However, the figures obtainable, of the imports and exports, are only approximate, and cannot be taken as an absolute indication of the state of trade. It is from the Returns of Shipping that a more correct estimate of the commercial prosperity of the Province can be formed, and these have shown for several years past a steady increase, more particularly in the amount of tonnage. [...]

The following was the number and tonnage of vessels of foreign nationalities which entered and cleared at Jaffa during the three months ended 31st December last, namely: Ottoman 43 — of which 40 were sailing vessels — (tonnage 4100 tons); Austrian 27 (tonnage 40,605); Russian 26 (tonnage 34,398); Italian 12 (tonnage 13,246) 3 being sailing vessels; French 11 (tonnage 26,369); German 8 (tonnage 10,586); Greek 3 (tonnage 2435); and Belgian 1 (1174 tons).[1]

The administrative state of this Province still showed a lamentable inefficiency in the Department of the Police and Gendarmerie. As was pointed out in previous reports it is hardly possible that a city like Jerusalem, with an annually growing population, should enjoy immunity from crime for any length of time. The number of petty thefts and robberies had considerably increased during the past Quarter, and in scarcely a single instance was there detection of the offenders. Foreign residents seem to have been the principal victims, and several have had their farm-yards swept clean of all their poultry in one night, or suffered the loss of other domestic animals. The inability, or inertness, of the police to arrest the thieves naturally induces house-holders to provide for their own protection. The result is that revolver shots are constantly heard during the night, the discharge of firearms being resorted to on the faintest alarm, and instances have been recorded in which innocent persons have had narrow escapes from stray bullets. More serious accidents of this nature would probably lead to acts of retaliation, and the public tranquility might thus become endangered. An efficient and vigilant police force is, therefore, all the more needed if future disorders are to be avoided.[2]

---

1    Cf. the data in a report from 1900 (see above, Nos. 82 and 84). According to the Consul's annual report for 1905, a total of 489 ships dropped anchor at Jaffa in all of 1904 (compared to 425 in 1903), of which 150 were British, 108 Russian, and 91 Austrian ("Trade of Palestine for the Year 1904," *Diplomatic and Consular Reports*, No. 3410).

2    This quarterly report does not refer to the lack of security in Jerusalem, but rather concentrates mainly on the general progress of the city: "The growing prosperity of

In the outlying districts the state of affairs was not very satisfactory. Accounts from Hebron and Gaza testify to mal-administration on the part of Government Officials, and to instances of a fanatical spirit among the Mohamedan inhabitants. In the former place the body of the Chief Rabbi of the Jewish Community, who had just died, was disinterred and exposed to insult,[3] and in the latter the Acting Caimakam manifested his ill-will to the English Medical Mission, long established there, by cruelly persecuting two Mohamedans — one an Egyptian — who (although not apostates from Islamism) were in the habit of frequenting the Mission. I regret to state that the Mutessarif of Jerusalem seemed rather inclined to endorse the proceedings of the Acting Caimakam, but as a new Caimakam has, in the meanwhile, been named to Gaza from Constantinople, it is to be hoped that matters will somewhat mend in that District.

John Dickson

# 100  J. Dickson to N. O'Conor
# Lighting Jerusalem at Night

In the absence of street lighting in the Old City of Jerusalem, every resident was required to carry a lantern while walking about at night, lest he be suspected of being a thief. Those who did not abide by the regulation were liable to arrest by soldiers and a fine. Only at the end of the nineteenth century did the City Council decide to erect several poles with glass-enclosed kerosene

Jerusalem and of Palestine generally, due in no small degree to the opening of the railway 12 years ago between here and Jaffa, and to the progress which is at present being made in the construction of the line between Haifa and Damascus, has caused a considerable increase in shipping at Jaffa, the seaport of Jerusalem, which is only 37 miles distant by carriage road and 54 miles by rail."
The annual report provides a detailed description of the progress of the Jewish and German colonies. Regarding the postal facilities, it states: "The opening in Jerusalem, within the last six years of three foreign post offices, in addition to one already existing, and to the Turkish Post Office, has facilitated correspondence with all parts of the world, and there is now almost a daily arrival and departure of mails to and from Europe." (See also the introduction to No. 97.)

3  The reference is most probably to Rabbi Hayyim Hezekiah Medini, the author of *Sedeh Hemed*, who was born in Jerusalem in 1832 and in 1901 was elected Chief Rabbi of Hebron, where he established a *yeshivah* (Talmudical academy). He died in October 1904. The incident described here is not mentioned in any other source. For Medini, see: *The Book of Hebron*, Jerusalem 1970, pp. 111–117 (Hebrew).

lamps on the main streets. These lamps were not, however, lit on a regular basis. In preparation for the visit of Kaiser Wilhelm II to the city in 1898, more lamps were added, and quarters outside the walls were illuminated as well. By 1905 most of Jerusalem's streets were lit, and it was no longer obligatory to carry a lamp when walking them at night.

Due to the importance of the subject, Dickson devoted a special despatch to street lighting in Jerusalem, which increased the security of the city's inhabitants, but also entailed the payment of a special levy.

FO 95/2199 — No. 31                                                    Jerusalem, July 31, 1905

Sir,

[...] In my report for the Quarter ended the 31st of March last, I referred to a proposal on the part of the Municipal Authorities of Jerusalem for properly lighting the city at night, and this measure has now been carried out. Besides being a convenience to the inhabitants, it will tend to diminish burglaries and night robberies, but the expenses of the measure are still the subject of discussion between the Mutessarif and the Consular body, and I may have to submit a special report to Your Excellency on the matter. The Municipality have decided to levy a tax on all holders of real property — foreigners as well as Ottoman Subjects — and with this object have taken as a basis a tariff appended to a Municipal regulation dated March 4/16 1305/1899, but they have doubled the tariff in question.[1]

The Consular Corps, whilst fully approving of the measure, contend that the increased tax, before it can be enforced on foreign subjects, needs the sanction of the Porte in conformity with Art. 39 of the Provincial Municipal regulations, as regards the imposition of taxes. The application of the increased tax to foreigners is, accordingly, still in abeyance. [...]

                                                                        John Dickson

1    At the end of the first decade of the twentieth century, the kerosene street lamps were
     replaced with 'Lux' (gas) lamps, which provided considerably more light; they constituted
     the greatest technological advancement in lighting prior to World War I.

# 101  J. Dickson to N. O'Conor
## The Jewish National Fund and its Aims

Upon the initiative of Prof. Hermann Schapira, the Jewish National Fund was established by the Fifth Zionist Congress (1901). The main objective of the JNF was to purchase lands in Palestine as a national asset, to administer these lands, and to allocate them for settlement needs by lease for a maximum period of 49 years. The JNF was to rely upon extensive contributions from all segments of the Jewish People. It was determined that it would begin functioning only upon the collection of a minimal sum of £200,000 and the attainment of a charter from the Ottoman government. However, the 'practical' Zionists, those who held that Zionist objectives in Palestine would be achieved by practical progress in the field rather than by political efforts, demanded that land acquisition begin even before the Fund had obtained a charter and raised this minimal initial sum. When the APC was established, it was authorized to act in the name of the JNF as well. The JNF began its activity only during the period of Herzl's successor, David Wolffsohn (1858–1914), second President of the Zionist Organization. The process of registration as a British company took a long time and had not been concluded by the time the following letter was written, the JNF being finally registered only in April 1907. Dickson, who closely followed the first steps of the JNF, was also aware of the political implications, of which he wrote in this letter.

FO 195/2199 — No. 53                              Jerusalem, November 23, 1905

Sir,

I have the honour to acknowledge the receipt of Mr Ronald Macleay's Despatch of the 27th ultimo, transmitting a Copy of a Despatch which Your Excellency had received from His Majesty's Principal Secretary of State for Foreign Affairs relative to 'Der Juedische National fonds', and asking for any observations I may have to make on the subject.

In reply I beg to state that after the formation of the great Scheme of the late Dr Herzl, under the name of 'Zionism', for the repatriation of the Jews to Palestine and the ultimate acquisition of the country, it was necessary to form a Company for the collection of funds and to deal generally with the financial questions involved in the undertaking.[1] With this object 'Der Juedische National fonds' was founded, which may be considered as the prospective

---

1   Dickson confused the Jewish National Fund with the Jewish Colonial Trust, which matched the definition given by the Consul.

Treasury of the Jewish State to be created in accordance with Dr Herzl's views.

'Der Juedische National fonds' lost no time in commencing operations in Palestine and the Company has already acquired in the vicinity of Jaffa and in Galilee, something like 15000 'deunums' of land, equal to 3368 acres.[2] As, however, by the laws of Turkey this land has had to be registered in the name of an individual member of 'Der Juedische National fonds', the managing Committee, to prevent difficulties in the future in the event of the death of the registered owners, has ceased for the present to make further purchases, hoping, no doubt, that when the Company is registered under section 23 of the Companies Act, 1867, an Imperial Iradé may be obtained from the Sultan, authorizing the property to be inscribed in the name of the President for the time being.

One of the promoters of the Company, namely, Dr Oscar Kokesch of Vienna, who was appointed on August 27th 1903 a member of Committee, has since died, and I am unaware who has been named his successor.[3] The object, however, of the Committee in desiring to have the Company registered in England, is to give it a status as an English Company, and to obtain for it British protection in the Ottoman Dominions, although it does not necessarily follow that it would be entitled as of right to receive such protection.

Presuming that the request of the petitioners be granted, and the proposed Company be registered under section 23 of the Companies' Act 1867, two questions would arise in reference to it, namely, (a) the possibility of its receiving British protection as an English Company, and (b) whether such a Company, which has identified itself with a scheme for the creation of a Jewish State in the Ottoman Empire, could exist without being involved in the political difficulties and complications, which must of necessity ensue in the attempt to form the State referred to.

As regards the possibility of the Company being under British protection, I would observe that an Association, although composed of foreign members, which is registered and has its head-quarters in England, is generally considered as under British protection, when it is incorporated as a bona fide

2     The first JNF acquisitions were: the site of Kiryat Sefer, an agricultural school for those orphaned during the Kishinev pogroms, in Beit 'Arif, east of Lydda (summer of 1904); the lands of Kfar Hittin, north of Tiberias (September 1904); the lands of Daleika and Umm-Djuni, later to become Kinneret and Deganyah (early 1905). In the summer of 1905, Levontin — the central figure in land transactions at the time — sold some of the land in Beit 'Arif to the Atid company, which began to build an olive oil factory.

3     This error of Dickson is strange, because Kokesch did not administer the JNF. The first Director was Johann Kremenetzky (1850–1934), a confidant of Herzl, who headed the JNF until 1907. He was succeeded as Director by Max Bodenheimer (1865–1940), one of the leaders of the Zionist movement in Germany, who held this post until 1914.

trading Company whose operations are to be carried on abroad, inasmuch as a Company in such a position must, to a large extent, have commercial transactions with mercantile firms in England, whose interests would indirectly be protected. The same remark holds good for certain purely philanthropic Societies whose head quarters are in the United Kingdom, although the majority of the members may be foreigners. I may mention as instances that the 'Anglo-Jewish Association',[4] and the 'Anglo-Palestine Company, Limited',[5] which was incorporated in 1902 and registered in London, are in the enjoyment of British Consular protection in this Country, whereas the 'Jewish Colonization Association' ('J.C.A.'), which, I understand, has its head-quarters in Paris,[6] and the newly formed 'Jewish Territorial Organization' ('J.T.O.'), are not.[7] Perhaps it would be desirable to draw up rules which would more clearly define the position of such Associations as regards their right to be entitled to British protection abroad.

With reference to the political aspect of the case, considering the objects which 'Der Juedische National fonds' has in view, I do not feel competent to offer any remarks on the subject, as the actual condition of the Jewish populations in Europe, which seems to call for the adoption of measures for the emigration and settlement of Jews in certain parts of the globe, is a matter to be dealt with by the Governments interested; but I would respectfully remark that if a company is formed under English protection for the acquisition of territory in Palestine, and the eventual creation of a Jewish state, important political questions must arise between the British and Turkish Governments, such questions practically involving dismemberment of the Ottoman Empire.

John Dickson

---

4    The Anglo-Jewish Association (AJA), a British organization, was founded in 1871 for the purpose of defending Jewish rights in "backward countries." It undertook educational and social work in Baghdad, Aden, Mogador, and other places. It also maintained the Evelina de Rothschild School in Jerusalem.
5    See above, No. 94.
6    See above, No. 81.
7    The Jewish Territorial Organization (JTO) was founded in 1905, after the rejection of the East Africa ('Uganda') proposal by the Zionist movement. Its main goal was the promotion of Jewish settlement on an autonomous basis in a suitable territory anywhere in the world.

# 102 J. Dickson to N. O'Conor
## Observations on the Egyptian Frontier at Rafah

Since the exact boundary between Palestine and Sinai was not delineated after the conclusion of the Egyptian conquest of Palestine, a royal Firman of 1 June 1841 established the El-Arish-Suez line as the border. A map, later lost, was appended to the Firman. In 1892, when Abbas Hilmi assumed the post of Khedive of Egypt, the Firman determining the boundary between Egypt, the Sanjak of Jerusalem, and the Hedjaz province was reaffirmed, as was the usual practice. When it was first determined on 8 April 1892 that all of the Sinai Peninsula would be administratively annexed to Egypt (see above, No. 89, n. 3), the de facto border was shifted eastward from El-Arish, on the initiative of Cromer (see above, No. 89, n. 5), and the border marker was moved to Rafah. The Turks turned a blind eye to the British interpretation regarding the boundary line, but in 1906 the border dispute erupted in full force. In January 1906 Cromer entrusted Bramley (see above, No. 89, n. 4) with the establishment of a border station in southern Sinai. The Turks reacted strongly, regarding the British act as an attack on Turkish territorial integrity. This incident constituted the beginning of an international dispute. After taking various threatening actions, and even some armed hostilities, an ultimatum was delivered to the Turkish government at the beginning of May, giving it ten days to recognize the delineation of the border along the Rafah-Akaba Bay line, on the pretext that Rafah had already served for years as the boundary marker. On 14 May 1906 the Turks submitted. Following negotiations, during the month of June the border was marked from Rafah to Ras-Tabba, about 10 km. from Akaba Bay.

On 1 May 1906 Dickson telegraphed the Embassy in Constantinople: "Consular Agent at Ghaza informs me privately that the Turks have removed the tree and two boundary pillars at Rafah and have advanced on Egyptian territory" (FO 195/2225).

Military units were concentrated at the spot, but in the meantime the two border markers had vanished and could not be returned. The Turks also removed eleven telegraph poles on Egyptian territory and replaced them with poles of their own, to demonstrate their sovereignty over the area (Dickson, *idem*, 7 May, 1906). On the 21st of the month, Dickson announced that the boundary pillars had been returned. After this, the following despatch was sent, which also attests to the thorough investigation conducted by the Consul regarding the Rafah boundary.

FO 195/2225 — No. 34 Jerusalem, June 5th 1906

Sir,

In my Despatch No. 22 of the 3rd ultimo, I had the honour to forward to Your Excellency a sketch of the boundary pillars marking the Syro-Egyptian frontier at Khurbet Rafah and a map of the locality, together with some remarks made by Mr Schumacher[1] who was working at the time in connection with the Palestine Exploration Fund. I now venture to submit to Your Excellency the following observations throwing still further light on the subject, and which may not be without some interest, at a moment when a Joint Commission is about to delimit the frontier from Rafah to Akaba.

Khurbet Rafah, the site of the boundary columns, together with Tell Rafah situated about half a mile to the west of it, and which no doubt was the acropolis of the town, has been identified with the Raphia of Polybius[2] (2.5.c.80) and of Josephus[3] (Wars, 1.4.2). The former, who wrote about 150 B.C., remarks that Raphia was the first Syrian town coming from Rhinocolura, which was considered an Egyptian town, and is probably the modern El-Arish. It is, therefore, evident that Raphia, the present Rafah, was from Ptolemaic times looked upon as a frontier town, and that the boundary between Egypt and Syria must have passed very close to, if not actually through, the place.

However, the foregoing argument would have no effect with the Turks, who naturally would contend that, since the conquest of Egypt and overthrow of the Mameluke power, by Sultan Selim the 1st, in the sixteenth century, all former boundary marks between the two countries, no matter how ancient, would be considered as obliterated, and that they, as conquerors, would be at liberty to place their boundaries wherever they pleased. Such a contention will no doubt carry some weight, but as far as can be ascertained, the Turks never seemed at any time to have troubled themselves to mark the frontier between Egypt and Syria, and one fact is quite certain, namely, that the two granite pillars at Khurbet Rafah were in existence in 1822, and may have stood there for years, if not for centuries previously. William Martin Leake, Acting

---

1     Gottlieb Schumacher (1857–1924), a German architect and archaeologist, lived in the German colony in Haifa and was a leader of the Templar sect. He served as the Acre District Engineer, and engaged in the planning of Jewish settlements and in archaeological researches on behalf of the 'Deutscher Verein zur Erforschung Palästinas' (the German Society for the Study of Palestine) and on behalf of the PEF.

2     Polybius (200–120 BCE), a Greek historian. The first five books of his *Histories* have survived. The quotation here is from Book V.

3     Josephus Flavius (c. 37–100 CE), an outstanding Jewish historian and one of the chief representatives of Jewish-Hellenistic literature.

Secretary of the Association for promoting the Discovery of the Interior parts of Africa, who edited Burckhardt's 'Travels in Syria and the Holy Land', published in 1822, states as follows: —

'And here the Editor may be permitted to add a few words on a third Roman route across these deserts (having travelled the greater part of it three times), namely, that from Gaza to Pelusium.' And he further goes on to say:

'The name of Rafah is still preserved near a well in the desert at six hours march to the southward of Gaza, where, among many remains of ancient buildings, two erect granite columns are supposed, by the natives, to mark the division between Africa and Asia.'

It will thus be seen that the boundary pillars were in existence in 1822, and the next point to be ascertained is, whether they were considered by the Firman of June 1. 1841, issued by the Sultan Abdul Mejid to Mehemet Ali, Viceroy of Egypt, as defining the boundaries between Syria and Egypt on the Mediterranean side. The Firman referred to states: — — 'I grant unto thee the Government of Egypt, within its ancient boundaries, such as they are to be found in the map which is sent unto thee by my Grand Vizier now in office, with a seal affixed to it.' This map has been lost or destroyed, and, therefore, it is impossible to know what were the 'ancient boundaries' of Egypt alluded to in the Firman.[4] As, however, the late Khedive, Ismail Pasha,[5] appears to have renewed the granite pillars at Khurbet Rafah, it is extremely probable they were marked on the map which has disappeared, and that Ismail Pasha had been aware of this fact.

In view of the foregoing remarks, the recent destruction of the pillars in question cannot but be considered as a wanton and arbitrary act on the part of the Turkish Officials, which cannot under any circumstances be justified.

As regards the delimitation of the frontier inland from Rafah to Akaba, difficulties will present themselves in ascertaining the exact line the boundary should follow, for the country is sparsely inhabited by different Arab tribes, — some considered as being on Turkish and others on Egyptian territory, — and in several places the tribal grounds interlace; but the Joint Commission appointed for the demarcation of the frontier is no doubt prepared to cope with any difficulties of this kind.

In conclusion, I beg to quote the following remarks from "Notes on Arabia Petraea, and the Country lying between Egypt and Palestine," by

4    For this matter, see: Gideon Biger, "The Rediscovery of the First Geographic-Political Map of Sinai," *Sinai*, 100/II (1987), pp. 907–910 (Hebrew); the collection of documents FO 371/11591.

5    Ismail Pasha (1830–1895), Khedive of Egypt, grandson of Muhammad Ali, Viceroy from 1863 and Khedive from 1867. In 1873 he obtained a Firman granting him much independence. He was forced to abdicate in 1879.

Colonel (now General) Sir Charles Warren, G.C.B., R.E., K.C.M.G., F.R.S., written in 1886,[6] for the 'Palestine Exploration Fund'. He states:

'The portion visited lies almost wholly between the Suez Canal and the Eastern Egyptian boundary. This boundary does not appear to have been clearly defined by treaty or otherwise. Several charts show it as a straight line drawn from El-Arish (on the Mediterranean) to Akaba; but, on the one hand, the Porte appears to assume a nominal control over some tribes of Bedouins to the west of this line (in Jebl Hilal for example); while on the other hand, the Egyptian territory on the coast of the Mediterranean extends up to Rephia, midway between El-Arish and Gaza. It seems probable that the boundary inland has never yet been demarked, and this uncertainty may at some future period be a source of difficulty, leading to a conflict of jurisdiction.'

John Dickson

# 103   Bishop Blyth to Sir E. Grey
   Appreciation of Consul Dickson

John Dickson's fifteen-year tenure as Consul in Jerusalem was not a period of peace and tranquility for him. His eldest son died of an illness in 1891, his first year in office. Dickson was himself a sickly person, and as time passed his health deteriorated further. From time to time he was forced to take sick leave, and the Consulate was left in the hands of an Acting Consul (see above, introduction to No. 76).

It was not only ill health that stood in his way. Suddenly, he was confronted by a new disagreeableness which caused him much bitterness and led to unbearable disputes. A new opponent arose from within the British community, a mentally disturbed young woman who did not cease to attack and slander him. She even gathered around herself some opposition to the Consul, with the aim of effecting his dismissal. Two files (FO 78/5253, 5470) were devoted to the "Complaints of Miss Charlotte Hussey against Consul J. Dickson."

Hussey had arrived in Jerusalem in 1892 as a worker in the mission of Ben-Oliel, but she unexpectedly left her place of employment after some time. She was well received in the Consul's house, and a love affair began between the young woman and W.H. Dunn, who had been sent to Jerusalem in 1897 by Mrs. Finn to represent her in legal proceedings regarding the various

6   *PEFQ* 1887, pp. 38 ff.

properties in dispute, which had served as a surety for the payment of her late husband's debts (see above, No. 53). The affair came to a sudden end after he had presumably proposed marriage, but his offer was found not to be serious. Hussey blamed Mrs. Dickson for meddling in the matter and causing the romantic tie to come to an end. This caused Miss Hussey to suffer from depression and paranoia, her mental distress leading her into personal quarrels with the Consul's wife.

The missionary Ben-Oliel had a very negative opinion of Hussey, calling her: "deceitful and untruthful, [a] snake in the grass" (see Dickson's letter of 8 March 1900, FO 78/5253, in which he relates the entire story).

The episode of the quarrel and the accusations against Dickson were even raised in Parliament. As a result, H.W. de Sausmarez, of the Consular Court in Constantinople, was sent to Jerusalem to investigate the charges that had been raised. On 18 April 1903 Sausmarez presented his report, in which he stated that all the charges against Dickson were unfounded. "She has been for some time suffering from monomania, consequent on breach with Mr. W.H. Dunn, Agent of Mrs. Finn, who has behaved in a most gentlemanly and proper way throughout" (FO 78/5470).

The judge determined that Miss Hussey, the cause of attacks and quarrels, was to be removed from Jerusalem. But Sausmarez also expressed his dissatisfaction with the Consulate: "With the very considerable and increasing amount of work to be done by him personally, he is unable to exercise a sufficient control over the employees. The Consul is not a strong man [he was already seriously ill] and he needs help."

It is on this background that we are to understand the following letter by the Bishop, head of the Anglican community in Jerusalem, to the Foreign Secretary, Sir E. Grey.

FO 369/45                                                        Jerusalem, July 20, 1906

Sir,

I hope it may not be considered out of my province[1] if I write a few lines to you, expressive of my sense of the loss to Jerusalem (and certainly to this very responsible Consular Service), by the death of John Dickson, Esq. He

---

[1]    George Francis Popham Blyth (1833–1914) served as a chaplain in Burma, and was appointed Bishop in Jerusalem "and the East" in 1887, after the Bishopric had been vacant for five years. He founded the 'Jerusalem and East Mission, to the dissatisfaction of the London Society and the CMS. In 1892 he began construction of St. George's Cathedral, which was consecrated in 1898. The conflicts with the LJS and the CMS intensified, but Blyth continued with his independent methods and succeeded in strengthening the Anglican Church and the British community in Jerusalem. His activities had a considerable influence on the Arab population, at the cost of poor relations with the Jews. He left Jerusalem in July 1914 and died in England some months later (see: Blyth, Introductory Chapter).

334

was the friend of the lowest and of the highest here; his loss is therefore great indeed; and personal character is also a *power* in a Consul. But I ought to confine myself, perhaps, to what he was officially. There was no Consul whose personal character was more influential than his. He was one of those quiet men, who are hard workers, who did not 'blow his own trumpet'; and I am sorry that I should have to undertake that office for him, because he has gone.

The Foreign Office is well aware of the baseless attacks which have been made upon him for a series of years, by two ladies who have been under the monomania that he was not doing his best for them in their eccentric fancies.[2] It has angered the whole Station; and his patience and gentlemanly conduct towards them won him general respect.[3] But the effect on Mr Dickson's system was serious; it lowered the tone of his health very greatly in this climate. But for that, he might well have undertaken the change to America, which the Foreign Office so kindly, and deservedly offered to him. It has told with fatal effect now, when the heavy business of the El-Arish incident came upon him so heavily, whilst suffering from an attack of illness.[4] I believe that the discovery and replacement of those boundary pillars, (which were never lost, but were displaced), was owing to Mr Dickson's experience of work, and personal power, and tact, applied in a most kindly manner to the local Governor, with whom he was on happy terms. The fact that his work, and official papers, were all signed and finished up to June 30, three days before

2   The second woman was Mrs. Theodore (Mabel) Bent, a widow, who came to Jerusalem with the avowed intent of championing her close friend, Miss Hussey. According to Sausmarez, she was "an unfortunate advisor, who does not hesitate to make the most scandalous and improper statements about Mr. & Mrs. Dickson [...] She is a mischievous and meddlesome woman."
On 5 January 1903 an anonymous letter was sent to the Foreign Office, stating: "We nine British householders representing the great majority of H.M.'s subjects in Jerusalem [...] dare not to sign our names as we feel convinced that they will be sent to Mr. Dickson to deal with as they wish; others who have complained, have been forced to leave the country or are still being persecuted" (FO 78/5470). Obviously, this slanderous letter against the Consul did not represent the majority of the British community in Jerusalem, but rather was instigated by the two women. As a counterweight, a letter supporting the Consul was sent to the Foreign Office, with the list of signatories headed by the Bishop, as well as members of the mission, many members of the community, and Jews, foremost among them Ms. Annie Landau, headmistress of the Evelina de Rothschild School.

3   On 6 February 1904 a delegation of the British community, headed by Bishop Blyth, gave Mr. Dickson a surprising presentation: "a beautifully illuminated address signed by 109 British subjects, and a handsome silver tea-service and two watch chains [...] with deep respect and regard how highly we appreciate your efforts to assist us in every way" (FO 195/2175, 10 February 1904; FO 78/5352, 8 April 1904). Dickson added to his report: "I have felt deeply touched and gratified by this manifestation of friendly feeling and confidence on the part of the English residents, the more so as it was intended as a surprise."

4   See above, No. 102.

his death, is thoroughly characteristic of Mr Dickson.[5] The doctor had ordered him away for change nearly three weeks before his death; and, after a consultation, had enforced his order; but Mr Dickson decided that his work must be completed, and unhappily for his family, and for us all, it was completed.

You will, I think, hold me justified in writing to you to mention what a loss we have had in this quiet but hardworking Servant of the Crown, when I tell you what he has been to myself officially: you know that at Jerusalem (which is a centre of the 'Eastern question,' and a centre of constant intrigue), political questions are very much fought with ecclesiastical weapons. England may have no ambition here, like that of some other Powers. But the future influence of the Anglican Communion, which I have the honour to represent here, (as the Bishops of all other Communions represent their Churches), often involves political matters. The Lands and Buildings I have been able to acquire, here and elsewhere in the country, being under 'Firmans', form, in certain aspects, a political *holding* for England; in the same sense that other such property is of recognized political value to other great Powers. In these matters, and in the keeping of Church matters from being mixed up with things political, Mr Dickson's advice and help have been beyond value to me; and most important things have been done with his aid. And in the question which arose about the 'British Cemetery' (which engaged the English and German Foreign Offices at intervals for several years), and which was by no means a simple burial ground question,[6] Mr Dickson and I have acted together, — the result being a very friendly accord between the English and German residents. Church questions in Palestine and Syria are often the envelope of political matters; and Mr Dickson was like an oracle on such points.

I conclude by venturing to express the hope that you may be able to select a member of the Church of England for Consul here, — for the same reason that Powers connected with the Greek or Latin Communions would

5    Following his death (from heart failure) on 4 July 1906, John Falanga, the Vice-Consul at Jaffa, was appointed to fill the position until the arrival of Frederick George Freeman, Acting Consul (1906–1907) (FO 195/2225, 20 July 1906).

6    The Protestant cemetery, which had been established in 1848, served both the British and the Germans. The question of the ownership of the property, which arose after the dissolution of the joint diocese, became more acute during Blyth's term. After negotiations which continued for several years, in which Blyth demonstrated a quite aggressive attitude, it was decided that both communities would continue to use the cemetery, under a joint management, and in 1904 they purchased additional land together for the expansion of the cemetery. Dickson was quite actively involved in all this. See: G. Mehnert, *Der Englisch-Deutsche Zionsfriedhof in Jerusalem*, Leiden 1971, pp. 15–32.

see the importance of such a selection in cases which affect their Churches, — not merely in Church matters, but politically.

G.F. Popham Blyth
Bishop in Jerusalem & the East

## 104 F.G. Freeman to N. O'Conor
## Death of Grand Rabbi J.S. Eliachar

Rabbi Jacob Saul Eliachar (1817–1906) was the last of the outstanding Sephardic Chief Rabbis prior to World War I. His death sparked the outbreak of an 'inheritance controversy' which was not resolved, but rather led to the appointment of compromise candidates, one after the other. The Sephardic Chief Rabbi, who bore the titles 'Hakham Bashi' and 'Rishon le-Zion', was regarded by the Ottoman authorities as the chief representative of the Jewish *Yishuv*, and it was he who appointed the Jewish member of the district council (*Medjles Idara*). The first Hakham Bashi in Jerusalem was appointed by the Sublime Porte in 1842. Rabbi Eliachar was revered by all circles in the *Yishuv*, and his writings constitue an extensive spiritual legacy. (See: R. Sharabi, *The Sephardic Community in Jerusalem 1893–1914*, Tel Aviv 1989, chap. 1 [Hebrew]).
Frederick George Freeman (1864–1933) was Acting Consul in Jerusalem, 1906–1907.

FO 195/2225 — No. 43

Jerusalem, August 3, 1906

Sir,

The Grand Rabbi of Jerusalem, Jacob Saul Eliaschar, died on Saturday the 21st ultimo, at the age of 92,[1] and was buried the following day in the presence of an immense concourse of people.

The late Grand Rabbi became president of the rabbinical council so long as fifty years ago, and retained office in that capacity until his election as Grand Rabbi in 1896.[2] He was under Italian protection until his appointment

1    This is a mistake. He died at the age of 89.
2    This is erroneous. In 1869 he was appointed Head of the Courts of the Sephardic community, and in 1893 was chosen to be the Hakham Bashi.

as Grand Rabbi, when he became naturalized as an Ottoman subject. I am told that he was popular and always tried to help the poor and distressed of his community. He was, however, opposed to modern ideas of education, especially as regarded females, and was at variance with the 'Alliance Israélite' in consequence of that body sending money for relief and educational work through their agents and not through him.

I understand that Rabbi Jacob Meyer, who is supported by the 'Alliance Israélite', is the probable successor of Eliaschar.[3] Meanwhile the chief rabbi of Hebron, Solomon Mani, has been appointed by the Mutessarif as locum teneus.[4]

F.G. Freeman

## 105 E.C. Blech to N. O'Conor
## Arabs and 'Arabia'

The new Consul, Edward Charles Blech, arrived in Jerusalem in June 1907. The following is one of his first political reports. The Consul did not appraise correctly the beginnings of the Arab nationalist movement, which expressed itself in opposition to Jewish immigration and settlement, as well as to Ottoman rule. Its first political declaration was *Le Reveil de la Nation Arabe*, a book published in 1905 by Negib Azouri, a Catholic Arab living in exile in Paris. From then on, Arab propaganda in Palestine proliferated, and national tensions increased between Arabs and Jews on the one hand, and between the Arabs and the Turks, on the other. Further on in the report, the Consul unsympathetically discusses the Jewish *Yishuv*.

3    Rabbi Eliachar's death sparked quarrels within the community. Rabbi Jacob Meir's candidacy was advanced by the progressive and enlightened circles, but his affinity for the Zionist movement and the Alliance Israélite Universelle spawned opposition, with the conservative elements supporting Rabbi Hayyim Moses Eliachar, the eldest son of the late Hakham Bashi. Rabbi Meir won the formal appointment in August 1906 (see: Hyamson, No. 447), but the Hakham Bashi in Constantinople, who had to confirm the appointment, invalidated Meir, who was forced to leave the post (*ibid.*, No. 449). In 1907 he was appointed Hakham Bashi in Salonika, and upon the establishment of the Chief Rabbinate for Palestine after World War I, he was chosen as the Sephardic Chief Rabbi.

4    In practice, Rabbi Suleiman Mani filled the post only until the appointment of Rabbi Jacob Meir, i.e., for only a few weeks.

FO 195/2255 — No. 32
Confidential

Sir,

For some time past a series of pamphlets, publications and newspaper articles has appeared advocating an autonomous administration for what is termed 'Arabia', and alleging that the population would welcome, and is ready to support, the establishment of such an administration.

Your Excellency is fully aware of the value to be attached to such statements, and has doubtless received exhaustive reports on the subject from other parts of the Empire. My own observation is limited to Jerusalem and Jaffa and their immediate neighbourhood, but I have availed myself of every opportunity for making discreet and confidential enquiry in this direction of various persons engaged in educational or missionary work both here and in outlying portions of Palestine, and the information which I have thus derived leads to the same conclusion as my own observations. All my informants agree in stating that while discontent, and dislike of the Turks and their administrative methods, prevail generally, no symptom is noticeable which would tend to support the belief that any cohesion exists between the different classes of people. Recent occurrences, though not within this district, have been reported to me which prove that religious differences are still as powerful as ever to effect a cleavage among neighbours and fellow-citizens: it is difficult to imagine the Moslems, Latins, Greeks, Greek Catholics and Protestants of Palestine uniting against any common enemy. Some have assured me that there exists a strong desire for a European — preferably, according to certain among them, an English — occupation of Palestine. Others assert that the Moslem notables of Palestine would be inclined to advise their co-religionists, who look to them for counsel, not to oppose a foreign occupation which could only tend to improve the condition of the country. But none are able to report the existence of anything like a homogeneous feeling of nationality among the people, who, if they use any generic name which could be held to cover all classes of the population, are inclined occasionally to describe themselves as Syrians, but never employ the term 'Arab', which seems here to be reserved for the Moslems alone.[1]

The discontent at the system of Government (which appears to me if anything to be rather less oppressive than in other parts of the Empire) finds vent in emigration, largely to America, both Northern and Southern. This is an undoubted loss to the country, as the outgoing Syrian peasant is not advan-

---

[1] The Consul's mistake was that he did not realize that the Arab national movement included both Muslims and Christians.

tageously replaced by the Jewish immigrant, returning in fulfilment of prophecy, as many Christians devoutly believe, to the land of his fathers. I understand that the tide of immigration is decidedly slacker than it was; from a well informed quarter I hear that during the last year some two thousand Jews landed in Palestine, of whom fifteen hundred left again in the course of the year.[2] Except for such as belong to the flourishing colonies founded in the plain of Sharon and elsewhere by the munificence of wealthy Jews in Europe, the lot of the Jewish immigrant is not an enviable one, and usually leads to his becoming a dependent on the supplies sent by the faithful in other countries.

I cannot help thinking that the System of Education pursued by the various missions, British and foreign alike, if not in part the cause of emigration, at least does nothing to prevent it. No attempt seems to me to be made to inspire the pupils, all Ottoman subjects, with any feeling of loyalty towards their Sovereign or patriotism to their country. The instruction which they receive, except in some of the Roman Catholic missions, is not such as to fit them for living useful lives in their own lands. [...]

E.C. Blech

## 106    E.C. Blech to N. O'Conor
The Anglo-Palestine Company

The status of the APC was questioned once again in 1907, when the President of the Commercial Court in Jaffa refused to acknowledge the Company's right to file a claim in his court. All the arguments used in 1903 (see above, Nos. 93–94) were raised again; in addition, the Governor of Jerusalem was unwilling to issue an explicit edict on behalf of the APC. Accordingly, the Consul requested the intercession of the Ambassador in Constantinople who, once again, attained concrete results after prolonged correspondence and vigorous action.

Though well aware that the government's harassment of the APC was due to its Zionist affiliation and the bank's efforts on behalf of Jewish settlement, nevertheless he was determined to protect a British company and extricate it from its difficulties.

2    A total exaggeration. Jewish emigration from Palestine reached serious proportions, but did not come to such a figure.

Sir

I have the honour to report that late on the 22nd instant I received from Mr Falanga[1] a telegram stating that, the Anglo-Palestine Company having brought an action against a debtor before the Mixed Commercial Court at Jaffa, the Court had refused to hear the case on the ground that without an Imperial Trade the company could not be recognised.[2] Mr. Falanga added that the Kaimmakam was applying for instructions to the Mutessarif,[3] and requested me to urge the latter to comply with the terms of the Porte's note, of which a copy was inclosed in Your Excellency's despatch of December 10, 1903. Although the next day was Friday, I went early to the Mutessarif's country residence, where he is spending the summer months, and endeavoured to induce him to instruct the Kaimmakam of Jaffa in the desired sense. His Excellency stated that no report on the subject had yet reached him from Jaffa, and that until he was acquainted with the Kaimmakam's version of the case he could express no opinion. I pointed out to him the inconsistency, to say no worse, of objecting on technical grounds (which moreover we could not admit as valid, not having agreed to the law on Joint Stock Companies)[4] to the existence of an Institution from which the Jerusalem Government had not scrupled to contract loans. His Excellency replied, with a frankness which disarmed criticism, that he was perfectly prepared to admit the Company's existence when desirous of borrowing money from it, but that this did not preclude him from refusing to acknowledge it whenever it so suited him. Eventually it was agreed to wait until the ensuing day, by which time the report from Jaffa might be expected. But as on the next day this report was not forthcoming, the Mutessarif telegraphed to Jaffa for information. On Monday (yesterday) the report was received: the Kaimmakam stated the facts and asked for instructions. But in spite of all my endeavours I was unable to induce the Mutessarif to give categorical instructions for the recognition of the Anglo-Palestine Company. Whereas on the previous Saturday he had stated that the terms of the Porte's note of November 24, 1903 had been received by the Government here and communicated to Jaffa, he now affirmed that no such instructions had ever reached Jerusalem; and his telegram sent last night to the Kaimmakam of Jaffa is couched in the following terms: 'On

1   John Falanga, Vice-Consul at Jaffa from 10 October 1903 until he resigned in August 1911.
2   See Dickson's letter, above, No. 94.
3   Ali Ekrem Bey, Governor of the Jerusalem district from December 1906 to September 1908. See: Kushner, *Governor*.
4   See above, No. 95.

October 9/22, 1319/1903 this Sanjak replied to an inquiry from the Ministry of the Interior to the effect that considering that the institution in question was an ordinary commercial house, no interference would take place with its operations of that nature. Latterly inquiries were again addressed here upon the opening by the Company of a branch at Beirout; the reply sent was to the effect that the institution was nominally a commercial house, and was in no respect a bank; that it had branches at Jerusalem[5] and Jaffa; and that before the establishment of the branch of the Imperial Ottoman Bank loans had been obtained from it as a commercial house. I have not been able to discover any other orders or instructions on the subject'.

As it seemed extremely unlikely that the Kaimmakam of Jaffa would regard this as an instruction to recognise the Anglo-Palestine Company, I ventured to telegraph to your Excellency requesting that orders might be sent to the Jaffa Commercial Court in that sense. The Anglo-Palestine Company, though possibly British only in name, has however during its four years of existence earned the right to protection. Its success has no doubt raised up for it many enemies, and these have sought to set the Authorities against it, by dwelling on its connection with the Zionist movement and thus exciting the suspicions of the Turks who are naturally hostile to any institution which may facilitate the immigration of Jews. It must, I think, be admitted that the Company does very little commercial business, except in connection with advances to Jewish firms, it is concerned chiefly with banking transactions and with granting loans to Jews for the purpose of enabling them to buy land. It has recently established branches at Hebron and Gaza,[6] and the opening of offices at Constantinople, Haiffa and Aleppo is in contemplation. I feel sure that the present refusal of the Mutessarif to accede to our request for the recognition of the Anglo-Palestine Company is based, not on the fact that it is an English Company, but on the denunciations of its efforts to extend Jewish colonisation, and not improbably on secret instructions to try to hamper its operations. I should add that this is the first case ever brought before the Courts by the Company.

It is clear that the action of the Authorities constitutes a direct violation of the undertaking contained in the Porte's note to Your Excellency No. 96 of November 24, 1903; and even if it be attempted to shew that the Company transacts banking business, the final paragraph in Your Excellency's reply to that communication is a sufficient answer to that contention. The Deutsche Palästina Bank and the Crédit Lyonnais both conduct their operations in

5    The Jerusalem branch, the second established by the APC, opened in August 1904.
6    The branch in Hebron was opened in 1909. In that year, only an agency was opened in Gaza.

Palestine without opposition,[7] though unprovided with Imperial authorisation; and British interests will undoubtedly suffer if an institution, nominally and as regards Palestine ostensibly English, is debarred from the enjoyment of rights exercised by its foreign rivals.[8]

E.C. Blech

*Translation.*
*To the Kaimmakam of Jaffa.*

The British Consul complains that hesitation is still being shewn in the matter of the hearing of the action brought by the commercial house known as the 'Anglo-Palestine Company' at Jaffa in the local commercial court. It appears from the correspondence exchanged at the time with the Sublime Porte that no opposition could be offered to the operations conducted by the commercial house in question under the name of a commercial establishment. You should therefore inform the President of the said court in categorical terms that there is no ground for hesitating to hear the case in question, and that if he thus continues to give occasion for complaints by delays unjustified by any order or law he will incur responsibility, and you should put an end to the affair.

Jerusalem. August 21. 1323 / September 3. 1907

Ekrem<br>Mutessarif of Jerusalem

# 107 E.C. Blech to Foreign Office
## Malaria in Jerusalem

A few months after Blech assumed the post of Consul in Jerusalem, he became aware of the harsh consequences for Europeans of its climate and sanitary conditions, the cause of protracted illnesses, the most serious among

7    See above, No. 94, n. 1. The French Crédit Lyonnais opened a branch in Jaffa in 1892, thus preceding the German bank.

8    On 3 September 1907, the Governor ordered the Caimakam of Jaffa to warn the President of the Commercial Court not to remain adamant in his refusal. When the latter still declined to deal with the case of the APC, the governor ordered "to dismiss Refik Effendi, the President of the Jaffa Commercial Court, after his refusal" (FO 195/2255). On 24 October 1907, David Levontin thanked the Consul for "the energetic steps taken by you." (*ibid.*).

them being malaria. It should be noted that seven Consuls representing several European Powers had passed away and been buried in Jerusalem, mostly of illnesses they had contracted while in the city. Many other Consuls, who had the good fortune not to die at their posts, had also fallen prey to sometimes lengthy illnesses caused by the climate and sanitary conditions. Accordingly, it was almost a universal practice of the Consuls to spend extended vacations in Europe. In the following letter, Blech attempted to have Jerusalem recognized as an "unhealthy" location, thereby entitling those who served in its Consulate to vacations longer than the standard two months. He based his arguments on the malaria epidemics that plagued the city's residents, especially the Europeans.

FO 369/107 (No. 36329)                                      Jerusalem, October 9th, 1907
No. 18

Sir,
    I have the honour to submit for your favourable consideration a request that this post may be added to the list of unhealthy places for purposes of leave of absence.
    The climate of Jerusalem, owing to the rapid changes from excessive heat to great cold, is exceptionally trying to Europeans, though even natives of mature years and strong constitutions are constantly suffering from malaria fever. For children it is particularly dangerous; the great heat of the day rendering them peculiarly susceptible to the violent fall in temperature at sunset, and I may state that since my arrival here in June, not one week has passed without one or more of my family being attacked by this insidious and debilitating malady, which eventually so weakens the system as in some cases to prove fatal. Moreover there is absolutely no place within the Consular district to which it is possible to resort even for a temporary change; the nearest 'villegiature' is the Lebanon which can only be reached by a long and costly journey.
    The place swarms with mosquitoes, including the germs recognized as the vehicle of the malaria bacillus, and there is no means of extirpating them in a city where every house has its own breeding ground in the cistern, which is its only water-supply.
    The inclosed certificate will give some idea of the views of medical men on the subject.[1] In his letter forwarding it, Dr. Cropper[2] states: 'In my second paper in the "Journal of Hygiene" I compared Jerusalem to the West Coast of

1    Not enclosed.
2    Dr. Cropper was a physician in the British missionary hospital.

Africa'; the same expression has been employed to me in conversation by a Missionary with great experience of this country.

If I make this request it is more in the interest of future occupants of the post than in my own, as my means would not permit of my availing myself of the annual two months' leave.[3]

Blech

## 108    E.C. Blech to N. O'Conor
## Report on Gaza

Already in a despatch of 7 February 1899, Consul Dickson had emphasized the rising importance of Gaza and requested that a Consular Agent be appointed for the region (see the introduction to No. 83, above). Only in 1905, however, was such an appointment approved, based on Dickson's proposal. The post was unsalaried, but after some time, the Agent asked that he at least be reimbursed for his expenses. The Consul, as had his predecessor, supported this request; however, in order to justify an expenditure of £50 over the course of one year, he saw fit to once again stress the importance of the "port" of Gaza and of the city, in terms of British interests.

FO 195/2255 — No. 67                                        Jerusalem, December 21, 1907

Sir,

With reference to Your Excellency's despatch of September 2 last, I have now the honour to report that having visited Gaza I am in a position to furnish certain additional information in connection with Mr Knesevich's application for an Office Allowance of £50 a year.[1]

Gaza is the port of a large and fertile grain-producing country. Its population, almost entirely Moslem, is about 40,000, though emigration to Egypt on account of the failure of last year's crop may have reduced it temporarily to 35,000. In years of ordinary prosperity some 40,000 tons of

---

3    On 9 November 1907, a favourable response was received: "The post will be added to the list of places which are considered unhealthy for purposes of leaves of absence." According to Foreign Office documents, it was Ambassador O'Conor who suggested that Consul Blech address the Foreign Office on this issue, that the former "had good grounds for the suggestion," and therefore, "we can hardly refuse to lay it before the Treasury" (the above FO file).

---

1    For Knesevich, see above, No. 83, n. 1.

barley are exported, chiefly to the United Kingdom, and the port is visited by some twenty-five British steamers in consequence, though none has called there this year, the circumstances being entirely exceptional. The Captains of such vessels as do come are entirely dependent on Mr. Knesevich as their intermediary in their dealings with the town, the almost constant violence of the sea makes it always possible that some accident may occur in which his assistance will be required (in 1906 the Captain of a British vessel was drowned in Gaza roads); the British subjects registered number nearly fifty; and the Church Missionary Society maintaines [sic] schools and a Hospital, with a staff of seven British-born missionaries. The school is attended by upwards of two hundred children and in the busy season I understand that there are often one hundred applicants at the Hospital. It is obvious that many circumstances may arise in which the intervention of Mr. Knesevich is called for: he has recently succeeded after a long struggle in obtaining for the material, etc., imported for the new hospital just completed exemption from the Gaza pier dues. The British subjects, Turkish officials, religious dignitaries and commercial notabilities with whom I came into contact were unanimous in praising Mr. Knesevich's tact and zeal and in recognising his services on behalf of foreign subjects generally, (he is the only Consular Officer at Gaza); and though I am aware that such eulogistic expressions are often of little value in the East, I think that in the present case they repose on solid foundation, and I could see for myself that he is respected by, and is on friendly terms with, all the officials and principal persons in the place. His position as Consular Agent undoubtedly entails on him some expenditure in the way of hospitality both to casual travellers and to the local authorities. He is well informed and makes it his special duty to keep this Consulate in possession of the latest news from the Turco-Egyptian frontier: indeed Your Excellency has been pleased to express your approval of his services in this respect.

I think in these circumstances that it would be inadvisable to suppress the Consular Agency at Gaza and that consequently it should be made possible for the Agent to exercise his functions without actual pecuniary loss. I venture therefore to express the hope that Your Excellency may see fit to recommend to the favourable notice of His Majesty's Principal Secretary of State for Foreign Affairs Mr Knesevich's request for an office allowance of £50 inclosed in Mr. Freeman's despatch No. 49 of September 24, 1906 and reiterated in the letter which I had the honour to forward to Your Excellency in my despatch No. 34 of August 19 last.[2]

E.C. Blech

2    After prolonged correspondence, a sum of £50 was approved "for office expenses per annum."

# 109 J. Falanga to E.C. Blech
## Riots in Jaffa

The bloody riots in Jaffa on the eve of the Purim holiday in 1908 were in fact an organized attack, with the active participation of soldiers and police, and even of the Caimakam himself, which led to the wounding of thirteen Jews. This episode is described in detail in: M. Eliav, "The Purim Riots in Jaffa — 1908," *Ha-Ziyonut* 3 (1974), pp. 152–174 (Hebrew). For reports on the riots by the German Vice-Consul at Jaffa, see: Eliav, *German Policy*, Nos. 191, 192, 194; for reports by the Austrian Vice-Consul see: idem, *Austrian Protection*, Nos. 154–156.

The version of the British Vice-Consul was significantly different, as he basically adopted the claims of the Arabs, who blamed the Jews for the outbreak of the rioting. However, the British report makes it is clear that there were thirteen innocent victims who had not been involved in the disturbances, but were injured by soldiers and police.

FO 371/541
Copy

Jaffa, March 18, 1908

Sir,

I have the honour to report the following incident that happened in the Jewish quarter of the town called Menshia during the night of the 16th inst.

Owing to a previous quarrel which had occured [sic] a few days ago between a Moslem and three or four young Jews (Russian emigrants)[1] passed the shop of the said Moslem & reprimanded him in harsh language for what he had done to them, the Moslem using also strong language shied an empty bottle of Soda and wounded one of the Jews on the head;[2] at the same moment five Jews rushed against the Moslem and inflicted on him twelve stabs with knives which they carried; the row attracted several Jews and Moslems on the spot and an open fight with heavy sticks began, this was at 8 o'clock at night when gendarmes arrived and put a stop to the fighting. The five Russian Jews who attacked the Moslem ran away in their domicile just opposite the place where they wounded the Moslem, this being a small hotel kept by a Russian

---

1   There is a lacuna of one or more words here. The writer does not mention that the dispute was caused by an Arab insulting a young Jewess, followed by a fracas in which the Arab was beaten.
2   According to the Austrian Vice-Consul, the Arab shopkeeper was "the provocateur of the entire affair" (Eliav, *Austrian Protection*, p. 339).

Jew;[3] in the interval of the fighting in the street ten soldiers with their guns (no cartridges) came to the spot and joining with the gendarmes they broke the door of the said hotel open and entered it;[4] several shots were heard in the house and some were fired out of the windows into the street, after 'a démilée' the soldiers succeeded in pulling the five culprits out of the house and they conducted them to the Serai where they were put to prison.[5]

Thirteen Jews were wounded and taken to the hospital, most of them are wounded on the heads with heavy blows of sticks, two of them were hurt by small bullets (revolver) in all three are in a dangerous state. The wounded Moslem is not expected to live according to the doctor of the Municipality.

I am not aware of the steps taken by the Russian Consulate. The incident caused a general panic among the Jews in Jaffa and some of our protected subjects addressed to me a petition which I inclose herewith in original.[6]

I saw the Kaimmakam on the matter who promised to do his best to repress any bad consequences of the incident; he has doubled the patrol and has imprisoned several Moslems who are apt to ferment the spirits of the low class of the population.

(Signed) J. Falanga[7]

# 110 E.C. Blech to N. O'Conor
# Riots in Jaffa

The Consul in Jerusalem decided to report to the Ambassador in Constantinople regarding the riots, and enclosed the report of Falanga, the Vice-Consul at Jaffa (see above, No. 109). The Consul's letter was also marked by a pronounced lack of sympathy for the *Yishuv*, especially for the immigrants of the Second Aliyah, whom he charged with provocative behaviour, and whose

3   The Spector Hotel housed pioneering Jewish immigrants who had recently arrived from Eastern Europe.
4   The Caimakam called in the soldiers for assistance after the police had not succeeded in entering the hotel. Not satisfied with forcibly entering the Spector Hotel, they also broke into another immigrant hotel.
5   This as well is debatable, and it is not at all certain that those arrested were indeed the attackers.
6   Not enclosed.
7   See above, No. 106, n. 1.

increased immigration, so he claimed, aroused the opposition of the Muslim and Christian populations (also see the report of the Austrian Consul from 26 March 1908, in which he stated that both the Governor of Jerusalem and the Caimakam of Jaffa present the immigration of Jews from Russia as a "social danger which must be fought," Eliav, *Austrian Protection*, p. 345). The British Consul clearly tended to accept the version of the Arabs regarding the incident, in contrast to his German and Austrian colleagues.

FO 371/541 — No. 16                                        Jerusalem, March 19, 1908
Copy

Sir,

I have the honour to report that on the 16th instant a somewhat serious riot took place at Jaffa between Russian Jews and Moslems, with the result that three of the former and one of the latter were dangerously wounded. The circumstances are described in the inclosed despatch from Mr. Falanga, the Acting Vice Consul at Jaffa; he has since then informed me that all is now quiet, though the Jews are somewhat perturbed and apprehensive, and the Russian Vice Consul has stated to him that the Authorities are not to blame in the matter.[1] I received this morning the visit of two Jews of British Nationality, who gave me what I consider a grossly exaggerated description of the incident and stated that the Jews both at Jaffa and here are afraid that they would be massacred. I endeavoured as far as possible to tranquillise them, and I see no reason whatever for apprehending that any untoward results will follow what appears to have been an ordinary disturbance in which the Jews were the aggressors.[2] At the same time, these Russian Jewish immigrants are turbulent and aggressive, saturated with socialistic ideas, and by their demeanour & by their growing numbers are likely to arouse the resentment of the natives of this country, both Christian and Moslem.

1    The Russian Vice-Consul at Jaffa, who presumably was supposed to protect his Jewish protégés, was a pronounced anti-Semite, and cooperated with the Caimakam, who was responsible in great measure for the attack on the Jews in the hotel. He added his voice to the false charge that the Jews had fired first. The Russian Consul-General in Jerusalem, Kruglow, resolved to provide a vigorous defense for the Jews under his protection, and severely criticized the actions of the Vice-Consul at Jaffa.
2    The British Consul attempted to allay the fears of his protégés in Jaffa, but, in this letter, he does not hesitate to lay the blame on the Jews as the aggressors in the incident; he also notes the opposition to the immigrants who possessed "socialist ideas." It is noteworthy that within the *Yishuv* itself, there were reservations regarding the behaviour of the Second Aliyah pioneers and their exaggerated self-confidence. See also the report of the Austrian Vice-Consul dated 25 March 1908 (Eliav, *Austrian Protection*, pp. 342–345).

No British interest having been involved, so far as I am aware, I have not deemed it necessary to make any representation to the Authorities.

E.C. Blech


## 111   E.C. Blech to G.H. Barclay
## Suspension of the Kaimakam at Jaffa

The Caimakam in Jaffa, Assaf Bey Assad, was appointed to this position in June 1907. He cooperated with the Governor of Jerusalem, Ali Ekrem Bey, who adopted a hostile policy toward the *Yishuv*, and especially against the immigrants (see: Kushner, *Governor*, index, and especially pp. 32, 167). He was even more radical then the Governor in his opposition to Jewish immigration. The considerable impact of the Jews on life in Jaffa was anathema to him. He also strictly enforced the prohibition against land purchases, and even incited the Arab populace against the Jewish settlers. This was followed by provocative acts against the Jews, accompanied by the violent incident described above. The Austrian and German Consuls demanded that he be removed, a protest supported by the Russian Consul-General. The leaders of the *Yishuv* and the Zionist Executive also demanded that the perpetrators be punished, specifically calling for the dismissal of the Caimakam. On 31 March 1908 the latter was summoned to Constantinople to deliver his report, following which he was relieved of his post. The dismissal order astounded the Arab population, while greatly satisfying the Jews. There was a radical change in the atmosphere, the tensions speedily decreased, and the provocations ceased totally. Although the events were forgotten after a while and no longer cast a shadow over Jewish-Arab relations in Jaffa, they are of importance as the first instance of organized riots and Jewish mobilization for self-defense.

The letter was sent to the Chargé d'Affaires, in the absence of the Ambassador.


FO 195/2287 — N° 20                                          Jerusalem, April 2, 1908

Sir,

In continuation of my despatch n° 18 of the 25th ultimo I have the honour to inclose herewith copy of a despatch which I have received from Mr. Falanga, reporting that the Kaimmakam of Jaffa has been summoned to Constantinople to explain his conduct in the affray between Jews and Moslems which occurred on March 16 last. This is a success for the Russian Consul

General, and I understand that the Mutessarif is much annoyed in consequence.[1]

Assaf Bey was transferred from Beersheba to Jaffa last June at the suggestion of Ekrem Bey himself. He has a courteous address and some knowledge of French, but neither his age nor his experience qualify him for so important a Kaza as Jaffa. Although my personal relations with him were uniformly cordial, I can hardly concur in Mr. Falanga's statement as to his willingness to assist us in the support of British interests. His return to Jaffa would be viewed with apprehension by the Jews, and I think it highly desirable that an older Kaimmakam more versed in official matters should be appointed.[2]

Abdul Kerim Bey, who was recently appointed as mouavin[3] of the Mutessarif to reside at Beer-Sheba, is acting as Kaimakam at Jaffa.

E.C. Blech

## 112   E.C. Blech to G.H. Barclay
## Proposal for Establishment of a British Post Office at Jerusalem

Four years after the proposal to open a British Post Office in Jerusalem was first discussed (see above, No. 97), it was raised once again. The stimulus this time apparently was the increased activity of foreign post offices, whose quiet competition was intended to enhance the influence of the Powers that operated the mail services. The four postal services operating in Jerusalem and in Jaffa were about to be joined by a fifth, that of Italy. This was the immediate cause for the resumed discussion of the proposal, which enjoyed the support of the Consul.

This despatch, too, was sent to the Chargé d'Affaires in the absence of the Ambassador at Constantinople.

1   Ekrem Bey attempted to defend his protégé in his report to Constantinople, and was especially irked by the demand by the Russian Consul-General for the immediate dismissal of the Caimakam, the punishment of the attackers, and the release of the Jewish prisoners. In practice, the steps taken by the Consul-General clashed with the position of the Governor, who expressed his displeasure at the acquiescence of the Sublime Porte to diplomatic pressure.
2   The deposed Assaf Bey continued to malign the Jewish public in order to justify his own actions. See his diplomatic report of 16 April 1908, published by David Farhi in M. Ma'oz (ed.), *Studies on Palestine during the Ottoman Period*, Jerusalem 1975, pp. 206–208.
3   Official assistant.

Sir,

I have the honour to acknowledge receipt this morning of your despatch of the 11th instant calling for my observations on the renewed proposal for the establishment of a British Post Office at Jerusalem.

In reply, I beg leave to invite attention to the late Mr Dickson's despatches n° 6 of January 22, 1904, n° 6 Commercial of Febrary 14, 1904, and n° 9 of April 11, 1905. In these despatches Mr Dickson estimated the annual cost of maintaining post offices here and at Jaffa at about £1000 per annum, and the probable yearly revenue at a sum slightly under that figure. I have not been able during my comparatively short residence here to collect any information which would justify me in suggesting any modification of these estimates, and see no reason to doubt their accuracy.

On the whole, I am of opinion that the establishment of a British Post Office would be welcomed by the British Community, and that its receipts would tend to increase. But this opinion is not universally held; only the other day Sir John Gray Hill[1] told me that he had refused to sign the petition in that sense, being persuaded that no British Post Office was required and that the Austrian Post Office offered adequate facilities and perfect security. There can be no doubt that this view of the Austrian Post Office is quite correct. It is true that quite recently I had occasion to report to His Majesty's Principal Secretary of State for Foreign Affairs the loss of a group of £2,800 while in course of transmission by the Austrian Post; but this might happen to any Post Office.

I am quite unable to see how the establishment of a British Post Office would facilitate British trade. Sufficient facilities exist for the transmission of letters, parcels, etc. through the Austrian, French, German and Russian offices, to which an Italian office is shortly to be added.[2] As far as numbers go,

---

1   In the late 1880s, Sir John Gray Hill, a barrister from Liverpool, purchased a sizable portion of the lands of Mount Scopus, where he built his home ("The centre of art and hospitality and wide philanthropy" — Goodrich-Freer, p. 12). From then on he would spend a considerable part of the year in his house in Jerusalem. In 1913 he conducted negotiations with Dr. Ruppin for the sale of his property on Mount Scopus to the Zionist movement. The transaction was concluded only in 1916, however, and with a donation by the philanthropist J.L. Goldberg a plot of 115 dunams was purchased, the site upon which the Hebrew University would be built.

2   The Italian Post Office in Jerusalem was opened on 1 June 1908. In his letter describing this, Blech added: "It is no uncommon occurrence for a tourist to send a hundred or two hundreds picture postcards from Jerusalem, while local Jews spend large sums on the postage of their appeals (often printed) to the charity of their co-religionists in foreign countries" (1 June 1908, FO 195/2287).

five foreign post offices added to the Turkish office are surely sufficient for an oriental city of 80,000 inhabitants. It is, I conceive, quite immaterial to the sender of a letter whether that letter is delivered at Jerusalem by a British Office, or, as is now the case, by the Austrian Post. Indeed the only practical advantage which I can see is that, if a British Post existed, I presume that the postal unit for letters forwarded from Jerusalem by it would be the ounce, that is, 28.35 grammes, whereas by the foreign offices the unit adopted is 20 grammes; and for this reason, if I am correct in this supposition, we might anticipate that a considerable amount of mail matter would be transferred to our hands.

But I am strongly of opinion that our prestige, if I may use a word which does not often figure in our official correspondence, is increased by the establishment of post-offices, hospitals, schools and the like. If this point is worthy of consideration, then I submit that the establishment of post-offices here and at Jaffa (for the former implies the latter) is desirable and is worth the slight expenditure which it would at first entail on the ratepayer. It is not for me to say whether the present moment is propitious, or whether it would be dignified for us to appear to be imitating the example of the Italians. But I submit that we have lost in the past in this country by not attributing more importance to outward show of this nature, which undoubtedly has weight with orientals.[3]

I have the honour to return herewith Sir Edward Grey's despatch forwarded to me in original.

E.C. Blech

## 113   E.C. Blech to G.H. Barclay
## British Protection for Jewish Companies

Blech's reservations regarding the *Yishuv*, and especially Zionist activity, were also expressed in the following despatch. The Consul was not pleased by the registration of Jewish firms as British companies in order to receive the protection of the Consulate in Jerusalem, especially since the duties involved in the handling of the companies and their problems "tend to increase the work of this Consulate." When, however, the company was an industrial one,

3    In the end, once again the matter remained unresolved, and the proposal was no longer current.

likely to reinforce British prestige and even to prove beneficial to the economy of Palestine, the Consul did not express any reservations. Blech's opposition as a matter of principle was in contrast with the more objective stance of his predecessor. Blech's stand was not accepted by the Foreign Office, which held that every British company was deserving of protection. English law did not establish any conditions regarding the nationality of the directors of companies registered in England, provided the companies paid taxes as required. The Consul in Jerusalem was left with no alternative but to accept this decision, while urging the directors of the APC to advance British commerce in Palestine.

FO 195/2287 — No. 33                                Jerusalem, June 29, 1908

Sir,
    I have the honour to report that it has recently come to my knowledge that three limited companies have just been registered in England, of which two are intended to conduct their operations in Palestine, while the third seems to contemplate undertaking business in other parts of the Ottoman Empire; their names are: the Anglo-Palestine Wine Company, Limited;[1] Stein & Co., Limited;[2] and the Anglo-Levantine Company, Limited.[3] Of these only the second seems to me likely to conduce to the advancement of British trade, being designed to facilitate the importation of machinery of British manufac-

---

1    There apparently is an error here, and reference is being made to the Palestine Wine Trading Company, which had been founded by English Jews in order to market wine from Palestine in England, having no connection with the APC. In 1907 the Vineyard Owner's Association (*Agudat ha-Kormim*), comprising the wineries of Rishon le-Zion and Zikhron Ya'akov, purchased the company as a means for exporting wine.

2    Leon Stein (died 1926) was a pioneer of industry in Palestine. He established workshops for metalworking in the Neveh Zedek quarter, north of Jaffa, in 1888. In 1905 a foundry was added to the factory, and he began to manufacture pumps and filters. On 25 May 1906 a stock company, 'L. Stein and Partners — Industrial Co.' was registered by two British subjects with the Consular Agent in Jaffa. The factory underwent various crises and was forced to close down. For the factory and industrial activity of Stein, see: S. Avitsur, "A Pioneer of Modern Industry in Eretz-Israel," *Cathedra*, no. 15 (April 1980), pp. 69–88 (Hebrew).

3    The Anglo-Levantine Banking Co. (ALBC) was founded on the initiative of David Wolffsohn, President of the Zionist Organization and one of the directors of the APC, at the end of 1907. Meant to represent the financial and political interests of the Zionist movement in the capital of the Ottoman Empire, tt was established as a small Jewish bank in Constantinople, with the JCT holding 60% of the shares. Dr. Victor Jacobson, formerly the director of the APC branch in Beirut and the brother-in-law of the Zionist leader Menahem Ussishkin, was appointed as Director. In practice, Jacobson acted as the Zionist political representative, and until World War I conducted negotiations on behalf of the Zionist Executive with the Turks.

354

ture. The first-named is merely the reconstruction of an already existing undertaking for the manufacture and export of wine, while the third is but another name for the Anglo-Palestine Co. The latter institution, the organ of the Zionist movement, seems to finance all three companies, and the signatories to the Articles of Association, mostly foreign Jews of apparently slight financial importance, are in nearly all cases the same.

It is clear that advantage is being taken of our Limited Companies' Law to obtain British protection for undertakings which have nothing English but their names. I do not know how far the mere act of registration at Somerset House can invest these and similar companies with a right to British protection, and a case decided not many months ago in Egypt would seem to indicate that this right is at least questionable. The Anglo-Palestine Company[4] is in the same position; very few of its employees are of British nationality, it has merely a nominal office in London, and so far my strong admonitions to their managers that we expect them to do something for British trade, in return for the protection which they enjoy, have led to very little result.

It is explained to me that the registration of these companies in London is due to a preference of British over foreign protection; the registration of a company under German laws, for instance, is stated to be both easier and less costly, but the Jews profess a predilection for British nationality. This statement may be exaggerated, and I can hardly think that non-German subjects would be allowed to register themselves as a German undertaking. But the promoters would experience no difficulty in finding the requisite number of Jews of German nationality to lend their names for purposes of registration, and I am led to the conclusion that British protection is really preferred. The establishment of these Companies will doubtless tend to increase the work of this Consulate, and to multiply its opportunities of tension with the Local Authorities. But, apart from the question whether it is desirable that aliens should through a mere technicality be entitled to our protection, I am not in principle averse to the increase of undertakings under British jurisdiction; and in the case of Stein & Company I certainly think satisfactory results may ensue.

E.C. Blech

---

4    See above, No. 94.

# 114  J. Falanga to E.C. Blech
## Hostilities against Austria

After the revolution of the Young Turks in July 1908, the Austrian government took advantage of the ensuing situation, and on 5 October 1908
proclaimed the annexation of the two provinces of Bosnia and Herzegovina,
which until then had been part of the Ottoman Empire but had been administered by the Austrians. The declaration of annexation generated a crisis in the
diplomatic relations with the adjacent kingdom of Serbia, and Turkey presented a stiff protest. France and England decided not to intervene, while
Germany supported the Austrian action. The Turks did not limit themselves
to a formal protest, and attempted to harass the Austrians as much as
possible. The ports of the Ottoman Empire were closed to Austrian ships and
goods, which led to demonstrations and hostile acts. On 13 October 1908 the
Austrian Vice-Consul at Jaffa registered a complaint with the Caimakam
concerning the boycott and acts of violence in Jaffa (see Eliav, *Austrian
Protection*, p. 160).

FO 195/2287                                           Jaffa, October 13, 1908
Telegram — Copy

British Consul
Jerusalem
    Upon political news received yesterday, a crowd assembled last night in
a Coffee-house at the head of which were several Hodjas who spoke against
the attitude of Austria, they succeeded in inducing the boatmen & lightermen
to refuse sending their boats along the Austrian steamer expected this morning.
This morning on the arrival of the steamer a crowd attacked the Austrian Post
Office, breaking the letter-box and a cart.[1] The boatmen refused to go on
board the ship and after long discussions they have permitted the steamer's
boat to land the post. Many Christian Ottoman Subjects encouraged the
boatmen of whom I have taken several names. Position at 10 o'ck.

Falanga

---

1    See also the report from 16 October 1908 of the director of the Austrian Post Office in Jaffa
    (Eliav, *Austrian Protection*, No. 161).

# 115 E.C. Blech to Sir G. Lowther
## Boycott of Austria

The telegram by Falanga (above, No. 114) was followed by a detailed report of the events in Jaffa harbour sent by the Consul on 13 October 1908. Even the passengers were not permitted to leave the ship. The agitation conducted by Muslim clerics at the instigation of the authorities, or, at the very least, with their silent acquiescence, led to disturbances by the masses and the categorical refusal of the stevedores to bring the cargo and passengers ashore. These were not spontaneous reactions, but rather organized and directed actions. The Consul already noted the repercussions of the boycott. The trade of other countries might possibly gain as a result of the boycott, but British interests could expect a good deal of inconvenience, because all British postal traffic went through the Austrian mail service. Also see the additional reports: Eliav, *Austrian Protection*, Nos. 164–165, in which England is mentioned as one of the countries attempting to replace the Austrians in the import trade. The boycott of Austrian goods and ships continued until 1 March 1909, when an agreement was signed between the Austrian and Turkish governments, in which the latter recognized the Austrian annexation of Bosnia and Herzegovina in return for a substantial monetary payment.

FO 195/2287 — No. 53                                    Jerusalem, October 15, 1908

Sir,

In continuation of my immediately preceding despatch, I have the honour to report that Mr Falanga informs me that the Austrian Lloyd steamship 'Enterpre' left Jaffa yesterday afternoon, without having been able to communicate with the port otherwise than by discharging her mails by means of her own boats. The local boatmen would not even consent to convey the Health Officer on board to carry out the disinfection and medical inspection imposed on arrivals from Egypt, and it was therefore impossible to disembark the passengers for Jaffa or the two thousand packages of goods destined for that port. The Health Officer on applying to the Acting Kaimakkam for assistance was merely told that nothing could be done.

Messages of approval and encouragement have been sent from here to the Jaffa boatmen (who are working freely in connection with French and Greek steamers now in harbour), and it is to be apprehended that they will continue their boycott of the Austrian flag unless strong instructions are sent from headquarters. The ultimate effect will no doubt be favourable to the trade of other countries, but meanwhile great inconvenience, will result to

Jaffa and Jerusalem, and our mail connections depend principally on the Austrian Lloyd steamers; thus letters for the Brindisi mail, the only rapid conveyance to Europe, are despatched on Saturday by Austrian Lloyd to Port Said, and great uncertainty now exists whether the mails can be put on board on the 17th instant. But I have thought it best to avoid further complicating the Mutessarif's difficult position by making representations to His Excellency, as I have every reason to suppose that my Austrian colleague is doing everything in his power in a matter which primarily concerns himself.[1]

E.C. Blech

# 116   J. Falanga to H.E. Satow
## Commercial Report on Jaffa for 1909

The following is the almost complete text of a commercial report of the Vice-Consul at Jaffa which reflects the economic activity during 1909. A comparison with a similar report for the same year by the Austrian Vice-Consul (Eliav, *Austrian Protection*, No. 172) is of interest. The latter provides an extensive description of the progress of Zionist activity: the beginnings of Tel Aviv and the developing Jewish settlements as well as developments in the German colonies. None of these topics are mentioned in the British report, which mentions economic progress, but concentrates on activity in the port and various public aspects.

JNUL 4°1513/47                                                    Jaffa, March 9th 1910

*General remarks*

The trade of Jaffa is on the increase in general. Imports show an increase of £165,515. as compared with 1908, and Exports an increase of £4,565. The receipts of the railway company Jaffa–Jerusalem exceeded by £4000 those for 1908. The goods traffic increased by 1300 tons while 26,700 more passengers of all classes were carried.[1]

1   After the conclusion of the boycott, merchants and customers returned to Austrian merchandise, so that Austrian trade suffered only minor damage. See Eliav, *Austrian Protection*, Nos. 166–167).

1   The numerical data in this section differ slightly from those in the commercial report on Jaffa appearing in the "Report for the Year 1909 on the Trade of the Consular District of Jerusalem" (*Diplomatic and Consular Reports*, No. 4471).

Round Jaffa the cultivation of cereals is being extended, — more orange groves are being planted, and experiments in cotton culture are being carried out. Industry which is only represented by the manufacture of soap remains stationary.

## Population

There has been a small increase of population quoted last year at 50,000 inhabitants for Jaffa and neighbouring German and Jewish colonies, the increase is due to the fact that immigration of Jews from Russia and to some extent from South Africa and Australia continues.[2] Most of these immigrants arrive with sufficient pecuniary means to establish themselves as shop keepers or cultivators.

Except for the influx of foreigners, the population would show a yearly decrease, this is seen in the case of the surrounding villages inhabited only by natives. The cause of the decrease is the neglect and carelessness of the parents in bringing up their children who are left altogether to nature and consequently suffer from the effects of a bad climate.

## Banking

The number of Banks represented in Jaffa is the same as last year viz The Imperial Ottoman Bank,[3] — The Crédit Lyonnais, — The Anglo-Palestine C° Ltd, — and The Deutsche-Palästina Bank.[4] They all realised more profits than in 1908. They worked on the basis of 8 p% discount up to the month of October when they raised the rate to 9 p% on account of the great rise of discount in London and kept at that rate until the end of the year. Advances against good securities were made at the rate of 6½ to 7% all the year round.

## Shipping

The same SS. companies as last year served in our roadstead of which the following sent regular mail and passengers steamers: 'The Messageries Maritimes'[5] with a fortnightly service from Egypt and then northward up the coast, and with a weekly service from Beirut and thence to Egypt.

2    The intent is not that there was a significant increase in the number of immigrants from South Africa and Australia, rather the two countries were mentioned because these immigrants enjoyed British protection.
3    The first branch of the Banque Impériale Ottomane was opened in Jaffa in 1904, and it later became the head branch of the bank in all of Palestine. In 1905 a branch was opened in Jerusalem. The establishment of the branches of the APC may possibly have spurred the Ottoman bank to open branches of its own.
4    See above, Nos. 94, 106.
5    The French company.

'The Austrian Lloyd' with weekly services from Egypt and northward and from Beirut to Egypt. 'The Italian C° Rubatino with the same ittinerary [sic], 'The Khedivial' calling every week on the same day, (Monday) one boat for Egypt and one for Beirut.

Besides the above mentioned five companies, Cargo boats of other companies call at Jaffa according to the needs of the export trade, among these are: 'The Prince', — 'Ellerman', — 'Moss', — and 'Papayanni Liverpool Liners', — 'the Asia Minor C°'', — 'Westcott & Laurence', — the 'Compagnie Royale Neerlandaise of Amsterdam', — the 'Deutsche Levante Line', — the 'Atlas SS. C°', — the 'Compagnie Russe du Nord', — the 'Hadji Daoud and Farkouf C°', formerly Turkish but lately transformed into an American Company under the name of the 'Archipelago American Line' (head office at Smyrna) — Freight on grain to British ports has been paid by the Jaffa shippers at from 9/ to 11/. per ton, — and from British ports to Jaffa at 20/. per measurement ton. [...]

*Crops*

In the district of Gaza the barley crop was a complete failure in 1909. Round Jaffa the cultivators were satisfied in general with their produce such as wheat, — sesame seed, — white millet, — water melons, — oranges &c. Prices in Europe were also favourable.

The olive crops of last autumn was an extra good one and there is consequently a great abundance of olive oil in the country so that the manufacture of soap will obtain its maximum quantity.

*Cotton cultivation*

The Jewish Colonists of Pettaktikwa [sic] continued their experiments in cotton growing: In February 1909 eighty acres of land were down with Egyptian seed; the picking begun on the first week of September and was finished at the end of December. The produce amounted to 36,000 Kilogrammes of unginned cotton giving 11,528 Kilogrammes of pure cotton and 24,300 Kilogrammes of seed which were sold by the owners at Haiffa for francs 29,259. The cotton was said to equal the best Egyptian quality and was valued at Frs 2.15c the Kilme sold on the spot at Haiffa. The cultivation was carried on with irrigation from May to middle of November.

A friend having sent me from Liverpool about half a pound of cotton tree seed, this has been distributed to several cultivators in different directions for experiments. — [...]

## Public works

Nothing has been done again this year to facilitate communications. Many schemes have been mooted, among which are those to construct roads and run electric cars on them; — to construct a quay in front of Jaffa along the seashore; — to work mines; — to canalise the river Houdja for irrigating the orange gardens and fields. So far however nothing has been done to carry out these schemes.

## Public health

The sanitary condition of the town of Jaffa was completely neglected, the result being that there were many cases of malarial fever in the autumn affecting perhaps 50% of the inhabitants who are are also liable to other epidemic diseases. [...]

J. Falanga

# 117 H.E. Satow to G. Lowther
# Purchase of Property by Jews

There were both stringent and lenient aspects to the prohibition of land acquisition by Jews. The authorities frequently turned a blind eye to real estate transactions — generally after the payment of bribes. When, however, a new Governor came to Jerusalem, he sought to demonstrate his determination to maintain the prohibitions, and once again it was necessary to turn to the Ambassador in Constantinople for the revocation of these arbitrary decrees, as in the case before us. For the actions of Consul Dickson against the prohibition of land purchases see above, No. 97; Hyamson, No. 439.

FO 195/2851 — No. 25

Jerusalem, May 21, 1910

Sir,

I have the honour to inform Your Excellency that recently Mr. M.M. Benin, a Jewish British subject, who has resided in Jerusalem uninterruptedly during the last eight years,[1] wished to purchase real property, as he has

1  A letter by Haim Amzalak dated 23 May 1899 reported the immigration to Palestine of a small group of Jews from Aden, headed by Moses Benin, his wife, and "two servants" (Hyamson, Enclosure to No. 430). The authorities demanded an undertaking that they

previously done without difficulty, and, furnished with the usual Consular Certificate, applied to the Dragoman of the Mutessarifat, as is customary, for the legalisation of my signature and official seal.

This official at first refused to comply with his request, so that recourse was had to the Mutessarif. The latter informed the Consular dragoman that before anything could be done he would be glad to have a statement in writing as to length of residence of the British subject.

I accordingly sent in an official note to the effect that Mr. Benin had been registered in this Consulate since 1902. To this I received a reply, translation of which is enclosed herewith, that renewed orders had been received in the year 1309 from both the Ministry of the Interior and the Grand Vizier that Jews who remained in Palestine after that date were to be considered as persons whose entry was forbidden, that the British subject in question belonged to this class of Jews who were not allowed to buy land and that, even if there had been neglect of these orders in the past, he could not now be permitted to acquire real property. It was further stated that the matter was to be reported to the Sublime Porte.

I contented myself in reply with expressing my astonishment at this answer in view of the first Article of the Law of 13 Sefer 1284 governing the acquisition by foreigners of land in Turkey which I quoted.

I understand that a similar refusal has been made to a Russian subject, who, although born in Jerusalem, had left it for a time and only returned some eight or ten years ago.

I venture to report this case to Your Excellency not only because the interests of a British subject are affected, but also because it would seem to show that the authorities at Constantinople, on whose orders Azmi Bey[2] is presumably acting, intend to take stricter measures in the future to prevent the acquisition of land by foreign Jews who, owing to the past neglect or acquiescence of the Local Authorities, have hitherto succeeded to a considerable extent in evading the prohibition aimed at them.

H.E. Satow

would not remain in the country for more than thirty days, but Amzalak refused to make such a commitment. There are no further reports regarding these immigrants. Benin had amassed a fortune from dealings in India and Egypt, and was already a wealthy man when he came to Jerusalem, where his business continued to flourish. He built a large house on Jaffa Road in the city.

2    Azmi Bey was Governor of Jerusalem from May 1910 to June 1911.

# 118  J. Morgan to Foreign Secretary
## Water-Supply for Jerusalem and other Schemes

In the absence of Consul Satow, the Acting Consul, J. Morgan, was required to deal with various proposals for the development of Jerusalem, primarily plans for the city's water supply, which various entrepreneurs raised with the authorities. Already in 1895 the Consul had sent a comprehensive report concerning a plan to improve the water supply. The proposal had been raised by the engineer G. Franghia, at the time the official in charge of public works in Palestine. It was based chiefly on bringing water from the Ayn Arroub springs (see above, No. 76). Nothing came of it because the capital required could not be raised. In November 1908 a new plan was put forth by the company of Carl Franke of Bremen, Germany, with a cost of 2,500,000 francs; it called for utilising the springs in Ayn Fara, located approximately 13 km. northeast of Jerusalem. During the negotiations between Dr. Arthur Ruppin, the head of the Palestine Office of the Zionist Organization, and the German firm, a proposal was raised for cooperation which would include mobilization of Jewish capital and the possible establishment of an Ottoman company that would apply for the concession, in order to overcome their competitors, who included, *inter alia*, a French company and an Italian-Belgian firm. Levontin, the director of the APC, also participated in the negotiations. In addition to the water supply programs, there also were plans for the installation of electric lighting, an electric transportation system, and even telephones. But while these discussions were continuing, it was learned in September 1909 that a representative of the German company had signed a contract with the municipality which had to be confirmed by the central government in Constantinople, and pressure began to be applied to the local and central governments to cancel the contract and transfer the concession to an Ottoman company in which the Jewish institutions would be represented. On the initiative of the Zionist Executive, a Dutch engineer, J. Meijers, was sent to Jerusalem at the beginning of 1910. After a thorough examination, he recommended concentrating on the springs of Ayn Fara, with a central electrical installation to operate steam pumps, to deal with the problem of height differentials; the details appear in the following despatch. Meijers held that approval should also be obtained for supplying electric light and an electrically-operated transportation system, with the central electric plant providing the power for all these projects. Meijers' report was published in the Hague in April 1910, accompanied by a detailed map of the water system and the plan of the electric trolley lines within the city: *Rapport sur l'adduction des eaux, l'établissement d'un réseau de tramways électriques et d'un eclairage électrique a Jérusalem.* See also: M. Eliav, *David Wolffsohn — The Man and His Times*, Jerusalem 1977, pp. 229–231 (Hebrew).

Jerusalem, August 11, 1910

Sir,

I have the honour to forward herewith a paper giving an outline of certain schemes devised by the Jerusalem Corporation[1] for the improvement of the town.

The Corporation seems to have rushed hastily into print for it was only after the paper outlining the schemes was printed that it was realised that a mass of further details would be needed if persons were deriously expected to put in tenders before October 1910.

These details are now being elaborated but some time must elapse before they can be published in their entirety.

In the meantime I have been able to obtain some information as to the various schemes which may give a rough idea of what is expected.

(1) *Supplying Jerusalem with water from the springs of Ain Fara and other springs in the vicinity.*

The question of utilising the springs of Ain Fara as a Jerusalem water-supply has been the subject of Mr. Blech's despatch No. 5 Commercial to Sir E. Grey of September 10, 1909 and of Mr. Satow's despatch No. / Commercial to Sir E. Grey of February 10, 1910 (copies of both of these despatches were sent to the Board of Trade).

In November 1909[2] a German engineer of the firm of Carl Franke, Bremen, drew up a report on the utilisation of the Ain Fara Springs. It seemed at one time probable that the concession for carrying out the scheme would be given to the German firm but after the contract had been drawn up, the terms (detailed in Mr. Blech's despatch mentioned above) seem to have been too onerous, and the German firm withdrew. At present the Corporation would prefer to pay outright for the execution of the project but does not exclude the possibility of its giving a concession for a term of years to the constructing company, if the latter plan seemed to it more advantageous.

The springs of Ain Fara are situated some 13 or 14 kilometres north east of Jerusalem, the springs in the vicinity, referred to, being those of Fawar some 7 kilometres beyond Ain Fara. Ain Fara springs are 350 metres below the mean level of Jerusalem (775 metres) and Fawar still lower. The reservoirs

---

1    An Ottoman company founded by the municipality to implement the plan.
2    According to other sources, the plan was raised in September 1908, and at the time this despatch was written, the German company had already withdrawn from its implementation.

and waterworks are to be constructed at a point some 40 metres above the mean level. It is estimated that for the first five years some 8000 cubic metres of water a day would be required. According to the Corporation Ain Fara alone can supply from 4000–7000 cubic metres a day. The selling price of the water whether sold by the Corporation or by the Concessionnaire is not to exceed 7¼d. per cubic metre.

An alternative scheme to the above viz. that of utilising the springs of Arroub —— some 20 kilometres from Jerusalem and situated at about the same altitude is favoured by the Chamber of Commerce of Jerusalem who are trying to convert the Corporation to their view.[3]

(2) *Electric tramways.*

Three lines are in contemplation. 1. From Jaffa Gate via Measharim–Syrian Orphanage–Town Hospital — back to Jaffa Gate some 10 to 12 kilometres, 2. A continuation of this line through the City walls as far as the Jewish Quarter — about half a kilometre, 3. From Jaffa Gate to station about 2 kilometres.[4]

The power station is to be constructed and all plant, cars, etc., to be supplied by the tenderer. There should be a double line and the current should be supplied from underneath the cars.

*Electric lighting.* Corporation wish to expend about 30,000 francs on electric lighting of the town.

It would prefer the lighting and transways to be undertaken by the same contractor.

(3) *Sewers.* To be constructed under the main roads at first.
   *Gutters.* Are to be constructed in every street.

(4) *Telephones.*

The Corporation will need some 40 installations and there will no doubt be many private persons who would become subscribers in the event of an exchange being constructed.

The funds at the disposal of the Corporation would not suffice to carry

---

3   In his report, Meijers discusses in detail the advantages and drawbacks of each of the two sources of water, and reaches the conclusion that the spring of Ayn Fara was preferable, after a detailed calculation of expenses.
4   According to Meijers, the lines would total 10-12 km. of trackage. The estimate of the length of the first line, obviously exaggerated, should not have been more than 5–6 km. His plan also delineates a fourth line, from the Augusta Victoria building on Mount Scopus to the Russian Compound.

out the above schemes but it has intimated to me its desire to contract a loan to put them in execution.[5]

James Morgan


1°   Adduction à Jérusalem des eaux d'Ain Fara & des sources avoisinantes.

2°   Construction d'un tramway électrique et éclairage de la ville de Jérusalem par l'électricité.

3°   Construction des égoûts et canalisation dans differents points de la ville de Jérusalem.

4°   Installation du téléphone à Jérusalem.

      La municipalité de Jérusalem ayant décidé de mettre en exécution les quatre projets ci-dessus, fait connaître au public qu'elle aura à adjuger définitivement les travaux que ces entreprises exigent, une fois les conditions ci-dessous exposées remplies:

1°   Ces travaux seront adjugés séparément ou en bloc.

2°   Les sociétés qui désireraient entreprendre les travaux en question auront à déposer leur proposition dans des feuilles signées et cachetées sous enveloppes.
    Celles-ci devront être remises à la Municipalité jusqu'au 30 Septembre 1526 (n.s. 15 Octobre 1910)

3°   A l'expiration de ce délai, une commission spéciale sera formée pour, qu'en sa présence, et à une époque fixe, soit procédé à l'ouverture de ces enveloppes.

4°   L'examen de ces feuilles durera un mois entier.

5°   Les sociétés dont les conditions seront jugées les plus avantageuses pour l'intérêt du pays devront produire des documents prouvant leur capacité technique et financière. Elles auront également à fournir une garantie de huit pour cent approximativement sur le total des frais de l'entreprise. En fois [sic] de quoi cet avis a été signé et publié

(sceau)


5   In the end, the decision was tabled, since the necessary capital could not be raised. Jerusalem had to wait until after World War I for an orderly water supply and the installation of electric lighting, while the plan for an electrically powered public transportation system was dropped completely. See the detailed enclosed tender of the Jerusalem municipality, from August 1910 in this file.

# 119  J. Morgan to Foreign Secretary
## Distribution of Charity from South Africa

South African Jewry, whose roots go back to the nineteenth century, numbered 45,000 in 1910, the year the Union of South Africa was established. Of these, approximately 26,000 lived in the Transvaal, and 16,500 in Cape Province. The first Jewish immigrants had come from England and Germany. They were joined at the beginning of the twentieth century by a stream of immigrants from Eastern Europe, principally Lithuania. This was a vibrant, traditional Jewish culture whose first language was Yiddish. Similar to the Jewish communities in other lands, South African Jewry also assumed the task of caring for the poor in Palestine, including the few immigrants from South Africa itself who were in need of assistance. The African Central Committee was established in Jerusalem for this purpose. The funds were not disbursed directly to the needy, but rather were transferred to various educational and charitable organisations, as is listed in the following report, to the Vilna Kollel, which included the immigrants from Lithuania, and to the General Committee of all the *kollelim*; these bodies were held responsible for caring for the needy among the immigrants from South Africa. The latter felt cheated, since they received very little aid. On 23 August 1910 David Goldblatt, editor of the Yiddish newspaper *Der Yiddishe Advokat* and an active member of the Cape Town community, complained to the Governor General of the South African Union about ten families "who need the assistance of the Consulate and do not receive it." He asked for an investigation of the matter (FO 369/332).

This complaint was forwarded to the Foreign Office in London which, on 18 October 1910, directed the Consulate in Jerusalem "to furnish Sir E. Grey [the Foreign Secretary] with any information on the subject which you may be able to obtain." See the following detailed response, from which it may be learned that no far-reaching changes were instituted in the methods by which funds from abroad were distributed. For South African Jewry during this period, see: G. Shimoni, *The South African Experience*, Cape Town 1980, chap. I.

FO 369/332                                              Jerusalem, December 14, 1910

Sir,

In reply to your despatch No. 7 of October 18th 1910 enclosing a copy of a letter from the Colonial Office respecting the desire of the Supervising Committee for Jerusalem Charities to obtain information with regard to the distribution of certain funds in Jerusalem, I have the honour to report that I have conducted an enquiry into this matter with the following result: —

All monies coming into Jerusalem from South Africa are received by a special Committee — The Africa Central Committee — appointed for that purpose. This committee is made up of six members, one representing the Bicur Holim Hospital[1] — a Jewish hospital in this town — one representing the Talmud Thora Jewish School,[2] two representing the Central Committee[3] and two representing the Vilna Society. The Central Committee is the most important alms-receiving committee in Jerusalem. On it depend the various minor committees formed for the receipt of money from various countries. Representatives of the Central Committee are appointed on each of the minor committees and a large proportion of the monies paid into the minor committees by particular countries is handed over to the Central Committee for general distribution among Jews in Jerusalem without reference to their country of origin.

The Vilna Committee is one of the minor committees which receives all money sent from Vilna in Russia and is responsible for relieving cases of distress among Jews originally from Vilna.

The Africa Central Committee receives all money sent from South Africa. All money so received is divided into 101 parts of which: —

| | |
|---|---|
| The Central Committee takes | 40 parts |
| The Vilna Committee takes | 27 parts |
| The Talmud Thora School and Etz Chaim College take | 14 parts |
| The Chai Olam College[4] takes | 5 parts |
| The Bicur Holim Hospital takes | 15 parts |

1 The Bikkur Holim Hospital, which opened its doors in 1857, was founded by the Perushim community in Jerusalem. The institution, which was under German protection, played an important role in the medical services provided in 1910. The cornerstone was laid for a new building, outside the walls of the Old City, which is still in use by the hospital to the present.

2 Reference is to the Etz Hayim institutions, the educational system of the Perushim community.

3 The 'General Committee' [ha-Vaad ha-Klali], which was established in 1866 as the coordinating body for a federation of the kollelim (organizations of European Jews, based on their country of origin). A representative of each kollel sat on the Committee. It dealt primarily with joint activities, such as the construction of neighbourhoods in the New City of Jerusalem and the maintenance of educational and charitable institutions. The Committee also aided the indigent who were not supported by any individual kollel. Eventually, the Committee served as a conduit for all the donations intended for the Ashkenazic community.

4 The Hayei Olam yeshivah [Talmudic academy] was founded in 1886 by the kollelim and existed for many years in the Muslim Quarter of the Old City.

The Africa Central Committee is supposed to sit regularly to hear applications of needy South African Jews for assistance. If a case is deemed a worthy one the applicant obtains relief either from the Central Committee or from the Vilna Committee who as mentioned above take 67 parts of the money sent from South Africa. If the applicant was born in Vilna, Zamut or Kurland in Russia he obtains relief from the Vilna Committee, if otherwise, from the Central Committee. The Central Committee and Vilna Committee must if necessary dispense to needy South African Jews one third of the monies received by them from the South African Committee. When one third of the monies so received has been dispensed, any further applications for relief will be met out of the general income of the Committees.

The conditions (as drawn up by the Central Committee) under which charity is dispensed to needy South African Jews, are that applicants should be deserving and should have resided in South Africa at least ten years. The reason of this last restriction is that many Jews emigrate from Russia, Germany or other countries to South Africa and, if they reside less than ten years in that country, are entitled to ask for relief from the Committee representing their country of origin.

In the course of my enquiry into this question I interviewed the members of the Africa Central Committee on the one hand and Mr. Barnet Shershewsky (mentioned in the memorandum of the Cape Town Committee) and as many South African Jews as I could obtain any information about. Their names and statements are given below. After taking down the depositions of the South African Jews I interviewed the Africa Central Committee and heard their defence. The result of the investigation is as follows: —

*Barnet Shershewsky* was over ten years in South Africa but not being in need of assistance has never applied for it. States however that complaints are continually reaching him that the Committee can rarely be seen and that it would be desirable that the ten years rule should be abolished and asks that a shorter period of residence in South Africa should entitle to the relief.

*Rabbi Lipschitz* was a collector for the charities in South Africa for five years. Has been several times to the Committee room and either found the Committee absent or the room closed. He receives a small sum from another Committee, the Kolel Minsk.

*Hirsch Traischman* — born in Russia, lived five years in Cape Town. In need; has never found the Committee room open despite frequent visits but has sometimes met the Shammas or factotum of the Committee in the street and explained his situation to him. Received this year three Napoleons from the Vilna Committee.[5]

5    60 francs = 3 Napoleons.

*Nathan Myers* — born in Russia — naturalised in South Africa, lived five years in Cape Town. Is in need but has not applied to the Committee. Received thirty francs a year ago from the Vilna Committee.

*J. Clark* — lived for some years in Cape Town. Saw some of the members of the Committee but got nothing from them. The members of the Committee say he receives money from the Chabad Committee.

*Solomon Ploter* — lived seven years in South Africa, is naturalised there, never found Committee room open or saw Committee but met Shammas in the street and received from the Committee 16/-three years ago and £1 : 12 :0[6] last year both sums being given him by the Shammas.

*Joseph Finkelstein* — was six or seven years in South Africa, is naturalised there. Went several times to the Committee room but found it closed. Got nothing from South Africa Committee but has received £2 : 0 : 0 from the Vilna Committee.

*Benjamin Moseson* — was thirteen years in South Africa and originally from Russia. Never applied for relief.

*Abraham Shaje Shapira* — was six years in South Africa and is a naturalised Colonial subject. African Committee says he receives aid from the Chabad Committee.

*Sam Wilson* — 13 years of age, was three years in South Africa. Father is at present in England, mother is in Cape Town. Is very poor, once received 3 lbs. of unleavened bread from the Committee.

At my request the Africa Central Committee furnished me with an account of the monies received from South Africa from September 16, 1909 to October 4, 1910 and of the sums disbursed to needy South Africans. In addition to Solomon Ploter who, as mentioned above, has received £1 : 12 : 0 the following were also helped: —

| | |
|---|---|
| *Aaron Schlomov* of Cape Town | £1 : 12 : 0 |
| *David Friedgut* of Cape Town | £2 : 8  : 0 |
| *Y.L. Zetlar* | £0 : 16 : 0 |
| *S. Israelson* | £1 : 1  : 0 |

Shershewski and the others confirm these figures.

The amount received by the Committee from South Africa between September 1909 and October 1910 was £352 : 12 : 0. It will be seen that the amount distributed directly on charity was £7 : 8 : 0 which seems a small amount in proportion to that received.

---

6     £1 was worth 25–30 francs. The pound was divided into 20 shillings.

As regards the Committee room being always closed the members of the Committee deny this. I am of opinion that the complaint was well-founded. The Committee has promised to sit regularly and to have a notice put up on the door showing the hours when the Committee will sit.

As the majority of the needy South African Jews in the town resided in South Africa less than ten years, no blame can attach to the South African Committee for not relieving them as long as the rule laying down the years' residence in a country as an essential condition for receiving relief from funds subscribed by that country, is in force. It seems to me that rule is rather a harsh one. I understand that the American Committee have reduced the period entitling to relief from ten years to a shorter one and I would recommend to the Committee in Cape Town to shorten the time also, if it be deemed expedient.

Summing up, the causes of complaint are as follows: —

(1) The harshness of the ten years rule.

(2) Irregularity in the sittings of the Africa Central Committee here. This the Committee have promised to remedy.

(3) The disproportion between the sums received from South Africa (£352 : 12 : 0) and the sums disbursed to needy South Africans (£7 : 8 : 9).

James Morgan

# 120    H.E. Satow to G. Lowther
# Difficulties of the Anglo-Palestine Company

The attempts to undermine the status of the APC and to limit its activity continued, even after the disputes in 1903 (above, Nos. 94-96) and in 1907 (above, No. 106). In December 1910 Levontin asked for a copy of the Note Verbale (the official written Turkish permit for the bank's activity), so that, with the document in hand, he could overcome the obstacles placed in the path of the APC by the courts and the authorities. The Embassy in Constantinople did not, however, send him a copy, knowing that the Note was not unequivocal and that it would not resolve any problems. Accordingly, from time to time the bank needed the assistance and protection of the Consulate against the attempts to obstruct it. On 23 October 1910 the Director of the APC complained to the Consul about difficulties in the operation of the Company, caused by "some Turkish officials," relating the episode described below (FO 195/2351). After the Consul's unsuccessful attempt to resolve the problem on the local level, he was forced to turn to the Ambassador, requesting that the latter take the necessary steps.

Sir,

I have the honour to report that recently 206 shares in the Jewish Colonial Trust Limited of London which had been sent by the Anglo-Palestine Company Limited of Jaffa, on behalf of some of its clients, to London for the renewal of the interest coupons were, on their return, seized by the Custom House in that town which now refuses to deliver them except by order from Constantinople.

The question of their delivery was referred by the Jaffa authorities to the Mutessarif.[1] I have endeavoured, but without success, to induce him to give the necessary orders, so that I have been obliged to refer the matter to Your Excellency by telegram of to-day's date.

The Mutessarif was at first inclined to raise the question of the right of the Anglo-Palestine Company to carry on banking business, but in view of the orders received from the Sublime Porte that the Company was allowed to carry on business as a commercial establishment and of the fact that cases in which it is concerned are heard before the Mixed Commercial Court he did not insist on this. He then attempted to maintain that the introduction into Turkey of shares in undertakings not recognised by the Ottoman Government was prohibited. Finally, after considerable argument, he stated that the question was after all one which he could not decide and that it must submitted to the Central Customs Administration at Constantinople.

I believe that the explanation of this unexampled interference with the business of a foreign commercial undertaking is due to the fact that the Anglo-Palestine Company is suspected by the authorities of being an organ of the Zionist Movement. My belief is strengthened by what I hear from the Jaffa Manager of the Company[2] who states that he notices some inclination on the part of the local authorities to call in question the right of the Company to conduct its business. It is, however, only right to say that, apart from the seizure of the shares, there has as yet been no overt act of opposition to the Company on the part of Government officials.

H.E. Satow

---

1     The Governor of Jerusalem was Azmi Bey (see above, No. 117, n. 2).
2     David Levontin (see above, the introduction to No. 94).

G. Lowther to Sir E. Grey
Anti-Zionist Resentments in Turkey


When the 'Young Turks' revolution broke out in July 1908, the Zionist leadership expected that it would lead to a change for the better in Ottoman policy towards the *Yishuv*, and to the abrogation, or — at the very least — alleviation of the prohibitions against immigration and land purchases by Jews. These hopes were quickly dashed, and the immigration laws remained in force. After the unsuccessful counterrevolution in April 1909, the opposition to Zionism even increased, the prohibitions becoming even more severe. Turkish suspicion towards any nationalist element increaded. Even Turkish Jews, who feared for their own status, became alienated from Zionist aspirations. The anti-Zionist bias within the central government, the Turkish parliament, and local officials in Palestine became stronger. Even protests by the representatives of the Powers, to the effect that the prohibition of land acquisiton by Jews under their protection contradicted the agreement of 1868, were to no avail. The following despatch, which describes the atmosphere and policy, also attests to the support of its writer for the claims against Zionism and to some degree of identification with the apprehensions of the Turks.

A few lines of this despatch were published by Hyamson (No. 455). Due to its importance, it is reproduced here almost in its entirety.


FO 371/1245 — No. 146                                    Pera, March 7th, 1911
Confidential

Sir,

In Mr. Marling's[1] despatch No. 992 Confidential of December 27th 1909, my 621 of August 31st 1910 and my No. 121 of the 21st ultimo, the question of Sionism or the unrestricted immigration of Jews into Turkey and more particularly into Palestine and Mesopotamia has been dwelt upon.

In 1909 the masses of the Turkish and other populations here began to notice the extent to which the influence of Jews and Salonica Crypto Jews[2]

---

[1]   Sir Charles Marling served as Councillor in the Embassy in Constantinople (1908–1913), and during the Ambassador's vacations he was appointed Chargé d'Affaires.

[2]   The reference is to the Doenmeh sect, the descendants of the Jewish families who accepted Islam after the pseudo-Messiah Shabbetai Zevi had converted to Islam. Their religious center was in Salonika, from where they spread to Constantinople and other locations. Although several generations had already passed, they had not forgotten their Jewish

were monopolising finance, commerce and the machinery of State, while during the last year the conviction has been growing that this influence is being used to further the objects of Sionism and that the political freemasonry which has been spreading its net over the capital and the Empire is indirectly connected with the same aim, as the inspiration of the lodges seems to be mainly Jewish.[3] Sionism has in fact become one of the main undercurrents of the political situation. To foreigners the movement may be interesting from the historical stand-point, but the natives and especially the Arabs regard it with some concern from the point of view of their own immediate interests.
[...]

The matter also affects foreign missions here owing to the fact that British and other foreign Jews are restricted as to the length of their stay in Palestine and their right to acquire real property in accordance with the protocol of 1868.

The Grand Vezier, during the discussion in the Chamber, ridiculed the whole movement as the fruit of the fancies of some Jewish idealists and incidentally referred to the red passports,[4] which foreign Jews are compelled to provide themselves with on arrival at Syrian Ports and which entitle them to a sojourn in Palestine of three months only. The foreign missions have frequently had difficulties on this point in the past and they are certain to recur. The restriction of the right to acquire real property is more serious, as it is, strictly speaking contrary to treaty, and, as a result of the complaints of foreign Jews, the various Embassies have recently addressed to the Porte an identic note verbale requesting the abolition of these disabilities as contrary to

origin and maintained certain Jewish traditions. They assimilated into Turkish society, filling central positions in economic life, and several prominent Turkish military leaders came from this sect.

3　The accusation of a connection between Zionism and Freemasonry had already appeared some time before in anti-Semitic literature.

4　Cf. Nos. 79 and 86, above. The Teskeré (the 'red paper') was instituted in 1901; anyone entering Palestine had to deposit his passport, and was provided with a Teskeré valid for three months. The implications of this arrangement was a total ban on Jewish immigration, although ways were found to circumvent the decree. The restrictions on land purchases also were enforced with an iron hand, and were even applied to Ottoman Jews. In March 1911 Arab leaders in Palestine called for a stop to land acquisition by foreign Jews and a halt to illegal entry into the country.

Zionism was strongly attacked in the debate in Parliament on 1 March 1911. The Grand Vezir Hakki Pasha proclaimed his hostility to the Zionist movement, because of its political designs in Palestine. He argued that the Zionist idea was a chimera, embraced by only a small group of people suffering from delusions. This was the sharpest declaration ever to be uttered by a leading member of the government circles. See also the conclusion of the report by the Ambassador of 24 April 1911 (Hyamson, No. 456).

international engagements.[5] It must, however, be allowed that the matter is one of special importance to the Turkish authorities and no mission has so far pressed the matter energetically. The Ottoman Government must, however, come to a definite decision on the matter and their only legal course would seem to be legislation on the lines of our 'indesirable Aliens Act' or the American, Canadian or other such immigration laws.

Gerard Lowther

## 122  H.E. Satow to G. Lowther
## Purchases of Land at Rafah

Already in 1906 a Jewish delegation had travelled to the El-Arish — Rafah area, on the Egyptian side of the border, in order to examine the possibilities of Jewish settlement. Due to the major events that occurred in the area in that year (see above, No. 102), activity connected with that proposal was suspended. The venture was resumed resumed in 1907 by the Jewish Anglo-Palestine Club, which had been founded by Jews in Jaffa who were British subjects, headed by Joseph Amzalak, the son of the former Consular Agent Haim Amzalak. As is related below, the group contacted the Consular Agent in Gaza, Knesevich (see above, No. 83, n. 1), who agreed to act as its representative and engage in land purchases, for a certain commission. According to the despatch of the Ambassador to the Foreign Secretary of 24 April 1911, he had been addressed by the British representative in Egypt, who defined Knesevich's actions "for many reasons undesirable and requesting that steps may be taken to restrain the Consular Agent's activity" (Hyamson, No. 456). The Ambassador also requested a detailed report from the Consul in Jerusalem. The following is the Consul's reply, which reviews developments in the matter from 1908 until the time of writing. In all stages of the matter, the plan proposed utilizing lands on the Egyptian side of the frontier. For the entire Rafah episode, see: Eliav, Rafah, pp. 117–208.

---

5  Only in September 1913 did the Turkish Minister of the Interior order the revocation of the Teskeré; the purchase of land also was facilitated. As a result of Arab pressure and anti-Zionist agitation, the official decree prohibiting Jewish immigration was renewed in July 1914, one month before the outbreak of World War I. Also see below, Nos. 130–131.

Sir,

In reply to Your Excellency's telegram No. 8 of the 17th instant and with reference to the last paragraph of my immediately preceding despatch, I have the honour to report as follows as to the purchases of land recently made at Rafah in the Sinai peninsula by the Consular Agent at Gaza.

In 1908 the Anglo-Palestine Development Company, a Jewish committee established at Jaffa, of which the majority of the members are said to be British subjects, entered into communication with Mr Knesevich with the object of obtaining land at Rafah on Egyptian territory on which to found an agricultural colony.[1]

This committee in March 1908 sent Mr Frumkin, a British subject and one of its secretaries, to Gaza with a letter of introduction to Mr Knesevich asking him to afford the bearer such assistance as lay in his power.[2]

Mr Knesevich advised Mr Frumkin to proceed to El-Arish to submit the matter to Kaimakam Beamish Bey, Inspector of the Sinai peninsula.[3] The latter in his turn submitted the question to His Excellency the Sirdar;[4] and, on August 8, wrote an official letter to Mr Frumkin in which he stated that 'with reference to your application to purchase land on behalf of your company in the El-Arish district, I have the honour to inform you that, provided the natives desire to sell, there is no objection to your so doing'.

Upon this the committee again approached Mr Knesevich and asked him to help them in buying the land at a commission of so much per cent per 'deunam'.

From 1908 up to the beginning of the present year the parties were in correspondence. Finally, some few months ago, a contract was entered into between Mr Knesevich and the following six persons, Messrs Shpekin, Kindrenski, Horodish, Levene, Ruppin and Barnett,[5] representing the committee,

---

1   The connection with Knesevich dated back to June 1907. In his reply, Knesevich expressed his joy over the proposal and promised to cooperate in its realization.
2   The delegation set out on 19 June 1907. Samuel Frumkin, an immigrant from South Africa, was an energetic and educated person. The Secretary was Moses Menahem Levine, a British subject.
3   H.B. Beamish served as District Superintendent in El-Arish until 1914.
4   Sir Eldon Gorst was British High Commissioner in Egypt, 1907–1911.
5   The reference is to Menahem Sheinkin (1871–1925), the director of the Information Bureau of Hovevei Zion; Joseph Koudranski (1863–1941) was a merchant and industrialist, the representative of the Bialystok society for the purchase of lands; Gershon Lewin (1865–1939) was one of the directors of the winery in Rishon le-Zion; Dr. Arthur Ruppin (1876–1943) headed the Palestine Office of the Zionist Organization; Zerah Barnet (1843–1936) was one of the founders of Petah Tikvah and of the Neveh Shalom quarter

by which the former was to buy for them land to the extent of 50,000 'deunams' at Rafah, at a distance of one square kilometre from the military frontier post. Up to date about 10,000 'deunams' of land have been bought.

No purchase of land on behalf of the committee has been made on the Turkish side of the frontier.

Mr Knesevich states that, believing that he was, as an unsalaried Consular officer, permitted to trade, he undertook the purchase of the land as a matter of business, being particularly glad of the opportunity as, owing to the bad harvests of the last three years, his ordinary business as a barley merchant had come practically to a standstill.

I do not believe that he has made use of his consular capacity to effect these land purchases. They have been made on Egyptian territory where he has no official position. His personal acquaintance with and knowledge of the natives have naturally been useful to him in the negociations.

I am of opinion that he believed that, as the Jews interested in the proposed colony were many of them British subjects, he was supporting British interests. He never made any secret of the project and referred to it with some pride in his last two Trade Reports. Thus in his report for 1908 he writes: 'The only hope of improvement here is the advent of Europeans and with them of European methods of agriculture. I have strongly recommended British Jews to start a colony in this district, and they empowered me to buy sufficient land for the purpose. I endeavoured to secure for them a tract of land near the frontier, but the present unsettled state of the Government prevented me from concluding the bargain. I still hope, however, to secure the land at a future date'.

In his report for 1909 he again refers to the project, as follows: 'The British Jewish Company that was in correspondence with me during 1908 as to colonisation in the district of Rafah, on the Turco-Egyptian frontier, was again in correspondence with me during 1909. During the last quarter of the year some members of the company came to Gaza and proceeded to Rafah with their engineers. They liked the place and are desirous of founding a colony. I think that possibly in the future they will found a British colony there'.

Mr Knesevich informs me that he has now handed over all the business connected with the purchase of the land to his son Emil.

H.E. Satow

near Jaffa. All these people, with the exception of Ruppin, who had joined in his official capacity, represented 'Agudat Yisrael' — a company established at the end of 1909 to purchase lands for settlement. The contract was signed in late 1910 (see: Eliav, *Rafah*, pp. 138–139, 174–175).

## 123 H.E. Satow to G. Lowther
## Purchases of Land at Rafah

It soon became obvious that the contract which had been signed could not be realized. Title to the land was unclear, and it was learned that various Bedouin were likely to claim ownership, thereby providing yet another difficulty for the negotiations. Similarly, the plots had never been surveyed, nor had their exact size been established. Knesevich encountered difficulties with the monies he had borrowed for land purchases; it was not possible to obtain deeds of sale, and it was quite doubtful if the sellers would be able to fulfill their commitments. In addition to all these, one more, decisive factor entered the picture and put paid to the entire project: the Egyptian government was adamantly opposed to Jewish settlement in the proposed area. This led to a more rigid British stance, who decided to prevent the entire transaction. Since this opposition did not become public knowledge, the Jewish organizations continued their feverish activity on behalf of the land transactions.

ISA 123/1/11 — No. 63 (Emb.79)                    Jerusalem, Aug. 23rd, 1911
Copy

Sir,

With reference to Mr. Marling's despatch No. 11 of the 17th ult.,[1] I have the honour to report that I duly informed the Consular Agent at Gaza of the dislike of the Egyptian Government to the establishment of Jewish colonies in its territory bordering on the Turkish frontier.

Mr. Knesevich has requested me to bring to Your Excellency's notice some points in connection with the purchases of land made by him on behalf of the Anglo-Pal. Development Co., purchases which were made in good faith and relying on a written communication from the Inspector of the Sinai Peninsula, that there were objections to this course.[2]

By his contract with the Company he and two partners, one a French

---

1    Charles Marling wrote on behalf of the Embassy to Satow: "I have to instruct you, in accordance with a request conveyed to the Foreign Office by the Egyptian Government, to use all proper means in your power to deter the agents of Jewish colonising associations from endeavouring to establish settlements in Egyptian territory bordering on the Turkish frontier" (ISA 123/1/11).

2    The Anglo-Palestine Development Company was founded in July 1907 upon the initiative of the members of the Anglo-Palestine Club (see the introduction to No. 122, above), for the purpose of land acquisition and settlement.

and the other a British subject, bound themselves to buy 50,000 dounams of land, besides a large area of sand and, if they failed to complete the purchase, to pay a penalty of 10,000 frcs. (£400). The actual amount bought up to the present is between 25,000 and 30,000 dounams of land and about 25,000 dounams of sand. To effect these purchases a sum exceeding 60,000 frcs. has been borrowed by Mr. Knesevich, in whose name the 'hendjets' for the land are made out, and his two partners who appear to have taken little active part in the proceedings. If the Egyptian Government refuses to allow the transfer of the 'hendjets' from the name of Mr. Knesevich into that of the Anglo-Palestine Co. Ltd. of Jaffa, as was proposed, he and his partners will have a dead loss, as the land is absolute unsaleable except to the Jewish Company.

I have advised him to proceed to Nakhal and interview the Mudir of Sinai,[3] and ask permission to complete the transfer from his name to that of the Anglo-Palestine Co. of the land already bought.[4]

I venture to submit that, as Mr. Knesevich took all reasonable precautions and had good reasons to believe that the Egyptian Government had no objection to the undertaking, it should either allow the transfer to be completed or indemnify Mr. Knesevich and his partners, who will otherwise suffer a loss, which he, at any rate, will be quite unable to meet.

I have the honour to request that Your excellency will, if see it fit, bring these considerations to the notice of His Majesty's Agency at Cairo.

H.E. Satow

## 124   H.E. Satow to Sir E. Grey
## Annual Report on Trade for the year 1911 (Extracts)

The following comprehensive commercial report, which was based on the report of the Vice-Consul at Jaffa, reflects economic developments in Palestine in the years preceding World War I. Special mention was made of the

3    A.C. Parker was Military Governor of Sinai, 1908–1912.
4    Knesevich continued in his attempt to persuade the Governor of Sinai to approve the transaction, but he learned that the Governor was not authorized to decide the fate of the purchase. On 30 November 1911 Parker wrote him that the clarifications were continuing, but in the meantime, "I hope it may be possible for you to refrain from any purchasing operations" (the above ISA file). Knesevich, however, did not despair, and persevered in his efforts to carry out the transaction.

increased influx of tourists and pilgrims. The Consul was also aware of emigration from Palestine, especially among the Jewish populace, whose economic position had not improved, and a sizable portion of which was still in need of the *Halukah*, charitable funds from abroad. In addition to data on the development of international trade, the author also reports of progress in transportation and road infrastructure.

Only a few sections of the report, containing tables and detailed numerical data, have been omitted.

ISA 123/1/12 — No. 2                      Jerusalem, March 12, 1912
Commercial (F.O. 18)

*Population and Industries*: — Although there are no reliable data available as to the population of Jerusalem, it seems unlikely that it has grown beyond the estimate of 80,000 souls given for the year 1910. There may even have been a slight decrease during 1911, as there was a certain amount of emigration, partly due to the extension to non-Muslims of the obligation to military service. The tendency among the younger and more enterprising Jews to leave Jerusalem for other lands where better openings exist and the earning of a livelihood is consequently easier was, probably for the same reason, more marked.

In this connection it should be noted that in Jerusalem, as in other towns in the Ottoman Dominions, the cost of living has enormously increased of late years. Within the last eight years the prices of meat, vegetables and other food-stuff have risen by 100 to 400 per cent, those of combustibles by about 100 per cent and the cost of house rent by 50 per cent.

The number of Jews is reckoned to be between fifty and sixty thousand.[1] Many of them are old, and most of them are poor, some extremely so. The majority of them eke out an existence on such savings as they may have supplemented by the alms, known as 'haluka', sent by their co-religionists in other countries and, in some cases, by a petty business. There was much distress among the poor Jews in 1911 owing to the financial collapse, in large measure due to mismanagement, of several local Jewish institutions of a charitable nature.

There are no industries except soap-making and the manufacture of the so-called 'religious articles', made of olive-wood and mother-of-pearl. The amount of soap exported from Jaffa shows an increase for the figures for 1910, although the value is less.

---

1    The number relates to the entire district, including the Jews of Jerusalem and Jaffa and the colonies in Judea.

The city of Jerusalem lives almost entirely by the tourist and pilgrim traffic. It is visited every year by large numbers of men, of all races and creeds. In the aggregate the amount of money left behind by them in the course of the year must be a large one.

The size of the British community, which numbers about 350 souls, is unchanged. Its members are for the most part either missionaries working in connection with various religious and charitable institutions or Jews.

There are two hospitals,[2] three churches and a number of schools in connection with British societies. Two of the principal hotels are also in England hands.

*Public Health* — There were no epidemies during 1911. Malaria was, as usual, prevalent. This disease can only be expected to decrease when, as the result of the establishment of a good water-supply, the practice of storing the rain-water in cisterns is abandoned. Although cholera was prevalent in Syria and Northern Palestine, as in other parts of the Ottoman Empire, it did not reach Jerusalem where special efforts in the direction of cleanliness were made by the Municipality. There were three officially declared cases of cholera at Jaffa in the month of November, but there is some reason for doubting the accuracy of the diagnosis.

*Commerce in 1911*: — The harvest was an improvement on that of 1910, but at the best can only be described as fair. There was consequently a large importation of flour at Jaffa during the early part of the year. The increase in the number of sacks was, as compared with 1910, 29,105 sacks and, as compared with 1909, 53,235 sacks. The orange crop was a good one, and 13,000 more cases were exported than 1910. The sesame crop was also good. There was an increased export of wine.

Of the total sum of £1,169,910 representing the year's imports at Jaffa, £146,000 worth is set down as coming from the United Kingdom and £49,000 worth from British Colonies. In addition, about £150,000 worth of goods of British origin, chiefly textiles, were, as they were imported from other towns in Turkey, considered by the Customs to be of Turkish origin. The total value of imports from the United Kingdom was thus about £296,000 being an increase as compared with 1910 of about £27,000. This increase may to some extent be explained on the ground that stocks of certain articles of British origin were low at the end of 1910. Nevertheless, even if it be conceded that the Turkish Custom House has not yet established a perfectly reliable system of classification by origin, there was undoubtedly an increase in British imports.

---

2    The missionary hospital, which moved to its new building outside the walls in 1897 and the ophthalmic hospital of St. John (see above, No. 69, n. 6).

*Imports.* There was an increase of about £167,000 as compared with the year 1910, of this about £50,000 was accounted for by the necessity of importing cattle and flour.

The sources of the chief articles of import remained unchanged. It should, however, be noted that owing to the Turco-Italian war the competition of Italian manufactured cotton goods has temporarily ceased [...]

*Exports.* [...] Exports to the United Kingdom showed an increase of £15,000 and those to British colonies an increase of £8000.

The difference between the value of imports and exports is, as is shewn in the annexed tables,[3] about £460,000. This difference is to a great extent to be accounted for by the larger remittances received from abroad by religious and charitable institutions and by the Jews, by the alms sent back by emigrants and by the money left in the country by the thousands of tourists and pilgrims. [...]

Owing to the prevalence of cholera in many parts of the Levant and Mediterranean shipping was during the greater part of 1911 hampered by quarantine regulations. There were for the greater part of the year enforced in Egypt against arrivals from the Syrian coast. For some time it was impossible to book a passage from Jaffa to Port Said and passengers for Europe had in many cases to proceed to Alexandria, undergo quarantine there on their return to Port Said. Quarantine in Egypt against Syria is apt to be disastrous for Palestine as the tourists who come on towards the end of the Egyptian season are kept away by fears and uncertainty as to their return to Europe. [...]

*Public works.* In the course of 1911 the concession for the establishment of a water-supply and for electric tramways and lighting was put up to competition and, according to the best information locally available, was awarded to a certain Mons. Fonquia of Constantinople, said to have been the only applicant.[4] Some doubt is now felt as to whether the matter has after all really been definitely settled, as it is stated, on what seems to be good authority, that the alleged concessionnaire has not deposited the necessary caution-money. In any case nothing has as yet been done locally.

Tenders for the construction of a port at Jaffa are said to have been asked for by the Ministry of Public Works at Constantinople. It is greatly to be desired that this long talked of scheme may now materialise and that some definite decision may be arrived at on the subject. As things are now the Customs administration refuses to take any serious measures to remedy the lack of space and consequent confusion which have long existed at the Jaffa

3    Not attached.
4    See above, No. 118.

Custom House on the ground that no decision as to the position of the very necessary new buildings can be come to unless it is known for certain whether or not a port is to be made.

It appears to be settled in principle that a branch line is to be built from Afuleh, on the Haiffa branch of the Hedjaz Railway, to Jerusalem via Nablous.[5] If this project is realised and if a port is built at Haiffa a serious blow will be dealt to the Jaffa passenger and transit traffic, while the imports and exports of Nablous, which at present pass chiefly by Jaffa, will presumably be diverted to Haiffa via the new line.

*Roads.* Some improvement in the state of the roads is to be recorded. Those to Hebron and Nablous are now in good condition, the former having been re-made during the past year. Repairs are being carried out on the Jericho road which is much used by tourists. The road to Jaffa is, on the other hand, worse than ever and in parts has ceased to exist. This state of things is greatly to the advantage of the railway company, competition by road being almost out of the question.

The Municipality of Jerusalem has shewn praiseworthy activity during the past year. The lighting of the main streets has been greatly improved,[6] some modern water-carts have been obtained from the United Kingdom, a motor road-roller and stone-crushes has been imported from the United States. [...]

*Tourists and pilgrims.* As already mentioned this traffic is of vital importance to Jerusalem. The approximate number of tourists and pilgrims of the better class who have visited the city during the last three seasons is as follows:

From June 1 1908 to May 31 1909 ... 5,595
June 1 1909 to May 31 1901 ... 7,196
June 1 1910 to May 31 1911 ... 5,759

of these 1626 were Americans, 957 British and 895 Germans.

*Jaffa–Jerusalem Railway.* The following are the figures giving the receipts and expenditure of this company for the years 1909–1911: —

|  | 1909 £ | 1910 £ | 1911 £ |
|---|---|---|---|
| Receipts | 47,444 | 53,200 | 54,000 |
| Expenditure | 13,444 | 20,000 | 20,000 |
| Net receipts | 34,000 | 33,200 | 34,000 |

5   See above, No. 73, n. 3.
6   See above, No. 100.

In the expenditure the expenses of the head office in Paris are not included. The number of passengers conveyed was: —

|  | 1909 | 1910 | 1911 |
|---|---|---|---|
| First Class ..... | 10,500 | 12,200 | 10,700 |
| Second Class .... | 138,700 | 156,000 | 158,000 |
| Total | 149,200 | 168,200 | 168,700 |

[...]

*Consular district. — Mutessarifat of Jerusalem*
Population —

| Approximate | 345,000 |
|---|---|
| Chief towns — | |
| Jerusalem | 80,000 |
| Jaffa (port)[7] | 55,000 |
| Gaza (port) | 30,000 |

Currency, with British equivalents —

| 23 piastres | = 1 medjidieh |
|---|---|
| 109 piastres | = 1 Napoleon |
| 124 piastres | = 1 pound Turkish |
| 136¼ piastres | = 1 pound (£1) |

Note. — The Turkish lira is very rare. The gold coin most in use is the Napoleon (20 frcs.). Commercial transactions with Europe are in francs. Rates of exchange per £1. —

|  | Buying rates | | Selling rates | |
|---|---|---|---|---|
|  | Fr. | c. | Fr. | c. |
| Maximum | 25. | 20 | 25. | 28 |
| Minimum | 24. | 80 | 25. | 15 |
| Average | 25. | 14 | 25. | 19 |

Weights and measures. —

| 1 okieh | = About ½ lb. |
|---|---|
| 1 rottel | = 5.6 lbs. |
| 1 kantar | = 560 lbs. |
| 1 pik or draa | = About 27 inches |
| 1,600 square piks | = 1 deunam |
| About 4½ deunams | = ¼ acre. |

7   In the enclosed report on the Jaffa Caza: "The total population of the Kaza is about 100,000 persons, of which some 50,000 are resident at Jaffa, while Lydda and Ramleh combined have a population of 15,000" (*Diplomatic and Consular Reports*, No. 4850).

# 125 H.E. Satow to Sir E. Grey
## New Building for Evelina de Rothschild School

The school for girls was founded in 1864. In 1867 Baron Lionel de Rothschild took it under his patronage and donated a large sum of money for its maintenance. The school was named after his daughter Evelina, who had died in 1866. It was the only Jewish school in Jerusalem in which the language of instruction was English. In 1894 the school came under the auspices of the Anglo-Jewish Association (see above, No. 100, n. 4). During the years 1896-1898 the Consulate in Jerusalem dealt with the registration of the building and the plot that had been purchased by the Association for the school (the building had initially served as the residence of banker Johannes Frutiger). Bureaucratic delays set in with the Governor of Jerusalem, and, following his lead, the Sublime Porte, which refused to register the building in the name of the Association. A solution was finally found: the property was registered in the name of a fictitious owner (see Hyamson, Nos. 379–382, 391, 398). Over the years, the school grew in size, with many improvements, and became one of the leading educational institutions in the city. The increasing student body grew too large for the building, so more extensive physical facilities were needed. In the final outcome, however, the existing building was renovated and enlarged; the building currently houses the Ministry of Education.

ISA 123/1/12 — No. 34 (Emb. 40)                                    March 19, 1912
(Draft)

Sir,

I have the honour to report that I have received from Miss Landau,[1] Headmistress of the Evelina de Rothschild School for Girls (Anglo-Jewish Association), a request that Your Excellency may be pleased to cause application to be made to the Sublime Porte for a Firman authorising the demolition of the present school and the erection in its place of a larger and modern building.

Miss Landau states that the school, which now contains 600 girls, has completely outgrown the present building which has accommodation for only

---

[1]  Miss Anna (Chana) Landau (1873–1945) immigrated from London in 1899 and directed the school from 1900 until her death. She was very active in the educational system in Palestine and in the British community. For the difficulties she experienced at the time of her immigration, see: Hyamson, Nos. 427–430.

385

250 children and is in every way unsuitable for the purpose for which it is used. She also expresses the hope that the Firman may be granted early enough, to enable the new building to be begun this summer.

I have the honour to enclose herewith two plans and an unofficial copy of the title-deed of the property belonging to the Association. If a further plan showing the details of the interior arrangements of the proposed building is required, I beg to request that in order not to lose time, direct application for this may be made to the architect Mr. Delissa Joseph, Portland House, 73 Basinghall str., London E.C., who will supply the same on demand.

H.E. Satow

# 126  J. McGregor to Ch. Marling
## Purchases of Land at Rafah

Efforts to purchase the lands of Rafah (see above, Nos. 122–123) became more complicated. Knesevich did not reveal to the Jewish parties involved the true extent of Egyptian opposition. In a letter dated 25 May 1912, Beamish, the British Governor in El-Arish, warned Knesevich not to deal with the sale of lands, some of which were state lands while ownership of the remainder might be claimed by individuals, a state of affairs that would entail lengthy judicial proceedings in Cairo. Moreover, these were small, noncontiguous plots. The British Governor adopted an even more severe stance; in a telegram from Constantinople to Jerusalem, dated 19 June 1912, the transaction was even termed an "illegal purchase of Government land from natives" (ISA 123/1/12). Though forbidden to proceed in his efforts, Knesevich did not renounce them and requested permission to enter Egyptian territory. In a report to the Embassy in Constantinople, McGregor, the new Consul in Jerusalem, described the financial imbroglio in which Knesevich found himself and availed himself of this opportunity to vehemently attack those Jews who had emigrated to England, thereby becoming naturalized subjects, and were now able to immigrate to Palestine and enjoy the protection of the Consulate.

ISA 123/1/12 — No. 24 (Emb. 79)                                    August 1, 1912
Copy

Sir,

With reference to Sir Gerard Lowther's telegram No. 13 of June 19,

1912,[1] I have the honour to report that Mr. Knesevich, Consular Agent at Gaza, is pressing for leave of absence in order to proceed to the Egyptian frontier in connection with the purchases of land which have formed the subject of Correspondence between the Consulate and H.M.'s Embassy during the past twelve months.

I have informed Mr. Knesevich that I cannot grant him leave without authorization from the Embassy, whose decision I am awaiting.

At the same time I beg to state that, while Mr. Knesevich is evidently still engaged in endeavouring to secure land for a Jewish Colonizing syndicate, I am in some perplexity as to the attitude to be assumed by this Consulate respecting these transactions, no reply having been received to Mr. Satow's despatch No. 63 of August 23, 1911,[2] in which he pointed out the difficult position of Mr. Knesevich in consequence of the Egyptian Government's having apparently changed its views with regard to the desirableness of Jewish settlements in the neighbourhood of the Sinai peninsula.

In the despatch above referred to, Mr. Satow submitted that, in consideration of Mr. Knesevich having acted throughout in evident good faith as with the general consent of the Egyptian Government, he had a reasonable claim to indemnification in the event of the Egyptian Government maintaining its objection to Jewish Colonization schemes, and I venture to add that, should such a course be adopted, H.M's Embassy would then be in a better position than it is at present the case, to second the views of the Egyptian Government by instructing Mr. Knesevich to do all in his power to oppose the purchase of land by Jews.

With reference, moreover to the instructions conveyed to the Consulate in the Embassy despatch No. 11 of July 17, 1911,[3] to use all proper means to deter the agents of Jewish colonizing associations from establishing settlements in Egyptian territory bordering on the Turkish frontier, I venture to remark that whereas it would be a matter of great difficulty to refuse ordinary assistance to a Jew having a claim to British protection, much might be accomplished, if measures could be devised for checking the influx of foreign Jews, who become naturalized in England, without any intention of residing in the U.K., but solely for the purpose of settling in Palestine under the British flag.

1   The telegram mentioned in the introduction, above.
2   See above, No. 121.
3   See above, No. 121, n. 1. After prolonged negotiations between the Foreign Office, the Embassy, and the Consulates, the recommendations of G. Jackson Eldridge, Consul-General in Beirut, were adopted in 1885. Eldridge called for a fundamental revision of the registration of protected individuals in Jerusalem, especially those from Russia, in order to drastically reduce the numbers on the list. The new regulations were put into effect in 1890 (see Hyamson, Nos. 309, 311–314, 327, 338).

The good effects of the removal from the Consular register some 30 or 40 years ago of the majority of Jews recognized as Protected Persons,[4] are being undone by the present infiltration of a pauperized, litigious and thoroughly discreditable Jewish element, whose members are entitled to all the rights and privileges of British subjects, despite the fact that there is usually nothing British about them except by their passports. These persons not only make no material or moral contribution to the well being of the Empire which protects them, but they furnish a continual source of friction with the local Authorities as well as with certain foreign Consulates, and as in the present case, their interests not unfrequently prove to run directly counter those of H.M.'s Government.[5]

Mc Gregor

## 127 G. Lowther to Sir E. Grey
## Purchases of Land at Rafah

In response to the letter from the Consul of 1 August 1912 (above, No. 126), on 14 August 1912 the Embassy rejected the granting of leave to Knesevich, emphasizing once again that this was an "illegal purchase of Government land from natives"; he would, however, be allowed to take a leave if "his object is to put an end to the whole business" (ISA 123/1/12).

In effect, this sealed the fate of the entire plan. Opposition to it was vigorous, reinforced by Lord Horatio Herbert Kitchener (1850–1916), the High Commissioner in Egypt from the end of 1911 to 1914. The Consul's proposal to compensate Knesevich for the great damage he had suffered went unanswered. Knesevich did not give up, mainly out of apprehension that his entire investment would be lost. He apparently did not understand that political considerations were decisive in this affair, and that the British government was adamant in its opposition to Jewish settlement in the border area. This position was not made known to Jewish parties involved, who continued to delude themselves that it would be possible to overcome all the obstacles.

---

4   The reference is to the new arrangements concerning the protection of former inhabitants of Russia, which led to the revocation of protégé status from a considerable number of these individuals (see Hyamson, Nos. 311–314, 320, 332).

5   McGregor's claims were thoroughly investigated by the Home Office. At the conclusion of the examination, the HO wrote to the Foreign Office on 19 May 1913: "It appears that the facts afford wholly insufficient foundation for Mr. McGregor's allegations" (FO 195/2453/2479).

Sir,

With reference to Mr. Marling's despatch No. 37 of August 14th last[1] on the subject of the attempts now being made by certain Jewish societies to acquire land for colonization purposes near the Egyptian frontier, I have the honour to report that I have been approached by Miss Margarete Palmer,[2] a British resident at Jerusalem with the object of learning whether the protection of this Consulate could be afforded to an association called the 'Palestine Land Purchase Company,' which is being formed for purchases of land in the neighbourhood of Rafa and El Arish.

In answer to my enquires, Miss Palmer informed me that her partners were Mr. Selim Ayub, an Ottoman subject, Persian Consul General at Jerusalem and Manager of the 'Banque Commerciale de Palestine' here,[3] Mr. Amush, a French Jew residing at Gaza,[4] and Mr. Knesevich, British Consular Agent at Gaza. It appears that Mr. Knesevich (who is an Austrian subject) and Mr. Amush have already bought 16,000 dunums of land situated in Eygptian and partly in Turkish territory, and that they are anxious to acquire 18,000 dunums in addition; but that funds are low and that Mr. Ayub has conse-

1   See the letter cited in the above introduction.
2   Miss Margaret Palmer, an eccentric woman of considerable means, arrived in Jerusalem at the beginning of the twentieth century, where she came under the influence of Solomon Feingold, a convert to Chrtistianity whose questionable occupations had gained him a bad reputation. He succeeded in gaining control of Margaret's money and property. On 17 January 1904 Consul Dickson reported: "Miss Palmer wants to open a printing office to teach young men the Printing Trade" (FO 195/2125), but she did not receive the concession. Four years later, on 18 January 1908, Consul Blech wrote: "Miss Margaret Palmer, an English lady of means, who resides chiefly at Jaffa, has decided to institute a life boat there at her own expense, facilitating the disembarkation of Jews." But Ekrem Bey, the Pasha of Jerusalem, refused to grant a permit (FO 195/2287).
    On 5 March 1908 Blech reported the Governor's refusal. As for Feingold, the Consul added that the latter had been without means at the time of their connection. But now he was "a land proprietor on large scale and interested with Miss Palmer in a variety of undertakings, and public rumours credit him with having absorbed the greater part of her fortune. It is unfortunate that Miss Palmer should be associated with him in any way" (ibid.).
3   Selim Ayub and his bank were the partners of Levontin and Ruppin in the attempts to obtain the concession for supplying water and electricity (see above, No. 118). Half of the shares of the bank were held by the APC.
4   David Amous, who resided in Gaza, was Knesevich's partner. The two succeeded in persuading Miss Palmer to participate in the establishment of the company, which would be under British protection. They argued that such a company would easily overcome the difficulties concerning the approval of the deeds of sale, and all the delays pertaining to the land transactions would come to an end.

quently agreed to put 12,000 frs. into the concern, while Miss Palmer has been begged to advance whatever further sums may be needed, both her and Mr. Ayub's advances being secured by a mortgage on Mr. Amush's property at Jerusalem.

The ultimate object of these transactions is the transfer of the land in question to a Jewish Colonization Syndicate, called the Anglo Palestine Development Co.,[5] and it is hoped that by securing Miss Palmer as a partner, the Company would obtain, not only her financial assistance, but also the protection of the British Consulate in connection with the transfer of the title deeds. The intention is to have the Company constituted and registered at Cairo, and to form a branch at Jerusalem under British protection; and the object of Miss Palmer's visit was to ascertain whether, in the event of her becoming a partner, the Company could be registered at this Consulate.

Miss Palmer is possessed of means, but is somewhat simple-minded, and she has fallen completely under the influence of a Jew of equivocal reputation called Feingold, who seems to have obtained absolute control over her affairs, so that she can hardly be considered as a free agent.

I have informed her that, if she decided to use her money in what might prove a troublesome undertaking, she must remember that, a company could only be constituted in Egypt under the legal conditions established in that country and that it would by no means necessarily follow that I could afford protection to a Jerusalem branch merely because she was concerned, — in fact, I thought the contrary to be the case, and could give her no assurance whatever.

I am unaware whatever Miss Palmer will eventually be persuaded to take a share in this scheme, but, as I conceive it to be my duty to withhold all encouragement from Jewish colonization near the Egyptian frontier, I have the honour to report what precedes, in case application should be made in Cairo or elsewhere for the registration of the Company and to request Y.E.'s instructions as to the attitude to be adopted here.[6]

McGregor

5   See above, No. 122.
6   According to a letter dated 22 November 1912, the Foreign Secretary changed his opinion, and was now willing to approve financial compensation for Knesevich's losses. McGregor also succeeded in persuading Miss Palmer not to join the company (ISA 123/1/12).
    In the end, Knesevich sold 10,000 dunams of land in the Rafah area to the Anglo-Egyptian Company, which was represented by the APC. The sale was registered in Cairo, but it transpired in March 1913 that the Egyptian government would not approve the sale. The response was totally negative, because the Egyptians had absolutely decided not to grant any concession for the purchase of land in the Sinai Peninsula. Efforts to acquire land in the Rafah region in 1903 suffered a fate similar to that of the El-Arish project (Eliav, Rafah, pp. 156–158).

# 128 Lowther to Sir E. Grey
## Ottoman Opposition to Zionism

The despatch of the Ambassador in Constantinople to the Foreign Secretary reflects the mood among British diplomatic representatives in the Ottoman Empire. In effect, the Ambassador defends, and even justifies, Turkish anti-Zionist policy. He regards the prohibition against immigration and the severe restrictions on land acquisition as being justified. He does not accept the political goals of Zionism, and it is doubtful whether this Ambassador was prepared to make any effort to counter these measures, as had his predecessors at the end of the nineteenth century. British public opinion regarded Zionist aspirations as serving German interests. See: P.A. Alsberg, "The Orientation of the Zionist Executive's Policy on the Eve of the First World War," *Zion* 22 (1957), pp. 149–176 (Hebrew).

FO 371/1794 — No. 218 (16925)                                   Pera, March 17, 1913

Sir,

After the coup d'état of January 23 last by which the Committee of Union and Progress seized power,[1] the Zionists again became active here and the Grand Rabbi of Turkey[2] addressed to the Minister of Justice and Cults two notes demanding the abolition of the 'red passport' with which non-Ottoman Jews have for a decade been obliged to provide themselves on entering Palestine and the removal of the restrictions against the acquisition by Ottoman Jews of larger tracts of land outside the towns and villages in Palestine and against the holding of land within the towns of Palestine by non-Ottoman Jews.[3]

1    In July 1912 the Committee of Union and Progress (CUP), the Young Turk leadership, that had held the reins of government almost uninterruptedly since the revolution in 1908, lost control of the government. The country was taken over by the 'Liberating Officers', who sought to return to a liberal and constitutional form of government and demanded the removal of the army from politics. On 23 January 1913, however, the CUP, led by Enver Pasha, launched a surprise attack against the government and seized power once again. The last remnants of freedom and democracy were swept away, and from then until 1918 the Empire was ruled by a military dictatorship.
2    Rabbi Haim Nahoum (1872–1960) was appointed Hakham Bashi of Turkey after the Young Turk revolution in 1908. He held this position until the collapse of Ottoman rule, and was quite active on behalf of Jews throughout the Empire. Though Nahoum was not an advocate of the Zionist movement, he saw fit to demand the revocation of the repressive decrees against the *Yishuv*.
3    See above, No. 121.

I have the honour to enclose the text of these two notes taken from the 'Aurore', the Local Zionist organ.[4] The Grand Rabbi describes the 'red passport' system and the other restrictions as 'deeply wounding to Jewish national and religious dignity', but it would appear that they were not so intended by the Ottoman Government, which has maintained similar restrictions in the case of Christians in the Vilayet of the Hejaz.

Jews are free to travel, reside and hold property etc. in other parts of the Ottoman Empire and it was only when the Zionist movement appeared from the language of its expounders to aim at the establishment of a Jewish polity in Palestine that the Turkish Government initiated the restrictive measures which it is now sought to be removed.

The disabilities in question are dealt with at length in Dr Max Nordau's long letter to the 'Times' of December 30 last.[5] From this and other writings on the subject it would appear that the Jewish problem from the Zionist point of view is not one of creed but of nationality and that it is perhaps one of the most important race problems with which Turkey has to deal in addition to those of the Arabs, Kurds, Armenians, etc.

Besides the political reasons which have led the Ottoman Government to oppose Zionism in the form of 'unrestricted immigration of non-Ottoman Jews into Palestine', it also felt it necessary to take this course owing to the Opposition of the local Moslem Arabs who on economic grounds objected to the large influx of foreign Jews backed up by subsidies from wealthy Jewish Associations, thus rendering it impossible for the native Arab to compete with the newcomers. Further the Ottoman Government is particularly sensitive in all matters connected with Jerusalem which also contains the Holy Sepulchre and other places to which Christians, and particularly those of the Oriental branch, attach such importance, especially in view of the causes which contributed to the Crimean War. It was consequently alarmed at Zionist projects as set forth by Dr Herzl in his book on the subject styled 'The Jewish State'.

Dr Max Nordau 'solicits the friendly interest' of European diplomacy in the matter, but it might be difficult to support projects of the kind without

4    Not enclosed.
5    On 28 September 1912, the London *Times* published an article about Jewish settlement in Palestine. It noted the congruence of Zionist and German interests in the land and concluded that England should not encourage the Zionist movement. An article by Max Nordau (1849–1923), one of the leaders of 'political Zionism', was published in the *Times* on 30 December 1912, signed by the "President of the Zionist Congress," thereby imparting to the article an official imprimatur. His essay dealt with the aspirations and goals of political Zionism and called for an end to the existing restrictions in Palestine and for the granting to the *Yishuv* a status equal to that of other nationalities in the Ottoman Empire. Nordau also criticized the CUP and its political program, thus causing a great deal of embarrassment to the Zionist leadership, which advocated 'practical' Zionism.

perhaps giving umbrage to the Arabs, and in view of our position in Egypt, H.M.'s Diplomatic Agent and Consul in Cairo,[6] to whom I am forwarding copy of this despatch, would doubtless be better able to judge of the attitude which His Majesty's Consular offices in Syria and Palestine should adopt in this matter. [...]

Gerard Lowther


## 129    Sir J. Gray Hill to Foreign Office
## Suggestions for Enhancing British Influence at Jerusalem

In the late 1880s, Sir John Gray Hill built his house on Mount Scopus (see above, No. 112, n. 1). He did not reside in Jerusalem on a permanent basis, but stayed there for a considerable period of time on each of his frequent visits. Over the course of twenty five years he came to know the different British consuls who served during this period, becoming acquainted with both their strong and weak points. In his letter to the Foreign Secretary, he raised several proposals to strengthen British influence in the city by enhancing the status of the Consulate, and called for greater care in the choice of Consuls.

FO 369/629                         Acre Hall, Birkenhead, 21 July 1913

Sir,

      Referring to my recent letter to you about the feeling in favour of England exhibited in Jerusalem, I beg to enclose an extract bearing on this subject from a letter to me of the 8th instant from my head servant George Mabbedy,[1] who writes to me every week, letters which often contain most interesting information about the state of Jerusalem and Palestine both West and East, with all of which he is well acquainted.

      I also take this opportunity of repeating in writing some suggestions

---

6    Lord Kitchener. See above, the introduction to No. 127.

---

1    Not attached to the letter in the file.

which I took the liberty of making to Lord Dufferin[2] when I had the pleasure of calling on him at the Foreign Office last week.

My suggestions are that the Consular Office at Jerusalem should be made more important and effective than it is at present in the following ways:

*1st.* That there should be a Consulate house built or hired that would be the permanent abode of British Consuls.[3]

France, Germany, Russia and less important Countries have such Consulates, and the comparison between these and the British Consulate has a great effect, to the detriment of our Country, upon the minds of the Government Officials, and the people of the City and neighbourhood.

At present the British Consulate is as Sir Frederick Treves mentioned in his recent book 'The land that is desolate'[4] situated in a back lane and in a poor looking place. Surely it should present an appearance which can fairly be compared with the Consulates of other Countries.

*2nd.* The Consul is too frequently changed. Since the death of Mr. Dickson there have been Mr. Blech, Mr. Satow and Mr. McGregor. Before a British Consul can properly get to know his work and the officials and people, he is removed.

*3rd.* I think the Consul should know Arabic in addition to Turkish. Without this knowledge he is at the mercy of the Dragoman or Janissaries.[5] Since Mr. Dickson's time, in all matters with which I have been concerned, the Consul has never been to the Serai in person, but only sent his dragoman and the man who formerly held that position, Mr. Tadros, was a rascal.[6]

*4th.* The Consul should have a larger salary.[7] Mr. Dickson suffered from poverty, and when the German Emperor visited Jerusalem in 1898 he had no horse to ride on. I suppose none could be hired at that time, and

2    Lord Terence Dufferin (1866–1918), the son of Lord Frederick Temple Dufferin, a prominent British diplomat who served as Ambassador in Constantinople, 1881–1884 (see above, No. 47), followed in his father's footsteps and held diplomatic posts in several countries. He was one of the leading figures in the Foreign Office prior to World War I.

3    During the entire period, the Foreign Office refused to invest money in a permanent building for the Consulate (see above, No. 43). Consul Moore built a house in the Mahaneh Yehudah quarter. The building served as his Residence and also of the Consuls who succeeded him. It was meant only for living quarters, and not for the Consulate offices, which were located in rented premises.

4    London 1912.

5    Janissaries = foot soldiers.

6    Constantin N. Tadrous ceased to be a Dragoman on 12 January 1910 (FO 195/2351).

7    The salary of the Consul at Jerusalem had always been a painful issue, all the Consuls complaining that it was insufficient for their living expenses. The salary of the Consuls was not significantly increased for more than sixty years, despite the considerable rise in expenses during this period.

Mabbedy had to lend him my horse in order that he might make a respectable appearance before the Emperor.

*5th.* He should always be a strong man. Mr. Dickson was a very weak one. Mr. Blech and Mr. Satow were strong. Mr. McGregor I know very little about as he is so new in Jerusalem.

The strongest and most efficient man in my time was Mr. Moore. I know the place is difficult to fill, and that the female Missionaries, and Jews claiming British protection are always a worry, but that makes it important that the Consul should be a man of tact as well as strong.

Jerusalem is growing fast, the Zionists are increasing, and they, especially the English Zionists, are buying much land, and if anything like decent Government should replace the utterly rotten and corrupt regime at present existing then Jerusalem would grow much faster.

At any rate the feeling of the people in favour of England is most remarkable, and alone would justify some expense being incurred, and the most careful selection being made in regard to the British Consulate at Jerusalem.[8]

John Gray Hill

Forgive the freedom of my remarks. I am speaking from a considerable experience. This is the 25th year in which I have visited Jerusalem.


# 130   W. Hough to J. McGregor
# The Abolishment of the 'Red Paper'


During the first half of 1913, there was an increase in Zionist pressure for the abrogation of restrictions in Palestine, with the active assistance of Rabbi Haim Nahoum (see above, No. 128, n. 2). The humiliating procedure of the 'red paper' placed a burden on the immigrants, although ways were found to circumvent it. After exhausting negotiations, it seemed that the Young Turks were willing to make concessions. On 24 September 1913 Tala'at Bey, the Minister of the Interior, ordered the authorities in Palestine to cancel the 'red paper', although nothing was said about removing the regulation restricting a stay in Palestine to three months. The Zionist leadership regarded this

---

8   In its response dated 31 July 1913, the Foreign Office thanked him for his proposals, noting that the Consul's salary had recently been raised to £800 and that an increase in the allocation for office expenses was currently under discussion (ibid.).

announcement as heralding a change in the anti-Zionist policy. It quickly became clear, however, that the restriction had not been lifted. For many months efforts were made to cancel it, but the Turks, in their usual fashion, evaded making a decision and refrained from revoking the restrictions on immigration and land purchases, for fear of fierce Arab opposition.

FO 195/2452/1254 — No. 67                                    Jaffa, October 27, 1913
Copy

Sir,

I have the honour to report that the Passport Officer at Jaffa recently received an order from the Local Authorities to discontinue the system of giving Red Papers to Jews entering the country as a receipt for their passports which were kept, on the ostensible grounds that this system had given rise to abuses and failed in its object of limiting Jewish immigration. He was further instructed to form a local commission in conjunction with the Local Authorities to decide on other more effective measures to prevent Jews from remaining in the country more than three months.

The latter part of these instructions is and will of course remain absolutely a dead letter; the order is simply due to Jewish influence in high quarters.

W. Hough[1]

## 131  Sir L. Mallet to Sir E. Grey
## The Abolishment of the 'Red Paper' and
## the Zionist Aims

Sir L. Mallet, the new Ambassador in Turkey, also credited the abrogation of the 'red paper' to Zionist pressure on the Turkish government. He took advantage of this opportunity to emphasize the Zionist struggle for the use of Hebrew and its recognition as the national language. When the 'Technikum' was about to be established in Haifa, upon the initiative of the leaders of the Hilfsverein of German Jewry, and German was chosen as the language of

---

[1]  William Hough was appointed Vice-Consul at Jaffa on 18 April 1912, after Nasri Fiani retired.

instruction, a 'language war' erupted, attacking the educational institutions of the Hilfsverein and the use of German. This controversy was at its height at the time this despatch was written, and therefore features prominently in the Ambassador's report. The language controversy ended on 22 February 1911 with a compromise; in practice, however, the Zionist movement and the Teacher's Federation won a decisive victory for the status of Hebrew in the Jewish educational system of Palestine, which now acquired a clearly national character.

After the abolition of the 'red paper', the Ambassador anticipated an increase in immigration and a gradual strengthening of Zionist influence, which, as the Yishuv became a majority of the population in Palestine, would lead to the appointment of a Jewish Governor in Jerusalem...

FO 195/2452/1254                            Pera, Dec. 21st 1913
Draft

Sir,

With ref. to despatch No 218 of March 17th last from this Embassy I have the honour to report that the Ottoman Government has abolished the 'red passport', which non-Ottoman Jews were obliged to take out on arrival in Palestine and which entitled them to stay there only three months. The Zionists have thus obtained the object for which they have long been thriving, viz. the unrestricted immigration of Jews into Palestine, and it is to be expected that a large influx of Jews into that region will soon begin.

As Zionism also means the Jewish National revival, great attention has lately been paid to the teaching and spread of the use of Hebrew as the national tongue.[1] It is taught, with German, in some fifty new schools established of late years in Palestine, by the Hilfsverein,[2] or German Jewish Zionist

---

1     The Ambassador had a (quite erroneous) negative opinion regarding the future of Hebrew in Palestine. On 23 December 1913 he wrote: "Modern Jews are not likely to take to talking Hebrew, whether at Jerusalem or elsewhere, however much it may be taught in schools. The attempt to galvanize dead languages into spoken ones is a fad of modern nationalism" (FO 371/1794).

2     The 'Hilfsverein der deutschen Juden' was founded in 1901 as a humanitarian organization, which began by extending assistance to the victims of the Russian pogroms. From 1904 on it began to develop extensive educational activity in Palestine, leading to the establishment of a large educational system in Jerusalem and in other cities. In 1911 about 3500 pupils attended the twenty five educational institutions of the organization, which employed about 100 teachers. It was the largest educational network in the country, and naturally gave priority to the German language. In contrast to what is written here, the organization had no connection to Zionism; on the contrary, the 'language war' that erupted in December 1913 led to a severe confrontation between the Hilfsverein and the Zionists.

organizations and there is considerable agitation in the Jewish world here against the use of German instead of Hebrew as the medium of instruction in the Jewish Polytechnic School recently, founded at Haifa.

The Italians have recently recognized Hebrew as an official language in Tripoli in Barbary and the Zionists aspire to have Hebrew similarly recognized by the Ottoman authorities as soon as Jews form the majority of the inhabitants in Jerusalem and Palestine.[3] The Committee of Union and Progress have agreed in principle that the local authorities should be acquainted with the language of the majority of the local population in different parts of the Ottoman Empire, so that it may one day be possible to have a Jewish Governor of Jerusalem.

[Sir L. Mallet]


## 132   W. Hough to J. McGregor
## Commercial Report of Jaffa for 1913 (Extracts)


The report by Hough, Vice-Consul at Jaffa, reflects the growth of that port city and its importance for the commercial activity of the entire country. Jaffa developed speedily, and important steps were taken for modernization, mainly by the growing *Yishuv*.
The following sections from this report describe the general development of Jaffa on the eve of World War I.


JNUL 4°1513/48                                                      Jaffa, April 11, 1914

*General remarks.* — The Caza of Jaffa has an area of about 350 square miles and a population of over 100,000. It is entirely situated in the historical plain of Sharon, a region of great fertility. In the south-westerly portion of the Caza the district is however subject to continual encroachments of sandhills, and more emergetic action than is at present being taken is necessary to prevent further marring of the fertility of the district.

The soil generally is of a light kind most suited to the cultivation of fruit trees. There are about a thousand orange gardens round Jaffa, and the

3   Since the *Yishuv* accounted for approxiamtely 12–13% of the entire population of Palestine in 1913–1914, the Ambassador's apprehensions were certainly exaggerated.

oranges produced, being both excellent in taste and having a thick skin which makes their transport for long distances possible, have become famous all over Europe. Vines, olive trees and almond trees also flourish. Sugar canes thrive on the banks of the river Auja, but are only used for chewing by the inhabitants, and their industrial possibilities are entirely neglected. [...]

The town of Jaffa has a population of about 50,000, which is increasing, mainly owing to Jewish immigration, which is entirely unchecked by the Turkish authorities. In the absence of reliable statistics it may be estimated that about half the population of the town is Mussulman and the remainder Christian and Jewish in about equal numbers.[1] It is noteworthy that the Jewish population of Jaffa is an entirely different element to the fanatical and pauperized Jews of Jerusalem. The Jaffa Jews are an intelligent and energetic class on the whole. It may be said that the Jewish quarter of Jaffa is the only part of the town showing any approach to the civilised conditions of a European town.[2]

The present population of the interior is mostly Mussulman. It is probably not increasing, but on the other hand the population and activities of the Jewish colonies, which contribute materially to the prosperity of the district, are increasing in importance [...]

*Public Works.* — The questions of the harbour and the Custom house stand at exactly the same point as they did last year, although a most circumstantial report was abroad in the summer that the concession had been finally signed. The matter of the harbour concession has unfortunately become involved in the general question of the financial relations between Turkey and France; if taken by itself there is no reason why it should not be settled at once, as a complete agreement has been reached on all questions both of principle and detail. I must regretfully observe that the town of Jaffa itself, which would naturally be the chief beneficiary by the scheme, neither takes nor seems likely to take the least initiative in the matter, although vigorous action on the part of the inhabitants might prove a decisive factor in the situation. Civic pride is non-existent, the Municipality is hopelessly corrupt, and the inhabitants have not learnt to trust each other sufficiently to embark on any corporate enterprise.

1   The number of Jews in Jaffa did not exceed 10,000, and it may be assumed that there were a similar number of Christian residents. Consequently, there were at least 30,000 Muslims.
2   The Jewish initiative led to expansion northward beyond the Old City, after the rapid growth in population had made living conditions in Jaffa unbearable. In 1888 the first northern Jewish neighbourhood, Neve Tzedek, was established, and three years later, nearby, the second neighbourhood — Neve Shalom. In 1909 the cornerstone was laid for a new suburb, even further to the north, named Ahuzzat Bayit, which would later develop into the city of Tel Aviv.

The recent concessions for public works at Jerusalem have stirred the imagination of the Jaffa people,[3] and there are rumours that concessions for tramways and electric lighting may be applied for. As I mentioned last year, the River Auja is a natural source of power which might well be employed and a tramway at least would stand a good chance of being a profitable enterprise, as the distances between various quarters of Jaffa are very great, and a brisk trade is now plied by diligences of an almost incredibly ramshackle description.

*Shipping.* — There was an increase in the total number of steamers calling at Jaffa, mostly due to the resumption of the Italian service after the war. British steamers were slightly less in number, but it may be noted that the falling off was not in the regular services of coasting vessels plying between Syrian ports and Egypt, nor in the regular Liverpool orange steamers which continue to hold their own well against the competing lines recently established. The figures for 1913 were 21 British and 20 foreign.

British lines continue to take the majority of passengers, as shown by the following table.

*Number of Passengers of all classes embarking at Jaffa during 1913*[4]

| | | | |
|---|---|---|---|
| British | steamers | . . . | 10215 |
| Russian | do. | . . . | 9032 |
| Austrian | do. | . . . | 8177 |
| French | do. | . . . | 6503 |
| Italian | do. | . . . | 1055 |
| American | do. | . . . | 680 |

Travellers embarking with return tickets previously issued are not included in the above table, except in the case of returning Russian pilgrims.

As a brief but sufficient instance of the difficulties under which shipping labours at Jaffa in the absence of a harbour, it may be mentioned that in December 1913 there was a period of 20 days during which communication with the shore was impossible, except on one occasion when the sea abated sufficiently to allow the mails to be landed and no more.

*Prospects for 1914.* — It is a difficult matter to give forecasts of any value, but owing to the mild winter and timely late rains at the beginning of April there is reason to believe that all crops have a good chance of doing well.

3    See above, No. 118.
4    The total of the numbers reveals that close to 38,000 entered Palestine. After deducting the number of pilgrims and tourists, the figures indicate increased Jewish immigration.

# 133 J. McGregor to Sir L. Mallet
## Arab Opposition to Zionism

*Falastin*, an Arabic newspaper which began publicaton in Jaffa in 1911, had blatantly anti-Zionist tendencies. It consistently attacked Jewish immigration and the settlement enterprise, warning of the Zionist goal to gain control of Palestine. The newspaper also criticized the abrogation of the 'red paper'. In October 1913 it lashed out at the relaxation of measures against immigration and settlement. When an article vehemently opposing Zionism was published, Zionist leaders in Jaffa exerted pressure on the Caimakam, who ordered the temporary closure of the periodical.

This letter by the Ambassador also exhibits his characteristically unsympathetic attitude towards Zionism.

FO 371/2134 — No. 22036                               Jerusalem, April 30, 1914

Sir,

I have the honour to transmit to Your Excellency copy, as marked in the margin, of a despatch[1] which I have received from H.M.'s Vice-Consul at Jaffa, reporting the suppression of the vernacular newspaper 'Falestin' in account of an article written in a sense hostile to Zionism.

There is no doubt that, as Mr. Hough says, the article from which an extract is given, faithfully mirrors the growing resentment among the Arabs against the Jewish invasion. I understand that assaults upon Jews in the outlying districts are increasingly frequent and it is conceivable that the jealousy created by the treatening economic preponderance of the Jewish element may become a source of serious embarrassment for the Government.

I am unable to confirm the statement that Mr. Morgenthau[2] openly championed the Zionist cause, and in fact, I have been assured that he studiously avoided taking sides; but as my information was necessarily derived from Jewish sources, I should hesitate to accept it unreservedly.

P.J.C. McGregor

1    Not enclosed.
2    Henry Morgenthau Sr. (1856–1946), financier and diplomat, served as U.S. Ambassador to Turkey from 1913 to 1916. His diplomatic efforts were largely concerned with the protection of Christian missionaries and Jews in the Ottoman Empire. During World War I he was especially active in organizing financial support by American Jews for their co-religionists in Palestine, who suffered from a shortage of food and were left without means.

Henry Alfred Cumberbatch served as Consul-General at Beirut from 1908 to 1914. Northern Palestine was included in the jurisdiction of this Consulate, and from time to time the Consul-General would conduct a survey of the area and report his findings (see, e.g., Hyamson, Nos. 267, 314). Cumberbatch's supervisory visit through northern Palestine in May 1914 was conducted with the explicit approval of the Foreign Office, apparently in response to a request by the Consul-General himself, who had not visited the area for quite some time.

He submitted a quite comprehensive report. Only the special memorandum on Safed is included here; the sections on Haifa and Nablus (Shechem) are deleted.

FO 195/2457/189 — No. 33                          Beirut, May 25, 1914
Confidential

Sir,

With reference to Foreign Office despatch No. 3 of February 9th (4750/14), sanctioning a tour of inspection by me in the Southern part of my Consular district, and to Your Excellency's telegram No. 4 of March 31st approving of my taking my annual local leave at the same time, I have the honour to forward herewith three Memoranda, the first and second on the organization etc. of the Vice Consulates at Haifa and Safed respectively and the third on the establishment of a Vice Consulate at Nablus as requested by British subjects residing there.

From these it will be seen that at Haifa I found things satisfactory[1] on the whole but that at Safed they were not quite as they should be, whilst at Nablus I found that no sufficient reasons existed for recommending the establishment of a Vice Consulate in that place.

The following general remarks, based on notes taken during my journey, may perhaps be of some interest to Your Excellency though they are not intended as an exhaustive report of matters of general knowledge.

The opportunity that offered itself of visiting Jerusalem decided me to

---

1   After J.H. Monahan, who served as Vice-Consul at Haifa until 1905 (see above, the introduction to No. 81), a local resident, Pietro Abella, was once again appointed — first as Acting Vice-Consul, and from 1909 as Vice-Consul.

take my local leave at this time and I went there before commencing my tour of inspection.

At Jaffa, I visited the new model Jewish dwelling compound[2] in course of construction under the auspices of the Jewish Colonization Societies, whose efforts to better the lot of their co-religionists forced to emigrate from Europe are becoming every year more visible all over Palestine. Some impetus has been given to the Zionist scheme by the recent visits of such influential Jewish personages as Baron Edmond de Rothschild[3] and H.E. Mr. Morgenthau,[4] the American Ambassador at Constantinople, the one leaving behind him a lot of money and the other many promises of personal help to the Zionist movement.

During the week I was in Jerusalem I had two interviews with the Anglican Bishop in Jerusalem[5] to discuss several pending questions connected with the properties of the Bishopric situated in my Consular district and to give him the advice he sought with regard to Anglican Church property at Aintab under the supervision of His Lordship's Chaplain at Beirut.

Apart from the historical and traditional interests concentrated in Jerusalem what struck me most, as an observer of the conflict of religious forces in Syria which formed the subject of my special report of November 6. 1911 (No. 64 Confidential), was the active rivalry in the erection of palatial buildings for pilgrims not only between the Orthodox and Roman Catholic Churches under Russian and French auspices respectively but also, since comparatively recent times, by German and Italian Catholics. The Protestant Church, represented by the buildings of the German and Anglican Cathedrals, makes a very small show in the midst of all these huge buildings which, like the fine old Mosque of Omar, are erected on commanding sites and do not fail to attract the attention of the crowds of pilgrims and tourists, and perforce must suggest speculation as to which of the Powers protecting the work centred in these grand edifices will ultimately replace the present administrative rulers of the Holy Places of Christianity, an eventuality which is, I think, more generally discussed in Syria and Palestine than in any other part of Turkey.

The excellent carriage road between Jerusalem and Jericho is perhaps

2    The reference is to Tel Aviv, which was founded in 1909 as a residential neighbourhood north of Jaffa.

3    Baron Edmond de Rothschild (1845–1934), patron of the First Aliyah colonies, which he funded until turning their administration over to the Jewish Colonisation Association in 1899, visited Palestine for the fourth time in February 1914 and toured the colonies in the south and north of the country. The visit profoundly stirred the *Yishuv*.

4    See above, No. 133, n. 2. For the visit to Jerusalem which was conducted in April 1914, see the report of Consul McGregor (Hyamson, No. 465).

5    Bishop Blyth (see above, No. 103, n. 1).

the best I have ever travelled over in Turkey and the only one I have seen on which the service of 'cantonniers' for keeping the road in a state of repair exists.

With my departure from Jerusalem and my arrival at Nablus (a short day's journey) my tour of inspection began. The only recent doings in the vicinity of Nablus worth noticing are the erection of a very large Greek Church over Jacob's well and the excavations by a German Archaeologist of the ruins of Shechem in the course of which he has so far only unearthered ancient pottery and old weapons of war.[6]

I visited the Church and hospital of the London Church Missionary Society in Nablus and during my visit to the Acting Mutessarif I secured his support of an arrangement I proposed for the settlement of a long standing boundary dispute between the Church Missionary Society and an influential Moslem neighbour.

The annual celebration of the Samaritan Passover on Mt Gerizim[7] was taking place during my stay and it was satisfactory to note the benevolent attitude of the Authorities and of the bigoted Moslem inhabitants towards this small remnant of a remarkable sect whose chief source of public revenue seems to be derived from the exhibition to tourists and other travellers of their famous Hebrew manuscripts.

The ruins of Samaria, partially laid open by the German Professor Reissner,[8] lie between Nablus and Nazareth at two hours distance from the former place.

The road to Nazareth bisects the immense fertile plain of Esdraelon in which can be seen here and there a few isolated small Jewish colonies of recent establishment and a very few native villages, the absence of which in such a vast expanse of cultivable land shows the room there is for further agricultural developments. [...]

At Tiberias I visited the hospital and the schools of the United Free Church of Scotland.

Dr Torrance M.D.[9] has spent 30 years in Tiberias and his fame extends far into the Syrian desert.

6   Prof. Ernst Sellin (1876–1946), who conducted the excavations at Jericho in 1907–1909 (see his book: *Jericho*, Leipzig 1913), began excavations at ancient Shechem in 1912 and renewed them in 1926–1927 (see: *Encyclopedia of Archaeological Excavations in the Holy Land [EAEHL]*, IV, Jerusalem 1978, pp. 1083–1086).
7   Cf. above, No. 45.
8   See: *EAEHL*, ibid., pp. 1032–1037.
9   Dr. David Watt Torrance (1862–1923) was quite an active member of the Scottish missionary expedition to Tiberias. He established a clinic, and later a hospital, in that city. His dedication to the provision of medical assistance and his vigourous public health

The British and French Jews at Tiberias having, of recent years, been giving trouble to their respective Consulates General at Beirut by their quarrels over the distribution of the relief funds sent by their co-religionists in India and France, I convened a special meeting of the British Rabbis and admonished them to live peacefully among themselves as well as with their French co-religionists.

I also later on requested the French Acting Consular Agent at Safed, whose district includes Tiberias, to convey the same admonition to the French Rabbis.

As Your Excellency is no doubt aware, in addition to the organized help of Colonization Societies, considerable sums of money are received by the Rabbis in Palestine from their co-religionists all over the world and as the Rabbis, who are very numerous, have full discretionary powers as to the distribution of this money and take the lion's share for themselves, they are able to lead an idle life in comparative ease.

The Hedjaz Railway authorities have recently placed a small steamer and a motor launch on the Sea of Galilee for the conveyance of passengers from their station at El-Samakh to Tiberias, Tabigha (Bethsaida) and Capernaum.

The bridle path from Tiberias to Safed passes through one of the oldest and most prosperous Jewish Colonies called Rosh-Pinah in which Baron Edmond de Rothshild is personally interested. I was courteously received by the French Acting Administrator who explained to me their methods for training the new Colonists and their children in agricultural and farming work.

I was also able to bring to a final satisfactory conclusion a long standing dispute between a Russian and a British Jew belonging to this Colony. [...]

Miss Newton[10] and her sister at Jaffa belong to a band of religious cranks with independent means of whom there are so many in Palestine and Mt Lebanon. They are generally not connected with any recognized Missionary Society and they start small Scholastic, Religious or Medical 'Missions' of their own which are not kept up after their death or withdrawal and the only

activity won him general acclaim. He died and was buried in Tiberias. For Torrance, see: W.R. Livingstone, *A Galilee Doctor, being a Sketch of the Career of Dr. Torrance*, New York 1927.

10    Frances E. Newton (1872-1950) arrived in Jaffa in 1889 as an assistant to her sister Edith, who was active on behalf of the Church Missionary Society. She returned to England for professional retraining and in 1895 began her work in the mission in Jaffa. In 1903 she began intensive missionary efforts, moving to Haifa in 1908. She engaged mainly in educational and medical activity among the Arab population. See her memoirs: Frances E. Newton, *Fifty Years in Palestine*, London 1948.

people who seem to benefit by their money are the native helpers, not always converts, who by some means or other succeed in getting hold of a substantial part of it.

The latest addition to the numerous foreign educational establishments at Haifa is the Jewish polytechnic Institution called 'Technikum' under German protection built with funds provided by Jews in Germany, Russia and America.

Some prominence was given by the local press to the recent dispute among the subscribers as to the language of the School, the local Jews desiring that it should be Hebrew and the Germans their language.[11] The matter has I understand been settled by the adoption of Hebrew for mathematics and physics and German for technical subjects. The study of English, French and Arabic will be optional.

H. Cumberbatch


Inc.
### Report by Consul General Cumberbatch on the organization etc. of the Vice Consulate at Safed (May 1914)

*Residence & Office.* The British Vice Consulate at Safed is situated in a comparatively new residential part of the town and is the property of the Vice Consul, Mr Micklasiewitz,[12] but the question of situation is of no importance as the town is small and distances are not great. The house is of respectable dimensions with a small garden on two sides, the private apartments and reception room are well furnished. The Consular office however is a very small, ill-lighted and badly furnished room off the front yard. The Consular flag is flown from a mast which is in good condition.

*Archives.* An inspection of the Archives showed that the requirements of Chap. XVI of 'General Instructions' had not been complied with notwithstanding a special Circular of mine on the subject addressed to Mr Micklasiewitz in 1909.

No proper register was kept and the correspondence of each year, whether received or sent, was all kept in one single bundle tight up with a piece of string. [...]


11   See above, the introduction to No. 131.
12   Joseph Miklasiewicz, a Polish Catholic, was appointed in 1890 as Vice-Consul without salary, in addition to his post as the Austrian Consular Agent (Eliav, *Austrian Protection*, p. 33 and document no. 32). He died in December 1906, succeeded on 1 July 1907 by his son, Carl Ladislaus; the Consul referred to the latter (see FO 369/105).

The direct trade with the United Kingdom at Safed is so insignificant that there are very few inquiries from British firms.

Mr Micklasiewitz' Chief duties consist in affording his official assistance and good offices to the few members of the London Society for the promotion of Christianity amongst the Jews and to the numerous British Jews at Safed.

*Fee Stamps.* I found that the Fee Account Book was improperly kept and that no regular account was kept of Fee Stamps though the quarterly returns have always been regularly transmitted to this Consulate General.

I showed Mr Micklasiewitz the correct way of keeping the Account Book and pointed out the necessity of retaining an office copy of his quarterly fee return.

*Official relations.* The relations, both official and private, of Mr Micklasiewitz with the Kaimakam and the few natural born British subjects at Safed are satisfactory but with regard to the large number of British Jews I had occasion to remind him that the existence of a British Vice Consulate at Safed is mainly due to the presence of those Jews and that he should show more zeal in the protection of their interests and not refer every small difficulty that arises between them and the authorities, and among themselves, to this Consulate General before using his best efforts to settle matters on the post.

*Office Allowance.* I do not consider it necessary to recommend an increase in the present office allowance of Twenty five pounds which is sufficient for providing all office requirements.

Among other minor non-observances I found that for some unaccountably [sic] reason Mr Micklasiewitz omitted to furnish a Quarterly account of expenses incurred for telegrams and postages on the Public Service.

H. Cumberbatch

# 135   W. Hough to Sir E. Grey
## Closing of the Consulate

When World War I broke out in August 1914, Turkey maintained its neutrality for the time being, despite a secret military alliance with Germany. However, relations between the Entente Powers and Turkey rapidly deteriorated. On 1 October 1914 the Capitulations, the privileges held by foreign subjects, were annulled, despite the vigourous protests of the Powers. This act led to the closure of the foreign post offices. At the beginning of November 1914 Turkey declared war, and the consulates of Great Britain, France, and

Russia were ordered to close down. From this moment, the American Consulate represented British interests. On 29 August 1914, almost a month after the outbreak hostilities, the Ambassador in Constantinople, Sir L. Mallet, received a communiqué that "The Consul at Jerusalem has broken down and the medical advisor suggests taking leave" (FO 369/774). The Vice-Consul at Jaffa, W. Hough, was instructed to take charge of the Consulate in Jerusalem (FO 369/775). It therefore fell to Hough to close the Consulate, and unfortunately, as is reported below, he burned a considerable portion of the Consulate records. Another part was apparently lost, and only fragments survived (see Hyamson, Preface, x).

FO 369/776 — No. 79910                                      Cairo, Nov. 21st 1914

Sir,
        I have the honour to report the circumstances attending my departure from Jerusalem.
        1. On receipt of a telegram from H.M.'s Embassy informing me that the rupture of diplomatic relations with Turkey was imminent, I immediately burnt the documents forming the subject of special instructions from the Embassy. The next morning (Oct. 31st) I received instructions to ask for my passports and called to this end on the Mutessarif. The Governor seemed much distressed at my request, saying that it had been his hope and that of a large party of Turkish statesmen that peace might be kept with England. He informed me, however, that a recently received order from the Sublime Porte instructed him not to give a safe conduct to any Consuls wishing to leave without referring first to Constantinople. I gathered later from the Governor's Secretary that this order had only been received two or three days previously.
        Thinking this most suspicious I immediately burnt the remainder of the Confidential archives. I have the honour to enclose a memorandum containing particulars of the documents destroyed.[1] [...]
        All Consular representatives of the Triple Entente Powers were detained at Jerusalem until November 16th, when I myself, the French Consul-General and Vice-Consuls of Jerusalem and Jaffa and their families were allowed to leave. [...] The Acting British Vice-Consul at Jaffa, Mr. N.H. Fiani, an Ottoman subject, was not included in the permit, but obtained the necessary authorization to leave as on private business from the military and civil authorities at Jerusalem. At the last moment, however, the Caimakam of Jaffa overrode the permission of these authorities and prevented Mr. Fiani from leaving. [...]

[1]    Unfortunately, no list was found of the documents destroyed at the end of October 1914, from which it would have been possible to learn of the contents of the Consulate archives.

I arrived at Cairo on Nov. 19th and I am now here awaiting orders.

2. The following incidents which came under my observation during the fortnight of my detention at Jerusalem are worthy of being reported. Practically all convents, religious institutions, schools, hospitals etc. under the protection of the Entente Powers were seized by the Military authorities, many of them being used as barracks, officers' quarters etc. Churches were mostly unmolested, but the English Cathedral Church of St. George was the object of a search after supposed hidden guns, in the course of which part of the floor was dug up and an altar removed. It seems certain that this wild goose chase was made on information received from a former serving-boy who knew very little English and had heard mention being made of the 'canons' of the Cathedral.

The Mission house at Jaffa is now serving as the Caimakam's private house and he drives his family about in a carriage requisitioned from a British subject. The English and French Banks (Anglo-Palestine and Crédit Lyonnais) were closed, while all funds belonging to enemy subjects were sequestered and removed to the Imperial Ottoman Bank. They were afterwards allowed to reopen on condition of doing no business with enemy subjects — a condition so irksome that their business is practically at a standstill.

I left shortly before Moharrem, the time when all house rents are paid for the ensuing year. There were threats that all rents falling due to enemy subjects would be sequestered, but the American Consul at Jerusalem, Dr Glazebrook,[2] who throughout displayed the utmost energy and goodwill in the protection of British subjects as far as he was able, promised to use his influence in opposing this measure, which would bring many British subjects face to face with starvation. He is in every respect a first class man.

Shortly before I left, an official proclamation from the Commandant at Damascus was circulated at Jerusalem, stating that all enemy subjects would be kept for the time being as hostages against the bombardement of open ports and that anybody trying to leave without permission would be shot without pity. I would urge that representations should be made through the American Government to allow all British subjects to leave, as their financial situation must inevitably be desperate after a few weeks in view of the embargo put upon the banks. [...]

William Hough

---

2    Dr. Otis A. Glazebrook served in Jerusalem during 1914–1917, until the entry of the United States into the war. As the Consul of a great Power which maintained neutrality, Glazebrook played an essential role in representing the interests of the Entente Powers, as well as occupying a central position in the provision of aid to the *Yishuv*, which suffered want and was in a state of distress.

# APPENDICES

## Appendix 1: Turkish Governors of Jerusalem

| | |
|---|---|
| Osman Agar (or Tahir) Pasha | July 1841–1842 |
| Mehemed Reshid Pasha | 1842–October 1843 |
| Ali Pasha | November 1843–October 1845 |
| Mehemed Pasha | November 1845–May 1847 |
| Zaarif Mustafa Pasha | June 1847–June 1848 |
| Bahri Pasha | July 1848–June 1849 |
| Adhem Pasha | July 1849–October 1851 |
| Hafiz Ahmed Pasha | November 1851–January 1854 |
| Kara Osman Yakub Pasha | March 1854–December 1854 |
| Kiamil Pasha | February 1855–March 1857 |
| Sureya Pasha | May 1857–April 1863 |
| Mehemed Khourshid Pasha | April 1863–February 1864 |
| Izzet Pasha | March 1864–February 1867 |
| Nazif Pasha | April 1867–September 1869 |
| Kiamil Pasha | September 1869–December 1870 |
| Ali Bey | March 1871–January 1872 |
| Mehemed Ra'ouf Pasha | February 1872–June 1872 |
| Sureya Pasha | July 1872–August 1872 |
| Nazif Pasha | October 1872–June 1873 |
| Kiamil Pasha | June 1873–December 1874 |
| Ali Bey | January 1875–December 1875 |
| Faik Farlallah Pasha | February 1876–May 1877 |
| Mehemed Ra'ouf Pasha | June 1877–April 1889 |
| Reshad Pasha | April 1889–October 1890 |
| Ibrahim Hakki Pasha | November 1890–November 1897 |
| Tewfik Pasha | November 1897–May 1901 |
| Mehemed Cevad Pasha | June 1901–February 1902 |
| Osman Kazim Pasha | February 1902–Summer 1904 |
| Ahmed Reshid Pasha | August 1904–November 1906 |
| Ali Ekrem Bey | December 1906–September 1908 |
| Subhi Bey | September 1908–November 1909 |
| Nazim Bey | December 1909–April 1910 |
| Azmi Bey | May 1910–June 1911 |
| Cevdet Bey | July 1911–July 1912 |
| Muhaddi Bey | July 1912–November 1912 |
| Tahir Hayreddin Bey | December 1912–February 1913 |
| Medjdid Cevket Bey | March 1913–End of 1914 |
| Midhad Pasha | February 1915–End of 1915 |
| Ahmed Munir Bey | January 1916–April 1917 |
| Izzet Pasha | May 1917–December 1917 |

*Appendix 2: British Subjects and Protégés in Palestine (Heads of Families)*

| Date | British Subjects | Protégés | Total | Number of Persons | Source |
|------|------------------|----------|-------|-------------------|--------|
| 22.7.1840 | 17 | | | | Hyamson, No. 22 |
| 29.12.1849 | | Jerusalem: 98; Hebron: 32; Safed: 161; Tiberias: 99 | 390 | 1500–1600 | Hyamson, No. 105 |
| 23.3.1854[1] | | Jerusalem: 190; Hebron: 19; Safed: 33; Tiberias: 16 | 258 | 1000–1100 | Hyamson, No. 160 |
| 1856[2] | 47 + 145 Colonial Subjects | Naturalized: 9; Jews from Russia: 301; Others: 195 | | 697 | ISA 123/1/6 |
| 1859 | 35 + 21 Colonial Subjects | 266 Jews — Jerusalem: 201; Nablous: 3; Hebron: 21; Safed: 25; Tiberias: 16 | 322 | 900–1000 | ISA 123/1/6 |
| 1866 | | Subjects and Protégés — Jerusalem and Hebron | 163 | 700–800 | FO 78/1929 |
| 1867 | | Protégés only — Jerusalem and Hebron | 135 | 500–600 | FO 78/1991 |
| 22.4.1870 | 22 adults+ 16 children | 294 adults and 44 children: Jerusalem and Hebron | | 775 | FO 195/944 Hyamson, No. 256 |
| 19.1.1871[3] | | Jerusalem: 139; Hebron: 16; Nablous: 2; Safed; 26; Tiberias: 17 | 200 | 800–1000 | Hyamson, No. 261 |
| 9.6.1871 | | Safed: 57 + 59 widows and orphans; Tiberias: 22; + 31 widows and orphans | 169 | 500–600 | Hyamson, No. 263 |
| 10.5.1872 | 17 + 3 | Haifa/Acre: 11; Safed: 125; Tiberias: 52 | 188 | 766 (68 British) | Hyamson, No. 267 |
| 19.6.1883 | | Subjects and Protégés — Northern Palestine | | 1000 | Document No. 67 |
| 1884 | | Jerusalem: 639; Jaffa: 50; Hebron: 121; Nablus: 11 | | 821 | FO 195/1477 |
| 28.5.1884 | | Subjects and Protégés — Northern Palestine | 229 | 900–1000 | Hyamson, No. 328 |
| 5.4.1888[4] | | Subjects and Protégés — Northern Palestine | 183 | 800–900 | Document No. 68 |
| 1891 | 215 | Naturalized: 18; Protégés: 171 + 34 for life (Jerusalem and Hebron) | | 438 | FO 195/1727 |
| 4.4.1911[5] | 162 | Naturalized: 211; Protégés: 21 (Jerusalem and Hebron) | | 394 | ISA 123/1/11 |

*General Remarks*: The number of British subjects is almost always omitted from the reports. Similarly, the number of protégés at Jaffa is generally missing. Certificates were not always issued only to heads of families, but to individuals as well. The total number of certificates, therefore, very often also includes individuals.

Whenever an exact number of persons is not stated, the figure given in the table is our estimation. The numbers of Jews in Safed and Tiberias supplied by the Consulate in Jerusalem are generally estimates and sometimes exaggerated.

1   Had Finn forgotten what he had reported five years earlier? The discrepancy between the two reports is probably a result of the re-examination of the certificates of protection and of the dismissal certificates presented by Jews in Safed and Tiberias. A certain number of them also preferred to come under Austrian protection. Therefore, the figures for 1854 seem to be more realistic. Furthermore, the increase in the number of protected families in Jerusalem reflects Finn's policy of bringing as many former Russian Jews as possible under his protection.
2   Most interesting is the division by religion: 59 Protestants, 448 Jews, 59 Roman Catholics, 109 Greek Orthodox, and 22 Moslems. Note the low number of Protestants.
3   Moore stated in his report: "The returns for Safed and Tiberias are taken from lists made by Consul Finn in 1856," i.e. fifteen years earlier!
4   The total number of protégés in the district of Jerusalem and in Northern Palestine was probably about 2000 in 1889. On 1 January 1890, protection was withdrawn from 1456 persons under the jurisdiction of the Consulates of Jerusalem, Beirut and Damascus, 842 of them in Jerusalem. It can be assumed, therefore, that the number of protégés was reduced by 1000–1200.
5   Many Jews emigrated from Russia to England. Some years later, after becoming naturalized British subjects, they immigrated to Palestine.

## Appendix 3: Ambassadors at Constantinople

| | |
|---|---|
| Viscount John Ponsonby | 1832–1841 |
| Sir Stratford Canning (Viscount Stratford de Redcliffe) | 1842–1858 |
| Sir Henry Lytton Bulwer | 1858–1865 |
| Earl Richard Bickerton of Lyons | 1865–1867 |
| Sir Austen Henry Layard | 1877–1881 |
| Earl Frederick of Dufferin | 1881–1884 |
| Sir H. Thorton | 1884 |
| Sir William A. White | 1885–1891 |
| Sir Frances Clare Ford | 1892–1893 |
| Sir Philip Henry W. Currie | 1893–1898 |
| Sir Nicholas O'Conor | 1898–1908 |
| Sir Gerard Lowther | 1908–1913 |
| Sir Louis de Pan Mallet | 1913–1914 |

## Appendix 4: Consuls and Consuls-General at Beirut

| | |
|---|---|
| Niven Moore, Consul | 1835–1841 |
| Colonel Hugh Henry Rose, Consul-General | 1841–1851 |
| Niven Moore, Consul | 1841–1852 |
| Niven Moore, Consul-General | 1853–1863 |
| George Jackson Eldridge, Consul-General | 1863–1890 |
| Lieutenant-Colonel Henry Trotter, Consul-General | 1890–1893 |
| Robert Drummond Hay, Consul-General | 1894–1908 |
| Henry Alfred Cumberbatch, Consul-General | 1908–1914 |

## Appendix 5: Foreign Secretaries

| | |
|---|---|
| Henry John Temple, Viscount Palmerston | April 1835–August 1841 |
| George Hamilton Gordon, Earl of Aberdeen | September 1841–June 1846 |
| Viscount Palmerston | July 1846–December 1851 |
| George Leveson Gower, Earl of Granville | December 1851–February 1852 |
| James Harris, Earl of Malmesbury | February 1852–December 1852 |
| Lord John Russell | December 1852–February 1853 |
| George William Frederick Villiers, Earl of Clarendon | February 1853–February 1858 |
| Earl of Malmesbury | February 1858–June 1859 |
| Lord John Russell | June 1859–October 1865 |
| Earl of Clarendon | November 1865–June 1866 |
| Lord Edward Henry Stanley (Earl of Derby) | July 1866–October 1868 |
| Earl of Granville | July 1870–February 1874 |
| Earl of Derby | February 1874–March 1878 |
| Robert Arthur Talbot Cecil, Marquess of Salisbury | April 1878–April 1880 |
| Earl of Granville | April 1880–June 1885 |
| Marquess of Salisbury | June 1885–January 1886 |
| Archibald Philip Primrose, Earl of Roseberry | February 1886–July 1886 |
| Stafford Henry Northcote, Earl of Iddesleigh | August 1886–January 1887 |
| Marquess of Salisbury | January 1887–August 1892 |
| Earl of Roseberry | August 1892–March 1894 |
| John Wodehouse, Earl of Kimberley | March 1894–June 1895 |
| Marquess of Salisbury | June 1895–November 1900 |
| Henry Charles Fitzmaurice, Marquess of Lansdowne | November 1900–November 1905 |
| Sir Edward Grey | December 1905–1916 |

# BIBLIOGRAPHY

## Archival Sources

(A) PUBLIC RECORD OFFICE (PRO), LONDON
Record Groups (Classes):
FO 78 — Foreign Office
FO 195 — Embassy in Constantinople
FO 369 — Consular Correspondence from 1906
FO 371 — General Political Correspondence from 1906
FO 617 — The British Consulate in Jerusalem

(B) ISRAEL STATE ARCHIVES (ISA), JERUSALEM
RG 67 — The German Consulate in Jerusalem
RG 123/1 — The British Consulate in Jerusalem

(C) JEWISH NATIONAL AND UNIVERSITY LIBRARY, DEPARTMENT OF MA-
NUSCRIPTS AND ARCHIVES, JERUSALEM
RG 4°1513 — The British Consulate in Jerusalem

(D) YAD IZHAK BEN-ZVI ARCHIVES, JERUSALEM
RG Finn Archive — Diaries of James Finn

## Published Books and Articles

Abu-Manneh = Boutrous Abu Manneh, "The Rise of the Sanjak of Jerusalem in the Late 19th
Century," G. Ben-Dor(ed.), *The Palestinians and the Middle East Conflict*, Ramat Gan 1979,
pp. 21–34.

Algernon = Cecil Algernon, "The Foreign Office," *The Cambridge History of Foreign Policy,
1783–1919*, III, Cambridge 1923.

Baldensperger = Philip J. Baldensperger, *The Immovable East*, London 1913.

Barclay = James Turner Barclay, *The City of the Great King, or — Jerusalem As it Was, As it Is
and As it Is to Be*, Philadelphia 1857 (repr. New York 1977).

Bartlett = William Henry Bartlett, *Jerusalem Revisited*, London 1855 (repr. Jerusalem 1977).

Bein = Alex Bein, "The Negotiations between Herzl and the Government of Great Britain
Concerning El-Arish," *Shivat Zion*, 1 (1950), pp. 179–220 (Hebrew).

Bell = Charles Bell, *Gleanings from a Tour in Palestine and the East*, London 1887.

Ben-Arieh = Yehoshua Ben-Arieh, *Jerusalem in the 19th Century*, I–II, Jerusalem 1984–1986.

Ben-Yaacov = Abraham Ben-Yaacov, *Jerusalem Within the Walls*, Jerusalem 1977 (Hebrew).

Biggs = Charles Biggs, *Six Months in Jerusalem*, Oxford 1896.

Blumberg, Consuls = Arnold Blumberg, "The British and Prussian Consuls at Jerusalem and
the Strange Last Will of Rabbi Herschell," *Zionism*, 1 (1980), pp. 1–8.

Blumberg, *View*, Arnold Blumberg, *A View from Jerusalem, 1849–1858: The Consulary Diary of James and E.A. Finn*, London–Toronto 1980.

Blumberg, *Zion* = Arnold Blumberg, *Zion before Zionism (1838–1880)*, Syracuse 1985.

Blyth = Estelle Blyth, *When We Lived in Jerusalem*, London 1927.

Bonar & McCheyne = Andrew Bonar and Robert McCheyne, *A Narrative of a Mission of Inquiry to the Jews from the Church of Scotland in 1839*, Edinburgh 1842.

Bost = Jean August Bost, *Souvenirs d'Orient*, Neuchâtel 1875.

Bourne = Kenneth Bourne, *Palmerston, the Early Years 1784–1841*, London 1982.

Braun = Stephan Braun, *Jerusalem: Bilder aus dem Orient*, Freiburg 1866.

Bremer = Frederika Bremer, *Travels in the Holy Land*, I–II, London 1862.

Buchanan = Robert Buchanan, *Notes of a Clerical Furlough, Spent Chiefly in the Holy Land*, London 1859.

Busch = Moritz Busch, *Eine Wallfahrt nach Jerusalem*, Leipzig 1881[3].

Buheiry = Marwan Buheiry, "British Consular Reports and the Economic Evolution of Palestine: The Mutasarrifya of Quds al-Sharif, 1885–1914," *The Third International Conference of Bilad al-Sham: Palestine, 19–24 April 1980, University of Jordan, I: Jerusalem*, Amman 1983, pp. 35–54.

Carmel, Activities = Alex Carmel, "The Activities of the European Powers in Palestine 1799–1914," *Asian and African Studies*, 19/1 (1985), pp. 43–91.

Carmel, *Christen* = Alex Carmel, *Christen als Pioniere im Heiligen Land*, Basel 1981.

Carmel, Competition = Alex Carmel, "Competition, Penetration and Presence: Christian Activity and its Influence in the Holy Land," Y. Ben-Arieh & I. Bartal (eds.), *The History of Eretz Israel, VIII: The Last Phase of Ottoman Rule (1799–1917)*, Jerusalem 1983, pp. 109–147 (Hebrew).

Carmel, German Community = Alex Carmel, "The German Protestant Community in Palestine, 1840–1914," *Cathedra*, no. 45 (September 1987), pp. 103–112 (Hebrew).

Carmel, Great Powers = Alex Carmel, "The Activities of the Great Powers in Eretz Israel, 1878–1914," I. Kolatt (ed.), *The History of the Jewish Community in Eretz Israel since 1882, I: The Ottoman Period*, Jerusalem 1989, pp. 143–213 (Hebrew).

Carmel, Palästina-Chronik = Alex Carmel (ed.), *Palästina-Chronik 1853–1914: Deutsche Zeitungsberichte [Süddeutsche Warte]*, I–II, Ulm 1978–1983.

Colbi = Saul P. Colbi, *Christianity in the Holy Land*, Tel Aviv 1969.

Crombie = Kelvin Crombie, *For the Love of Zion: Christian Witness and the Restoration of Israel*, London 1991.

Dupuis = Hanmer L. Dupuis, *The Holy Places: A Narrative of Two Years Residence in Jerusalem and Palestine*, London 1856.

Egerton, *Journal* = Harriet F. Egerton, *Journal of a Tour in the Holy Land*, London 1841.

Eliav, *Austrian Protection* = Mordechai Eliav, *Under Imperial Austrian Protection: Selected Documents from the Archives of the Austrian Consulate in Jerusalem, 1849–1917*, Jerusalem 1985 (Hebrew).

Eliav, Diplomatic = Mordechai Eliav, "Diplomatic Intervention concerning Restrictions on Jewish Immigration and Purchase of Land at the End of the Nineteenth Century," *Cathedra*, no. 26 (December 1982), pp. 117–132 (Hebrew).

Eliav, Finn = Mordechai Eliav, "The Rise and Fall of Consul James Finn," *Cathedra*, no. 65 (September 1992), pp. 37–81 (Hebrew).

Eliav, *German Policy* = Mordechai Eliav, *The Jews of Palestine in German Policy: Selected Documents from the Archives of the German Consulate in Jerusalem, 1842–1914*, I–II, Tel Aviv 1973 (Hebrew & German).

Eliav, Rafah = Mordechai Eliav, "The Rafah Approaches in the History of the Jewish Settlement," *Cathedra*, no. 3 (February 1977), pp. 117–208 (Hebrew).

Eliav, Shimon Rosenthal = Mordechai Eliav, "The Case of Shimon Rosenthal— Apostacy, Return to Judaism and Relapse," *Cathedra*, no. 61 (September 1991), pp. 113–132 (Hebrew).

Eliav, Women = Mordechai Eliav, "By Virture of Women: The Role of Women in the Conversion Attempts by the British Mission," *Cathedra*, no. 76 (July 1995), pp. 96–115 (Hebrew).

Eliav, *Yishuv* = Mordechai Eliav, *Eretz Israel and its Yishuv in the 19th Century, 1777–1917*, Jerusalem 1978 (Hebrew).

Ewald = Ferdinand C. Ewald, *Journal of Missionary Labours in the City of Jerusalem (1842–1844)*, London 1846.

Finn E., *Home* = Elizabeth Anne Finn, *Home in the Holy Land*, London 1866.

Finn E., *Reminiscences* = Elizabeth Anne Finn, *Reminiscences*, London 1929.

Finn J., *Byeways* = James Finn, *Byeways in Palestine*, London 1868.

Finn J., *Stirring Times* = James Finn, *Stirring Times*, I–II, London 1878.

Fisk = George Fisk, *A Pastor's Memorial of ... Jerusalem and other Principal Localities of the Holy Land*, London 1843.

Frankl = Ludwig August Frankl, *Nach Jerusalem*, II, Leipzig 1858.

Friedman, British Schemes = Isaiah Friedman, "British Schemes for the Restoration of Jews to Palestine, 1840–1850," *Cathedra*, no. 56 (June 1990), pp. 42–69 (Hebrew).

Friedman, Palmerston = Isaiah Friedman, "Lord Palmerston and the Protection of Jews in Palestine, 1839–1851," *Jewish Social Studies*, 30 (1968), pp. 23–41.

Fürst = Aaron Fürst, *New Jerusalem*, Jerusalem 1946 (Hebrew).

Gatt = Benzion Gatt, *The Jewish Yishuv in Eretz-Israel, 1840–1881*, Jerusalem 1963 (Hebrew).

Gerber = Haim Gerber, *Ottoman Rule in Jerusalem 1890–1914*, Berlin 1985.

Gidney, *At Home* = William T. Gidney, *At Home and Abroad: A Description of the English and Continental Missions*, London 1900.

Gidney, *London Society* = William T. Gidney, *The History of the London Society for Promoting Christianity Amongst the Jews, 1809–1908*, London 1908.

Gidney, *Missions* = William T. Gidney, *Missions to Jews — A Handbook*, 11th rev. ed., London 1914.

Gidney, *Sites* = William T. Gidney, *Sites and Scenes: A Description of the Oriental Missions of the London Society...*, II, London 1899.

Ginat = Shalom Ginat, "The Activity of the London Society for the Promotion of Christianity Amongst the Jews Inside the Jewish Yishuv in Jerusalem (1825–1914)," Master's thesis, University of Haifa, 1986 (Hebrew).

Glass = Joseph B. Glass, "Jospeh Navon Bey's Contributions to the Development of Eretz Israel," *Cathedra*, no. 66 (December 1992), pp. 87–110 (Hebrew).

Glass & Kark = Joseph B. Glass & Ruth Kark, *Sephardic Entrepreneurs in Eretz Israel: The Amzalak Family, 1816–1918*, Jerusalem 1991.

*Gobat = Samuel Gobat, Sein Leben und Werk*, ed. Heinrich Thiersch, Basel 1884.

Goodrich-Freer = Adele Goodrich-Freer, *Inner Jerusalem*, London 1904.

Grajewski = Pinchas Grajewski, *The Struggle of the Jews against the Mission from 1824 till our Times*, Jerusalem 1935 (Hebrew).

Gross = Nachum T. Gross, "The Anglo-Palestine Company: The Formative Years," Gad. G. Gilbar (ed.), *Ottoman Palestine 1800–1914*, Leiden 1990, pp. 219–254.

Hajjar = Joseph Hajjar, *L'Europe et les destinées du Proche Orient, 1815–1848*, [Belgium] 1970.

Halsted = Thomas Halsted, *Our Missions*, London 1866.

Hanauer = J.E. Hanauer, "Notes on the History of Modern Colonisation in Palestine," *PEFQSt* 1900, pp. 124–142.

Hannam, Britons = Michael Hannam, "Some Nineteenth-Century Britons in Jerusalem," *PEQ* 1982, pp. 53–65.

Hannam, Jerusalem Bishopric = Michael Hannam, "The Jerusalem Bishopric," *Britain and the Holy Land, 1800–1914: [Symposium]*, London 1989, [no paging].

Hermel = Gideon Hermel, "The Protestant Cemetery on Mount Zion," *Ariel*, nos. 57–58 (January 1988), pp. 174–185 (Hebrew).

Herschell = Ridley H. Herschell, *A Visit to My Father-Land*, London 1844.

Hertslet = Edward Hertslet, *Recollections of the Old Foreign Office*, London 1901.

Hodder = Edwin Hodder, *The Life and Work of the Seventh Earl of Shaftesbury*, I–III, London 1887.

Holmes = Reed M. Holmes, *The Forerunners*, Independence MO 1981.

Horn-Elbaum = Shlomit Horn-Elbaum, "The Jerusalem Bishopric, 1841," Ph.D. diss., University of Minnesota, 1978.

Hornby = Edmund Hornby, *An Autobiography*, London 1929.

Hornus = Jean Michel Hornus, "L'évêché anglo-prussien à Jérusalem (1841–1881)," *Proche Orient Chrétien*, 12 (1962), pp. 255–269.

Hough = William Hough, "The History of the British Consulate in Jerusalem," *Journal of the Middle East Society*, 1, no. 1 (Oct.–Dec. 1946), pp. 3–14.

Hyamson, *British Consulate* = Albert M. Hyamson, *The British Consulate in Jerusalem in Relation to the Jews in Palestine*, I–II, London 1939–1941.

Hyamson, *British Projects, 1917* = Albert M. Hyamson, *British Projects for the Restoration of the Jews to Palestine*, London 1917.

Hyamson, *British Projects, 1918* = Albert M. Hyamson, *British Projects for the Restoration of the Jews to Palestine*, New York 1918.

Hyamson, *Palestine* = Albert M. Hyamson, *Palestine — The Rebirth of an Ancient People*, London 1917.

Ilan = Zvi Ilan, "On the History of the Finn House in 'Abraham's Vineyard'," *Kardom*, nos. 21–23 (July 1982), pp. 175–185 (Hebrew).

Ilan & Amit = Zvi Ilan & David Amit, "The Farm of Consul Finn in the Village of Fa'our," *Cathedra*, no. 32 (July 1984), pp. 175–181 (Hebrew).

Iseminger = Gordon L. Iseminger, "The Old Turkish Hands: The British Levantine Consuls, 1856–1876," *Middle East Journal*, 22 (1968), pp. 297–316.

Jack = Sybil M. Jack, "Imperial Pawns: The Role of the British Consul," D.M. Schreuder (ed.), *Imperialisms*, Sydney 1991, pp. 33–63.

*Jerusalem Medical Mission* = *The Jerusalem Medical Mission*, London 1911.

Jones = Ray Jones, *The Nineteenth Century Foreign Office: Administrative History*, London 1971.

Kark, Changing Patterns = Ruth Kark, "Changing Patterns of Landowership in the Nineteenth-Century Palestine: The European Influence," *Journal of Historical Geography*, 10 (1984), pp. 357–384.

Kark, *American Consuls* = Ruth Kark, *American Consuls in the Holy Land 1832–1914*, Jerusalem 1994.

Kark, Millenarism = Ruth Kark, "Millenarism and Agricultural Settlement in the Holy Land in the Nineteenth Century," *Journal of Historical Geography*, 9 (1983), pp. 47–62.

Karkar = Yakub N. Karkar, *Railway Development in the Ottoman Empire 1856–1914*, New York 1972.

Katzburg = Nathaniel Katzburg, "Some Early Despatches by the First British Vice-Consul in Jerusalem (1839–1841)," H.Z. Hirschberg (ed.), *Vatiqin*, Ramat Gan 1975, pp. ix–xxix (Hebrew).

419

Kent = *The Great Powers and the End of the Ottoman Empire*, Marion Kent (ed.), London 1984.

Kushner, *Governor* = David Kushner, *A Governor in Jerusalem: The City and the Province in the Eyes of Ali Ekrem Bey, 1906–1908*, Jerusalem 1995 (Hebrew).

Kushner, Governors = David Kushner, "The 'Foreign Relations' of the Governors of Jerusalem Toward the End of the Ottoman Period," D. Kushner (ed.), *Palestine in the Late Ottoman Period*, Jerusalem 1986, pp. 307–319.

Kushner, Intercommunal = David Kushner, "Intercommunal Strife in Palestine during the Late Ottoman Period, *Asian and African Studies*, 18 (1984), pp. 187–204.

Kushner, Ottoman Government = David Kushner, "The Ottoman Government of Palestine, 1864–1914," *Middle Eastern Studies*, 23 (1987), pp. 274–290.

Lambert, *Time is at Hand* = Richard S. Lambert, *For the Time is at Hand: An Account of the Prophecies of Henry Wentworth Monk*, London 1947.

Lask-Abrahams = Beth-Zion Lask-Abrahams, "James Finn, Her Britannic Majesty's Consul at Jerusalem, 1846–1863," *Transactions of the Jewish Historical Society of England*, 27 (1982), pp. 40–50.

Le Roi, *Christenheit* = J.F.A. de Le Roi, *Die evangelische Christenheit und die Juden*, I–III, Leipzig-Berlin 1884–1892.

Le Roi, *Ewald* = J.F.A. de Le Roi, *Ferdinand Christian Ewald — Ein Lebensbild der neueren Judenmission*, Gütersloh, 1896.

Lieber = Sherman Lieber, *Mystics and Missionaries: the Jews in Palestine 1799–1840*, Salt Lake City 1992.

Liebetrut = Friedrich Liebtrut, *Reise nach dem Morgenlande*, II, Hamburg 1858.

Lipman, America-Holy Land = Vivian D. Lipman, "America-Holy Land Material in British Archives, 1820–1930," M. Davis (ed.), *With Eyes Toward Zion*, II, New York 1986, pp. 25–34.

Lipman, *Americans* = Vivian D. Lipman, *Americans and the Holy Land through British Eyes, 1820–1917: A Documentary History*, London 1989.

Lipman, Britain = Vivian D. Lipman, "Britain and the Holy Land, 1830–1914," M. Davis & Y. Ben-Arieh (eds.), *With Eyes Toward Zion, III: Western Societies and the Holy Land*, New York 1991, pp. 195–205.

Lipman, British Consulate = Vivian D. Lipman, "The British Consulate in Jerusalem 1838–1914," *Britain and the Holy Land 1800–1914: [Symposium]*, London 1989, pp. 1–23.

Macleod = Norman Macleod, *Eastward*, London and New York 1866.

Ma'oz = Moshe Ma'oz, *Ottoman Reform in Syria and Palestine, 1840–1861*, Oxford 1961.

Mandel = Neville J. Mandel, "Ottoman Policy and Restriction on Jewish Settlement in Palestine (1881–1908)," *Middle Eastern Studies*, 10 (1974), pp. 312–332; 11 (1975), pp. 33–46.

Marlowe = John Marlowe, *Perfidious Albion: The Origins of Anglo-French Rivalry in the Levant*, London 1971.

Minor = [Clorinda Minor], *Meshullam, or Tidings from Jerusalem: From the Journal of a Believer Recently Returned from the Holy Land*, Philadelphia 1851 (repr. New York 1977).

Montefiore = *Diaries of Sir Moses and Lady Montefiore*, ed. L. Loewe, London 1983².

Morgenstern, *Messianism* = Arieh Morgenstern, *Messianism and the Settlement of Eretz Israel*, Jerusalem 1985 (Hebrew).

Morgenstern, Perushim = Arieh Morgenstern, "The Perushim, the London Society and the Opening of the British Consulate in Jerusalem," *Shalem*, 5 (1987), pp. 115–138 (Hebrew).

Neil = James Neil, *Palestine Re-peopled*, London 1877.

Neumann = Bernhard Neumann, *Die heilige Stadt und deren Bewohner*, Hamburg 1877.

Öke = Mim Kemal Öke, "The Ottoman Empire, Zionism and the Question of Palestine," *International Journal of Middle East Studies*, 14 (1982), pp. 329–341.

Parfitt = Tudor Parfitt, *The Jews in Palestine 1800–1882*, London 1987.

Petermann = Johann Heinrich Petermann, *Reisen im Orient*, I, Leipzig 1865.

Platt, *Cinderella Service* = D.C.M. Platt, *The Cinderella Service: British Consuls since 1825*, London 1971.

Platt, *Finance* = D.C.M. Platt, *Finance, Trade and Politics in British Foreign Policy 1815–1914*, Oxford 1968.

Plitt = Theodor Plitt, *Skizzen aus einer Reise nach dem Heiligen Land*, Karlsruhe 1853.

Rhodes = Albert Rhodes, *Jerusalem As it Is*, London 1865.

Richter = Julius Richter, *A History of Protestant Missions in the Near East*, Edinburgh–London 1910.

Rodkey = F.S. Rodkey, "Lord Palmerston and the Rejuvenation of Turkey, 1830–1841," *Journal of Modern History*, June 1930, pp. 193–225.

Rogers = Mary Eliza Rogers, *Domestic Life in Palestine*, London 1862.

Rubin = Rehav Rubin, "History of the Colonization of Artas," *Zev Vilnay's Jubilee Volume*, I, Jerusalem 1984, pp. 325–331 (Hebrew).

Salibi = Kamal S. Salibi, "The Two Worlds of Assad Kayat," B. Braude & B. Lewis (eds.), *Christians and Jews in the Ottoman Empire*, New York–London 1982, pp. 135–158.

Salzbacher = Joseph Salzbacher, *Erinnerungen aus meiner Pilgerreise im Jahre 1837*, Wien 1839.

Samuel = Sydney Montagu Samuel, *Jewish Life in the East*, London 1881.

Sapir, Blyth = Shaul Sapir, "Bishop Blyth and his Jerusalem Legacy: St. John's College," *Cathedra*, no. 46 (December 1987), pp. 45–64 (Hebrew).

Sapir, Contribution = Shaul Sapir, "The Contribution of the Anglican Missionary Societies to the Development of Jerusalem at the End of the Ottoman Rule," Master's thesis, Hebrew University of Jerusalem, 1979 (Hebrew).

Schölch = Alexander Schölch, *Palestine in Transformation, 1856–1882*, Washington 1993.

Schütz = Christine Schütz, *Preussen in Jerusalem, 1800–1861*, Berlin 1988.

Schulz = E.W. Schulz, *Reise in das gelobte Land im Jahre 1851*, Mülheim 1854.

Schur, Finn = Nathan Schur, "Consul Finn's Last Years in Jerusalem," *Cathedra*, no. 30 (December 1983), pp. 64–90 (Hebrew).

Schur, *Jerusalem* = Nathan Schur, *History of Jerusalem*, III, Tel Aviv 1987 (Hebrew).

Schwake = Norbert Schwake, *Die Entwicklung des Krankenhauswesens der Stadt Jerusalem vom Ende des 18. bis zum Beginn des 20. Jahrhunderts*, I–II, Herzogenrath 1983.

Scult = Mel Scult, "English Missions to the Jews: Conversion in the Age of Emancipation," *Jewish Social Studies*, 35 (1973), pp. 3–17.

Searight = Sarah Searight, *The British in the Middle East*, London 1979.

Shepherd = Naomi Shepherd, *The Zealous Intruders: The Western Discovery of the Holy Land*, London 1987.

Smith = Robert Michael Smith, "The London Jews' Society and Patterns of Jewish Conversion in England," *Jewish Social Studies*, 43 (1981), pp. 275–286.

Spyridon = S.N. Spyridon, *Annals of Palestine 1821–1841*, Jerusalem 1938.

Stanley = Arthur P. Stanley, *Sermons Preached before H.R.H. the Prince of Wales during his Tour in the East in the Spring 1862*, London 1863.

Stavrou = Theofanis J. Stavrou, "Russian Interests in the Levant, 1743–1848," *Middle East Journal*, 17 (1963), pp. 91–103.

Strauss = Friedrich Adolph Strauss, *Sinai und Golgotha: Reisen in das Morgenland*, Berlin 1859.

Temperley = Harold Temperley, *England and the Near East: Crimea*, London 1936.

Tennenbaum, Consul = Mark Tennenbaum, "The British Consul in Jerusalem, 1838–1890," Master's thesis, Hebrew University of Jerusalem, 1972 (Hebrew).

Tennenbaum, Consulate = Mark Tennenbaum, "The British Consulate in Jerusalem, 1858–1890," *Cathedra*, no. 5 (October 1977), pp. 83–108 (Hebrew).

Thomas = Margaret Thomas, *Two Years in Palestine and Syria*, London 1900.

Thompson = Albert E. Thompson, *A Century of Jewish Missions*, New York 1902.

Tibawi = Abdul Latif Tibawi, *British Interests in Palestine 1800–1901*, Oxford 1961.

Tilley & Gasellee = John Tilley & Stephen Gasellee, *The Foreign Office*, London 1933.

Tischendorf = Constantin von Tischendorf, *Reise in dem Orient*, II, Leipzig 1846.

Titmarsh = M.A. Titmarsh [W.M. Thackeray], *Notes of a Journey from Cornhill to Grand Cairo, by Way of... Jerusalem*, New York 1848.

Tobler, *Dritte Wanderung* = Titus Tobler, *Dritte Wanderung nach Palästina im Jahre 1857*, Gotha 1859.

Tobler, *Topographie* = Titus Tobler, *Topographie von Jerusalem und seine Umgebung*, I–II, Berlin 1853.

Tristram = Henry Baker Tristram, *The Land of Israel: A Journal of Travels in Palestine*, London 1865.

Tuchman = Barbara Tuchman, *Bible and Sword*, London 1957.

Vereté = Mayir Vereté, "Why was a British Consulate Established in Jerusalem?" *English Historical Review*, 35 (1970), pp. 316–345. (Hebrew version: *Zion*, 26 (1961), pp. 215–237).

Verney-Dambmann = Noel Verney & George Dambmann, *Les puissances étrangères dans le Levant et en Palestine*, Paris 1900.

Warren = Charles Warren, *Underground Jerusalem*, London 1876.

Webster = Charles Webster, *The Foreign Policy of Palmerston 1830–1841*, London 1951.

Wilde = William R. Wilde, *Narrative of a Voyage to Madeira, Teneriffe and along the Shores of the Mediterranean, including a Visit to ... Palestine*, II, Dublin–London 1840.

Wilson = John Wilson, *The Land of the Bible Visited*, II, Edinburgh 1847.

Wood = Alfred Wood, *A History of the Levant Company*, Oxford 1935.

Yellin = Yehoshua Yellin, *Memoirs of a Jerusalemite*, Jerusalem 1924 (Hebrew).

Zitron = Samuel Leib Zitron, *Behind the Curtain: Converts, Traitors and Deniers*, Vilna 1923 (Hebrew).

# INDEX

The index does not include references to: Britain (England); Foreign Office; London; Jerusalem (when the city is mentioned in general); Palestine (Holy Land); Ottoman Empire (Turkey)